THE CAMBRIDGE CONSTITUTIONAL HISTORY OF
THE UNITED KINGDOM

*

VOLUME I

Exploring the Constitution

THE CAMBRIDGE CONSTITUTIONAL HISTORY OF THE UNITED KINGDOM

*

VOLUME I

Exploring the Constitution

*

Edited by
PETER CANE
Christ's College, Cambridge and Australian National University

H. KUMARASINGHAM
University of Edinburgh

University Printing House, Cambridge CB2 8BS, United Kingdom

One Liberty Plaza, 20th Floor, New York, NY 10006, USA

477 Williamstown Road, Port Melbourne, VIC 3207, Australia

314–321, 3rd Floor, Plot 3, Splendor Forum, Jasola District Centre, New Delhi – 110025, India

103 Penang Road, #05-06/07, Visioncrest Commercial, Singapore 238467

Cambridge University Press is part of Cambridge University Press & Assessment, a department of the University of Cambridge.

We share the University's mission to contribute to society through the pursuit of education, learning and research at the highest international levels of excellence.

www.cambridge.org
Information on this title: www.cambridge.org/9781009277754

DOI: 10.1017/9781009277778

© Cambridge University Press & Assessment 2023

This publication is in copyright. Subject to statutory exception and to the provisions of relevant collective licensing agreements, no reproduction of any part may take place without the written permission of Cambridge University Press & Assessment.

First published 2023

Printed in the United Kingdom by TJ Books Limited, Padstow Cornwall

9781108474214
9781009277754
9781009277099

A catalogue record for this publication is available from the British Library.

ISBN 978-1-009-27775-4 Hardback

Cambridge University Press & Assessment has no responsibility for the persistence or accuracy of URLs for external or third-party internet websites referred to in this publication and does not guarantee that any content on such websites is, or will remain, accurate or appropriate.

A cumulative index of both volumes is available for download on Cambridge Core and via www.cambridge.org/constitutionalhistoryindex

Contents

List of Contributors *page* viii
Editors' Preface to Volumes I and II xi
PETER CANE AND H. KUMARASINGHAM

PART I
PERSPECTIVES

1 · The Historical Constitution 3
H. KUMARASINGHAM

2 · Law and the Constitution 35
PETER CANE

3 · Political Constitutionalism 59
RICHARD BELLAMY

4 · The Economic Constitution 88
TONY PROSSER

5 · Religion and the Constitution to 1688 113
PIPPA CATTERALL

6 · Religion and the Constitution since the Glorious Revolution 140
PIPPA CATTERALL

7 · The Social Democratic Constitution 168
K. D. EWING

CONTENTS

8 · The Constitution of Rights *195*
PETER CANE

9 · The People and the Constitution *221*
VERNON BOGDANOR

10 · Constitutional Theory and Thought *254*
JEFFREY GOLDSWORTHY

PART II
ACTORS AND INSTITUTIONS

11 · Monarchy *285*
EDWARD CAVANAGH

12 · Legislatures *309*
MICHAEL GORDON

13 · The Executive and the Administration *335*
JANET MCLEAN

14 · Judiciaries *359*
JOSHUA GETZLER

15 · Coercive Institutions *386*
BRICE DICKSON

16 · Locality, Regionality and Centrality *406*
LUKE BLAXILL

17 · Political Parties *431*
ROBERT CROWCROFT

PART III
POLITICS

18 · Conservatism *457*
ASANGA WELIKALA

Contents

19 · Liberalism   480
EMILY JONES

20 · Socialism   499
STEPHEN SEDLEY

21 · Unionism   520
JAMES MITCHELL AND ALAN CONVERY

22 · Nationalism   540
MICHAEL KEATING

Index   561

Contributors

RICHARD BELLAMY is Professor of Political Science at University College, London. He is a Fellow of the British Academy and of the Academy of Social Sciences. His many publications include *Political Constitutionalism: A Republican Defense of the Constitutionality of Democracy* (Cambridge University Press, 2007) and *A Republican Europe of States: Cosmopolitanism, Intergovernmentalism and Democracy in the EU* (Cambridge University Press, 2019). With Jeff King he is co-editing *The Cambridge Handbook of Constitutional Theory*.

LUKE BLAXILL is College Lecturer in Modern British History at Hertford College, University of Oxford. His expertise is British electoral politics, and the computational and traditional analysis of political language in the nineteenth and twentieth centuries. He has previously published on the local and national dimensions of electoral politics, and published his first book *The War of Words: the Language of British Elections* with the Royal Historical Society in 2020.

VERNON BOGDANOR CBE is Professor of Government, King's College London, and was formerly Professor of Government at Oxford University. He is a Fellow of the British Academy, an Honorary Fellow of the Institute for Advanced Legal Studies, a Fellow of the Royal Historical Society and a Fellow of the Academy of the Social Sciences. He has been an adviser to a number of governments, including Albania, Czech Republic, Hungary, Kosovo, Israel, Mauritius, Slovakia and Trinidad. He has written widely on constitutional issues and is a frequent contributor to TV, radio and the press. In 2008, he was awarded the Sir Isaiah Berlin Award by the Political Studies Association for Lifetime Contribution to Political Studies. He is a Chevalier de la Legion d'Honneur, an Honorary Fellow of the Queen's College, Oxford, an Honorary D. Litt. of the University of Kent, and an Honorary Bencher of the Middle Temple.

PETER CANE is Senior Research Fellow at Christ's College, Cambridge, and Emeritus Distinguished Professor of Law at the Australian National University. His main interests are in public law and its theory, diversity and history. He is a Corresponding Fellow of the British Academy and a Fellow of the Academy of the Social Sciences in Australia and the Australian Academy of Law. Recent publications include *Controlling Administrative Power: An Historical Comparison* (Cambridge University Press, 2016).

List of Contributors

PIPPA CATTERALL is Professor of History and Policy at the University of Westminster and editor of *National Identities*. Her publications include *Labour and the Free Churches 1918–1939: Radicalism, Righteousness and Religion* (Bloomsbury, 2016), and her current research explores the intellectual and constitutional history of ecumenism.

EDWARD CAVANAGH was a scholar who researched and wrote at the crossroads of history and law.

ALAN CONVERY is Senior Lecturer in Politics at the University of Edinburgh. He writes about conservatism, the Conservative Party and territorial politics in the UK.

ROBERT CROWCROFT is Senior Lecturer in History at the University of Edinburgh. He works on modern political history and statecraft. His most recent book is *The End is Nigh: British Politics, Power, and the Road to the Second World War* (Oxford University Press, 2019), and he co-edited *The Oxford Handbook of Modern British Political History, 1800–2000* (Oxford University Press, 2018).

BRICE DICKSON is Emeritus Professor of International and Comparative Law at Queen's University Belfast. He was Chief Commissioner of the Northern Ireland Human Rights Commission from 1999 to 2005 and an independent member of the Northern Ireland Policing Board from 2012 to 2020. He has also served as a custody visitor to police stations. His latest book is *International Human Rights Monitoring Mechanisms: A Study of their Impact in the UK* (Elgar Publishing, 2022).

K. D. EWING has been Professor of Public Law at King's College London since 1989, having taught previously at the Universities of Edinburgh (1978–83) and Cambridge (1983–89). His research and writing focus in part on the boundary between constitutional law and labour law, and the contribution of trade unions to economic and political democracy.

JOSHUA GETZLER is Fellow of St Hugh's College, Professor of Law and Legal History at the University of Oxford, and Conjoint Professor at UNSW Law. Educated in law and history at the Australian National University and Oxford, he researches on land and water law, native title, trusts, equity, companies and financial law, combining doctrinal, historical and economic analysis. He co-edits *Oxford Legal History* and the *American Journal of Legal History*.

JEFFREY GOLDSWORTHY is an Emeritus Professor at Monash University; a Professorial Fellow at the University of Melbourne; and an Adjunct Professor at the University of Adelaide. His expertise is in constitutional law, theory, and history, and legal philosophy. He is the author of *The Sovereignty of Parliament, History and Philosophy* (Oxford University Press, 1999) and *Parliamentary Sovereignty, Contemporary Debates* (Cambridge University Press, 2010), and the editor of *Interpreting Constitutions, A Comparative Study* (Oxford University Press, 2006).

MICHAEL GORDON is Professor of Constitutional Law, School of Law and Social Justice, University of Liverpool. Michael specialises in constitutional law, theory and reform, with a focus on the UK and particular expertise relating to parliamentary sovereignty, political constitutionalism, and democratic accountability.

EMILY JONES is Lecturer in Modern British History at the University of Manchester. She is the author of *Edmund Burke and the Invention of Modern Conservatism, 1830–1914: An Intellectual History* (Oxford University Press, 2017), which was awarded the Longman-History Today prize in 2018. She is currently writing a history of the construction of 'One Nation' conservatism following the death of Disraeli in 1881.

MICHAEL KEATING is Emeritus Professor of Politics at the University of Aberdeen and a Fellow of the Royal Society of Edinburgh, the British Academy, the Academy of Social Sciences and the Academia Europea. He has published widely on European politics, nationalism, and territorial politics. His most recent book is *State and Nation in the United Kingdom: The Fractured Union* (Oxford University Press 2021).

H. KUMARASINGHAM is Senior Lecturer in British Politics at the University of Edinburgh. His work and interests cover the history and politics of the United Kingdom, the late British Empire and the Commonwealth. His publications include the collections *Constitution-Maker – Selected Writings of Sir Ivor Jennings* (Cambridge University Press, 2015) and *Viceregalism – The Crown as Head of State in Political Crises in the Postwar Commonwealth* (Palgrave Macmillan, 2020). He is Co-Editor of the *Transactions of the Royal Historical Society*.

JANET McLEAN is Professor of Law at the University of Auckland where she specialises in constitutional history and theory. She is a King's Counsel (KC) and a Fellow of the Royal Society of New Zealand.

JAMES MITCHELL is Professor of Public Policy at the University of Edinburgh. His areas of interest include government, devolution, the constitution, and public policy.

TONY PROSSER is Professor Emeritus of Public Law at the University of Bristol, having previously been John Millar Professor of Law at the University of Glasgow and visiting professor at a number of European universities. His interests are in regulation, especially economic regulation, and the relationship between regulation and public law in a comparative perspective. His teaching interests are in public law, and social and legal theory.

STEPHEN SEDLEY practised as a barrister, principally in public law. In 1992 he was appointed a judge of the Queen's Bench, and in 1999 a Lord Justice of Appeal. He also sat as a judge ad hoc on the Judicial Committee of the Privy Council and the European Court of Human Rights. On retirement in 2011 he was appointed a visiting professor of law at Oxford.

ASANGA WELIKALA is a Senior Lecturer in Public Law and the Head of the Public Law subject area at the School of Law, University of Edinburgh, and the Director of the Edinburgh Centre for Constitutional Law. His teaching and research interests lie in British and Scots public law, comparative constitutional law and theory, and Commonwealth constitutional history.

Editors' Preface

The History, Law and Politics of the Constitution

One of our main motivations for undertaking this large project was a conviction that constitutional history is a subject that receives less attention than it deserves from lawyers, historians and students of politics alike. This is not to say that lawyers are uninterested in the constitutional past; but they tend to focus on its legal aspects and their relevance to, and significance for, constitutional law present and future, rather than on the history of the constitution as a topic of interest and importance in its own right. As a disciplinary group, historians have neglected the constitution for the past fifty years and more. Constitutional and political history were pre-eminent strands of British historical studies in the nineteenth and early twentieth centuries. New approaches to history that examine cultural, social, environmental and regional themes, and focus on issues such as gender and race, were as much a reaction against constitutional and political history as a concerted attempt to enhance under-researched fields of historical enquiry. While the emergence of these new areas is obviously welcome, the decline of constitutional history has meant that knowledge of the political and legal workings, and the historical foundations, of government and society is no longer within the expertise of many modern practitioners and students of history. Nevertheless, in a broad sense of 'constitution', covering the whole system of government including its norms, usages and traditions, its history lies at the core of the discipline because the constitution frames and regulates the political, the political frames and shapes the social, and the social frames and shapes the personal.

As for students and scholars of politics, they typically start with the day-to-day practice of politics and the quotidian conduct of government. They are also often concerned with ethical and moral aspects of government and politics. The modern progenitor of this sort of approach was, perhaps, Walter Bagehot, who famously distinguished between the 'dignified' and 'efficient' parts of constitutions.[1] As understood by A. V. Dicey, Bagehot's concern with how politics and government ought to be conducted, as opposed to the way it actually was conducted, extended only to norms of political conduct (which Dicey dubbed 'conventions of the constitution'), and did not embrace legal norms, which were the object of Dicey's interest.[2] The legal framework of politics is typically left to the lawyers.

In planning this constitutional history our aim was to bring together the disciplines of history, law and politics in understanding the way public power is created, allocated, exercised and controlled. In our view, the politics of a society cannot be adequately understood without taking account of its constitution; and neither the constitution nor the law of the constitution can be adequately understood without studying the constitution's history and its surrounding politics. Politics, law and history are inextricably intertwined. The over-arching objective of *The Cambridge Constitutional History of the United Kingdom* is to bring the disciplinary preoccupations, methods and insights of history, law and politics together to enable readers to appreciate not only the historical development, legal nature and political importance of the constitution but also its general relevance to all aspects of human social life. Very recently, Brexit and Covid-19 (for instance) have borne stark witness to the ubiquitous and continuous significance of public power, its creation, allocation, exercise and control, to social and personal life. The history of the constitution is also part of public affairs. Within hours of his accession to the throne in September 2022, King Charles III in his first public address as monarch spoke of valuing dearly 'the precious traditions, freedoms and responsibilities of our unique history and our system of parliamentary government'. The new King, in the style of sovereigns past, 'solemnly' pledged 'to uphold the constitutional principles at the heart of our nation'. This constitutional history seeks to uncover what those changing principles are and the history and context behind them and more.

Innovation

In seeking insights from law, politics and history, the *Cambridge Constitutional History of the United Kingdom* aims to innovate in various ways. First, this is

---

[1] Walter Bagehot, *The English Constitution*, Miles Taylor, ed. (Oxford: Oxford University Press, 2001 [1867]), 7–13.
[2] A. V. Dicey, *The Law of the Constitution*, J. W. F. Allison, ed. (Oxford: Oxford University Press, 2013), 18.

the only book-length 'constitutional history' of Britain to have been published for more than fifty years. We think that an updated account, incorporating recent developments in legal, political, historical and historiographical research, is both justified and needed.

Second, the volume breaks new ground in extending its gaze to the United Kingdom. Typically, monographic constitutional histories have been concerned primarily or exclusively with England. An important reason for extending the focus to encompass the other components of the UK is that some of the most important constitutional developments and issues of the last twenty-five years have related to the internal structure of the UK. Put crudely, it is difficult properly to appreciate the process of 'devolution' to units of the UK without understanding the evolution of the UK. However, space considerations (alone) rule out providing constitutional histories of the various components of the UK of the length, breadth and depth that each deserves. Perhaps inevitably, and certainly predictably, England receives preferential treatment. However, in addition to many chapters that cover themes and viewpoints of other parts of the UK, there are two chapters specifically devoted to the constitutional histories, respectively, of Ireland, Scotland and Wales – one dealing with the period before, and a second dealing with the period after, amalgamation or union with England.

Third, traditional constitutional histories have little or nothing to say about empire. Yet colonisation is an integral part of the history of British and UK constitutionalism – and vice versa. Once again, however, space has not allowed us to provide a comprehensive history of the constitution of the empire and colonisation. The two chapters on empire focus particularly on the relationships between constitutionalism at the centre and constitutionalism at the periphery.

Fourth, from the legal perspective, this *Cambridge History* is innovative in its approach to control of political power. For over a century, lawyers have distinguished, within public law, between constitutional and administrative law. Administrative law is typically understood as being concerned particularly with administrative (executive) power and, especially, control of its exercise. The identification of this discrete area of public law can be explained historically as a product of the growth of the 'administrative state' since the mid-nineteenth century. However, for this project, the distinction between constitutional law and administrative law is of no relevance. A constitution is as much concerned with administrative power as with legislative, judicial, and other, public power. Indeed, the very idea that there are different types of public power can itself be historically situated (in the seventeenth and eighteenth centuries) and is part of the history of the constitution.

Finally, the *Cambridge Constitutional History of the United Kingdom* aims to revive history's role in constitutional studies. However, unlike previous accounts from the nineteenth century, it will employ history to investigate power and society from multiple perspectives. A critical objective is to demonstrate that constitutional history is relevant for all fields of history. By bringing together scholars of wide-ranging expertise in law, politics and history, we hope to have shown the reach and relevance of constitutional history, its centrality to understanding the governmental and political world of the United Kingdom and its influence on society.

The Shape of This *Cambridge History*

This two-volume *Cambridge History* is obviously the work of many minds and hands. Traditionally, constitutional histories were the work of a single author. However, in the present intellectual climate it is hard to imagine that any single scholar would be brave – or foolhardy – enough to attempt to bring historical, political, and legal perspectives to bear on a millennium of the governance of a particular polity. Some will, no doubt, also question the wisdom of recruiting more than forty scholars to participate in such a project. How even to begin to give some shape to such a kaleidoscope of human social life? Changing the metaphor, our solution to this problem has been to cut the cloth in various different ways and, as it were, to produce several different garments. Inevitably, because we had only rather undeveloped ideas about how each garment should look and gave the manufacturing scholars correspondingly vague instructions, the final result is a patchwork rather than piece of finely tailored *haute couture* – but all the more versatile and stimulating for that. These volumes are not meant, in any sense, to be comprehensive or 'authoritative' or the last word. The best way to describe the final result may be as a set of essays contributing to our understanding of the history of the UK constitution. For this reason, alone, it may be helpful to provide the reader with brief summaries of each chapter.

The Cambridge Constitutional History of the United Kingdom was originally conceived as a single volume. However, for technical reasons, the decision was made to distribute the various chapters between two separate volumes available both individually and as a set. In the original plan, the chapters now in Volume II were located between Parts I and II of what is now Volume I. This positioning was intended to suggest to the reader that the surrounding 'contextualising' chapters were, in our minds, as important as the periodised, chronological chapters in painting a rounded picture of the history of the constitution as a dynamic and evolving phenomenon. However, when it came to allocating chapters and parts between two volumes, the neatest, most practical solution seemed to be to transfer the periodised accounts into a volume of their own. At the same time, by allocating the 'contextualising' chapters to Volume I we hope to encourage readers to take them as seriously as the chapters in Volume II. Both volumes contain this Preface and list the contributors to both. In our minds, each of the two volumes is an integral component of a single project.

Volume I

The chapters in Part I of Volume I explore various aspects of and approaches to the constitution and constitutionalism. In Chapter 1 ('The Historical Constitution'), H. Kumarasingham explains the central place of the constitution in British history through three interrelated themes: that the constitution is as much a matter of culture and ideas as of documents and legislation; that its history underpins traditions of governance and understandings of power across society; and that its practices have long been matters of contestation. In Chapter 2 ('Law and the Constitution'), Peter Cane tells a story about the complex interplay, over a millennium, between law understood as both norm and artefact, and constitution understood both organically and synthetically. He argues that law has always played a significant role in the constitution and increasingly so since the mid-twentieth century. He also suggests a positive correlation between the invention of the written constitution and the constitutional role of law.

In Chapter 3 ('Political Constitutionalism'), Richard Bellamy sketches the genesis of three main versions of political constitutionalism based on parliamentary sovereignty: the mixed constitution, parliamentary government, and representative democracy. Today, he says, political constitutionalism is mainly identified with representative democracy. However, he argues that this version is currently challenged on one side by ideas of popular sovereignty and, on another, by the growing dominance of law in constitutional thinking; and that it is currently unclear whether it will be replaced by one of the other versions or a new form of political constitutionalism. Tony Prosser's argument in Chapter 4 ('The Economic Constitution') is that the economic focus of the UK constitution has always been on scrutiny of government financial activity rather than on regulation of the economy. He examines the role of various scrutineers, including Parliament, the courts, and the executive itself. Prosser also discusses the development of regulatory bodies that operate at arm's length from government and the impact of EU membership on the UK's 'economic constitution'.

In her two contributions, Chapters 5 ('Religion and the Constitution to 1688') and 6 ('Religion and the Constitution since the Glorious Revolution'), Pippa Catterall traces the history of relations between Church and State and between religion and the constitution. Although those relations have changed dramatically over the past millennium in response to factors such as the Reformation, the Glorious Revolution and the rise of secularism, phenomena such as the Global War on Terror witness to the continuing constitutional significance of religion. In Chapter 7 ('The Social Democratic Constitution'), K. D. Ewing traces the birth, life and death of social democratic structures of government, and the constitutional position of trade unions; and he examines tensions between liberal constitutional values of the nineteenth century and social democratic values of the twentieth century. The high-water mark of representation of workers' interests in government was the Social Contract of the 1970s. The chapter concludes with an assessment of the reasons for the decline and collapse of the social democratic constitution.

Peter Cane's main argument in Chapter 8 ('The Constitution of Rights') is that in historical terms, constitutional rights may be understood as claims (always political and sometimes legal) made by the governed on the governors; but, also, that the content and foundations of such claims are moulded by circumstances of time and place. As ideas change about the nature, make-up and functions of political communities, so do claims, in the name of rights, for inclusion within, and good governance of, the community. In Chapter 9 ('The People and the Constitution') Vernon Bogdanor starts with the claim that although democracy is sometimes defined as government by the people, in almost every democracy – including Britain – the role of the people is very limited. Nevertheless, he explains, there has been limited acceptance of the doctrine of the mandate, and a long debate on whether the referendum is or is not compatible with the British constitution. Further, there have been experiments with primary elections, recall of MPs, and e-petitions. However, in Bogdanor's opinion there is probably more scope for direct democracy at local level than nationally.

Part I of Volume I is rounded out by Jeffrey Goldsworthy's survey in Chapter 10 ('Constitutional Theory and Thought') of constitutional theory since the twelfth century. He shows how contending theories have attempted to reconcile the need for strong central authority to maintain order and justice with the desire to control that authority. He describes a gradual transition from theories of monarchical rule to theories of mixed government and, finally, theories of parliamentary democracy; and he explains how each theory understood the place and role of the monarch, the Church, the Houses of Parliament, statute and common law, 'the community', and 'the people'.

Part II of Volume I contains chapters that variously examine aspects of the historical development of constitutional offices and institutions. As Edward Cavanagh points out in Chapter 11 ('Monarchy'), monarchy is a medieval institution that has become subject to statutory and legal limitations. Between the thirteenth and nineteenth centuries, first in England and then across the United Kingdom, the most important of these limitations were imposed during periods of regency administration or uncertainty and/or crisis surrounding the succession. This history has unfolded in sometimes startling ways to leave us with the 'constitutional monarchy' that we have today. Cavanagh explains how this has happened and hints at how the crown might advance into a future of possibly uncertain constitutional politics. In Chapter 12 ('Legislatures') Michael Gordon identifies core functions of a legislature, considering how these various functions emerged and developed in the case of the UK Parliament. Gordon argues that while its functions, legislative authority, and democratic legitimacy have evolved, the Parliament at Westminster has provided a degree of continuity in the UK's political system. Yet, he continues, there has recently been momentous change: the UK Parliament has dispersed some of its power through devolution so that it is now the central legislature within a wider constellation. Although this new paradigm for legislative activity has become quickly embedded in the UK's constitutional architecture, wider uncertainties about the trajectory of devolution mean that the stability of the relationships between the UK's legislatures cannot be taken for granted.

Moving on to the executive, Janet McLean (in Chapter 13 'The Executive and the Administration') considers changing understandings, from the seventeenth century onwards, about the nature of executive power itself and the relationship between executive power and administration. She identifies the concept of 'office' as a central organising principle for pre-democratic administration, and discusses the relationship between sovereignty and office, the incomplete separation of those office-holders who make the law from those who execute it, and the messy distinction between high political office and subordinate office-holders. McLean then focuses on those subordinate officials and their relationship with the centre, and the changes wrought to these relationships with the advent of modern democracy. In Chapter 14 ('Judiciaries') Joshua Getzler suggests that judiciaries in England emerged from four interacting historical sources. At the foundation lay the authority of monarchs empowered, by virtue of regal office, to judge their subjects' rights, duties and status. The second source was royal delegation to dedicated judges sitting in permanent courts of common law, or to executive courts with a more political mandate. A third source was local and widely distributed decision-making by groups or associations or sub-units of government, contributing to the particular entity's self-direction. The fourth source was Parliament, which issued legislation, conducted trials, and reviewed and settled points of law from all other jurisdictions. The dialogue between royal, common-law, local, and parliamentary justice drove the constitutional development of the nation, as principles had to be devised to distribute the wielding of power in the various law-making and law-enforcing institutions. The constitutional role of the courts was often contested, particularly during times of political and social tension, from the medieval period down to the present day.

In Chapter 15 ('Coercive Institutions'), Brice Dickson reviews the development of the UK's armed forces and police services from a constitutional point of view. He charts how these coercive institutions began to be regulated, highlighting the consequences for the army of the civil wars of the seventeenth century and of the reforms introduced in the early twentieth century. Dickson outlines the concepts of martial law and military law, and discusses constitutional issues concerning the deployment of armed forces abroad. He also briefly outlines the history of policing, emphasising the principles promoted by Robert Peel, the perceived need for police officers to be politically independent, and the frequency with which public confidence in policing was easily shaken. Dickson sketches present-day police powers and the system for holding the police to account for their actions through the investigation of complaints, regular inspection and auditing, and the pursuit of litigation.

Luke Blaxill's claim in Chapter 16 ('Locality, Regionality, and Centrality') is that the evolution of local institutions, principles and precedents, laws and governance, form a major pillar of the evolution of the British constitution. Local governance bodies were frequently integral to the lived constitutional experience of British subjects. While the rise of the modern British state has generally been a story of centralisation and the corresponding disempowerment of local government, the role of Parliament – sitting between the centre and the localities – has always remained somewhat ambiguous. Blaxill traces the development of local government, its rise, brief Victorian apogee, and twentieth-century decline. He then explores the analytical concept of 'constitutional communities', reflecting the fact that the constitution could mean different things to different groups, even at times when all were, in theory, stakeholders in a single national constitution. Finally, Blaxill focuses on the relationship between Parliament and the localities, paying special attention to the Member of Parliament as a bridge between them, and how this role has changed and evolved.

Rounding off Part II, in Chapter 17 ('Political Parties') Robert Crowcroft turns our attention to political parties. He argues that parties have been a primary vehicle for constitutional contestation and innovation. As Edmund Burke grasped, parties are integral to the practical operation of the constitution and the parameters within which politics are carried out. Deep antagonisms could be fought to a resolution – and a legitimate one at that – through the mechanism of party conflict. Constitutional questions summoned parties into existence, tore them asunder, and proved a natural hunting ground for ambitious individuals. Crowcroft examines the highly interactive relationship between parties and the constitution; demonstrates the primacy of high-political manoeuvring in constitutional conflict; and ponders the impact of individual leaders on the constitution-party linkage. He concludes that party-political competition has strengthened Parliament as a national institution in ways that have contributed to the stability of British life.

The chapters in the final Part III of Volume I adopt historical perspectives on political concepts at the heart of constitutional history and constitutionalism. In Chapter 18 ('Conservatism'), Asanga Welikala offers a conservative approach to British constitutionalism. He argues that conservatism has provided the intellectually dominant conception of constitutional self-understanding in British constitutional history, both in terms of substantive ideology and the approach to constitutional change. He outlines a history of British conservative ideas about self, state, and society as they were shaped by the crucial debates of the European Enlightenment, and how those ideas formed the basis of a constitutional ideology that evolved through successive stages of constitutional development from absolutism to constitutional government and mass democracy. Welikala's central thesis is that British constitutional conservatism is defined more by its incrementalist theory of constitutional evolution than by its commitments to any particular set of institutions. In the view of Emily Jones (in Chapter 19, 'Liberalism'), the significance of liberalism in the constitutional history of the United Kingdom stretches deep into the past, extending not merely to the giants of the historic Liberal Party in the nineteenth century, but also to the Whig inheritance from seventeenth- and eighteenth-century constitutional disputes. Hence, while Jones concludes by referring to the modern Liberal Party – an alliance, from 1981, between historic Liberalism and the Social Democratic Party that fused formally in 1988 – she primarily considers the longer history of Liberalism and the British Constitution. In this 'historic' reading, Jones demonstrates the significance of Whig-Liberal ideas, people and histories to the construction of national and political identities that reached forwards far into the twentieth century, and which has had important consequences for current debates on sovereignty and the relationship between Britain, Northern Ireland, and Europe. In Chapter 20 ('Socialism'), Stephen Sedley seeks to situate the movement for a more equitable society in the political and juridical history of a capitalist democracy. He considers the tension between constitutionalism and revolution, focusing on the electoral capture of power by the Labour government of 1945–1951, and contrasting it with both the neglected Co-operative Movement and the case for workers' control.

In Chapter 21 ('Unionism') James Mitchell and Alan Convery neatly describe the UK as an evolved state that has become a devolved state; created by a series of bilateral arrangements, it has become a 'state of unions'. The authors argue that the rationale for each union has changed over time, reflecting changing views of how the UK should stay together as a multi-national state. Over the centuries, unionism has been characterised by flexibility, ambiguity, and contingency. According to Mitchell and Convery, the UK has been strongest when and where national identity and loyalty to the state have been taken for granted, unquestioned, uncontested and requiring no name. Unionism has reflected the challenges it has faced, often mimicking but sometimes offering a mirror image of nationalist and other challenges. Unionists have supported diverse means of maintaining the UK state of unions. Finally, and on the other side of the coin, in Chapter 22 ('Nationalism') Michael Keating argues that although the concept of nation has no constitutional standing in the United Kingdom, it has featured in constitutional debates for some three hundred years. While the dominant view of the UK is that it is based on the absolute sovereignty of the Westminster Parliament, the constitution also creates a union of nations joined in different ways. While nationalists in the peripheral nations argue that the fact of nationality points to statehood, or at least self-government, for their own territories, unionists argue that it is consistent with membership of a wider British union. In recent years, Keating argues, British nationalism and that of the smaller nations have become competitors, putting strains on the union. The UK's withdrawal from the European Union has increased centri-fugal tensions within the UK's own union and allowed nationalists in

Scotland, Wales and Northern Ireland to appropriate the language of union, applied to the EU, to justify secession.

Volume II

The title of Volume II ('The Changing Constitution') reflects our understanding of the constitution as a 'living tree'. The rings that witness its past form an integral part of its present state and future life. Our tree has its roots in post-Roman, Anglo-Saxon soil. In his account of 'The Kingdoms of Anglo-Saxon England (450–1066)' (in Chapter 1), Simon Keynes uses diverse documentary, literary and archaeological evidence to piece together the political history of England from around 450 to the Norman Conquest (and, in a brief epilogue, its after-life in the English imagination). Perhaps the strongest and clearest themes running through the more or less shadowy events of this 600-year period are, first, the complex relationship between religious and secular power; and, second, the pivotal achievements of Alfred the Great in laying the foundations of the larger polity that the Normans would first conquer by force and then claim as theirs by lawful inheritance.

In 'England after the Conquest' (Chapter 2) George Garnett echoes F. W. Maitland's aphorism that land law and constitutional law were inextricably linked in the period after 1066. Central to William's claim to the throne was the assertion that the whole of the kingdom had been bequeathed to him by Edward the Confessor, thus establishing continuity of rule and the dependence of all titles to land on the king's inheritance. This, the most important consequence of the Conquest, was foundational to the inquiry that produced the Domesday Book. In the first decades of the reign of Henry II, new legal procedures were made available in royal courts to enforce tenurial continuity and dependence. These remedies benefitted sub-tenants at the expense of tenants-in-chief, who could not sue their lord, the king, in his own courts. King John's exploitation of this situation created the conditions for the transformation, in Magna Carta, of the inherited law from a source of royal legitimacy to a constraint on royal power.

In Chapter 3 ('England in the Thirteenth Century) Paul Brand focuses on the monarchy and its finances, and on the development of the main institutions of government: the royal courts, the council and Parliament. The goal of Christine Carpenter and Andrew Spencer in Chapter 4 ('England in the Fourteenth Century') is to locate the history of governance and politics within a constitutional frame. The authors examine, in turn, political ideas, the central and local institutions of government and law, and the political society of nobles, gentry, towns and church. Then they offer an account of the major problems of fourteenth-century kingship and how they were addressed: organising and paying for war while continuing to deepen the reach of royal government, both for war and in response to subjects' demands, all this in a time of great demographic, economic and social change. Carpenter and Spencer show that this resulted in a major governmental and constitutional transformation. In David J. Seipp's telling in Chapter 5 ('England in the Fifteenth Century'), difficulties in governing England, ambiguities about power and authority, and a fundamental lack of consensus about what constituted rule and who had a legitimate right to exercise it, persisted throughout the fifteenth century. Lacking the ordinary indicia of legitimacy, weak English kings needed to cobble together support where they could find or buy it. Local lords often wielded more effective power than a distant king. In the view of lawyers, there was a need to enhance, not to restrain, royal authority. The difficulty was to find a way to check the power of those whom chief justice Fortescue called 'over-mighty subjects'. Only at the end of the century could Henry VII begin to restore royal authority. However, argues David Chan Smith (in Chapter 6, 'England in the Sixteenth Century'), Henry's dramatic usurpation in 1485 ushered in a period in which dynastic crises raised new constitutional questions, about legitimacy and the authority of the monarch, that were aggravated by religious strife following the Reformation. Added to this instability were new issues raised by the expansion of the central legal system and the weaknesses of royal finance. Smith suggests that while the Tudors arguably created a stronger monarchy, it was also one whose powers were increasingly questioned.

Glenn Burgess continues the theme in Chapter 7 ('The English Constitution in the Seventeenth Century: Crises of Inadequacy'). He observes that England, culturally divided (especially by religion) and part of an unstable multiple monarchy, saw a bloody civil war, popular insurrection, and fear. These exposed the weakness of a constitution whose ambiguities and silences made it inadequate to restrain misgovernment and maintain peace. Constitutional weakness also spurred imaginative attempts – sometimes democratic or republican – to repair or replace the flawed constitution. From this process, argues Burgess, there emerged both a stronger sense of what a constitution was and a series of constitutional adjustments that made the nation more securely Protestant. Radical change was masked by the myth that all this was achieved by making only minimal alterations to the ancient constitution and preserving its long continuity.

The next three chapters provide some 'spatial' context for the story of England told so far. In Chapter 8 ('A European Perspective') Tamar Herzog questions ideas of the exceptionalism of English constitutionalism by placing it in conversation with early developments in other parts of Europe. Herzog interrogates three aspects: the centrality of common law in most narratives of English legal history, its identification as an immemorial customary law, and the history of the English parliament. She demonstrates that the refashioning of local norms as customary, the insistence that they included a constitutional pact that was immemorial, and the wish to use both to place checks on kings as well as on the growing powers of parliament, were common throughout late-medieval and early-modern Europe.

Robin Chapman Stacey's main aim in Chapter 9 ('Wales before Annexation') is to complicate the seeming inevitability of the constitutional order referred to in the chapter's title. Instead of focusing on the usual constitutional hallmarks of the period, the Statute of Wales of 1284 and the Act of Union of 1536 (revised in 1543), Stacey challenges the teleology of the traditional narrative by examining not only what did happen but also what might have happened, both within native Wales and in its relationships with England and the March. Among other issues, she considers the complex nature of alliances and governance in the period leading up to 1284, in which ethnicity was not always the determining factor; the possibility that political fragmentation might have been able to survive as a long-term form of 'nationhood', both internally within Wales and externally with respect to England; and the increasing hybridity of identities and allegiances amongst inhabitants of Wales even before the Act of Union. In a similar vein, in Chapter 10 ('The Scottish Constitution before 1707') Laura A. M. Stewart argues that early modern Scotland, like many of its neighbours, witnessed intense debate over its constitutional forms and function. At the heart of these debates were contested views on the nature of royal power and what limits, if any, could legitimately be placed upon it. According to Stewart, what has been termed Scotland's 'aristocratic-conciliarist' constitution, to which noble counsel-giving was integral, arguably reached its apogee in the 1638 National Covenant. The subsequent conquest of Scotland by an English army, and the aggressive reassertion of an absolutist ideology after the Restoration of the British monarchy, put such ideas under enormous strain.

R. A. Melikan's Chapter 11 ('The Eighteenth-Century Constitution: Settlement and Resettlement') moves the story on into the eighteenth century. She argues that the Act of Settlement 1701 – which changed the royal succession, reinforced the other branches of government, and entrenched both the

Anglican Church and individual liberties – was, perhaps, the most significant piece of constitutional legislation enacted in the eighteenth century. Some of its objectives were not achieved, however, as the Privy Council gave way to the cabinet, and Parliament was not insulated from royal or ministerial influence. The support offered to the Anglican Church and to individual liberties, moreover, was so broadly phrased that, in Melikan's view, its effectiveness is difficult to judge. Nevertheless, the Act of Settlement responded to a looming threat by embracing necessary change while fortifying all that remained in an organic and gradualist fashion. Like England, as Thomas Bartlett points out in Chapter 12 ('The Constitutional and Parliamentary History of Ireland till the Union'), Ireland lacked a written constitution in the centuries before 1800. It had a parliament consisting of a House of Commons and a House of Lords, and there were law courts modelled on those in England. However, what is striking is the contrast in constitutional development between the two countries. This divergence may be explained by Poynings' Law which, for over four hundred years, governed the summoning, role and function of the Irish parliament. Bartlett explores the evolution of parliament in Ireland from an occasional event in the medieval and early modern periods to a key institution in the eighteenth century. He examines the reasons why that parliament voted itself out of existence in 1800.

Ewen A. Cameron's Chapter 13 ('The United Kingdom in the Nineteenth Century') covers the years from 1800 to 1921, the period of the maximum extent of the UK resulting from the unions with Wales, Scotland and Ireland. Cameron's main theme is the interplay between constitutional and political issues in the nations of the United Kingdom. He examines the relationship between the churches and the state; the extension of the franchise; local government; and the imperial dimension of constitutional debates. Cameron explores both elite and popular understandings of the constitution, and various attempts to widen the sections of society that were recognised as having constitutional rights. In doing so, he emphasises the ways in which the constitution was at the heart of politics in the long nineteenth century.

Andrew Blick takes the Parliament Act 1911 as the starting point of his discussion, in Chapter 14, of 'The United Kingdom in the Twentieth Century'. Blick considers themes including House of Lords reform; referendums; devolution; the impact of war; European integration; and the possibility of movement towards a 'written' constitution – all within the context of the ascendancy of the concept of democracy and perceptions of threats to it. He argues that the traditional interpretation of the UK constitution, as having a capacity for piecemeal change that has enabled it to avoid more fundamental breaks in continuity, is unhelpful because the dichotomy between gradual and fundamental alteration fails to represent the subtle nature of constitutional change in the UK. Vernon Bogdanor's perspective on constitutional change, in Chapter 15 ('The Twenty-First Century Constitution'), is somewhat different from Blick's. He argues that the twenty-first century constitution, which he considers to have been inaugurated in 1997, would have been unrecognisable in the middle of the twentieth century. The new constitution's leitmotiv, says Bogdanor, is diffusion of power both territorially, through devolution, and centrally, as a result of the Human Rights Act, which has emphasised the separation of powers between the executive and legislature, and the judiciary. Diffusion of power, he argues, has been assisted by political developments, particularly the fragmentation of the party system, itself largely a product of the introduction of proportional representation for elections to subordinate bodies. In Bogdanor's opinion, the massive constitutional changes of the twenty-first century raise the issue of whether Britain can long remain one of just three democracies that lack a codified constitution.

Like Chapters 8–10, the last four chapters of Volume II add important context to those that have preceded. In Chapter 16 ('Wales since the Annexation') Matthew Cragoe traces the constitutional history of Wales from conquered medieval province to its contemporary state of – somewhat ambivalent – nationhood. He argues that the small size of Wales – it has only some 6 per cent of seats at Westminster – has ensured that its constitutional identity has been contingent on the activities of other partners within the shifting British state. England has naturally been a dominant influence but, in the nineteenth century, Ireland became a touchstone for those seeking constitutional reform in Wales, whilst in the twentieth, Scotland played this role. In constitutional terms, therefore, 'Wales' is a very 'British' creation. For Stephen Tierney in Chapter 17 ('Scotland in the Union') the constitutional union between England and Scotland is central to our understanding of the nature of the British state today. Tierney argues that the union of crowns in 1603 and of parliaments in 1707 left a legacy of Scottish national distinctiveness that began to play out dramatically only with the rise of Scottish nationalism in the 1960s. Tierney addresses how the creation of the parliamentary union produced a tradition of constitutional thinking that challenged the orthodox story of the British constitution and how, after 300 years, the Union continues to face an existential threat in the form of secessionist Scottish nationalism.

In Chapter 18 ('Ireland in the Union') Donal K. Coffey discusses both the development of constitutional rule within Ireland and the influence of Irish constitutionalism on the United Kingdom's constitution. The theoretically and technically complex constitutional arrangements developed to ensure Ireland's place within the Union created room for contestation over the franchise, land, Home Rule, independence, and other matters. The question of whether Britain was willing, or indeed able, to extend constitutionalism to Ireland was the subject of much debate at the time. Coffey ends with a brief consideration of the diverging constitutional histories of the Irish Free State, latterly Ireland, and Northern Ireland in the overall context of British and imperial legal history.

Empire is the subject of the last two chapters in Volume II. According to Coel Kirkby in Chapter 19 ('The Making of Empire'), the British constitution has always been an imperial constitution. The institutional structure and ideological discourse of the British constitution always extended beyond the pale of England and the English people. The British constituted themselves and their empire through institutions of government sustained by a single system of law; and they and their subjects constantly argued over the nature of their common constitution: its past, present and future. This British constitutional discourse connected metropole to colony in a complicated global network of ideological debate that shaped the institutional evolution of England's expansion into the British empire. In similar vein, in Chapter 20 ('Constitution and Empire') H. Kumarasingham suggests that the constitutional history of Britain would be drastically diminished in importance if not for empire. Concentrating on the period from the mid-nineteenth century until the last days of colonial rule in the twentieth century, he focuses on three key matters: first, the resonance of empire in British constitutional thinking as well as the contradictions and limitations of the late imperial constitutional project; second, the divergent ways in which Britain sought to govern its vast empire, especially the marked difference between the minority of increasingly autonomous settler-dominated states and the majority whose indigenous populations were deemed unable to govern themselves; and third, in the last stage of imperial rule when self-government was demanded, how British constitutional traditions, concepts and institutions fared in the colonial context and what this meant for those living under the British Empire.

As editors, we are delighted to be able to present to the reader a collection of essays of such depth, breadth and rigour. We are extremely grateful to and proud of all our contributors and trust that they, and other readers, will find the volume valuable and stimulating, and that some will be encouraged to join what we hope will be a twenty-first century renaissance of constitutional history in the UK and beyond.

Preface

Although each author is responsible for his or her own contribution, as editors we both read and commented on all the chapters and (in rare cases, participated more actively in the process of composition). The overall shape and contents of the volume are the responsibility of the editors. We readily admit that discharging this responsibility presented us with significant challenges of both form and substance. We are very pleased that many of our contributors were able to meet in Edinburgh in October 2018 and in Cambridge in March 2019 and, on those occasions, to urge us to broaden the coverage of the volume in various beneficial directions. Nevertheless, we have (no doubt) made editorial decisions with which some readers will disagree. Our motto throughout has been to avoid allowing the best to be the enemy of the good. F. W. Maitland once warned that 'Life I know is short, and law is long, very long, and we cannot study everything at once'.[3] This is even more the case with constitutional history; and while we have endeavoured to cover a great deal in two volumes, we make no claim to be comprehensive in our coverage.

Our thanks are due to Cambridge University Press and the Cambridge Centre for Public Law for supporting the two workshops financially. The project owes its birth to the enthusiasm and vision of Finola O'Sullivan. We owe her a great debt. We are also very grateful for the assistance of Marianne Nield and the other members of the production team at Cambridge University Press. Special thanks are owed to Fiona Cole for her meticulous, friendly and excellent copy editing. Peter Cane thanks Christ's College, Cambridge for providing a congenial and stimulating environment for undertaking this project. H. Kumarasingham thanks Gary Gerstle, Peter Mandler and Paul Seaward for their advice regarding the volume and its contents; and also his colleagues at the University of Edinburgh for their support.

---

[3] F. W. Maitland, *The Constitutional History of England*, H. A. L. Fisher, ed. (Cambridge: Cambridge University Press, 2007 [1908]), 539.

PART I

★

PERSPECTIVES

I

The Historical Constitution*

H. KUMARASINGHAM

Introduction

All constitutions rely on history. Without constitutional history the political affairs of the United Kingdom would be unintelligible. As J. R. Seeley aphorised in his inaugural lecture as Regius Professor of Modern History at Cambridge in 1885: 'History without Political Science has no fruit; Political Science without History has no root.'[1] For such reasons the United Kingdom's constitutional history is as much the concern of the politician as it is of the historian or lawyer. Constitutional history exists to speak precedent unto power.

The United Kingdom, for much of its history, has made an art, or perhaps a muddle, of the ambiguity, conjecture and utility its constitutional system affords. British history for generations was taught and studied through its constitution. Its centrality to the discipline and its influence on identity and ideas is real and extensive. A symbiotic relationship exists between history and the constitution.

The British constitution was seen as intrinsic to the status and rights of not only the state, but also of those who lived in it. In 1803 Edward Christian, the first Downing Professor of the Laws of England at Cambridge, wrote of the 'English' constitution, that other than 'some slight and perhaps inevitable imperfections' – a sentiment that resonated throughout British history –

---

* I would like to thank Ewen Cameron, James Mitchell, Laura Stewart and Asanga Welikala for their help with certain queries of mine. I am very grateful to Donal Lowry and Stuart Ward for the astute and detailed comments they generously provided on earlier drafts. Peter Cane proved an excellent and constructive person to test the ideas in this chapter and without doubt his questions and advice helped improve it.
[1] J. R. Seeley, *Introduction to Political Science: Two Series of Lectures* (London: Macmillan, 1896), p. 4.

that to be free, is to be born and to live under the English constitution.[2]

Christian's words bring a feel of the vanity and prejudice inspired by the constitution and its history. This is apparent when considering how such history is used to inform and influence power, law and society. The writing, studying and teaching of constitutional history means more than covering a set of official texts and edicts. It also compels a study of the forces and passions in society as well as the manifestation of England's and then Britain's ideals and later the United Kingdom's through its institutions and political customs. Constitutional history is therefore not narrowly confined to debates in ivory towers among historians and lawyers, but is of wider significance. The constitution can more usefully be understood through the wider horizon of the state and its machinations. This extension of the constitution's purview, while necessary, requires a command and appreciation of numerous sources and spheres of intellectual and empirical material.

This chapter on the historical constitution seeks to interrogate these ideas and show the extensive nature and form that constitutional history has taken. The chapter aims to explore the multiple facets and expanse of constitutional history by focusing on three interrelated themes. First, the history of the constitution will be covered to show that rather than seeing constitutional history purely as one of documents, institutions and events it is valuable to explore how constitutional history is indelibly one of culture and ideas that have had a powerful hold over British history, law and politics. Second, constitutional history is central to an understanding of how the constitution gave or withheld power and also of the people that sought its refuge or reform with varied results. Finally, the theme of law and utility will be explored to see the synergy of law, politics and constitutional expedience, which creates ongoing tension between the exercise of power and will on the one hand, and compliance with norms and standards on the other. Studying the constitution and its history is studying this interactive tension. Collectively these three sets of connected themes are put forward to show the breadth, variety and consequence of constitutional history and its importance for greater historical inquiry. History is needed to penetrate the

---

[2] Christian also approvingly quoted Cicero to further emphasise his claim: 'Hanc retinete, quaeso, Quirites, quam vobis tanquam hereditatem, majores vestry reliquerunt'. [Preserve, I beseech ye, O Romans, this liberty, which your ancestors have left ye as an inheritance]. Sir Ivor Jennings, 'Magna Carta and Constitutionalism in the Commonwealth' in H. Kumarasingham (ed.), *Constitution-Maker: Selected Writings of Sir Ivor Jennings* (Cambridge: Cambridge University Press, 2015), pp. 284–285.

constitutional fog that falls on governance, politics and law. F. W. Maitland explained that whereas in some countries, questions of constitutional rules and duties would be ones of constitutional law, in England they 'would be questions of convenience' since all that can be called 'constitutional' had 'no special sanctity' in law.[3] This characteristic presents the United Kingdom's constitution instead as a necessary mixture of history, law and politics. It is therefore more than a convenience to study constitutional history.

Culture and Ideas

The constitutional history of the United Kingdom would be meaningless without acknowledgment of the powerful role culture plays in its image and influence. It is a characteristic of many British constitutional histories written before the twenty-first century to have legislative, legal and institutional details prefaced with a national and patriotic dimension of the constitution, which often veered into the uniqueness and superiority of the English and their constitution. In 1966 Keith Thomas decried English historical writing as warped by the Victorian era's pride in British ascendency and consequent faith in the superior verity of its institutions. This legacy and climate saw English constitutional history as a flag-waving, pedagogic tool since many historians in the United Kingdom, well into the twentieth century, believed and taught that 'the constitution was England's greatest contribution to the world'.[4] The Irish-Australian constitutional historian William Edward Hearn, for example, in his popular scholarly late nineteenth-century book praised by figures like A. V. Dicey, could on one hand, describe and list in great breadth many constitutional and legal precedents with detailed analysis on issues like ecclesiastical representation or taxation powers and, at the same time, wax lyrical about the inherent excellence of the British constitution and its history. The constitution, Hearn swooned, was like 'the stateliest oak that now graces the green fields of England', a 'wondrous Constitution, so old, yet stretching forward (if Heaven pleases) to such indefinite futurity' tracing back to King Ine of Wessex's seventh-century Code of Laws. Hearn, like other constitutional writers throughout British history sought to show the idea and continuous lineage of the constitution as essential to British culture.

---

[3] F. W. Maitland, *The Constitutional History of England*, H. A. L. Fisher (ed.) (Cambridge: Cambridge University Press, [1908] 2007), pp. 535–537.
[4] Keith Thomas, 'The Tools and the Job', *Times Literary Supplement*, 7 Apr. 1966, pp. 275–276.

Such histories promoted a powerful message. To look back was to see how the constitution should be. Change was not the object, but past work on constitutional reform by political leaders was viewed as a matter of

> restoration, not of change. They desired to remove the unsightly excrescences of our Constitution, the gilding and the plaster with which profane and inartistic hands had deformed the grand old temple of liberty that lay sullied but uninjured beneath. Not a stone of the original structure did they wish to move; not a fragment of the time-honoured edifice that they did not regard with affectionate veneration and pious solicitude.[5]

Constitutions became, Linda Colley argues, a global political and cultural technology in the eighteenth century and gained iconic importance as a signifier of national status and civilisational affectations. For Britain this constitutional icon was the Magna Carta: a 'reviving cult around this liberty text (as some imagined it to be) was less a celebration of ancient constitutionalism' than a recognition of the growing worldwide symbolism of a constitution as a projection of history and nationalism.[6] Edmund Burke expressed this belief in 1775 when he spoke of the British constitution as the instrument that enabled the country's triumphs of liberal and enlightened good by forging 'the spirit and the power which conducted us to this greatness'.[7] These accounts were highly effective in promoting, for contemporary consumption, a culture of British constitutional hegemony and the rite of reading retrospective merit into the constitutional past. A certain amazement with the constitution was not restricted to the English. As Isaiah Berlin observed, for political thinkers like Joseph de Maistre and Montesquieu the British Constitution was a 'marvel': 'The very absurdities and conflicts of British laws and customs are evidence of divine power guiding the faltering hands of men. For there can be no doubt that the British constitution would have collapsed long ago had it been of merely human origin.' Berlin concludes that 'this is an argument in a circle with a vengeance'.[8]

---

[5] William Edward Hearn, *Government of England: Its Structure and Development*, 2nd ed. (Melbourne: George Robertson, 1886), pp. 4–5.
[6] Linda Colley, *The Gun, the Ship & the Pen: Warfare, Constitutions and the Making of the Modern World* (London: Profile Books, 2021), pp. 96–101.
[7] Richard Bourke, *Empire and Revolution: The Political Life of Edmund Burke* (Oxford: Princeton University Press, 2015), p. 8.
[8] Isaiah Berlin, *The Crooked Timber of Humanity: Chapters in the History of Ideas*, Henry Hardy (ed.), 2nd ed. (London: Pimlico, 2013), p. 168.

Not all saw a celestial constitution of perplexity and wonder. Humans were very much at the fore. The Edinburgh historian and philosopher David Hume, who would write his own multi-volume constitutional history of Britain, opined in 1741 that the best way to think of the constitution and system of government was to recognise that 'every man ought to be supposed a knave' acting in private self-interest.[9] It was in the interests of Britain to present its constitutional history as laudable and instructive of its power. Beyond England, Scottish unionist historians like William Robertson in his *History of Scotland* (1759) described the 1707 union of England and Scotland as one of equals, which made neither 'feudatory to the other'; if that were not the case, no 'treaty of union' could have been concluded. An alternate reading of the union's constitutional importance by the Scots would render their interests irrelevant and exposed accordingly.[10] Welsh affairs in contrast were to be considered England's from the time of the annexation of the territory by Edward I. From 1747, it was ruled that any mention of England in an Act of Parliament was synonymous with Wales. The following century would see the Welsh Courts of Great Sessions abolished and the Principality's laws placed under English jurisdiction.[11] Westminster was there to subsume the private and corporate interests of all parts of the union. In practice, naturally, this was, and is, disputed. The politics of autonomy have long been a feature of constitutional debates, especially at times of crisis such as over the issue of 'Home Rule' for Ireland. In the summer of 1913, Ireland seemed on the verge of war with armed militias like the Ulster Volunteer Force and Irish Citizen Army ready to attack the other in order to defend their competing interests in what Ireland should be. Figures like George V, fearing that conflict could spread to the British mainland, appealed to political leaders for a constitutional settlement, building on earlier ideas on 'devolution' by the Earl of Dunraven, a sympathetic Anglo-Irish landlord, to provide autonomy in order to placate the various interests within the union. Beyond a parliament and executive for 'Southern Ireland' and a parliament and executive for 'Ulster', ideas circulated during this tense period that anticipated devolution reforms in the late 1990s by the Blair government, for new parliaments in Scotland, Wales and even for England itself. Westminster

---

[9] David Hume, 'Of the Independency of Parliament' in Knud Haakonssen (ed.), *Hume: Political Essays* (Cambridge: Cambridge University Press, 1994), p. 24.
[10] Colin Kidd, *Union and Unionism: Political Thought in Scotland, 1500–2000* (Cambridge: Cambridge University Press, 2008), pp. 96–97.
[11] William R. Anson, *The Law and Custom of the Constitution, Part II: The Crown*, 2nd ed. (London: Stevens & Sons, 1896), pp. 217–218.

would remain the paramount legislature. Austen Chamberlain wrote in November 1913 of these plans, 'Four or five Parliaments ... may be a nuisance but can hardly be a serious danger to Westminster sovereignty'.[12] Whether Chamberlain was right or wrong, the ability and appeal of the British constitution to house those beyond England, whether by conquest or convention, was a crucial feature.

The constitution was also undeniably a powerful emblem beyond the British Isles, especially when imperial Britain was the world's foremost power. It found admirers in unlikely places. Simon Bolívar, El Liberator of the Spanish American Empire, advised the delegates and constitutional drafters of the new Venezuelan state: 'Representatives, I suggest that you study the British constitution, which is the one that seems destined to bring the greatest good to the peoples who adopt it.' As Colley explains, Bolívar was not attempting to copy the British constitution, but saw the selective utility of its elements, during the tumultuous creation of Latin America, to balance executive power with societal consent. Britain's 'popular constitution' was one despite being a monarchy, which Bolívar believed 'recognizes popular sovereignty, the division and balance of powers, civil liberty, freedom of conscience, freedom of the press, and all that is sublime in politics'.[13]

As Britain's empire and might expanded so did the culture of constitutional hagiography. A certain disquiet occasionally surfaced. The poet, Robert Burns, could on one side, declare 'the British Constitution, as settled at the [1688] Revolution, to be the most glorious Constitution on earth, or that perhaps the wit of man can frame'. Yet at the same time, Burns, who sympathised with the American and French revolutionaries, could complain that Britain had 'a good deal deviated from the original principles of that Constitution', especially as 'an alarming System of Corruption has pervaded the connection between the Executive Power and the House of Commons'.[14] Prejudice against foreign constitutions was a strong trait of Britons; and no more so than in the case of the French. Sir Henry Maine believed, perhaps conservatively, that 'detestation for the [French] Revolution did not cease to influence politics till 1830'.[15] Burke famously attacked the ideals and actions of

---

[12] Harold Nicolson, *King George the Fifth: His Life and Reign* (London: Constable & Co Ltd, 1952), pp. 218–229.
[13] Colley, *The Gun, the Ship & the Pen*, p. 233.
[14] Philip Butcher, 'Robert Burns and the Democratic Spirit', *Phylon*, vol. 10, no. 3, 1949, p. 267.
[15] Henry Sumner Maine, *Popular Government: Four Essays*, new ed. (London: John Murray, 1890), pp. 12–13.

the French Revolution as dangerous and ill-conceived. He implored the need to preserve 'the firm ground of the British constitution' rather than attempt 'to follow in their desperate flights the aëronauts of France' in their dangerous constitutional innovations.[16] In her stinging 1790 pamphlet *A Vindication of the Rights of Men*, Mary Wollstonecraft publicly disagreed with the reverential cult surrounding the constitution that Burke asserted. The constitution of the state was not one of 'religion and piety'. Instead, to Wollstonecraft, it was one that worshipped property, the rich, and men using the false constitutional deities of Crown, Parliament and Church. She refused 'to reverence the rust of antiquity' that the constitution and English history conjured for Burke with its fatal propensity to

> term unnatural customs, which ignorance and mistaken self-interest have consolidated, the sage fruit of experience: nay, that, if we do discover some errors, our feelings should lead us to excuse, with blind love, or unprincipled filial affection, the venerable vestiges of ancient days. These are gothic notions of beauty – the ivy is beautiful, but, when it insidiously destroys the trunk from which it receives support, who would not grub it up?[17]

In his 1912 history of English government, A. Lawrence Lowell wrote from Harvard that England had a 'peculiar veneration for custom' that meant constitutional 'tinkering' was the preferred method of constitutional change rather than radical reform.[18] Such accounts, however, hide Britain's constitutional furnace, belching out actions and policies that not only challenged the status quo, but often took the state into directions and actions that had hitherto seemed implausible and contradictory judged by historical practice. The so called 'Glorious' Revolution of 1688, celebrated as a sensible corrective to monarchical absolutism, was, in reality, more a spectacular fix utilised by politicians, lawyers and historians alike. The expulsion of a legitimate sovereign, James II, because of his open Catholicism and his replacement by a Protestant pair in his daughter and Dutch son-in-law, Mary and William, risked full-scale civil war, the violation of legal norms and the collapse of institutions and offices of state. Indeed, the seventeenth century saw the execution of James's father, Charles I, a republic and military dictatorship

---

[16] Iain Hampsher Monk (ed.), *Burke: Revolutionary Writings* (Cambridge: Cambridge University Press, 2014), p. 249.
[17] Sylvana Tomaselli, *Mary Wollstonecraft: A Vindication of the Rights of Men and a Vindication of the Rights of Woman and Hints* (Cambridge: Cambridge University Press, 1995), p. 8.
[18] A. Lawrence Lowell, *The Government of England*, vol. 1 (New York: Macmillan, 1912), p. 14.

under Oliver Cromwell, civil wars, extensive and armed religious turmoil, fundamental disagreements over principles of government, major revolts in Ireland and Scotland and foreign invasion. All of this clearly undermined the constitutional bedrocks of the state, but also posed challenges to scholarly explanation of the traditional historical continuum of the constitution. As J. G. A. Pocock argues, it suited England to see 1688 as a bloodless revolution achieved under the 'fabric of an ancient constitution' instead of the reality of destructive havoc, divided allegiances, weaponised positions, contested dogma and transactional replacement of kings.[19]

The narrative encouraged the belief that the constitution and its history were supported by heaven's command and the people's will. When the constitution was attacked, the forces of God and nature would correct any extremes. Even the legend, that James II had petulantly tossed the Great Seal ('emblem of sovereign sway' as a later Lord Chancellor, John Campbell, described it) into the Thames just prior to his flight to France to impede any moves against him, was further mythologised to explain the indestructible constitution and its symbols. 'Heaven' intervened, the Lord Chancellor wrote, so that the seal was netted by a fisherman who 'restored it to the Government' and thus ensured the divine continuity of the constitution, which did 'not depend on the frailty of man'.[20] All of this was sustained by elastic constitutional history. William of Orange summoned 'Convention' parliaments in England and Scotland which, though dismayed by James II, had various interpretations of the dramatic events and what to do about them. The Tory belief in hereditary monarchical succession was tested, as were hopes among their number that James II could recant, reform and return. When this did not happen, it was read conveniently as abdication of the throne. The Whigs took a different view, soon after notably theorised by John Locke in his *Two Treatises of Government* (1690) in terms of the 'contract' argument, that James II had reneged in his responsibilities to the people and violated the rights and fundamental laws having 'abdicated the government' and abandoned the kingdom. As a result, for the Whigs, the throne was vacant; and this legitimised the dramatic succession of Mary and William. While not a condition of the enthronement, the royal couple accepted the Declaration of Rights (the 'Claim of Right' in Scotland), which would

---

[19] J. G. A. Pocock, *The Discovery of Islands: Essays in British History* (Cambridge: Cambridge University Press, 2005), pp. 120–121.
[20] See Hilary Jenkinson, 'What Happened to the Great Seal of James II?', *The Antiquaries Journal*, vol. xxiii, nos. 1–2, 1943, pp. 1–13.

become the 1689 Bill of Rights. The language of the law was purposely ambiguous to overcome party and personal rancour. It did, nonetheless, set out to prevent royal abuse of legal proceedings, taxation and direction of the armed forces. It also committed to frequent and free elections and the right of petition; but it also constitutionalised a sectarian principle of barring Roman Catholics from many offices of state including, most obviously, the throne. Yet, it is misleading to read the events of 1688–1689 as establishing a constitutional compact of subdued monarchy and enhanced parliaments of the people. Most of the participants were interested just as much, if not more, in the immediate protection of landed property that underwrote their constitutional privileges as in the long-term constitutional legacy the 'revolution' provided or the parliamentary rights that emerged.[21]

Constitution worship was an attractive idea and style of history despite its obvious shortcomings. Sir Ivor Jennings adduced 'very little in the theory of "the wisdom of our ancestors"'. He believed, instead, that a pragmatic theory operated in British constitutional history which, in essence, showed 'that slow evolution wraps our institutions in the fabric of society'.[22] Yet even the idea of evolutionary pragmatism is found wanting in the quest to conceptualise the state and its history. Historians, especially looked to German constitutional 'science' to help form British constitutional history. From the eighteenth-century German academics developed the term *Staatswissenschaft*, which implied a science of the state that used economic, political, legal, social and historical factors to study, and prepare for, government and statecraft. In the early nineteenth century, the influential German historian, Leopold von Ranke, famously stated that facts were paramount to an historian. Ranke judged that the duty of the historian was to avoid 'moralising' and rather 'simply to show how it really was (*wie es eigentlich gewesen*)'. As E. H. Carr reflected well over a century later 'this not very profound aphorism had an astonishing success'.[23] Constitutional history in the British tradition tried to follow the German example and incorporate elements of the science of the state and produce a factual record. H. A. L. Fisher stated in his biography of his brother-in-law, the legal historian F. W. Maitland, that two books greatly affected the early 'intellectual virility' of the famed Cambridge constitutional historian. One of those works was

---

[21] Mark Kishlansky, *Monarchy Transformed: Britain 1603–1714* (London: Penguin, 1997).
[22] H. Kumarasingham, 'Sir Ivor Jennings' "The Conversion of History into Law"', *American Journal of Legal History*, vol. 56, no. 1, March 2016, pp. 126–127.
[23] E. H. Carr, *What Is History?* (London: Penguin, 1990), pp. 8–9.

Friedrich Carl von Savigny's multi-volume *Geschichte des Römischen Rechts im Mittelalter* (1815–1831). Maitland found the German jurist's history of Roman law impressive for its framework of historical jurisprudence and legal reasoning of medieval and 'Teutonic civilization', and even started a translation into English. The other book we are told was 'found in a London club'.[24] It was William Stubbs' three volume *Constitutional History of England* (1875–1878). Stubbs, a nineteenth-century historian and bishop, also looked to German historical methods and called his famous constitutional texts both a 'treasury of reference' and a 'manual for teachers and scholars' so that the British could become well versed in the machinery of state of their own land and not just ancient Athens and Rome.[25] Constitutional history in this rendering became instructional. Stubbs was admired by a successor in the Regius Chair of Modern History at Oxford as being a 'scientific historian' whom he directly compared to Darwin in that his *Constitutional History* 'textbook' was 'one of the finest examples of the process of evolution ever worked out'.[26] It is no great stretch to find an almost biological exclusivity of the constitution and nation in these once celebrated styles of history as being the subjective property of 'virtuous' Englishmen to the exclusion of others on account of gender, race and class.[27]

In 1901, the scholar-politician, James Bryce, attempted to classify political systems, including Britain's, in order to identify their constitutional characteristics. Rejecting 'written' and 'unwritten' as categories, he saw the constitutions of older states, such as Britain with its common-law traditions and consequent 'elasticity', as being of the 'flexible' type that can be bent and altered in form while retaining [its] main features', as opposed to the 'rigid' type predominantly found in newer states. Yet Bryce, like many, struggled to differentiate between laws that are constitutional and those that are not. The Scottish Universities Act of 1852 would not be considered a constitutional

---

[24] H. A. L. Fisher, *Frederick William Maitland, Downing Professor of the Laws of England: A Biographical Sketch* (Cambridge: Cambridge University Press, 1910), pp. 48–50.

[25] William Stubbs, *Select Charters and Other Illustrations of English Constitutional History: From the Earliest Times to the Reign of Edward the First*, 8th ed. (Oxford: Clarendon Press, 1895), pp. v–vi.

[26] This was Fredrick York Powell. James Campbell, 'Stubbs, Maitland and Constitutional History' in B. Stuchkey and P. Wende (eds.), *British and German Historiography, 1750–1950: Traditions, Perceptions and Transfers* (Oxford: Oxford University Press, 2000), p. 103.

[27] Catherine Hall, Keith McClelland and Jane Rendall, *Defining the Victorian Nation: Class, Race, Gender and the Reform Act of 1867* (Cambridge: Cambridge University Press, 2000), pp. 25–28.

statute and yet it modified the constitutionally critical Act of Union; however, there was technically no difference between the status of these statutes.[28]

The constitution stretched far in its historical and legal reach. Constitutional theories and ideas are useless without context and culture. Linked to this is the attention constitutional history gives to politics and behaviour. Legal and political theorists like Burke, Locke and Montesquieu saw this and all considered that laws should be made to underscore the civilisation of the state. William Blackstone even wrote, in the 1769 edition of his famous *Commentaries of the Laws of England*, that individuals were legally 'bound to conform their general behaviour to the rules of propriety, good neighbourhood, and good manners, and to be decent, industrious and, inoffensive in their respective stations'.[29] Yet there were those who believed that scandalous behaviour at the highest 'stations' littered British history and corrupted the state. The republican historian Catherine Macaulay in her multi-volume *History of England*, which appeared from 1763, critiqued the personal 'imperfections and vices' of the British establishment, especially royalty, and the calamity their peccadillos, lovers and favourites inflicted on the constitution. Such analysis had an underlying theme of reform to remedy the constitutional and societal rot in favour of normal citizens. The radical libertine, John Wilkes, popularised Macaulay's intellectual points on the constitution to a wider spectrum of society by peddling vivid sexual innuendos and xenophobic abuse about figures such as the Scottish nobleman, John Stuart, 3rd Earl of Bute, who was personally chosen by George III, whom he had closely tutored as a young man, to be prime minister in 1762. Wilkes graphically spread lurid and nationalistic rumours that Bute was having an affair with the King's mother and insinuated a Stuart Scottish plot to rule England. These smears were used to showcase that scandal and corruption lay at the heart of the constitution and were, in Bute's case, part of Wilkes' attempt to question the rights of the King to select a prime minister that did not enjoy support of parliament, the readers of his newspaper the *North Briton*, or from crowds of 'middling and inferior sorts of people' whom he stoked on the streets of London.[30] Accepted conduct and societal norms were powerful themes in British constitutional history designed to distinguish those who deserved power and those who did not.

[28] James Bryce, *Studies in History and Jurisprudence*, vol. I (New York: Oxford University Press, 1901), pp. 126–134.
[29] Keith Thomas, *In Pursuit of Civility: Manners and Civilization in Early Modern England* (New Haven and London: Yale University Press, 2018), pp. 338–339.
[30] Anna Clark, *Scandal: The Sexual Politics of the British Constitution* (Oxford: Princeton University Press, 2006), pp. 19–52.

Power and People

Early modern political thinkers articulated a common belief that the interests of the people were represented by others, especially through the responsible leadership of the sovereign. The fifteenth-century jurist and thinker, Sir John Fortescue, was dismissive of the idea that the people were a distinct political community since 'a people beynge headless is not worthye to be called a bodie'. The people needed a head. In the sixteenth century, scholars employed and popularised the idea of 'mixed monarchy', which saw the monarch, lords and commons as collectively representing the people and all united under one constitution.[31] Three hundred years after the 1567 English translation of Fortescue's *A Learned Commendation of the Politique Lawes of Englande*, in 1867 Walter Bagehot explained, in his famous *The English Constitution*, that it was no 'defect' to have the 'effective exclusion of the working classes from effective representation'. Bagehot, echoing Fortescue, explained stylishly that the constitution's symbolic power and 'dignified' parts were crafted to 'impress the many' in order that the elite could with 'efficient' power discreetly 'govern the many'.[32] Richard Crossman perceived that Plato's 'Noble Lie' was used by writers on the British constitution, like Bagehot, where a version of history was given not just to describe the history of the development of the constitution, but also a feeling of respect, if not deference. While criticisms and flaws are highlighted, the people must be persuaded not to overthrow the constitution and its institutions. In thus being descriptive and prescriptive the constitutional historian and writer, perpetuates, 'the acquiescence of the many in the rule of the few'.[33] However, as the twelfth century cleric and scholar John of Salisbury recognised in his *Policraticus* (1159) while the ruler 'holds the place of the head' and is 'rightly preferred before others', the church guides the body as the soul, the ruler's counsellors being the heart, the tax collector and soldier forming the two hands, it is the peasantry as the feet 'who raise, sustain and move forward the entire weight of the body' and despite the different and unequal functions of these and other parts only in cooperation can the body politic function in the collective good of the whole.[34]

---

[31] Quentin Skinner, *From Humanism to Hobbes: Studies in Rhetoric and Politics* (Cambridge: Cambridge University Press, 2018), pp. 341–383.
[32] Walter Bagehot, *The English Constitution* (London: Fontana, 1978), p. 176.
[33] Ibid. R. H. S. Crossman, 'Introduction', pp. 26–28.
[34] Cary J. Nederman, 'The Physiological Significance of the Organic Metaphor in John of Salisbury's "Policraticus"', *History of Political Thought*, vol. 8, no. 2, 1987, pp. 212–217.

Finding power in the formal, historical constitution was not straightforward. It would not be until the Chequers Estate Act 1917 that statutory reference was made to the most powerful person within the modern constitution: the Prime Minister. The person commonly taken to be the first holder of the title, Sir Robert Walpole, was at pains to reject the label. In a motion of 13 February 1741 to remove Walpole, Samuel Sandys, a leading member of the opposition, argued that 'According to our constitution we can have no sole or prime minister.' He charged the resident of 10 Downing Street with committing 'the most heinous offence against our constitution' having 'monopolized all the favours of the crown' by irresponsibly assuming 'sole direction of all public affairs' instead of sharing power. Walpole, who had effectively functioned as prime minister since 1721, stated in refutation: 'I unequivocally deny that I am sole and prime minister, and that to my influence and direction all the measures of government must be attributed.' In mitigation Walpole said that he only functioned at the King's pleasure and was ready to depart should confidence in him be withdrawn.[35] The location and nature of power may have been obscure in statute and constitutional law, but it was clear in practice and in the popular imagination that Walpole and his successors were indeed the *prime* minister. Constitutional history would be redundant without the analysis of power even though for much of British history statute and law barely recognised the reality of the political executive. Near the end of the eighteenth century, James Gillray's caricature, of an obscenely huge prime minister, William Pitt, literally straddling over the chamber of the House of Commons, flattening his great rivals Charles James Fox, Thomas Erskine and Richard Sheridan with one foot while the other is held up by Henry Dundas and William Wilberforce, depicted in satire what the law had yet to recognise namely the reality of prime ministerial power. Political personalities were critical because they had the power to direct and deflect the constitution. As Samuel Taylor Coleridge remarked, the nimble George Canning 'flashed such a light around the constitution that it was difficult to see the ruins of the fabric through it'.[36] Several politicians fitted this description.

Maitland, was someone who, with great elegance, rejected the idea that people in the medieval period used the word 'liberty' or thought of 'sovereignty'

---

[35] *English Historical Documents, c1714–1783*, vol. vii (London: Routledge, 1996 [1957]), documents 19B and 19C.
[36] Boyd Hilton, *A Mad, Bad and Dangerous People? England 1783–1846* (Oxford: Oxford University Press, 2006), footnote 394, p. 308.

in the same way as those in more modern eras might. Despite this straightforward revelation and the eminence of Maitland's historical influence, the idea of constitutional constancy has been near irresistible for many scholars through the ages.[37] For E. A. Freeman the continuity of the constitution and its institutions, and their ancient pedigree, were as obvious as the Whig view of progress. This historical narrative gave power to institutions and people who ran them by giving them an ancient and continuous legitimacy. In a tellingly titled article in the *Edinburgh Review* in July 1860 called 'The Continuity of English History', Freeman claimed 'from the thirteenth century onwards we have a veritable Parliament, essentially as we see it before our own eyes. In the course of the fourteenth century every fundamental constitutional principle becomes fully recognised. The best worthies of the seventeenth century struggled, not for the establishment of anything new, but for the preservation of what even then was already old.' Even at the time of the Norman Conquest, England possessed, in her 'barbaric greatness and barbaric freedom' the 'germs' of 'every institution which we most dearly prize'.[38] In this Freeman, like other historians of that period especially, looked back into the political and constitutional history of England to give credence to the idea of having institutions and a constitution of near divine significance that needed conserving not abandoning.

However, Freeman, who served as Regius Professor of Modern History at Oxford, was no Conservative. Instead, he was a firm Liberal, who used his popular historical narrative to patriotically explain the 'origin of the national tradition of liberty' in Britain, an idea persuasively parroted in countless history faculties at the time.[39] Constitutional history was written with party politics in mind. Henry Hallam, considered to be the first writer to use the term 'constitutional history', in his influential *Constitutional History of England* published in 1828, was perceived as promoting history and philosophy aligned with the Whig party. A review of it by Robert Southey in the Tory *Quarterly Review* damned the book as full of 'prejudices of party'.[40] Historians like G. M. Trevelyan and his great-uncle, Thomas Babington Macaulay, (who penned an admiring review of Hallam), wrote their popular and rich histories with the partisan Whiggish idea of progression as its central theme. The

---

[37] John Hudson, *F. W. Maitland and the Englishness of English Law* (London: Selden Society, 2007).
[38] E. A. Freeman, 'The Continuity of English History', *Edinburgh Review*, July 1860 in *Historical Essays*, Series 1 (London: Macmillan, 1871), pp. 42–43.
[39] John Burrow, *A History of Histories: Epics, Chronicles, Romances and Inquiries from Herodotus and Thucydides to the Twentieth Century* (London: Allen Lane, 2007), p. 407.
[40] Michael Bentley, 'Henry Hallam Revisited', *The Historical Journal*, vol. 55, no. 2, 2012, pp. 454–456.

narrative was alluring. Yet, Herbert Butterfield thought it 'strange' that Macaulay 'should ever have imagined his *History of England* as transcending party prejudice'. From the seventeenth century, Butterfield continued, parties and historians did not want to be 'innovators', even if they were but, instead, to be seen as 'restorers of ancient ways' using history to 'discover what they wished to discover'.[41] A tendency that has not ended, especially on vexed subjects such as sovereignty. Trevelyan, who had begun as an 'angry young Whig', had by the end of his career in the mid-twentieth century, shifted to seeing the Liberals and Tories as necessary to each other in order to act as guardians of Britain's great institutions. Only together had they contributed to make Britain 'exceptional', and its constitution, history and liberties 'the envy of "less happier" lands'.[42] Party interests unquestionably propelled the constitution and its control was an accepted ambition to further political aims. Authors of constitutional histories were often adorned by party rosettes since such works provided an historical frame which either justified a party's record in government or explained the perils of not being so. It should come as no surprise that politicians as varied as Earl Grey, Lord John Russell, Benjamin Disraeli and Harold Wilson penned works of political and constitutional history.

The much-used school textbook, *The Groundwork of British History*, by two History masters from Harrow and Eton respectively, written and revised throughout the first half of the twentieth century, astutely asserted that 'the Constitution develops most when the Crown is for any reason ineffective'.[43] The monarch was a constant and active presence in the constitution, but changes in the eighteenth century saw the constitution move away from the sovereign's sway. This change was driven, in part, by the development of parties, as the Crown retreated from ruling without them. The Crown had not, however, become ceremonial. Between June 1710 and June 1711 alone, Queen Anne and her consort, attended sixty-four meetings of the Cabinet (but never of cabinet committees) dispelling impressions of a 'leisured' past.[44] The Queen was popular and able to appeal to the Tories as an Anglican Stuart and to the Whigs as a contractual monarch; and this versatility helped

---

[41] H. Butterfield, *The Englishman and His History* (Cambridge: Cambridge University Press, 1944), pp. 4–6.
[42] David Cannadine, *G. M. Trevelyan: A Life in History* (London: Penguin, 1997), p. 108 and generally pp. 95–140.
[43] George Townsend Warner and C. H. K. Marten, *The Groundwork of British History* (London: Blackie and Son, 1924), p. 100.
[44] J. H. Plumb, 'The Organisation of the Cabinet in the Reign of Queen Anne', *Transactions of the Royal Historical Society*, vol. 7, 1957, p. 142.

foster the growth of party politics. Even Anne's famous withholding of the royal assent to the Scottish Militia Bill in 1708 was on the advice of ministers rather than as an arbitrary projection of royal power. Anne died in 1714 without any surviving children, which meant that the Act of Settlement 1701 bypassed her Catholic half-siblings. Into the breach came Georg Ludwig von Braunschweig-Lüneburg, electoral prince of Hanover, who would become George I. The constitutional history of the state from the Hanoverian period began to assert styles of government that would have lasting impact on our historical understanding, if not the practice, of political power. Despite his inaptitude in the English language and early inexperience of the affairs of his new British realm, George I did not entirely leave the running of government to others, but he did rely on his advisers. Many key conventions of cabinet government and parliament emerged from the early eighteenth century that saw the sovereign become less of a force in the executive powers of the constitution. Instead, beginning with Sir Robert Walpole, monarchs delegated their instructions to a *prime* minister chosen on the basis of their ability to deliver royal policy preferences in cabinet and parliament. In consequence, the decisions of cabinet and statutes of parliament assumed greater significance.

However, it would be almost two hundred years after the Hanoverian dynasty took the throne before systematic record keeping of the apex of government became routine. In December 1916, in part due to the demands of war, a Secretary to the Cabinet from the Civil Service was appointed for the first time and the production of cabinet minutes and an office to serve the most important decision-making body in the land became a regular and mandated function. Like much of the constitutional history of the state this seemingly logical development of a cabinet office and secretary was in fact driven by exigencies and the vision of key personalities, in this case David Lloyd George and Sir Maurice Hankey.[45] On the other hand, while a cabinet secretariat might well be relatively new, the office of the Privy Council, which was seen by many historians as the original critical administrative organ of the state, can trace a systematic recording of its decisions to the Tudor period when the Council, in 1540, decided to appoint a clerk to administer its official activities.[46]

---

[45] Anthony Seldon, *The Cabinet Office 1916–2016: The Birth of Modern Government* (London: Biteback, 2016).
[46] See David J. Crankshaw, 'The Tudor Privy Council c.1540–1603' (Cengage Learning EMEA, 2009).

To some the highest levels of the state had forgotten the constitution's compact with the people. 'Originally the constitution must have been free', speculated John Baxter, a silversmith from Shoreditch, a politically active radical, and author of the 1796 text *New and Impartial History of England*, a work which sought to see in history the rights of ordinary people. As E. P. Thompson observed of such thinking on the constitution 'History was the history of its corruption', which gave ordinary working people, the right to 'defy the constitution', which no longer upheld their liberties and rights as 'free-born Englishmen' but favoured degraded aristocratic rule.[47] In the opinion of the famed Thomas Paine, who shared many of these critical constitutional views, the constitution had rotted and needed radical reform. As it stood it was only good for

> courtiers, placemen, pensioners, borough-holders, and the leaders of the Parties . . .; but it is a bad Constitution for at least ninety-nine parts of the nation out of a hundred.[48]

A narrow and formal analysis of constitutional history would see the limited position of women in the long eighteenth century. Lord Mansfield, as Lord Chief Justice from 1756, extended the 'exceptions' to the common-law rule that married women had no legal personality separate from that of their husbands. Yet this concentration ignored the broader and richer constitutional history of assertion by women and their contribution and reaction to the state. During this period, Mary Wollstonecraft challenged the patriarchal underpinnings of the constitution and argued that gender equality was essential and justified. In fact, the active participation of women could in fact be seen not only in roles such as political hostesses, but through involvement in local government and in political and reform movements, including seventy-three female associations working across Britain in the anti-slavery campaigns of the 1820s and 1830s. George IV's attempt, in 1820, to divorce his first cousin, Queen Caroline, and the proposed Pains and Penalties Bill that aimed to strip the Queen of her title and position, generated considerable political agitation. While the high politics of the trial of the Queen were conducted in the House of Lords, all manner of classes and people protested on the streets and by speeches and letters. Conceivably, these feelings were motivated by the restricted constitutional position of women in the state, even at the very top.[49]

---

[47] E. P. Thompson, *The Making of the English Working Class* (London: Penguin, 1991), p. 94.
[48] Ibid., pp. 100–101.
[49] Frank O'Gorman, *The Long Eighteenth Century: British Political and Social History 1688–1832*, 2nd ed. (London: Bloomsbury, 2017), pp. 353–357.

Throughout British history, the constitution seemed not to reach all in society. An ordinary northern Englishman in 1838 argued that the 'truth is we have no constitution, and it is high time the people set about making a constitution for themselves'.[50] Perhaps the most significant organised movement of popular protest concerning the constitution and the state of Britain was Chartism. The Chartists were a loose assemblage of disparate groups and individuals such as Scottish universal suffragists, Irish independence fighters, trade unionists, temperance campaigners and education reformers. Emanating from core groups like the London Working Men's Association and Radical MPs, they produced in May 1838 a People's Charter, drawn up by William Lovett and Francis Place, respectively a cabinet maker and a tailor, which contained six demands: universal manhood suffrage, secret ballots, constituencies of equal size, abolition of property qualifications for MPs, payment of MPs, and annual parliaments. The Commons needed to become, the Chartists proclaimed, 'the People's House'. Over the next decade the Chartists petitioned parliament three times with demands near constant to those published in 1838. The second petition presented to parliament in May 1842 reputedly listed more than 3 million signatures, while the Irish Protestant MP, lawyer and publisher, Feargus O'Conner, boastfully claimed that the third one, delivered in April 1848, contained over 5 million (though the House of the Commons disputed such high numbers). The new industrial heartlands of Glasgow, Manchester, Leeds, Birmingham, and the working and occupational labour classes of London, were particularly in evidence in their support. Nevertheless, each petition failed to convince more than a small minority of MPs in the Commons. The rejections were predicted to cause revolution which, in 1848, was raging across Europe, seeing popular upheavals demanding constitutional change and political rights. The Royal Family left London for the Isle of Wight at the Government's request when around 150,000 Chartist supporters descended upon Kennington Common in April 1848, who were met by a heavy and menacing military and police presence including 85,000 special constables. However, no revolution occurred and no coronets tumbled. Instead, the movement faded from consciousness, and while episodes of violence occurred and intensive discord openly existed, there was no bloody repression from the state and no armed militia determined to overthrow it. The Chartist message, while not completely adopted, was finding voice in key

---

[50] Colley, *The Gun, the Ship & the Pen*, p. 250.

laws and policies such as the Income Tax Act (1842), the Mining Act (1842), the Ten Hours Act (1847) and, most importantly, Sir Robert Peel's repeal of the Corn Laws, which had favoured landed interests by maintaining high grain prices to the detriment of others in society. Some historians argue that these reforms contributed to the weakening of the belief that the state was the enemy and indicated that society and constitution were moving away from serving only the interests of the landed oligarchy.[51] Eventually, all of the Chartist demands, except annual parliaments, would become reality and thus shedding their 'radical' label in constitutional history, despite earlier views to the contrary.

However, it would be a leap too far to read this as a victorious insertion of the people into the constitution. It is conventional to place great store on the electorate, and the reforms to expand it are heralded as critical achievements. The 'Great' Reform Act of 1832 created an electorate where just 3 per cent of the total population could register to vote and the Second Reform Act of 1867 increased this to about 10 per cent of the adult population (those who had reached the age of majority of twenty-one). In 1918 women were partially enfranchised and in 1928, when they finally had the same conditions to vote as men and same voting age of twenty-one, the electorate became around 90 per cent of the total adult population. By 1970 when the voting age was lowered to eighteen years the electorate had risen to almost 100 per cent of the total adult population.[52] There were, nonetheless, still some who, like the 3rd Marquess of Salisbury, rebuffed the idea of 'the people as an acting, deciding, accessible authority' and saw social reforms such as the 1884 Reform Act, which he helped to draft, as necessary only in order to protect property and prevent revolution.[53] His rival, William Gladstone, albeit with suitable ambiguity, captured a growing sentiment when he declared that 'every man' is 'morally entitled to come within the pale of the Constitution'. For all his successful platform hustings on the needs for change, the Liberal leader had his limits. Gladstone's constitutional reform attempts in his 1866 bill excluded the 'residuum', as the urban poor were

---

[51] See Robert Tombs, *The English and Their History* (London: Penguin, 2015), pp. 450–453; and more generally on the significance of the Chartists David Cannadine, *Victorious Century: The United Kingdom, 1800–1906* (London: Penguin, 2017), pp. 240–241; Malcolm Chase, *Chartism: A New History* (Manchester: Manchester University Press), pp. 300–303; and Hilton, *A Mad, Bad, and Dangerous People?*, pp. 612–621

[52] S. E. Finer, *The History of Government*, vol. I (Oxford: Oxford University Press, 1997), pp. 44–45.

[53] Andrew Roberts, *Salisbury: Victorian Titan* (London: Weidenfeld & Nicolson, 1999), p. 840.

termed, from the constitution's embrace.[54] In the context of decolonisation of the British Empire, Jennings observed that little could be done regarding the creation of a new state 'until someone decides who are the people'.[55] The United Kingdom was no different. The union between England and Scotland caused the construction of a new national identity of 'Britishness' defined in part as being against France, Catholicism, the Irish and the Jews.[56]

Access to the British constitution and its privileges in history therefore was culturally and legally restrictive, based on what David Cesarani argues as assumptions that migrant groups coming in the late nineteenth and early twentieth centuries, such as Russian Jews, Chinese or Blacks, 'could not fully belong to the nation'. Various acts, like the 1919 Aliens Restriction (Amendment) Act gave the state huge power to remove civic and employment rights from such communities even if naturalised since they were perceived as the racialised 'other' with their rights dependent on the interests of the government.[57] The history and law of the British constitution was, therefore, critical to racial and cultural discourse. As Paul Gilroy argues, statements like those of Sir Kenneth Newman, Metropolitan Commissioner of Police 1982–1987 – stating that in 'Jamaicans, you have a people who are constitutionally disorderly ... It's simply in their make up, they're constitutionally disposed to be anti-authority' – pushed a far from uncommon racial narrative in history and law that Britain was being 'violated' by Blacks and others unable to appreciate or adhere to Britain's constitution and the rule of law. In this way prejudices, like Newman's, emerge of the 'national constitution ... distorted and destroyed by the presence of the alien blacks' threatening British identity and civilisation.[58] This tendency to label such 'outsiders' as incompatible with national constitutional probity arguably highlights what David Armitage has observed from the late eighteenth century onwards of the 'persistent reluctance' to politically and academically

---

[54] Jon Lawrence, *Electing Our Masters: The Hustings in British Politics from Hogarth to Blair* (Oxford: Oxford University Press, 2009), p. 43.
[55] Ivor Jennings, *The Approach to Self-Government* (Cambridge: Cambridge University Press, 1956), pp. 20–21.
[56] See generally Linda Colley, *Britons: Forging the Nation 1707–1837* (London: Yale University Press, 1992).
[57] David Cesarani, 'The Changing Character of Citizenship and Nationality in Britain' in David Cesarani and Mary Fulbrook (eds.), *Citizenship, Nationality and Migration in Europe* (London: Routledge, 2003), pp. 61–68.
[58] Paul Gilroy, *There Ain't No Black in the Union Jack: The Cultural Politics of Race and Nation*, 2nd ed. (London: Routledge, 2002), pp. 84–91.

incorporate empire into studies of the British state due to narratives of domestic *libertas* sitting uncomfortably with *imperium* abroad.[59]

Typically, in chronicles of the constitution, there appear figures resembling the omnipresent English gentleman. It suited an historical narrative that the state preferred the dabbler over the professional. This history embraced and venerated a Queensbury Constitution, where the game of politics was run by eternal norms and fair-play verities. The leftist constitutional scholar, Harold Laski, decried the 'gentleman' theory of British history that government and state were the patriarchal preserve of a certain type of Englishman. This, Laski argued, was based on 'two hundred years and more of instruction in the thesis that only the gentleman is fit to govern'.[60] Interestingly, John Austin, writing in 1859 believed that because of the flexible and wide application of the word 'gentlemen' in British society, the House of Commons was in fact 'an aristocracy of independent gentleman', that enabled a more porous avenue for political participation in contrast to the closed aristocracies of Europe, which led to 'fatal consequences' for those states. This is also perhaps due to the tendency seen by Elizabeth I's trusted counsellor, Sir Thomas Smith, that 'gentlemen ... they be made cheap in England'.[61]

It is thereby tempting to see Britain as having 'government by amateurs'. This idea of the 'amateur' is augmented by ordinary citizens 'unlerned and lewed' (as Sir Sidney Low imagined Chaucer would see freeholders) doing their duty in the county court, burgesses and knights in the Commons, justices of the peace, members of school boards, guardians of the poor and other lay people holding various governmental or civic roles upheld in turn by an 'amateur electorate'.[62] In this rendering constitutional history was also social history in that it provided an idealised portrait of the governing characters and their society, which was equally important to the constitution, as, if not more than, legislation and laws. While not historically as rigid in its membership as its European neighbours, the political and social class found at the highest and middling levels of British government were conscious of their position and adept at maintaining their influence with a cloistered and

---

[59] David Armitage, *The Ideological Origins of the British Empire* (Cambridge: Cambridge University Press, 2004), p. 11. On this point and on the links between empire and the constitution see Kirkby and Kumarasingham's chapters 19 and 20 respectively in Volume 2.

[60] Harold J. Laski, *The Danger of Being a Gentleman and Other Essays* (London: George Unwin, 1940), p. 28.

[61] John Austin, *A Plea for the Constitution*, 2nd ed. (London: John Murray, 1859), pp. 10–12.

[62] Sidney Low, *The Governance of England* (London: T. Fisher Unwin, 1904), p. 201.

practised rigour that ensured government and bureaucracy were filled by those who shared comparable educational and social qualifications. Though there was no 'grand design' of detailed planning, the constitutional ethos of the public-spirited dilettante was a powerful historical tool popularised to deflect attention from the carefully constructed cultural and institutional edifice that the constitution provided British society. The 1853 Northcote-Trevelyan Report, for example, which led to the introduction of open competition for entry into the hitherto socially closed Civil Service, was the product of Victorian reformers who, Asa Briggs argued, saw the need for 'a plentiful supply of informed gentlemen'. The social spectrum from this reform indeed expanded and saw, for instance, the son of a carpenter, P. J. Grigg, and an heir to a dukedom, Sir George Murray, both rise on merit to head the War Office and Treasury respectively. Nonetheless, while background and emphasis on competition over class had changed, the reforms were still geared to foster an expanded professional cadre of gentlemen with 'proficiency in history, jurisprudence, political economy', well versed and invested in British constitutional history and the preservation of its values in order to deliver public service and run the state.[63] Therefore, through acculturation and training, the number of those versed in the constitution's mores expanded into the age of democratisation.

In Whitehall there existed what Clive Priestley called in the mid-1980s 'the good chap theory of government' where unwritten mantras of constitutional courtesies reigned to underwrite the running of the state. This amusing description of 'good chaps' masked a more cohesive, sensitive and historically grounded understanding and professional handling of the constitution.[64] The hazards, however, of relying on the 'good chaps theory' was only too real and can be illustrated when this was tested in the Federal Court of Pakistan over the scandalous use of the Royal Prerogative to forcibly dissolve the legislature in 1954 without advice to stop it from passing measures to curb the Crown's powers. In decrying the abuse of British conventions by the Governor-General, the counsel for the President of the Assembly informed the Court that such an action went against the tenets of British constitutional

---

[63] Cited in Peter Hennessy, *Whitehall* (London: Pimlico, 2001), pp. 31–51.
[64] Priestley explained the good chap theory to visiting American civil servants as the Whitehall equivalent of the 'Code of the Woosters'. Peter Hennessy, '"Harvesting the Cupboards": Why Britain Has Produced No Administrative Theory or Ideology in the Twentieth Century', *Transactions of the Royal Historical Society*, vol. 4, 1994, p. 205.

history and accepted behaviour: 'After all, one has to rely on the words of a gentleman'. This was not enough to prevent this blatant abuse of power.[65] Nonetheless, the amateur and gentlemanly versions of constitutional history shrouded a deep, pervasive and shrewd appreciation of the social dynamic of the British constitution's power strategies as well as the essential and sensitive manoeuvrability of the constitution to adapt for crisis and immediate need.

Law and Utility

The Liberal grandee Sir William Harcourt, who served for a time as both Home Secretary and Whewell Professor of International Law at Cambridge, was incensed by the 1910–1911 parliamentary crisis that saw the two Houses of Parliament engage in a deeply partisan conflict that threatened many of the principles and conventions of the pre-1914 constitution. Harcourt colourfully exclaimed to his party colleagues who sought to reform the constitution that they should avoid such indulgences, 'We must stick tight to principles and not go a' whoreing after false constitutions.'[66] The problem was that the constitution embraced many conflicting principles. Constitutional history and law provide ample evidence that norms are easily replaced. Henry VIII radically overturned key understandings of the ecclesiastical foundations of the state and used the law to do it. The King's dynastic ambitions saw a social and religious tumult in the state's constitutional affairs. Finding that Pope Clement VII was unwilling to endorse the Tudor monarch's marital choices, Henry, the once loyal servant of Rome, removed papal legal jurisdiction over England. This led to a chaotic and long-felt constitutional revolution. The Pope was sensationally replaced by the Sovereign as Head of the Church and Catholicism's divine and exclusive constitutional status was dramatically revoked by the Act of Supremacy 1534, with deep institutional, financial, and social ramifications. This included transforming English rule in Ireland, which was taken to be endorsed by the 1159 papal bull *Laudabiliter*, embellished to serve the Angevin desires for conquering the territory. The English

---

[65] S. S. Pirzada, *Dissolution of Constituent Assembly of Pakistan and the Legal Battles of Maulvi Tamizuddin Khan* (Karachi: Asia Law House, 1995), p. 291 and H. Kumarasingham, 'A Transnational Actor on a Dramatic Stage: Sir Ivor Jennings and the Manipulation of Westminster Style Democracy in Pakistan' in Gregory Shaffer, Tom Ginsburg and Terrence C. Halliday (eds.), *Constitution-Making and Transnational Legal Order* (Cambridge: Cambridge University Press, 2019), pp. 55–84.
[66] Roy Jenkins, *Asquith* (London: Collins, 1964), p. 205.

monarch's ambiguous twelfth-century title of Lord of Ireland was replaced with King of Ireland in 1541 in order to affirm the English crown's complete legal sovereignty over the Irish and render papal supremacy *ultra vires*. The Irish reformation was no less a major constitutional revolution than its English counterpart.[67] Henry's desires had lasting import and illustrated how the bedchamber is an essential source in constitutional history.

The expanse and variety of the common law made many political actions possible. Henry II sought to unify the different courts and laws in the kingdom so that there could be a common system of the King's justice administered by royal judges and courts. This was disputed, particularly by the Church. Nonetheless local customs and principles did not die as long as the Crown was acknowledged and justice administered in its name. While the Crown wanted centralisation of the rule of law, there was inherent scope for variety. This system of law, relying on historical precedent and judicial interpretation, encouraged legal thinking to look to history to inform contemporary and local disputes. The common law abetted a sovereign's desire for control across their dominions, but it also gave certain benchmarks from which to check royal and state intrusion. As G. M. Trevelyan put it, from the thirteenth century 'Our constitution was the child of Feudalism married to the Common Law.'[68] Doctrines and laws had their limits. In the late thirteenth century, Edward I suspected that some lands in England held by nobles were in fact originally Crown lands; and in an attempt to reverse a perceived decline in royal authority, he used writs of *quo warranto* to demand proof of the legal pedigree of the landholder's claim; and if it could not be satisfactorily established, the tenurial rights would revert to the King. The Earl Warenne, for one, did not respond with parchments, but instead flourished his rusty sword to the King's Justices as his alternative authorisation.

> Here my lords, here is my warrant! My ancestors came with William the Bastard and conquered their lands with the sword, and I shall defend them with the sword against anyone who tries to usurp them.[69]

---

[67] Nicholas Vincent, 'Angevin Ireland' in Brendan Smith (ed.), *The Cambridge History of Ireland: Volume I 600–1550* (Cambridge: Cambridge University Press, 2018), pp. 185–221 and Brendan Bradshaw, *The Irish Constitutional Revolution of the Sixteenth Century* (Cambridge: Cambridge University Press, 1979), pp. 231–257.

[68] G. M. Trevelyan, *Illustrated History of England*, Illustrated ed. (London: Longmans, Green and Co, 1956), p. 167.

[69] Andrew M. Spencer, *Nobility and Kinship in Medieval England: The Earls and Edward I, 1272–1307* (Cambridge: Cambridge University Press, 2013), pp. 72–73.

Much of traditional constitutional history was told through law and institutions. The generally ready archival availability of legal and legislative acts as well as the identifiable reality of Crown, Lords, Commons and Courts provided institutional and legal bones for the state's body. However, as Jennings memorably diagnosed, it is conventions, which we may think of as political and legal norms formed by contextual utility, which give the constitution and the body politic its 'flesh'.[70] All of this is to say that laws and institutions, along with historical norms and political context, are collectively needed to understand and study the constitution. Removing one part would undermine the relevance of constitutional history. Nonetheless, this has not always been apparent in constitutional texts. A popular English history book published in the late nineteenth century complained that 'our constitutional history has been perverted at the hands of lawyers'. If History was to look to law at all, it conceded, then it should be seen from the statute book, 'but it must be in a Statute Book which begins at no point later than the Dooms of Æthelbehrt'.[71] For their part legal scholars, too, had reservations about the use of history. One of the most famous, A. V. Dicey, saw constitutional history, while possibly 'fascinating', as 'mere antiquarianism' not remotely linked to the modern constitution or its law; instead, such history dangerously engaged in 'retrogressive progress'. Dicey was by no means against history, but saw it having limited worth in producing law. History was not law.

> [T]he appeal of precedent is in the law courts merely a useful fiction by which judicial decision conceals its transformation into judicial legislation; and a fiction is none the less a fiction because it has emerged from the Courts into the field of politics or of history. Here, then, the astuteness of lawyers has imposed upon the simplicity of historians. Formalism and antiquarianism, have, so to speak, joined hands; they have united to mislead students in search for the law of the constitution.[72]

Nonetheless, and inevitably, Dicey used history. Interestingly, Dicey's most famous articulation of constitutional principle, made in 1885, namely the principle of parliamentary sovereignty, being parliament's right 'to make or unmake any law whatever', while drawing on ideas of Coke, Blackstone and

---

[70] Ivor Jennings, *The Law and the Constitution*, 5th ed. (London: University of London Press, 1959), p. 81.
[71] E. A. Freeman, *The Growth of the English Constitution from Earliest Times*, 3rd ed. (London: Macmillan), pp. x–xi.
[72] A. V. Dicey, *The Law of the Constitution*, J. W. F. Allison, ed. (Oxford: Oxford University Press, 2013), pp. 17–18.

Burke, also uses histories of the British constitution by outsiders to validate his theory. Judged by the written histories of the eighteenth century 'foreign observers' such as Swiss theorist Jean-Louis De Lolme, the nineteenth century German jurist Rudolf von Gneist and the French man of letters Alexis De Tocqueville, saw what locals did not. To Dicey these international scholars were 'as is natural, clearer sighted than Englishmen' in detecting 'at once the sovereignty of Parliament as a salient feature of the English constitution'.[73] These legal and historical ideas helped cement parliament in popular and scholarly thinking as the seminal institution of the British constitution. Key histories, such as A. F. Pollard's influential 1920 work, *The Evolution of Parliament*, which used the Tudor legislatures as its pivot, consciously looked to parliament as the focus and explanation of Britain's history. Parliament's wider representative function was prominent in constitutional history. While challenging earlier ideas of 'model' parliaments, later histories still promoted the historical Whiggish idea of development of the constitution as the growth and evolution of parliament sustained by a liberal sentiment found within the English character.[74] Laski who, in earlier writings, argued for major decentralisation of British institutions and fundamental transformation of the state, with Labour in power in 1950 robustly defended the power of parliament, cabinet and the civil service to be in the national interest. Critics of the constitution, who argued for reform of the system, like his contemporary Leo Amery, the Tory writer and politician, suffered from 'distorted historical perspective' in not seeing the transformation of Britain from an agricultural state to an industrial one; and that the House of Commons, now out of the hands of the oligarchy, had evolved to enable positive government intervention reaching and representing a wider electorate and society. Laski, the one-time radical saw parliament, now with his party finally in clear majority from the 'most mature electorate in the world', as the historical culmination of the British constitution. He dismissed the critics of parliament with the stark judgement that they 'would, if pressed, admit the real alternative to the House of Commons is the concentration camp'.[75]

The jurist Sir Edward Coke's creative and instructive use of constitutional history are among the most famous in British history and hugely influential on the development of the constitution and the common law. Coke, in his

---

[73] Ibid., pp. 51–52.
[74] Michael Bentley, *Modernizing England's Past: English Historiography in the Age of Modernism, 1870–1970* (Cambridge: Cambridge University Press, 2005), pp. 19–44.
[75] Harold J. Laski, *Reflections on the Constitution: The House of Commons, The Cabinet, The Civil Service* (Manchester: Manchester University Press, 1951), p. 16.

legal and political roles in the eras of Elizabeth I and James I, sought protection and natural justice against arbitrary absolutism. In the Magna Carta, Coke found his historical vessel to bring life into his arguments. His reinvention gave the Charter, which was hitherto hardly discussed in the Tudor period, an assumed fundamental and emotional power as the fountain head of Anglo-Saxon liberty, despite the limited legal practicality of the majority of its chapters. Indeed, were it not for its reinvention in the seventeenth century it is plausible that the document would have been of interest only to medievalists and not an object of international celebration. Coke, 'the supreme figure in weaponizing the common law', as Mark Goldie has labelled him, 'constructed a canon' to defend his views, which harnessed ideas such as those of Henry de Bracton's thirteenth-century espousal of England's predilection for *lex non scripta*, 'unwritten law rooted in usage'. Such was the power of Coke's interpretation, as written in his *Reports* and *Institutes*, that Charles I confiscated them on his death. Later, the Long Parliament ordered their publication, which helped cement their historical status.[76] Pocock notably argued that the 'common-law mind' interpretation of history produced a picture of an ancient constitution in existence before the Norman Conquest that bequeathed the common law, courts and trial by jury, and parliament itself. The 'immemorial' nature of the constitution intensified the 'radical' tendency of the 'English mind' to 'read existing law into the remote past'.[77] As Coke himself put it

> The Lawes of England are of much more antiquity, then they are reported to be, and more then any of the constitutions or lawes Imperiall of the Romaine Emperours.[78]

As John Baker argues, the fact that Coke and others mythologised and reinvented the past, as in the case of Magna Carta, is not sufficient to erode their significance: 'Coke may have got some of the early history wrong, but his constitutional conclusions have thrived down the centuries because they seemed right'.[79]

---

[76] Mark Goldie, 'The Ancient Constitution and the Languages of Political Thought', *Historical Journal*, vol. 62, no. 1, 2019, p. 10.
[77] J. G. A. Pocock, *The Ancient Constitution and the Feudal Law: A Study of English Historical Thought in the Seventeenth Century – A Reissue with a Retrospect* (Cambridge: Cambridge University Press, 1987), pp. 30–31.
[78] Butterfield, *The Englishman and His History*, p. 50.
[79] John Baker, *The Reinvention of Magna Carta 1216–1616* (Cambridge: Cambridge University Press, 2017), p. 444.

Edmund Burke identified the contradictory forays of history and the common law. In *An Essay towards an History of the Laws of England* he perceived the esteemed writings of the jurist and legal historian, Sir Matthew Hale, and the historian polemicist, Henry St John Bolingbroke, as united in two incompatible historical assertions. Hale and Bolingbroke wrote of the 'eternity' of English law as well as placing faith in its constant 'improvement'. For Burke the common law and the constitution, far from being eternal, were instead based on contingencies and struggles between liberty and authority and could, without vigilance, crumble away. Burke believed the people's ultimate welfare in fact needed contestation or the branches of state could be ranged against them: 'the People cannot suffer a great deal whilst there is a Contest between different Parts of the Constitution.'[80] Contestation of legal principles has always been at the heart of key constitutional clashes and their history. The ability to make law and, thus, rule is a fundamental part of governance. Constitutional history is often an account of disputations of which institution or institutions has this power to make law. In *Trew Lawe of Free Monarchies*, published in 1598, James VI asserted that kings alone by divine right were the 'authors and makers' of law. The Scottish cleric Samuel Rutherford challenged this idea in his 1644 work *Lex, Rex, or, The Law and the Prince* arguing that kings, in practice, needed to work with parliament in 'the power of making Lawes'. The powerful intellectual George Buchanan, who had been James's childhood tutor, also believed that kings were subject to law and not God alone.[81] These were critical and volatile themes in Scottish constitutional history and political thought and, of course, in the kingdoms of England and Ireland, which James assumed in addition to his Scottish one in 1603. In June 1616, sitting atop his new realms, James declared to the judges of the Star Chamber that the 'absolute Prerogative of the Crown is no Subject for the tongue of a Lawyer'. The seventeenth-century judiciary, while not rejecting this regal rule of law, sought to navigate it by accepting wide governance functions assigned to the Crown, which was different from allowing arbitrary and autocratic power. Over 300 years later the Lord Chief Justice, Gordon Hewart, published *The New Despotism* in 1929, which argued that this judicial forbearance of executive discretion had gone too far and eroded the rule of law.[82]

---

[80] Bourke, *Empire and Revolution*, pp. 191–195.
[81] Laura A. M. Stewart and Janay Nugent, *Union and Revolution: Scotland and Beyond, 1625–1745* (Edinburgh: Edinburgh University Press, 2021), pp. 124–125.
[82] Martin Loughlin draws this link also between James and Hewart in *Foundations of Public Law* (Oxford: Oxford University Press, 2010), pp. 379–380, 398 and fn. 121. Lord Hewart, *The New Despotism* (London: Ernest Benn, 1929).

Lord Melbourne believed the conduct of executive government 'rested so much on practice, on usage, on understanding, that there is no particular publication to which reference can be made for the explanation and description of it. It is to be sought in debates, in protests, in letters, in memoirs, and wherever it can be picked up'. Even a cursory examination of the nineteenth century, which saw the active phase of Melbourne's political career, shows how practices and principles though deeply historical and intrinsic to the constitution are, in fact, of more recent innovation and expedience. As G. H. L. Le May shows, key conventions, which many consider akin to constitutional law took shape only in Queen Victoria's reign. Conventions that only came about in the Victorian age include: a parliamentary majority is a condition of taking office; a ruling party enjoys autonomy in cabinet selection; the speech from the throne, and matters of defence and foreign policy are the government's responsibility unshared with the monarch; the House of Commons is the dominant institution of the constitution; the cabinet is collectively responsible; and the monarch is obliged to follow the advice of the incumbent administration, only came of age under the Victorian Constitution. It would be remiss to ignore the fact that the person behind this eponymous constitution did not always move with the times. Queen Victoria still believed she needed to give to her heir the constitution that she 'inherited' in 1837 from William IV, despite the coming of a very different era of constitutional usage and custom. Perhaps this explains Victoria's solution for avoiding undesirable counsel from William Gladstone. The Sovereign simply told her Prime Minister 'she did not wish to receive advice'.[83] This also illustrates how emotion and human nature invest themselves in constitutional norms. Sir Henry Maine sensed this. To him the British constitution

> if not (as some call it) a holy thing, is a thing unique and remarkable. A series of undesigned changes brought it to such a condition, that satisfaction and impatience, the two great sources of political conduct, were both reasonably gratified under it.[84]

As Sir Courtney Ilbert, Clerk to the House of Commons, elegantly, but with steely appreciation, explained, in a letter in November 1909 to prime minister Herbert Asquith during a time of political crisis, 'There are occasions when respect for the constitution must override respect for the law.'[85]

---

[83] G. H. L. Le May, *The Victorian Constitution: Conventions, Usages and Contingencies* (London: Duckworth, 1979), pp. 63–84.
[84] Maine, *Popular Government*, p. 54.   [85] Jenkins, *Asquith*, p. 201.

Ilbert's analysis provides a neat statement of the constitution's generous allowance for expedience. This feature was also crucially attractive to various groups from foreign dynasties on the throne, to trades unions and outsiders, who reasoned that constitutional power could be theirs. Both Monarchists and Marxists could utilise such history. A close reading of British constitutional history showed how the constitution enabled levers of state to be used in extraordinary ways, but also largely imperceptibly since, outwardly, institutions such as parliament remained, and traditions, invented and real, were honoured and remarketed. John Locke argued in 1690, a critical English constitutional principle, namely the 'power to act according to discretion, for the public good, without the prescription of the law, and sometimes even against it'. Clinton Rossiter believed this to be a classic statement of the constitution's historical power to allow the rise of dictatorial powers within the established customs of the state.[86]

The institutions and laws of the state enabled considerable reforms and changes to British society. William Beveridge, for example, saw the constitution's ability to create the welfare state, or 'social service state' as he preferred to call it, and formalise his principle of 'bread and health for all before cake and circuses for any', despite disappointments in application.[87] The Welsh Labour party titan, Aneurin Bevan, spoke approvingly of the British constitution's 'revolutionary quality' since it affords 'a flexibility enjoyed by few nations' to transform society without appeal. To Bevan, the 'British constitution, with its adult suffrage, exposes all rights and privileges, properties and powers, to the popular will'.[88] In periods of crisis and dramatic reform across British history, law was still craved to legitimise that which seemed irredeemable. Of the Cromwellian Commonwealth, with its brutal and violent battles at home and across the Irish sea, it was said 'they wished ... to fix a legal wig upon the point of a soldier's sword'.[89] The constitutional history of Britain is one that shows a symbiotic relationship between law, convention and political behaviour. The law is both a check and an instrument of politics. Statutes, conventions, and the common law operate not just under the burden of history, but also for the needs of a society and state used to finding a solution for its ever-changing requirements

---

[86] Clinton Rossiter, *Constitutional Dictatorship: Crisis Government in the Modern Democracies* (London, Transaction Publishers, [1948], 2009), pp. 138–139.
[87] José Harris, *William Beveridge: A Biography* (Oxford: Clarendon Press, 1977), pp. 458–461.
[88] Vernon Bogdanor, *The New British Constitution* (Oxford: Hart, 2009), p. 40.
[89] Warner and Marten, *Groundwork*, p. 392.

within its constitutional corpus. As Sidney Low argued, the constitution 'enshrines within its being the principle of Life and the principle of Law. Its capacity for growth, its rhythmical flexibility, have not left it'.[90]

Conclusion

At the beginning of the twentieth century a student doing the History Tripos at Cambridge could expect around seventy lectures in 'English' constitutional history and likely another fifteen in comparative constitutions. In earlier times students crammed the 'sacred' texts by the likes of Bishop Stubbs, which 'were approached by the devout disciple in much the same spirit as that in which the youthful Brahmin draws near to the Vedas'.[91] At times the craft of constitutional history has been dominant and unavoidable while at other periods, including more recently, training in constitutional history evades entry in the historian's manual. The field of constitutional history is not for a rarefied scholarly caste, and nor are there sacred texts, which must be read to uncover its revelations. Instead, constitutional history is critical to understanding so many areas of life, society and government. Constitutional history's wider importance is reflected in it being grounded in, and best engaged via a multi-disciplinary vantage, especially History, Law and Politics. The constitution's role in history requires a broad thematic approach to appreciate its deep ubiquity. It has been argued in this chapter that the historical constitution can be usefully recognised through three sets of connected themes. The theme of culture and ideas is essential to understanding the historical constitution since the constitution has been central to debates over identity and legitimacy. In this, the constitution's history is shown to be more than documents and institutions: it is also pivotal to the culture of society and ideas of governance. Power and people are at the heart of the constitution's history and a theme of enduring relevance. Too often constitutional history has been characterised as one of antiquarianism at the edge of history, yet in fact it is mandatory in evaluating the exercise of power as well as how people of all levels have been affected by the constitution's influence. Through the theme of law and utility we are witness to contestation over constitutional norms and the use of institutions. The tension between changing canons of the constitution and the assorted practices of

---

[90] Low, *Governance of England*, p. 311.
[91] J. R. Tanner, 'The Teaching of Constitutional History' in W. A. J. Archbold (ed.), *Essays on the Teaching of History* (Cambridge: Cambridge University Press, 1901), pp. 51–68.

the state are a fundamental theme of constitutional history. Together these themes give an impression of the wide-ranging reach of constitutional history and its influence and relationship with the state. If nothing else, the historical constitution inherently binds the tangled fabric of the United Kingdom and its parts.

2

Law and the Constitution

PETER CANE

Introduction

'Law' and 'constitution', like other concepts we use to make sense of the world, have a history.[1] In the case of law, part of that history is the ongoing interplay between two different ideas. One is that law concerns what people should, should not and may do. In other words, law is 'normative'. Another is that law is a product of human activity. Human beings and institutions can and do make and enforce legal norms. In Western legal and political theory, these two ideas are often crystallised into rival schools of thought about the nature of law: natural law and positivism. However, historically rather than theoretically, the focus of this chapter is on the age-old interaction between the two aspects of law. A further persistent strand in thinking about law concerns whether law tells us not only what we ought, ought not and may do but also what we *really* ought, ought not and may do. This chapter says nothing about this debate or its history. The chapter's starting point is that an important aspect of the history of law and its relationship to the constitution is the interplay between the ideas of law as norm and law as artefact.

The history of the concept of 'constitution' also chronicles an interplay between two different understandings of what a constitution is: one 'organic' and the other 'synthetic'. In the organic sense everything, including individuals, groups, institutions, states, nations, has a 'constitution', a 'nature', a 'make-up'. In the synthetic sense, a constitution is a written document: the United States Constitution of 1789 is paradigmatic. These two understandings

---

[1] I owe a great debt of thanks to H. Kumarasingham for helping me frame the argument of this chapter.

exist side by side throughout the period covered by this volume. In the medieval period, the word 'constitution' was sometimes used in the synthetic sense, as in the so-called Constitutions of Clarendon of 1164. With the benefit of hindsight, Magna Carta is sometimes thought of as England's first constitution. In discussion of politics and government since the eighteenth century, the synthetic sense has eclipsed the organic sense. In the history of the UK, however, the interplay between the two senses has occupied and continues to occupy a central place.

This chapter makes a risky attempt to tell a plausible, coherent and worthwhile story about the interplay, over a millennium, between law understood bi-focally as norm and artefact, and constitution understood bi-focally as organic and synthetic. The first of the following sections covers a period beginning with Magna Carta and ending in the late nineteenth century. The second and third sections focus on the scholarship of A. V. Dicey, whose contribution to and influence on the study of the UK constitution and, within it, the role of law, have been immeasurable. The fourth section considers the period after Dicey flowing into the present and the future. The conclusion returns to the starting point by arguing (in light of the history) that law (understood as both norm and artefact) has always played a significant role in the constitution, but more so at certain times than at others, and increasingly so since the mid-twentieth century. In the UK context, however, the essentially organic nature of the legal constitution (despite significant synthetic accretions) suggests that law may play a larger role in limitation and control of political power than in its creation, exercise and maintenance.

The Development of the Legal Constitution: From Magna Carta to A. V. Dicey

Law, as norm and artefact, has always played a central role in the English polity. One of the main strands in the development of the English state after the Norman Conquest was the creation, under the auspices of the monarchy, of a unified (though partly de-centralised) court system and a 'common law' for the whole country. The provision of legal services was, at one and the same time, both an obligation of monarchy and a source of its power and legitimacy. Magna Carta – for centuries treated as the first 'statute of the realm' and a foundational constitutional document (in both the organic and synthetic senses) – is saturated with law talk. Most famously, chapters 39 and 40 of Magna Carta 1215 (amalgamated into chapter 29 in all subsequent versions, and still on the statute book as one of three remaining provisions of the 1297 enrolled version) went as follows:[2]

> No free man shall be seized or imprisoned, or stripped of his rights or possessions, or outlawed or exiled, or deprived of his standing in any way, nor will we proceed with force against him, or send others to do so, except by the lawful judgement of his equals or by the law of the land. To no one will we sell, to no one deny or delay right or justice.

Over a period of several decades in the mid-fourteenth century, Parliament played around with various elements of chapter 29.[3] A provision of 1351 was directed against creation and operation of criminal courts that did not follow 'common-law' procedure by indictment or writ but allowed complaint by simple petition. A statute of 1354 introduced the phrase 'due process of law' to describe the standard against which the acceptability of criminal proceedings was to be assessed. In a petition for confirmation of the Charter in 1362, Parliament complained about arrests by royal command in disregard of common-law procedures; and in 1369, it legislated against arrest and charge 'without presentment before justices, or matter of record, or by due process and writ original, according to the old law of the land'.

Other, less famous, provisions of the 1215 Charter include chapter 17: 'Ordinary lawsuits shall not follow the royal court around, but shall be held in a fixed place'; chapter 18: 'Inquests of novel disseisin, mort d'ancestor, and darrein presentment shall be taken only in their proper county court'; chapter 24: 'No sheriff, constable, coroners, or other royal officials are to hold lawsuits that should be held by the royal justices'; chapter 34: 'The writ called *precipe* shall not in future be issued to anyone in respect of any holding of land, if a free man could thereby be deprived of the right of trial in his own lord's court'; and chapter 44: 'People who live outside the forest need not in future appear before the royal justices of the forest in answer to general summonses, unless they are actually involved in proceedings or are sureties for someone who has been seized for a forest offence.'

These provisions were concerned with procedural and institutional matters, not substantive law; and, in this sense at least, they were 'constitutional'. Chapter 17 foreshadowed the establishment at Westminster of what came to

---

[2] I have used the British Library translation reproduced in R. Hazell and J. Melton (eds.), *Magna Carta and Its Modern Legacy* (Cambridge: Cambridge University Press, 2015), 233–242; also available at www.bl.uk/magna-carta/articles/magna-carta-english-translation.

[3] R. V. Turner, *Magna Carta through the Ages* (London: Routledge, 2003), 123–124.

be called the 'Court of Common Pleas' – in other words, a court dealing with litigation between subject and subject. Together with the Court of Exchequer and the Court of King's Bench, which were particularly concerned with matters that involved or affected the interests (rights and duties) of the monarch, it formed what became known as 'the common-law courts', staffed by 'the common-law judges' (or 'justices'). The processes and procedures of these courts and the law they administered collectively came to be called 'the common law of England'. This was distinguished from civil and canon law and procedure, associated with ecclesiastical and admiralty courts, for instance. As chapter 29 of Magna Carta suggests, the common law of the land was meant to bind monarch and subject alike. There was a sort of contract under which both sides mutually promised to respect and comply with the common law of the land and the processes and procedures through which it was administered: the monarch as governor and the people as governed.

The establishment of permanent courts at Westminster began a long and gradual process of separation of the administration of justice from other governmental activities and recognition of the constitutional role of courts as controllers, not just organs, of government. In the wake of curial settlement at Westminster there also appeared a profession of lawyers who represented litigants and discoursed with judges about the cases in which their clients were involved. They included individuals, called 'Serjeants' or 'Attorneys', appointed and employed by the monarch to represent royal interests before the courts. In the middle of the fifteenth century, a new permanent office of Attorney General was created to supplement, but not replace, the office of King's Serjeant and to provide the monarch with 'general legal counsel', somewhat in the modern corporate sense.

The creation of courts that were institutionally distinct from the rest of government, which was identified with the monarch's various councils, did not spell the end of the involvement of the monarch and councillors in the provision of legal services and the judicial enforcement of law. Sometime in the fifteenth century, a conciliar group that met in the Star Chamber of the old Palace of Westminster developed a sideline in judicial services, which grew in popularity and success until things went off the rails during the reign of Charles II, leading to the abolition of the Court of Star Chamber (and other conciliar courts) by Parliament in 1641. This marked the culmination of a long battle by common-law judges and, latterly, MPs, to stamp out competition to the common-law courts not only by monarch and council but also the Church (although after the split with Rome, ecclesiastical courts theoretically came under royal control). One of the weapons used by the common lawyers against rival jurisdictions was the writ of habeas corpus, which could be deployed both to secure the physical presence of a litigant before a common-law court and to prohibit their physical appearance before any but a common-law court – in other words, to move people around the justice system. The personal involvement of the monarch in the administration of justice also became highly controversial in the early seventeenth century. In 1607, Sir Edward Coke, who was then Chief Justice of the Court of Common Pleas, advised the King that he could not, 'in his own person . . . adjudge any case, either criminal or betwixt party and party; but it ought to be determined and adjudged in some Court of Justice, according to the law and custom of England'.[4] The expression of such opinions eventually led to Coke's translation from the Court of Common Pleas to the (less important) Court of King's Bench and, then, to his dismissal from the judiciary in 1616. Coke continued his campaign as a member of the House of Commons and leading proponent of the Petition of Right of 1628.

The new constitutional settlement put in place by the Glorious Revolution, the Bill of Rights 1689 and the Act of Settlement 1701 kick-started a transformation of the position and role of law and the courts in governmental arrangements. The monarch no longer had any right of personal, direct participation in the administration of justice; and the monarch's formal role in the legislative process was reduced to a right of veto (necessitating recourse by the Crown to informal modes of influence). The monarch's power to dismiss judges was conditioned upon a request for dismissal by both Houses of Parliament; and, from the mid-eighteenth century, judicial appointments were no longer terminated by the death of the monarch. Courts were now to be understood as agents of Parliament, not the monarch; and, in that capacity, they assumed a monopoly over authoritative interpretation of Parliamentary legislation. The separate and independent role of the courts in handling matters between subject and subject was untouched by these events. Moreover, legal rules applicable between subjects (contract and tort law, for example) could apply in cases against government officials, who were, despite their position and function, treated – for these purposes and in this context – as ordinary citizens: 'citizens in uniform' as John Gardner felicitously called them.[5] The monarch, personally,

---

[4] *Prohibitions del Roy* [1607] EWHC KB J23; 12 Co Rep 64.
[5] J. Gardner, 'Criminals in Uniform' in R. A. Duff, L. Farmer, S. E. Marshall, M. Renzo and V. Tadros (eds.), *The Constitution of the Criminal Law* (Oxford: Oxford University Press, 2013), 98.

had never been subject to such law, and (reflecting the shift of power from monarchy to legislature) Article 9 of the Bill of Rights 1689 protected (and protects) MPs from being sued, as ordinary citizens, for the tort of defamation (for instance) on the basis of things said in the course of 'proceedings in Parliament'. Throughout the seventeenth century, the Court of King's Bench developed the pre-existing administrative writs of mandamus, prohibition and certiorari as judicial mechanisms for exercising control, in the name of law, over government administration, especially at the local level.[6] The Court of Star Chamber had also been much involved in exercising control, in the name of the Crown, over administrative government at both central and local levels. Its abolition in 1641 left a hole that, in the case of central government, was not to be fully plugged until the late twentieth century.

The dramatic events of the seventeenth century stimulated much thought and debate about the nature, structure and functions of government. Law and courts were more or less invisible to early theorists, such as John Locke, who were interested primarily in the distribution of legislative power (the power to make general rules), on the one hand, and administrative or executive power to manage the country's affairs both at home and abroad, on the other. Unsurprisingly, perhaps, given long-standing identification of the monarch as the fount of justice, settling disputes and exercising jurisdiction and judgment were thought of essentially as aspects of administration. Similarly, although Montesquieu noticed courts in the English constitutional set-up, he thought that they had (or should have) no distinct function separate from that of the legislative and executive organs of government.

William Blackstone was instrumental in shifting the paradigm. He innovated in two crucial ways. First, he stressed the importance of the judiciary and its independence in maintaining a balanced constitution. In his account, judging is not merely an aspect of administration (as it was for Locke) and courts are not mechanical adjuncts of the legislature and the executive (as they were for Montesquieu).[7] Second, Blackstone's declared purpose was to explain the substance of English law.[8] Ever since the Norman Conquest, thinking and writing about the English legal system had been concerned predominantly with matters of institutional structure and interaction, and

---

[6] R. G. Henderson, *Foundations of English Administrative Law: Certiorari and Mandamus in the Seventeenth Century* (Cambridge, MA: Harvard University Press, 1963).

[7] A. M. Cohler, B. C. Miller and H. S. Stone, *Montesquieu: The Spirit of the Laws* (Cambridge: Cambridge University Press, 1989) (hereafter '*Montesquieu*'), 158.

[8] D. Lemmings (ed.), *William Blackstone Commentaries on the Law of England, Book I* (Oxford: Oxford University Press, 2016), 9–32.

issues of process and procedure. Works that focused on what the law was, as opposed to how it was created, administered and enforced, were quite rare. In this sense, legal knowledge was essentially 'constitutional': what was most important was to know how the system worked and could be worked. Outcomes and their substance (whether in the form of statutes, decrees, regulations or court decisions) were a sort of by-product. Law and justice were, essentially, matters of institutional structure and procedure. Blackstone thought that legal knowledge of how the system was structured and worked was interesting and comprehensible only to those actively involved in the system: legislators, administrators, judges and lawyers. What the ordinary educated punter most wanted and needed to know was what the law said, not how it worked.

Blackstone framed his substantive account of English law with three distinctions. First, he said, law is about rights and wrongs. Second, there are two types of rights: rights of persons and rights of (in and over) things. Third, there are two types of wrongs: public (criminal) and private (non-criminal or 'civil'). The distinction between persons and things comes from Roman law. A third heading under which Roman law was organised was the law of actions – procedural law. Blackstone did his best to translate the procedural law of actions into the substantive law of public and private wrongs.[9] In the volume dealing with the rights of persons, Blackstone dealt not only with the 'absolute rights of individuals' and with relationships such as master and servant, and husband and wife but also (at great length) with the rights of Parliament, the King, the King's Councils and Prerogatives, subordinate magistrates, the clergy, the civil state and so on – in summary, what we would now call 'constitutional law'.

As Linda Colley has recently chronicled,[10] the eighteenth century also witnessed the invention of the modern written, canonical constitutional document called 'The Constitution'. In *Federalist No 1*, Alexander Hamilton described the process of constitution-making in terms of 'establishing good government from reflection and choice ... [not] accident and force'.[11] This new technology was widely adopted in the nineteenth century and has

---

[9] Radical reform of the English law of actions, which shifted the focus from process and procedure to substance, did not start in earnest until the 1830s and was not complete until 1875. However, English law still carries many of the marks of its origins as a system of process and procedure for resolving disputes.

[10] L. Colley, *The Gun, the Ship and the Pen: Warfare, Constitutions, and the Making of the Modern World* (London: Profile Books, 2021).

[11] A. Hamilton, J. Madison and J. Jay, *The Federalist Papers* (Oxford: Oxford University Press, 2008), 11.

proved so successful that the UK is one of only a very few states that have not, to date, employed it. Despite this 'UK exceptionalism', the invention of the written constitution is relevant to our story in two ways. First, it gave rise to a new usage of the word 'constitution' – what I have called the 'synthetic' sense. Previously, this word had typically (though not exclusively) been used in an organic sense to refer to the nature or make-up of a polity and the way it was governed. For instance, Montesquieu said that 'political laws ... [concerned with] the relation between those who govern and those who are governed ... should be related [inter alia] to the degree of liberty that the constitution can maintain'.[12] Second, the US Constitution came to be understood as a legal document in the sense that (at least some of) its provisions were enforceable by the Supreme Court.[13] Moreover, the theory was that the Constitution expressed the sovereignty of 'the people' and was, therefore, 'fundamental law' from which all other laws (provided they were consistent with the Constitution) derived their force, and from which all governmental institutions derived their power and authority as delegates of the people. These were conceptual and theoretical changes of deep and wide significance.

A. V. Dicey on Laws and Conventions of the Constitution

Colley posits various factors to explain why advocacy for a written constitution did not succeed in Britain in the eighteenth and nineteenth centuries: 'an early curbing of royal power, a setting out in law of certain religious and civil rights, a precocious entrenchment of the powers and position of the Westminster Parliament ... a strong financial system ... substantial immunity after 1700 from major civil wars and successful invasions, plus a generally high level of warlike success'.[14] All of these factors may have played a part; but I would argue that the roots of the matter lie deeper in the constitutional soil. Prominent early in the seventeenth-century English constitutional crisis was Coke's ideological use of the concept of an ancient constitution and its reassertion to resist the strengthening of the monarchy. Similarly, Coke espoused the idea that change in the common law was not a matter of looking to a better future but of tracking changes that had already taken place in the customary life of the community. The constitutional crisis

---

[12] Montesquieu, 8–9.   [13] Marbury v. Madison (1803).
[14] Colley, The Gun, the Ship and the Pen, 215.

was punctuated by a civil war and a short-lived experiment in 'republicanism' that included an ill-fated attempt, in the Instrument of Government, to reduce the English constitution to writing. The aptly named 'Restoration' of 1660 more or less erased the Interregnum from the political zeitgeist; and the Bill of Rights 1689 was not dissimilar in tone and spirit to Magna Carta – both identified the main political problem facing the country not as the need to change the world but to set it to rights. A century later, shorn of its Whiggish tone of celebration, Edmund Burke's conservative and incrementalist reaction to the French Revolution reflected and expressed a strong historical strand in the English approach to constitutional change.

Over the course of the next century, the English constitution went through a process of change at least as dramatic as what had been achieved in short order by the North American colonists. By some sort of constitutional alchemy, the constitution of 1900 was essentially the same as, but also utterly different from, the constitution of 1800, let alone 1600. Statutes had played their part in this transformation, particularly in the nineteenth century, as the relative strength of the legislature in the constitution gradually increased. However, written documents were only a small part of the story. To understand why, we need to think about the ways various types of norms are made and changed.

'Customary' norms change as a result of changing patterns of what we might call 'normative behaviour' – human social behaviour expressive of and driven by shared value judgments. Although evidenced by writing, common law is a form of customary law in this sense: as Coke might have put it, the common law is the product of the practices of the common-law courts – judges and advocates – concerned, in turn, faithfully to express community norms and normative practices. The making and changing of custom are ongoing, incremental processes. By contrast, the making and changing of statutes and Constitutions are episodic and punctuated. Statutes and synthetic Constitutions do not emerge over time: they are deliberately made at specific points in time. Statutes and synthetic Constitutions do not evolve over time: they are deliberately amended or repealed at specific points in time. Moreover, one of the most significant differences between statutes and Constitutions is that Constitutions are typically made and changed by different, and more elaborate, demanding and time-consuming procedures than statutes. In informal parlance, Constitutional norms are more 'rigid'[15] or 'sticky', less flexible

---

[15] This was the term used, in preference to 'written', by James Bryce, *Studies in History and Jurisprudence* (New York: Oxford University Press, 1901), 124–215.

and malleable, than statutory norms. The US Constitution, for instance, has been formally amended only twenty-nine times since 1789 and more than a third of those amendments were made in one hit in 1791. Again, because the conditions of success are very strict, only a small minority of attempts to amend the Australian Constitution have succeeded.

The distinction between customary law and deliberately manufactured law is blurred when Constitutions and statutes are interpreted and applied by courts in individual cases. Interpretation by courts of statutory and Constitutional texts has the same customary quality as common law. As a result, it introduces an element of incrementalism into the processes of statutory and Constitutional change. Moreover, and importantly, except by the courts themselves, authoritative judicial interpretations of statutes and Constitutions can be deliberately changed or abrogated only by the same episodic and punctuated processes as statutes and Constitutions are, themselves, deliberately made and changed. The practice of authoritative judicial interpretation of Constitutions, in particular, effectively provides a route to amendment alternative to that provided by the Constitution itself – namely, litigation. This helps to explain why the US Supreme Court plays such an important role in relation to the US Constitution which, as we have seen, is very rigid and sticky.

With this theoretical digression in mind, we can now return to our story of the English constitution. One of the effects of the rise of the written Constitution was the creation of a strong association between deliberate, rigid, sticky law-making and the idea of a 'constitution'. This led to the invention of a new concept of 'constitutional law' referring, first and foremost, to the contents of a canonical Constitution. Could this new concept be applied to a system that lacked a canonical Constitution? The first and most influential attempt, to analyse the relationship between the concepts of law and the constitution in the English system in the age of written constitutions, was, and still is, that of A. V. Dicey in his *Introduction to the Study of the Law of the Constitution*, first published in 1885. By this time, the word 'constitution' was being used – by Walter Bagehot, for instance[16] – to describe the English system of government. It was clear to Dicey both that law was part of the English constitution but also that there was much more to it than that. Indeed, Dicey called Bagehot a 'political theorist' concerned 'mainly with

---

[16] In *The English Constitution*, first published in 1867.

political understandings and not with rules of law':[17] with (as Bagehot put it) the 'efficient' as opposed to the 'dignified' institutions of government. Dicey distinguished between constitutional law and such 'political understandings', dubbing the latter 'conventions of the constitution'. Although, in his view, conventions, like laws, were prescriptive rather than merely descriptive of political practice, they were not enforceable by a court and, thus, were not laws 'strictly so called'.

Leaving aside for the moment the issue of court enforceability, this was a brilliant and enduring insight about constitutions. Constitutions contain norms – that is, statements about the way things ought, ought not and may be done constitutionally – that frame and regulate the conduct of politics and the exercise of governmental power. Some of those norms may be deliberately made, rigid and sticky to varying degrees; but (leaving aside judicial interpretations) others may be customary, the product of ongoing normative practices. In the case of constitutional conventions, the salient practices are not those of society at large or of courts but of those engaged in government and politics – especially legislative and executive politics and government. This insight is not uniquely applicable to a constitution of the English type: customary norms (whether legal or political) are a feature of all constitutions. However, the existence and importance of non-legal, political norms have proved to be much harder to appreciate in systems crowned by a canonical, legal constitution. For instance, only in relatively recent years have US constitutional scholars begun to give 'conventions' (customary constitutional norms) the attention they deserve.

Laws and conventions of the constitution are similar to one another in being prescriptive; but how do they differ? Dicey's answer to this question has proven much less successful than his basic insight. As already noted, Dicey argued that laws are, but conventions are not, enforceable by a court. Nevertheless, he claimed, while conventions are not 'strictly' law, they are dependent on law in the sense that a breach of convention will, sooner rather than later, lead to a breach of law which is enforceable by a court. The first of these propositions was fatally undermined as long ago as 1880 by the Austrian public lawyer, Georg Jellinek,[18] who pointed out that much

---

[17] J. Allison (ed.), *A.V. Dicey, The Law of the Constitution* (Oxford: Oxford University Press, 2013), 18.
[18] M. Koskenniemi, 'A History of International Law Histories' in B. Fassbender and A. Peters (eds.), *The Oxford Handbook of the History of International Law* (Oxford: Oxford University Press, 2012), 958.

constitutional law is, like much international law, unenforceable.[19] Even in a system with a canonical, legal Constitution, certain provisions of the Constitution may be considered 'non-justiciable' because they raise purely 'political questions' beyond the jurisdiction of a court to resolve.[20] The second proposition is also false: for instance, it is (at the very least) highly unlikely that a breach by the monarch, of the convention that the advice of the Prime Minister to prorogue Parliament must be accepted, would (by itself) lead to a breach of any law.

If laws and conventions cannot be distinguished in terms of their enforceability, how then? It may be tempting to say that laws are (deliberately) 'written' (down) but conventions are not. However, conventions may be reduced to writing in forms similar to provisions of Constitutions and statutes (and unlike the forms of reasoning recorded in written reports of court decisions). This has happened in the UK increasingly in recent years.[21] As already suggested, the most significant distinction between laws and conventions of the constitution is not their form or how (if at all) they are enforced but, rather, who makes and can change them. In the English system, Parliament and senior courts can make constitutional law – statutory in the former case and common law in the latter. The practices of Parliament and the senior courts may also generate conventions in situations in which they do not purport to be exercising their law-making powers. This, we may say, is because, even when they are not making law, they are political, governmental and constitutional actors. Moreover, the practices of political, governmental and constitutional actors that lack law-making power can generate conventions.

The Diceyan analysis of the constitution raises another fundamental question. We have already noted that the invention of the written, canonical Constitution made it possible to define 'constitutional law' in terms of the contents of the Constitution. But how is 'constitutional law' to be defined and distinguished from non-constitutional law in a system that lacks a large-C Constitution? Dicey answered this question by claiming that '[t]he true law of the constitution is ... to be gathered from the same sources whence we collect the law of England in respect of any other topic'.[22] For Dicey, in other

---

[19] C. A. Whytock, 'Thinking beyond the Domestic-International Divide: Toward a Unified Concept of Public Law' (2004) 36 *Georgetown Journal of International Law* 155.
[20] M. Tushnet, *The Constitution of the United States of America: A Contextual Analysis*, 2nd ed. (Oxford: Hart Publishing, 2015), 145–149.
[21] A. Blick, *The Codes of the Constitution* (Oxford: Hart Publishing, 2016).
[22] J. W. F. Allison (ed.), A. V. Dicey, *The Law of the Constitution* (Oxford: Oxford University Press, 2013) (hereafter '*Dicey*'), 25.

words, the only difference between constitutional and non-constitutional law was that they deal with different topics. Constitutional law is an area of 'ordinary' law, not an extraordinary, fundamental type of law. In his words, it consists of 'all rules which directly or indirectly affect the distribution or the exercise of the sovereign power in the state'.[23] These may include not only what Montesquieu called 'political laws', which deal with 'the relation between those who govern and those who are governed' but also 'civil laws' dealing with 'the relation that all citizens have with one another'.[24] For example, tort law is a branch of 'civil law'; but rules of tort law dealing with trespass to the person and to land, and false imprisonment, have for centuries played an important 'constitutional' role in controlling government power to search, seize and detain.[25]

A. V. Dicey on Courts and the Rule of Law

Dicey argued that the English constitution embodied three basic principles, summarily expressible as follows: Parliamentary sovereignty, the coexistence of laws and conventions, and the rule of law. He broke down the rule of law into three propositions that can loosely be stated as follows: first, that state coercion may be used against subjects only in response to a breach of the law; second, that government officials, like ordinary citizens, are subject to the 'ordinary' law administered by the 'ordinary' courts that administer law as between citizen and citizen as opposed to a separate set of courts administering law as between citizens and government; and third, that the legal, civil and political rights of the citizen are the product of the same processes of law-making as any other legal provision: they are not conferred by a documentary bill of rights.[26] The rule of law, so understood, places courts at the very heart of the constitution. The principle of Parliamentary supremacy meant that courts had no power to strike down an Act of Parliament; but apart from that, they could invalidate any governmental action that did not comply with the law of the land as they (subject to Parliamentary reversal) said it to be. Law made by courts is just as much law as law made by Parliament even though, in case of conflict, the latter prevails over the former. Law made by courts does not owe its status as such to

---

[23] *Dicey*, 20. [24] *Montesquieu*, 7.
[25] E.g., *Entick* v. *Carrington* (1765) 19 St Tr 1030; 95 ER 807.
[26] This aspect of Dicey's work is discussed in more detail in Chapter 9 of this volume.

powers conferred by Parliament. At the same time, because constitutional conventions are not strictly law, compliance with a recognised convention cannot 'cure' breach of a law.

Although Dicey described his *magnum opus* as being about 'constitutional' law, the second element of his account of the rule of law is centrally concerned with an area of law now called 'administrative law'. Whereas (I have argued) the concept of constitutional law was a product of the invention of the canonical, written constitution in the eighteenth century, the separate category of administrative law was being invented (in England at any rate) only around the time Dicey was writing.[27] It was a product of the rapid and ongoing expansion of the executive branch of central government and dramatic growth of its administrative functions. One feature of the new, so-called 'administrative state' was extensive conferral by Parliament on Ministers of power to make 'subordinate' (or 'secondary' or 'delegated') legislation. The term 'administrative law' is sometimes used to describe law made by the executive as delegate of the legislature. More commonly, however, the term is used to refer to law that, on the one hand, grants powers (including rule-making powers) to the executive and, on the other, regulates the use of such powers in the name of law. A very common view about Dicey is that when he said something along the lines that there is no administrative law in England, he was using 'administrative law' in this latter sense. A more plausible interpretation is that he was referring to the absence, in England, of a set of courts, separate and distinct from the 'ordinary' courts, that dealt exclusively with relations between citizens and government as opposed to relations between citizens amongst themselves. Dicey devoted significant attention to habeas corpus – one of the main mechanisms used by courts to control administrative government. In that context, he said that '[t]he judges therefore are in truth, though not in name, invested with the means of hampering or supervising the whole administrative action of government, and of at once putting a veto on any proceeding not authorised by the letter of the law'.[28] However, he more or less ignored the other mechanisms – notably the writs of mandamus, prohibition and certiorari – that, over the preceding three centuries, the Court of King's/Queen's Bench had utilised and developed to exercise control over the administration, especially at the local level.

---

[27] The first English book on what we now call administrative law did not appear until 1929: F. J. Port, *Administrative Law* (London: Longmans, Green & Co, 1929).
[28] Dicey, 130.

Why Dicey restricted his coverage in this way is unclear, as are the reasons why he remained, for about 30 years, unable or unwilling to explain his approach. Be that as it may, the obvious question is why administrative law is put into a separate legal category and not treated as part of the law of the constitution (as Dicey seems to have been inclined to do)? In my opinion, the best explanations are historical and pedagogical rather than theoretical. In the West, with the notable exception of Germany, the growth spurt of the executive, and of the administrative functions of government associated with administrative law, post-dated the events that gave rise to the concept of constitutional law. If what lawyers call 'administrative law' were treated as part of the law of the constitution, law would loom much larger in 'the constitution' than it is currently perceived to do.

After Dicey

An alleged consequence of the standard interpretation of Dicey's attitude to administrative law is that the development of judicial review of government administration and the significance of courts as constitutional actors were significantly delayed. The standard story is that courts were quite unwilling to interfere with the conduct of government during the first half of the twentieth century.[29] However, in a series of cases in the 1960s the (judicial) House of Lords signalled a willingness to review government action more searchingly to assess its lawfulness.[30] Moreover, the constitutional position of courts was very considerably strengthened by Britain's membership of the EU from 1973 to 2020. Under EU law, courts of Member States have the power and obligation to invalidate laws of their Member States, including sovereign legislation, that are inconsistent with directly applicable EU laws.[31] Even though, under English law, this power was derived ultimately from the European Communities Act enacted by the Westminster Parliament itself in 1972, it gave rise to a new concept of 'higher' law with which all other law, including Parliamentary legislation, had to comply. In this sense, it could be

---

[29] S. Sedley, 'The Long Sleep' in M. Andenas and D. Fairgrieve (eds.), *Tom Bingham and the Transformation of the Law: A Liber Amicorum* (Oxford: Oxford University Press, 2009).

[30] T. T. Arvind, R. Kirkham, D. MacSíthigh and L. Stirton (eds.), *Executive Decision-Making and the Courts: Revisiting the Origins of Modern Judicial Review* (Oxford: Hart Publishing, 2021).

[31] R v. *Secretary of State for Transport, ex parte Factortame Ltd* [1991] 1 AC 603.

said that (between 1973 and 2020) 'directly applicable' EU law[32] effectively enjoyed large-C Constitutional status in the UK legal system.

Accession by the UK government to the European Convention on Human Rights (ECHR) in 1952 followed, in 1964, by its acceptance of the right of individual petition to the European Court of Human Rights (ECtHR), also had a significant effect on the constitutional position of the courts.[33] In the 1970s and 1980s the increasingly common 'spectacle' of the UK government being successfully sued for human rights breaches in Strasbourg not only led to high-profile campaigns for a UK bill of rights as part of a written constitution. It also played a part in encouraging the courts to attempt to strengthen domestic protection of human rights by inventing a new concept of 'fundamental common-law rights' according to which such judicially created or recognised rights could be abridged or abrogated by Parliament only by using the clearest and most specific statutory language and not, as it were, 'by a side wind'. This is an exception to the general rule that statute can displace common law impliedly – express words are not needed provided the words that are used can reasonably be interpreted as implying abrogation.

This technique for protecting common law from statutory encroachment was rendered more or less redundant by enactment of the Human Rights Act 1998, which effectively superseded the common law as a source of rights because English courts generally assume that Convention rights cover at least as much ground as common-law rights. This Act does not empower courts to invalidate Parliamentary legislation on the ground of inconsistency with the ECHR. However, if a legislative provision cannot be interpreted consistently with the ECHR, the Supreme Court may declare that the provision is incompatible with Convention rights. The effect of this provision has been to encourage the courts to go to extreme lengths to interpret legislation consistently with Convention rights. A legislative attempt to infringe such rights will succeed only if the words of the statute leave, in the court's opinion, absolutely no room for doubt that infringement was the goal of the legislature. Indeed, a court may even add words to a statute to render it compliant. At this point, the distinction between interpreting law and making law becomes, at least, very blurred. A declaration of invalidity imposes an obligation on the government either to bring the provision into line with the ECHR, by amendment or repeal, or to take the political risk of ignoring the declaration and facing fresh litigation before the ECtHR (or defeat at the polls).

---

[32] Not all EU law was directly applicable.   [33] See also Chapter 9 in this volume.

The European Communities Act 1972 (now repealed) and the Human Rights Act 1998 are examples of what are now called 'constitutional' statutes. The development of this concept has given the distinction, between constitutional and non-constitutional law, legal significance it did not have for Dicey. What distinguishes constitutional statutes from their non-constitutional cousins is not who made them or how they were made but rather their effect. The basic common-law rule of statutory interpretation is that a more recently made statute that is inconsistent with an older statute 'impliedly repeals' the older statute, even if it does not do so expressly: the later in time prevails. A different rule now applies to constitutional statutes: a later statute will be effective to repeal an earlier provision of a constitutional statute only if the intention to repeal is expressly stated in the clearest terms. In other words, the approach applied in the human rights context is now also applied to constitutional statutes. Other examples of constitutional statutes include the Bill of Rights 1689 and the Parliament Acts of 1911 and 1949. However, there is no precise definition of 'constitutional statute' and the category remains open.[34]

It was noted earlier that written Constitutions tend to be relatively rigid, sticky and difficult to change both because they have the status of 'law' and also because they are typically 'entrenched' – that is, more difficult to change than written, non-constitutional laws. Rigidity can be dysfunctional if it effectively prevents constitutional law keeping pace with social, political and economic development and change. On the other hand, adoption by English courts of the concepts of 'fundamental common-law rights' and 'constitutional statutes' suggest that flexibility may also be dysfunctional to the extent that it allows lawmakers to change the law in ways that do not reflect social, political and economic pressures for stability. The issue of how, and how easily, constitutional arrangements can be made and changed and, historically, have been made and changed, lies at the heart of questions about the role of legal and other norms in practices of politics and the conduct of government. To return to Colley's speculations about why the UK did not acquire a large-C Constitution in the eighteenth and nineteenth centuries (and, indeed, has still not done so), I have argued that the explanation goes beyond the sorts of empirical factors mentioned by Colley to the very nature of constitutions and Constitutions: the extent to which politics and government are framed by norms rather than being matters of mere habit or brute

---

[34] See, e.g., F. Ahmed and A. Perry, 'Constitutional Statutes' (2017) 37 *Oxford Journal of Legal Studies* 461.

power; and the mix, in any particular set of constitutional arrangements, of different types of norms.

The sorts of changes in the role of courts and law in the constitution chronicled in this section have been mirrored around the globe since the Second World War and have been variously described as the 'legalisation' or 'judicialisation' or 'juridification' of the constitution. Such developments have generated considerable debate about the nature of the UK constitution. Some would say that they have transformed the UK's constitution from being more appropriately described as 'political' to being best described as 'legal'.

The term 'the political constitution', as used in contemporary debates about the nature of the constitution and its relationship to law, seems to have been invented by (then) LSE law professor, John Griffith. In an article entitled 'The Political Constitution', he notoriously declared that,

> The constitution of the United Kingdom lives on, changing from day to day for the constitution is no more and no less than what happens. Everything that happens is constitutional. And if nothing happened that would be constitutional also.[35]

This rather opaque pronouncement raises two related questions: first, are practices of politics and the conduct of government part of the constitution? Second, if so, are they all there is to the constitution? Griffith is sometimes interpreted as answering the second question in the positive and being committed to a radical reduction of the constitution to practices of politics and the conduct of government. However, he continues,

> I am arguing for a highly positivist view of the constitution: of recognising that Ministers and others in high positions of authority are men and women who happen to exercise political power but without any such right to that power which could give them a superior moral position; the laws made by those in authority derive validity from no other fact or principle, and so impose no moral obligation of obedience on others; that so-called individual or human rights are no more and no less than political claims made by individuals on those in authority; that a society is endemically in a state of conflict between warring interest groups, having no consensus or unifying principles sufficiently precise to be the basis of a theory of legislation.

This passage makes clear that Griffith was not an empirical reductionist. The claim, that he was taking a 'highly positivist view' of the constitution, is not

---

[35] Griffith, 'The Political Constitution', 19.

most plausibly read as implying that the constitution consists purely of what politicians and governors do and say, and that norms about what they ought, ought not and may do and say are no part of the constitution. Put differently, it seems unlikely that Griffith was using the term 'constitution' in a purely organic sense somewhat in the way that Montesquieu did when he said (as quoted earlier) that a polity's 'laws' are or should be reflective of its 'constitution'. Although the UK lacks a written, canonical, large-C Constitution, the invention of that technology had a radical effect on the way people thought about the constitution; and that effect has lasted to the present. The change was reflected in Dicey's search for legal principles of the constitution; and fruit of that search was the recognition that certain laws and conventions are integral parts of the constitution.

So, if the doings and sayings of politicians and governors are not the sum total of what we now mean by 'the constitution', are they even part of what we mean? Lawyers and non-lawyers respectively might answer this question differently. Lawyers educated since 1900 would take it for granted, following Dicey, that law and legal norms are not all there is to the UK constitution: Conventions and political norms, they would say, are also part of the constitution. Some might be prepared to go further and include within the term norms of political 'morality' that have the status neither of law nor convention. In this view, the constitution could be understood as a set of norms that frame and regulate the practices of politics and the conduct of government. This way of thinking is reflected in dichotomies such as 'law and politics', 'might and right', 'is and ought'. In these contrasts, the constitution is coded as 'law', 'right' (or 'justice' or 'morality') and 'ought'. By contrast, non-lawyers – historians, political scientists and so on – might be inclined to turn this picture upside down and place the practices of politics and the conduct of government at the very core of the constitution. In extreme versions of such an approach, law, conventions and other norms may even be treated as superfluous to understanding and explaining the constitution, as heuristically and motivationally irrelevant and inert. Human behaviour, it might be said, is fully explicable in terms of needs and desires, and beliefs about the way things are; and that norms and values are merely epiphenomenal on needs, beliefs and desires. In such a view, norms do not motivate or explain behaviour but, on the contrary, serve only to rationalise and justify things said and done in the service of need, desire, belief and power.

There is a middle way between these two approaches, which is to understand the constitution as a matter of both law and politics, might and right, is and ought. In this view, norms make no sense independently of the conduct and behaviours they frame and regulate. Conversely, as evolutionary psychologists now tell us, human social behaviour can best be accounted for by recourse to some concept of interpersonal ought.[36] In this sense, fact and value are intertwined. In the terms used earlier, law is (at one and the same time) both norm and artefact; and the constitution is (at one and the same time) both organic and synthetic. I do not mean to say that such a capacious understanding of the constitution, as intertwined fact and value, is what 'constitution', in the phrase 'the UK constitution', currently means or ever meant. It meant, and means, different things to different people. But those various meanings all involve putting fact and value, is and ought, norm and action into some sort of relationship with one another. The way such relationships have been understood in these islands over the past millennium has not only varied from person to person and place to place, but also from time to time: historically, as it were.

If we think of the UK constitution as a matter of both is and ought, might and right, law and politics, what can we make of debates amongst lawyers (in particular), sparked by Griffith's intervention, about whether the UK has a 'legal' *or* a 'political' constitution? Note, first, that constitutional norms, legal and otherwise, look in two directions at once: on the one hand they 'confer' ('create', 'allocate', 'constitute') governmental power; and on the other hand, they impose limits on the exercise of governmental power. Political constitutionalists argue that ultimately, governmental power is rooted in politics, not law; and on the other, that historically, governmental power in the UK has been limited and controlled by political means and institutions, not by law and courts. They celebrate this fact and bemoan the increasing role of courts in recent times. They (like Griffith) tend to oppose written constitutions and bills of rights on the ground that they effectively transfer power, to decide how society should be organised and run, from politicians and governors to judges and courts. Legal constitutionalists, by contrast, argue that for centuries courts have played a central role not only in the conferral and allocation of governmental power (such as prerogative power) but also in its control (through the writs of mandamus, prohibition, certiorari and habeas corpus). They celebrate the role of courts and argue that 'the rule of law' (of which courts are the guardians, servants and enforcers) is as vital a component of the constitution as the powers of the legislature and the executive.

---

[36] M. Tomasello, *A Natural History of Human Morality* (Cambridge, MA: Harvard University Press, 2016).

Related to this debate between political and legal constitutionalists is one between those who assert and those who deny that the UK has a 'common-law constitution' in the sense of a constitution the ultimate legal foundation of which is the common law. For instance, some common-law constitutionalists might say that the foundational principle of the sovereignty of Parliament is, itself, a common-law norm. Their opponents, by contrast, would say that the ultimate source of power (and its control) in the English constitution is Parliament – an institution, not a norm.

However neat and compelling such dichotomies may be in theory, approaching the constitution historically suggests that it would be more accurate to view the UK's constitution as *both* legal *and* political. The executive, Parliament and the courts have, for centuries, all been involved in the creation and distribution, limitation and control of governmental power. Theoretically messy as it may be, Parliament, the executive and the courts have all been sources of law, including constitutional law. Of course, relationships between the legislature, the executive and the courts have changed over time. In high medieval theory, Parliament and the courts were part of the royal machinery of government and administration, and they worked together in various ways. The Revolution Settlement changed these relationships: legislature and executive were institutionally separated even though functionally integrated by reason of the royal veto. The courts were removed from royal control and gradually assumed a place outside the legislative-executive axis as 'independent' constitutional actors, albeit appointed by the executive and dismissible (in theory, anyway) by the legislature and the executive acting in concert. By the time Dicey was writing, legislature and executive had become effectively integrated under the principle of responsible government while the courts, in various ways, consolidated their position outside the axis of the executive (including a rapidly growing civil service bureaucracy) and the legislature. To all intents and purposes, (as a result of the development of conventional norms) the monarch had dropped out of the picture. With the benefit of hindsight, this made Dicey's bipolar account of the constitution seem almost obvious: in his view, the two fundamental principles of the English constitution were the sovereignty of Parliament and the rule of law – 'ordinary law' made and enforced by 'ordinary' courts.

The power of this bipolar picture has increased even more since Dicey's time as a result of the advent of universal adult suffrage, the development of strong political parties in the country at large and strong party discipline within the Commons, and increasing popular demand for robust, coordinated government in the face of threats, disasters and emergencies. In light of the concentration of power in the executive (the effective master of both Parliament and the civil service) the growth of judicial assertiveness and power in the twentieth century may be understood as the creation of a new constitutional balance. In the eighteenth century, the English constitution was admired for the balance it struck between social interests: monarch, aristocracy and commons. Significantly, however, this concept of balance gave no distinct place to courts. It was not an institutional/functional balance of powers but a balance of socio-political-economic interests. The shift from socio-political-economic balance to institutional-functional balance may be understood as a function of increasing democratisation and the invention of multi-level modes of political and governmental organisation. In the American system of government developed by the Founders in the late eighteenth century, a balance of interests was replaced by a balance of powers. American settler society was flatter and more 'democratic' (with wider suffrage and less hierarchical differentiation – slavery and the treatment of First Nations aside) than English society at the time. The desire for group identity within a larger polity was sublimated into federalism – geo-political division of power. In the UK, too, in the past century or so, democratisation has had a flattening tendency and, in the past thirty years, pressure for geo-political division of power has been mounting – by the time of writing, almost to boiling point.

At the same time, the balance of institutional and functional powers has changed. In the eighteenth century, in the transition from socio-political-economic balance to institutional-functional balance, the association between interests and institutions – the monarchical executive, the aristocratic House of Lords and the 'people's' House of Commons – maintained a certain degree of tension amongst institutions that allowed them to 'check and balance' one another. A combination of factors including democratic flattening or, at least, softening of socio-political-economic differences; marginalisation and, eventually, complete depoliticisation of the monarchy; the development of responsible government; the widening of the suffrage; and a first-past-the-post electoral system, has reduced the tension by producing an agglomeration of governmental power and functions – legislative, executive and bureaucratic – in the government of the day.

Viewing recent events through the lens of such changes brings them into sharper focus. In the course of deciding the 2019 challenge to the prorogation of Parliament by Prime Minister, Boris Johnson,[37] the Supreme Court agreed

---

[37] *R (Miller)* v. *Prime Minister* (2019).

that the monarch could not but accept the Prime Minister's (Privy Council's) advice to prorogue Parliament. Although the court did not say so, the subservience of the monarch to the government in respect of the exercise of politically important prerogative powers which, at the end of the nineteenth century, was considered to be conventional, appears effectively to have become a matter of law. Put differently, the division of power and potential constitutional tension arising from separation of the role of Head of State from that of Head of Government has, in the UK, been replaced by an effective merger of the two roles. At the same time, as a Parliamentary system of responsible government, the UK lacks various checks and balances central to the operation of a presidential system, such as the US, in which the two roles are formally fused. In that light, the Supreme Court's decision that the Prime Minister had acted unlawfully may be interpreted as based on an admittedly controversial and contested assessment by the judges that they should step in to provide the sort of check and balance that, in other parliamentary systems, the Head of State might provide. In this view, the UK again has a balanced constitution, but in the pans of the balance are the law and courts on the one side and the government (legislature, bureaucracy and executive) on the other. The UK constitution, we might say, has acquired – or is in the process of acquiring – a legal constitution because the political constitution is no longer considered to be effective (or susceptible to being made effective) to regulate the exercise of political and governmental power.

Conclusion

Law as artefact is a significant tool of political power and a product of the activities of lawmaking institutions: legislatures and legislators, courts and judges. Law and lawmakers have always played a role in the constitution, more at certain times than at others. The history of the constitution is, necessarily, partly a history of the use of law as a tool of power and of the activities of lawmakers of various sorts. Law as norm takes its place alongside other types of norms – customary and moral, for instance – as one of the essential building blocks of social and political life: without norms, politics is brute power and human life is no more than the survival of the fittest. In the period covered by this volume, lawmaking institutions have always been identifiable features of social and political life, and law has always taken its place alongside customary, religious and moral norms as both social stabilisers and facilitators of change. Successful human social life may not require law as an institutionalised phenomenon; but it is an inescapable aspect of the social arrangements and phenomena examined historically in this volume.

It seems undeniable that the social and political significance of law as both artefact and norm, and of public institutions that make, administer and enforce law, has increased significantly in the past 200 years and more. Many and varied social, political and economic changes, both local and global, have greatly increased the demand for (and subsequent supply of) state-based and state-backed normativity. It is widely recognised that the period since the end of WWII has witnessed dramatic 'legalisation' and 'judicialisation' of politics both domestically and internationally. The near-universal supersession of organic constitutionalism by synthetic constitutionalism has fuelled such developments. Written constitutions and bills of rights are typically conceived and operated as legal artefacts and norms. One of the reasons why law may be less visible to students of the UK's constitution and its history is that the UK's constitution has always been, and remains, essentially organic. If and when the UK adopts a synthetic constitution and bill of rights, it will be impossible to marginalise the role of law and courts in the ongoing story of government and politics. Another factor that operates to conceal the constitutional and historical significance of law is that lawyers themselves treat the law of the executive and administration – 'administrative law' – as sub-constitutional. One hundred and fifty years ago, Dicey gave Parliamentary Sovereignty pride of place in his analysis of the English constitution. Since then, despite democratisation, there has been a massive transfer of power from Parliament to the Executive. In Dicey's terms, we might now want to say that the premier legal principle of the constitution is the Rule of Law. Law may not be crucial for the creation, exercise and maintenance of political and governmental power but it has become critical to its limitation and control and, as importantly, to its legitimation. Of course, this is no new phenomenon: Magna Carta was primarily concerned with control and legitimation, not creation, of power. It may be that it is in the history of the control of political and governmental power that law has its most profound constitutional significance. That said, control of power is much too important to be left to the lawyers! The constitutional role of law and lawyers demands the attention of constitutional historians and students of politics.

3
Political Constitutionalism

RICHARD BELLAMY

Introduction: On Legal and Political Constitutionalism

The British Constitution possesses many distinctive features: from its uncodified character and lack of entrenchment to the status as ordinary statutes rather than 'higher' law of those written rules that comprise it. However, all these features can be regarded as manifestations of its most distinguishing characteristic – its quality as a predominantly 'political' rather than a 'legal' constitution.[1] Whereas codification, and those other features that the British Constitution notoriously lacks, comprise essential elements of a legal form of constitutionalism, their absence has traditionally been deemed necessary for the integrity of the UK's political constitution.

On the legal account of constitutionalism, of which the USA has become the exemplar, a constitution necessarily consists of a codified legal document or documents, that together with certain legal norms or conventions, be they written or unwritten, are designated as higher law that legal institutions, notably constitutional courts, are responsible for upholding. According to this legal conception of constitutionalism, constitutional law frames the operation of politics. It allows politicians and public servants to be held accountable by citizens, and other individuals, who are subject to their authority, and obliged to abide by the terms of the constitution via the courts. Legal constitutionalism has become especially associated with so-called 'strong form' rights-based judicial review, whereby judges can either strike down legislation or executive acts as incompatible with constitutional rights, or 'read in' their interpretation of these rights into laws.[2]

---

[1] A. Tomkins, *Our Republican Constitution* (Oxford: Hart, 2005), 6–10.
[2] R. Dworkin, *Freedom's Law: The Moral Reading of the American Constitution* (Cambridge, MA: Harvard University Press, 1997), Introduction.

By contrast, a political account of constitutionalism designates an approach that locates the constitution in the character and design of the political system and the modus operandi of its component political processes.[3] According to this political conception, citizens can hold governments and the administration accountable via political institutions – in the British case, indirectly through elections and directly by elected parliaments and the need for the government to abide by existing laws and to govern and legislate with the support of a plurality of the population and a majority of MPs.[4] On this account, there can be no higher laws other than the laws that emerge from a duly constitutive and constitutional political process. Even the very contours of this process may be politically reconstituted should Parliament choose to do so. Parliament rather than the law is constitutionally sovereign because not only does it make the law, but also the democratic cast of its operations produce those attributes we associate with constitutional government, such as the restraint on arbitrary rule or the need to accord equal concern and respect to individual citizens in both the framing and administration of law and in executive actions.

This distinction between legal and political constitutionalism may seem too sharp. It will be objected that legal constitutions typically detail how the political system should operate, while political constitutionalists regard courts as necessary components of any complex political community, allowing laws to be impartially applied to particular cases, including against the executive and individual MPs should they infringe them. Does that not mean that any constitution is both political and legal? In some sense, that will necessarily be the case. The key distinguishing factor consists in where final authority concerning the operation of the legal and the political system ultimately lies.

Political constitutionalists contend that the qualities of the law and legal system reflect those of the political system more generally. That is not just a descriptive contention but also a normative proposition.[5] Political constitutionalists see law not as framing the political system, as we saw legal constitutionalists propose, but as being rightly framed by politics. In their view, identifying and upholding the rights and obligations of those subject to the law is a political act that can only be legitimately undertaken via a

---

[3] R. Bellamy, *Political Constitutionalism: A Republican Defence of the Constitutionality of Democracy* (Cambridge: Cambridge University Press, 2007).

[4] J. A. G. Griffith, 'The Political Constitution', *Modern Law Review* (1979) 42 (1): 1–21; Tomkins, *Our Republican Constitution*, 1–6.

[5] Bellamy, *Political Constitutionalism*, 4–5.

political process by those politically authorised to do so by these self-same subjects of the law, to whom they must ultimately remain accountable.[6] The constitution of a polity consists precisely in the way the processes of authorisation and accountability frame the exercise of authority and the degree to which its members regard these processes as legitimate.[7] The task of the legal system becomes to implement politically determined laws, the effective and equitable fulfilment of which may be fostered by its officials possessing a degree of political independence, as is likely to be true of the state bureaucracy more generally. From this perspective, legal constitutionalism, and in particular 'strong form' rights-based judicial review, involves judges illegitimately adopting a political role without either authorisation or accountability by those subject to their judgments, so that they become judge and jury over their own authority.[8] However, it is compatible with 'weak form' review, whereby the legality under existing law of certain administrative acts and laws can be challenged in the courts so long as the ultimate decision on their constitutionality lies with parliament, including through the enactment of new law.[9]

It might be objected that the authority of parliament to rule must rest itself on some extra-political and ultimately legally recognised norm akin to what the English philosopher of law H. L. A. Hart termed a 'rule of recognition' or the Austrian jurist Hans Kelsen the legal and political system's 'basic norm'.[10] If so, that would suggest that the UK does have a legal constitution, albeit one that consists of a partly conventional and unwritten common-law framework of political rules about the making of collective decisions and the exercise of executive power by virtue of the sovereignty of parliament.[11] This is a powerful argument, one (as we shall see) raised most recently in the Supreme Court's decision in *Miller 2*. However, the political account takes its cue from Thomas Hobbes in regarding all norms of law and morality, including human rights, as only possible through the creation of a sovereign

---

[6] J. Waldron, *Law and Disagreement* (Oxford: Clarendon Press, 1999), chs. 10, 11.
[7] Waldron, *Law and Disagreement*, ch. 5 and Bellamy, *Political Constitutionalism*, ch. 6.
[8] J. Waldron, 'The Core of the Case against Judicial Review', *Yale Law Journal* (2006) 115: 1346–1406; Bellamy, *Political Constitutionalism*, ch. 1.
[9] Waldron, 'Core Case'; R. Bellamy, 'Political Constitutionalism and the Human Rights Act', *International Journal of Constitutional Law (I-Con)* (2011) 9 (1): 86–111.
[10] H. L. A. Hart, *The Concept of Law*, 2nd ed. (Oxford: Clarendon Press, 1994), 94–95; H. Kelsen, *Introduction to the Problems of Legal Theory* (Oxford: Clarendon Press, 1992), 54–55.
[11] T. R. Allan, *Law, Liberty and Justice: The Foundations of British Constitutionalism* (Oxford: Clarendon Press, 1993).

political order that can uphold and define them in impartial ways.[12] The reasons urging us to do so are prudential and rational rather than moral or legal.[13] On this account, the right of parliament to rule was established in the seventeenth century through the consummate political act of a civil war and the beheading of King Charles I, the prior claimant to sovereign power. Since then, parliament has gradually altered its own constitutive rules under pressure from citizens either claiming or exercising their political rights.

This chapter offers a genealogy of the UK's political constitution from the seventeenth century to the present, noting how it has drawn on different ideas and taken different forms over time, and highlighting the contingent nature of its current representative and parliamentary character. The next section explores how the English system of government came to be conceived as embodying the classical idea of mixed government in a novel form, that of the balanced constitution. Involving elements of what became the separation of powers, it located sovereignty in the Crown in Parliament: that is, in the combined rule of the monarch and his or her Ministers, the House of Lords and the House of Commons. The subsequent section traces how Montesquieu offered a canonical account of this mixture as a form of constitutional government that preserves liberty and generates the rule of law. Adopted by Blackstone, later thinkers such as Hume, Bagehot and Dicey then adapted this account into a theory of parliamentary government to accommodate the emerging superiority of the Commons, whereby this mix became expressed through the influence of crown and aristocracy on parties within the lower house. In the process, as the succeeding section shows, the conceptual basis was established for a democratic version of parliamentary government based on representation through electoral competition between parties. Developed over the twentieth century, this version is most commonly associated with political constitutionalism today. A final section looks at the prospects for the political constitution in the twenty-first century, and whether we are seeing the emergence of popular constitutionalism as a new form of the political constitution.

---

[12] T. Hobbes, *Leviathan*, R. Tuck (ed.) (Cambridge: Cambridge University Press, 1991), 90. See too B. Williams, 'Realism and Moralism in Political Theory', in *In the Beginning Was the Deed* (Princeton: Princeton University Press, 2005), 1–17 and R. Bellamy, 'Turtles All the Way Down? Is the Political Constitutionalist Appeal to Disagreement Self-Defeating? A Reply to Cormac Mac Amhlaigh', *International Journal of Constitutional Law (I-Con)*, (2016) 14 (1): 204–216.

[13] Q. Skinner, 'The Context of Hobbes's Theory of Political Obligation', in M. Cranston and R. Peters (eds.), *Hobbes and Rousseau: A Collection of Critical Essays* (New York: Doubleday, 1972), 109–142.

From Mixed Government to the Balanced Constitution: Checks, Balances and the Separation of Powers

The idea of a political constitution has its origins in the classical account of mixed government to be found in ancient Greek and Roman political thought.[14] The theory of mixed government originated from the classification of political systems on the basis of whether One, a Few or Many ruled. According to this theory, the three basic types of polity – monarchy, aristocracy and democracy – were liable to degenerate into tyranny, oligarchy and anarchy respectively. This corruption stemmed from the concentration of power in the hands of a single person or group, which created a temptation to its abuse in arbitrary or self-interested rule. The solution, which received its canonical expression in book VI of Polybius's *Histories*, was to ensure moderation and proportion by combining or mixing various types.[15] As a result, the virtues of each form of government, namely a strong executive, the involvement of the better elements of society and popular legitimacy, could be obtained without the corresponding vices.[16] Moreover, this mixture was credited with constitutional properties – most notably the curbing of arbitrary power by forcing the different sections of society to consult each other's interests.

Three related constitutional mechanisms have become associated with a mixed form of government. First, there is the conception of the dispersal of power. Second, there is the notion of checks and balances on power. Third, and developed somewhat later, there is the thesis of the separation of powers. Many analyses of these mechanisms, especially those focused on the last, tend to conflate the three.[17] This tendency was fostered by Montesquieu's combination of the second and third in particular within his canonical account of the English constitution in Book 11 chapter 6 of the *Spirit of the Laws*, and compounded by James Madison when he added the first idea to the mix in his defence of the federal scheme of the US constitution in *The Federalist* 47. All three serve a parallel purpose, that of reducing the possibility of arbitrary

---

[14] M. Vile, *Constitutionalism and the Separation of Powers* (Oxford: Clarendon Press, 1967), 2.
[15] Polybius, *Rise of the Roman Empire*, F. W. Walbank (ed.), trans. I Scott-Kilvert (Harmondsworth: Penguin, 1979), Bk VI, chs. 3, 4, 10.
[16] Polybius, *Rise*, Bk VI, chs. 11–18.
[17] J. Waldron, *Political Political Theory: Essays in Institutions* (Cambridge, MA: Harvard University Press, 2016), 49.

exercises of power, and can be combined. However, as Jeremy Waldron has noted, they do so in different ways that should be kept analytically distinct.[18]

The dispersal of power need not involve either checking and balancing or the separation of different functions of governance, merely that not all power is held in the same hands. A federal system disperses power in this sense, for example. Such a dispersal might be regarded as serving the need to ensure that governance reflects local conditions and preferences, and so does not involve the arbitrary imposition of uniform rules and regulations on a diverse and heterogeneous political community. Yet, all the relevant powers might be unified in the hands of a single local authority and be neither separated nor checked. As Madison noted in *The Federalist* 51, a federal dispersal of power can provide a new dimension to a system of mixed government. However, it is not a requirement of the doctrine.

That proves important in the British context. Although the UK is a plurinational state, it has resisted moves towards such a dispersal of power. Rather, it developed through the incorporation of Wales, Scotland and Ireland into the governance structure of the British state, through granting these component parts representation in the sovereign British Parliament. True, the powers of local relative to central government have played an important, if neglected, part in the English, and later British, constitution from the Middle Ages, and fed dissatisfaction with Charles I. However, within the UK the devolution of authority to make certain specified decisions from the central to the local level has tended to be conceived as an administrative convenience rather than a form of dispersed power that extends mixed government to the sharing of sovereign authority between the nations of the UK. That remains the case even with the re-establishment of parliaments in Scotland, Wales and Northern Ireland. For example, the decision to leave the EU was ultimately a matter for the British parliament, with the devolved governments having little say in the process outside the largely consultative (and erratically convened) Joint Ministerial Committee EU.

In the UK, mixed government has been more associated with the second and third ideas of checks and balances and the separation of powers. The former idea was crucial to the original formulation of mixed government, the crux of which involved different social groups governing concurrently, yet not only predated but also was independent from the latter idea. As Wilfried Nippel has remarked, Polybius's conception of mixed government did not

---

[18] Waldron, *Political*, 49–53.

involve 'normative ideas of a necessary differentiation of governmental functions'.[19] Its prime purpose was to ensure that the exercise of political power reflected the 'natural' balance of the different social classes and interests within the political 'body', and to provide mechanisms whereby each could check the other. Although the Polybian version of the argument came to predominate, it diverged in important respects from the Aristotelian account. Aristotle had regarded kingship as the best form, and democracy as a corruption of what he called Polity. However, he thought the ideal was almost impossible to obtain, and was highly likely to degenerate into tyranny, which was the worst possible option. Consequently, he advocated Polity as the most generalisable form of government. This consisted of a mixture of two corrupt forms – democracy and oligarchy. Unlike Polybius, Aristotle had not considered that different political bodies should represent different groups and he had thought that citizens should be directly involved in government. His aim had been to employ devices, such as a combination of election and lot, to ensure a social mixture amongst the political officers. Whereas Polybius conceived mixed government as a balance of classes, therefore, Aristotle had interpreted it as meaning a mingling of them. He had believed that whilst democracy and oligarchy undermined the common interest by placing government exclusively in the hands of either those without means or those with them respectively, a Polity resulted when those with moderate wealth predominated and tempered the conflict between rich and poor.[20]

The importance of balancing social power was given especial emphasis by Machiavelli, whose *Discorsi* can in many respects be read as a radical version of the Polybian argument, obtained via an Aristotelian appreciation of an active citizenry. Continuing the organic imagery of the ancients, he observed that all political bodies contain two classes, the nobles (grandi) and the people (popolo), whose 'humours' (umori) or desires conflict. He contended that the prime advantage of the Roman 'mixed constitution' admired by Polybius was the balance it achieved amongst these two humours by dividing power between the respective classes. Indeed, he claimed that their discord, far from being destructive, had actively promoted 'all the laws made in favour of

---

[19] W. Nippel, 'Ancient and Modern Republicanism: Mixed Constitution and "Ephors"', in B. Fontana (ed.), *The Invention of the Modern Republic* (Cambridge: Cambridge University Press, 1994), 9.

[20] Aristotle, *The Politics*, trans. T. A. Sinclair, rev. ed. (Harmondsworth: Penguin, 1981), Bk III ch 7.

liberty'.[21] The republic had only collapsed when the economic struggle finally subverted this political balance and the patricians overthrew it in order to recover the privileges taken away from them by the Gracchi's attempt to enforce the Agrarian Law.[22]

Machiavelli's analysis involved a sociological insight that linked the relative merits of different political institutions or ordini to the social conditions – what he called the materia – of the polity in which they operated. 'Good laws' and 'good customs' were interdependent, and only 'extreme force', which had dangers of its own, could create the second through the imposition of the first.[23] He related the process of corruption and the attendant Polybian cycle of constitutional change, which ultimately affected even mixed governments, to changes in society at large.[24] Differences in manners and the degree of equality between citizens were particularly important in this regard. Thus, republics were more suited to egalitarian societies in which there was a general concern for the common good amongst the citizenry, whilst principalities were more appropriate to conditions of social inequality.[25] Machiavelli disputed classic fears of the inconstancy and unreliability of the multitude. He believed that the greater equality of republics made the people more prudent, law-abiding and caused them to identify their interest more closely with the common welfare. In particular, there was a greater preparedness to bear arms and hence no need for mercenaries. These features rendered republican governments more stable and secure than principalities, in which the temptation to abuse one's power was greater.[26]

This Machiavellian sociological understanding of the role of the balance of power proves central to the operation of a political constitution. To achieve the requisite procedural legitimacy, the organisation and operation of a political constitution needs to be tied to the character of the political society to which it applies – such as the pattern of social cleavages, the degree of economic development and so forth that determine the political community's material constitution. The aim of this congruence between the political and the material constitution is to ensure the various groups and interests within society gain sufficient influence and control to be accorded equal concern and respect in the formulation of collective policies. It would prove crucial to ways the political constitution in the nineteenth and twentieth

---

[21] N. Machiavelli, 'Discorsi', in S. Bertelli (ed.), Il Principe e Discorsi (Milan: Feltrinelli, 1960), Bk 1 ch. 4.
[22] Machiavelli, 'Discorsi', Bk 1 ch. 37.   [23] Machiavelli, 'Discorsi', Bk 1 ch. 17.
[24] Machiavelli, 'Discorsi', Bk 1 chs. 16–18.   [25] Machiavelli, 'Discorsi', Bk 1 ch. 55.
[26] Machiavelli, 'Discorsi', Bk 1 ch. 58, Bk 2 ch. 2.

centuries came to encompass the representative institutions of mass democracy in response to the demand for universal suffrage.

The republican interpretation of mixed government as involving a balance of social groups first entered English constitutional discourse in Charles I's Answer to Parliament's Nineteen Propositions of 1642, where it served to characterise the parliamentary system as combining King, Lords and Commons. It may seem paradoxical that it was royalists who introduced the view that monarchical power should be limited by the nobility and the people as part of a balanced constitution.[27] Yet, the move was forced on them by the insistence of the Nineteen Propositions on the need for the King's ministers and judicial appointees to be approved by and responsible to Parliament. It offered a way of insisting that the King also played a necessary and legitimate role and possessed appropriate entitlements within a scheme of parliamentary governance. The Answer's authors maintained that 'the experience and wisdom of your ancestors' had 'moulded' a mixture 'as to give to this kingdom (as far as humane prudence can contrive) the conveniences of all three, without the inconveniences of anyone, as long as the balance hangs even between the three estates ...',[28] and warned how to disturb this hard-won balance risked unleashing the 'vices' of 'tyranny ... faction and division [and] tumults, violence and licentiousness' to which monarchy, aristocracy and democracy respectively were prone.[29] Meanwhile, although the Answer drew on the writings of Sir Edward Coke to assert the 'immemorial' character of this arrangement, this move also reveals how the ascription to Coke and his followers of a common-law constitutionalism[30] – whereby a distant fundamental law grounded and constrained the authority of king and parliament alike – goes too far. Not only had common lawyers granted the ancient status of parliament's ability to enact law, but also statute had proved more effective than judicial 'discovered' law to bind the king to a petition of right.[31] In the Answer, the ancient constitution now became the product of an immemorial constitutive political act, wherein sovereignty and the right of law-making was constituted within the king in Parliament. Common law thereby became

---

[27] Vile, *Constitutionalism*, 36–40.
[28] 'The King's Answer to the Nineteen Propositions, 18 June 1642', in J. P. Kenyon (ed.), *The Stuart Constitution: Documents and Commentary* (Cambridge: Cambridge University Press, 1966), 22.
[29] 'King's Answer', 21.
[30] J. G. A. Pocock, *The Ancient Constitution and the Feudal Law*, 2nd ed. (Cambridge: Cambridge University Press, 1987), 49–50, 234.
[31] G. Burgess, *The Politics of the Ancient Constitution: An Introduction to English Political Thought 1603–1642* (London: Macmillan, 1992), ch. 8.

subordinated to parliamentary sovereignty as the embodiment of an ancient political constitution.[32]

However, this proved a dangerous argument to employ. Not only did it undermine the absolute authority of the king by suggesting that power was shared, as Robert Filmer pointed out,[33] it was also open to the radical Machiavellian argument of James Harrington.[34] Harrington claimed that the mixed constitution was unstable precisely because it no longer reflected a social balance. The undermining of the feudal system and the gradual transferral of property, and with it military and political power, to the commons meant that the only stable political system was a republic in which property and military responsibilities were shared amongst them alone, rather than with the king and aristocracy.[35] Harrington's consequent advocacy of economic and institutional 'superstructures' capable of inducing civic virtue within a single social group proved important,[36] as we shall see, when it came to elaborating a democratic version of the separation of powers.

Unfortunately, Cromwell failed to institute the Harringtonian republic. Nevertheless, the problem of controlling government in a society without distinctions of rank remained. It was these circumstances that helped to crystallise the essential elements of what became the theory of the separation of powers: namely, the notion that different agencies should perform distinct functions and the belief that the judicial branch especially should be independent. Lack of space prohibits an account of this history here.[37] Suffice it to say, that the struggle between King and Parliament, the experience of the Long Parliament, and the setting up of the Protectorate, all served in different ways to raise the issues of the respective roles, limits and relations of legislature and executive. On the one hand, it emerged that large assemblies were inefficient for the implementation of laws and policy. On the other hand, it became apparent that legislative functions should not be entrusted to those executing or judging violations of the law if legislation was to be made in the common

---

[32] C. C. Weston, 'England: Ancient Constitution and Law', in J. H. Burns (ed.), *The Cambridge History of Political Thought 1450–1700* (Cambridge: Cambridge University Press, 1991), 388–390, 397–398.

[33] R. Filmer, 'The Anarchy of a Limited or Mixed Monarchy', in J. Somerville (ed.), *Patriarcha and Other Political Writings*, (Cambridge: Cambridge University Press, 1991).

[34] J. G. A. Pocock, *The Machiavellian Moment Florentine Political Thought and the Atlantic Republican Tradition* (Princeton, NJ: Princeton University Press, 1975), 15–42.

[35] J. Harrington, *Political Works*, J. G. A. Pocock (ed.) (Cambridge: Cambridge University Press, 1977), 163–165.

[36] Harrington, *Political Works*, 171–174.   [37] Vile, *Constitutionalism*, 37–52.

interest, administered impartially, and officials held to account. A separation of legislative and executive powers appeared justified on both counts.

This doctrine was a commonplace, therefore, by the time of the Restoration and John Locke's seminal analysis of the 'powers of government' in the *Second Treatise*.[38] However, Locke elaborated the doctrine in ways that were to be crucial to political constitutionalism. First, Locke noted that legislation was more likely to be in the public interest, apply equally to all, and treat all those subject to it with equal concern and respect, if it was made on an equal basis by an assembly of those – or their representatives – who would have to live under these laws. Second, this mechanism will be undermined if legislators can control the application of the law and be able to exempt themselves or their supporters from it – hence the need to separate the legislative from the executive branch. Third, while an executive branch was required for general legislation to be efficiently and effectively administered, transposed into policies and applied to particular cases, to avoid arbitrary, discretionary rule that branch had to operate under the law. As a result, the legislative branch could be regarded as the 'supreme power'; since it set down the 'positive laws' and 'common rule' that are to be executed. Moreover, though the judiciary tends to be treated as an aspect of the executive branch in Locke's account, a key aspect of his conception of political society was that the executors of the law were not judges in their own case as to whether they had implemented the law or not: that possibility was the very definition of a tyrannous form of arbitrary rule. Finally, the exception was the 'federative power' of peace and war and international treaty making and negotiations, that Locke contended could not be law governed given the need for flexibility and dispatch to deal with unforeseeable situations. However, although this federative power was most appropriately held by the executive branch it needed to be separated from the executive power proper.

As Waldron notes,[39] the separation of powers operates here as a mode of articulated governance that operates in the service of the rule of law as a curb on arbitrary rule. However, although an independent judiciary plays an important role in this account, the rule of law is not the rule of constitutional law or of judges as its interpreters, as in legal constitutionalism, but the rule of legislation and the legislature, the primacy of which binds the judiciary as

---

[38] J. Locke, *Two Treatises of Government* (Cambridge: Cambridge University Press, 1988), II paras 143–144.
[39] Waldron, *Political*, 57.

it does the executive. This account of the rule of law as involving the primacy of legislation, and hence of the legislature, with executive action needing to be authorised by duly made law and responsible to the legislature – sometimes indirectly via the judiciary, became the hallmark of political constitutionalism. However, to achieve this result the separation of powers needed to be assimilated to a view of the English constitution as a model of the 'balance' to be achieved in mixed monarchy. While hinted at in Locke, it only became established doctrine with the constitutional settlement expressed in the Bill of Rights of 1689 that affirmed not only the Protestant character of the English state but also established a constitutional monarchy by asserting the absolute legislative authority of free and regular Parliaments, including the power to abolish royal prerogatives by Act of Parliament.

Montesquieu to Dicey: From the Balanced Constitution to 'Parliamentary Government'

This settlement attained its canonical expression in Montesquieu's account of the English constitution in the *Spirit of the Laws* of 1748. Montesquieu began by enunciating some of the basic premises of constitutional government. Political liberty, he asserted, differed from self-defeating licence by requiring acceptance of the rule of law.[40] However, law and liberty went together 'only when there is no abuse of power'. Since 'all experience proves that every man with power is led to abuse it', all power must be kept within bounds by so framing the constitution 'that power checks [arrete] power'.[41] His innovation lay in modifying the idea of functional separation so that it operates as a check.

Montesquieu's initial description of the separation of powers followed the Lockean distinction between legislative and executive, the latter being further subdivided into internal and external affairs. However, he immediately restated the doctrine introducing this time a third 'power of judging'.[42] Although not the first to do so, this tripartite division only gained wide currency with Montesquieu. The vast majority of earlier writers had classified judicial power under the domestic duties of the executive, though they did argue that those who decided civil and criminal cases ought not to

---

[40] C.-L. De S Montesquieu, *De l'esprit des lois*, 2 vols (Paris: Garnier-Flammarion, 1979), I Bk XI ch 3.
[41] Montesquieu, *De l'esprit*, I Bk XI ch 4.
[42] Montesquieu, *De l'esprit*, I Bk XI ch 6, from which all the quotes that follow also come.

exercise other executive functions. He then drew not only the standard conclusion that uniting the executive and legislative endangered liberty by allowing a monarch or senate to make 'tyrannical laws in order to execute them in a tyrannical way', but also argued that an even greater danger of oppression followed if the judicial power was united to either of the other two, or worse still all three came together in the same person or body. His reasoning was that whilst the legislature was concerned solely with declaring 'the general will of the state' and the executive with 'nothing more than the execution of that general will', only the judiciary applied the laws to particular persons. Consequently, the true definition of despotism was the uniting of this power with the other two.

Montesquieu did not believe that formal separation alone would allow each to check the others. Criticising the Venetian republic, he observed that although the legislative, executive and judicial power were divided between the Supreme Council, the 'pregardi' and the 'quarantia' respectively, 'all these tribunals are formed from magistrates who belong to the same social estate, which virtually turns them into one and the same power'. A material and procedural basis had to be given to the distinction, therefore.

Mixed government partially resolved this difficulty, since making the executive an hereditary monarch ensured its separation from the legislature. Departing, as he often did, from the reality of the English situation, he argued against ministers being taken from the legislature on the grounds that in this case 'the two powers would be united' and 'there would no longer be any liberty'. This arrangement also served the efficiency aspect of the separation of power, 'because this part of government, which almost always requires rapid action, is better administered by one person than many'. However, mixed government added an additional dimension by dividing the legislature between two assemblies – the one consisting of the nobles and the other of the representatives of the people. Separate representation for the nobility was warranted by the need to protect their distinct interests and views stemming from the advantages of 'birth, riches or honours'. But bicameralism also operated as part of a checking mechanism. Montesquieu advocated that both the executive and the upper chamber should be able to check the power of the legislature by having the right of veto. Likewise, he believed that the legislature should have the power to investigate how the executive officers had carried out the law and impeach them if found corrupt. But he thought the monarch ought to be distinguished from his 'evil counsellors' in this respect, otherwise his independence would be jeopardised. These suggestions partially undermined a pure separation, since they gave the executive a negative share in legislation. However, they helped strengthen the weaker parts of the constitution against the growing strength of the legislature, whose wider and logically prior role of law-making made it the most powerful body and so the most in need of restraining from going beyond its remit.

Montesquieu's most novel argument in this regard was his reworking of the republican thesis that the best way of ensuring that legislation reflected the common interest was to have it made by the people. In a 'free state', he affirmed, 'every man who is considered a free citizen ought to be governed by himself. Hence the people as an estate ought to have the legislative power'. However, this republican point did not lead to advocacy of republican forms of government. He criticised ancient direct democracy for confusing the power of the people with its liberty. Such radical participation subverted the distinction between legislative and executive powers. Besides being unworkable in large states, even in small ones it involved many people in decisions they were 'unfit' to make. Representative democracy remedied these defects by introducing checks into the democratic process. It involved selecting only the more capable citizens and reducing those involved in debating public business to manageable proportions. It exploited the fact that people were better able to choose suitable candidates and, if necessary, reject them, than to propose laws. As Harrington had noticed, this division between proposers and resolvers could offer a perfect procedural guarantee of fairness.[43] Organising constituencies geographically rather than according to estates, thereby removing the case for mandation, provided a further check against class-based legislation. Finally, in book XIX chapter 27 Montesquieu introduced a related social foundation to the constitution in the customs of a free people. The habit of saying and thinking what one liked, led citizens to divide into parties supporting either the legislature or the executive. Self-interest motivated those favoured by the executive to support it, those with nothing to hope for to attack it. The effect of liberty, he contended, was for citizens always to favour the weaker side. The jealousy of the people and their representatives in the legislature was in this respect the surest way to check the executive.

The fusion of the separation of powers and mixed government produced a socially and politically balanced and mutually checking constitution.[44] Although such an arrangement might lead to 'inaction', he claimed the 'necessary

[43] Harrington, Political Works, 172, 174.   [44] Montesquieu, De l'esprit, I Bk XI ch. 6.

movement of things' forced the various parts to work together'. The system served to distil the public interest out of certain disparate private ones, and to gain the advantage of the better elements in society in its enactment as law. Note, the judicial power remained hard to assimilate to this scheme, since it added a potential fourth department within the theory of mixed government. As we saw, Montesquieu believed this power would be especially dangerous if linked to either of the other two. He thought its independence was best achieved through the jury system and lay magistrates so that it did not become attached to any estate or profession. This lack of a social base or permanent cadre rendered it the weakest power. It became 'invisible' having 'in a sense, no force', at least in the political sense.

The influence of Locke notwithstanding, Montequieu's view of the constitution remained essentially organic rather than contractual. He emphasised mixed government and the balancing of the various parts of the body politic. He did not treat the constitution as a compact between the people that established government. As Thomas Paine remarked in his *Rights of Man* of 1791,[45] it was this conception of a constitution as a popular contract that lay behind the 'modern' legal model of a constitution of the United States, as a codified and comprehensive fundamental law that was antecedent to government.

By contrast, the British constitution continued to be conceived in ancient terms as a form of governing. The two main constitutional texts of the eighteenth and nineteenth century, Blackstone's *Commentaries of the Laws of England* (1765–1769) and A. V. Dicey's *Lectures on the Law of the Constitution* (1885), both remain within Montesquieu's framework. They consider the British constitution a form of mixed government – that of Crown-in Parliament – that combines the advantages of a system of checks and balances and the separation of powers that taken together ensure the rule of law conceived as the primacy of legislation. As Dicey summarised it, 'the sovereignty of Parliament, as contrasted with other forms of sovereign power, favours the supremacy of law' because 'the commands of Parliament ... can be uttered only through the combined actions of its three constituent parts', with the need for an accommodation between monarch, Lords and commons providing a series of checks and balances. Meanwhile, the need to rule through law made by a sovereign Parliament 'constantly hampers ... the action of the executive' so that 'the government can escape

---

[45] T. Paine, 'Rights of Man Part 1', in B. Kuklick (ed.), *Political Writings* (Cambridge: Cambridge University Press, 1989), 78–92.

only by obtaining from Parliament the discretionary authority which is denied to the Crown by the law of the land.'[46]

An important upshot of this approach was that 'the constitution is the result of the ordinary law of the land', so that 'the law of the constitution ... [is] not the source but the consequence of the rights of individuals'.[47] Dicey's argument has been dismissed as an 'outburst of Anglo-Saxon parochialism'.[48] Yet, the most glaring weakness is that the endorsement of the mixed constitution in the seminal legal texts of the period had little or no basis in reality, as political analysts of the actual working of the constitution had long pointed out. Three related aspects of this reality had preoccupied eighteenth-century political analysts of the constitution:[49] first, the 'influence' of the Crown in elections and the Commons through what was known as 'Old Corruption'; second, the role of parties that could not be understood either in the classical or Machiavellian terms of a struggle between different classes or branches of the legislature, but cut across both; and finally the primacy of the Commons, predominantly through its control over supply but also via the associated convention of the need for ministers to command a parliamentary majority and the effective disuse of the royal veto, and which had buttressed its independence through the Septennial Act. The distinction between 'Court' and 'Country' parties offered no real help in this regard, given that they could not be regarded as the 'grandi' or nobles and the 'plebs' respectively. Even if the latter liked to portray themselves as representing the people, they were hardly of, and only very imperfectly elected by, the people, while the former was if anything the King's rather than aristocracy's party. Indeed, the two groups were not so much what David Hume came to term 'parties of interest', as 'parties of affection' and to some degree 'of principle,' more accurately associated with the alternative terms of Whigs and Tories.[50]

The intellectual task confronting contemporary observers of this reality was how to assimilate it to the mixed constitution. One solution was to suggest that all three elements – Crown, aristocracy and commons – were

---

[46] A. V. Dicey, *Introduction to the Study of the Law of the Constitution*, 8th ed. (London: MacMillan, 1915), Part II, ch. 13, 402, 405.
[47] Dicey, *Introduction*, Part II, ch. 4, 198–99.
[48] J. Shklar, 'Political Theory and the Rule of Law', in A. C. Hutchinson and P. Monahan (eds.), *The Rule of Law: Ideal or Ideology* (Toronto: University of Toronto Press, 1987), 5.
[49] J. A. W. Gunn, 'Influence, Parties and the Constitution: Changing Attitudes, 1783–1832', *Historical Journal* (1974) 17(2): 301–328.
[50] D. Hume, *Essays Moral, Political and Literary*, E. F. Miller (ed.) (Indianapolis: Liberty Fund, 1987), Part I Essays 7 and 8.

present within the Commons and existed in balance there. As Hume argued, this involved a justification of the Crown's influence over the Commons via the members of the executive and its supporters, which he saw as having the salutary effect of transforming parties of principle and affection – both of which he regarded as prone to factionalism and irrationality, and as such sources of instability – into parties of interest, which tended to be more constant and rational.[51] Others observed that the aristocracy also operated as a distinct influence within the lower house, through the presence of their retainers. Meanwhile, the commons proper was represented by those elected without and in opposition to influence. In this way, the commons became the arena in which the contest between the three estates took place. Hume viewed this transformation as an adaptation of the mixed constitution to a commercial age. The institutionalisation of balance based on interests placed virtue in stable political arrangements rather than in the uncertain disposition of particular individuals, such as the monarch, and so supported a regular system of justice that upheld property rights and contract, the necessary prerequisites of a commercial republic.

Unsurprisingly, this defence of influence came under increasing attack from those denied office by such means, notably the radicals and the Whig politician Charles James Fox, who became a champion of electoral reform.[52] Throughout the eighteenth century no administration ever lost an election – ministries fell largely because they lost the support of the King, who managed the composition of the Commons to comply with his choice of ministers and whose prerogative to choose them went largely unchallenged. Only two resigned due to a failure to win a vote in the Commons. That became increasingly untenable with the mishandling of the American War of Independence and the questioning of the established order posed by the French Revolution. Yet the prospect of reform, supported by both Foxite Whigs and radicals such as Paine and Jeremy Bentham, albeit from different perspectives, raised a different threat to the balance of the constitution – that of democracy.

The early and mid-nineteenth century debate thereby came to centre on defending the encroachment of popular sovereignty on parliamentary sovereignty and its distinctive balance between commons, lords and monarch, without in the process succumbing to monarchical sovereignty through the

---

[51] Hume, *Essays*, Part 1 Essay 6.   [52] Gunn, 'Influence', 310–311.

use of influence and the royal prerogative.[53] The solution was seen in making the authority of the executive, as organised in the Cabinet, dependent on parliament, without making parliament dependent on the people. This argument found its defining statement in Earl Grey's essay *Parliamentary Government Considered with Reference to Reform of Parliament* (1858), and was adopted by contemporary constitutional authorities, such as Sir Thomas Erskine May's *Constitutional History of England* (1861–1863).[54] Again parties played a crucial role. As May noted, that 'a form of government so composite, and combining so many conflicting forces, has generally been maintained in harmonious action, is mainly due to the organization of parties'[55] Parties offered a degree of cohesion that could discipline individual MPs both in and out of office. To the extent they formed groups bound by shared ideals, they became a constraint on corruption via the royal prerogative. But at the same time, they needed to be sufficiently loose not to rest on an electoral mandate, so that a ministry could fall without necessitating dissolution. It is this version of party that lies behind Burke's famous defence of representation as trusteeship based on Parliament offering a virtual representation of the national interest.[56] Parties in this account were parliamentary groups under aristocratic leadership not electoral organisations responsive to popular demands, which represented the interests within the country without giving them a direct voice. As a result, a mix between people, aristocracy and monarch continued, with the new balance that encapsulated this mix being that between the competing parties of government and opposition.[57]

This doctrine of 'parliamentary government' underlies Dicey's famous account of parliamentary sovereignty outlined above. Yet, by the 1880s parliamentary government had largely given way to the two-party system. If the 1832 Reform Act had been an attempt to maintain this arrangement in the face of demands for electoral reform, the reforms of 1867 and 1884 promoted the shift towards parties that were much more akin to electoral machines.[58] In a political analysis of *The English Constitution* of 1867, Walter

---

[53] A. Hawkins, '"Parliamentary Government" and Victorian Political Parties c 1830–1880', *English Historical Review*, (1989) July, 645, 660.
[54] Hawkins, 'Parliamentary Government', 657, 661.
[55] Thomas Erskine May, *The Constitutional History of England since the Accession of George III*, 2 vols (Boston: Crosby and Nicols, 1863), Vol. II, ch. VIII: 17.
[56] E. Burke, 'Speech to the Electors of Bristol', in I. Hampshire-Monk (ed.), *The Political Philosophy of Edmund Burke* (Harlow: Longman, 1987), 108–110.
[57] Hawkins, '"Parliamentary Government"', 647.
[58] A. Hawkins, *Victorian Political Culture: 'Habits of Heart and Mind'* (Oxford: Oxford University Press, 2015), ch. 10.

Bagehot had already questioned the continued relevance of the mixed constitution. Bagehot made a key distinction between the 'dignified' and the 'efficient' elements of the constitution which he deployed to call into question the reality of both checks and balances and the separation of powers within the British system of government, and with it the existence of the rule of law. If the monarchy and the doctrine of the Crown in Parliament formed the 'dignified' parts of the constitution, which gave it a certain mystique and popular legitimacy, the 'efficient' parts 'by which it, in fact, works and rules' involved 'the nearly complete fusion of the legislative and executive powers' in the hands of the Queen's ministers through the government's control of a parliamentary majority. Moreover, after 1886 governments possessed office as a result of winning a parliamentary majority in elections. Bagehot, like Dicey, was an unenthusiastic democrat and worried that without the 'dignified' façade the result would produce the 'democratic despotism' or 'unmoderated democracy' that many adherents of parliamentary government and the mixed constitution feared would result from the fusing of parliamentary with popular sovereignty.[59]

Yet, as Montesquieu had hinted, representative democracy had the potential to offer a new and 'efficient' mechanism of checks and balances through electoral competition between parties reflecting contrasting interests and ideologies. That shift had begun in 1841, when Sir Robert Peel's Tories returned more members to the Commons than the governing Liberals and, for that reason, were invited by Queen Victoria to replace them and form a government. This period also saw the term Her Majesty's Loyal Opposition enter common usage,[60] signalling a new electorally based parliamentary balance between the government and a government in waiting. The 1880s completed this process with the ideological consolidation of the Liberal Party post the Home Rule crisis and the Liberal and Conservative Parties full transformation into electoral machines, thereby finishing the process begun in the 1860s towards the modern two-party system.[61] The Parliament Act of 1911 finally brought the end to the remaining 'effective' elements of the mixed constitution by removing the veto of both the Lords and the monarch on the Commons and the will of an elected government. Occasioned by the House of Lords rejection of the Liberal Administration's 'People's Budget', introducing both a supertax on the wealthy and death duties to fund its social

---

[59] A. L. Lowell, *The Government of England*, 2 vols (London: Macmillan, 1908), 1, 447.
[60] The first use, as a quip, was by Sir John Cam Hobhouse in 1826, Waldron, *Political*, 103.
[61] Hawkins, *Victorian Political Culture*, 325–328.

reforms and pensions, and the King's refusal to appoint new Liberal Peers to overcome the Lord's opposition, it led to two elections in 1910 that confirmed the government's authority. Consequently, the legislative authority of the Commons was now tightly linked to its being an elected chamber where the government of the day commanded a majority of MPs. Over the ensuing thirty years, the two-party system – during which Labour was eventually to supplant the Liberals – effectively became the new political constitution.

Representative Democracy and Party Competition: Towards a New Balance of Power

The balance of the mixed constitution involved an explicit check against popular majorities. The 'majority' was simply that social class that involved the 'most' people, but their interests had at best to be weighed and balanced against those of the few – the aristocracy – and the one – the monarch. Although it proved flexible enough to adapt to changes in the social and economic material constitution, it involved an explicit bias towards upholding the prevailing class divisions, even if these had altered with the passage from a landed to a commercial society. As such, it had a tendency towards preserving the existing balance of society.

The gradual extension of the suffrage to encompass the whole adult population by 1928 meant that the majority now referred to a majority of the population as a whole. Political equality on the basis of one person, one vote brought to the centre of politics what became known as the 'social question'. It was also associated with an expansion of the social and economic role of the state. A modern economy involved not only greater regulation but also the provision of a more extensive infrastructure, all of which required higher taxation and public borrowing. The displacement of the Liberal Party by a Labour Party rooted in the Trade Union movement may not have been inevitable, but the need to make a credible appeal to the working population was.[62]

As both Max Weber and Joseph Schumpeter noted, among other mainly foreign observers of the evolution of party systems,[63] electoral party competition promotes a dynamic balance, akin in certain respects to market

---

[62] Hawkins, *Victorian Political Culture*, ch. 10.
[63] M. Weber, 'The Profession and Vocation of Politics', in P. Lassman and R. Speirs (eds.), *Political Writings*, trans. R. Speirs (Cambridge: Cambridge University Press, 1994), 309–369; J. A. Schumpeter, *Capitalism, Socialism and Democracy* (London: Routledge, 1976), chs. 21 and 22.

competition among firms and entrepreneurs. As a result, the character of parties also changed. Organised mass parties to some degree preserved elite rule but encouraged leading politicians to develop certain campaigning skills that enabled them to recruit a following. Building a majority now involved cross-party alliances of interest that were tied to competing ideational conceptions of the national interest. Although these could have – and largely came to possess – a class basis, as favouring the interests of capital or labour, the need to fish for votes more broadly meant that parties also built support around an ideological claim that policies favouring such interests were either more just and/or more beneficial to all. As a result, the balance came to be between competing programmes for government that encompassed, but were not simply defined by, competing affective or interest groups.

Reinforced by the mass mobilisation and high taxation required to fight two world wars, these trends led Britain, in common with the rest of Western Europe, to be transformed from a liberal to a social democracy over the first half of the twentieth century. It was in this context that the contemporary debate arose over Britain's anomalous political constitution and proposals came forward that it adopt a 'modern' legal constitution.[64] Despite the new circumstances, these critiques reflected earlier worries that democracy undermined parliamentary government by empowering an executive that was unrepresentative of the people as a whole. Echoing Bagehot, Lowell and the literature of the 1860s–1880s bemoaning the decline of 'parliamentary government' and the triumph of the philosophic radicals' agenda of Jeremy Bentham and James and John Stuart Mill, critics argued that MPs who owed their legitimacy to being members of a popularly elected party were mere lobby fodder, voting as directed by the party leadership. The efficient part of the constitution was the Cabinet, itself emasculated by secrecy and collective responsibility, and possibly just the Prime Minister, with the legislature but a dignified rubber stamp of an ever-growing and more intrusive body of legislation.[65] The supposed result was what Lord Hailsham famously termed 'an elective dictatorship', whereby 'a bare majority in a single chamber' can 'assert its will over a whole people whatever that will may be'. Indicating the immediate and particular ideological motivation underlying this apparently general constitutional concern, he continued: 'It will end in a rigid economic plan, and I believe a siege economy, a curbed

---

[64] L. Scarman, *English Law: The New Dimension* (London: Stevens and Sons, 1974).
[65] R. H. S. Crossman, 'Introduction' to Bagehot *The English Constitution* (Glasgow: Collins, 1963).

and subservient judiciary and a regulated press. It will impose uniformity on the whole nation in the interest of what it claims to be social justice'.[66]

As with his nineteenth-century forebears, Hailsham's view traded on regarding electoral competition as lacking balance and involving the victory of a purely sectoral interest. He ignored how even in two-party systems a majority party is usually a coalition of different interests and ideological views that may fail to vote consistently along government lines. Nor did he note the parliamentary scrutiny of ministers and legislation performed by opposition parties, an aspect of parliament likewise passed over by Bagehot. His remarks on the danger to the judiciary and a free press notwithstanding, his account contained no mention of the class and political biases prevalent in media ownership or membership of the judiciary.

Meanwhile, his solution was a revamped version of the mixed constitution, designed to 'so rearrange the balance of forces within the separate organs of the constitution as to make dominance by any one of them impossible'.[67] This new constitutional arrangement was to include a proportionately elected second chamber and a federal structure involving devolution to Scotland, Wales, Northern Ireland and the English regions. Such counter-majoritarian arrangements can have a pronounced anti-egalitarian bias in giving extra weight to certain sectoral interests and favouring the status quo by making any change dependent on a super-majority or even consensus. However, this was Hailsham's explicit intention. 'Fundamental changes', he affirmed, 'ought only to be imposed, if at all, in the light of an unmistakeable national consensus'.[68] Indeed, not content with so diffusing power as to make such change politically unlikely, he sought to render it legally impossible by entrenching a doctrine of 'limited government or freedom under law' through a bill of rights that would guard against both 'equality' and 'the common good' and 'offer protections against the oppressiveness of unions and corporations' by upholding those entitlements of individuals and minorities that reflect 'the instructed conscience of the commonality'.[69]

Hailsham's thesis met with a spirited counterblast from J. A. G. Griffith in his Chorley Lecture of 1978 entitled 'The Political Constitution'. Griffith sought to defend the modern democratic constitution. At the heart of his

---

[66] Lord Hailsham, *The Dilemma of Democracy: Diagnosis and Prescription* (Glasgow: Collins, 1978), 9–10.
[67] Hailsham, *The Dilemma*, 68.   [68] Hailsham, *The Dilemma*, 21–22.
[69] Hailsham, *The Dilemma*, 9–10, 13.

defence was the claim that the constitutional doctrine of equilibrium in defence of the 'general conscience of mankind' hid the genuine conflicts and disagreements that animated politics. In Benthamite manner, he viewed talk of natural or human rights as metaphysical nonsense. They were simply political claims that reflected the political prejudices of those making them.[70] Asking courts to decide difficult policy questions with reference to necessarily abstract concepts of rights involved not the rule of law so much as the rule of judges and their political views. The only legitimate way to resolve differences over rights was through an explicitly political process – one where those making such decisions were political actors who were responsible and accountable to the people who would be subject to them.[71]

Griffith contended this did not entail any disrespect for law or the judiciary. On the contrary, it involved upholding the proper role of both. Griffith insisted that 'only an outlaw' would regard a regular system of law upheld by an independent judiciary, which applied equally to all – including the government of the day – as undesirable.[72] However, rights became more certain in their judicial application through being incorporated into concrete legislation embodying a determinate and democratically authorised political policy choice aimed at addressing a specific issue or set of issues. Invoking a democratic version of Dicey's view of the rule of law, he argued that democratically elected governments could rightfully and non-arbitrarily enact such legislation so long as it met the two key conditions imposed by the British political constitution: that they did not infringe existing legal entitlements of individuals unless expressly authorised to do so by statute, and that any change to the law or their powers under it obtained the assent of a democratically elected Parliament. That did not mean he thought the current political process by any means perfect. He argued for a more open and accessible system of government, with greater scope for debate. However, he contended the aim had to be to improve the democratic qualities of governance, not to further diminish democracy through the legal constraints of a written constitution.[73]

Ironically, by the time Griffith's lecture was published a Conservative administration under Mrs Thatcher had been elected which was to use the very powers Hailsham, her new Lord Chancellor, had decried to promote changes he found congenial but others would regard every bit as fundamental an attack on the existing social consensus as those he had feared from a

[70] Griffith, 'Political Constitution', 17.
[71] Griffith, 'Political Constitution', 16–19.
[72] Griffith, 'Political Constitution', 15.
[73] Griffith, 'Political Constitution', 15–17.

Labour government. Far from diffusing power, she used her parliamentary majority – achieved with never more than 43.9 per cent of the vote – to centralise it, curtailing the independence of local authorities in the process. She also weakened considerably the rights of labour to organise and strike through the Trade Union Act of 1984 and the Employment Act of 1988 and oversaw a significant increase in inequality.[74]

Griffith had noted how the contemporaneous constitutional proposals of Liberals and Progressives, such as Lord Scarmen and Ronald Dworkin, had been remarkably similar in their details and philosophical basis, if not their political motivation, to the now shelved plans of Lord Hailsham.[75] Unsurprisingly, the ensuing eighteen years of Conservative rule made these plans increasingly attractive to a Labour party that feared the terms of the British political constitution might condemn them to permanent opposition.[76] Public law networks, such as the Venice Commission, also promoted legal constitutionalism not only for new democracies in Central and Eastern Europe and elsewhere, but also within established democracies such as the Nordic and Commonwealth countries, that like the UK had strong political constitutional traditions, and influenced movements such as Charter 88 within the UK. Tony Blair's first Labour administration in 1997 was to see the introduction of the Human Rights Act (HRA) in 1998, the creation of a Supreme Court, a strengthening of local government in London and other metropolitan areas, and considerable devolution to Scotland, Wales and Northern Ireland. Meanwhile, the impact of the European Convention of Human Rights (ECHR), which, for example, curbed the use of certain procedures to interrogate terrorist suspects in Northern Ireland under the Thatcher administration, and of European Community law post the *Factortame* litigation, were held to have fashioned a European legal constitutional constraint on the sovereignty of parliament.

These moves were not without their critics, who revived and developed many elements of Griffith's earlier argument. Labour lawyers, such as Keith Ewing,[77] documented the mixed judicial record – including that of the European Court of Human Rights – in defending the rights of workers,

---

[74] S. Fredman, 'The New Rights: Labour Law and Ideology in the Thatcher Years', *Oxford Journal of Legal Studies* (1992) 12 (1): 24–44.
[75] Griffith, 'Political Constitution', 9, 10–12.
[76] A. Lester (ed.), *A British Bill of Rights* (London: IPPR, 1990); R. Dworkin, *A Bill of Rights for Britain* (London: Chatto, 1990).
[77] K. Ewing, *Bonfire of the Liberties: New Labour, Human Rights, and the Rule of Law* (Oxford: Oxford University Press, 2010).

whistle blowers and asylum seekers against executive actions based on reason of state. Waldron argued how a democratic vote on the basis of majority rule offered a fair mechanism for resolving disagreements about rights,[78] and defended the dignity of legislation as a more legitimate and deliberative way of deciding rights issues than judicial review. Adam Tomkins drew on the writings of Quentin Skinner to relate the historical origins of parliamentary sovereignty in the seventeenth century to a distinctively republican conception of liberty as non-domination, which he contrasted with the liberal view of liberty as non-interference that he associated with the doctrine of limited government informing many legal constitutionalist proposals, such as Hailsham's.[79] Finally, I developed a number of these strands in my own neo-republican account of political constitutionalism,[80] stressing in particular the relationship between non-domination and political equality, and noting the role of party competition as involving a dynamic form of balance promotive of certain constitutional values, such as equality under law and minority rights.

Despite these criticisms, it might be argued that Labour's constitutional reforms had moved Britain decisively towards a legal constitution. In particular, a number of judges, most explicitly and programmatically Sir John Laws, but also implicitly in key judgments by Lords Hoffmann in *R v. Home Secretary, ex parte Simms* [2000], and Steyn in *Jackson v. Attorney General* [2005] among others, argued that legality and rights rather than parliamentary sovereignty formed the cornerstone of Britain's 'common-law constitution'. Contra Dicey, they claimed the law was the source not the consequence of our rights. Of course, this was not a new claim, and it might be objected the role of the common law has been conspicuous by its absence throughout this account. Yet, not only does the political constitution play a distinct and autonomous role, which rests on foundations independent of the common law and retains a capacity to shape its judicial interpretation, but also the Thatcher period gives the lie to claims that the common law has ever contained rights comparable to those found in modern bills of rights. Instead, these rights derive from the HRA, which has the status of an ordinary statute and institutionalises a system of 'weak' review where Parliament has the last word.[81] As such, the recent prominence of rights in British legal culture reflects a democratic version of Dicey's dictum of how

---

[78] Waldron, *Law and Disagreement*, Part III. [79] Tomkins, *Our Republican*.
[80] Bellamy, *Political Constitutionalism*.
[81] Bellamy, 'Political Constitutionalism and the Human Rights Act'.

the exercise of our political rights can give rise to legal rights. Indeed, this was Lord Bingham's argument in *A. v. Secretary of State for the Home Department* (Belmarsh Prison) [2004].

Meanwhile, I have argued that if one conceives both the Council of Europe, within which the ECHR operates, and the EU as associations of democratic states, that are under the mutual control of the democratically elected representatives of their constituent states, then far from undercutting parliamentary sovereignty these arrangements can be seen as mechanisms for maintaining it in the circumstances of an interconnected and globalising world.[82] After all, that the UK's withdrawal from the EU was possible, underscores the degree to which parliament remained sovereign.

Whither the Political Constitution?

Since the return of the Conservatives to power in 2010, a vocal section of the party has argued that not only EU law but also the ECHR, the HRA and the UK Supreme Court place illegitimate legal constitutional constraints on parliamentary sovereignty. As Home Secretary, Theresa May argued for withdrawal from the ECHR (if not, pre-referendum, from the EU) and the scrapping of the HRA. Many of these supposed constraints related to executive powers to arrest and detain without trial or to deport alleged terrorist suspects (e.g. *Othman (Abu Qatada) v. the United Kingdom* [2012]). Parliamentary sovereignty was more directly involved in the *Hirst* case concerning prisoner's voting rights, where Parliament explicitly took the view that citizens forfeited such a right when committing any crime that merited a jail sentence, a position the European court viewed as disproportionate. Yet other complaints, such as those of Jonathan Sumption,[83] seem aimed more broadly at a rights culture that turns issues of individual morality and responsibility into litigable matters requiring ever-greater state regulation.

These new Conservative critiques contrast with Hailsham's earlier argument, which had viewed rights-based judicial review as defending limited government. Now, judges are criticised, on the one hand, for threatening legitimate government action to protect citizens by favouring the terrorist

---

[82] R. Bellamy, 'The Democratic Legitimacy of International Human Rights Conventions: Political Constitutionalism and the ECHR', *European Journal of International Law* (2014) 25 (4): 1019–1042; *A Republican Europe of States: Cosmopolitanism, Intergovernmentalism and Democracy in the EU* (Cambridge: Cambridge University Press, 2019).

[83] J. Sumption, *Trials of the State: Law and the Decline of Politics* (London: Profile Books, 2019).

and criminal against their potential or actual victims; and, on the other hand, for promoting a 'nanny state' that is overprotective by treating issues of health and safety and individual morality as matters of fundamental rights.

These criticisms seem as much a complaint about liberal judges as a concern with the encroachment of an emergent legal on the political constitution. Sumption's conception of politics resembles the 'parliamentary government' of the mid-Victorian era, with its invocation of Burke's understanding of the role of MPs. Moreover, he seems happy for judges to uphold classic liberal rights to property and freedom of contract should a Labour Party committed to 'social justice' ever come to power.[84] A similar conviction animates those Conservatives who consider repeal of the HRA would return the judiciary to the Thatcher era, when they upheld the allegedly 'traditional' British liberties of the common law.

Meanwhile, representative democracy and the related case for parliamentary sovereignty has also come under criticism. Parties are claimed to have transformed into governing cartels of professional politicians.[85] These parties may compete for office on technocratic grounds of competence and responsibility but not on democratic grounds of partisan ideologies and responsiveness to the electorate. As a result, the political constitution has taken on many of the characteristics of 'parliamentary government', with parties representing little beyond their respective prospective office-holders. As in other democracies, dissatisfaction with parliamentary politics has fed into populism, which in the UK as elsewhere in Europe became closely linked to Euro scepticism. However, in the UK senior members of the governing Conservative Party, including former Ministers, proved willing to deploy these criticisms of party 'elites' to support a referendum on EU membership, which was eventually held in June 2016.

The ambiguities of recent Conservative defences of the political constitution became apparent in the aftermath of the referendum result. The Conservatives had made the EU a core issue in the 2001 and 2005 elections, with largely disastrous results. However, it had grown in salience following the financial crisis of 2008, with a referendum seen by a vocal section of the Conservative Party, and a much smaller section of the Labour Party, as a way of appealing beyond the party cartels within Parliament. The direct appeal to

---

[84] R. Bellamy, 'The Limits of Lord Sumption: Limited Legal Constitutionalism and the Political Form of the ECHR', in N. Barber, R. Ekins and P. Yowell (eds.), *Lord Sumption and Human Rights* (Oxford: Hart, 2016), 193–212.
[85] P. Mair, *Ruling the Void: The Hollowing Out of Western Democracy* (London: Verso, 2013).

popular sovereignty suggests a new form of political constitutionalism – popular constitutionalism.[86] Yet, the appeal to the British 'people' had become increasingly problematic in the UK as a result of devolution – itself legitimised through the popular constitutionalist mechanism of a referendum and reflecting dissatisfaction in Scotland particularly with representation at Westminster. In the event, only popular majorities in England and Wales supported leaving the EU, with Scotland and Northern Ireland, together with Greater London, voting to remain. However, leave won over all by 51.9–48.1 per cent on a 73 per cent turnout.[87]

The result placed the prevailing parliamentary form of the political constitution under great strain given a majority of MPs had favoured remaining in the EU. Though technically advisory, few MPs felt the vote could be ignored. However, the terms of leaving remained deeply contested between the advocates of various 'soft' and 'hard' Brexits. With no deal commanding a parliamentary majority, the post-referendum Conservative administrations of first May and then of Boris Johnson attempted to push one through by appealing to a popular majority. This provoked legal moves to defend parliamentary sovereignty. In two key judgements (*Miller* 1 and 2) involving May's and Johnson's first administrations respectively, the Supreme Court insisted that the British constitution rested on parliamentary sovereignty. Some have seen these judgments as proof that a common-law constitution underlies the political constitution. However, *Miller* 1 can be seen as upholding a politically established norm that governments act with the consent of parliament, unless they have gained explicit parliamentary assent to do otherwise – most notably by calling an election, as May did in 2017 and Boris Johnson was to do in 2019. *Miller* 2 is more complex yet could be viewed as articulating the political limits to prorogue within a democratic political constitution. Fittingly, it returns us to our starting point of 1642, echoing Charles I's acceptance in the Answer that sovereignty, and hence prerogative power, lay not with the king or his ministers but with the king in Parliament, as ordained by an ancient political constitutive act as 'immemorial' as the common law, which it grounds.

In fact, the tribulations of Johnson's first administration came mainly from the difficulties posed by parliamentary procedure and the Fixed-term Parliaments Act rather than the Court. Despite winning a large parliamentary

---

[86] For a general defense of popular constitutionalism, see B. Ackerman, *Revolutionary Constitutions* (Cambridge, MA: Harvard University Press, 2019). I criticise such approaches in *Political Constitutionalism*, 129–141.

[87] I discuss the vexed issue of the legitimacy of the EU referendum in R. Bellamy, 'Was the Brexit Referendum Legitimate, and Would a Second One Be So?', *European Political Science* (2019), 18(1): 126–133.

majority in the 2019 election, the main constraint on his second administration came not from the judiciary but from the prospect of a successful electoral challenge by the opposition parties due to popular dissatisfaction with his flouting of lock down rules during the pandemic (the so-called 'party gate' scandal), and various allegations of ineptitude, corruption and mendacity more generally. His growing unpopularity led MPs from his own party to withdraw their support for his leadership, and Johnson resigned as PM on 7 July 2022 – less than three years after his electoral victory. Arguably, this episode illustrates the continued effectiveness of the democratic checks and balances of the modern representative political constitution in the face of populism. How long they will remain so only time will tell.

Conclusion

This chapter has sketched three main versions of the political constitution within the UK – the mixed constitution, parliamentary government, and representative democracy, and the prospects of a fourth, populist constitutionalism. Each has proved able to accommodate governments of very different ideological leanings and both adapt to and partly shape changing social and economic cleavages and conflicts. Legal constitutions are sometimes portrayed as standing outside and constraining politics, and by implication the social, economic and ideational conflicts that give rise to political activity. In practice, they either reflect or not infrequently succumb to those conflicts (the average life span of a legal constitution is seventeen years).[88] A political constitution operates by creating a self-enforcing equilibrium between the disagreements and clashes of different parties and groups by generating different kinds of checks and balances. However, such equilibriums need not be egalitarian, and historically have not been so. The contemporary challenge is to retain the democratic credentials of political constitutionalism at a time of increased social inequality and global interconnectedness, and a growing disaffection with politics in general and political parties in particular. The result is a system that frequently appears closer to 'parliamentary government' than representative democracy, a shift that has fed populism in the form of referendums, on the one hand, and mixed government, in the form of devolution, on the other. How far either can promote the constitutional values of equality and rights remains an open question.

---

[88] Z. Elkins, T. Ginsburg and J. Melton, *The Endurance of National Constitutions* (Cambridge: Cambridge University Press, 2009).

4
The Economic Constitution

TONY PROSSER

Introduction

The terminology of an 'economic constitution' is little used in the UK, and coverage of the constitutional aspects of economic management finds only limited (and diminishing) space in the standard constitutional law texts. This is in marked contrast to other European jurisdictions, where the economic constitution is a familiar analytical concept for both domestic and EU law.[1] The absence is surprising given how central economic questions have been to our constitutional development. The seventeenth-century struggles which shaped our constitution were largely about economic issues in the form of Parliamentary scrutiny of the Crown raising and spending financial resources. The development of regulatory institutions was relatively unconstrained by constitutional norms, but it raised difficult questions of the extent and meaning of the central doctrine of ministerial responsibility. In this chapter I shall inevitably have to be selective and so shall examine these two examples, of scrutiny of public expenditure and of economic regulation, to draw some broader themes still relevant today, about the nature and requirements of our constitutional order.[2]

As the concept of an economic constitution is unfamiliar in the UK it will be helpful to begin by discussing different conceptions of such a constitution

---

[1] Sabino Cassese, *La Nuova Costituzione Economica*, 5th ed. (Editori Laterza, 2017); in the EU context H.-W. Micklitz, ed., 'La Constitution Economique Européenne Revisiteé' (2011) XXV(4) *Revue Internationale de Droit Economique* 411.

[2] The two areas chosen reflect Daintith's seminal distinction between dominium and imperium as policy instruments in economic management. Dominium is the deployment of wealth by government, and imperium the deployment of force or the threat of force. In this chapter, however, I shall limit my discussion of dominium to the ability of government to raise and spend finance so that it can undertake economic activity rather than its actual deployment by government to achieve public purposes, for example, through contractual means (T. C. Daintith, 'Legal Analysis of Economic Policy' (1982) 9 *Journal of Law and Society* 191, esp. 211–216).

which might be employed for analytical purposes before applying them to the UK's historical experience.

Two Models of Economic Constitution

My first type of economic constitution I shall term the 'substantive' economic constitution. It sets out principles of substance of how the economy should be organised. A largely historical usage was in the constitutions of socialist countries requiring, for example, public ownership and administration of public services.[3] A vivid example was Article 83(1) of the 1976 Portuguese constitution, stating that nationalisation measures carried out since the revolution were 'irreversible conquests by the working class'. Provisions of this kind have largely disappeared with economic liberalisation and privatisation, though the French constitution still has traces of this approach in its incorporation of the principle from the 1946 constitution requiring that enterprises with the character of a national public service or monopoly must become public property; this has not prevented substantial privatisation. This type of economic constitution can be conceived in terms derived from Rousseau; the economic constitution reflects the general will, or, in modern-day terms, the 'will of the people'.[4] More recent versions of a substantive economic constitution would include, for example, that associated with the German ordoliberalism of the post–Second World War period.[5] In this group of theories a common claim is that the constitution should establish the basic elements constituting the economic system; it translates economic philosophy into law by providing the basic elements of economic conduct. Most famously these include competition law, but may also involve constitutional recognition of property rights, stability of the currency and a balanced budget. Further examples of advocacy of such a substantive economic constitution are that of Hayek on the constitutional conditions for markets to work freely and those of economic constitutionalists such as James Buchanan drawing on rational choice principles to develop substantive constitutional norms, notably through advocacy of a balanced

---

[3] Terence Daintith and Monica Sah, 'Privatisation and the Economic Neutrality of the Constitution' (1993) *PL* 465.
[4] Philip Pettit, *Republicanism: A Theory of Freedom and Government* (Oxford University Press, 1997) 30–31; cf 252–253.
[5] David Gerber, 'Constitutionalizing the Economy: German Neo-liberalism, Competition Law and the "New" Europe' (1994) 42 *American Journal of Comparative Law* 25.

budget rule.[6] In such cases the normative concern is to develop principles on *a priori* grounds to protect economic freedoms or to facilitate the assumed rational choices of individuals and the efficient economic allocation of goods.

The UK has never had a substantive economic constitution of this kind. Of course, this is in part due to the lack of codification of UK constitutional arrangements, but it also reflects a reluctance to treat substantive economic policy as a matter of law rather than of politics. In fact, the nearest the UK has come to such substantive principles is at the end of the period to be examined here through membership of the European Union, which does have a number of high-level economic principles inscribed in the Treaties. These have been of very limited effect in shaping substantive economic management, however, as evidenced by the minimal practical importance of the removal of the objective of undistorted competition contained in the former Article 3(1)(g) EC repealed by the Lisbon Treaty.[7] The EU commitment which went furthest in requiring substantive constitutional norms was the Fiscal Compact of 2011, to which the UK was not a party.[8] Nor has recognition of fundamental rights such as a right to property played a major role in shaping economic management; advocacy of a 'property-owning democracy' was always a political rather than legal programme.[9] Of course, the four freedoms of the EU have been fundamental to our recent economy, but the influence of the European Convention on Human Rights on substance has been limited with a wide margin of appreciation given to national authorities on matters of economic decision-making.[10]

There is another type of economic constitution which is far closer to the UK's historical experience. This derives from a different form of Republican tradition from that of Rousseau and does not attempt to set out any substantive 'general will'. It sees the economic constitution as creating a means for contesting and scrutinising government economic management,

---

[6] F. A. Hayek, *The Constitution of Liberty* (Routledge, 1960), esp. ch. 12; James M. Buchanan and Gordon Tulloch, *The Calculus of Consent: Logical Foundations of Constitutional Democracy* (University of Michigan Press, 1962).
[7] Natalia Fiedziuk, 'Services of General Interest and the Treaty of Lisbon: Opening Doors to a Whole New Approach of Maintaining the "Status Quo"' (2011) 36(2) *European Law Review* 226.
[8] Paul Craig, 'The Stability, Coordination and Governance Treaty: Principle, Politics and Pragmatism' (2012) 37 *European Law Review* 231.
[9] For the development of this idea see Ron Amit, 'Visions of Democracy in "Property-Owning Democracy": Skelton to Rawls and Beyond' (2008) 29 *History of Political Thought* 89.
[10] E.g., in *International Transport Roth GmbH v. Secretary of State for the Home Department* [2002] EWCA Civ 158, [2003] QB 728, paras 83–87.

not setting any substantive direction to it. This model is not majoritarian but contestatory. Its concerns are with the creation and management of institutions, and with procedures and opportunities for scrutiny and deliberation. Its character has been put succinctly by Philip Pettit:

> [t]his points us towards the ideal of a democracy based, not on the alleged consent of the people, but rather on the contestability by the people of everything that government does: the important thing to ensure is that government doings are fit to provide popular contestation, not that they are the product of popular will.[11]

As a convenient shorthand, one can call this the 'contestatory' model of economic constitution (following Pettit). It includes procedures for economic management but goes far beyond procedure in any restricted legal sense, encompassing the building of institutions, their interrelationships, and the provision of means for scrutiny and deliberation in the development and application of economic policy.

We shall see that the seventeenth-century settlement put Parliament squarely in the centre of this role. However, developments since have meant that a variety of institutions other than Parliament have become central to this model of economic constitution. This shift is partly due to internal political changes in Parliament itself, where the dominance of party has seriously limited its opportunities for scrutiny of the executive in economic management, especially in the planning of public expenditure. It is also due to developments outside Parliament, where a wide range of regulatory and other institutions has been developed for scrutiny purposes, thus providing an essentially pluralistic form of economic constitution and downgrading the constitutional role of ministerial responsibility to Parliament.[12]

Not least, much scrutiny is carried out within the executive itself.[13] For example, the role of the Treasury is central to the management of public expenditure and attempting to secure financial stability. As the leading account of its work has emphasised, it sits in complex networks of interaction and interdependencies with other governmental institutions which have

---

[11] Pettit, *Republicanism*, 277; for the importance of these ideas in UK historical experience see Adam Tomkins, *Our Republican Constitution* (Oxford University Press, 2005) esp. 51–52.
[12] Tony Prosser, *The Economic Constitution* (Oxford University Press, 2014).
[13] This point is made in detail in Terence Daintith and Alan Page, *The Executive in the Constitution: Structure, Autonomy and Internal Control* (Oxford University Press, 1999).

changed over time.[14] Nor will scrutiny be limited to formal legal rules as there is a vast array of internal, informal rules and processes which also need examination. Similarly, the role of the Bank of England is also central to economic management. The Bank was founded as a private institution in 1694 and nationalised by the Bank of England Act 1946. Very importantly, the Bank's Monetary Policy Committee gained responsibility for setting interest rates under the Bank of England Act 1998. It is thus clear that in all areas of economic management the interaction, formal and informal, of institutions is crucial. The failure of such interaction was a major problem in the Government's response to the economic crisis of 2008–2009.[15]

Having set the scene through identification of these two models of economic constitution, it is now possible to examine the two selected aspects of UK historical experience.

Raising and Spending Public Money

The Development of Parliamentary Scrutiny

The establishment of Parliamentary powers over Crown spending in the seventeenth century is of course central to any discussion of our constitutional history. It also underlies other areas of democratic scrutiny of the executive. As Tomkins has put it

> The most significant curtailment of the monarchy's powers, of its independence and of its room for manoeuvre came not as much through the formal enactments of legislation as from its permanent shortage of money. That there has been a Parliament in England every year since the 1690s is principally due not to any statutory provision but to the fact that government is prohibitively expensive.... Without parliamentary supply there can be no government: it is as simple as that.[16]

Of course, this reflected older developments, with the gradual establishment of a Parliamentary role in the authorisation of expenditure from the thirteenth century onwards. Magna Carta in 1215 prohibited the levying of some forms of aid without the common consent of the realm. These provisions

---

[14] Colin Thain and Maurice Wright, *The Treasury and Whitehall: The Planning and Control of Public Expenditure, 1976–1993* (Oxford University Press, 1995).
[15] For a detailed account of the Bank of England see David Kynaston, *Till Time's Last Sand: A History of the Bank of England 1694–2013* (Bloomsbury, 2017). for a brief account of institutional relations during the financial crisis see Prosser, *The Economic Constitution*, 22–36.
[16] Tomkins, *Our Republican Constitution*, 107.

were later withdrawn, but in practice they were observed, and in 1295 the representatives of the commons and the clergy began to meet regularly to consider taxes. In 1297 Edward I was forced to withdraw a tax at a time of crisis and, according to Maitland, 'we may fairly say that after 1295 the imposition of any direct tax without the common consent of the realm was against the very letter of the law. ... And the common consent of the realm was now no vague phrase; that consent had now its appropriate organ in a parliament of the three estates'.[17] From 1362 there was some requirement of Parliamentary assent to indirect taxation, and in 1407 Henry IV agreed to the principle that grants were initiated by the Commons with assent of the Lords, a basic principle underlying Parliamentary authorisation since.[18] By the middle of the fourteenth century there was some appropriation of funds for specified purposes, and early in the next century the King was made to submit accounts of expenditure. However, as Maitland remarked, 'the principle had to be contested over and over again; it was a principle of no value unless parliament had a will of its own which it would exert year by year ...'.[19] Under the Tudors Parliament was submissive. For example, Henry VIII exacted heavy loans and then Parliament wiped out his debts; Parliament played only a very limited role in this respect under Elizabeth I.[20]

These events laid the basis for the major struggles of the seventeenth century between king and Parliament, and the English revolution. It is not necessary here to describe all the complex ways in which Parliament gradually reinforced its constitutional role as many accounts are available elsewhere.[21] It may be useful however to note some landmark events in relation to finance; those relating to regulation will be considered later in this chapter. Both the courts and Parliament itself were to play major, and often conflicting, roles in the determination of the Crown's financial powers. For example, *Bate's Case* in 1606 arose when a merchant refused to pay a levy imposed by James I on imported currants on the grounds that it amounted to indirect taxation without the consent of Parliament.[22] The Court of Exchequer held that this was justified by the Crown's extraordinary prerogative to regulate

---

[17] F. W. Maitland, *The Constitutional History of England* (first published 1908, Cambridge University Press, 1961) 92–96.
[18] Ibid, 182.   [19] Ibid, 184.   [20] Ibid, 251.
[21] For background see Christopher Hill, *The Century of Revolution 1603–1714* (Sphere Books, 1978); for more details Maitland, *The Constitutional History*, Period III; J. P. Kenyon, *The Stuart Constitution 1603–1688: Documents and Commentary*, 2nd ed. (Cambridge University Press, 1986); Tomkins, *Our Republican Constitution*, ch. 3 and Elizabeth Wicks, *The Evolution of a Constitution* (Hart Publishing, 2006) ch. 1.
[22] (1606) 2 St. Tr. 371.

foreign affairs, and there were broad *dicta* to the effect that the Crown's prerogative was not reviewable. When it was reconvened in 1610, Parliament undertook a major debate on impositions which resulted in an agreement with the King; this included a commitment that future impositions without Parliamentary consent would be declared illegal by statute. However, Parliament was dissolved before this could be implemented.[23] After further skirmishes between Crown and Parliament, the Commons passed the Petition of Right in the Parliament of 1628–1629. The Petition provided that no impositions were to be levied by the King without the consent of Parliament, effectively reversing *Bate's Case*.[24] King Charles I assented to the Petition but its legal status remained uncertain, and the issue re-emerged in the *Case of Ship Money* in 1637.[25] The case concerned funding and the provision of ships for a navy to protect trade, levied without the consent of Parliament. John Hampden refused to pay on the basis that the financial resources necessary for defence had to be raised through Parliament. The majority of the court held that the King had sole responsibility for the defence of the realm and that this included the raising of taxation in this field which could not be restricted by Parliament.[26] The case 'finally wrecked the reputation of the bench'[27] and the Long Parliament responded vigorously; in 1641 it passed a statute pronouncing the decision void, declared the writs for the collection of ship-money unlawful, and impeached two of the judges. In the same year the Triennial Act had been passed requiring Parliament to be called at least every three years. Thus '[by] the time of the Long Parliament it had become clear that conflicts between the prerogative and the exclusive right of Parliament to tax would be resolved in favour of the latter, and in that sense Parliament ultimately won.'[28]

Civil War intervened, and a final and authoritative statement of Parliament's role had to wait until after the Glorious Revolution of 1688 and the Bill of Rights of 1689.[29] The key provisions are well known; Article 4 provides that 'levying of money for or to the use of the Crown, by pretence of prerogative, without grant of Parliament for longer time, or in other

---

[23] Kenyon, *The Stuart Constitution*, 48–49.
[24] Tomkins, *Our Republican Constitution*, 77–81; Kenyon, *The Stuart Constitution*, 52–53, 68–71.
[25] *R v. Hampden* (1637) 3 St. Tr. 825.   [26] Tomkins, *Our Republican Constitution*, 83–87.
[27] Kenyon, *The Stuart Constitution*, 90.
[28] Paul Craig, 'Prerogative, Precedent and Power', in Christopher Forsyth and Ivan Hare (eds.), *The Golden Metwand and the Crooked Cord* (Oxford University Press, 1998), 65 (footnote omitted).
[29] For more details see Wicks, *The Evolution of a Constitution*, ch. 1.

manner than the same is or shall be granted, is illegal'. There is no equivalent statement relating to the authorisation of expenditure but there was recognition of a similar principle based on the redress of grievances before supply. As the Judicial Committee of the Privy Council put it in 1924 'it has been a principle of the British Constitution now for more than two centuries ... that no money can be taken out of the consolidated Fund into which the revenues of the State have been paid, excepting under a distinct authorization from Parliament itself'.[30] Hill summarises the position after 1689 as follows; 'Parliament's control was exercised through finance. ... from 1690 government policy was controlled by specific appropriations. The King, a courtier complained in that year, was kept "as it were at board wages".... By the end of Anne's reign the Treasury was as a matter of routine drawing up annual budgets for submission to Parliament. We are in the modern world.'[31]

The Absence of Parliamentary 'Control'

Clearly, the successful assertion of Parliamentary authority in relation to supply of funds to the Crown was central to our constitutional history. It has, however, to be treated carefully. Apart from the fact that, of course, it predated universal suffrage by centuries, it was not an assertion of Parliamentary 'control' in the substantive Rousseau sense explained above.[32] It fell into the second of our models of economic constitution. Thus it was concerned with the inter-relationship of institutions; '[t]he financial *context* of government meant that, irrespective of the text of statute law, no government could survive without parliamentary support.'[33] The bases for Parliament's claims were to a large extent that traditional liberties under common law (the 'ancient constitution'), and even a classical vision of liberties, were threatened and so it was necessary to provide institutional means for their protection.[34] In Maitland's terms, it was not an assertion of the divine right of majorities over that of the monarch, but 'a protest against arbitrary power or, more accurately, against the exercise of power in

---

[30] *Auckland Harbour Board* v. *R* [1924] AC 318, 326–327.
[31] Hill, *The Century of Revolution*, 239.
[32] Insofar as there was a substantive constitutional agenda in the Glorious Revolution and Bill of Rights, it was that of the entrenchment of discrimination against Roman Catholics in public life, since thankfully forgotten in favour of the institutional developments.
[33] Tomkins, *Our Republican Constitution*, 108.
[34] Kenyon, *The Stuart Constitution*, 7; Quentin Skinner, 'John Milton and the Politics of Slavery' and 'Classical Liberty, Renaissance Translation and the English Civil War' in Quentin Skinner, *Visions of Politics, Volume II: Renaissance Virtues* (Cambridge University Press, 2002) 286, 308.

arbitrary ways'. Insofar as there was any 'democratic' element, this was not based on any notion of general will but rather because 'it may be argued *a priori* that a democracy is less likely to exercise arbitrary power than is a monarchy. The many minds of many men check each other, one would go this way, another that, so that the steady consistency which is required of those who would exercise power arbitrarily in the face of opposition must be wanting.'[35]

This means that it is seriously misleading to speak of Parliament having powers of control of public spending.[36] One exemplification of this is the Crown's monopoly of initiative of spending proposals through which 'this House will receive no Petitions for any Sum of Money, relating to publick service, but what is recommended by the Crown'. This was reaffirmed in the late seventeenth century, passed in the form of a resolution in 1706 and made a standing order in 1713, thereby preventing any form of 'rule by financial assembly'.[37] The rule is now contained in Standing Order 48. The inappropriateness of viewing Parliament's financial powers as powers of control can also be seen in the later development of our constitution. A familiar feature is, of course, the growth of political parties and associated internal discipline in the House of Commons.[38] One outcome is that the supply procedure by which expenditure is authorised is almost wholly a formality; the Hansard Society observed in a 2006 inquiry that '[t]he majority of people who gave evidence to this inquiry were of the view that the supply process as it currently operates, while being very complex, is little more than a "rubber stamp".'[39] No estimate has been rejected since 1919 (referring to the provision of a second bathroom for the Lord Chancellor).[40] Moreover, much public

---

[35] F. W. Maitland, 'A Historical Sketch of Liberty and Equality as Ideals of English Political Philosophy from the Time of Hobbes to the Time of Coleridge' in H. A. L. Fisher (ed.) *Collected Papers of Frederic William Maitland*, Vol 1 (Cambridge University Press, 1911) 1, 38–39, 79–85. For contemporary statements of this theme from, among others, Harrington and Milton, see Philip Pettit, 'Republican Theory and Political Trust' in Valerie Braithwaite and Margaret Levi (eds.) *Trust and Governance* (Russell Sage, 1998) 295, 303, 309.
[36] For a fuller statement of this theme see William Bateman, *Public Finance and Parliamentary Constitutionalism* (Cambridge University Press, 2020). For reasons of space I shall concentrate on Parliamentary scrutiny of spending rather than of taxation here; for the latter see Dominic de Cogan, *Tax Law, State-Building and the Constitution* (Hart Publishing, 2020).
[37] Kenyon, *The Stuart Constitution*, 417–418, 424.
[38] Walter Bagehot, *The English Constitution* (first published 1867, Fontana 1963) 155–161.
[39] Alex Brazier and Vidya Ram, *The Fiscal Maze: Parliament, Government and Public Money* (Hansard Society, 2006) para. 4.7.
[40] Liaison Committee, *Parliament and Government Finance: Recreating Financial Scrutiny* (HC 2007–2008, 426) para. 19; HC Deb 24 June 1919, vol 117, cols 113–116.

expenditure (around a third) falls outside parliamentary supply procedure. Indeed, powers of control would be incompatible with effective and democratic government through enabling Parliament to use finance as a means of leverage against government on unrelated matters, as experience in the United States has vividly shown.

Even Dicey was reluctant to portray Parliament as possessing powers of control over public expenditure. His discussion of 'The Revenue', including authority for expending revenue, is contained in the section of his *Law of the Constitution* relating to 'The Rule of Law: Its Application' rather than that on 'The Sovereignty of Parliament'. It makes just one explicit reference to parliamentary 'control' in the context of misapplication of funds, and even this did not appear in later editions.[41] Bagehot is more explicit; '[i]n truth, when a Cabinet is made the sole executive, it follows it must have the sole financial charge, for all action costs money, all policy depends on money, and it is in adjusting the relative goodness of action and policies that the executive is employed.'[42]

The obverse of lack of Parliamentary *control* is Parliamentary *scrutiny* of public spending. More specifically in relation to economic management, 'Parliament, in the British system, should not be viewed as the maker or possessor of economic policies. Its role is rather one of scrutiny, discussion and legitimation of policies formed elsewhere. ... [T]he legislative process secures the civic benefits of comprehensive discussion, democratic consent, publicity and formal promulgation for governmental measures.'[43] This contestatory role can be undertaken in different ways. By far the most successful is examination of the use of public funds *ex post facto* by Parliamentary committees and the audit of government expenditure on Parliament's behalf.[44] Although the role of a public official auditing government expenditure dates back to at least 1314, the major initiative to ensure that such an audit was institutionally supported came during Gladstone's Chancellorship, from 1859 to 1866.

The Exchequer and Audit Departments Act 1866 required that all departments produce annual appropriation accounts, and that these should be audited by the Comptroller and Auditor General supported by the Exchequer and Audit

---

[41] A. V. Dicey, *Lectures Introductory to the Study of the Law of the Constitution*, 1st ed. (Macmillan, 1885) 322; cf A. V. Dicey, *Lectures Introductory to the Study of the Law of the Constitution*, 8th ed. (Macmillan, 1915) 205.
[42] Bagehot, *The English Constitution*, 155.
[43] Daintith, 'Legal Analysis of Economic Policy', 197, 213.
[44] For a detailed account see Daintith and Page, *The Executive in the Constitution*, ch. 6.

Department. This official was made responsible for granting consent for the issue of public money to government departments, having satisfied himself that it fell within Parliamentary authorisation, and for the auditing of the actual expenditure. Gladstone also established a specialist committee of the House of Commons, the Committee of Public Accounts, to consider audit reports and to take evidence from senior officials. The system was considerably strengthened by the National Audit Act 1983, providing greater Parliamentary involvement in the renamed National Audit Office and statutory backing for value for money audit, going far beyond traditional financial audit. This has given Parliament a major and high-profile role in the *ex post facto* scrutiny of public spending; it has been further enhanced by the growth of the work of departmental select committees of both Houses, established in a more rational and comprehensive fashion by resolution of Parliament in 1979. As a result, scrutiny of financial expenditure by Parliament after it has taken place has grown in strength over the last fifty years, and it is now closely allied to internal control by the Executive, especially within the Treasury, which of course has its own complex system of approvals and delegations of authority for expenditure. Indeed, the latter relies heavily on National Audit scrutiny as a basis for its own role in control.[45]

The Growth of Other Types of Institutional Scrutiny

The discussion so far has emphasised the legacy from the seventeenth century in which the House of Commons is the central actor in financial scrutiny. However, we shall see that other institutional fora have developed apart from the House. A good example is the planning of public expenditure and scrutiny of planned expenditure before it takes place, in which the Parliamentary role is much less impressive. Moreover, a substantial proportion of public finance escapes the procedures for Parliamentary authorisation of funds; for example, the ability to use funding under the Banking Act 2009 to rescue failed banks after the 2008–2009 financial crisis.[46] Parliamentary scrutiny of borrowing is particularly restricted.

One important means of scrutiny is through processes developed by and operating within the Executive itself. At the beginning of the new millennium, major changes took place in the arrangements for planning public expenditure. This can be seen in the development of the Comprehensive Spending Review system, building on earlier reforms and intended to permit

---

[45] Daintith and Page, *The Executive in the Constitution*, 169–206, 380–398.
[46] See the Banking Act 2009 s 228.

a review of spending in the round that would be valid for longer than the annual budgeting period. It culminated in the 2010 Spending Review attempting to set spending for a full Parliament which was of immense importance as the means by which the politics of austerity was implemented in the UK.[47] The involvement of Parliament was extremely limited and the spending review process took the form of negotiation within government itself; the key decisions were taken by the quadrilateral steering group of the leaders of the Coalition parties and their deputies. It represented a culmination of the process of executive self-regulation described by Daintith and Page and referred to above.[48] Parliament's role was restricted to scrutiny by select committee (the Treasury Committee was particularly active here) and very limited debate rather than meaningful input into the process itself.

In terms of scrutiny of these decisions by institutions outside the executive, two developments were of importance. The first was the creation of the Office for Budget Responsibility, established shortly after the 2010 election and given a statutory basis by the Budget Responsibility and National Audit Act 2011. This took over from the Treasury the drawing up of the official five-year forecasts for the economy and is also responsible for assessing whether the Government is on course to meet its financial targets, reporting on the financial implications of tax and spending measures, the health of the public sector balance sheet and the long-term sustainability of public finances. It is a body corporate acting on behalf of the Crown and is robustly independent of government.[49] The Office's creation reflects a broader move towards creating bodies with major economic responsibilities at arms-length from government; another example is that of the Monetary Policy Committee of the Bank of England responsible for setting interest rates within a remit set by the Chancellor.[50] What we see here, then, is that responsibility for scrutiny of government fiscal and monetary policy is for the executive itself and institutions set up at arm's length, rather than being the direct responsibility of Parliament, the role of which is one of *ex post facto* scrutiny of propriety and efficiency of spending. Of course, the UK economic constitution has been further complicated by territorial devolution with varied degrees of responsibility for economic development and expenditure being passed to the devolved nations, thereby further increasing institutional

---

[47] HM Treasury, *Spending Review* 2010 (Cm 7942, 2010); for background see Tony Prosser, '"An Opportunity to Take a More Fundamental Look at the Role of Government in Society": The Spending Review as Regulation' [2011] PL 596.
[48] Daintith and Page, *The Executive in the Constitution*, chs. 4–6.
[49] Budget Responsibility and National Audit Act 2011, s 3 and sch. 1.
[50] Bank of England Act 1998, Part II.

complexity. I shall not consider the effects of devolution here as they are covered in later chapters.

The second important development has been that external scrutiny of government borrowing and spending passed not to Parliament but to the institutions of the European Union. Although the UK did not join the eurozone nor the Fiscal Compact, it was part of the Stability and Growth Pact adopted in 1997 together with the Excessive Deficit Procedure now contained in Article 126 of the Treaty on the Functioning of the European Union. Though no sanctions could be issued under the latter against the UK given its opt-out from full monetary union, it nevertheless remained subject to the 'Europe 2020' strategy for enhanced coordination of national fiscal frameworks and financial procedures. This includes the 'European Semester', a six-month strategy permitting unified surveillance of budgetary and structural policies through review by the Commission.[51] A further important means of scrutiny of some types of government spending was detailed assessment by the Commission of state aid.

The scrutiny role of Parliament has, then, been increasingly shared with other institutions, both domestic and European. What has been the role of the courts as the other Diceyan constitutional actors here? In other European nations audit has been conceived as in part a quasi-judicial function and has been entrusted to institutions with some of the characteristics of courts. Given Dicey's treatment of 'The Revenue' under the section of his *Law of the Constitution* dealing with the application of the rule of law, and his suggestion that mandamus could be issued to ensure that money was properly spent under statutory authority, it might have been assumed that there would be a judicial role in policing the use of public funds.[52] However, the role of the courts in the seventeenth century struggles to hold the Crown accountable in financial matters was hardly impressive, and, although the courts have taken a major role in tax law, both on substance and on procedure, their role in relation to spending has been restricted. They will of course police the normal boundaries of statutory authority as part of review of *vires*, and this may occasionally have some importance in backing up Parliamentary authority for spending.[53] Decisions relating to human rights may also have relevance to some aspects of taxation, but they have not had a role to play in relation to spending decisions. There were suggestions that the courts might have begun to assume a role alongside that of the National

---

[51] See Prosser, *The Economic Constitution*, 105–106.
[52] Dicey 1885, *Lectures Introductory*, 329.
[53] See notably *Auckland Harbour Board* v. *R* [1924] AC 318, 326–327.

Audit Office in examination of value for money after the decision in the 'Pergau Dam' case in 1995. Here the High Court held that a grossly uneconomic use of public funds was *ultra vires*.[54] However scrutiny of value for money is not a role the courts have assumed since, and that decision was based on its own very particular facts.

In the discussion of public spending, what we see is an assertion of Parliament's powers of scrutiny over the Crown in the seventeenth century and the development of complex procedures to secure this. It needs to be emphasised once more, however, that this does not in any way represent a role for Parliament in representing a popular will, nor in exercising control over government in the crude sense of issuing orders or vetoing spending policy in advance. Instead, it represented the development of contestatory institutions for scrutiny and deliberation in relation to spending. Insofar as any credible commitments could be made to protect property rights, these were institutional commitments, not principles of constitutional substance.[55] Parliament does still exercise important functions of *ex post facto* scrutiny of spending through committees and through the work of the National Audit Office, but in relation to the planning of expenditure what has become much more important is the role of internal processes within the executive itself, now partially institutionalised in the form of spending reviews, and scrutiny by other institutions, including the Office for Budget Responsibility and (pre-Brexit) the European Union institutions. Constitutional scrutiny is plural, using a mix of different institutions. There is an irony that the promise of the seventeenth-century constitutional revolution is now realised by institutions far from any which could then have been envisaged.

Regulatory Institutions and the Limits of Ministerial Responsibility

Early Regulatory Institutions

It is now time to turn away from the way in which the constitution treats the spending of public money by government and to look instead at how it approaches the regulation of other actors in the economy. This is also

---

[54] *R v. Secretary of State for Foreign and Commonwealth Affairs, ex parte The World Development Movement Ltd.* [1995] 1 All ER 611; Ian Harden, Fidelma White and Kathryn Hollingworth, 'Value for Money and Administrative Law' [1996] PL 661.

[55] Douglas North and Barry Weinglass, 'Constitutions and Commitment: The Evolution of Institutions Governing Public Choice in Seventeenth-Century England' (1989) 49 *The Journal of Economic History* 803.

essentially a question of institutions; the UK has not developed, at least in the legal sphere, a set of principles like those of the French *service public* which provide a unifying and distinctive source for the performance of the state's economic tasks, including those delegated to private actors.[56] One noticeable theme will be the degree of flexibility and experimentation permitted by the UK constitution in the design of regulatory institutions. A second will be that the Diceyan constitutional dualism of Parliament and the courts does not work here. The central concept of ministerial responsibility to Parliament has been increasingly modified and, indeed, abandoned; instead more complex and subtle patterns of institutional relations have developed.

Regulation is not a modern development but has been central to economic management since before the Middle Ages, and it has encompassed a wide range of rationales, instruments and institutions. In the medieval period regulation included extensive price and lending controls in different forms, undertaken by the Crown: 'Monarchs did not aspire to ensuring that every bargain was completely equal, or obeyed church law and teachings, but they went beyond their own self-interest and acted when it became apparent that the profiteering of certain persons was producing outrage or seriously deleterious effects, particularly if those effects went beyond the parties to a bargain.'[57] Later on, '[a]t no time in English legal history has the law governing industry and commerce been so extensively and intensively penetrated by regulation as in the Tudor and Stuart periods.'[58]

A bewildering range of different techniques was used for regulation in these periods, including professional self-regulation, most notably through guilds; the sale of monopolies; control of trade; and price regulation. Much regulation involved the use of royal prerogative powers, and such powers played a part in the seventeenth-century legal struggles. The *Case of Proclamations* related to two proclamations made by James I, to prohibit new buildings in and about London, and to prohibit the making of starch from wheat.[59] It was held that the King could not by proclamation change the common law, statute or custom, nor create a new offence by way of proclamation; the King 'hath no prerogative, but that which the law of the

---

[56] For an outline see Tony Prosser, *The Limits of Competition Law: Markets and Public Services* (Oxford University Press, 2005) 98–108.
[57] Gwen Seabourne, 'Law Morals and Money: Royal Regulation of the Substance of Subjects' Sales and Loans in England, 1272–1399' in Anthony Musson (ed.), *Expectations of the Law in the Middle Ages* (Boydell Press, 2001) 117, 129.
[58] A. I. Ogus, 'Regulatory Law: Some Lessons from the Past' (1992) 12 *Legal Studies* 1, 17.
[59] (1616) 12 Co. Rep. 74 (for discussion see Craig, 'Prerogative, Precedent and Power', 67–69).

land allows him'.[60] As Craig has emphasised, the effect was to deny the King's exercise of a claimed power to regulate commerce as he thought fit whilst by-passing Parliament.[61]

The sale of monopolies also became a major area of controversy involving the Crown.[62] Although their major purpose was as a means of solving governmental fiscal problems, monopolies might also have a regulatory function. The famous *Case of Monopolies* in 1602 ostensibly involved a form of social regulation; it was concerned with the exclusive right to make, import and sell playing cards and was presented to the court as a way of protecting public morals by making the price of cards so high that they could not be bought by the poor.[63] The court held that monopolies were in most circumstances contrary to common law and to the liberty of the subject. James I, however, granted monopolies after he had succeeded to the throne; in 1624 Parliament passed an Act prohibiting them, subject to a number of exceptions.[64] This case thus combined fiscal policy, competition policy and social regulation; together with the 1624 Act it has been seen as 'a great step forward in popular rights' and as leading to modification of other areas of law restricting competition.[65]

It would be a mistake to see regulation as withering away with the growth of economic liberalism culminating in a *laissez faire* Victorian age, despite Dicey's claim in 1860 that the extensive state intervention of the sixteenth century was 'an evil ... now too well established to need the confirmation of further arguments'.[66] Indeed, the industrial revolution and new technologies such as the railways resulted in new forms of regulation. What is most interesting from a public lawyer's perspective is the sort of institutional arrangements adopted. As with regulatory techniques, we can identify a wide range of different institutional forms. Much early regulation was administered locally through Justices of the Peace, reflecting the lack of

---

[60] 76.   [61] Craig, 'Prerogative, Precedent and Power', 68–69.
[62] For background see Hill, *The Century of Revolution*, 37–40.
[63] *Darcy v. Allein* (1602) 74 ER 1131, discussed in detail in Sidney T. Miller, 'The Case of Monopolies: Some of Its Results and Suggestions' (1907) 6 *Michigan Law Review* 1. He observes, in the context of the protection of the morals of the poor, that '[u]nder the patent the price of the cards was so high that they would be beyond the reach of any except the very wealthy whose morals were either beyond reproach or past repair, so the cards could do no hurt in either case' (5, footnote omitted).
[64] 21 & 22 Jac. I, c. 3.   [65] Miller, 'The Case of Monopolies', 12.
[66] A. V. Dicey, *The Privy Council* (Macmillan, 1860) 190, quoted in H. W. Arthurs, *'Without the Law': Administrative Justice and Legal Pluralism in Nineteenth-Century England* (University of Toronto Press, 1985) 90.

effective central administration.[67] There was also an extensive role for self-regulation by domestic tribunals.[68]

The highly pluralistic landscape of regulation was confronted by moves during the nineteenth century to assert the dominant role of the courts and of Parliament as regulatory bodies. This was based on conservative constitutional principle, but neither institution proved effective as a regulator. A particularly important example was that of rail regulation, encompassing both economic regulation of charges, particularly to avoid undue discrimination, and social regulation on safety grounds and on the basis of what we would now call 'universal service'.[69] Regulation of railway rates was, in the words of Arthurs, 'exiled, in 1854, into the wilderness of a reluctant and inept Court of Common Pleas'. This was an attempt to apply the separation of powers but proved a dismal failure.[70] A new Railway and Canal Commission was established in 1873, but this was dogged by the effects of its highly legalistic procedures and by judicial review, resulting in its 'virtual paralysis'; this continued to be a problem for its successor Railway Rates Tribunal.[71] Nor was regulation by Parliament more successful; for the railways this took the form of private acts setting out detailed conditions for their operation, forming the equivalent of a modern licence. However such a regulatory device obviously proved highly inflexible in a rapidly changing economic environment, faced enforcement difficulties given the inadequacies of the JPs to whom this was delegated, and was undermined by the strength of the railway lobby in Parliament.[72] An ambitious attempt to regulate profits and to impose social obligations was undertaken through Gladstone's Regulation of the Railways Act of 1844, but this also proved inadequate and was 'emasculated by the railway interest'.[73] Using the traditional constitutional organs of courts and Parliament as regulatory institutions was clearly inappropriate.

The Use of Boards and Agencies

A much more influential development was the growth of specialist boards of different types to carry out regulatory functions. Such boards had a long history; for example, in the field of agriculture permanent commissioners had

---

[67] Arthurs, 'Without the Law', 91.   [68] Ibid, 96–97.
[69] For details see C. D. Foster, *Privatization, Public Ownership and the Regulation of Natural Monopoly* (Blackwell, 1992) chs. 1–2.
[70] Arthurs, 'Without the Law', 126; for a detailed account of the treatment of one such category of cases see R. W. Kostal, *Law and English Railway Capitalism 1825–1875* (Clarendon Press, 1994) ch. 5.
[71] Foster, *Privatization*, 46, 59; Arthurs, 'Without the Law', 176.
[72] Foster, *Privatization*, 35–36.   [73] Ibid, 35.

been established as long ago as 1555 to enforce statutes where necessary but with a discretion not to do so where appropriate.[74] There was a big growth of such boards in the early nineteenth century, responsible for new forms of regulatory law, including, for example, both economic and social forms of railway regulation. A further related innovation was the creation of factory inspectors under the Factories Act 1833. The use of these forms of regulatory institution did, however, raise constitutional problems. In many cases they continued to rely on courts for enforcement and this was often difficult to secure for reasons which included the predominance of employers in the local bench.[75] Most importantly, they fell outside the doctrine of ministerial responsibility; how could an independent board be held accountable to Parliament for its decisions? This came to a head with the entrusting of the administration of the Poor Law to the Poor Law Commission, none of whose members could sit in Parliament, under the Poor Law Amendment Act 1834. Its administration of the law was highly divisive and unpopular. In 1847 it was replaced by a body of commissioners presided over by a senior Cabinet minister, and this heralded a move towards ministerial administration.

Although independent regulatory boards continued in use in some areas, a privileging of ministerial responsibility as the core means of accountability remained central to constitutional understanding, and this was one of the reasons for the adoption of nationalisation in the UK form of public corporations, themselves responsible to a minister.[76] This created a dilemma. On the one hand, ministerial responsibility meant that there was little use of innovative institutional forms, such as the tripartite form of governance for public enterprises adopted in France or forms of management involving the workforce. On the other, ministers were not to be involved in the day-to-day management of businesses, and this was the basis for the 'Morrisonian' model of a public corporation operating at 'arm's length' from central government.[77] The outcome was continuing uncertainty as to the legitimate spheres of operation for ministers and for boards. The rudimentary statutory arrangements to create a framework for cooperation and a clearer division of functions were ignored in favour of informal and secretive relations. Arrangements for accountability to the broader public and for public scrutiny of the operations of the nationalised industries were minimal, and later

---

[74] Ogus, 'Regulatory Law', 11.   [75] Arthurs, 'Without the Law', 103–115.
[76] This is covered in detail in Tony Prosser, *Nationalised Industries and Public Control* (Blackwell, 1986) esp ch. 2.
[77] The most influential work was Herbert Morrison, *Socialisation and Transport* (Constable, 1933).

attempts to set out clearer relationships based on economic principles were doomed to failure because of the impossibility of separating economics from politics.[78]

The Disintegration of Ministerial Responsibility

Of course, things changed dramatically with the privatisation of public enterprises under the Thatcher and Major Governments from 1983 onwards. The privatisation process itself benefited from the openness of the UK's economic constitution. Thus there was no need to engage in constitutional amendment to permit privatisation of enterprises constitutionally required to be in public ownership or under public administration, as was required in, for example, Portugal and Germany.[79] The latitude permitted to government in the privatisation process was also extremely wide, especially given its ability to secure a majority in the House of Commons. There was nothing equivalent to the decision of the French *Conseil Constitutionnel* making the constitutional legitimacy of privatisation of public services conditional on independent valuation to ensure that public assets were not sold at below their true value, thereby breaching the principle of equality.[80] Scrutiny of the process was once more *ex post facto* by the National Audit Office and Parliamentary committees.

In the creation of regulatory institutions, the UK Government also benefited from the openness of its economic constitution. There was a major revival in the use of agencies operating at arm's length from central government. In some cases they took the legal form of non-ministerial government departments, but in practice they were granted a considerable degree of independence in order to give 'credible commitment', a stable environment distanced from direct political intervention in order to attract investors.[81] Despite this objective, inevitably the regulators were granted extensive discretion and this grew with time, facilitated by the fact that the UK has never had an equivalent of the former US non-delegation doctrine limiting

---

[78] Prosser, *Nationalised Industries*, ch. 3.
[79] Daintith and Sah, 'Privatisation and the Economic Neutrality'.
[80] Conseil Constitutionnel, déc. 86–207, 25–26 Juin 198; for detailed discussion see Cosmo Graham and Tony Prosser, *Privatizing Public Enterprise* (Oxford University Press, 1991) 97–104.
[81] Brian Levy and Pablo T. Spiller, 'A Framework for Resolving the Regulatory Problem' in Brian Levy and Pablo T. Spiller (eds.), *Regulation, Institutions and Commitment* (Cambridge University Press, 1996) 1; the various agencies are discussed in Tony Prosser, *Law and the Regulators* (Oxford University Press, 1997).

the power to give substantive discretion to agencies of this kind.[82] Nor were there the constitutional restrictions which existed in some Continental European countries limiting the ability to confer broad governmental powers on independent authorities.[83]

The major constitutional issue was the lack of direct ministerial responsibility to Parliament for the work of the agencies. However, if one recognises that the role of Parliament is to scrutinise rather than to control, it became evident that a number of important mechanisms exist for such scrutiny of agencies of this kind. Agencies will in many cases fall within the ambit of the National Audit Office's value for money studies and so may also find themselves the subject of inquiries by the Public Accounts Committee.[84] This has permitted detailed examination of financial aspects of their work. They are also subject to examination by departmental select committees if their boards are appointed by ministers so making them associated public bodies to the department, and once more this has permitted important studies of their work to be carried out. Most strikingly of all, the Constitution Select Committee of the House of Lords undertook a far-reaching study of the accountability of regulatory bodies in general.[85] This report emphasised the degree to which agencies could be held accountable by Parliament and other institutions, and it developed the concept of the '360° View of Accountability' to emphasise the different ways in which such accountability could work. Once one interprets the role of Parliament as one of scrutiny rather than control or instruction, it is possible to address questions of ministerial responsibility in this more nuanced and subtle way.

The creation of regulatory agencies may raise tricky constitutional questions as the role of the regulators has clearly never been a purely technical one but has involved key social issues; and there may be major political implications from their actions or failures to act. What are the limits to regulatory independence in a framework where government is responsible for broader economic and social policies? A low point was reached in the case

---

[82] *Panama Refining Co.* v. *Ryan*, 293 US 388 (1935); *Schechter Poultry Corp.* v. *United States*, 295 US 495 (1963).
[83] Jeanette Bougrab, 'Independent Administrative Authorities in France' and Anne van Aaken, 'Independent Administrative Agencies in Germany' in Roberto Caranta, Mads Andenas and Duncan Fairgrieve (eds.) *Independent Administrative Authorities* (British Institute of International and Comparative Law, 2004) 47 and 65.
[84] For an account of the work of the National Audit Office in this context see Ed Humpherson, 'Auditing Regulatory Reform' in Dawn Oliver, Tony Prosser and Richard Rawlings (eds.) *The Regulatory State: Constitutional Implications* (Oxford University Press, 2010) 267.
[85] *The Regulatory State: Ensuring Its Accountability* (HL, 2003–2004, 68).

of rail in 2001 in the context of the collapse of Railtrack, the privatised rail infrastructure company. The minister threatened the regulator that, should he introduce an emergency interim review of Railtrack's charges, the Government would force through Parliament emergency legislation to remove his power to do so.[86] However, in other circumstances more structured means of providing the governmental context for the operation of the regulator have been provided, including the publication of statutory environmental and social guidance and relevant government objectives.[87]

The major development from the mid-1980s has thus been towards the use of independent agencies with complex and multiple forms of relations to Parliament and to core government. Not only has this been characteristic of the UK; it has also been important in the EU. The Union's own strict non-delegation doctrine limited its direct regulatory capacities, and it has instead relied on networks of National Regulatory Authorities required to act with independence both from market actors and from national governments.[88] This multi-level network regulation also clearly represents a major change in institutional geography and is likely to remain influential even after Brexit.

Finally in this section, there should be some mention of the arrangements for policing competition. The role of the courts in applying the doctrine of restraint of trade was limited and inconsistent as a means of promoting open competition.[89] Instead this was entrusted to a highly complex mix of different institutions under the Monopolies and Restrictive Practices (Inquiry and Control) Act 1948 and the Restrictive Trade Practices Act 1956.[90] The former established a Monopolies and Restrictive Practices Commission to investigate oligopolies and cartels (with mergers added later), reporting to the Board of Trade which would then decide what action to take. The latter legislation established the Restrictive Practices Court, a specialist adjudicator on cartel

---

[86] For the then regulator's account of events see Tom Winsor, 'The Future of the Railways: Sir Robert Reid Memorial Lecture 2004' (2003–2004) 13 *Utilities Law Review* 145.

[87] E.g., Energy Act 2013 s. 131; see generally Tony Prosser, *The Regulatory Enterprise* (Oxford University Press, 2010) 179–184.

[88] From an extensive literature see Saskia Lavrijssen and Annetje Ottow, 'Independent Supervisory Authorities: A Fragile Concept' (2012) 9 *Legal Issues of Economic Integration* 419. For the origins of the non-delegation doctrine see Case 9/56, *Meroni & Co. Industrie Metallurgiche S.p.A. v. High Authority of the ECSC* [1957–1958] ECR 133.

[89] Daintith, 'Legal Analysis of Economic Policy', 198–199.

[90] For a succinct history of early institutional developments in competition law see Paul Craig, 'The Monopolies and Mergers Commission: Competition and Administrative Rationality' in Robert Baldwin and Christopher McCrudden (eds.) *Regulation and Public Law* (Weidenfeld and Nicolson, 1987) 201.

policy required to apply broad public interest tests in deciding whether cartels were to be prohibited. Otherwise, the role of the minister remained central, for example in determining whether to refer a merger to the Monopolies Commission and whether to follow its views. According to the historian of the Monopolies Commission, '[t]he Secretary of State for Trade and Industry [was] the sun around which British competition policy orbits.'[91]

This was to change dramatically, in part reflecting the move to the use of independent agencies described above but most importantly reflecting the important role of EU law and institutions. In brief, from the Competition Act 1998 onwards the vast majority of ministerial discretion was removed and instead independent authorities were employed to take decisions on the basis of economic tests rather than exercising a broad public interest discretion. The process was taken further as a result of the decentralisation of EU competition law to national competition authorities operating through a European Competition Network by Regulation 1/2003.[92] As Wilks has argued, this represented an 'extraordinary coup' on the part of the European Commission, delegating tasks to national authorities which reflected the Commission's own economics-based approach to competition policy.[93] The relevant UK authority is now the Competition and Markets Authority, a non-ministerial government department established under the Enterprise and Regulatory Reform Act 2013.

What conclusions can be drawn from this account of the development of institutions for economic regulation in the UK? The first is that, as Arthurs demonstrated clearly for the nineteenth century, the system has always been highly pluralist and attempts to impose a more constraining institutional framework on it through entrusting regulation to courts and Parliament were clearly unsuccessful. Instead, institutional trial and error has been employed and this has been facilitated by the relative openness of the UK constitution in relation to economic management. The second lesson is that of the disintegration of ministerial responsibility as a central principle of economic management. This may be seen as part of more general 'hollowing out' of the central state; there is a large political science literature on this

---

[91] Stephen Wilks, 'The Prolonged Reform of United Kingdom Competition Law' in G. Bruce Doern and Stephen Wilks (eds.) *Comparative Competition Policy: National Institutions in a Global Market* (Oxford University Press, 1996) 139, 150.
[92] Council Regulation Implementing Articles 81 and 82, OJ L1/1.
[93] Stephen Wilks, 'Agency Escape: Decentralization or Dominance of the European Commission in the Modernization of Competition Policy?' (2005) 18 *Governance* 431.

theme.[94] In constitutional terms, what is most striking is the replacement of ministerial responsibility by a wide range of different types of institutions for managing the economy with complex inter-relationships between each other and with a variety of different means for securing scrutiny and accountability. This has happened by a process of trial and error and certainly has not reflected any grand constitutional plan. It has also been influenced strongly by the role of the European Union, especially in the context of competition law.

Conclusions

The first conclusion is an obvious one. Especially in the UK, in the absence of any overarching constitutional court having responsibility for the explicit development of constitutional principle, the economic constitution has been the result of a gradual and incremental development of different types of institutions and norms. The courts have played only a limited role and have not attempted to lay down general principles; even review on the basis of infringement of fundamental rights has been limited. High politics has been important, especially in the seventeenth century; clearly it would be a mistake to dismiss the central role of the Treasury, but in practice many of the most important developments have been through informal institutional design and the growth of assorted arrangements for scrutiny. Administrative self-regulation and internal rule-making have played a major role in constitutional development, which suggests that any analysis of our economic constitution must be as much sociological as legal.

Second, the development of a range of different institutions and their complex inter-relations is central to our constitutional history. I have emphasised throughout this chapter that the UK's economic constitution has never been concerned to set out constitutional principles of substantive economic management, still less to reflect any popular 'general will' in the form of fundamental economic norms. It has instead been about arrangements for scrutiny of economic management. Understanding this is the key to appreciating the historical developments set out here, especially those of the seventeenth century and more recent organisational and institutional aspects

---

[94] See, for example, R. A. W. Rhodes, 'The Hollowing Out of the State: The Changing Nature of the Public Service in Britain' (1994) 65 *The Political Quarterly* 138; Michael Moran, *The British Regulatory State: High Modernism and Hyper-Innovation* (Oxford University Press, 2003).

of regulation. The emphasis has been on what Pettit termed 'contestability' and Maitland the 'avoidance of arbitrariness'.[95]

What has changed dramatically is the type of institutional form utilised to secure such scrutiny. The seventeenth-century struggles placed it firmly within Parliament and the role of the House of Commons in particular was bolstered by the later development of ministerial responsibility. However, a variety of circumstances reflecting both the growth of party discipline within Parliament itself and the increased complexity of economic management meant that Parliament was not an effective institution to offer the sole or even the main means of scrutiny. At first sight the apparent centralisation of economic management in the Treasury might seem to provide a central institutional focus, and there is no doubt that executive self-regulation through the Treasury has been central to the operation of public expenditure systems. However, even here the literature makes it clear that the Treasury has operated through networks, both in policy implementation and in scrutinising other governmental institutions. The role of the Treasury has been highly complex and cannot be reduced to simple dominance over other departments.[96]

What happened instead was the growth of 'countervailing institutions' providing other means of scrutiny, covering monetary and fiscal policy and also regulation. They provide a form of what John Keane has termed 'monitory democracy'; 'a new historical form of democracy, a variety of "post-parliamentary" politics defined by the rapid growth of many different kinds of extra-parliamentary, power-scrutinising mechanisms'.[97] The proliferation of such institutions may limit the overall coordination and coherence of our constitutional arrangements, though coherent design has never been a characteristic of the UK constitution. They may also offer important improvements in constitutional openness and scrutiny, creating opportunities for dialogue and deliberation between institutions.

There is one final irony here. On this account of the UK constitution, emphasising the importance of scrutiny of economic management, important contributions have been made by European Union institutions where Parliament is inadequate to oversee a modern internationalised economy. These include scrutiny of aspects of fiscal policy, especially public borrowing,

---

[95] Pettit, *Republicanism*; Maitland, 'A Historical Sketch of Liberty'.
[96] See Thain and Wright, *The Treasury and Whitehall*; Daintith and Page, *The Executive in the Constitution*.
[97] John Keane, *The Life and Death of Democracy* (Pocket Books, 2009) 688, 736–742.

and the development of regulation, especially in the context of competition law. Under the approach taken here, this has not been some sort of alien imposition on a UK Parliamentary-based system, but a means of meeting the promise of contestability offered by our constitutional arrangements in a complex and globalised economic system.[98] It remains to be seen what can be offered after Brexit to ensure that this promise continues to be met.

---

[98] For a similar argument see Athanasios Psygkas, *From the 'Democratic Deficit' to a 'Democratic Surplus': Constructing Administrative Democracy in Europe* (Oxford University Press, 2017).

5
Religion and the Constitution to 1688

PIPPA CATTERALL

It is time to put God back into readings of the British constitution. Writings about that constitution since 1945 have often focused on technicalities and processes of the constitutional order – whether the law, Parliament, or territorial politics – rather than the constitution as a lived idea. Yet states, beneath the daily reality of their role as legal entities claiming monopolies of violence over the territories they purportedly control, are fundamentally ideas. They are legal constructs which humans invest with imagination and to some extent anthropomorphise in the process of making them meaningful. The constitution – that web of the rules of the game structuring the orders and governance of a society – is therefore founded upon ideas of the identity and personality of the state which constitutional procedures merely animate. Legal processes thus rest upon often unspoken assumptions about the authority and derivation of that law. For instance, when (until the 1960s) the British state impacted on certain of its citizens in the most onerous way it can through the death penalty, in invoking 'and may God have mercy on your soul' judges referenced a more fundamental system of divine justice of which theirs was merely a shadow.[1]

Introduction: Religion and the Pre-Conquest Framing of the Constitution

Religion shapes concepts of trust, not least through the swearing of oaths. Its role in the British constitution is much more than the formal continuing place that the very different established Churches of England and Scotland occupy in state structures. Indeed, religion both pre-dates and helped to

---

[1] The relationships between the moral economy of the parish, the nation and the cosmos are nicely evoked in George Eliot's 1859 novel *Adam Bede* edited by Stephen Gill (Harmondsworth: Penguin, 1980) especially chapter 40 and appendix 2.

shape the emerging British state and constitution in various significant ways. First, religion seeks to express the fundamental nature of a cosmic order established and ordained by God, and the implications of that order for human society.

Second, it thereby provides framing devices for the moral values and codes applied, if inadequately, to the ordering and practices of societies and states. It thus shapes the truths a society lives by, from the social order to moral economy, which is here understood as the framework for spiritual, moral, social and economic relations. On the one hand, this was reflected in the sacredness of oaths sworn, either in giving testimony or allegiance, at peril to the soul if broken. On the other, allegiance to those higher truths could conflict with the allegiances rulers and states demanded, hence the refusal of groups such as Quakers to make pledges to earthly authorities.

Third, the state can thus see religion as a potentially challenging power within, preferably to be harnessed to its own activities. If this can be accomplished, by giving a sense of permanence and meaning to it, the state is itself invested with religious qualities. This might seem absurd, as states are obviously impermanent and flawed human institutions, with the British state only dating back as far as 1921 within the boundaries of its current jurisdiction. Yet states do often acquire religious characteristics, both in a Durkheimian sense as the ontological framework for the society they govern, and as institutions which nonetheless are invested with personality, ideals, and values. States are thereby able to command the loyalty of their subjects. In this sense, forms of patriotism transcend the imagining of some kind of national community and become a belief system and focus for devotion through which the state and/or nation becomes itself the fundamental ontological reality, with God either replaced or subordinated to a supporting role.

Fourth, this instrumental use of religion to bolster and legitimate the state's power and authority has a long history. An example is the title *Pontifex Maximus* arrogated by Roman emperors from Augustus onwards, including Constantine when he was proclaimed emperor in York in 306.

Fifth, Constantine's subsequent adoption of Christianity and its emergence as the official religion of the Roman Empire by the end of the fourth century was important because it informed the subsequent imagination of what a state is and how it relates to the Church in Latin Christianity. England, in particular, was incorporated into the thought-world of Latin Christianity during the seventh century. This gave, as Bede in the following century emphasised, a cosmological framework for understanding human existence among the Anglo-Saxon nobles evangelised by missionaries from Rome. Moreover, as Bede indicates by his inclusion, in his *Historia ecclesiastica gentis Anglorum*, of numerous letters from Pope Gregory I to his emissaries, it established a framework for kingship as well as social conduct. This included a sense of the religious responsibilities of kings who held their office by grace of God. Church and state began to be conceived as in a symbiotic relationship.

Sixth, Anglo-Saxon kingdoms which early converted to Christianity relied upon the Church for more than divine sanction. At a time when Britain was not much more than the redundant name of a long-abandoned Roman province, the Church was the one institutional link with that past. This gave it prestige, access to learning and transnational connections and language, including identity and authority structures which did not always sit well with the pretensions of local rulers. Meanwhile, the Church's drive to cure souls at the most local of levels also meant that it imported the parish system already developing during the late Roman Empire. This meant that the Church was the most ubiquitous of institutions. In what remained a largely oral society right down to the nineteenth century, its pulpits were therefore crucial means of news disseminations and official pronouncements, ensuring their political as well as spiritual significance.

Furthermore, at a time when government was weak and kingship generally peripatetic, the parish system established a territorial structure of governance that was potentially administrative as well as ecclesiastical. That structure extended throughout the various Anglo-Saxon kingdoms, though it was not to be widely established in Scotland until the twelfth-century reign of David I. The levying of tithes at parish level – consisting of a tenth of produce in cash or kind from landowners in order to support the clergy, maintain church buildings, and assist the poor – was also introduced and, from the mid tenth century in England, enforced by royal sanction. This was significant, even if its potential administrative use was not fully developed until after the sixteenth-century Reformation, particularly in terms of the delivery of poor relief and local infrastructure.

Generally predating the parish as a superior territorial unit of the Church was the diocese administrated by a bishop under the separate archdiocesan provinces established in England at Canterbury and York in the eighth century. The diocese did not become a territorial unit of the state in the way the parish did. The provinces, however, interacted with the state. Their respective Convocations, membership of which was regularised in the late thirteenth century, not only discussed church matters and canon law, but also the taxes exacted from them by the Crown and Papacy. This was not least because the authority, learning and wealth that bishops and their monastic counterparts, the abbots, were able to wield ensured they became both territorial magnates and valued advisers from Anglo-Saxon times. Their abbeys, such as Repton where the kings of Mercia were buried, also became important in the rituals of these kingdoms. Iona played if anything an even more important role in eighth-century Scotland. Religion thus became fundamental to the running and financing as well as the meaning and function of the state.

Seventh, the Church's centrality in the development of scribal culture ensured its importance to both administration and institutional and public memory. The written word established a formal memory for these kingdoms and, through the impressive dissemination of Bede's work, helped to reify the concept of an 'English people', not least among their elites. It also enshrined the highest form of knowledge – that revealed in holy scripture. Furthermore, it facilitated the fixing of legal meaning in place of the oral customary rules hitherto practiced. The two were indeed brought together in Alfred's law code, prefaced as it was by reference to a spiritual and legal inheritance from Mosaic law. The legal certainty such law codes provided was fundamental to the emergence of abstract conceptualisation – reinforced by the rediscovery of Aristotle in the twelfth century – through which law, and thus the constitution, became sets of ideas as well as human relationships.[2]

Eighth, the role of religion in limiting the application of secular law was established long before the articulation of the British constitution began. The idea of separate ecclesiastical courts sanctioned by the state dates back to the reign of Constantine and this was followed by the increasing codification of a system of canon law. By the end of the fourth century the Church had also adopted the pre-existing pagan practice of providing sanctuary for fugitives from the state. Nonetheless, this did not significantly constrain the exercise of royal power. The rules as developed in England from the twelfth century, for instance, allowed the accused only forty days either to prove their innocence or negotiate with their opponents before being sent permanently into exile, except in the unlikely event of a royal pardon.

Ninth, religion thus played a role in determining who was and who was not included in the state. Heterodox beliefs and folk magical practices may

---

[2] Brian Stock, *The Uses of Literacy* (Princeton, NJ: Princeton University Press, 1983).

have been widely ignored or tolerated both in late Antiquity and throughout much of the medieval period in Britain. Indeed, Gregory had enjoined a strategy of accommodation with pagan traditions upon his missionaries. Yet beliefs which appeared to cast doubt upon loyalty could certainly be seen as problematic, not least because religion served to create and reinforce group identities and allegiances. An obvious example is Alfred's requirement that Guthrum and his Danish army of pagan followers convert to Christianity as part of the Treaty of Wedmore in 878. Jews, in contrast, were almost unknown in the Anglo-Saxon era and could be safely admired from afar. It was only with the advent of a small but significant community after the Norman Conquest that their position as distinctive outsiders became an issue. This was not least because of their role in a tenth and crucial factor shaping relations between Church and state, the exigencies of royal finances.

Medieval Conflicts over Royal and Ecclesiastical Authority and Revenues

For all these reasons religion fundamentally shaped understandings of what the state was and how it operated by the start of the eleventh century. It located that state within a transnational Christian community centred on Rome, a process very much cemented by the Norman Conquest and the wholesale changes in leading ecclesiastical positions that followed. If anything, the Church subsequently became even more central to the operation of the English state, not least because of the frequent absence of the king in his French territories.

There were also significant refinements of the understanding of the relationship between Church and king. The latter, understandably, wished to use the Church as an agent of power, rather than seeing it as a rival centre of authority. Strong partnerships, such as those between William the Conqueror and Archbishop Lanfranc of Canterbury or David I and Bishop John of Glasgow, were exemplary of close, collaborative relations between Church and state. Without such personal relationships the Church remained both a source of royal advisers and rich offices with which to reward them. Senior ecclesiastical offices brought land and temporal power as well as spiritual authority. This could make bishops potential powerbrokers, as witnessed by the role played by Henry of Blois, Bishop of Winchester, in supporting his brother King Stephen during the mid-twelfth century Anarchy. Some could also become powerful opponents as well as supporters – consider the conspiratorial role played in power-politics during Richard

I's reign by Hugh of Nonant, Bishop of Coventry – hence the desire of kings to control appointments to these important positions. A ruler's authority to do so, however, was challenged by Pope Gregory VII in the 1070s. In England, this conflict was compounded by royal demands on and willingness to seize church revenues. The Investiture Controversy (1100–1107) at the start of the reign of Henry I exemplified these struggles over who could appoint to ecclesiastical office and of where their incumbents' loyalties lay, with the Crown or the Pope in Rome. The crisis was only resolved after Archbishop Anselm, of Canterbury – having threatened the removal of the favour of that higher authority of God in this world and the next by the sanction of excommunicating the King – secured Henry's agreement to relinquish royal control of appointments in return for bishops offering homage for their lands; a compromise which did little to prevent continuing royal interference in appointments.[3]

Anselm also played a leading role in the 1102 Council of London, which condemned the 'infamous business ... of selling men like animals'. At least 10 per cent of the Anglo-Saxon population were slaves, even including priests, and ports such as Bristol had a thriving slave trade. Lanfranc had, however, led growing condemnation of slavery which, with royal support, had largely disappeared by the 1120s.[4]

Throughout the Investiture Controversy Anselm was in regular communication with Pope Paschal II. Their role as keepers of the keys to heaven and dispenser of legitimacy on earth ensured popes played an indispensable, if frequently supplementary, role in medieval power politics. For instance, their legitimate interest in reforming church order could be used as both a justification and a pretext for military expansion, as exemplified by Henry II's intervention in Ireland in 1171. Yet it could also be a source of friction within the kingdom, hence Henry's abortive attempt to prevent appeals to the Papacy in 1164. For the other significant twelfth-century development was in the relationship between canon and royal law. This proved a potent source of church-state conflict. A revived interest in written Roman law led to canon law becoming regularised, more focused on due process, and more thoroughly enforced. However, Henry felt that it was doing so at the expense of royal jurisdiction and revenues. This developed into a contest over the

---

[3] Consider, for instance, the reign of Henry II. As well as appointing his illegitimate son Geoffrey as Bishop of Lincoln, he told the monks of Winchester in 1173, 'I order you to hold free elections, but nevertheless, I forbid you to elect anyone [as abbot] except Richard my clerk.' Cited in David Boyle, *Blondel's Song* (London: Penguin, 2006), p. 186.
[4] Marc Morris, 'Normans and Slavery: Breaking the Bonds' *History Today* 63/2 (2013).

Church's management of its own affairs and tendency to less savage sentencing, though couched in more grandiloquent language of defence of the laws of God against royal encroachment. This contest peaked in the confrontation between Henry II and the Archbishop of Canterbury, Thomas Becket, from 1163. It culminated in the latter's murder in his cathedral in 1170. It was only resolved by the Compromise of Avranches in 1172, whereby the King made cosmetic concessions over canon law, while retaining considerable royal control over the temporalities of the Church.[5] Although Henry was not directly implicated in the murder, he followed up this agreement with Pope Alexander III with a grand gesture of repentance at Becket's shrine in 1174. Problems in relations between Church and king, not least over episcopal appointments and royal finances, nonetheless continued into the reigns of his sons, especially John.

John's refusal to accept the papal appointment of Stephen Langton to Canterbury in 1207 left the new archbishop, like Becket, in exile in France for six years. This led Innocent III in 1208 to impose the interdiction that had merely been threatened against Henry II, effectively banning all religious services except for baptism and services for the dying throughout the realm. A recalcitrant John was then personally excommunicated in 1209. The King retaliated by distraining Church revenues for his unsuccessful conflict with France. It was only under threat of French invasion in 1213 that John relented, surrendering his territories of England and Ireland to the Papacy and offering to recompense the Church's purloined funds.

Meanwhile Langton – well aware from his studies in Paris that controlling the depredations of bad kings had been a problem frequently addressed in the Old Testament – formulated ideas that shaped his role as mediator between heavily taxed barons and John in the run-up to the signing of *Magna Carta* in 1215. The need to control bad kings was not new: at least two kings were effectively deposed by their councils with clerical encouragement in Anglo-Saxon times. Nor was much of *Magna Carta* new either, recapitulating as it did ideas or chunks of text from other recent similar treaties. It subsequently gained talismanic importance, more as a piece of legal imaginary than as law in practice, particularly during the seventeenth century. At the time it reflected principally the interests of the various stakeholders involved. Langton's hand is most clear in its opening clause, one of only four still on the statute book: that the Church shall be free.

---

[5] Frank Barlow, *Thomas Becket* (London: Phoenix, 2000).

Enshrining this in written law, however, did not ensure its justiciability, as continuing controversies over political interference in ecclesiastical appointments into the twenty-first century bear witness.

More significant was Langton's role in the definitive version of *Magna Carta* promulgated by Henry III in 1225. This was issued in return for tax revenues from the Church and barons. It emphasised reciprocity between ruler and ruled, putting constraints on the arbitrary conduct of both. Reflecting long-standing concern among canon lawyers about the relative absence of due process in royal courts, it also reiterated the relevant 1215 clause, one of the others that remain in force. Langton backed this up by ensuring that cathedrals held a number of copies and by pronouncing excommunication on all who broke the Charter. Thereby a temporary agreement between a king and the most significant of his subjects became a constitutional innovation, periodically reinforced by further threats of excommunication from Langton's successors.

Often overlooked among the provisions of 1215 are the restrictions on Jews, followed three years later by an order that Jews wear a marking badge. This hostility was reflective of battles around royal finances. Restrictions essentially confining Jews to money-lending activities were balanced by royal protection of an important source of taxes and loans, including the grant of their own *Beth Din* under Henry II. Their importance to the Treasury was such that, when the coronation of Henry's son, Richard I, was marked by a series of pogroms around England, the new King responded by issuing a charter of special protection. With blood libel allegations of Jewish sacrifices of Christians and crusading fervour – greatly heightened following the fall of Jerusalem to Saladin in 1187 – driving hostility to Jews, this made them overly dependent upon royal favour. Jews were also a target of resentment against royal impositions and their distinctive position compared to other taxpayers. In the thirteenth century, anger among the lower baronage at onerous debts contracted to Jews to fulfil feudal military duties to Henry III spilled over into the wholesale slaughter of Jews during the civil conflict of the 1260s.

Imposition of taxes and feudal dues, not least military services, also had two other significant effects. One was to incentivise transfers of land to the Church in order to avoid taxes, it being cheaper for the donor to lease land back from the Church. This problem was already apparent in the twelfth century. Ineffective attempts were made in 1217 to limit this and prevent alienation of land in order to avoid services. Redressing the effects on the tax base led to various significant adjustments in the late thirteenth century to finance Edward I's wars. First, the over-dependence on heavy taxation of a diminished and impoverished Jewry was reduced. Instead, Edward traded restrictions on Jewish usury – culminating in their expulsion from England in 1290 – for increased taxation from the recently conceded Parliament and, in 1297, from the clergy.[6] Second, the system of land tenure was reformed in 1290. While *Quia Emptores* regularised land sales, the Statutes of Mortmain (1279 and 1290) sought, if unsuccessfully, to prevent transfers of land to the Church. The effective establishment of trusts through the practice of *cestui que*, continued to be a shelter from royal taxes down to the Reformation.

Tax issues therefore remained central to church-state relations, especially in times of war. The reluctance of the archbishops to summon Convocations to grant these revenues led Edward I to compel clerical representation in Parliament instead from 1290. This new arrangement was to break down at the start of the Hundred Years' War. Clerical objections came to a head when in February 1338 a Parliament in which only a few prelates were present granted Edward III half of the kingdom's wool to meet his dire financial needs. The clergy then refused to supply wool granted in their absence, prompting recourse to Convocation as a source of less draconic, but still enormous, taxation.[7]

As the long war against France wore on, the increasingly nationalistic tone used to justify such exactions also had effects. The removal of the Papacy to Avignon after 1309 had already led to it being seen as the tool of the French monarchy. It also undermined the transnational character of the Church. This was already being challenged by the 1306 Statute of Provisors, forbidding clergy from sending levies out of the kingdom. Suspicion of papal simony and corruption in appointments to English benefices only deepened thereafter. The Franciscan philosopher William of Occam, who spent several unhappy years at Avignon in the 1320s, began formulating the idea of separating church and state in the 1330s, in order to preserve the independence and integrity of the former.

The Hundred Years' War more generally, however, instead reinforced the trend towards subservience to the state developing under the earlier Plantagenets. As the conflict continued Edward III and his successors

---

[6] Paul Brand, 'Jews and the Law in England 1275–90' *English Historical Review* 115 (2000), 1138–1158.
[7] T. F. T. Plucknett, 'Parliament 1327–36' in E. B. Fryde and Edward Miller (eds.) *Historical Studies of the English Parliament: I Origins to 1399* (Cambridge: Cambridge University Press, 1970), 212–214; F. R. Barnes, 'The Taxation of Wool 1327–1348' in George Unwin (ed.) *Finance and Trade under Edward III: The London Lay Subsidy of 1332* (Manchester: Manchester University Press, 1918), 137–177.

demanded prayers for the success of their campaigns and encouraged the clergy to promote nationalistic propaganda.[8] The Statute of Provisors 1351 furthermore emphasised that the church in England had been founded by sovereigns to inform them and the people of the laws of God and forbade papal interference in ecclesiastical appointments. This was accompanied by Statutes of *Praemunire* in 1351, 1365 and 1393, which sought to prevent recourse to papal courts and effectively determined the superiority of royal law.

An episode in these disputes was the inconclusive meeting between papal and English envoys in Bruges in 1374. Among the latter was the Oxford scholar, John Wyclif. Wyclif criticised ecclesiastical abuse and property-holding, emphasising instead the secular authority of the king held by the grace of Christ. This brought him temporarily to the fore during the war-induced crises of the 1370s. His conception of grace was central to Wyclif's thinking. All legitimate dominion derived from it and the source of the knowledge of grace was scripture. This thinking led to an exaltation of royal authority, with Wyclif defending the murderous violation of Westminster Abbey in 1378 on the grounds that sanctuary should not be used to harbour criminals. The emphasis on scripture, meanwhile, led Wyclif to undertake the first translation of the Bible into English during the 1380s.

Wyclif's views on kingship found ready support at court. His teachings on returning the Church to the poverty of apostolic times encouraged sometimes covetous support among the gentry. The more radical implications of his views on dominion led contemporary opponents to associate them with the Peasant's Revolt in 1381. Wyclif's criticisms of ecclesiastical wealth and abuse, however, were different. Unlike the radical preachers of the Revolt, exemplified by John Ball, he did not seek to overturn established order in favour of groups whose aspirations to take advantage of labour scarcity following the Black Death had been firmly checked by the authorities and hit by draconic taxation. Nonetheless, subsequent concerns about the subversive effects of social mobility and heterodox teachings were easily conflated. Itinerant preachers, labelled Lollards, and itinerant labourers were presented as similar threats. Targeting both was Henry IV's expedient tactic to consolidate support for his rule, particularly amongst the clergy, following his ousting of Richard II in 1399. Legislation in 1401 led to clampdowns on Lollard teaching and the burning of obstinate heretics, while Sir John Oldcastle's revolt in 1414 provided opportunity for Henry V, in the context

---

[8] Rory Cox, 'The Hundred Years' War and the Church' in Anne Curry (ed.) *The Hundred Years War Revisited* (Basingstoke: Palgrave, 2019), 85–110.

of renewed war with France, to suppress Lollardy with the willing support of the Church hierarchy. Lollardy was now associated with treason, so Henry V's campaign included the enforcement of orthodoxy in public worship, extending royal control over the Church.[9]

His early death in 1422, however, meant that the throne passed to his baby son. Henry VI's chaotic reign did not prove opportunity to further consolidate royal control over the Church. Indeed, papal support remained significant for ambitious clergy in fifteenth-century England. Once preferment was secured, however, careful navigation of the factional politics of the court became an important consideration, especially when in-fighting grew as defeat in France turned to rout. This was even more so with the descent into civil war that ensued. Thomas Bourchier's anointing of successive kings, as the tides of the Wars of the Roses shifted during his long tenure as Archbishop of Canterbury from 1454 to 1486, marks his personal success in managing these challenges, as a veritable fifteenth-century Vicar of Bray. It also indicates the relative irrelevance of the Church in that conflict.

Nonetheless, the last of the kings crowned by Bourchier, Henry VII in 1485, did actively seek papal support for his somewhat dubious claims to the throne. One of his key advisers was his Lord Chancellor, Bourchier's successor as archbishop, John Morton. Changes in the position of religion in England were more marked at popular level. Lollardy may have been driven underground, but there was a growing market among the burgeoning merchant classes during the fifteenth century for works of personal piety in the vernacular. These developments, however, did not suggest that change in the position of religion in the constitution was imminent. It also remained very much the case that such changes would be driven by its relationship to the Crown, as the Church had ceased to be the prop of royal power, becoming instead its tool.

The Reformation and the Constitution

This position was concealed under Morton's long archbishopric, and the subsequent lengthy ascendancy of Thomas Wolsey during the early years of Henry VIII's reign. Wolsey may have been Papal legate, but he was very much the servant of the Crown. His royal master, moreover, had ambitions to regain lands and power-broking influence on the other side of the

---

[9] Jeremy Catto, 'Religious Change under Henry V' in G. L. Harriss (ed.) *Henry V: The Practice of Kingship* (Oxford: Oxford University Press, 1985), 97–115.

Channel. Wolsey, for instance, was the instrument of trying to raise the necessary funds for invasion of France in 1525 to take advantage of the capture of Francis I at the battle of Pavia, bypassing a reluctant Parliament in the process. It was the clergy, religious houses and townspeople who either could not or would not pay.

That year was also marked by the publication of William Tyndale's incomplete translation into English of the New Testament – a different version from Wyclif's – while in exile in Cologne. In the short term it was the growing difficulties that Wolsey – who condemned Tyndale as a heretic – experienced after 1525 that proved more significant. His foreign policy of switching from alliance with France to alliance with the Holy Roman Empire failed to win Henry lasting diplomatic triumphs or lasting continental friends. The latter failure became important in 1527, when Wolsey was charged with resolving the King's 'Great Matter'. This was Henry's attempt to secure papal dispensation for release from the dynastic marriage with Catherine of Aragon he had inherited from his deceased elder brother, which had failed to produce a male heir. Securing annulment was not an impossible task: Henry's sister Mary's second marriage was annulled by Pope Clement VII in February that year. Henry's chances of securing a similar annulment were, however, unlikely to win the support of Catherine's nephew, the Holy Roman emperor, Charles V. After Charles captured the Pope and Rome in May 1527, nor was it likely to gain papal support. This eventuality became even more certain with the subsequent peace Charles concluded with France in August 1529. This was accordingly swiftly followed by Wolsey's dismissal from the Lord Chancellorship.

These developments, frustrating as they were to the King's ambitions, were accompanied by Henry's growing conviction that he should become the head of the Church in England.[10] He therefore deployed the *Praemunire* laws to deny the jurisdiction of the papal curia. When Clement then forbade the English clergy from trying the divorce case, in January 1531 Henry invoked *Praemunire* against the entire English clergy. Henry then used Parliament to declare his royal supremacy over the English Church.

Allegations of clerical abuses, not least during Wolsey's long ascendancy, were also used to justify the Supplication against the Ordinaries of 1532 attacking the fees, powers and operation of clerical courts and offices. In May 1532 Henry

---

[10] Richard Rex, 'The Religion of Henry VIII' *Historical Journal* 57/1 (2014), 1–32.

was presented with a Papal bull threatening excommunication. Two days later a rump Convocation of Canterbury renounced its ability to make canon law without royal licence and agreed to subject all existing canons to royal consent in what was known as the Submission of the Clergy. Furthermore, the ecclesiastical revenues called Annates, which had been regularly paid to the Papacy since the early fourteenth century, were now claimed by the Crown. The Great Matter had thus become an assertion of royal doctrinal, legal and financial authority over the Church.

It was, however, still unresolved. Throughout it had been a major problem that Catherine could appeal to the Papacy against any divorce. This situation became even more acute when Henry married Anne Boleyn secretly late in 1532 and his new wife conceived. Accordingly, an Act of Restraint of Appeals was passed in April 1533. The following month a court under the new Archbishop of Canterbury, Thomas Cranmer, determined that the King's earlier marriage was invalid. Clement's subsequent excommunication of the King was too late to change the course of events, particularly when Charles V proved unwilling to back it up with force. Instead, the Act of Succession, passed in March 1534, emphasised the legality of the King's second marriage. This was followed by a further suppression of Annates and, in November 1534, by the Act of Supremacy declaring royal headship of the Church of England.

A Reformation in the constitution of the Church, rather than in its doctrine, had been effected. It was a church established by statute, not God. Allegiance to the new order was enforced and those elites and clergy who refused to take the oath faced imprisonment or worse. Royal power was also asserted over transnational institutions known as religious orders. The problem that monasteries might owe their allegiance and pay taxes outside the realm was not a new one. Alien priories, particularly those headquartered in France, had been targeted under Edward I. Ensuing suppressions had set a precedent for transfers of assets to the Crown or to fund activities such as educational provision. Bishops used the endowments from the occasional suppression of monasteries to establish university colleges or grammar schools. Justified by contemporary criticisms of monasticism, such suppressions had also occurred earlier in Henry's reign. His newly established ecclesiastical supremacy provided for a much more thoroughgoing approach under Thomas Cromwell. The abuses that the visitation of the monasteries in 1534–1535 allegedly uncovered became the basis for the first legislation to suppress monasteries with assets of a yearly value less than £200. Despite the popular risings in autumn 1536 in

Lincolnshire and Yorkshire against this asset-stripping, further legislation was enacted in 1539. The immediate context for this reassertion of royal authority over the church was Pope Paul III's reiteration of Henry's excommunication and a temporary alliance between Charles and Francis that potentially threatened invasion. By early 1540 nearly all the religious houses in England had been suppressed.

This despoliation consolidated Crown authority and revenues and led to newly enriched local elites. There was also a parallel consolidation of national identity through the Church and the English language. First, three years after Tyndale's execution in the Low Countries, a translation of the scriptures based on his work was issued with royal authority as the Great Bible. Henry's Six Articles were also to be read out in each church once a quarter. This homogenisation of religious experience in the vernacular across the parishes of England was followed ten years later by the Acts of Uniformity of 1549 and 1552. This legislation imposed commonalty of worship and belonging through compulsory use of Cranmer's much more Protestant *Book of Common Prayer* (especially the 1552 edition) and, in 1552, penalties for non-attendance. Aided by the recent introduction of the printing press, this standardised a liturgy in English which sacralised the nation and the monarch, thereby engendering a print Protestantism designed to consolidate English identity under the Crown.

These developments occurred during the short reign of Edward VI. They were not, however, set in stone, as became clear when he was succeeded in 1553 by his elder half-sister, Catherine of Aragon's staunchly Catholic daughter, Mary I. Indeed, Mary's rule suggests that the *ius reformandi* – that the religion of the state was that of its ruler – certainly was followed up to this point in England, particularly given the power of the Crown over the Church. The Acts of Repeal 1553 and 1555 demonstrated that a quiescent Parliament would willingly carry out Mary's policy of largely reversing the religious changes of the preceding decades, once property-owners who had benefited from the despoiling of monastic lands were reassured that this was the one aspect of the recent past not to be reversed. Her entanglement, however, in the continuing struggle between France and the realms of her Spanish husband, Charles V's son Philip II, drew her kingdom into costly and unpopular foreign wars. Nor was Parliament entirely subservient, demonstrated not least in a refusal to rule out the succession of her Protestant half-sister Elizabeth, a succession that Mary's failure to produce an heir and early death in 1558 made inevitable.

A Broad Church Settlement?

This succession and the long reign that followed consolidated the Reformation in England. The Act of Supremacy immediately reversed Mary's legislation, restated the monarch's governorship of the Church, and criminalised allegiance to foreign authorities, especially the Papacy. Supplementary legislation in 1562 made refusal to swear the oath of allegiance a treasonable offence. Ensuring that allegiance through a Broad Church settlement that would command the support of the widest range of her subjects was what Elizabeth sought. It was on this basis that the Archbishop of Canterbury, Matthew Parker, in 1563 initiated discussions on a reformulation of the articles of faith on which this consolidation of church and nation would rest.

At local level this consolidation occurred through the development of the parish vestry. In theory this body met monthly, with all parishioners who paid church rates – regardless of sex – entitled to attend or be elected to the vestry. This allowed a selection of society locally to engage in the business of both church and state. The latter included the regulation and oversight of the local population and tax-base through the registration of births, marriages and deaths introduced in 1538, the surveying of highways and other infrastructure, enforcement of the militia ballot and, consolidated in the Poor Law of 1598, the oversight of the poor and the travelling vagrants whose numbers had been swollen by Tudor enclosures of formerly common land. Through the device of the parish vestry, local society was thus incorporated institutionally into the post-Reformation church-state nexus.

At national level Elizabeth's Broad Church aspiration was, however, threatened by Catholic responses to the 1568 flight south of Elizabeth's deposed cousin, the Catholic former Queen Mary of Scotland. Their sympathy with Mary, particularly after the Northern rebellion of 1569–1570 in her favour, led to the purging of Catholics who had hitherto served on Elizabeth's Privy Council. This in turn was cited in the Papal bull *Regnans in Excelsis* of 1570 as among the grounds for condemning Elizabeth as a heretic, releasing all her subjects from allegiance to her and excommunicating all who obeyed her. It was in this context that the Thirty-Nine Articles were adopted in 1571 as the statement of the Church of England's doctrine. Religion was thus articulated as a key determinant of loyalty to the Crown. Although many conformist Catholics accepted this development, it also led to a militant core of recusants who were regularly fined for their refusal to attend Protestant services.

Meanwhile, international events such as growing conflict with Spain hardened the conflation of Protestantism and national identity. This helped to consolidate the English character of the Elizabethan Reformation.[11] It became a treasonable offence to claim that Elizabeth was a heretic. All laity were required to take communion at least once a year according to the rites of the *Book of Common Prayer*. Additionally, the annual services introduced in the 1570s to commemorate Elizabeth's accession gave thanks that 'vpon this day' God 'diddest deliuer thy people of England from daunger of warre and oppression', thus opening an era of 'peace and true religion'.[12] Here religion was rhetorically incorporated into the providentially ordained state and nation over which Elizabeth ruled.

Those groups increasingly labelled Puritan, who had been influenced by fifty years of various strands of Reformed thinking coming from the Continent, could nonetheless prove hostile to what they saw as the compromises of the Elizabethan Broad Church settlement. Having thrown off the Bishop of Rome, many wished to throw off the authority of bishops in England and their associated vestments and rituals as well and move towards Presbyterian forms of church government. They also favoured a revival of preaching, which had been suppressed since Lollardy. The apparent risk of a Catholic resurgence in 1569–1570 led to a hardening of their position, expressed in the 1572 *Admonition to the Parliament* demanding a Calvinistic restoration of the purity of New Testament worship. The Queen forbade Parliament to debate this subversive document that threatened her authority in the Church. Separatist Puritans, such as Robert Browne, were denounced in a royal proclamation of 1583 as 'lewd and evil persons ... ready to violate and break the peace of the church, the realm, and the quietness of the people'.[13]

It was in the midst of the ensuing controversies that Richard Hooker's magisterial *Of the Lawes of Ecclesiastical Politie* appeared in the 1590s. At a time when the Broad Church settlement was being reinforced by further repressive legislation, Hooker's work was significant for several reasons. He and contemporaries answered Puritans by arguing that no particular church

---

[11] Neil Younger, 'How Protestant was the Elizabethan Regime?' *English Historical Review* 133/564 (2018), 1060–1092.

[12] Cited in Alec Ryrie, '*Prologue*: When Did the English Reformation Happen? A Historiographical Curiosity and Its Interpretative Consequences' *Études Epistémè: Revue de Littérature et de la civilisation (XVIe–XVIIIe siècles)* 32 (2017).

[13] Cited in John Coffey, 'Church and State 1550–1750: The Emergence of Dissent' in Robert Pope (ed.) *Companion to Nonconformity* (London: T&T Clark, 2013), 51.

order was ordained in scripture. Authority could not be exclusively derived from an individual's conscientious response to holy writ. Hooker refuted Machiavelli as well as the Puritans, making it clear that 'The law of the state as here conceived is no command of an irresponsible king or prince, for the power to make such laws rests with the inhabitants of the state and may be exercised only by them or by their duly appointed representatives.'[14] In defending the Elizabethan settlement Hooker thus also articulated the concept of government by consent through the Crown in Parliament.

The Reformation elsewhere had different effects on relations between religion and state. For instance, although Wales was formally incorporated into the English kingdom under Henry VIII, most of its inhabitants spoke Welsh. The Tudor nation-building project had limited purchase there until the first Welsh translation of the Bible in 1588. This development helped to ensure that Welsh became a printed language in which powerful biblical imagery could, in due course, be used to express a sense of Welsh identity.

Henry VIII also consolidated his rule over Ireland as a result of the Reformation. The rebellion of Thomas FitzGerald, 10th Earl of Kildare in 1534–1535, including swearing allegiance to the Pope rather than the Crown, furnished a reason to reassert English power there. Additionally, as English lordship over Ireland rested on a papal grant to Henry II, Henry's break with Rome required him to claim Ireland as his own kingdom, an act confirmed by the Irish Parliament in 1541. Initially the Reformation was extended to those parts of Ireland where English rule was effective. However, imposing the radical shifts of Edward VI's reign proved a much more protracted process than in England, not least because of the absence from Ireland until 1551 of that handmaiden of Protestantism, the printing-press. The predominance of Irish rather than English speaking outside the Pale around Dublin did not help either.

The lack of progress of Protestantism in Ireland became even more marked after Elizabeth's accession. The oath of supremacy was resisted by officials as well as clergy, and liturgy disrupted. An Irish Ecclesiastical Commission established in 1564 to encourage respectful attendance at Protestant services had, if anything, the opposite effect. In 1579, attempts to compel such attendance led to rebellion with the willing complicity of recalcitrant Irish elites. This experience demonstrates that the *ius reformandi* did not apply throughout the Tudor realms: indeed, even in England,

---

[14] Richard Hooker, *Of the Lawes of Ecclesiastical Politie* (London, 1594), Book 1, 58–59.

Protestantism was only able to take hold through vernacular bibles, the spread of Reformed ideas and pamphlets, the determined training of preachers and the prior condemnation of Romish practices and superstitions. None of these factors were significantly present in Ireland. Furthermore, the English character of the Reformation, particularly under Elizabeth, may have helped its adoption in England itself, but positively hampered its advance in Ireland.

Religion and the Crises of the Stuart Realms

The Scottish Reformation was different again. There was no Lollardy in Ireland, but a centre of their activities emerged in Ayrshire. There were also far more Protestant preachers and martyrs in early sixteenth-century Scotland than in Ireland. James V, however, was no Henry VIII. He resisted the efforts of the English king, his uncle, to bully him into breaking both with Rome and with the longstanding Scottish alliance with France. Scottish defeat at Solway Moss in 1542 was followed by James's early death and the succession of his only legitimate child, a six-day-old baby called Mary. Henry then saw the opportunity for a dynastic union of the two kingdoms through a marriage of his great-niece to his son, the future Edward VI. The faction led by the vehemently pro-French Cardinal David Beaton, Archbishop of St Andrews, nevertheless won out and led the rejection of the marriage treaty in the Scottish Parliament in December 1543, prompting an English resumption of war. Around the same time, the Protestant preacher, George Wishart, returned with John Knox to his native Scotland with doctrines he had imbibed in Geneva and Cambridge. Beaton did not move against him until December 1545. In the meantime, Wishart had won sympathy among disgruntled and anti-clerical elements in the Scottish nobility. His martyrdom in March 1546 was followed swiftly by Beaton's murder.

In such circumstances the Anglo-Scottish war, which continued with short intervals until 1550, featured much Protestant propaganda. This included contributions from figures such as the Scottish merchant James Henrisoun – who had acquired Protestantism when trading in the Low Countries – in favour of a divinely sanctioned union of the kingdoms of England and Scotland. East coast mercantile elites, who looked to Protestant Northern Europe, were perhaps particularly inclined to take this line. Nonetheless, French domination of Scottish affairs survived Beaton's death under the tutelage of James V's French widow, Mary of Guise. Attempts to reform the Church were led by Beaton's successor, John Hamilton. Then a second decisive phase of the Scottish Reformation was triggered by the queen's marriage to the heir to the French throne in 1558. Resistance to French influence combined with Protestantism coalesced the opposition to Mary of Guise's regency under the leadership of a group of nobles who designated themselves the Lords of the Congregation. Civil conflict came out into the open when fiery preaching by John Knox catalysed a series of local riots and Protestant takeovers of towns in the summer of 1559. After they solicited English intervention, and Mary of Guise's sudden death, the Lords of the Congregation called the Scottish Reformation Parliament of 1560.

When Mary returned to her native kingdom in 1561, following the death of her French husband, Scotland demonstrated the opposite of the *ius reformandi*. The queen did not attempt to reverse the dramatic shift to Protestantism of 1559–1560 as her namesake had earlier done in England. Instead, there was a further shift towards Calvinist doctrine within Scotland following Mary's deposition in 1567 after a crisis-ridden reign. The Reformers' victory in the ensuing civil war was then followed by the emphasis on Presbyterian ecclesiastical government in the *Second Book of Discipline* of 1578. Its principal author, Andrew Melville, like Knox before him, argued that the Kirk should be self-governing, organised around a revitalised parish structure that elected its own ministers and cared for education and the local poor, disciplined by thirteen presbyteries under a General Assembly.

Moves towards Presbyterianism, however, were to be limited by Mary's son, James VI. Succeeding his mother as an infant, he was brought up a Protestant, but was reluctant to see the episcopal function taken over by presbyteries he could not control. His brief captivity in 1582–1583 prompted James to respond with the 'Black Acts' in 1584, which reasserted royal control over the Kirk, and a restoration of episcopacy. This combination of Reformation and royal power was used to justify James's interventions in the Western Isles in the 1590s – where the prevalence of Gaelic had aided resistance to Protestantism's 'civilising' mission – and the Plantation of Ulster in the following decade.

James also shared the drive to assert control, authority and discipline embedded in Protestantism's emphasis on individual, masculine virtues. This had been marked by Knox's view that women should not exercise authority, expressed most trenchantly in his 1558 imprecations against the 'monstrous regiment of women'. Similar gender bias was also marked by the witchcraft legislation passed in 1542 in England and 1563 in Scotland. This followed attacks on Catholic superstition with the outlawing of folk religion and supposedly magical practices, penalties that largely fell upon women.

James enthusiastically supported laws which only gradually fell into desuetude during the seventeenth century as a result of growing juridical concerns about the validity of prosecutions, the conduct of witchcraft trials and the veracity of claims of demonic possession, though anti-witchcraft legislation would not be repealed until 1736.[15]

Particularly significant was James's rejection of the advice of his one-time tutor, George Buchanan, that a king should rule by consent of the people and subject to the rule of law. James instead argued in *The True Law of Free Monarchies* (1598) that the king's authority comes from God. On succeeding Elizabeth to the English and Irish thrones in 1603 James sought to exert this authority by consolidating his kingdoms into one nation under God, officially unified both by liturgy and text and enforced by mandatory church attendance. Political union foundered, not least on the problems of consolidating the laws of England and Scotland. Ecclesiastical unity proved equally elusive among parties disinclined to compromise. The large Puritan faction in 1603 immediately petitioned James, optimistic that he might promote their religious views. James's response was to convene a conference at Hampton Court in 1604 at which he tried to broker a Broad Church agreement. This proved, however, only to raise impossible expectations. Some recusant extremists, finding their hopes of greater toleration dashed, responded with the Gunpowder Plot of 1605. The Puritans, meanwhile, ran into the determination of Richard Bancroft – soon to be translated to Canterbury – to enforce church discipline. The main fruits of the Hampton Court conference were thus Bancroft's 1604 canons regulating religious life in England and the commissioning of the Authorised Version of the Bible which appeared in 1611.

Under James's son Charles I, Bancroft's anti-Puritanism was replaced by the more thoroughgoing and ritualistic policies of William Laud. Because of his closeness to the Duke of Buckingham, the unpopular royal favourite assassinated in 1628, Laud was already an object of suspicion before his appointment to Canterbury in 1633. Thereafter he extended across England the rooting out of Puritanism and restoration of sacerdotal ritual, vestments and clerical authority he had already pursued as Bishop of London. These activities challenged the authority local gentry had grown accustomed to exercise at parish level. Laud's zealous pursuit of such policies also prompted much opposition, associated as they were with the ongoing Counter-Reformation elsewhere in Europe.

---

[15] Edward Bever, 'Witchcraft Prosecutions and the Decline of Magic' *Journal of Interdisciplinary History* 40/2 (2009), 263–293.

As in the previous century, the international context remained important. Still caught in the struggles between France and the Habsburgs, James attempted to break out of his strategic limitations by dynastic marriages. Instead, these drew Charles, at the start of his reign in 1625, into a costly and unpopular war alongside France, the home of his Catholic bride, Maria Henrietta. Parliamentary criticism culminated in the 1628 Petition of Right. Although Charles accepted this, from 1629 he ruled without Parliament, attempting to break out of his strategic dilemma by building up a fleet. Conveniently, he could use the medieval practice of raising ship money as a non-Parliamentary form of taxation to finance both objectives.

Religion and the War of the Three Kingdoms

Charles' policies came to grief in Scotland. The Scottish nobility were alienated by the revocation in 1625 of all the grants of royal and church lands since 1540, on which they now had to pay rent. Additionally, the attempt to extend Laudianism to Scotland from 1637 led to riots in Edinburgh. In 1638 the General Assembly instead expelled the bishops from the Kirk. In biblically infused language the notion of a National Covenant to protect Protestantism, first used in 1581, was also revived. Charles responded by attempting to impose his religious changes by force in what became known as the Bishops' War. His resulting need for finance led the King to recall the English Parliament in 1640. Faced with their complaints against Laudianism and the ship money, he swiftly dissolved it again. However, further defeat at Scottish hands led the impoverished King to summon what became known as the Long Parliament. By the time Charles had conceded the Covenanters' demands in the Treaty of London signed in August 1641 he was experiencing growing difficulties with these English counterparts. Thomas Wentworth, who had served Charles as his deputy in Ireland during the years of personal rule, was arrested and executed. Laud followed him to the scaffold in 1645.

Ireland might not have converted to Protestantism under Elizabeth I, but it was laboriously subjugated. Protestant plantations were established, and Catholic disabilities increased. Charles' French marriage prompted Catholic nobles to press for relief. Central to their requests for 51 'graces' was security of property from the depredations of the Crown. Wentworth's determination to secure the revenues of the Crown and support for a plantation in Connacht as thorough as that in Ulster led him, however, to reject the two key graces in 1634. The possibility that the graces might yet be granted nonetheless could still be used to solicit Irish Catholic assistance for Charles in his other realms at the time of the Bishops' War. Indeed, the suspicion that this might happen led to talk of a Protestant invasion of Ireland. To forestall this, a number of Irish Catholic landlords planned to seize Dublin Castle. Their leader, Sir Phelim O'Neill, claimed to have been given a commission by Charles to lead Irish Catholics against the designs of English Protestants.

Although O'Neill's proclamation was almost certainly a forgery, it demonstrated that the King, far from controlling events in the manner some of his opponents ascribed to him, had become in some ways a pawn in the machinations and mutual suspicions of the competing elites of his kingdoms. His religious policies, meanwhile, though they flowed logically both from the state and nation-building strategies of the Reformation and the high doctrines of kingship imparted by his father, had divided rather than united his realms, and strengthened his opponents. For instance, propaganda about Catholic atrocities in the ongoing upheavals in Ireland only increased suspicion of Charles, culminating in the accusations of a Catholic plot around the queen and Charles' ham-fisted retaliatory attempt to arrest a group of MPs in January 1642.

Ecclesiastical reform was accordingly a key target of his Parliamentary critics in the Grand Remonstrance of November 1641. Charles particularly objected to demands for the exclusion of bishops from Parliament, a Parliamentary veto over the appointment of royal ministers, and the establishment of a national assembly of divines on church reform. Parliament nonetheless went ahead with appointing this assembly in 1642. Losing control of the situation, Charles resorted to war.

Faced by the Solemn League and Covenant the Scots concluded with his English opponents in 1643, and with ineffective support from the Catholic nobles who had gained control of Ireland, it was a conflict Charles was to lose. His defeat had a number of significant consequences. It re-established the ascendancy of Reformers in the Church, with episcopacy abolished in 1646. Following renewed conflict, it also led to the trial and execution of the King in January 1649. Many who were not Laudians were appalled by this action, including Scots who now switched sides. Even among his erstwhile opponents many who did not share Charles' sense of his divine right – and duty – to rule nonetheless feared that the killing of the King would incur divine wrath. The heightened sense of divine providence that had emerged from the Reformation and concomitant existential conflicts with Catholic Spain, in which Puritans fully shared, had been used against Charles earlier in his reign.[16] After his death it could be played upon by royalist propaganda portraying the return of the monarchy as a means of restoring both constitutional order and divine favour.

This propaganda found purchase because the faction around Oliver Cromwell who determined the King's death was not able to establish their new Commonwealth on a wider basis. Cromwell's creation of the New Model Army may have secured the king's defeat, Cromwell's subsequent military triumphs over the Scots and Irish and the position he attained in 1653 as Lord Protector. The Calvinism he espoused, however, proved no more a religious basis for the state than Laudianism. The factionalism that bedevilled the Westminster Assembly similarly stymied its attempts to find an alternative. The ferment of millenarianism unleashed by the turmoil of the 1640s and 1650s instead led to a range of positions, including Fifth Monarchism, which looked to the coming of King Jesus. Such groups could attack Cromwell's authority with as much vigour as he had attacked that of Charles. The difference is that Cromwell crushed them in a way Charles proved incapable of. Cromwell did tolerate the private re-emergence of Jewish groups in London, partly for commercial reasons and partly because of millenarian beliefs. What he did not succeed in doing was establishing a new sustainable institutional basis for the legitimate authority of the state without a king. The chaos that ensued after Cromwell's death accordingly paved the way for the restoration of the monarchy – with the support of the Presbyterian factions in the Church – in the person of Charles II in 1660.

The new King promised religious toleration in his preceding Declaration of Breda. This was aimed more at the Catholic monarchs, particularly Louis XIV of France, who supported him in exile than the various Protestant groups that had emerged in Britain over previous decades. The latter included Puritans. Their development of more democratic structures of Presbyterianism or congregational independency asserted spiritual independence from the unscriptural and Romish associations of church leadership exercised by bishops appointed according to apostolic succession. However, the new regime's clerical fixer, Gilbert Sheldon, insisted on acceptance of episcopacy as a condition of clerical appointment over Charles' more cautious approach. Clergy were accordingly required to conform to the new *Book of Common Prayer* and Act of Uniformity issued in 1662. Nearly 2,000 lost their positions. The exclusion of these dissenters from the state was defined

---

[16] Christopher Hill, 'God and the English Revolution' *History Workshop* 17 (1984), 19–31.

and reinforced by associated legislation which required all office-holders to take the sacrament according to Anglican rites at least once a year and effectively made all religious services in England and Wales other than those of the purged Church of England illegal, enforced by fines and imprisonment. Episcopacy was also restored in Scotland.

Two years later Sheldon, by then Archbishop of Canterbury, agreed to surrender the right to tax the clergy through Convocation in return for a clerical right to vote in Parliamentary elections. This rid his office of the task of collecting taxes from the clergy. Just as the 1662 Act undermined the claim of the Church of England to be comprehensive, this diminished the political significance of Sheldon's own role and that of Convocation. With the Crown no longer having a financial interest in summoning it, Convocation ceased to play a role in representing the Church as one of the estates of the realm, or to enact canons to govern moral issues in the ecclesiastical courts.

Meanwhile, Charles' sympathies with Rome led him to renewed attempts to promote toleration of both Protestant dissenters and Catholic recusants. His 1672 Declaration of Indulgence was, however, firmly quashed by Parliament. The Anglican elites returned to Parliament after the Restoration reacted by instead passing the Test Act 1673, requiring office-holders to abjure transubstantiation. One of the first to be caught by the new legislation was James, the King's brother and successor, whose resignation from the office of Lord High Admiral made public his conversion to Catholicism. In the hysteria resulting from the fabricated allegations of a Popish Plot in 1678, Catholics were excluded from Parliament. This was followed by repeated attempts in 1679–1681 to pass legislation excluding James from the succession, while open rebellion broke out among Covenanters in lowland Scotland. In the end Charles II resorted to ruling without Parliament for the rest of his reign.

James VII and II found the English Parliament no more amenable on his succession in 1685. He prorogued it after November 1685 when it refused to pass legislation promoting religious toleration. The Anglican elites embedded in Parliament may have withheld consent to a measure that threatened their monopoly on power, but the promise of toleration won over dissenters like the Quaker William Penn, who supported James issuing royal Declarations of Indulgence in 1687. This dissenting support and the risk that it could be used to strengthen the authority of a Catholic monarch was one among several concerns for the Anglican elites. James's attempt to come up with a new variant of the *ius reformandi* whereby the king presided over a more tolerant spectrum of beliefs, as a way of incorporating his own into those officially sanctioned, also foundered on two other factors. First, suspicions that toleration was a covert means arbitrarily to favour James's co-religionists were stoked at local government level by the actions of his Catholic confederates in Scotland and by James's previous suspension of the Test and Corporation Acts for certain Catholics in England. Second, James's Declarations posed a threat to the authority of both Parliament and the Church of England as institutions. This led to passive resistance when James tried to force Anglican clergy to read this non-Parliamentary proclamation from their pulpits in April 1688. Refusal to read the Declarations of Indulgence was led by the seven bishops prosecuted for seditious libel at James's behest. In an age of growing material culture this led to widespread representation of James not as an architect of toleration but as a Catholicising threat to the established constitutional and social order. With Huguenots flooding in from France following the revocation of the Edict of Nantes in 1685, the risk of a return to Catholic persecution on the English side of the Channel at the time seemed very real.

This threat appeared more palpable when James's second wife, Mary of Modena, gave birth to a Catholic heir in June 1688, shortly before the bishops were acquitted. Hitherto the succession had been expected to pass to Mary, James's Protestant daughter from his first marriage. As anti-Catholic riots broke out in England, her husband, the Dutch ruler William of Orange, received a despatch inviting him to oust his father-in-law. His widely distributed Declaration of the Hague appealed to a sense of the threats to institutions and order James had posed by endeavouring to introduce a religion 'which is contrary to law', helping to pave the way for a successful invasion. James's discarding of the Great Seal was interpreted as abdication. A recalled Parliament justified this so-called Glorious Revolution in the Bill of Rights of 1689 on grounds of the threat James posed to the Protestant religion, though it would be more accurate to talk of the threat to the Church of England and the Anglican elites in the English Parliament. In Scotland, more radically, Parliament concluded that James had forfeited the throne by his flight.

Some had merely sought the restoration of the status quo of 1685, rather than this new dispensation and monarchy. The manner of James's overthrow caused particular problems for those who had conscientiously sworn allegiance to their king before God. Among the 400 Anglican clergy who refused to break that oath was William Sancroft, the Archbishop of Canterbury and former leader of the seven bishops, who was ejected from office for his pains. Some of these non-jurors ended up supporting a Jacobite restoration, an eventuality the English Parliament sought specifically to avoid by ruling out Catholic monarchs in the 1701 Act of Settlement.

Catholicism was now a dynastic as well as an internal threat, represented in both cases by James's Jacobite supporters. James's invasion of Ireland in 1689 and Catholic risings in the Highlands reinforced awareness of this threat. James's defeat was followed by much tougher anti-Catholic legislation in Ireland and the flight of many of the local elites who had supported him. In Scotland Presbyterianism was re-imposed in 1690. Everywhere there was renewed ejection of clergy of suspect loyalty to those institutions of Church and state whose position had been bolstered by 1688 and over which William III (II in Scotland) and Mary II now sought to preside. Passive resistance, exemplified by Quaker refusals to swear the oath of allegiance, was met with persecution. Active resistance, as in the Jacobite assassination plot against William in 1696, led to punitive legislation in the form of the 1698 Popery Act outlawing the celebration of Mass, Catholic education and banning Catholics from purchasing land.

Conclusions

The Glorious Revolution and its immediate aftermath thus has some claim to mark the culmination of Britain's long and distinctly state-led Reformation. In its sixteenth-century origins, the Reformation built upon existing church-state relations in England, reflected in Henry VIII's use of medieval legislation. Langton may have written the freedom of the Church into *Magna Carta*, yet in practice ecclesiastical revenues and preferment had become increasingly subject to royal authority. Henry consolidated these processes, and further transferred authority over moral and sexual conduct, for instance through the 1533 Buggery Act, to the royal courts. This was followed by propaganda that associated Protestantism with manliness and Catholicism with effeminacy and sexual deviance.

The Church was also used to bolster the sense of the nation under the Crown, a process which came to full fruition under Elizabeth I. Yet the alignment of a moral, legal and authoritative community into a providentially ordained order of church, crown and nation proved elusive. Hooker's harmonious framework went unrealised under Elizabeth's Stuart successors' rejection of his and Buchanan's advice that this order necessarily rested upon the consent of the governed. Royal policy around particular types of churchmanship engendered dissent. The mid seventeenth century struggles that engulfed the Stuart realms then made clear how difficult it was to recreate an ecclesiastical institution that could incorporate all the disparate elements and act as the source of a unifying source of identity across those territories.

Cromwell, like Charles I, failed to establish such a framework. After the Restoration, the ejections that accompanied the Act of Uniformity indicated that this was no longer a feasible goal. In a final variation on the applications of the *ius reformandi* in Britain, it was the English Parliament that imposed this last attempt at uniformity, in despite of a king who had personal as well as political reasons to favour moves towards religious pluralism. Parliament followed this assertion of its authority by attempting to rule out a Catholic succession in 1679–1681, a goal actually achieved in 1701. The kingdom may still have been under God, but who that king was, henceforward, was determined by statute.

6

Religion and the Constitution since the Glorious Revolution

PIPPA CATTERALL

Before the Glorious Revolution attitudes towards religion's position in the state had already helped to define the groupings coming to be known as Tories and Whigs that emerged from pro- and anti-court positions during the 1679–1681 exclusion crisis. Both groups had, however, felt threatened by James VII and II's circumvention of Parliament and the apparent threat to the Anglican monopoly on power represented by his attempts at religious toleration. The overthrow of the monarch in 1688 made plain the power these elites now wielded through the instrument of Parliament. In the aftermath, however, there was a political imperative to return to the subject of toleration. After James's wooing of Dissenters in 1687, William III and II needed to secure the unity and loyalty of his Protestant subjects, not least to enable him to subjugate the Jacobite rising in Ireland. Both from personal preference – as someone from a Calvinist background with Dutch followers of similar churchmanship to reward – as well as expediency, William sought a broad-church solution which would comprehend most Protestants. Gilbert Burnet, rewarded with the bishopric of Salisbury in 1689, also argued that diplomatic considerations, not least the wellbeing of Protestants elsewhere under Catholic rule, militated against a punitive approach to Catholics. This stance only shifted following the Jacobite attempt on William's life in 1696.

The Glorious Revolution, Toleration and the Emergence of Dissent

This Broad Church 'Comprehension' Scheme, despite the sympathies of men like Burnet, foundered on a range of objections, including the impact 'bringing in so great a body as the Presbyterians' would have on Church practices and doctrines. With it went the attempt to recast the relationship between church, crown and nation. Burnet, however, claims that he had more success in persuading Queen Anne to make provision for the increased effectiveness of the Church. Noting the small benefices available to many clergy he lamented: 'Where the encouragement is so small, what can it be expected clergymen should be?' His solution was that the Annates revenues taken by Henry VIII should be applied to the support of poor clergy by the creation in 1704 of Queen Anne's Bounty. Because the supplementary income was intended to come in the form of land grants, this was accompanied by repeal of the Statute of Mortmain.[1]

Such measures were designed to strengthen the Church, particularly at local level where the parish remained very much the most visible sign of authority and – through the continuation of practices like beating the bounds – the prime unit of community. The breach in the church-state nexus was thus very limited in intent. What emerged from the 1688 settlement and its aftermath was a compromise with those Anglican elites who had already stymied toleration attempts in 1672 and 1687. Toleration, for instance, was only extended to Trinitarian Protestants who swore the oath of allegiance, took the sacrament in an Anglican church and subscribed to thirty-six of the Thirty-Nine Articles.

This limited toleration was enough to complete the removal of those many Dissenters from the established Church who had frequently continued, if only to escape persecution, to practice occasional conformity. The Toleration Act of 1689 thus formalised the split in English Protestantism and achieved the very opposite of Comprehension. This was apparent from the ensuing rapid growth in the registrations of now tolerated meeting houses. In such circumstances even leading Presbyterians such as Edmund Calamy, in his *Defence of Moderate Nonconformity* (1704), came to articulate the virtues of toleration, calling for freedom of conscience in religion 'as long as the Civil Interests of Mankind ... remain untouch'd'.[2] This was, as contemporary propagandists swiftly pointed out, in marked contrast to the position taken by his grandfather in the 1640s. Then Presbyterians had aspired to control the Church of England. Now they were excluded from it. The settlement of 1688 and the concomitant failure of Comprehension ensured that England and Wales henceforth had an unusually large Protestant minority. Meanwhile, the contemporaneous triumph of Presbyterianism in Scotland produced a smaller group of Episcopalian dissenters there.

---

[1] Gilbert Burnet (abridged by Thomas Stackhouse), *History of His Own Time* (London: Dent, 1979), vii, 304–306, 398.
[2] Cited in John Coffey, 'Church and State 1550–1750: The Emergence of Dissent' in Robert Pope (ed.) *Companion to Nonconformity* (London: Bloomsbury, 2013), 66.

Calamy's formulation suggested that toleration could only really be achieved by a separation of religious and civil interests. However, this was not something the Anglican establishment was ready to concede. Indeed, such doctrines could themselves be seen as dangerous. Nonconformists remained largely excluded from public offices and their meeting houses were seen, as John Locke acknowledged in his *Letter Concerning Toleration* (1689), as 'nurseries of factions and seditions'. They were simply more within the pale of the constitution than those explicitly excluded, including Catholics, Jews, atheists and Unitarians. While Catholics and Jews were seen as of suspect allegiance, the latter two groups were seen as subversive of the very basis of law and society. As Lord Chief Justice Hales earlier emphasised in the Taylor case (1676) 'to say religion is a cheat, is to dissolve all those obligations whereby the civil societies are preserved'. Locke, whatever his sympathies with Trinitarian Dissenters, concurred, noting 'those are not at all to be tolerated who *deny the being of a God*. Promises, covenants, and oaths, which are the bonds of human society, can have no hold upon an atheist.'[3]

Such positions were thus as much about reinforcing social order and trust as religious orthodoxy. The two certainly overlapped: it was in an atmosphere of moral panic about the undermining of these pillars of order by non-Trinitarian Deism in the 1690s that no less a figure than William's new Archbishop of Canterbury, John Tillotson, was accused of sympathy with those who denied the Trinitarian doctrines of Christianity. The consequence was the strictures against Unitarianism in the 1697 Blasphemy Act. Though this legislation was little used, it still established a clear warning of what was deemed acceptable.

Dissenters more generally were also not so much tolerated after 1689 as made the beneficiaries of non-enforcement of disabilities. Many were able to qualify for public office by taking the sacrament once a year. Such practices could nonetheless be seen as making a mockery of both sacrament and conscience by High Church Tories. It was not just that many of them continued to believe in the absolute necessity, for civil order, of the homogeneous unity of both church and state under a beneficent providence. They also saw Dissenters as existential threats to that order. Allowing occasional conformity, in the incendiary preaching of Henry Sacheverell, gave official authority to those schooled in the doctrines of regicide, fanaticism and anarchy. The rabble-rousing sermon Sacheverell preached in St Paul's

---

[3] Taylor's Case (1676) 1 Vent 293, (1676) 86 ER 189; John Locke, *Letter Concerning Toleration* (London, 1689), 93.

cathedral in London on the portentous anniversary date of 5 November 1709 darkly warned that these enemies within were sapping the Church's character. He also hinted at all kinds of syncretistic threats whereby toleration would eventually be extended to Jews and Muslims as well as Quakers. This colourful invocation of cultural politics, together with the then Whig ministry's decision to prosecute him, turned Sacheverell into both a celebrity and a martyr, and a talismanic figure for the Tories in their election triumph the following year. More important than the immediate political effects, however, was the palpable identification between the Church and membership of civil society that Sacheverell, above all, articulated.

The Tories were therefore equally opposed to the naturalisation of foreign Protestants (who might inspire costly foreign wars) and the role of Dissenters in education. The apparent growth of Dissent after 1689 only heightened their anxieties. Tory ministries therefore outlawed occasional conformity in 1711, and in 1714 they attempted to suppress Dissenting academies that had been growing steadily since the 1660s. Concerns about the 'Church in Danger' also led to major attacks on Dissenters' places of worship when the best-qualified Protestant claimant to the throne, George I, the Lutheran Elector of Hanover, was crowned in 1714, prompting the subsequent passage of the 1714 Riot Act. These riots were good examples of the privileged attacking the oppressed on the grounds that their privileges were threatened; by no means the last example of aggression fuelled by fears of relative deprivation during the eighteenth century. Tory concerns were, however, misplaced. Dissenters might bear witness for liberty of conscience before God, but their marginal social position also led them to emphasise their loyalty to the Crown. Indeed, it was arguably only as they came to feel more secure that in 1732 they set up the Protestant Dissenting Deputies to lobby Sir Robert Walpole's Whig ministry discreetly for repeal of their civil and religious disabilities.

The scene for this development was partly set by the events that followed George I's accession. First, the Tory willingness to sign peace with the French who menaced his Hanoverian domain had not endeared them to their new monarch, who promptly turned them out of office. Second, the threat of a Jacobite rising to secure the accession of James's son in George's place, proved easier to contain than imagination had previously suggested when it actually arose in 1715. Third, this rising also weakened the effectiveness of Tory High Anglican scaremongering about supposed threats to the Church. Tories, many of whom preferred the Pretender if only he turned Anglican, thus were tarred with the brush of Jacobitism and consigned to long years of opposition.

The now-dominant Whigs repealed the Tory impositions on Dissenters in 1719 and instead promoted so-called latitudinarians more accommodating of Dissent within and without the Church. The view of the non-jurors (those who had refused to swear loyalty to William and his successors) that the Church was ordered and endowed with authority by God was most controversially challenged by the Bishop of Bangor, Benjamin Hoadly, in 1717. Hoadly identified the Church as a spiritual organisation which should not seek to wield temporal authority or, by implication, discriminate against those who were not its adherents. This sermon was apparently preached with royal encouragement, and it certainly chimed with George's warning of 1714 against the clergy presuming to meddle in affairs of state. The King followed this up by suspending Convocation in 1717 when it attempted to pronounce against Hoadly. The corollary was Lord Chief Justice Hardwicke's judgement in 1736 in *Middleton* v. *Crofts* that effectively confirmed Parliamentary sovereignty in legislation concerning the laity. Limitations to liberalisation were nonetheless marked by successful resistance in the same year to attempts to repeal the Test and Corporation Acts, and by the defeat of the Jewish Naturalisation Bill in 1753.

Jacobitism and After

By then Jacobitism was a spent force after the failure of a final major Jacobite rising in 1745–1746. This rebellion was fronted by James's grandson and centred, like its 1715 predecessor, in Scotland. Dynastic issues were thus the occasion, if not the cause, of political conflict between the two kingdoms. These were exacerbated by the failure of the English Parliament even to consult their Scottish counterparts in 1701 over the Act of Settlement. In riposte, the Scottish Act of Security 1704 threatened the succession unless Scottish Parliamentary, religious and commercial freedoms were guaranteed. The dynastic risk this posed ensured that, whereas James VI and I's efforts to unite his kingdoms in 1607 had foundered upon English opposition, exactly a hundred years later the English were the driving force. English gold helped to prevail upon the Scottish Parliament to vote itself out of existence, but this did not end Scottish discontent. Embittered men, like the earl of Mar, who lost office with the Tories in 1714 and sparked the rising a year later, could instead find in the idea of a Stuart restoration an apparent means also to restore Scotland. This was particularly the case in the Highlands, where Catholicism and Gaelic continued to predominate. Indeed, state attempts in the 1720s to promote Protestant education in the region to undermine such rebelliousness were limited by failure to adopt Gaelic as the language of instruction. It was following the 1745 rising that the power and traditions of the clans was broken, not least through the much more brutal interventions of the Highland clearances.

Catholicism could nonetheless still be seen as a sinister threat in the empire Britain had carved out in North America, especially following the capture of French Canada in 1759. The expedient recognition given to the Catholic Church and the accompanying exemptions from the Test and Corporation Acts in the 1774 Quebec Act proved significant factors in the rebellion of Britain's North American colonies that broke out the following year. Across the Atlantic, however, the military emergency this created led to limited Catholic relief measures. The 1778 Papists Act separated allegiance from churchmanship, allowing Catholics to join the army. In practice the restrictions of 1698 thus repealed had, like the Blasphemy Act, long been more symbolic than real. Toleration of a kind had advanced by stealth through the non-application of penal laws against Catholics and Dissenters. Leading Catholics nonetheless rightly feared a populist reaction against formal legislative admission of relief. This came in the form of the Gordon riots in London of June 1780.

These reflected a number of factors. A long-standing critique levelled at the 'Court Whig' factions in power was that they had used the authority and patronage of the Crown for their own benefit, not least through their close interest in and increasing control of ecclesiastical appointments. This critique had been particularly catalysed by the political instability of the first decade of George III's reign in the 1760s. Lord George Gordon's allegations in 1780 that Catholics sought a return to absolute monarchy played upon such fears. These were heightened by the rise of print culture in an expanding public sphere, not least through the scandalous journalism of John Wilkes. Wilkes' Nonconformist background was reflected in a religious tolerance that led him to contemplate cathedrals, minarets, synagogues and pagodas sharing the English skyline.[4] The mobs who followed him in the 1760s, and those he opposed in 1780, however, expressed a concatenation of economic and cultural grievances. In the latter case these included suspicions that advancement of Catholic rights would be at the expense of people who saw themselves as of marginal status.

---

[4] Arthur H. Cash, *John Wilkes: The Scandalous Father of English Liberty* (New Haven, CT: Yale University Press, 2006), 30.

Similar fears of relative deprivation were also palpable among Ulster Protestants. The non-enforcement of penal laws had facilitated the emergence of a wealthier Catholic class and their growing involvement in industries, such as the linen trade, where they competed with Protestants. The resulting backlash culminated in the founding in 1795 of the Orange Order, named in memory of the Protestant king from Holland.

Liberty, Conscience and Slavery

Although Presbyterians were involved in this development, not all shared in it. Indeed, a shift in thinking among Dissenters more generally about what they meant by liberty was discernible during the eighteenth century from Calamy onwards. Non-enforcement of their legal disabilities led them to move from simply pursuing freedom to practice their faith in peace to making wider claims about liberty of conscience for all people, not just themselves, as a natural right. As early as the 1720s the Scottish philosopher Gershom Carmichael was arguing 'men are not among the objects over which God has allowed the human race to enjoy dominion'.[5] Under the influence of his successors such as Francis Hutcheson and Adam Smith, such views became embedded in the improving literature of sentiment of the growing Georgian public sphere.

One fruit of this was positive assertion of the moral dictates of conscience in the political sphere, including a growing critique of slavery among the figures of the Scottish enlightenment. From the sixteenth century, the labour requirements of North American and Caribbean plantations had been increasingly met in the racialised form of black chattel slavery. By the eighteenth century this was the foundation of the fortunes of many contemporary self-proclaimed friends of liberty, such as the prominent Wilkesite, William Beckford. Liberty for them was embedded in the political discourses developed in the seventeenth century of resistance to royal power and indicated their Country Whig tradition of opposition to aristocratic elites and Court Whig influence-peddling. This was despite the active encouragement the slave trade was given by the Crown, first under Elizabeth I and then more actively from the Restoration. The irony of slavers invoking liberty was only to be gradually highlighted from the 1760s and 1770s – at a

---

[5] James Moore and Michael Silverthorne (eds.), *Natural Rights on the Threshold of the Scottish Enlightenment: The Writings of Gershom Carmichael* (Indianapolis, IN: Liberty Fund, 2002), 100.

time when the English involvement in the trade was coming to its height – partly through the anti-slavery legal cases of Granville Sharp. These were initially adventitious developments in response to maltreatment, not critiques of the institution itself. It was only in 1769 that Sharp published the first anti-slavery tract in England. Notwithstanding Sharp's Anglicanism (his father was archdeacon of Northumberland), this denounced slavery on grounds of human liberty much more than on grounds of religion.

This was forty years after Hardwick and Charles Talbot, the then Attorney General and Solicitor-General, had determined 'that baptism doth not bestow freedom' on a slave.[6] Nonetheless, it was widely believed among the enslaved that baptism did grant manumission, as had often been early Christian practice. It was also widely believed among the slave-owners in the seventeenth and eighteenth centuries that Christian conversion – and the literacy and advocacy skills acquired in consequence – would prompt slave rebellions. Missionary activities and the threat to power and property they posed were, therefore, long opposed in the slave colonies of the Caribbean and North America.

One missionary who served in the then non-slave colony of Georgia in the 1730s was John Wesley. Following his return to England Wesley promoted a 'religion of the heart' and founded the evangelical group of Methodism that was only to formally split from the Church of England after his death in 1791. Wesley was criticising man-stealing slavers by the 1750s, but it was only in 1774 that he published the first substantial religious tract to attack slavery (though other prominent evangelicals, notably George Whitefield, owned slaves). Wesley's publications drew on those of the Philadelphia Quaker, Anthony Bezenet, yet the proximate impulse appears to have been the Somerset case in 1772. Brought by Sharp, this culminated in the Lord Chief Justice, Lord Mansfield, ruling not that slavery was illegal in England, but that 'no master was ever allowed here to take a slave by force to be sold abroad'. A formal anti-slavery movement may only have emerged in 1787; three years after James Ramsay had used his experience as an Anglican missionary in the Caribbean to publish his *Essay on the treatment and conversion of African slaves in the British Sugar Colonies*. Yet Wesley's work was important, and not just in the conversion to Methodism in 1774 of Olaudah

---

[6] Granville Sharp, *A Representation of the Injustice and Dangerous Tendency of Tolerating Slavery* (London: White and Horsfield, 1769), 2. See also Katherine Gerbner, *Christian Slavery: Conversion and Race in the Protestant Atlantic World* (Philadelphia: University of Pennsylvania Press, 2019).

Equiano, the author of the most influential memoir by a former slave of the late eighteenth century. One aspect of this was the realisation of the distinctive and racialised horrors of black chattel slavery: Wesley noted 'it infinitely exceeds, in every instance of barbarity, whatever Christian slaves suffer in Mahometan countries'. Slavery was thus both an affront to Christianity as a whole and a blot on the conscience of the individual. Wesley thereby incorporated the prevailing literary trope of sentiment to urge sympathy with the suffering of slaves, and this theme thereafter was a fundamental characteristic of the anti-slavery movement.[7]

Freedom from oppression thus became framed as a personal responsibility. Some of those influenced by early eighteenth-century Presbyterian philosophers, such as Hutcheson, took this further than more conservative figures like Wesley, emphasising the duty to exercise political and religious liberty, not least as a people rather than as subjects. For those Presbyterians in Ulster who followed Wolfe Tone rather than the nascent Orange Order, this led them towards the broad-based nationalism espoused by the United Irishmen founded in 1791. One of their first actions was the Catholic convention Tone organised in Dublin in 1792. By such measures, the Anglican Ascendancy in Ireland was threatened with an alliance of liberal Dissenters co-opting the Catholic peasantry to their cause. This aimed at replacing the existing Irish Parliament with one that was the express image of the Irish people, enabling 'a prosperity established on civil, political and religious liberty'.[8] These developments prompted a series of limited and ineffective attempts to contain Catholic grievances in Ireland, including the concession of their right to vote for the first time since 1728.

Emancipation and the Dissolution of the Church-State Nexus

By the 1780s radical Dissenters were re-interpreting the revolution of 1688 as not going far enough to secure liberty, particularly in light of the revolutions first in America and then, in 1789, in France. The time, the veteran Unitarian divine Richard Price asserted, was ripe for the assertion of inalienable rights. His opponents, however, feared the dissolution of a socially and morally desirable unitary public sphere underpinned by religion, leaving chaos in its

---

[7] Cited in Brycchan Carey, 'John Wesley's *Thoughts upon Slavery* and the Language of the Heart' *Bulletin of John Rylands University Library of Manchester* 85, 2–3 (2003), 269–284.
[8] *Northern Star*, 7 Jan. 1794, 4.

place. A dinner in Birmingham to mark the second anniversary of the storming of the Bastille provoked anti-Dissent riots that ended with four chapels torched. Dissenters were widely seen as more dangerous than Catholics. This was certainly the view of John Reeves, who in face of the wars against Revolutionary France after 1793, sought to rally public opinion in defence of those bastions of the constitution – Church and Crown – through his Association for Preserving Liberty and Property against Republicans and Levellers.

As French revolutionaries moved increasingly against Catholicism, sympathies with English Catholics discernibly grew. The 1791 Catholic Relief Act was followed by the repatriation of English religious houses from France and Flanders and their re-establishment in England. Even the bloodily suppressed rebellion in Ireland in 1798, brought about by an incendiary combination of radical Presbyterian thinking, plots with revolutionary France and Catholic agrarian grievances, did not immediately stem this rising tide. The 1800 Act of Union with Ireland, intended to contain such outbreaks, was originally supposed to include Catholic Emancipation safely within the confines of a Protestant-dominated Parliament at Westminster. Those among the ruling Pittite coalition who argued for this saw it as a pragmatic shift to securing loyalty to the state as an institution, rather than through religion as a system of organising society. Their purposes, however, foundered on George III's objections to breaking his coronation oath. The King clearly maintained the view that the 'happy Constitution' he presided over rested upon a still fundamental state-church nexus, amendment of which would result in 'the complete overthrow of the whole fabric'.[9]

The incorporation of Ireland, transforming Catholics from a tiny minority to a third of the population, encouraged others to share the King's anti-Catholicism. A minority of William Pitt the Younger's cabinet shifted their ground on the issue after 1798. Anti-Catholicism was also revived by the rapprochement between the Papacy and Napoléon after 1804 and, after Napoléon's defeat, the re-emergence of Bourbon absolutism in France and Spain in the 1820s. Additionally, while Nonconformity – as it was increasingly termed – had been swollen by the emergence of Methodism in the eighteenth century and the evangelical revival it helped to spark, these new recruits were often vehemently anti-Catholic. The first successful attempt to mobilise Catholics politically in Ireland, the Catholic Association founded

---

[9] The National Archives, London (henceforward TNA): Chatham Papers, C.IV, George III to Pitt, 1 Feb. 1801.

in 1823 by Daniel O'Connell to push for Catholic Emancipation, thus not only challenged – though it did not expunge – longstanding Protestant and English prejudices about disorganised Irish Catholics. The anti-emancipation petitions repeatedly presented to the Lords by Anglican bishops in the later 1820s made clear the continuance of these prejudices.

Nonconformists were also concerned lest the more numerous Catholics should have their grievances addressed first. When the pro-emancipationist Pittite, George Canning, succeeded to the premiership in 1827, Nonconformists, practised in the arts of propaganda by their role in anti-slavery campaigns since the 1780s, therefore launched a vigorous campaign for removal of their own disabilities. This was orchestrated by the veteran Unitarian MP, William Smith, whose leadership of the Protestant Dissenting Deputies had already succeeded, in 1813, in removing the moribund Trinitarian stipulations of the Blasphemy Act.

The Whig opposition spotted the political opportunity, as well as the fragility of the case for continued, weakly applied discrimination against Nonconformity. As Lord John Russell argued in the Commons, if Nonconformists 'were dangerous, they ought to have been excluded altogether; and, if not, they should have been fully admitted'.[10] The Test and Corporation Acts were repealed in 1828. Russell crowed: 'It is really a gratifying thing to force the enemy to give up his first line, that none but Churchmen are worthy to serve the State, and I trust we shall soon make him give up the second, that none but Protestants are.'[11]

It was the second line that was seen as more important for most of those who voted on this repeal. That this line continued to be stoutly defended was clear when an Emancipation bill was defeated in the Lords early in 1828. What broke it was an adventitious by-election in County Clare that summer where O'Connell secured two-thirds of the votes. The support the Catholic Association was able to offer, bolstered by priestly threats of excommunication, trumped the ability of Protestant landlords to direct the votes of their Catholic tenants through fear of eviction. The Wellington ministry now in power was markedly less pro-emancipation than the recently deceased Canning. However, Wellington feared that the Catholic Association was becoming a surrogate government of Ireland, a situation exacerbated by the election of a Catholic who would not be able to take his seat. In these

---

[10] *House of Commons Debates* 2nd ser., vol. 18, c.683 (26 Feb. 1828).
[11] Rollo Russell (ed.), *Early Correspondence of Lord John Russell 1805–40* (London: Fisher Unwin, 1913) i 272.

circumstances even Sir Robert Peel, the Home Secretary and long the leading defender of the existing church-state nexus in Parliament, concluded that conceding emancipation was now expedient. George IV objected but, unlike his father in 1801, had no alternative ministry to turn to in defence of the Protestant constitution. Catholic Emancipation passed in April 1829 at the expense of widespread disenfranchisement of smaller freeholders in Ireland.

The upheaval of 1828–1829 was recognised by High Tories as terminating their efforts to maintain the church-state nexus. Beneath the level of high politics, this nexus was also being disrupted. The Church of England was still seen as central to social order and national unity into the 1820s, reflected in state financing of the church-building programme in burgeoning urban areas. Indeed, it and its parish officers were, for most of the population, the most visible emanations of authority and the state in what had hitherto remained a society principally both governed and taxed locally. Nonetheless, the development and gradual spread of the select vestry from the late sixteenth century onwards undermined the notionally open and accessible nature of this local institution. In theory, putting the affairs of a large and complex parish into the hands of a select few was administratively rational, hence the early adoption of this model in London. In practice, it was a recipe for the capture of the vestry by vested interests. From 1693 there were periodic, unsuccessful attempts at reform. By the 1820s the greed of select vestrymen and women was a key part of the attacks on the jobbery of the unreformed system regularly deployed by satirical cartoonists in the burgeoning print culture of the time. This 'Old Corruption' as it was labelled by radical journalists like William Cobbett, was depicted as a morass of oligarchic and unaccountable sinecures.

Would-be reformers in Parliament were, however, more impressed by the cost of the rising local rates. Tutored by the Anglican clergyman Thomas Malthus to be alarmed about the financial and demographic pressures caused by a swelling population, political elites were more concerned about the perverse incentives they felt were created by generous Poor Law provisions. To tilt the balance back in favour of those who funded the Poor Law, in the reforms introduced by William Sturges-Bourne, the Tory son of a clergyman, in 1818–1819 the wealthy were given additional votes in the election of open vestries and the incumbent's role in enforcing the distinction between the 'deserving' and 'undeserving' poor was reinforced. The supposed irrationality – and expense – of the old system of popular management of parish affairs was thus apparently to be made more administratively efficient and, most crucially, cheaper for the ratepayers. Sturges-Bourne's Acts, along with the Church Building Commission, might be seen as the final throes of the old church-state nexus. The Church had always had a role in social control. Now, however, in face of a growing population at a time of changing labour markets and privation, the role of the local parish in such processes became more palpable.

Social tensions at parish level were also being exacerbated by other developments. Many parish clergy from the mid eighteenth century increasingly came into conflict with their parishioners over tithes, not least because agricultural improvements and new crops led clergymen to demand their share of increased yields. Such conflicts were sometimes assuaged by the practice of commuting tithes for land grants, which accompanied the spread of enclosures, lifting many clergy into the ranks of the minor gentry. This made them among those socially eligible to act as the local arm of the state and social order on the magistrates' bench. The percentage of the magistracy who were clergy peaked in the 1830s at 25 per cent.[12] Local incumbents were, for instance, prominently involved in calling out the yeomanry to bloodily suppress the Parliamentary reform meeting in Manchester in 1819 commonly known as Peterloo. The oxymoronic nature of the clerical-magistrate – with 'the cross in one hand, and the gibbet in the other' – was a subject of much comment at the time of the convulsions during the passage of the Reform Act at the start of the 1830s.[13]

That reform ushered in a period of substantial change and rationalisation under the Whig governments of the 1830s, altering the relationship of church and state. At national level, the inferiority of canon law was made clear in 1833 when the judicial committee of the Privy Council was made the final court of appeal. The diminished value of Queen Anne's Bounty was supplemented by suppressing various of the ecclesiastical offices that had been highlighted by the critics of 'Old Corruption'.[14] Meanwhile, at local level legislation to replace select vestries in large London parishes with vestries elected by all male and female ratepayers was passed in 1831, though the select vestries were not to be more generally abolished until 1855. What the vestries could do, however, was dramatically altered by the 1834 Poor Law as

---

[12] John W. B. Tomlinson, 'The Decline of the Clerical Magistracy in the Nineteenth Century English Midlands' *Studies in Church History* 56 (2020), 421.

[13] Richard Fryer, MP for Wolverhampton 1832–1835, cited in Roger Swift, 'The English Urban Magistracy and the Administration of Justice during the Early Nineteenth Century' *Midland History* 17/1 (1992), 75–92.

[14] This led to the founding of the Ecclesiastical Commissioners in 1836, which was merged with Queen Anne's Bounty to form the Church Commissioners in 1948.

parish level administration was replaced by civil Boards of Guardians. The parish church's role in the physical well-being of its inhabitants was thus attenuated. Furthermore, its role in the registration of births, marriages and deaths was replaced by civil registration in England and Wales in 1836 (and in Scotland in 1855). The inadequacy of the existing parish register system dating from 1538 had been a bone of contention for some years previously, not least because of its questionable admissibility in court in inheritance cases. The resulting legal uncertainty was exacerbated by the frequent absence of Nonconformists and Catholics, and the poor from these records.[15] The objections of the Archbishop of Canterbury, William Howley, to the greater intrusion the new system would involve in community life were swept aside in favour of this rationalisation of administration around property rights. A similar shift to civil administration around property rights was marked in the same year by legislation commuting tithes in England into a state-regulated money payment.[16] The informal social structures Howley sought to defend were thus steadily replaced by a state apparatus growing in functions. The state was effectively decoupling itself from the church-state nexus. It now had administrative means other than the churches to connect to local communities, bind society and promote identity, loyalty and belonging. These developments also moved political and constitutional debates to national level within a rapidly expanding public sphere.

Changing Church-State Relations

One consequence of this transition effected in the 1820s and 1830s was re-examination within the churches of their functions in relation to society and the state. Liberal Anglicans like Thomas Arnold sought, in his *Principles of Church Reform* (1833), to justify the church as a force for social good rather than the light of truth. For others, this 'fashionable liberality' was precisely the problem. A growing indifference to fundamental matters of faith 'forced on the Legislature by public opinion' was likened to national apostasy in John Keble's famous 1833 sermon.[17] Keble, who had published an edition of Hooker's works in 1830, saw that the harmonious juncture of church and state lauded by the Elizabethan divine no longer existed. Many of those

---

[15] Edward Higgs, *Life, Death and Statistics: Civil Registration, Censuses and the Work of the General Register Office 1836–1852* (Hatfield: University of Hertfordshire Press, 2004), 3–18.
[16] A form of commutation of tithes (called teinds there) had applied in Scotland since 1633.
[17] John Keble, *The Christian Year* (London: Oxford University Press, 1914), 549.

around Keble in the emergent Oxford movement looked back instead to the pre-Reformation period for inspiration to revive the spirituality of the church. For some of them, this could only be accomplished by separating it from the state.

The bifurcation of church and state also proved disruptive in Scotland. The catalyst was the determination of the Court of Session in 1834, in response to conflict over the right of nomination of ministers to parishes contrary to the will of the local congregation, that the Kirk was ultimately governed by the state through Act of Parliament. This trammelled long-held views that the Kirk was primarily a self-governing, spiritual body whose first allegiance was to Christ. Those unwilling to accept this situation walked out of the General Assembly to form the Free Church of Scotland in the 'Great Disruption' of 1843. The following year Nonconformists in England formed the Anti-State Church Association to press for disestablishment there.

Three trends were set in train by the disruption to the post-Reformation church-state nexus that occurred in the early nineteenth century. First, Anglicans sought to balance the desiderata of the 'spiritual independence of the Church' and 'the national recognition of religion'. This was partly because of Parliamentary intrusion into doctrinal matters, but even more because lack of Parliamentary time meant much ecclesiastical business was not attended to. The restoration of the Convocations of Canterbury and York in 1852 and 1861 respectively did not effectively address this problem. The solution proffered in the 1916 report on *Church and State* was to provide a body which could legislate for the Church, retaining the historic relationship with the state through giving Parliament powers of scrutiny and veto.[18] The result was the founding of the new National Assembly of the Church of England in 1919.

The previous year an ecumenical report suggested that a condition for other Protestant churches reuniting with the Church of England would be if the ancient practice of election of bishops by clergy and people were revived. After all, similar arrangements were introduced to the Church in Wales on disestablishment in 1920. In England, however, episcopal appointments continued to be managed by the state. Furthermore, although it was increasingly recognised that the Crown might be explicitly Christian, even if Parliament was not, the latter retained a major role in managing ecclesiastical legislation, most famously when rejecting the new Prayer Book put forward in

---

[18] The Archbishops' Committee on Church and State *Report* (London: SPCK, 1916), I, 28–29.

1927–1928. The result of this debacle was a new enquiry into church-state relations that reported in 1935. One solution canvassed was based on the Scottish legislation in 1921 recognising the spiritual independence of the Kirk. This had paved the way for a reunion of the Church of Scotland in 1929 that ended the schism of 1843.

Achieving consensus about what was a spiritual measure outside the purview of Parliament proved much more difficult within the Church of England given the much greater degree of doctrinal differences therein. The attempts of the 1935 *Church and State* report to resolve these issues therefore proved abortive. In 1964 it remained the case, as a leading member of the Treasury Solicitor's Department put, that in law 'Fundamentally the Church of England is the English people engaged in Christian worship and service. It is the sacred counterpart of the secular state'.[19] Indeed, in English law other churches did not exist but were simply voluntary bodies.

The Church of England was nonetheless to achieve greater spiritual autonomy from the state in 1970 with the formal subordination of the doctrinal and liturgical functions of the Convocations to the newly reconstituted General Synod. In the same year Owen Chadwick's committee recommended changes to the appointment of bishops. Henceforth, the Church would nominate two names for the prime minister to choose between before recommending preferment. James Callaghan, the prime minister who implemented these changes in 1977, reminded Parliament that as the monarch remained the governor of the Church of England and bishops continued to sit in the Lords the state retained a legitimate interest in their appointment.

The ensuing decade of Mrs Thatcher's Conservative rule was to be marked by sharp conflict between Church and State. The critical approach to nuclear weapons taken in *The Church and the Bomb* (1982) was followed by the strictures against the role of government policy in creating urban poverty and decay in *Faith in the City* (1985). It was, however, the intemperate reaction of the Thatcher government that turned a report mainly addressed to the inner-city mission of the Church into a crisis in Church-State relations; suggesting that ministers saw the Church of England as having a continuing cultural, if not constitutional, significance. The Church may still have been part of the state and the Archbishop of Canterbury a member of the Privy Council. Yet the brief controversy over Rowan Williams as Archbishop using

---

[19] Oxford Centre for Methodism and Church History: DAMUC HW2/1: Henry Woodhouse, 'A Note on the Church of England by a Methodist Lawyer', 28 Oct. 1964.

the unusual pulpit of the *New Statesman* in 2011 to accuse David Cameron's government of reviving Poor Law concepts of the deserving and undeserving poor showed that its role had shifted towards heckling from the sidelines.[20]

Religion and Social Order

The second significant development that emerged after 1828–1829 was a growing focus on how to christianise the social and political order (as opposed to the state) in light of the readily visible deprivation in a rapidly urbanising society, the increasing intrusion of legislation into social life, the impact of the mid-century cholera outbreaks and the evidence of the 1851 religious census that many of the urban working classes were unchurched. This prompted more activist forms of social intervention building on and broadening out from the anti-slavery campaign of the late eighteenth century. Radical Tory Anglicans such as Richard Oastler in the 1830s denounced the changes to the Poor Law as unchristian. The national impact of this legislation, passed by a Parliament whose oligarchic nature became even clearer in the aftermath of the 1832 Reform Act in its patchy response to popular agitation and petitioning, led him and others to call for further reform of the franchise.

Religious campaigners for a more righteous constitutional order instead tended to focus on the slavery issue until its abolition was enacted in 1833. Accordingly, when it came to Parliamentary reform, their emphasis was initially on removing the rotten boroughs that they suspected helped to bolster slaving interests in the Commons. Nonconformists may have felt that they practised democracy among their congregations, but their enthusiasm for it at Parliamentary level was curbed by Anti-Catholicism, a focus on salvation, fears of state suppression and democracy's association with mob rule.[21] The bishops in the Lords, meanwhile, generally divided against the reform legislation.

In the later 1830s the campaign for further Parliamentary reform coalesced around the calls for the Great Charter. This was a portmanteau set of demands for the expunging of many of the abuses of 'Old Corruption' that continued to be associated with the reformed Parliament, not least through

---

[20] Rowan Williams, 'Leader: The Government Needs to Know How Afraid People Are' *New Statesman* 9 June 2011.
[21] Michael Brock, *The Great Reform Act* (London: Hutchinson, 1973), 40, 80; Pippa Catterall, 'Religion and the Rise of Mass Democracy in Britain' *Contemporary British History* 34/1 (2020), 510–528.

making Parliament and the government more accountable to the people by devices such as universal (usually manhood) suffrage, recall of MPs and annual Parliaments. It was also seen as a means to secure measures to tackle existing deprivation. Speaking of the clergy, one local Chartist leader proclaimed: 'They preached Christ and a crust ... Let them go to those men who preached Christ and a full belly ... Christ and Universal Suffrage'.[22]

References to Christ or texts from the Bible had always provided a readily recognisable language of social and political protest that could be used to denounce the existing order. Now this language was attached to the new, nationally organised, political movements that print culture, the penny post and railways helped to make possible from the 1830s. As well as adapting some of the organisational practices of Methodism, in using scripture groups such as the Chartists both harnessed its power and emphasised the righteousness of their cause against the unchristian existing order. For instance, in 1839 they occupied various parish churches and enjoined – usually unsuccessfully – the incumbents to preach on specially chosen texts.

Although Chartism was a national movement, such actions reflect the extent to which it encompassed continuing local, social and denominational tensions, given the numbers of working-class Nonconformists who seem to have been prominent in the Chartist leadership at grassroots level. There were, however, only sufficient of them on the electoral roll to secure a solitary MP in Nottingham in 1847. After the Chartists presented their third monster petition to Parliament in 1848 – drawing on a means of popular pressure dating back to medieval times which had rapidly grown as a result of the anti-slavery agitation – the movement went into a decline. The existing political parties adjusted to Parliamentary reform and became even more dominant. Both Chartists and the churches ended up responding to this situation. For instance, Nonconformity became widely associated with the Liberal party that emerged from Whiggery in the mid nineteenth century as a political vehicle for both tackling continuing civil disabilities and advancing reformist goals.

Simply promoting evangelism was coming to be seen as not enough. Sympathy with Chartist attacks on 'unsocial Christians' led the maverick Anglican cleric, F. D. Maurice, to launch the short-lived *Christian Socialist* in 1848 and experiment with establishing co-operatives as means of addressing the needs of the working classes. Co-operation, rather than the competition

---

[22] Abram Hanson cited in Malcolm Chase, *Chartism: A New History* (Manchester: Manchester University Press, 2007), 23.

emphasised by contemporary followers of Malthus, or the provident habits inculcated by nineteenth-century adherents of Adam Smith, was Maurice's theme.[23]

From the 1860s views about the insufficiency of encouraging piety and providence among the working classes began steadily to be more widely voiced among the leadership of the churches. As the prominent Birmingham Congregational minister, R. W. Dale, pointed out, 'if the drainage is bad and the water, praying will never save ... from typhoid'.[24] Local churches, both Nonconformist and Anglican, therefore pioneered a range of social welfare activities, which only made those involved even more aware of the inadequacy of such interventions. Individual and social morality coincided in the mobilisation of church opinion in the struggle against the sexual doublestandards of the Contagious Diseases Acts 1864–1866. This campaign demonstrated to Nonconformists – hitherto often understandably suspicious of state intervention – that if the state could make social conditions worse, it could also make them better. Reflections on the social conditions fostering sexual immorality also led the London Congregational Association's pamphlet *The Bitter Cry of Outcast London* (1883) to emphasise that the state must 'secure for the poorest the rights of citizenship'.[25] During the 1880s the state was increasingly conceived as a device for protecting society not only from external and domestic threats, which for much of the post-Reformation era had meant Catholics, but also as a means of positively promoting welfare.

Anglicans shared in these developments. Among the High Church heirs of Keble there were attempts to envisage a distinctively Christian social order or even, as the maldistribution of social goods and periodic unemployment under late nineteenth-century capitalism became more apparent, a Christian Socialist economic one. These efforts were further stimulated by the impacts of the First World War on society, economics and ecumenical relations between the churches. A coherent statement of what a Christian Order in Politics, Economics and Citizenship might look like did not, however, emerge from the eponymous conference held in Birmingham in 1924. This was a deficiency its moving spirit, William Temple, was to play a major part

---

[23] R. A. Seligman, 'Owen and the Christian Socialists' *Political Science Quarterly* 1/2 (1886), 231–232. An influential promoter of the local providence movement was Thomas Chalmers, the first Moderator of the Free Church of Scotland.

[24] Cited in David M. Thompson, 'R. W. Dale and the "Civic Gospel"' in Alan P. F. Sell (ed.), *Protestant Nonconformists and the West Midlands of England* (Keele: Keele University Press, 1996), 103.

[25] *The Bitter Cry of Outcast London* (London: London Congregational Union, 1883), 24.

in addressing in the national emergency of the Second World War. Temple's understanding of the Church's duty 'to lay down principles which should govern the order of society' found fullest expression in his *Christianity and the Social Order*, which sold some 140,000 copies when published in 1942, the year he became Archbishop of Canterbury.[26] In particular, the principles Temple set out in his wartime writings were to popularise the concept of the welfare state developed, after his untimely death in 1944, by the post-war Labour government of Clement Attlee.

The state was thus turned into a risk pool that sought to provide a safety net of social security for its citizenry. To its Christian advocates, however, this was not an end in itself. There was anxiety that welfarism, by creating a culture of entitlement, could promote selfishness, rather than a fuller life for both individuals and society. This concern was accompanied by growing critical scrutiny of the impact on individuals of the stifling rules of nineteenth-century respectability whereby the state had sought to police moral order through legislation rather than through the Church. An example, a century on from the Offences Against the Person Act 1861, was widespread support for abortion reform among Protestant churches, driven not least by concern about backstreet abortionists. The development and well-being of the individual rather than moral discipline received more emphasis. Radical Christian thinkers argued in the 1960s that their role was to inclusively redeem people through unconditional love, rather than mechanistically policing social mores – not least homosexuality – through the state.[27] The churches nonetheless generally remained wedded to heteronormative models of family elevated in Victorian discourse. Although limited decriminalisation was enacted in 1967, it was only as the moral panic over the AIDs/HIV epidemic in the 1980s receded towards the end of that decade that homophobia discernibly declined in the churches, though openly gay Anglican bishops remained taboo.

Religion and the Public Sphere

The third development marked from the 1830s was the way in which the ruling elites hesitantly, often unwillingly, largely removed the state from

---

[26] Cited in Edward Carpenter, *Cantuar: The Archbishops in Their Office*, 2nd ed. (Oxford: Mowbray, 1988), 478–479.
[27] Sam Brewitt-Taylor, *Christian Radicalism in the Church of England and the Invention of the British Sixties 1957–1970* (Oxford: Oxford University Press, 2018).

direct involvement in the religious adherence or behaviour of its subjects. For instance, mandatory church attendance, long unenforced, was finally ended in 1846. The civil and ecclesiastical parishes were formally separated twenty years later. This process was assisted by the concurrent growth of modern political parties as civil society institutions for socio-economic mobilisation in an emergent democratic framework. These parties may have been differentially aligned with one religious group or another, but religion itself gradually became a lesser defining feature of socio-political differences.

This was a slow process. Despite his support for Catholic Emancipation, Russell himself was directly involved as Prime Minister in the last piece of deliberately anti-Catholic legislation passed in Britain, the 1851 Ecclesiastical Titles Act. This responded to Pius IX's ineptly communicated decision to take advantage of a diplomatic rapprochement with Russell's government and restore a Catholic episcopacy in England, with an equally maladroit riposte from Russell about papal aggression. 'No Popery' demonstrations, indicative of continuing popular anti-Catholicism, may have triggered Russell's actions. In contrast, the 'tendencies of the age towards religious liberty' meant for William Gladstone that 'It is our business to control and guide their application.'[28] Twenty years later, Gladstone's first administration repealed Russell's ineffective legislation.

Gladstone was the dominant statesman of the later nineteenth century. A High Anglican, he certainly believed that these tendencies towards religious liberty needed guiding. He argued in *The State in its Relations with the Church* (1839), that the nexus between state, church and society sought since the Reformation was ideal. However, since that had proved impossible, his best alternative was social recognition of religion to turn individuals into citizens by 'destroying that law of self-will and self-worship'. For him, that social recognition nevertheless remained centred on the historic Church of England as the moral guide for both state and society.[29] Toleration was thus more by the indulgent removal of disabilities from certain heterodox groups, rather than their admission to full citizenship. However, they could not be coerced into compliance. Accordingly, it was a civil injustice if the state meddled in the internal affairs of non-established religious communities. This

---

[28] Cited in John Morley, *The Life of William Ewart Gladstone I: 1809–1859* (Cambridge: Cambridge University Press, 2011 [1903]), 413.

[29] Cited in David J. Lorenzo, 'Gladstone, Religious Freedom and Practical Reasoning' *History of Political Thought* 26/1 (2005), 96.

view informed Gladstone's arguments for Jewish Emancipation after Lionel de Rothschild was elected for the City of London in 1847.

Jewish Emancipation was eventually won in 1858. It was followed by a third problematic election in 1880 with the return of the prominent atheist, Charles Bradlaugh, for Northampton. Bradlaugh, like O'Connell and Rothschild before him, was disbarred from taking his seat. Dropping the reference to religion from the Parliamentary oath for his benefit, argued the maverick Tory MP Sir Henry Drummond Wolff, would 'divorce the House from the very elements of religion'. Gladstone retorted that the previous admission of Catholics and Jews had cut the link between religion and eligibility for office.[30] Coercing conscience through a religious test did nothing either for religion or to protect loyalty to a state which no longer actively sought to discriminate between those of differing religious beliefs. It was not, however, until 1886 that Bradlaugh was allowed to take his seat.

This guided retreat unfolded under Gladstone on a case-by-case basis in response to challenge. For him it never entailed disestablishment for the Church of England. However, its sister church in Ireland did not fulfil the role Gladstone argued establishment in England played of promoting spiritual well-being for a population many of whom were voluntarily its adherents. Indeed, its continuing establishment threatened both the British state, as demonstrated by the Fenian bombings of the 1860s and, through this indefensible association, the Church of England

Gladstone's guided retreat thus involved an Anglican core combined with concessions at the periphery. Accordingly, Irish disestablishment in 1869 was followed by Gladstone's attempts from 1885 to enact Irish Home Rule. As a result of the extensions to the franchise of 1884, a revived Irish Parliament was likely to be Catholic-dominated. Resulting fears of coercion into a Romish, illiberal and agrarian Ireland prompted the hostility of Irish Protestants, while consequent delays radicalised opinion among the Irish majority. Eventual descent into civil conflict during and after the First World War culminated in the partition of Ireland and the emergence of a rump Ulster statelet with a Protestant majority population as part of the continuing United Kingdom in 1921.

The differential effects of economic change and emerging public spheres in the various parts of the realm were by then already starting to affect local nationalisms. Gladstone's core and periphery religious strategy, combined

---

[30] *House of Commons Debates* 3rd ser., vol. 278, cc.1168–1173 (26 Apr. 1883).

with the consequences of resistance to it by a Conservative establishment (and the Conservative party), tended to accentuate these fissiparous tendencies emerging within the British state by drawing attention to differences in treatment. For instance, Gladstone deemed the case made for Irish disestablishment, but not for the Church in Wales. Irish disestablishment, however, prompted demands for similar concessions from Welsh MPs who, from the 1860s, began to draw attention to Nonconformity's numerical strength there. They were at the forefront of efforts to tackle continuing Nonconformist grievances, exemplified by the eventual passage of the Burials Act 1880. Welsh nationalism and Nonconformity became entwined, not least in the 1905 survey underpinning the successful Welsh demand for their own education board, which demonstrated the preponderance of Nonconformists in Wales. Welsh Liberals were able, like their Irish Home Rule counterparts, to wring Parliamentary time from the Liberal minority government after 1910. Disestablishment of the Church in Wales was enacted in 1914, though only carried out after the First World War in 1920.

Towards Pluralism

In England, in contrast, the creation of the Church Assembly reduced pressure for disestablishment. Controversy instead focused on tithes. Abolished in Wales at disestablishment, they remained a potent source of conflict in England, not least because of the effects of the 1925 Tithe Act. Growing non-compliance led to further legislation to curtail tithes in 1936, though it was not until 1977 (and only in 2000 in Scotland) that they were finally abolished. The 1960s and 1970s also saw the dismantling of other elements, often fallen into desuetude, of the old state-church nexus. The Blasphemy Act, for instance, was repealed in 1967. It remained, however, a common-law offence, albeit one long considered moribund until the moral campaigner Mary Whitehouse successfully revived it in 1977 by prosecuting *Gay News* over a poem about Christ's crucifixion. This common-law offence was only removed in 2008.

Meanwhile, public debate about blasphemy revived. The common-law offence historically only protected Christianity. This potential problem had briefly surfaced in 1938. There were widespread riots in a British empire which contained over half the world's Muslim population in response to recent derogatory remarks about the Prophet by the well-known author, H. G. Wells. Indeed, there were disturbances in London, where there had been an organised Muslim presence – as well as of a number of other non-

Christian faith groups – of some kind since the later nineteenth century. The Muslim convert, Lord Headley, in 1916 urged official recognition of this presence through building, at national expense, a mosque in commemoration of the thousands of Muslim soldiers – mainly from India – who died fighting for the empire in the First World War. At the time, this received short shrift: the India Office official, Sir Arthur Hirtzel, noted how unthinkable he found the idea of a Christian government erecting a mosque in a Christian country.[31] By 1940, however, the Colonial Secretary, Lord Lloyd, agreed that establishing such a mosque 'would serve as a tribute to the loyalty of the Moslems of the Empire and would have a good effect on Arab countries of the Middle East'.[32] The resulting Islamic Cultural Centre opened by George VI in 1944 in Regent's Park was subsequently augmented by the grand adjacent mosque opened in 1977.

Post-war immigration from the former empire greatly increased the number of Muslims in Britain as part of a wave that also augmented the British population of other faiths, notably Hindus and Sikhs. A similar wave of Jewish immigration from Eastern Europe in the late nineteenth century had prompted growing anti-Semitism and culminated in the passage of the 1905 Aliens Act. This, however, did not address Commonwealth immigration. Despite growing concern among their backbenchers, the Conservative government of Harold Macmillan nonetheless avoided raising the issue of immigration during their successful election campaign in 1959. A surge in arrival numbers over the next two years prompted renewed backbench clamour. Explicit references to religion were rare and tended to come from the few extreme restrictionist Tory MPs, such as Cyril Osborne. In August 1961 Osborne warned that the conversion of a Smethwick church into a Sikh temple indicated the risk of Britain ceasing to be a Christian country. Increasing numbers of his colleagues were nonetheless raising anxieties that immigrants should be 'easily assimilated', which presumably coded a preference for those who were Christian and white.[33] The resulting Commonwealth Immigrants Act passed in 1962, though it did not immediately impact on the rate of arrivals.

---

[31] Humayun Ansari (ed.), *The Making of the East London Mosque 1910–1951* (Cambridge: Cambridge University Press, 2011), 11.

[32] TNA: Lord Lloyd, 'Proposal that His Majesty's Government should provide a site for a mosque in London', WP(G)(40)268, 18 Oct. 1940.

[33] James McKay, 'The Passage of the 1962 Commonwealth Immigrants Act: A Case Study of Backbench Power' *Observatoire de la Société britannique* 6 (2008), 89–108.

Further tightening of immigration law followed, accompanied by a series of pieces of race relations legislation from 1965 intended to help manage this process of assimilation. In the debates surrounding these processes, even the most ardent restrictionists tended to avoid following Osborne in explicitly acknowledging that they had a religious as well as racial dimension. This was partly because much of the moral panic from the 1950s to the 1980s revolved around West Indian immigration and focused upon cultural differences with an immigrant population who were largely Christian in faith. Other faith communities, largely from South Asia, tended to occupy geographically distinct areas within towns, often as a result of racist housing allocation processes and, in the 1960s and 1970s, were socially separated by even bigger cultural barriers and endogamy.

It was the 1989 Rushdie affair, and the issues around blasphemy that it raised, that brought the risk of religious tensions explicitly onto the agenda. Burnings of Salman Rushdie's novel *The Satanic Verses* in various towns and cities with a large Muslim presence culminated in the issuing of a *fatwā* by the Iranian religious leader, Ayatollah Khomeini, sentencing to death all those involved in its publication. The Iranian revolution, ten years earlier, had already undermined the long-standing tendency among British elites to see Islam as a conservative force. The Rushdie affair strongly revived in the British imaginary the trope of a fanatical Islam that had flourished in response to encounters on the imperial frontier in the late nineteenth century, most notably in Sudan against the forces of the Mahdi in 1885. The difference was that now this imaginary was relocated onto Britain's streets.

Parallels with past fears of the subversive threat of Catholicism were observed in Edward Kemp's 2006 drama *5/11*. Ostensibly staged to mark the 400th anniversary of the Gunpowder Plot, its punning title also referenced the Islamophobia stimulated by the 9/11 terrorist attacks in New York in 2001. Suspicions that Muslims owed their primary allegiance to external powers and sought to recast British society through the introduction of *Sharia* law, reinforced by the theocratic language of some radical Muslim preachers, only heightened these parallels. As with Catholics in the past, there was also a misplaced tendency to treat a heterogeneous Muslim presence as a monolithic community. The modern British state's handling of the situation was, however, rather different from its early modern predecessor.

On one level a religious dimension to racial tensions was henceforth explicitly emphasised. In the counter-terrorism legislation and programmes introduced since 9/11, parallels between Islam and this risk of politicised violence were drawn much more explicitly than was the case with Catholic links to the IRA during the Troubles in Northern Ireland between 1969 and 1998. This helped to feed popular Islamophobia. The complexities of terrorist action and the motives that underpin it were obscured by simplistic rhetoric that – in developing a sense of an existential threat from Islam, briefly if improbably given popular credence by the emergence of Islamic State around 2014 – incubated some of the elements that would feed the authoritarian populism palpable, particularly in England, in the second decade of the twenty-first century.

This othering of Muslims has, however, also been accompanied by efforts at protection. In particular, religion was among the categories covered by the 2010 Equality Act which consolidated and extended the anti-discrimination laws introduced since the 1960s to protect various historically excluded or disadvantaged groups. The state, having gradually withdrawn from actively discriminating against particular groups because of their religion, was also now preventing other actors within society from doing so. This could be fraught with difficulties when one set of protected characteristics clashed with another.[34]

Conclusions

These various developments have still not reduced the Church of England, as Keble put it in 1833, to one sect among many. Nevertheless, the linkage between church, state and nation constructed in the post-Reformation period was substantially attenuated by the incremental, guided retreat following the upheaval in church-state relations of the early nineteenth century. Religion was no longer fundamental to the moral order Lord Chief Justice Hales invoked in 1676. Instead, the Supreme Court in *Lee* v. *Ashers Bakery* (2018) spoke of freedom of religious expression by individuals. Religion had ceased to be a socio-political framework and become a personal choice. As the introduction of a religious question on the census from 2001 indicated, this operated within a pluralistic environment in which considerable numbers of the British population adhered to all kinds of faith or, increasingly, to none.

A series of phases can be observed in this history of church-state relations in Britain. In the medieval period, within the framework of a divinely ordained order, there was – particularly in England – a growing struggle between the monarchy and the Church over the temporalities of the latter,

---

[34] See *Lee* v. *Ashers Bakery* (2018) UKSC 49, www.supremecourt.uk/cases/uksc-2017-0020.html (accessed 13 July 2022).

not least in terms of access to tax revenues from the clergy. John's reign exacerbated conflicts with the Papacy, culminating in the assertion of English royal power and Crown-centred national identity in the sixteenth century. As the Church was the key institution of civil society, controlling it was central to the consolidation of the post-Reformation state. However, trying to consolidate a single reformed church order within a united state conflicted with the very different trajectories of the Reformation across the realms of the Tudors and Stuarts. Yet attempts to do so continued until the late seventeenth century. Notwithstanding the latitudinarianism of the Hanoverian bishops' bench, moves towards more religious pluralism were delayed by the threat Jacobitism apparently posed. Jacobitism's demise, together with the strategic rationale behind the incorporation of Ireland into the United Kingdom in 1800, paved the way for Catholic Emancipation. Emancipation's eventual passage in 1829 – and the removal of Nonconformist disabilities the previous year – ended the post-Reformation church-state nexus. Yet it left Anglicans in a privileged position and religious minorities merely tolerated. The guided retreat that ensued shifted the balance between these groups, whilst increasing the contradictions of the British state across its various territories, culminating in the secession of most of Ireland in 1921. Meanwhile the established churches, particularly in the early twentieth century, sought to assert their spiritual independence. Religion has moved from the realm of social order to one of individual conscience, so long as it does not threaten the integrity or existing order of the state.

As the twenty-first century dawned there was considerable debate about whether Britain remained a 'Christian country'. By then the confident assertion of a committee on the Establishment chaired by the Bishop of London, Robert Stopford, in 1967 that 'It can be safely stated that the English people have an inarticulate but no less definite wish to remain a Christian nation with a government and law resting firmly on divine sanction and Christian principles' may have seemed more doubtful.[35] Nonetheless, Britain certainly was neither a secular nor a multi-faith state. It might be more apt to invoke the suggestion of King Charles III that the title 'Defender of the Faith', ironically given to his ancestor Henry VIII by the Pope in 1521 and proudly borne by monarchs ever since, be interpreted as the Church of

---

[35] DAMUC HW 2/2: 'Constitutional Issues and Matters of the Establishment', 27 Apr. 1967.

England's 'duty to protect the free practice of all faiths in this country'.[36] This protection continues to be combined with recognition and status for religious institutions, particularly the Church of England. Religious groups, including Muslim ones, can run their own schools largely at taxpayers' expense. Indeed, the continuing role of the Church of England in running 25 per cent of English schools made it impossible on grounds of equity to refuse to allow other faith communities to establish state-aided schools. Religious groups can also discriminate on certain grounds, as reflected in the protection given to the Church of England from having to break its canons and perform gay marriages when these were legalised in 2013.

Subject to such distinctions Britain has, in a Durkheimian sense of the state's narrative of itself, moved to a new situation. A long common-law tradition of granting negative rights has culminated in religious non-discrimination being, in theory though not always in law or practice, enshrined among the core values of the state. Respect and tolerance for those of other faiths is one of the five key principles of the fundamental 'British values' that in 2012–2014 became required teaching in England's schools. However, far from being a considered statement of what officially is seen as the core values of contemporary British society, the accompanying guidance notes make clear that these were introduced as part of the ongoing counter-terrorism strategy and that they were intended, in a coded reference to Islamicism, to counter 'opinions or behaviours in school that are contrary to fundamental British values'.[37] Indeed, the very term 'British values' was regarded as othering in Scotland, implying that there is an inherent conflict between being British and being Muslim. The term, 'shared values' was instead preferred. It was certainly more inclusive than the terminology in England. There, the focus covertly remained on who was included or not included in the state. This inclusion, as the term 'British values' suggests, has rhetorically moved from being structured around belonging through a shared religious identity, towards instead elevating the false god of 'the nation'.

---

[36] www.princeofwales.gov.uk/will-prince-wales-be-defender-faith-or-defender-faith (accessed 26 Apr. 2020).

[37] *Promoting fundamental values as part of SMSC in schools* Department for Education (Nov. 2014), 5. These 'values' specifically only relate to the law in England, while values such as welfare provision seem to have been designedly excluded.

7
The Social Democratic Constitution

K. D. EWING

Introduction

This chapter is concerned with the constitutional position of trade unions in the United Kingdom. Modern trade unionism emerged from the industrial revolution to protect the interests of workers, and from the late eighteenth century increased in membership and influence, both of which peaked in the 1970s. There were then about 13 million trade unionists, representing some 60 per cent of the working population. But trade union influence extended more widely, touching the lives of almost every worker in the country, either through the coverage of collective agreements negotiated with employers or employers' associations, or through legislation on a wide range of matters that trade unions had persuaded governments to introduce. Trade unions in the 1970s were also at the heart of government, influencing the direction of social, economic and fiscal policy.

This now seems a distant memory: the gradual ascent of trade unions to political power and constitutional engagement has been matched since 1979 by a swift decline and marginalisation of trade unionism, the speed of the decline only briefly delayed by the New Labour governments from 1997 to 2010. Now trade union membership is about half of what it was in 1980, only 23.4 per cent of the workforce is unionised, and collective bargaining coverage has fallen from about 82 per cent of the working population to only 26 per cent, which is lower than all but one of the twenty-seven EU member states.[1] Legal support for trade union activity has been diminished, and many workers currently work in precarious economic circumstances, as trade union political influence has been greatly reduced, and levels of economic inequality have correspondingly increased.

---

[1] Department for Business, Energy & Industrial Strategy, 'Trade Union Statistics 2018', 30 May 2019 (available online). According to the government's statistics, female employees are more likely to be unionised than male employees.

The erstwhile constitutional role for trade unions is a feature of the different functions they perform. In earlier writing I have described these as being a service function, a representative function, a regulatory function, a government function, and a public administration function.[2] Some of these different functions have a constitutional dimension, particularly where they involve parliamentary representation, participation in the process of government, and the delegated or devolved power to regulate working conditions. In other countries this would be seen as part of a process of economic democracy and industrial citizenship constitutionally entrenched, which would endorse the legitimacy of trade union demands to be involved in national policy-making, and to be participants in determining the rules by which workers are governed.[3]

In this chapter the 'social constitution' is the term used primarily to explain the process of trade union participation in the political arena and in particular in the conduct of government. But the term is also used to explain the process of trade union involvement in the government of industry, as a feature of economic democracy and industrial citizenship.[4] The idea of a social constitution and the practice of social constitutionalism are thus based in part on developing ideological understandings about the nature of democracy; the erstwhile need for the containment of shifting sources of power in what were Keynesian demand-led political economies; and more recently at EU level the need for inclusivity to encourage support for European integration. As such, social constitutionalism was a product of social democracy and social justice, and of Social Europe and the EU's 'social market'.[5]

In the pages that follow, we begin with an account of the emancipation of organised labour from legal restriction, and the unleashing of its latent power (Part II). Thereafter we are concerned with the representation of trade union interests in Parliament (Part III), together with the direct representation of labour interests more specifically in government (Part IV). The two are obviously closely related, if only because the representation *in* government would be much more congenial for organised labour if its own party was also

---

[2] K. D. Ewing, 'The Function of Trade Unions' (2005) 34 *Industrial Law Journal* 1.
[3] See K. D. Ewing, 'Economic Rights', in M. Rosenfeld and A. Sajo (eds.), *The Oxford Companion of Comparative Constitutional Law* (Oxford University Press, 2012), ch. 50. Note also, the Weimar Constitution, Art 165. For a sobering assessment of the latter, see O. Kahn-Freund, 'The Weimar Constitution' (1944) 15 *Political Quarterly* 229.
[4] On this dimension, see especially R. Dukes, *Labour's Constitution: The Enduring Idea of Labour Law* (Oxford University Press, 2014). Albeit a secondary theme in this chapter, it is addressed specifically in Part IV below.
[5] Treaty on European Union, Art 3(3).

the party *of* government. A third concern addressed in this chapter is participation by labour as a feature of social constitutionalism (Part V), a process said by Alan Fox as being 'apt to cause alarm in some quarters as 'bypassing' Parliament and subverting its sovereignty'.[6] This is an alarm to be heard loudly during the Social Contract era of the 1970s in particular.

Despite its informality and apparent flexibility, Fox's observation suggests that the British constitution may have had difficulty in adapting to these new methods of government. Indeed, social constitutionalism raised several questions of legitimacy for those schooled in liberal traditions, and it helped to expose a counter-intuitive inflexibility of the British Constitution, and paradoxically the powerful restraining influence of the underlying principles in our unwritten arrangements. These questions of legitimacy related to the role of trade unions, and in particular their role as representative institutions in the conduct of government. We consider the disruptive role of the liberal constitution for the Social Contract in Part VI, before considering in Part VII the contrasting approach in a later era to law-making by 'Social Dialogue', widely accepted as an integral to 'Social Europe'. We conclude in Part VIII.

Emancipation

The first requirement of a social constitution is the presence of social institutions through which social representation and participation can develop. The major interest for this purpose is the organisation of workers and the emancipation of trade unions from legal restraint. The development of the social constitution has constantly been frustrated by the legal values of the liberal constitution, and the principles of economic liberalism these values betrayed. In his classic text, Wedderburn wrote of trade unions being hampered by three restraints, of which the first was wage-fixing by magistrates that continued until abolished in 1824, giving way to 'the new ideology of free competition'.[7] These wage-fixing measures had been accompanied by legislation 'regularly passed to make illegal workers' combinations either generally or in various trades'.[8]

---

[6] A. Fox, *History and Heritage: The Social Origins of the British Industrial Relations System* (Allen and Unwin, 1985), p. 291.

[7] K. W. Wedderburn, *The Worker and the Law* (Penguin, 1965), p. 215. There were two subsequent editions (1971 and 1986). Wedderburn was a leading labour law scholar, who became a government adviser and Labour peer during the Social Contract era discussed below. For an account of his work, see A. Bogg, 'The Hero's Journey: Lord Wedderburn and the "Political Constitution" of Labour Law' (2015) 44 *Industrial Law Journal* 299.

[8] Ibid, pp. 215–216.

Second, Wedderburn refers to the judges who saw 'union organisation as a common-law crime, namely that of conspiracy'.[9] Here he discusses *R v. Mawbey*,[10] where Mr Justice Grose is recorded as saying that while the journeyman 'may insist on raising his wages if he can', if 'several meet for the same purpose it is illegal and the parties may be indicted for a conspiracy'.[11] And third, Wedderburn refers to the Combination Acts of 1799 and 1800 passed at the time of the French Revolution, which was said to encourage governments 'to see all organisations of workers as a potential source of Jacobin revolution', the Acts of 1799 and 1800 consequently rendering criminal all combinations to improve working conditions, as well as the attendance of meetings for such purposes. So set in motion a recurring suspicion of trade unionists as 'rebels and revolutionaries'.[12]

These criminal liabilities were removed in 1824 but restored the following year, and it was not until 1859 and 1871 that there was a significant relaxation of statutory criminal liability for engaging in trade union activity. That said, the Criminal Law Amendment Act 1871 was met almost immediately by a display of judicial muscle when in the following year striking gas workers were indicted for criminal conspiracy at common law, and having been found guilty sentenced to two years' imprisonment.[13] The essence of the common-law offence as explained by Mr Justice Brett was that it is 'an unjustifiable annoyance and interference with the masters in the conduct of their business' of such a nature that it 'would be likely to have a deterring effect upon masters of ordinary nerve'.[14] So set in motion what has been referred to by Hugh Collins as a game of 'cat and mouse' between Parliament and the judges.[15]

The Conspiracy and Protection of Property Act 1875 was important for several reasons. But principally for present purposes because it removed criminal liability at common law for taking trade union action, provided the acts in question were done 'in contemplation of furtherance of a trade dispute'.[16] This was not complete emancipation, revealing the continuing

---

[9] Ibid, p. 216.　[10] (1796) 6 T R 619.　[11] Ibid, p. 636.
[12] This is a point made forcefully in A. Bogg, K. D. Ewing and A. Moretta, 'The Persistence of Criminal Law and Police in Collective Labour Relations', in A. Bogg, J. Collins, M. Freedland and J. Herring (eds.), *Criminality at Work* (Oxford University Press, 2020).
[13] (1872) 12 Cox CC 316. The defendants were released after four months.
[14] Ibid, pp. 348–339.
[15] H. G. Collins, 'Judicial Control and the Betterment Test' (1978) 7 *Industrial Law Journal* 126.
[16] Conspiracy and Protection of Property Act 1875, section 3.

suspicion about the political motives of trade unions, and a desire to confine them to the industrial sphere. Notably too when contemplating a rights-based social constitution, the language used was not a right to strike, but an excuse from liability where the action would otherwise be unlawful. This was to set the foundations of a parliamentary approach that was adopted in relation to the civil law, to which we are about to turn. Provisions similar to the 1875 Act remain to this day as the essence of trade union protection from criminal liability.[17]

Criminal liabilities imposed by Parliament and the courts gave way to civil liability created by the courts, developing doctrines of restraint of trade and conspiracy to injure for application to trade unions.[18] The development of these liabilities – which emerged in the period after 1875 – reached a climax with two major decisions of the House of Lords in 1900. As Graeme Lockwood records, *Taff Vale Railway Company v. Amalgamated Society of Railway Servants*,[19] was the culmination of a very aggressive anti-union campaign by the railway company.[20] A large scale strike appears to have been smouldering for some time and was precipitated by the victimisation of a shop steward. In the course of legal proceedings, the company established the existence of tortious liability for inducing workers to act in breach of their contracts of employment.

Liability for the latter arose when the union instructed its members to take strike action in breach of their contracts of employment, for which the unions were liable to the employer. But the decision was even more significant for holding that the union was vicariously liable for the tortious acts of its servants and agents, with the result that substantial damages could be enforced against the union as if it were a legal person. The practical effect of what was a massive

---

[17] Trade Union and Labour Relations (Consolidation) Act 1992, section 242, with protection from liability under the Criminal Law Act 1977, which replaces the common-law offence.

[18] See *Hornby v. Close* (1867) 2 QB 153 and *Quinn v. Leathem* [1901] AC 495, respectively. In *Hornby v. Close*, the Court of Queen's Bench held that because trade unions were organisations in restraint of trade, they could not make use of statutory procedures for the purposes of recovering money which had been embezzled by a corrupt branch official. Apart from the risk to trade union organisation and finances, this was a reminder to trade unions that their very existence was inconsistent with common-law rules then in force. *Hornby v. Close* was reversed by the Trade Union Act 1871, the provisions of which are still needed: Trade Union and Labour Relations (Consolidation) Act 1992, s 11.

[19] [1901] AC 426.

[20] G. Lockwood, 'Taff Vale and the Trade Disputes Act 1906', in K. D. Ewing (ed.), *The Right to Strike: From the Trade Disputes Act 1906 to a Trade Union Freedom Bill 2006* (Institute of Employment Rights, 2007), ch. 2.

judicial blow in favour of employers was to constrain trade union freedom generally, and the 'right to strike' in particular: no trade union could contemplate calling industrial action if it meant unlimited liability in damages. There are few judicial decisions that can have had such dramatic consequences, one of which was the formation of what became the Labour Party.

Taff Vale was followed a few months later by *Quinn v. Leathem*,[21] where trade union action was held also to be an unlawful conspiracy at common law, actionable in civil proceedings by the employer. The essence of liability was the conspiracy – there was no need otherwise to show the violation of any legal rights or duties. An act done by two or more people which would be lawful if done by one person acting alone was unlawful, the essence of the illegality being the combination (or 'conspiracy'). John McIlroy highlights the strong language of the House of Lords in *Quinn v. Leathem*, which provides an insight into the hostility trade unions continued to face from the courts despite the retreat of the criminal law.[22] So although more restrained than the language of the lower court, the appellants were nevertheless attacked in the House of Lords for 'inflicting acts of wanton aggression', and perpetrating 'organised and ruinous oppression'.[23]

These and other judicial attacks on trade union freedom led to demands for legislation to overturn the decisions, demands which led almost immediately to the Trade Disputes Act 1906.[24] But although badged as organised labour's 'Magna Carta', the 1906 Act did not confer rights. In emancipating trade unions, the Act adopted the pattern set in 1875, the Liberal government of the day following the example of a Conservative predecessor in providing trade unions with a limited immunity from common-law liability, on this occasion arising in the civil rather than the criminal law. There was no question of trade unions being given legal rights, and no question either of the abolition of the underlying common-law liabilities. Although welcomed by trade unionists, the 1906 Act in truth did the minimum required to protect trade union action, though as discussed in Part VI below even this was to prove constitutionally highly contentious.

---

[21] [1901] AC 495.
[22] At the heart of the case was a principle of the common law, which can be seen to run through the jurisprudence of the nineteenth century, namely the 'right of every trader to carry on his business in his own manner' (Lord Brampton). There was no countervailing right of workers or trade unions.
[23] J. McIlroy, 'The Belfast Butchers: *Quinn v. Leathem* after a Hundred Years', in Ewing (ed.), *The Right to Strike*, p. 50.
[24] For background and context, see F. Bealey and H. Pelling, *Labour and Politics 1900–1906* (Macmillan, 1958). Also J. Saville, 'The Trade Disputes Act of 1906' (1996) 1 *Historical Studies in Industrial Relations* 11.

Political Representation

The formation of the Labour Party in 1906 provided trade unions with a voice in Parliament to press for legislation to secure their freedom and to improve working conditions. But the existence of the Labour Party itself was to face a legal challenge, financed it is believed by the railway companies smarting from the statutory reversal of the *Taff Vale* decision. Trade unions affiliated to the Labour Party had imposed a compulsory parliamentary levy on their members to enable the union in question to engage in political work, including support for the Labour Representation Committee and subsequently the Labour Party. The money was used in part for payments to MPs, at a time when there were no parliamentary salaries. In *Osborne* v. *Amalgamated Society of Railway Servants*,[25] it was held that trade union funding of the Labour Party was unlawful, thereby creating a risk to the Party's survival.

The *Osborne* judgment is infamous in Labour folklore as an attempt to strangle the Party at birth, in what is the most eloquent yet most overlooked judicial account of the liberal constitution. It is true that the majority decided the case on the ground that trade union support for the Labour Party was ultra vires the legislation legalising trade unions in the 1870s. In defining the purposes of trade unions, Parliament made no reference to political activity, which could not be implied as a way of implementing statutory objectives. Often overlooked by legal historians, however, is the claim by Sir George Farwell in the Court of Appeal that the structure of the Labour Party was 'utterly unconstitutional',[26] a line of argument sustained by two members of the House of Lords. According to Lord Shaw of Dunfermline

> The proposed additional rule of the Society that 'all candidates shall sign and respect the conditions of the Labour party, and be subject to their whip , the rule that candidates are to be 'responsible to and paid by the society', and, in particular, the provision in the constitution of the Labour party that 'candidates and members must accept this constitution, and agree to be bound by the decision of the parliamentary party in carrying out the aims of this constitution', are all fundamentally illegal, because they are in violation of that sound public policy which is essential to the working of representative government.[27]

For the Labour Party and its MPs, infanticide was avoided by the gracious intervention of the Liberal government which not only introduced

---

[25] [1910] AC 87.
[26] *Amalgamated Society of Railway Servants* v. *Osborne* [1909] 1 Ch. 163, at p. 196.
[27] [1910] AC 87, pp. 114–115.

parliamentary salaries as life support almost immediately,[28] but eventually also partially reversed the *Osborne* decision by legislation. The Trade Union Act 1913 provided the legal foundations for the continuing relationship between the trade unions and the Labour Party, though in doing so the Act did not reverse *Osborne* completely. Rather, it infused the relationship between trade unions and the Labour Party with liberal legal principles, in the sense that trade unions could engage in political activities only with the consent of their members voting in a ballot. Armed with this approval:

- trade unions were required to finance their political activities by a separate levy of the members which had to be paid into a separate political fund; and
- trade union rules were to provide that members who objected to paying the levy had a right to opt out of the obligation to do so.

These conditions were strongly resisted by both the trade unions and the Labour Party. But they were a fair compromise at a time when trade union membership was very often a condition of employment, either formally or informally as result of closed shop agreements and practices. These conditions also had the effect of creating large pools of money in the form of trade union political funds to be used only for political purposes, with the unintended consequence of providing the Labour Party with a significant measure of financial security. The money generated by trade union political levies in this way would be used for several purposes set out rather inelegantly in the 1913 Act, but mainly in affiliation fees and election grants to the Labour Party, on which the Party relied for the great bulk of its income for the best part of the twentieth century.

The 1913 Act also enabled the Labour Party to operate as it had done previously, subject to a number of changes to reflect judicial criticism of the obligations of its MPs. But it remained a political party of affiliated organisations only, with no individual members. It was not until the Party's constitutional reforms famously drafted by Sidney Webb in 1918 that Labour ceased being what Maurice Duverger has classified as an 'indirect party',[29] indirect in the sense that it was a party of intermediate bodies only. As Duverger points out, under this model these union members 'do not belong to the party itself: they belong to an organisation that is a collective member

---

[28] W. B. Gwyn, *Democracy and the Cost of Politics* (Athlone Press, 1962).
[29] M. Duverger, *Party Politics and Pressure Groups* (Nelson, 1972), pp. 16–17.

of the party', not the same thing as individual membership.[30] Since 1918 it has been a mixed party of affiliated organisations (trade unions and socialist societies) and individual members organised in Constituency Labour Parties.

As an organisational member of the Party, a union would pay an affiliation fee based on the number of its political levy-paying members, which would give each union a measure of aggregated power within the Party. Under the Party constitution, affiliated organisations have thus enjoyed representation and influence within the policy-making processes, as well as an important role in Party administration, the selection of parliamentary candidates, and latterly the election of Party Leader. These arrangements provided a unique forum for influence and power through the constitutional structures of the Party, and through the Party within government itself.[31] It was, however, a framework that was based on a cross-party political consensus that accepted the legitimacy of trade unionism, the legitimacy of trade unions as political actors, and the legitimacy of the Labour Party's system of collective affiliation.

As events have unfolded, none of this could be taken for granted, with questions as to the legitimacy of one or more of the foregoing leading to legislative steps being taken by Conservative administrations to reduce the role of trade unions in the Labour Party.[32] Initially, this was simply a self-confessed partisan attack, as Cabinet Ministers made clear.[33] More recently, Conservative-led attacks on the Labour Party reveal a deeper concern about the political influence of organised labour at a time when governments were seeking to marginalise its role economically. This concern is to be seen in Hayek's perceptive remark that 'a political party in which trade unions have a major constitutional role cannot strike at the source of their power',[34] and

---

[30] Ibid, p. 17.
[31] For the restrained use of the power, typically to support the Party Leader, see L. Minkin, *The Contentious Alliance: Trade Unions and the Labour Party* (Edinburgh University Press, 1991). See subsequently L. Minkin, *The Blair Supremacy* (Manchester University Press, 2014).
[32] The statutory compromise was thus amended by Conservative administrations in 1927 though the 1913 settlement was restored by the Attlee government in 1946. Additional restraints that so far have not been revoked were introduced in 1984 (periodic review ballots) and 2016 (opting in for new members, rather than opting out).
[33] See K. D. Ewing, *Trade Unions, the Labour Party and the Law: A Study of the Trade Union Act 1913* (Edinburgh University Press, 1983), citing a Cabinet memorandum in which the Minister of Labour openly acknowledges that the purpose of changing the law was 'a desire to hit the Socialist party through their pockets' (p. 51).
[34] F. A. Hayek, 1980s *Unemployment and the Unions*, with a Postscript on *British Trade Unions and the Law: From Taff Vale to Tebbit*, C. G. Hanson (ed.), 2nd ed. (Institute of Economic Affairs, 1984), p. 57.

Thatcher's reported ambition to displace Labour with what was then the SDP-Liberal Alliance as Her Majesty's Opposition.[35]

The battle for the recognition of the Labour Party's constitutional form and its principle of collective affiliation is thus still constitutionally contested,[36] with the result that the legal foundations of this relationship have proved now to be very unstable. What this may tell us is that while trade union political representation through a political party was not an essential precondition, it was nevertheless a form of representation that greatly enriched the practice of social constitutionalism. Political representation through the Labour Party was understood by its critics as a barrier to the displacement of the social constitution as the latter had developed through patterns of participation. It did so by giving trade unions through the Party close access to the levers of political power, and with it the economic policy and legal arrangements by which their authority was sustained.

Representation in Government

If a key element of the social constitution was the representation of worker interests in the Labour Party, a second element was the representation of worker interests in the machinery of government (regardless of the party of government), a need recognised by early socialist pioneers and their colleagues in the trade union movement. Rodney Lowe records that in the years since 1892, there had been fifteen bills and two amendments to the Address proposing the establishment of a Ministry of Labour, the issue also examined by two royal commissions.[37] Apart from Keir Hardie, the proposal was supported by Dockers' Union leader Ben Tillett, who demanded a minister 'who for the first time in history would be able to speak in the name of the workers, as the President of the Board of Trade does of trade, as the President of the Board of Agriculture does of agricultural interests'.[38]

The cause was taken up by the Trades Union Congress (TUC) which had been directly engaged with government during the First World War. The TUC's demand was that these patterns of representation and participation in

---

[35] *The Observer*, 1 May 1983.
[36] House of Lords, Report of Select Committee on Trade Union Political Funds and Political Party Funding, HL Paper 106, 2015–2016.
[37] R. Lowe, *Adjusting to Democracy: The Role of the Ministry of Labour in British Politics 1916–1939* (Oxford University Press, 1986), p. 15. See also K. D. Ewing, 'Socialism and the Constitution' [2020] 73 *Current Legal Problems* 27, on which this part draws.
[38] Lowe, *Adjusting to Democracy*, p. 16.

government should continue after the war had ended, and that the establishment of a Ministry of Labour would be a 'fitting recognition' of 'labour's co-operation during the war'. This would 'enable the workers to realise that at last they were taking a direct, active and real part in the administrative affairs of the country'.[39]

These demands were met when the Ministry of Labour was set up by statute in 1916,[40] Lloyd George acknowledging that

> The department would be one of the most important departments of the government because, however important a Labour ministry would be in time of peace – and it would essentially be a department whose decisions would very materially affect the lives of millions of people in this country – in times of war it is almost doubly important.[41]

So a dedicated department was not only about representation as Tillett demanded, or participation as the TUC insisted upon. It was also about policy, doing things that would benefit workers by consistently meeting rising expectations for better working conditions and improved standards of living. As a statutory body, the Ministry of Labour thus had a number of responsibilities transferred to it from other departments (including the Board of Trade). Its greatest achievement, however, was in implementing J. H. Whitley's programme for economic democracy and industrial citizenship,[42] at a time when universal male suffrage was being introduced politically, and steps were being taken to protect Labour internationally. The latter included the formation of the International Labour Organisation at Versailles in 1919, a unique tripartite body now an agency of the United Nations.

J. H. Whitley was a Liberal MP and also Deputy Speaker of the House of Commons who as part of the post-war reconstruction had been asked in 1916 to chair a Committee on the Relations between Employers and Employed. The Committee produced five reports, with 'far-reaching recommendations',[43] including (a) the formation of Joint Industrial Councils in well-organised industries; (b) the creation of works committees of management and workers in individual enterprises; and (c) the regulation of wages by

---

[39] Ibid.
[40] New Ministries and Secretaries Act 1916, ss 1 and 2. This would now be done by a combination of prerogative powers and secondary legislation, in the latter case under the authority of the Ministers of the Crown Act 1975.
[41] Lowe, *Adjusting to Democracy*, p. 14.
[42] On which see K. D. Ewing, 'The State and Industrial Relations: "Collective Laissez Faire" Revisited' (1988) 5 *Historical Studies in Industrial Relations* 1.
[43] Ministry of Labour, *Industrial Relations Handbook* (HMSO, 1961 ed.), p. 21.

statutory trade boards in industries where trade union organisation was weak. Underpinning these and other recommendations relating to the resolution of disputes between trade unions and employers was the belief that there should be a continuation of the policy that industries should 'make their own agreements and settle their differences themselves'.[44]

From 1917 onwards, the Ministry of Labour set about promoting these recommendations with alacrity, so that by 1921 an additional five million workers had been brought into some kind of collective wage regulation system, either through a Joint Industrial Council or a trade board. The former were joint councils of trade unions and employers' associations operating industry or sector wide. They were established on a 'voluntary' basis, where necessary the product of administrative pressure applied by Ministry officials. The latter in contrast were established under the Trade Boards Act 1918. Following the Whitley recommendations, the trade boards were tripartite in nature, thereby ensuring trade union and employer representation respectively on the boards in question, with government nominees helping to resolve differences.

Commitment to these procedures waned from 1921 following the implementation of the government's austerity programme. True, the Ministry of Labour survived and the Whitley legacy was not actively dismantled. But it is nevertheless clear from the Ministry's annual reports that Whitley's legacy was allowed gradually to decay for lack of support. It was not until the mid-1930s that survival was to lead to revival, with the radical change in direction of economic policy leading successive governments to recall the reasons why the Ministry of Labour had been created in the first place.[45] The need to raise wages and stimulate demand led to renewed government support for collective bargaining, with the intervention of Ministry officials, the new policy of the department acknowledged by Ernest Brown, the Liberal Unionist Minister of Labour in the Baldwin government:

> The development of individual freedom in this country has gone side by side with industrial freedom, and it is becoming increasingly recognised that our voluntary collective bargaining system is one of the most potent instruments for the stability of our national life. That being so, it is our duty to foster and encourage the establishment of such machinery over an ever-widening field.[46]

---

[44] Ibid, p. 21.   [45] See Ewing, 'The State and Industrial Relations'.
[46] HC Deb, 11 May 1938, col 1621.

The policy of promoting collective bargaining in this way involved the creation of autonomous systems of rule-making on an industry or sector wide basis by trade unions and employers' associations, in what was a de facto delegation or devolution of regulatory activity from the State to what are now referred to as the social partners. At its peak, the system nurtured in this way by the administrative and legislative power of the State was said by the Ministry of Labour to apply to 86 per cent of British workers,[47] all the more impressive for the absence of what the Italian constitution refers to as the mandatory effects of collective agreements.[48] In practice, however, such formalities were largely unnecessary, as British trade unions had other ways of ensuring that rules were observed, including the power of trade unions themselves to impose industrial sanctions on recalcitrant employers.[49]

The role of the Ministry of Labour in promoting greater economic democracy and industrial citizenship vindicated the insight of the early socialist pioneers for labour representation in government. That said, while a dedicated government department may be important for ensuring the effective representation of workers, it was perhaps naïve not to anticipate that such a department can also be the instrument for undermining workers' interests. In the early years of the Thatcher administration, there is evidence that what was now the Department of Employment had operated as a restraint on the emerging market-oriented initiatives of the new government. But that was to change with new ministerial appointments, the Department to become a willing party in dismantling the infrastructure of participation and citizenship previously nurtured and nourished by its predecessors.

---

[47] Ewing, 'The State and Industrial Relations'.
[48] The Italian constitution provides, for example, that trade unions 'may enter into collective labour agreements that have a mandatory effect for all persons belonging to the categories under the agreement': Constitution of the Italian Republic 1946, Art 39.
[49] The quasi-legislative, regulatory nature of industry wide bargaining of the kind operating in the United Kingdom and other EU member states (where it has not been abandoned) is laid bare in the Posted Workers Directive (Council Directive 96/71/EC) where by Art 3 collective agreements declared universally applicable are given the same legal status as legislation passed by the Parliaments of Member States. Curiously, Hepple nevertheless considered as a solecism the characterisation of this activity as a delegated or devolved State function, notwithstanding the clear evidence of State support which created and sustained it. See B. A. Hepple, 'The Future of Labour Law' (1995) 24 *Industrial Law Journal* 303.

Participation in Government

Beyond emancipation and representation in Parliament and in government, there is also the question of participation in government, with some form of tri-partism being on the agenda at least since 1915. The starting point is the 'Treasury Agreement' of 1915, under the terms of which trade union leaders agreed to relax what would be referred to today as restrictive trade practices in order to support the war effort, said to be one of the first antecedents of the Social Contract considered below.[50] Initiatives of this kind continued after the First World War, and included the National Industrial Conference, whose representatives of capital and labour were in the words of one commentator convinced that their recommendations 'would become law'.[51] The initiative quickly collapsed, however, with some employers reported to be alarmed by the proposals of the National Industrial Conference on rights of union membership, working time and a legal minimum wage.[52]

Although this experiment in the direction of participation in government thus failed to ignite, trade unions continued to be consulted by governments in the post-war period, though it was the Second World War that led to a recognition of the need for 'permanent formal machinery'.[53] These developments continued in the post-war era, being variously described as 'tri-partism', 'bargained corporatism', and 'quasi-corporatism',[54] and were a direct consequence of the post-war policy of full employment and the acceptance of trade unions as legitimate actors in raising wages and improving working conditions. These forms of government were formally tripartite in nature, though given its inauspicious title, the significance of National Joint Advisory Council might easily be overlooked. Nevertheless, as explained by the *Ministry of Labour Handbook*:

> When the war ended it was obvious that regular consultation with the two sides of industry would have an equally important role in peacetime. It was therefore decided, in 1946, that the National Joint Advisory Committee

---

[50] Fox, *History and Heritage*, p. 291.
[51] R. Charles, *The Development of Industrial Relations in Britain 1911–1939* (Hutchinson, 1973), p. 249.
[52] Ibid. On the National Industrial Conference, see also R. Martin, *TUC: The Growth of a Pressure Group 1868–1976* (Oxford University Press, 1980), p. 165.
[53] Ministry of Labour, *Industrial Relations Handbook*, p. 16.
[54] See respectively W. Grant and D. Marsh, *The Confederation of British Industry* (Hodder and Stoughton, 1977); C. Crouch, *The Politics of Industrial Relations* (Fontana, 1979), and S. H. Beer, 'Pressure Groups and Parties in Britain' (1956) 50 *American Political Science Review* 1.

should be reconstituted and each side was invited to send seventeen representatives. It had been evident for some time that, unless special measures could be taken, there was a danger that, with the nationalisation of certain industries, the Council would become unrepresentative of industry as a whole. Accordingly, in 1949, a third side, namely the nationalised industries, was represented. In this form, the Council has held quarterly meetings under the chairmanship of the Minister of Labour and has continued to give consideration to matters affecting employers and workers. The Council has examined and advised upon many important problems in the field of employment and of industrial relations including automation, practices impeding the full and efficient use of manpower, the recruitment and training of young workers in industry, and the establishment of joint consultative machinery in industry.[55]

In addition to procedures such as the foregoing, there were various other forms of trade union participation at the highest levels of government. The TUC was consulted by government on a wide range of issues of interest to trade unions, with deference to the views of the TUC being displayed in Cabinet and elsewhere. Thus it was the TUC that vetoed legislation to make it unlawful to take strike action to disrupt military supplies during the Korean war, and it was the TUC that vetoed the proposal to ban trade unions at GCHQ in the mid-1950s.[56] More significantly, however, we see alternative forms of governance and rule-making on matters of economic management, most notably in the wage work bargain of 1948 by which the TUC agreed a programme of wage restraint with the Attlee government. According to Samuel Beer in a passage which was revealing as much for its insight into the informality of government processes as for their outcome:

> The bargain was not itself embodied in any legislative instrument such as a statute or statutory order. Yet it achieved the regulation of an important aspect of the British economy that no such legislative instrument by itself could have done. Indeed, one may think of it as a kind of extra-governmental legislation.[57]

One of the problems with informal processes of this kind, however, is the problem of compliance, and despite its significance this was a 'bargain' that the TUC had difficulty in maintaining. Unofficial strike action by key groups

---

[55] Ministry of Labour, *Industrial Relations Handbook*, p. 16.
[56] See respectively, K. D. Ewing, J. Mahoney and A. Moretta, 'Civil Liberties and the Korean War' (2018) 81 *Modern Law Review* 395, and K. D. Ewing, J. Mahoney and A. Moretta, *MI5, the Cold War and the Rule of Law* (Oxford University Press, 2020), ch. 12.
[57] S. H. Beer, *Modern British Politics* (Faber and Faber, 1965), p. 205.

of workers unhappy with the restraints imposed led to the ill-judged prosecution of striking gas-workers and the unsuccessful prosecution of dock workers in what was another strike-hit industry.[58] The process was nevertheless repeated under the Social Contract in the 1970s, the description suggesting a greater degree of formality than in the 1940s. The description nevertheless disguises the fact that this too was undertaken without being 'embodied in any legislative instrument such as a statute or statutory order',[59] the Social Contract being announced in the Labour Party election manifesto – *Britain will win with Labour* – in October 1974:

> At the heart of our manifesto and our programme to save the nation lies the Social Contract between the Labour Government and the trade unions, an idea derided by our enemies, but certainly to become widely accepted by those who genuinely believe in government by consent – that is, in the democratic process itself as opposed to the authoritarian and bureaucratic system of wage control imposed by the Heath Government and removed by Labour. The Social Contract is no mere paper agreement approved by politicians and trade unions. It is not concerned solely or even primarily with wages. It covers the whole range of national policies. It is the agreed basis upon which the Labour Party and the trade unions define their common purpose.[60]

As I have explained elsewhere, this was a dynamic 'contract' that led subsequently to agreements on a wide range of social and economic questions, and to legislation that would assist trade unions.[61] It was soon extended to apply to the annual rate of wage growth, with the TUC also closely involved in negotiations over the Budget, setting up what was in effect an autonomous process of government that was denied complete autonomy by the need to govern through Parliament. An example of how this was done is the Remuneration, Charges and Grants Act 1975, one purpose of which was to render unenforceable any term of a contract of employment in breach of the pay policy agreed between the Government and the TUC on wage restraint.[62] Thus, in a complex but legally significant provision the Act provided that

---

[58] Ewing et al., *MI5, the Cold War and the Rule of Law*, pp. 75–76. [59] Ibid.
[60] Labour Party, *Britain Will Win with Labour* (Labour Party, 1974).
[61] See K. D. Ewing, 'The Politics of the British Constitution' [2001] *PL* 405, and Ewing, 'Socialism and the Constitution', on which this section draws.
[62] HC Deb, 22 July 1975, col 51 (Denis Healey, Chancellor of the Exchequer).

> Where an employer limits the remuneration paid to him by any person for any period while this section is in force and the limitation is no greater than necessary to keep the remuneration within the *limits imposed by the policy set out in the document laid before Parliament by command of Her Majesty in July 1975 (Cmnd 6151)* he shall not be liable for breach of contract by reason only that the remuneration is less than would, apart from this section, be payable under any agreement entered into before the commencement of this Act.[63]

We can put to one side for present purposes the fact that this was a curious provision for a trade union organisation representing workers to agree to. This was not the concern of those who challenged the constitutional propriety of these arrangements. The social constitution – or at least this manifestation of it – was seen to undermine two core principles of the liberal constitution, the first being the sovereignty of Parliament and the other being the rule of law, with the Conservative peer Lord Hailsham leading the charge in the House of Lords.[64] According to Hailsham, clearly troubled by the formal and express incorporation of the Command Paper into the 1975 Act:

> What is depriving the workman of his contractual right is a document which is not an Act of Parliament. It has not even had the approval of both Houses of Parliament. It has not gone through three readings. It has never been capable of amendment and it has no legal force at all. I ventured to call this another nail in the coffin of the rule of law, and that is what is.[65]

But it was not government by Command Paper. The legislation embracing the Command Paper was passed by Parliament in the normal way, and it was open to Parliament to amend the Bill as it made its way through both Houses, Labour notably having a bare majority in the Commons and no majority in the Lords. Nevertheless, it was hard to shake off the sense that the role of the TUC in government generally and the Social Contract in particular was in some – albeit inarticulate and unconvincing – way incompatible with the principles of the liberal constitution referred to above, revealing a paradoxical rigidity in the operation of these principles. Hostility was to come significantly also from *The Times* (taken more seriously then under different ownership than it is now), critical of the Budget in 1976 in which the Chancellor of the Exchequer announced income tax cuts on the condition that the TUC agreed to accept wage restraint. According to *The Times*:

---

[63] Remuneration, Charges and Grants Act 1975, s 1. Emphasis added.
[64] HL Deb, 31 July 1975, col 1189 et seq.   [65] Ibid, col 1191.

For the first time the Budget has ceased to be an act of Government, dependent for its authority only on Parliament and has become a matter of negotiation between the Government and an outside body representative of only one section of the community, an important minority, but a minority nevertheless. This constitutional innovation must tend to increase the authority and prestige of the TUC and correspondingly to reduce the authority and prestige of the Government and of the House of Commons . . . [T]here is no country in which the Budget is announced in a conditional form subject to negotiations with the trade unions. It is as though the TUC had by virtue of their power become a second House of Parliament, a second chamber with power and authority the House of Lords has long since lost . . . In the modern world governments governed by armies are common, but governments governed by trade unions are a rarity.[66]

Constitutional Tensions Reinforced

Critiques of the Social Contract from the Right based on constitutional principle barely concealed more fundamental conflicts between the emerging social constitution and the established values of the liberal constitution. The concern was as much with outcomes as it was with process, and in particular the steps taken to underpin trade union and worker power. The legislative benefits for trade unions under the Social Contract were significant, and included a raft of legislation designed to empower trade unions in the workplace, as well as extend freedom from common-law restraint. Paradoxically, the contradiction of the Social Contract was that while the government was to acknowledge by legislation the full legal autonomy and freedom of trade unions, it also sought by agreement to contain the exercise of the power thus conferred.

It is self-evident that unlike post-war continental constitutions, in the British system there were no fundamental social rights to underpin, validate or sustain trade union freedom or the social, economic and political power derived from such freedom. In Dicey's constitution, it was the common law that was the source of liberty.[67] But as we saw in Part II above, trade unions were unlawful at common law as being in restraint of trade, while their activities invited prosecution and thereafter liability in tort on grounds that

---

[66] *The Times*, 7 Apr. 1976.
[67] A. V. Dicey, *Introduction to the Study of the Law of the Constitution* E. C. S. Wade (ed.), 10th ed. (Macmillan, 1959), pp. 202–203.

continued to expand. It was a very partial sort of liberty that the common law protected. Trade unions thus stood in direct conflict with the orthodox economic liberalism of the common law, leading to hostility from the judges, and to the need for statutory protection – a need that survives to this day.

The conflict with economic liberalism was to transition very quickly into a conflict with the liberal constitution, as lawyers took strong exception to what was to become one of the legal foundations of the social constitution, namely the Trade Disputes Act 1906, which as we saw in Part II reversed *Taff Vale* and much else besides. That hostility was on open display in the first case to reached the Court of Appeal following the passing of the 1906 Act. In *Taff Vale*, Sir George Farwell at first instance had justified his decision that trade unions were vicariously liable for the torts of their servants and agents on the ground that trade unions were 'engines with great capacity for evil'.[68] In *Conway* v. *Wade* two years after the 1906 Act was enacted, Lord Justice Farwell reflected that while Parliament cannot make good that which is evil, it can nevertheless make evil non-actionable.[69]

It was not only that the emancipation of trade unions violated the prevailing economic orthodoxy, it also violated the constitutional principles which supported that orthodoxy. Here the key principle was the rule of law, enlisted not to protect liberty but to attack it, the substance of the attack being concealed by an anxiety about legal form.[70] Thus the Trade Disputes Act 1906 did not confer rights on trade unions or their officials, but insulted the judges by conferring what was subsequently portrayed as an immunity from common-law liabilities. The torts survived but did not apply to those for whom they had principally been created. More importantly, the 1906 Act provided by section 4(1) that

> An action against a trade union, whether of workmen or masters or against any members or officials thereof on behalf of themselves and all other members of the trade union in respect of any tortious act alleged to have been committed by or on behalf of the trade union, shall not be entertained by any court.[71]

---

[68] [1901] AC 426, at p. 431.
[69] *Conway* v. *Wade* [1908] 2 KB 844, p. 856. See subsequently [1909] AC 606.
[70] See A. V. Dicey, *Law and Public Opinion in England*, 2nd ed. (Macmillan, 1914). According to Dicey, the Act 'makes a trade union a privileged body exempted from the ordinary law of the land. No such privileged body has ever before been deliberately created by an English [sic] Parliament' (p. xlvi).
[71] Trade Disputes Act 1906, s 4(2) provided that the trustees of a trade union could be sued in prescribed circumstances.

Claims that these provisions conferred an immunity on trade unions were not quite right. But both economic liberals and common lawyers united to condemn them, and with their condemnation the legal foundations of the social constitution.[72] It is indeed very difficult to find any judicial acknowledgement of the legitimacy of trade unions or the trade union role, with Lord Wright's famous war-time dictum in the *Crofter* case being notable as much for its exceptionalism as its content.[73] Much of the twentieth century was thus spent by the courts in labour cases in undermining the trade union power that sustained the social constitution, the courts being invited by plaintiff lawyers controversially to work around the legal protections Parliament had created for trade unions, judicial activism being particularly prominent in the period after the Second World War.

The legislation empowering trade unions and thereby underpinning the architecture of the Social Contract unleashed a ferocious judicial attack, in the wake of new legislation in the 1970s which renewed, refreshed and expanded trade union freedom from common-law liability. That said, the new measures were designed mainly to restore the law to what had been intended in 1906 (which was not without its limitations), and to remove some of the judicial restraints that had been imposed on trade unions by the courts in the 1960s in particular. The legislation was simply a reflection that corporatist arrangements such as the Social Contract were based on the autonomy of countervailing sources of power, which – as we have seen – in some countries would be underpinned by formal constitutional guarantees but which in the United Kingdom had by necessity to be secured by legislation.[74]

---

[72] See especially F. A. Hayek, *The Road to Serfdom* (Routledge, 1944); F. A. Hayek, *The Constitution of Liberty* (University of Chicago Press, 1960); and Hayek, 1980s *Unemployment and the Unions*.

[73] *Crofter Hand Woven Harris Tweed* v. *Veitch* (1942) SC (HL) 1: 'The right of workmen to strike is an essential element in the principle of collective bargaining' (at p. 24).

[74] This was a point made forcefully by Lord Wedderburn, *Employment Rights in Britain and Europe* (Institute of Employment Rights, 1991), ch. 4, a lecture delivered at Durham University in response to what were then heretical views to the contrary in P. Elias and K. D. Ewing, 'Economic Torts and Labour Law: Old Principle and New Liabilities' [1982] 41 *Cambridge Law Journal* 321. As a principle academic architect of the Social Contract, he failed however to explain persuasively why we continued with this model in place of a rights-based model. See Bogg, 'The Hero's Journey', for a penetrating analysis. For an account of contemporary European states where there is formal constitutional protection of labour rights, see K. D. Ewing, 'Social Rights and Constitutional Law' [1999] *Public Law* 104.

The judicial attack on this legislation was led in the Court of Appeal by Lord Denning, who writing extra-judicially expressed concern that empowered by statutory immunity from common-law liability, trade unions presented the 'greatest threat to the rule of law'. He was also to write of his wish that 'we had had some doctrine – authorising the judicial review of statutes when we had the recent spate of cases on the Trade Union Acts of 1974 and 1976'.[75] In the absence of a power of judicial review to undermine trade union freedom and the constitutional arrangements they sustained, the struggle against trade unions had to be fought in the Court of Appeal by using other powers, notably the power of statutory interpretation to read down the scope of the protection, in a series of controversial decisions that were often contrived and generally inconsistent with the clear intention of Parliament.

In the end, Lord Denning's vision of the rule of law had to give way to an even more fundamental constitutional principle, the Court of Appeal's continuing reluctance to give effect to the wishes of Parliament being trumped by parliamentary sovereignty. Lord Denning's persistent failure to apply the legislation earned the following rebuke from Lord Diplock in one of several successful appeals:

> Where the meaning of the statutory words is plain and unambiguous it is not for the judges to invent fancied ambiguities as an excuse for failing to give effect to its plain meaning because they themselves consider that the consequences of doing so would be inexpedient, or even unjust or immoral. In controversial matters such as are involved in industrial relations there is room for differences of opinion as to what is expedient, what is just and what is morally justifiable. Under our constitution it is Parliament's opinion on these matters that is paramount . . .[76]

This, however, was not an endorsement for the Labour government's legislation of 1974–1976 extending trade union freedom. Lord Diplock was also to say that the legislation in question 'was intrinsically repugnant to anyone who has spent his life in the practice of the law or the administration of justice'.[77] By this stage the Social Contract was in tatters, a new Conservative government preparing to butcher its legacy.

---

[75] Lord Denning, *What Next in the Law* (Butterworths, 1982), p. 321.
[76] *Duport Steels Ltd* v. *Sirs* [1980] 1 WLR 142.
[77] *Express Newspapers Ltd* v. *McShane* [1980] ICR 43, at p. 57.

From Social Contract to Social Dialogue

The election of the Conservative government in 1979 put an end to what *The Times* had referred to in its attack on the Social Contract as the 'corporate constitution'. There was little prospect of the Thatcher regime adopting such practices, despite the willingness of previous Conservative governments to embrace both formal and informal corporatist arrangements. These included the National Economic Development Council which had been set up in 1962,[78] a tripartite body of contestable effect which was wound up by Norman Lamont as Chancellor of the Exchequer in 1992, as 'the last vestiges of tripartite economic management'.[79] The policy of government was not to collaborate with organised labour but to undermine it, by dismantling not only the architecture of the social constitution, but also the economic policy and legal regime by which it was underpinned. There was no *need* for such arrangements in the years after 1979.

Nor was there any *desire* on the part of governments – whether Conservative or Labour – to embrace such arrangements. It is true that Labour held office between 1997 and 2010; but New Labour was an ideologically different beast from the Labour Party of the 1970s. So although close to trade unions which had easy access to government, New Labour struggled to find the unions a formal governmental role,[80] and generally failed to avoid disappointing its trade union friends on questions of policy. It could not ever be said that Britain was 'governed by the trade unions' under New Labour – of either the Blair or Brown variety. The trade union role was one of electoral mobilisation, and they had to make do with a diluted role within the policy-making machinery within the Party following important constitutional reforms during the Blair years in particular.[81]

There was thus no representation in government (through the restoration of the Ministry of Labour or equivalent), and no participation in government, except on an informal ad hoc basis. To which there was one important caveat arising as a result of membership of the EU and the decision of the Blair government to accept the Social Protocol to the EC Treaty concluded at Maastricht in 1992.[82] This was a procedure whereby eleven of the then

---

[78] For a constitutional analysis of the role of the NEDC, see Grant and March, *Confederation of British Industry*, ch. 7.
[79] J. Major, *The Autobiography* (Harper Collins, 1999), p. 667.
[80] See Ewing, 'The Function of Trade Unions'. [81] Minkin, *The Blair Supremacy*.
[82] Though the caveat may be more important for its method than its outcomes.

twelve Member States were authorised to use the procedures of the EC to develop the social agenda set out in the Charter of the Fundamental Rights of Workers concluded in 1989, from which the United Kingdom initially opted out. When, however, the opt-out was revoked in 1997, the United Kingdom became part of a process which led to the making of social rights, but also a process whereby such rights could be created by Social Dialogue.

These arrangements are now to be found in the Treaty on the Functioning of the European Union (TFEU), which in Part X confers a limited power on the EU institutions in relation to social rights, a power diminished by the requirement that its exercise requires the unanimity of the Council in relation to multiple (though admittedly not all) important questions. Part X also includes the Social Dialogue procedure, reinforcing the sense that a social constitution is as much about procedures as it is about substantive outcomes. Social Dialogue is different from the participatory forms outlined above, though it does invite reflections on the *The Times*' criticism of the Social Contract as having created a functionally new parliamentary chamber. Nevertheless, the Social Contract was about participation in executive government, whereas Social Dialogue also carries with it a direct legislative role for trade unions, albeit within a carefully confined area.

The legislative nature of Social Dialogue is thus different from the quasi-legislative role of industry-wide collective bargaining described in Part IV above, not least because it leads to outcomes that have the same legal effects as legislation made by traditional parliamentary procedures. Thus, TFEU, Article 154 imposes a duty on the Commission to consult 'management and labour at Union level', and to 'take any relevant measure to facilitate their dialogue by ensuring balanced support for the parties'. To this end, the Commission must consult the social partners about the future development of social policy, as well as on proposals for any particular legislative initiative. In either case the social partners may inform the Commission that they would like to take ownership of the question and seek to conclude an agreement in relation to its subject matter.

Thereafter, the treaty provides that Social Dialogue agreements may be implemented 'at the joint request of the signatory parties, by a Council decision on a proposal from the Commission'.[83] Despite the fact that the European Parliament has no formal role in this process other than to be 'informed',[84] Social Dialogue agreements typically have been implemented in the form of Directives. Thereafter it is possible under EU law for the

---

[83] TFEU, Art 155(2).   [84] Ibid.

Directives to be implemented at national level by collective agreement between management and labour, thereby maintaining the role of the social partners in a legislative process wholly autonomous at all levels from traditional parliamentary procedures.[85] The rapid decline of collective bargaining procedures in the United Kingdom since 1979, however, means that the latter was not an option for the United Kingdom.

As a result, Directives giving effect to Social Dialogue agreements had of necessity to be implemented in the United Kingdom by statutory instrument, in the same way as a Directive channelled through the typical law-making procedures. In this way, Parliament was required to implement Directives created by agreements between management and labour rather than by European parliamentary institutions. Yet despite the constitutional criticisms of the Social Contract referred to above, Social Dialogue as a legislative procedure attracted very little – if any – criticism on constitutional grounds in the United Kingdom. This is curious: if the Social Contract strained liberal constitutional procedures, so too does Social Dialogue, strains laid bare in litigation challenging the first agreement under the Social Dialogue procedures, on the question of rights of workers to parental leave.

The latter agreement was made between the European Trade Union Confederation representing workers on one side, and two organisations representing European employers on the other. In a direct challenge to the agreement and the procedures by which it was made, another organisation – one representing small employers in Europe – complained before the Court of First Instance that it had been excluded from the process, and that the views of its members had not been properly represented.[86] In a remarkable decision, however, the Court provided judicial benediction to the process of legislation by Social Dialogue on the ground that

> the principle of democracy on which the Union is founded requires – in the absence of the participation of the European Parliament in the legislative process – that the participation of the people be otherwise secured, in this instance through the parties representative of management and labour.[87]

---

[85] The first Social Dialogue Agreement (on parental leave) provided that 'Member States shall adopt the laws, regulations and administrative provisions necessary to comply with the Council decision within a period of two years from its adoption *or shall ensure that management and labour introduce the necessary measures by way of agreement by the end of this period*' (italics added): Council Directive 96/34/EC of 3 June 1996.

[86] *Case T-55/98, European Association of Craft, Small and Medium Sized Enterprises (UEAPME) v. Council* [1998] ECR II – 2335.

[87] Ibid, para 89. See B. Bercusson, 'Democratic Legitimacy and European Labour Law' (1999) 28 *Industrial Law Journal* 153.

This is in sharp contrast to the constitutional experience of the United Kingdom under the Social Contract.[88] Although the United Kingdom is no longer a member of the EU, the legacy of this form of rule-making nevertheless remains part of British law, at least for the time being.[89] As for Social Dialogue, it has been the victim of the death of Social Europe following the economic crisis in 2008, though there are now attempts to revive it.

Conclusion

The United Kingdom's experiment with social constitutionalism is over, at least for the time being. Although the Labour Party survives, its trade union base has been greatly diminished with the decline in trade union membership. The Ministry of Labour/Department of Employment no longer exist, their functions transferred to other Whitehall departments, now the Department for Work and Pensions, and the Department for Business, Energy and Industrial Strategy. While trade unions may continue to be consulted by government departments, there is no question of them having the type of role that they enjoyed in the 1970s, the importance of organised labour reflected not only in grand schemes such as the Social Contract, but also in small gestures such as the conferring of Privy Council status on the General Secretary of the TUC.

One reason for the eclipse is that what has been referred to as the social constitution was no longer needed, in the sense that the social constitution was to large extent the consequence of economic power: that is to say the post-war economic policy that empowered organised labour, which had to be accommodated and contained. The general election in 1979 led to an express repudiation of that post-war economic policy in favour of an

---

[88] Notably, the issue was not whether law-making by management and labour was a legitimate process for making law of universal application, but whether the organisations of management and labour were sufficiently representative. Concerned in this case with the representativity of the management side, the CFI took the view that the organisations involved were well placed to represent the views of all employers. UEAPME were nevertheless involved in the negotiations for the revised Agreement and Directive. However, there are more serious questions of legitimacy on the workers' side, concerns reinforced by declining levels of trade union membership.

[89] European Union (Withdrawal) Act 2018, ss 2–7. See now EU–UK Trade and Co-operation Agreement, Art 399(7): 'Each Party shall protect and promote social dialogue on labour matters among workers and employers, and their respective organisations, and with relevant government authorities.'

approach that emphasised the free functioning of markets and the removal of barriers to their unobstructed operation. Along with major industrial restructuring, this anticipated a much different role for trade unions which lost many of their regulatory functions in favour of a more limited representative role.[90] Within the redefined role for trade unions, the Thatcher governments found more coercive means of containment.

While it is true that elements of social constitutionalism continued to be deployed in the EU and thus to affect the United Kingdom indirectly, the paradox of more recent years has been that the attention of the 'social' in the constitution (and with it the attention of constitutional lawyers with sufficient interest) has moved from representation and participation to rights.[91] Although social rights may be more tangible and more visible, this nevertheless represents a significant regression. Indeed, to the extent that social rights are now relied on by organised labour as shields against political attack from hostile governments, they are a symptom of the weakness of trade unions which in the 1970s had been said improperly to have been given an exaggerated constitutional role. Rarely can constitutional actors have been so radically and so quickly disempowered or disenfranchised.

The emerging recognition of labour rights as human rights has yet to translate into labour power in a way that would encourage governments to adapt economic policy and/or constitutional structures. It is true that there has been a radical transformation of the jurisprudence of the ECtHR in the sense that it has been read dramatically to include a suite of labour rights, including the right to organise, the right to bargain, and the right to strike.[92] But for reasons about which we can only speculate,[93] the same court has resolutely refused in recent years to apply this jurisprudence to the United Kingdom, despite many invitations to do so.[94] And in view of the foregoing, we ought not to be surprised that the domestic courts have refused to allow

---

[90] This reflected strongly the theorising of economists such as Hayek, for whom the then Prime Minister openly expressed her admiration. On Hayek and the role of trade unions, see Hayek, *The Constitution of Liberty*, and subsequently Hayek, *1980s Unemployment and the Unions*, pp. 39–64.
[91] A notable exposition of social rights analysis is Jeff King, *Judging Social Rights* (Cambridge University Press, 2012).
[92] See especially *Demir and Baycara* v. *Turkey* [2008] ECHR 1345.
[93] See K. D. Ewing and J. Hendy, 'Article 11(3) of the European Convention on Human Rights' [2017] EHRLR 356.
[94] See especially *RMT* v. *United Kingdom* [2014] ECHR 366.

the Human Rights Act 1998 to be a Trojan horse to transform what has been hitherto the economic liberalism of the common law.[95]

Other indications that the social rights revolution has failed to protect core trade union freedoms is to be seen in EU law, where in the *Viking* case the European Court of Justice gave priority to the economic freedoms of business over the fundamental rights of labour, which would prevail only in very exceptional circumstances.[96] The conflicts between capital and labour contested in the trenches of the common law in the late nineteenth century, were now being contested on the much more elevated plain of the TFEU over one hundred years and several revolutions later.[97] But the result was the same. And although the EU Charter of Fundamental Rights has since been given full legal status and although that Charter includes labour rights, the subordination of labour rights to corporate freedoms has been – inadvertently or otherwise – tailored into the text.[98]

If social constitutionalism is to be restored, it will require an epochal shift in the direction of social democracy and social justice, and the political economy necessary to sustain both. While lawyers may seek to encourage social rights advocacy, social rights are a consequence not the cause of social democracy or social justice. Social constitutionalism is thus to be celebrated for its processes and structures: for its emancipation and representation of citizens as workers and their participation (through their representatives) in the decisions at all levels that affect their lives. Social constitutionalism is to be celebrated also for having contributed in the 1970s to the creation of what social epidemiologists tell us was the decade of lowest income inequality in the United Kingdom,[99] a decade which others may choose to remember for other reasons.

---

[95] The best we have been able to manage is a recognition that some basic assumptions in favour of common-law liability and against statutory protection now need to be revised: see *RMT* v. *Serco Ltd and ASLEF* v. *London & Birmingham Railway* [2011] EWCA Civ 226. But there has been no engagement yet with the argument that the Human Rights Act 1998 provides a new and wider basis of protection from common-law liability than the Trade Union and Labour Relations (Consolidation) Act 1992. See K. D. Ewing and J. Hendy, *Days of Action: The Legality of Protest Strikes against Government Cuts* (Institute of Employment Rights, 2011).

[96] Case C-438/05, *International Transport Workers* v. *Viking Line ABP* [2007] ECR I-10779.

[97] The parallel between *Taff Vale*, above, and *Viking Line*, above, is striking, in both senses of the term.

[98] See for example, EUCFR, Art 28 – right to collective action 'in accordance with Union law'. This would include the jurisprudence giving priority to the economic freedoms in the TFEU.

[99] R. Wilkinson and K. Pickett, *The Spirit Level: Why More Equal Societies Almost Always Do Better* (Penguin, 2010).

8

The Constitution of Rights

PETER CANE

The year 2015 witnessed celebrations around the world of an event that took place 800 years earlier in a meadow west of the city of London near what is now Heathrow Airport. Then, the main participants were King John on the one side, and leading barons and prelates on the other. They had gathered to sign up formally to a document (which came to be known as Magna Carta) with the aim of forestalling violent rebellion against the monarchy. Eight centuries later, four provisions of the 1297 re-issue of Magna Carta still decorate the United Kingdom's statute book even though the document was not a 'statute' (or, for that matter, a 'law') in the modern sense and the surviving provisions are of no practical significance. It is remarkable that such a document still stands as a sort of proto-typical declaration of rights at a time when dominant cultural understandings of 'human rights' in the UK revolve around the European Convention on Human Rights and the Human Rights Act 1998 (HRA). This chapter aims to tell a story of the journey from Magna Carta to the HRA and beyond.

The story is about an idea, the language(s) in which it has been expressed, the documents in which it has been embodied, and the political and legal uses to which it has been put, in various places, at various times, and by diverse groups and individuals.[1] It focuses on the rhetoric rather than the actuality of rights, on their recognition rather than their realisation. Rhetorically, constitutional rights may generically be understood as claims (always political and sometimes legal) made by the governed on the governors; but the content and foundations of such claims are moulded by circumstances of time and place. As ideas change about the nature, make-up and functions of political communities, so do claims, in the name of rights, for inclusion within, and good governance of, the community.

---

[1] Many thanks to H. Kumarasingham for perceptive and constructive comments on an earlier draft.

The first part of the chapter is concerned with Magna Carta and its 'reinvention', twice, over a period of more than 500 years. The second section discusses the development of a new approach to constitutional rights in the wake of the Glorious Revolution of 1688. Third, the chapter surveys developments in the twentieth century culminating in the enactment of the Human Rights Act in 1998. The conclusion draws threads together in a discussion of continuities and discontinuities in understandings of rights.

Magna Carta

The First Three Centuries

Even though Magna Carta still inspires some, it is, to all intents and purposes, a spent political and legal force. Nevertheless, in the Anglophone historical tradition, Magna Carta is the documentary *fons et origo* of constitutional protection of rights. For this reason, alone, its story must be told.

Magna Carta presents itself as a sort of settlement agreement or peace treaty between disputing parties – on the one side, King John and, on the other, church leaders and a group of the most wealthy and powerful of the King's subjects. Apparently, the agreement was primarily designed to reassert and re-establish norms and practices from which (by his own admission) the King had departed, and obligations that he had failed to fulfil. However, there may have been an element of real novelty in some of its provisions. Notably, the Charter created an enforcement mechanism (never used) to underwrite the king's compliance (Chapter 61 of the 1215 version).

Magna Carta 1215 was formally addressed to 'free men of our kingdom', and some of its specific provisions are expressed to be for the benefit of 'all free men' or, even, 'all men'.[2] Most famously, chapter 39 (of 1215) undertook that 'no freeman shall be seized or imprisoned, or stripped of his rights or possessions, or outlawed or exiled, or deprived of his standing in any way, nor will we proceed with force against him, or send others to do so, except by the lawful judgement of his equals or by the law of the land'. In chapter 40, the king promised that 'to no one will we sell, to no one deny or delay right or justice'.[3] Other provisions were more limited in scope. For instance, chapter 8 concerned 'widows', chapter 29 'knights', and chapter 40 'merchants'. In some

---

[2] I have used the British Library translation reproduced in R. Hazell and J. Melton, *Magna Carta and Its Modern Legacy* (Cambridge: Cambridge University Press, 2105), 233–242.
[3] Chapters 39 and 40 of the 1215 version were amalgamated into chapter 29 of the 1225 and all subsequent versions.

provisions, the king undertook obligations (such as not to 'seize any land or rent in payment of a debt, so long as the debtor has movable goods sufficient to discharge the debt' (chapter 9)) without explicit reference to their beneficiaries.

As for its content, Magna Carta addresses a large and miscellaneous collection of grievances, great and small. Chapter 1, for instance, guaranteed the 'rights and liberties' of the English Church and freedom from royal interference with its elections. A significant number of chapters addressed the property-based relationship between the monarch, and the earls and barons who held land directly from the king as tenants-in-chief. Another group of provisions concerned the administration of royal justice. For instance, chapter 17 provided that 'ordinary lawsuits shall not follow the Royal Court around, but shall be held in a fixed place'. This clause witnesses increasing demand for easy access to royal (as opposed to local) courts.

Although Pope Innocent III, whose overlordship King John had acknowledged in 1213 in return for aid against France, initially encouraged the King to accede to the rebels' demands, he annulled the charter only about two months after it was issued.[4] Following the King's unexpected death in 1216, a version of the charter was issued on behalf of the nine-year-old Henry III in an attempt to secure his position on the throne. A significant number of provisions of the 1215 charter were omitted from the 1216 version and subsequent versions. Notably, they included the enforcement provision (chapter 61 of the 1215 charter) and two chapters (12 and 14 of 1215) requiring (in modern terms) consent to taxation. Another version was issued in 1217 and this was reconfirmed by Henry III in 1225. The 1225 version was thereafter treated as definitive, being reissued and reconfirmed many times in the thirteenth and fourteenth centuries. The charter was also widely distributed, read and publicised throughout the realm. When the charter was reconfirmed by Edward I in 1297, it was officially enrolled in Chancery and has since been treated as the first English 'statute'. Whereas the 1215, 1216 and 1217 versions had been issued in attempts to forestall violent rebellion, subsequent re-confirmations were typically made in return for grants of taxation by Parliament. As Parliament became more representative and assumed a stronger institutional identity, it took the place of the barons and prelates as the champion of royal restraint. The charter played a significant symbolic role in this process.

---

[4] R. Helmholz, 'Pope Innocent III and the Annulment of Magna Carta' (2018) 69 *Journal of Ecclesiastical History* 1.

Magna Carta Revived

According to Sir Ivor Jennings, '[t]he last known confirmation was in 1416'.[5] By this time, many of Magna Carta's provisions were no longer of significant contemporary relevance. Indeed, already '[i]n the fourteenth century, chapter 29[6] was ... coming to be seen as the most important of the provisions in Magna Carta'.[7] A statute of 1354 extended the scope of chapter 29 from 'no free man' to 'no man of whatever estate or condition may be' and introduced the phrase 'due process' to describe the standard against which exercises of power were to be judged.[8] However, Magna Carta figured primarily in political debates and made very few appearances in strictly legal contexts. Moreover, '[n]o-one thought of it as a bill of rights in the seventeenth-century sense, let alone as a constitution for England or a charter of human rights.'[9] It was more about asserting and re-asserting standards of good and faithful kingship against the monarch.

Ironically, then, revival of interest in chapter 29 of Magna Carta and, indeed, the creation of the constitutional 'myth' around the charter, which persists to this day, is largely attributable to lawyers.[10] The political context was the growing strength of the monarchy during the Tudor period. One manifestation of this new royal assertiveness was increasing exercise of the prerogative power to arrest and detain individuals 'for reasons of state', without charge and without trial. In an application for a writ of habeas corpus in 1572 the judge 'explicitly linked the writ to chapter 29 of Magna Carta'.[11] Since the early part of the thirteenth century (even before 1215), the writ of habeas corpus had been used in support of judicial process, to get people into court.[12] By the fourteenth century, it was also being used by the common-law judges[13] to force transfer to their courts of cases started in other

---

[5] I. Jennings, *Magna Carta and Its Influence in the World Today* (London: Central Office of Information, 1965), 11.
[6] See Hazell and Melton, *Magna Carta and Its Modern Legacy*.
[7] J. Baker, *The Reinvention of Magna Carta 1216–1616* (Cambridge: Cambridge University Press, 2017), 40.
[8] R. V. Turner, *Magna Carta: Through the Ages* (London: Routledge, 2003), 123.
[9] Baker, *Reinvention of Magna Carta*, 86.
[10] J. Baker, 'Magna Carta: The Emergence of the Myth' in C. Macmillan and C. Smith (eds.), *Challenges to Authority and the Recognition of Rights: From Magna Carta to Modernity* (Cambridge: Cambridge University Press, 2018).
[11] Baker, *Reinvention of Magna Carta*, 26.
[12] J. Farbey and R. J. Sharpe, *The Law of Habeas Corpus*, 3rd ed. (Oxford: Oxford University Press, 2011), 2.
[13] This term refers to the justices of the royal courts of Common Pleas, King's Bench and Exchequer.

courts – local courts for instance, and (in the sixteenth century) conciliar jurisdictions such as Star Chamber[14] and High Commission.[15] In this context, 'due process' and 'the law of the land' came to be associated with procedure in the common-law courts, including jury trial, in contrast to the less formal and resource-intensive procedures adopted by most other courts and the practice, in the Court of High Commission in particular, of compulsorily exposing litigants to the risk of self-incrimination.[16] The association of habeas corpus with Magna Carta suggested that the writ might be used not to move people around the justice system but to protect their freedom of movement.

At around the same time, other well-established writs, such as prohibition and mandamus (respectively prohibiting and requiring action), were being adapted by King's Bench as mechanisms for judicial review of conduct of executive and administrative bodies. In 1616 a lawyer, Francis Ashley, attributed all this to Magna Carta.[17] Ashley's claim reflects a process in which interpretations of chapter 29 became increasingly broad. In a treatise written in 1604, Sir Edward Coke, then Attorney General to James I, said of chapter 29 that,

> Everything that anyone has in this world, or that concerns the freedom and liberty of his body or his freehold, or the benefit of the law to which he is inheritable, or his native country in which he was born, or the preservation of his reputation goods, or his life, blood and posterity – to all these things this act extends.[18]

Despite the increasingly broad scope attributed to Magna Carta, freedom of movement and personal liberty were the practical foci of attention. On the other hand, because detention was such a widely used tool of power, habeas corpus might indirectly protect other interests, such as freedom of speech and freedom from torture. Economic freedom was implicated in the power given to holders of royal monopolies to imprison those who infringed their privileges.[19] Even so, the various writs – prohibition, mandamus, habeas

---

[14] Baker, *Reinvention of Magna Carta*, 402–406.
[15] J. Baker, 'Magna Carta and Personal Liberty' in R. Griffith-Jones and M. Hill (eds.), *Magna Carta, Religion and the Rule of Law* (Cambridge: Cambridge University Press, 2015).
[16] Baker, *Reinvention of Magna Carta*, 289–298. High Commission was established to enforce religious uniformity on Catholics and Protestant non-conformists. Henry VIII's assumption of the headship of the English Church coupled with the English Reformation effectively stripped chapter 1 of Magna Carta of any potential as a foundation for protecting religious freedom.
[17] Baker, *Reinvention of Magna Carta*, 35. [18] Quoted in Ibid, 34. [19] Ibid, 311–323.

corpus and so on – were understood not in terms of protecting rights but, in the name of the monarch, as controlling the use of power.[20] In this period, the conceptual foundation of chapter 29 of Magna Carta and the prerogative writs was – in modern terms – 'the rule of law', not 'rights'.

Of course, this begs the question of what 'law' means. In particular, it leaves open the choice (and productive tension) between 'customary', 'voluntarist' and 'positivist' images of law based on exercises of human authority and consent, on the one hand, and 'moralistic', 'natural/divine law' images grounded in practice-independent ideas of right and wrong, on the other.[21] Is law a purely political phenomenon or is it rooted in something more enduring and less contestable? Coke's conservative historicism was predominantly positivist whereas radicals were, unsurprisingly, more attracted to ideas of 'natural rights'. Coke was content to derive the powers of the ruler and the 'liberties' of the ruled from the same source – the customary common law.[22] Radicals (such as Richard Overton),[23] on the other hand, thought more asymmetrically: 'nature' conferred rights on individuals while rulers, far from possessing anything like 'Divine right', were merely delegates of the people for the time being.

Magna Carta had originally been the product of internecine struggles between factions within a small political elite.[24] In modern terms, the legal form of the settlement was contract; and other social groups were third-party beneficiaries of the agreement. Similarly, chapter 29 of the Charter was reinvented in the seventeenth century amidst conflict between elite factions: the monarchy (which had effectively absorbed the church), the House of Commons (which was, itself, sometimes in conflict with the House of Lords) and (a few of) the common-law judges. The context had shifted from ideas of reciprocal agreement to claims about the allocation of governmental power. Members of what we would now call 'civil society' figured as subjects of power. Appeals to Magna Carta enabled elite power-holders to claim that they were acting in the interests of power's subjects.

---

[20] Regarding habeas corpus, see P. D. Halliday, *Habeas Corpus: From England to Empire* (Cambridge, MA: Belknap Press, 2010), ch. 1.

[21] Regarding the fifteenth century, see, e.g. N. Doe, *Fundamental Authority in Late Medieval English Law* (Cambridge: Cambridge University Press, 1990).

[22] D. C. Smith, *Sir Edward Coke and the Reformation of the Laws: Religion, Politics and Jurisprudence, 1578–1636* (Cambridge: Cambridge University Press, 2014).

[23] J. Witte Jr, 'Towards a New Magna Carta for Early Modern England' in Griffith-Jones and Hill (eds.), *Magna Carta, Religion and the Rule of Law*, 115–116.

[24] For a contrary view see, e.g., D. Carpenter, 'Magna Carta 1215: Its Social and Political Context' in C. Breay and J. Harrison (eds.), *Magna Carta: Law, Liberty, Legacy* (London: The British Library, 2013), 21–22.

Magna Carta and the Petition of Right

The association between chapter 29 of Magna Carta and habeas corpus played a central role in the cause celebre of *Darnel's Case* in 1627, in the arguments on behalf of five knights imprisoned by Charles I for refusal to satisfy a royal demand for a compulsory loan. The judges decided in the king's favour; but in the face of increasing Parliamentary unrest and opposition, Charles agreed to reconfirm Magna Carta,[25] although without the addition of various clauses requested by Parliament. Dissatisfied with this offer, in 1628 Parliament presented Charles with a petition 'concerning divers Rights and Liberties of the Subjects'. The Petition of Right addressed three main grievances: prerogative taxation without the consent of Parliament; the use of martial law, in disregard of the common law, to condemn or exonerate alleged offenders; and imprisonment without cause shown.

Regarding taxation, although monarchs were chronically short of money, in the early seventeenth century, for various reasons, the financial situation of the monarchy became particularly dire. Parliament's parsimony was based partly on the fact that once supply was granted, it could exercise little or no control over the way the money was spent. Refusal of supply was often motivated by disagreements over foreign and religious policy.[26] The concerns about martial law perhaps reflect the wider campaign of the leading proponent of the Petition of Right, Sir Edward Coke, to establish a monopoly for the common-law courts in the provision of 'justice'.

In relation to unexplained imprisonment, the Petition recites chapter 29 of Magna Carta, although it does not explicitly mention habeas corpus. The Petition's concern was to control the use by the government, for political purposes, of prerogative powers of detention. Ironically, each of the Houses also claimed a 'privilege' of 'committal' into custody to protect its dignity and authority, and its 'debates and proceedings'. As Parliament's (and particularly the Commons') strength and confidence increased in the course of the seventeenth century, so did its willingness to detain opponents for alleged breaches of 'the law of Parliament' (as opposed to 'the law of the land'). The Habeas Corpus Act of 1679, which aimed to reform various aspects of the writ's operation in favour of applicants, applied only to imprisonment for

---

[25] According to George Garnett, no king since Henry V in 1422 had 'proposed defusing opposition in this way': G. Garnett, 'Sir Edward Coke's Resurrection of Magna Carta' in L. Goldman (ed.), *Magna Carta: History, Context and Influence* (London: University of London Press, 2018), 51, 57.

[26] J. P. Kenyon, *The Stuart Constitution 1603–1688: Documents and Commentary* (Cambridge: Cambridge University Press, 1966), 89.

felony or treason and, so, did not regulate imprisonment for 'contempt of Parliament', which remained a matter for the common law. As it had been since the sixteenth century, arrest without cause shown remained a political and legal battle ground in the eighteenth century, except that now the aggressor was as likely to be Parliament as the government. The constitutional upheavals of the seventeenth century established the principle that the monarch enjoyed only such prerogatives as the courts (and Parliament) were prepared to recognise.[27] That the same principle applied to the privileges of Parliament was not firmly established until the nineteenth century.[28] The House of Lords last exercised the power of committal in the early nineteenth century, and the House of Commons in 1880.[29]

By the end of the nineteenth century, A. V. Dicey could confidently announce that 'When we say that ... the rule of law is a characteristic of the English constitution ... [w]e mean, in the first place, that no man is punishable or can be lawfully made to suffer in body or goods except for a distinct breach of law established in the ordinary legal manner before the ordinary courts of the land.'[30] In other words, Dicey considered non-punitive, preventive detention by the executive (or Parliament) to be contrary to the common law. Of course, statutes are part of the law and, to the extent that the executive controls the legislative process, it has the means to free itself of the common-law constraints of habeas corpus by giving itself statutory power to detain and imprison 'for reasons of state'. In twenty-first-century Britain, immigration control and anti-terrorism measures are two sites of continuing contestation about the use of statutory detention for non-punitive purposes. Even more recently, measures to control the Covid-19 pandemic have raised concerns about pre-emptive constraints on personal liberty and freedom of movement.

---

[27] Recognised as landmarks are *The Case of Prohibitions* (1607) and *The Case of Proclamations* (1610). Neither involved a litigated dispute but rather a rendering of advice in conference by Sir Edward Coke, then Chief Justice of the Court of Common Pleas, at the request of the monarch. Such activity led to his dismissal from Common Pleas and his appointment as Chief Justice of the Court of King's Bench, in which capacity he continued his campaign against royal overreach, leading to his dismissal from the bench in 1616. Coke promoted the Petition of Right in his capacity as a member of the House of Commons.

[28] E. N. Williams, *The Eighteenth-Century Constitution 1688–1815: Documents and Commentary* (Cambridge: Cambridge University Press, 1960), 386; Joint Parliamentary Committee on Parliamentary Privilege, *First Report*, 1999, paras 23–26 (https://publications.parliament.uk/pa/jt199899/jtselect/jtpriv/43/4305.htm).

[29] Joint Parliamentary Committee on Parliamentary Privilege, para 22. See also C. Wittke, *The History of English Parliamentary Privilege* (Columbus: Ohio State University, 1921).

[30] A. V. Dicey, *The Law of the Constitution* (J. W. F Allison ed.) (Oxford: Oxford University Press, 2013), 97.

The Constitution of Rights

Magna Carta and the Bill of Rights

Magna Carta was 'granted' in 1215 (and reissued in 1216 and 1217) to forestall violent rebellion. Thereafter, it was frequently re-confirmed in return for Parliamentary grants of supply; and Charles I accepted the Petition of Right for similar reasons. Not until 1642 did negotiation give way to civil war. Despite the Restoration in 1660, the Interregnum fundamentally altered the political dynamics of the kingdom. In 1689, the Bill of Rights was enacted, with the assent of William and Mary, not to head off a rebellion or in return for grants of supply but, in part at least, as the price for the very Crown itself. This was a political transaction. Support for natural law theories of kingship lingered in some quarters but evaporated by the middle of the eighteenth century. Parliament's new-found dominance was not rooted in natural law or natural rights but in changing social and economic realities. Sovereignty no longer belonged to the monarch; but neither had it moved to the people. It remained with the rich and powerful, even as the make-up of the elite was changing.

This is reflected in the main provisions of the Bill of Rights. Amongst other things, it declares illegal: the 'pretended' royal power to suspend or dispense with laws; ecclesiastical courts created by the Crown; and, without Parliamentary consent, levying taxation, and raising and keeping a standing army in peacetime. Elections of members of Parliament are to be 'free'; Parliaments are to be held 'frequently'; and 'freedom of speech and debates or proceedings in Parliament' are 'not to be impeached or questioned in any court or place outside Parliament'. Most of the provisions of the Bill of Rights that directly benefited individuals concerned the criminal process and were directed, for instance, at corrupt jury selection, circumvention of habeas corpus by requiring excessive bail, outsized fines and 'cruel and unusual punishment'.

The Second Revival of Magna Carta

Perhaps surprisingly, the shift in power from the monarchy to Parliament, especially in the 150 years after the Glorious Revolution, did not dull the appeal of Magna Carta, which was reinvented a second time as a result of its adoption by myriad radical proponents of democratic, libertarian, egalitarian and populist ideas beginning with the Levellers (especially John Lilburne) in the late 1640s,[31] and including John Wilkes and followers in the 1760s, the

---

[31] See, e.g., A. Pallister, *Magna Carta: The Heritage of Liberty* (Oxford: Oxford University Press, 1971), 14–25; R. Foxley, '"More Precious in Your Esteem than It Deserveth": Magna Carta and Seventeenth-Century Politics' in Goldman (ed.), *Magna Carta: History, Context and Influence*.

Chartists in the 1830s and 1840s, and the suffragettes in the early twentieth century. The core issue for these groups was not the division of the spoils amongst those seated at the table but the much more basic question of who could take a seat and who would have to be satisfied with fallen crumbs. In this context, in the seventeenth century, political philosophers such as John Locke and Thomas Hobbes invented the idea of the 'social contract' to replace the more individualised notions of reciprocal agreement that apparently underpinned the Charter, thus laying (as we will see later) the foundation for subsequent conceptions of rights. The apotheosis of the Charter's second reinvention was, perhaps, the presentation of the Great Reform Act 1832 as a new Magna Carta.[32] Even the gradual repeal of most of its provisions over the course of the nineteenth and twentieth centuries did not kill the Charter. What started out as a detailed response to specific grievances about excesses of royal governance and denial of 'liberties' previously granted, ended up as a non-specific rallying point for political radicals of many stripes and, even, a tourist attraction.[33]

The Creation of a Constitutional Theory of Rights: Blackstone and Dicey

The Revolution Settlement of 1688, and the political and governmental changes that followed, created a new environment for thinking about ideas of rights and liberties. William Blackstone's approach to Magna Carta was legal and historical (or, as is often said, 'antiquarian'),[34] not political or radical. In 1759 he published the first critical edition of Magna Carta, consisting of fourteen charters from the reigns of John, Henry III and Edward I, and a long editorial introduction. In his *Commentaries on the Laws of England* (1765), which is littered with references to Magna Carta,[35] Blackstone represented it as a significant milestone along the road from the Conquest (by which the Normans crushed the 'rights and liberties' enjoyed by the English before the Conquest) to the state of near-perfect liberty that he saw re-established

---

[32] A. Lock and J. Champion, 'Radicalism and Reform' in Breay and J. Harrison (eds.), *Magna Carta: Law, Liberty, Legacy*, 165. See also A. Lock, 'Reform, Radicalism and Revolution: Magna Carta in Eighteenth- and Nineteenth-Century Britain' in Goldman (ed.), *Magna Carta: History, Context and Influence*, 114.
[33] L. Colley, *The Gun, the Ship and the Pen: Warfare, Constitutions and the Making of the Modern World* (London: Profile Books, 2021), 97.
[34] E.g. W. Prest, *William Blackstone: Law and Letters in the Eighteenth Century* (Oxford: Oxford University Press, 2008), 166.
[35] W. Prest, 'Blackstone's Magna Carta' (2016) 94 *North Carolina Law Review* 1495.

around him.³⁶ Blackstone bases his account in the *Commentaries* on an understanding that law commands 'right(s)' and prohibits 'wrong(s)'.³⁷ Following Roman precedents, Blackstone distinguishes between rights of persons and rights in and over things. The rights of persons include their 'civil duties'. 'Persons' include Parliament, the king, 'subordinate magistrates', the clergy, and the civil (i.e. non-clerical) state.

The principal right and duty of the monarch-in-Parliament (says Blackstone) is to make laws,³⁸ including laws that specify the degree to which every person retains their 'natural liberty'. According to Blackstone, there are two sorts of natural liberty: absolute and relative. Absolute liberty belongs to individuals as human beings; relative liberty belongs to individuals as members of society. Absolute rights may be limited by law 'so far ... (and no farther) as is necessary and expedient for the general advantage of the public'.³⁹ Natural rights, so limited, 'may be reduced', he says, 'to three principal ... articles; the right of personal security, the right of personal liberty; and the right of private property'.⁴⁰ The right of personal security encompasses life, body, health and reputation. Blackstone traces the right of personal liberty back to chapter 29 of Magna Carta. 'The right of private property ... consists in the use, enjoyment, and disposal of all ... acquisitions.'⁴¹ These three rights (says Blackstone) are supported by a number of auxiliary rights designed 'to secure their actual enjoyment':⁴² '[t]he constitution, powers, and privileges of parliament', '[t]he limitation of the king's prerogative', the right 'of applying to the courts of justice for redress of injuries',⁴³ 'the right of petitioning the king, or either house of parliament, for the redress of grievances',⁴⁴ and the subject's right 'of having arms for their defence, suitable to their condition and degree'.⁴⁵

In Blackstone's view, the 'absolute rights of every Englishman (which ... are usually called their liberties) ... are founded on nature and reason ... though subject at times to fluctuate and change; their establishment ... being still human ... they have been from time to time asserted in Parliament, as often as they were thought to be in danger'.⁴⁶ At the same time, Parliament, as legislator, can 'do everything that is not naturally impossible'; and 'being the highest and greatest court, over which none other can have jurisdiction in

---

³⁶ R. Paley (ed.), *William Blackstone: Commentaries on the Laws of England, Book IV* (Oxford: Oxford University Press, 2016), 273–274.
³⁷ D. Lemmings and W. Prest (eds.), *William Blackstone: Commentaries on the Laws of England, Book I* (Oxford: Oxford University Press, 2016), 83.
³⁸ Ibid, 42. ³⁹ Ibid, 85. ⁴⁰ Ibid, 88. ⁴¹ Ibid, 93. ⁴² Ibid, 95.
⁴³ Ibid, 95. ⁴⁴ Ibid, 96. ⁴⁵ Ibid, 97. ⁴⁶ Ibid, 86.

the kingdom, if by any means a misgovernment should anyway fall upon it, the subjects of this kingdom are left without all manner of remedy'.[47] On the other hand, Blackstone also stressed the importance of interpretation of statutes, independent of the legislator, as a protection against 'partiality and oppression'.[48] He laid much emphasis on the value of judicial independence, and (unlike Montesquieu, by whom he was much influenced) understood the power of courts in the English tradition and their consequent potential to play an active role in maintaining the balance of the constitution.[49]

Blackstone's account hovers precariously between natural law thinking and the positivism of Parliamentary sovereignty; but in it we have a constitutional theory of civil and political rights that, in its essence, survives to this day. Shorn of its naturalistic element and fortified with a good dose of consequentialism, Blackstone's theory of rights is essentially similar to Dicey's account of the rule of law in his classic restatement of English constitutional law published more than a century later.[50] By the time Dicey was writing, the world had been made over by the invention, in America and France, of the modern written constitution and bill of rights, and by significant progress towards universal adult suffrage. Moreover, the balance of the post-1688 constitution had changed, most notably as a result of the shift of executive power from the monarch to the government. On the other hand, the House of Lords still had significant political muscle, and parliamentary party discipline was not yet strong enough reliably to secure the position of the executive vis-à-vis the House of Commons. The courts were adjusting to changed circumstances partly by developing their control over the newly empowered central executive while, at the same time, acknowledging the dominance of Parliament by adopting literalist, textual modes of statutory interpretation and (through the doctrines of precedent – specifying a hierarchy of courts, and *stare decisis* – discouraging judicial creativity) by channelling active judging into the senior courts.

The three main pillars of Dicey's constitution were Parliamentary supremacy; the distinction between constitutional law and non-legal, conventional norms of the constitution; and the rule of law. For him, the rule of law had concrete implications for the protection of rights such as the right to

---

[47] Ibid, 107.
[48] Ibid, 45–47, 64–67. See also H. L. Lubert, 'Sovereignty and Liberty in William Blackstone's Commentaries on the Laws of England (2010) 72 *Review of Politics* 271.
[49] M. J. C. Vile, *Constitutionalism and the Separation of Powers*, 2nd ed. (Indianapolis, IN: Liberty Fund, 1998), 113–114.
[50] Dicey, *The Law of the Constitution*.

personal liberty and the right of public meeting.[51] It is a 'special attribute of English institutions' (he wrote) that rights 'are the result [by generalisation] of judicial decisions determining the rights of private persons in particular cases brought before the Courts'.[52] By contrast, 'under many foreign constitutions the security (such as it is) given to the rights of individuals results, or appears to result, [deductively] from general principles of the constitution'.[53] At one level, Dicey conceded, '[t]his is ... merely a formal difference.' However, he believed that it had at least three important ramifications. First, he claimed that the English approach put much more emphasis on effective remedies for interference with rights than the 'foreign' approach.[54] Second, the foreign approach (he said) was apt to generate a distinction between more important-and-secure 'constitutional' rights, and less important-and-secure 'non-constitutional' rights.[55] Third, Dicey claimed that foreign, constitutional rights were more likely to be 'suspended' than English rights.[56] He considered 'suspension' of the Habeas Corpus Act (in the context of security 'emergencies') to be less drastic because it only affected one of the citizens' rights (personal liberty) and only in limited respects; it did not, *ipso facto*, affect the availability of the (common-law) writ of habeas corpus.[57]

Now, juxtapose Dicey's account of the rights and the rule of law with his rendering of Parliamentary sovereignty: Parliament has 'the right to make or unmake any law whatever; and, further, no person or body is recognised ... as having a right to override or set aside the legislation of Parliament'.[58] Implication: Parliament has ultimate control over the rights of individuals and therefore, constitutionally, has it within its power to erode individual liberty.[59] Dicey, like Blackstone, understood and insisted upon the role and significance of courts as a check on the exercise of power by the executive,[60] but disabled them vis-à-vis the legislature. Instead, citing Burke, he put his faith

---

[51] Ibid, 115–119.   [52] Ibid, 115.
[53] Ibid, 115. The words in square brackets in this and the previous quotation have been interpolated from a different formulation of the point: ibid, 116.
[54] Ibid, 117.   [55] Ibid, 118.   [56] Ibid.
[57] A very important theme not explored here is the relationship between talk of rights and the rule of law in the domestic context on the one hand and the colonial context on the other. Regarding Dicey in particular see D. Lino, 'The Rule of Law and the Rule of Empire: A. V. Dicey in Imperial Context (2018) 81 *Modern Law Review* 739. Re habeas corpus see Halliday, *Habeas Corpus: From England to Empire*, especially ch. 8.
[58] Dicey, *Law of the Constitution*, 27.
[59] Ibid, 31–33. Of course, this implication in turn raises another: that there is some concept of 'personal liberty' that pre-exists Parliamentary specification.
[60] 'The judges therefore are, in truth, though not in name, invested with the means of hampering or supervising the whole administrative action of government, and of at once putting a veto on any proceeding not authorised by the letter of the law': ibid, 130.

in the idea, embedded in English constitutional thinking since the thirteenth century, that the House of Commons *represented* the whole nation.[61] Representation, in this sense, is not a function of the nature or width of the franchise but, rather, a product of ideas about the role of Parliament and the relationship between members of Parliament and 'the people'.[62]

The Invention of Human Rights

Dicey's *Law of the Constitution* attracted a barrage of criticism on many fronts, but his account of rights was not one of them. Indeed, Sir Ivor Jennings, perhaps Dicey's most systematic early critic, thought that so far as securing 'liberty' was concerned, 'we do the job better than any country which has a Bill of Rights'.[63] On the other hand, the first half of the twentieth century witnessed two catastrophic world wars, and a global pandemic and economic depression that resulted in large and, to a significant extent, permanent extensions of governmental regulation of and intervention in social and economic life.[64] Pressure for expansion of government was also increased by the progress and eventual completion of the project of 'democracy' in the sense of representative government based on universal adult suffrage. By and large, English courts acquiesced in the growth of executive discretionary power.[65] Off the bench, however, in 1929 the Lord Chief Justice of England, Lord Hewart,[66] published a book bluntly entitled *The New Despotism* in which, amongst other things, he attacked increasing delegation of broad legislative (and judicial) powers by Parliament to Ministers. In a pre-emptive strike, the (Labour) government appointed a Committee on Ministers' Powers (the Donoughmore Committee). In its report,[67] the Committee (of which, interestingly, Harold Laski was a member) expressed the view that 'the [wholesale and almost indiscriminate][68] delegation of legislative powers

---

[61] Ibid, 48.
[62] See, e.g., W. Selinger, *Parliamentarism: From Burke to Weber* (Cambridge: Cambridge University Press, 2019).
[63] Quoted in A. W. B. Simpson, *Human Rights and the End of Empire: Britain and the Genesis of the European Convention* (Oxford: Oxford University Press, 2001), 17; see also ibid, 22.
[64] For a helpful brief account in the legal context of habeas corpus see Farbey and Sharpe, *Law of Habeas Corpus*, 90–114.
[65] See, e.g., S. Sedley, 'The Long Sleep' in M. Andenas and D. Fairgrieve (eds.), *Tom Bingham and the Transformation of the Law: A Liber Amicorum* (Oxford: Oxford University Press, 2009); A. W. B. Simpson, *In the Highest Degree Odious* (Oxford: Oxford University Press, 1992).
[66] London: Ernest Benn, 1929.   [67] Cmd 4060 (1932).
[68] The bracketed words are interpolated from p. 23 of the Report.

is at the present day inevitable'.[69] However, the Committee concluded that there was no justification for 'an alarmist view of the constitutional situation. What the system lacks is coherence and uniformity in operation'.[70] The Committee 'venture[d] to express a hope'[71] that powers to legislate on 'matters of principle' or to impose taxation would be delegated only in exceptional circumstances[72] and in the clearest possible language; and it recommended that powers to amend Parliamentary legislation should only exceptionally be delegated.[73] It also recommended the establishment of a standing Parliamentary committee on delegated legislation and greater consultation of stakeholders in the drafting process; and that judicial review of delegated legislation should be excluded only in exceptional circumstances and then expressly, not impliedly. The conceptual framework of the Report was Diceyan, based on the principles of Parliamentary supremacy and the rule of law, with no mention of rights.

At the same time, in some places widespread desires and demands for a better life were catastrophically exploited by populist, nationalistic and genocidal dictators. In particular, the rise of Nazism and the implementation of Nazi ideas of legality[74] provoked debates about whether naturalistic ways of thinking about law might not provide more effective protection than positivism against government overreach and totalitarianism.[75] An upshot of such debates was the United Nations' Universal Declaration of Human Rights of 1948 (UDHR).[76] Given the standing of the UK in world affairs at the time, it is unsurprising that it played a significant role in the promotion and drafting of the UDHR. Although senior officials were nervous about its implications for the empire,[77] it had little, if any, domestic impact. The Declaration was not a treaty; it had no binding legal force either internationally or in the UK, and it provided no enforcement mechanism. Its supplementation by binding Conventions and the construction of a supporting set of international institutions to monitor and enforce compliance began only in the mid-1960s. Nevertheless, the UDHR deserves attention here for several

---

[69] Ibid, 15. [70] Ibid, 54. [71] Ibid, 58. [72] Ibid, 59. [73] Ibid, 65.
[74] See, e.g., J. Meierhenrich, *The Remnants of the Rechtstaat: An Ethnography of Nazi Law* (Oxford: Oxford University Press, 2018). In 1958, Hart and American jurist, Lon Fuller, debated the issue in the pages of the *Harvard Law Review* on which see, e.g. P. Cane (ed.), *The Hart-Fuller Debate in the Twenty-First Century* (Oxford: Hart Publishing, 2010).
[75] The most well-known English intervention is, perhaps, that of H. L. A. Hart in *The Concept of Law*, first published in 1961. See H. L. A. Hart, *The Concept of Law*, 3rd ed. (with an Introduction by Leslie Green) (Oxford: Oxford University Press, 2012), 207–212, 303–304.
[76] Simpson, *Human Rights and the End of Empire*, ch. 4. [77] Ibid, chs. 7 and 8.

reasons. First, it was founded on the novel premise that 'all human beings are born free and equal in dignity and rights' (Article 1). The UDHR focuses on individuals: it broke new ground in its coverage of all human beings 'without distinction of any kind' (Article 7).[78] Rights, it presupposed, are incidents of membership of the human species, not of a polity. The Declaration gave rise to a new concept of 'fundamental human rights' that knew nothing of national borders. Second, it was not until much later in the twentieth century that international law started to recognise interests of minorities and indigenous groups as 'rights'.[79] Genocide, for instance, was not dealt with in the UDHR but in a separate Convention; and genocide is now considered part of international criminal law, not human rights law.

Third, the UDHR was innovative in its declaration of certain 'global' rights, such as every person's right 'to leave any country, including his own, and to return to his country' (Art 13); the right to asylum (Art 14) and the right to a nationality (Art 15). Fourth, further adding to the civil and political rights that had been established to a greater or lesser extent in many polities over the preceding centuries, the UDHR announced that everyone 'is entitled to realisation ... in accordance with the organization and resources of each State, of the economic, social and cultural rights indispensable for his dignity and the free development of his personality' (Art 22). Such rights include a right to representative governmental institutions and to free and fair elections based on universal suffrage (Art 21); rights to work and equal pay (Art 23); a right to 'a standard of living adequate for the health and well-being ... and to security in case of unemployment, sickness, disability, widowhood old age or other lack of livelihood in circumstances beyond his control' (Art 25); and a 'right to education' (Art 26). Such rights could be limited but only 'by law solely for the purpose of securing due recognition and respect for the rights and freedoms of others and of meeting the just requirements of morality, public order and the general welfare in a democratic society.' (Art 29).

Fifth, in the twenty-first century, the concept of 'human rights' has generated a large historical and historiographical literature.[80] Differences of

---

[78] The first UN treaty directed specifically against discrimination was the Convention on the Elimination of All Forms of Racial Discrimination of 1965.
[79] See, e.g., W. Kymlicka, 'Minority Rights' in C. Brown and R. Eckersley (eds.), *The Oxford Handbook of International Political Theory* (Oxford: Oxford University Press, 2018).
[80] Including L. Hunt, *Inventing Human Rights: A History* (New York: W. W. Norton, 2007); S. Moyn, *The Last Utopia: Human Rights in History* (Cambridge, MA: Belknap Press, 2010); P. Alston, 'Does the Past Matter? On the Origins of Human Rights' (2013) 126

opinion about the 'origins' of the concept typically turn on what is meant by 'human rights'. Some look back as far as the ancient world, and many consider the eighteenth-century revolutions to have been central in the story, while Samuel Moyn – at the other extreme – fixes the birthday of human rights in the late 1970s.[81] Whatever their antecedents, developments during and after World War II reflected genuinely new thinking about the nature of rights and their role in constituting the relationship between the governors and the governed. Rights were no longer thought of as 'liberties' extended by the governors to the governed, nor as limitations on government power but as entitlements of the governed against the governors.

The European Convention on Human Rights, the Human Rights Act 1998 and Beyond

Sixth and, perhaps, most importantly for our story, taking 'the first steps for the collective enforcement of certain of the rights stated in the Universal Declaration' is one of the aims stated in the Preamble of the European Convention on Human Rights and Fundamental Freedoms (ECHR). The ECHR, the most significant regional human rights treaty in operation today, was signed by the eleven states of the Council of Europe, including the United Kingdom, in 1950.

Various features of the ECHR deserve comment. First, the Convention embodies a thoroughly positivist and 'political' conception of rights. The aims of the ECHR include achieving 'greater unity' between signatories and fostering 'a common understanding and observance of the Human Rights upon which ... justice and peace in the world depend'. A second feature is related to the first: a significant number of the rights established by the ECHR are qualified by a proviso permitting such interference with the right as is 'necessary in a democratic society' in the interests (variously) of national security, public safety, the economic well-being of the country, the prevention of disorder or crime, the protection of health and morals, and the protection of the rights and freedoms of others. Third, the ECHR typically specifies rights in much more detail than traditional national bills of rights or the Universal Declaration.

Harvard Law Review 2043; S. Moyn, *Human Rights and the Uses of History*, 2nd ed. (London: Verso, 2017); C. McCrudden, 'Human Rights Histories' (2015) 35 *Oxford Journal of Legal Studies* 179; M. Halme-Tuomisaari and P. Slotte, 'Revisiting the Origins of Human Rights: Introduction' in P. Slotte and M. Halme-Tuomisaari (eds.), *Revisiting the Origins of Human Rights*.

[81] S. Moyn, *The Last Utopia: Human Rights in History* (Harvard, MA: Belknap Press, 2010).

Fourth, the language of the ECHR is not uniformly or exclusively rights-based. For instance, freedom of expression is said to carry 'duties and responsibilities' (Art 10.2); Article 2 of the First Protocol does not confer a right to education but states that 'no person shall be denied the right to education'; Article 3 of the First Protocol does not confer a right to vote but rather records an undertaking by states to hold 'free elections at reasonable intervals by secret ballot'; married spouses 'shall enjoy equality of rights and responsibilities of a private law character between them' (Protocol 7, Art 5). The ECHR twice declares that 'the death penalty shall be abolished' (Protocol 6, Art 1; Protocol 13, Art 1); and those that are wrongly convicted 'shall be compensated' (Protocol 7, Art 3). Perhaps most significantly, the ECHR imposes an obligation on states to secure Convention rights and freedoms 'without discrimination on any ground such as sex, race, colour, language, religion, political or other opinion, national or social origin, association with a national minority, property, birth or other status' (Art 14; Protocol 12, Art 1). The idea that rights are things that government has a positive obligation to secure, not merely a negative obligation to respect, goes beyond both natural-law thinking, in which rights pre-exist government, and the Diceyan view that everyone has a right to do anything that government has not prohibited by law. It plays an especially important part in conceptualising and operationalising economic and social (as opposed to civil and political) rights. Fifth, given this positive governmental obligation, the ECHR creates a dual enforcement mechanism: it creates a right to an effective domestic remedy for breaches of Convention rights (Art 13) and it establishes the European Court of Human Rights (ECtHR) (Arts 19–51), accessible by both states and individuals. At first, the UK did not allow individuals access to the Court; but it changed its mind in 1966. Because the ECHR was (and is) an international treaty, it generates obligations that bind the government in international law but, by itself, creates no rights in domestic law even in favour of an individual who successfully challenges UK government action in the ECtHR.

As in the case of the UDHR, the UK government played a leading role in the conception and drafting of the ECHR. Given the dominance of the Diceyan approach to rights, Simpson argues that the UK's sponsorship of documentary human rights is to be understood as a foreign-relations exercise in good international citizenship designed to export to other countries, including British colonies and overseas dependencies, the freedom and liberties already enjoyed by the UK population.[82] In practice, however, UK imperial policy in the 1950s and 1960s was more concerned with maintaining law and order in the scramble to decolonialise than with promoting individual rights.[83] The same was true of policy in relation to Northern Ireland during the 'troubles' in the 1970s and 1980s. Domestically, governments in the early post-war years were more focused on building the welfare state than on promoting individual rights. Energy was also devoted to imposing duties of non-discrimination (and affording remedies for their breach) in favour of groups such as racial minorities (in the Race Relations Act 1965), homosexuals (in the Sexual Offences Act 1967), women (in the Sex Discrimination Act 1975) and people suspected of or charged with criminal offences (in the Police and Criminal Evidence Act 1984). Disability discrimination was tackled in the 1990s, and the duties-based approach has generally and more recently been reinforced in the Equality Act 2010.

The issue of a domestic Bill of Rights was debated in Parliament on various occasions from the late-1960s and through the 1970s.[84] Outside Parliament, as early as 1969, high-profile figures from across the political spectrum were coming out in favour of such a development.[85] As in the early-modern period, lawyers – such as Law Lord Leslie Scarman in his 1974 Hamlyn Lectures – were prominent in advocacy for protection of rights.[86] Scarman was embarrassed by the spectacle of the UK being tried in a foreign court.[87] In 1978, Lord Hailsham, while Shadow Lord Chancellor, founded his case for a written constitution and an entrenched Bill of Rights not on any notion of human rights but on a preference for (what he called) 'freedom under law' over 'elective dictatorship'. Hailsham associated freedom under law with the tradition of limited government traceable as far back

---

[82] Simpson, *Human Rights and the End of Empire*, ch. 1.
[83] C. O. H. Parkinson, *Bills of Rights and Decolonization: The Emergence of Domestic Human Rights Instruments in British Overseas Territories* (Oxford: Oxford University Press, 2007).
[84] M. Lippman, 'The Debate over a Bill of Rights in Great Britain: The View from Parliament' (1980) 2 *Universal Human Rights* 25.
[85] For a detailed historical account see D. Erdos, 'Ideology, Power Orientation and Policy Drag: Explaining the Elite Politics of Britain's Bill of Rights Debate' (2000) 44 *Government and Opposition* 20; 'Smoke but No Fire? The Politics of a "British" Bill of Rights' (2010) 81 *The Political Quarterly* 188; *Delegating Rights Protection: The Rise of Bills of Rights in the Westminster World* (Oxford: Oxford University Press, 2010), ch. 7. See also M. R. Madsen, 'France, the UK, and the "Boomerang" of the Internationalisation of Human Rights (1945–2000)' in S. Halliday and P. Schmidt (eds.), *Human Rights Brought Home: Socio-Legal Perspectives on Human Rights in the National Context* (Oxford: Hart Publishing, 2004).
[86] L. Scarman, *English Law: The New Dimension* (London: Stevens, 1974), Part II.
[87] Ibid, 19.

as Bracton in the thirteenth century. By contrast, he associated elective dictatorship with the political left[88] and claimed that it was made possible by various structural features of the governmental system, notably universal adult suffrage combined with first-past-the-post elections; and concentration of executive and bureaucratic power in the government, and effective legislative power in the House of Commons.

The 1980s was the decade of new-right Thatcherism. The Conservative's second electoral victory in 1987 led to the formation, the next year, of Charter 88, a centre-left organisation supported initially by 'over 200 leading members of the political, literary and academic intelligentsia'.[89] The Charter adopted Hailsham's trope of the elective dictatorship and 'reasserted a tradition of demands for constitutional rights in Britain, which stretches from the barons who forced the Magna Carta on King John, to the working men who drew up the People's Charter in 1838, to the women at the beginning of this century who demanded universal suffrage'. 'We are united', its sponsors declared, 'in one opinion only, that British society stands in need of a constitution which protects individual rights and of the institutions of a modern and pluralist democracy'.[90] In addition to a written constitution incorporating a Bill of Rights, Charter 88 called for subjection of executive and prerogative powers to the rule of law, regimes of freedom of information and proportional representation, democratisation of the second chamber, a democratically renewed Parliament to control the executive, and 'equitable distribution of power between local, regional and national government'. Thus, the Charter's proponents sought to diffuse power in two directions – towards the people on the one hand, and the courts (that would enforce a Bill of Rights) on the other. Enactment of a Bill of Rights became official Labour policy under John Smith's brief leadership of the Party in the early 1990s.

The Human Rights Act 1998 (HRA) formed part of a large package of constitutional changes made under Tony Blair's New Labour, which also included devolution to Scotland, Wales and Northern Ireland, freedom of information legislation, the replacement of the judicial House of Lords by the UK Supreme Court, and limited reform of the legislative House of Lords that

---

[88] Labour was in power from 1964 to 1970 and again from 1974 to 1979.
[89] D. Erdos, 'Charter 88 and the Constitutional Reform Movement: A Retrospective' (2009) 62 *Parliamentary Affairs* 537. In 1991, the human-rights organisation, Liberty, published a draft bill of rights: *A People's Charter: Liberty's Bill of Rights: A Consultation Document* (London: National Council for Civil Liberties, 1991).
[90] https://unlockdemocracy.org.uk/resources-index/2016/07/04/charter-88.

saw its hereditary (as opposed to its appointed) element greatly reduced in absolute and relative size. In a very significant sense, the HRA neither involved nor required fundamental structural change to the UK's constitutional arrangements. It did not 'incorporate' the ECHR into UK law although, ironically, the various devolution statutes do incorporate it into the respective legal systems of the devolved nations; and as a result, their assemblies' legislation can be invalidated for inconsistency with the Convention whereas Westminster legislation cannot. The HRA is not 'entrenched' and could, therefore, be repealed by Parliament. In another irony, however, such repeal would not, by itself, affect the impact of the ECHR on the UK under international law – that would entail withdrawal by the UK government from the Convention and the Council of Europe which might, itself, (as did withdrawal from the EU treaties) require an Act of Parliament to be effective, even if it were politically and diplomatically feasible. The purpose and effect of the HRA is to provide a domestic mechanism for enforcement by UK courts of certain Convention rights. This mechanism is additional to the Convention's own enforcement mechanism, not in substitution for it. Decisions of the UK Supreme Court can be challenged in the European Court of Human Rights for inconsistency with the Convention; and an adverse decision would impose on the UK government an obligation in international law to bring UK law into line with the Convention.

As noted, the HRA does not give UK courts power to invalidate UK legislation (that is, legislation made by the UK Parliament at Westminster) for inconsistency with Convention rights (although executive action, including delegated legislation, can be struck down). Instead, the Act imposes on courts an obligation, 'so far as possible ... to read and give effect to legislation in a way which is compatible with the Convention'. In doing so, the court must 'take into account' the case-law of the ECtHR. Statutory interpretation has long been a pressure point in the relationship between senior courts and Parliament. Before the Glorious Revolution, the line between making and interpreting law was not sharply drawn and senior judges were involved in both activities. In this period, courts tended to interpret legislation in a 'purposive' as opposed to a 'literalist' or 'textualist' way. Purposive modes of interpretation place individual words and phrases within a broader context of the aims and objectives of the statute as a whole or, going even further, within the context of circumstances, beyond the statute, that effect its operation. In the eighteenth century, theorists such as Montesquieu and Blackstone explicitly distinguished the role of the legislator in making law from that of the judge in applying the law. By the late nineteenth century, in response to the growing strength and legislative activity of Parliament, the courts were adopting a much more text-bound approach to statutory interpretation.

A century later, a discernible shift back to more purposive approaches occurred, first, in the context of the courts' power and obligation, under the European Communities Act 1972 (in force from 1973 to 2020), to invalidate Acts of Parliament that could not be interpreted consistently with EU legislation. Courts became more inclined to read provisions of UK legislation non-literally in order to save them from incompatibility, unless the words of the UK legislation were so clearly and unambiguously in conflict with EU law that they could not reasonably be read in any other way. This basic approach was carried over to the issue of the compatibility of UK legislation with the ECHR. It is also applied to questions about the consistency of other UK statutes with the HRA itself on the basis that the HRA is a 'constitutional statute', a concept invented by the judges to make it more difficult for the government to alter the law by legislation without doing so reflectively, clearly and unambiguously. However, there is no authoritative definition of 'constitutional statute',[91] and it is unclear whether the term includes, for instance, equality and anti-discrimination legislation or legislation that promotes what are now commonly recognised as social and economic rights, such as access to education and health care.

In case a statutory provision cannot be read compatibly with the ECHR, the court has (as already noted) no power to invalidate the provision but may make a 'declaration of incompatibility'. In that case, the HRA confers on a Minister the power to amend the offending statutory provision by delegated legislation to render it compatible where there are 'compelling reasons' to do so. Arrangements of this type have come to be known as 'soft judicial review of legislation' to distinguish them from the US model under which courts have the power to strike down statutory provisions that are inconsistent with a Bill of Rights. They are also referred to as 'the Commonwealth model of judicial review' because they were pioneered in the old Commonwealth, not in the UK.[92]

---

[91] See, e.g., F. Ahmed and A. Perry, 'Constitutional Statutes' (2017) 37 *Oxford Journal of Legal Studies* 461.
[92] S. Gardbaum, *The New Commonwealth Model of Constitutionalism* (Oxford: Oxford University Press, 2013).

In the decade before the HRA came into operation in 2002 and, some would say, in anticipation of that event, the judges also applied this basic interpretative strategy to so-called 'fundamental common-law rights'. If a right recognised by the courts is 'fundamental', legislation is not to be read as impinging on the right unless it does so explicitly and unambiguously. The catalogue of fundamental common-law rights is still open and includes, for instance, a right of access to justice. However, it seems clear that the ECHR and the HRA give effect to rights (such as a right to privacy) not (yet) recognised by the courts as fundamental. The 'fundamental common-law rights strategy' is significant in light of the fact that there is some political support for repeal of the HRA and its replacement by a 'British Bill of Rights'. By itself, such a move would not free the UK from the obligations under international law derived from the ECHR or from the jurisdiction of the ECtHR.[93] Furthermore, unless it expressly so provided, enactment of a home-grown (statutory) Bill of Rights would not prevent its supplementation by the courts if it was judged to fall short of the fundamental requirements of the common law. On the other hand, there is considerable scepticism about the willingness and ability of the courts to develop the common law as a robust protector of many of the rights that international and regional regimes recognise, if not realise.[94]

Conclusion: Continuities and Discontinuities

This whistle-stop tour of the past eight centuries of development of 'rights' in the UK constitution (and its predecessors) reveals both radical change and underlying continuity. One continuous thread is found in the distinction between recognition of rights and their enforcement and realisation. The mere fact of recognition, whether in a formal document or not, is of subsidiary significance independently of structural mechanisms for the protection, enforcement and promotion of rights. This was as true of Magna Carta as it is of the ECHR and the HRA. It helps to explain the prominence of the remedy of habeas corpus in the story of rights in the UK constitution.

---

[93] Before 31 December 2020, the UK was also bound by rights recognised by EU law. It was often, though incorrectly, said that withdrawal from the EU would end rights-protection in the UK. This statement ignored the continuing operation of the HRA and the ECHR, which provide a much more significant avenue for protection of rights than EU law did.

[94] M. Elliott and K. Hughes (eds.), *Common Law Constitutional Rights* (Oxford: Hart Publishing, 2020).

Perhaps the most significant distinction between the ECHR and the UDHR was that the former created an enforcement mechanism that the latter lacked; and what most significantly distinguishes the current international human rights regime from the ECHR is that the ECHR enforcement mechanism is much stronger than international counterparts.

Another element of continuity in our story is the co-existence at all periods of various views about the foundation of rights. The basic divide is between viewing rights as pre-legal or extra-legal or 'natural' on the one hand, and in positivist terms of the rule of law on the other. The rule-of-law approach dominates the UK tradition, although naturalistic views have been strong at various times. Blackstone (as noted earlier) equivocated between the two approaches. On the whole, legislative supremacy as understood by Dicey has been found inconsistent with naturalism about rights. Some modern English constitutional theorists, of a non-positivist frame of mind, have sought a reconciliation between the two approaches by offering a 'thick', substantive account of the rule of law in place of a 'thin', proceduralist account.[95]

On the other hand, our survey also reveals some major discontinuities. Perhaps the most obvious is the extension of rights discourse beyond national borders and the creation, after World War II, of international human rights law and regional human rights regimes. The ECHR has imposed entirely new external constraints on the UK government and, by extension, the UK Parliament. Another dramatic change in recent times has been a divorce between rights and duties. For much of the period we have surveyed, rights and duties were treated as correlative in the sense that anything said about the rights of one person could alternatively be phrased in terms of the duties of another person. Moreover, rights were often coupled with duties: for instance, a feudal lord with the right to hold court was also considered to be under a duty to do so: 'liberties' carried responsibilities. The monarch had both a right and duty to govern (well) and the monarch's subjects had both a duty and a right to be governed (well). Today, by contrast, rights and duties tend to be treated separately in thinking about relations between governors and the governed. For instance, the development of the welfare state was inspired politically more by understandings of the duties of government and society than of the rights of citizens. In the UK,

---

[95] Most notably T. R. S. Allan in, for example, *Constitutional Justice: A Liberal Theory of the Rule of Law* (Oxford: Oxford University Press, 2001). For general discussion see B. Z. Tamanaha, *On the Rule of Law: History, Politics, Theory* (Cambridge: Cambridge University Press, 2004).

the conceptual foundations of free universal healthcare and free universal education are duties of government. Again, partly because it operates horizontally between citizen and citizen as well as vertically between citizen and government, equality and anti-discrimination law focuses on obligations and duties of equal treatment and non-discrimination. The effective invention of social and economic 'rights' post-dates the development of the features of the welfare state that they mirror. In UK law, it is an entirely open question whether duties can have 'fundamental' or 'constitutional' status in the way that rights can. Similarly, the effective (international) recognition of group and minority rights has post-dated many domestic measures to create and enforce obligations of equal treatment and non-discrimination. Thus, although both the UDHR and the ECHR prohibit discrimination in the giving effect to the rights they respectively recognise and establish, neither creates free-standing rights (or obligations) of non-discrimination.

Finally, consider the role of the judiciary in the recognition and enforcement of rights. Magna Carta's contemplated enforcers were the barons. They were succeeded by Parliament. The courts early established the principle that although the monarch could not be held accountable to a court for breach of the law (including infringements of rights), those who acted in the monarch's name could be. In the eyes of the law, the monarch could not do wrong; but the monarch's delegates certainly could and, if they did, could be ordered by a court to make amends. In the sixteenth and seventeenth centuries the common-law courts developed the 'prerogative writs' that were specifically (although not exclusively) directed against official, government illegality and could be deployed to secure the release of people illegally detained, require legal duties to be performed, prohibit illegal conduct and deprive illegal actions of purported legal effect. Substitute 'the monarch-in-Parliament' for 'the monarch' and you have the system Dicey described in 1885 and that is, in its essentials, still operating in the UK today. However, the eighteenth and nineteenth centuries brought major shifts in power from the monarch to the executive; and the twentieth century witnessed a further dramatic shift of power, driven by the broadening of the franchise, from (the two Houses of) Parliament to the executive.

The judges have reacted to these developments by gradually strengthening judicial control over the administration and subjecting to the rule of law powers that were originally prerogatives of the monarch. This is not to say that courts are the most important institutional guardians of rights but only that, relatively, their political significance has increased as that of Parliament has decreased and as democratisation has fuelled rising social expectations of the willingness and ability of governments, whether local, national, regional or global, to make people's lives better. The more power we grant to government or it takes for itself, the more we seek to protect ourselves by the assertion of rights. Such contestation is the thread that runs through the many changes documented in this chapter.

9

The People and the Constitution[*]

VERNON BOGDANOR

Direct Democracy

Democracy is a form of government in which ultimate power rests with the people. Indeed, Aristotle in his *Politics*, Book 3, argued that only those who participated in government could be called citizens in the full and complete definition of that term. The word 'democracy' derives from the Greek 'demos' and 'kratos' meaning rule by the people. The Greeks, admittedly, held a very limited view of who was entitled to be involved in decision-making. Only male citizens could participate; women and slaves were excluded. But for those who were entitled to participate, more was required than is asked of those living in modern democracies. For the Athenians practised, not representative democracy, but direct democracy in which all male citizens gathered together to make decisions for the city. Such direct democracy still survives in two small cantons in Switzerland – Appenzell Inner Rhodes and Glarus – in town meetings in the United States, and, in an attenuated form, in some parish meetings in England. The Greeks participated in their government on a continuous and regular basis. In Britain today, by contrast, participation is very limited indeed. A man or woman lucky enough to live a long life will vote around twelve times at national level and perhaps around fifty times in local elections – activities which probably take up perhaps less than twenty hours of time in total, less than the time some spend watching television every week.

In every modern democracy, with the exception perhaps of Switzerland, the role of the people is severely limited if not entirely negative. Many modern constitutions, however, do prescribe a role for the people, with whom sovereign power is presumed to lie, primarily in referendums. For a

[*] I am grateful for criticism of an earlier draft to Professors Bruce Ackerman and Peter Cane, Sandy Sullivan and Jonathan Owen, Chief Executive of the National Association of Local Councils. But they are not responsible for my arguments or conclusions.

brief period in the seventeenth century, it seemed that the sovereignty of the people would also come to be a principle of the British constitution. The Levellers, a faction of Cromwell's New Model Army, were the first to advocate this principle, the first to believe that the people not Parliament should have the final word in government. The Leveller tract, known as the third Agreement of the People, published in 1649, can justifiably be regarded as the first written constitution in modern European history, a title often given to Oliver Cromwell's constitution of 1653, the Instrument of Government, a document which declared that legislative power resided in the person of the Lord Protector 'and the people'. But the Lord Protector abolished the House of Lords, and refused to summon the Commons. It is not clear what power the people in fact had during Cromwell's dictatorship.

Under the terms of the third Agreement of the People, by contrast, the people themselves would create their government by means of a constitutive act.[1] 'An Agreement of the People', declared John Lilburne, the Leveller leader, 'is not proper to come from Parliament, because it comes from thence – with a command – it ought not so to do, but to be voluntary and free. Besides, that which is done by one Parliament – may be undone by the next – but an Agreement of the People begun and ended by the People, can never come justly within the Parliament's cognizance to destroy'.[2]

It followed, therefore, in the words of the Leveller, Richard Overton, that 'an appeal from them [Parliament] to the people is not anti-parliamentary, anti magisterial; not *from* the sovereign power, but *to* that sovereign power'.[3]

The Levellers also implied that there should be judicial review of legislation. But they believed that judges could not be relied upon to undertake impartial review. Therefore, the task of review should, in accordance with the Leveller doctrine of the sovereignty of the people, lie with 'the whole People of England', as represented by juries.[4]

After the Restoration, the concept of fundamental law receded. Yet it was to be resurrected across the Atlantic by the American revolutionaries, and some of the ideas of the Levellers came to be embodied in the American

---

[1] Perez Zagorin, *The English Revolution: Politics, Events, Ideas* (Aldershot: Ashgate, 1998), p. x.
[2] Perez Zagorin, *A History of Political Thought in the English Revolution*, (1954) (Bristol: Thoemmes Press, 1997), p. 14.
[3] Richard Overton, An Appeal from the Commons to the Free People, 1647, cited in A. H. Birch, *Representative and Responsible Government: An Essay on the British Constitution* (London: George Allen and Unwin, 1964), p. 37.
[4] T. C. Pease, *The Leveller Movement: A Study in the Historical and Political Theory of the English Great Civil War*, (1916) (Washington, DC: Peter, Smith, 1965), pp. 317-318.

constitution. But in Britain, the concept of fundamental law was replaced by that of parliamentary sovereignty, and, until recently at least, the British constitution, so it seemed, knew nothing of the people. It may have been government for the people, but it was not by the people.

It is not, however, wholly clear what is meant by saying that the constitution 'knew nothing of the people'. It seems to have meant no more than that the people were not part of the legislative process. But the same is true, for example, in the United States and India even though their constitutions declare that they derive from 'the people'. And indeed, some British commentators have been perfectly happy to declare that the people are in fact part of the constitution. Blackstone, for example, wrote in his *Commentaries* that. 'Every man is in judgment of law party to making an Act of Parliament'.[5] Austin insisted that 'speaking accurately, the members of the commons' house are merely trustees for the body by which they are elected or appointed'. The trust, however, was tacit rather than express. 'It arises from the relation between the bodies as delegating and representing parties rather than from oral or written instructions given by the former to the latter, but since it arises from that relation, the trust is general and vague. The representatives are merely bound generally and vaguely, to abstain from any such exercise of the delegated sovereign powers as would tend to defeat the purposes for which they are elected and appointed. The trust is simply enforced by moral sanctions'.[6] Dicey, the first to advocate use of the referendum in Britain, agreed with this view, writing of 'the doctrine which lies at the basis of English democracy – that a law depends at bottom for its enactment on the consent of the nation as represented by the electors'.[7] Of course this doctrine has no legal force. As Sir Frederick Pollock declared, at the beginning of the twentieth century, an identical resolution passed by the electors of every constituency would have no legal force and no court would pay any attention to it.[8] It remains the case that, in Dicey's words, 'the judges know nothing about any will of the people except in so far as that will is expressed by an Act of Parliament, and would never suffer the validity of a statute to be questioned on the ground of its having been passed or being

---

[5] William Blackstone, 1 *Commentaries*, p. 184, quoted in Geoffrey Marshall and Graeme C. Moodie, *Some Problems of the Constitution*, [1959] 5th ed. (London: Hutchinson, 1971), p. 15.
[6] John Austin, *The Province of Jurisprudence Determined*, Lecture VI, [1832] 2nd ed. (London: John Murray, 1861), pp. 203–204.
[7] Albert Venn Dicey, *A Leap in the Dark*, 2nd ed. (London: John Murray, 1911), p. 190.
[8] Frederick Pollock, *A First Book of Jurisprudence*, 5th ed. (London: Macmillan, 1923), p. 274.

kept alive in opposition to the wishes of the electors'.[9] Nevertheless, this does not prove that the people are not 'part of the constitution'. Political parties, the civil service and local government do not enjoy legal sovereignty either, but few would suggest that they are not part of the constitution. The law says nothing of responsible government, although this principle is clearly a fundamental part of the constitution. Saying that a body is 'part of the constitution' could mean one of two things, either that it is part of the procedure for making and reviewing law – Parliament and the courts – or that it is part of the wider system of government. Clearly, the people are not part of the constitution in the first sense, but for many centuries, the people – or at least a section of them – have long been thought to be part of the constitution in the wider sense, since legislation is, after all, an outcome of the process of election rather than some other process such as the will of a hereditary monarch or a dictator. And the 1832 Reform Acts and similar Acts are entitled 'Representation of the People' Acts. Being part of the constitution is wider, therefore, than being part of the legislature.

It is, however, undoubtedly true that, until recently, the people played a less active role in British government than in many other liberal societies. That, no doubt, is largely due to the culture of deference so much celebrated by Bagehot, the 'habit of authority', which one authority has traced back to the Norman Conquest. 'England's history', it has been argued, 'is the history of a certain tradition and practice of governance – a tradition of successful paternalism'. 'Democracy', Richard Cobden, the mid nineteenth century crusader against the Corn Laws, believed, 'forms no element in the materials of English character'.[10]

Constitutional lawyers and political scientists have been divided as to whether the people are or have been in fact part of the constitution in the wider sense, and, in particular, whether the doctrine of the mandate is part of the constitution. This doctrine entails either that a government is required to follow instructions given by voters in a general election, that it is indeed under a duty to follow such instructions; or, alternatively, that major new policies should not be introduced without the sanction of the voters; that a government has no right to introduce major new policies without such a sanction. MacIver in 1926, Pulzer in 1967 and Birch in 1973 roundly declared that the mandate was an untenable doctrine. Jennings declared in *The Law*

---

[9] A. V. Dicey, *Law of the Constitution*, 8th ed. (London: Macmillan, 1915), pp. 57, 72.
[10] A. P. Thornton, *The Habit of Authority: Paternalism in British History* (Toronto: University of Toronto Press, 1966), p. 16.

and the Constitution that the doctrine 'cannot be said to be a convention until the present century'. In *Cabinet Government*, however, he declared that it was 'part of the political cant. It is a stick used by the Opposition to beat the Government'.[11] By contrast, one authority has insisted that 'The principle of the people's mandate has been recognized as operative by statesmen and by constitutional experts for the best part of a century'.[12]

The Mandate and the Referendum

The idea of submitting a clear issue of policy for the approval of the electorate was, according to this view, established in 1831 when the Whigs appealed to the people on the question of whether Parliament should be reformed; and many candidates gave pledges for or against reform. MPs returned in this election seemed to be delegates rather than mere representatives. The doctrine of the mandate came to be explicitly formalised by Disraeli. In 1835, he argued in his *Vindication of the English Constitution*, that the divine right of kings ought not to be succeeded 'by the divine right of the House of Commons'.[13] In 1868 he objected to Gladstone raising the issue of disestablishment of the Irish Church without having first brought it before the country. He denied the 'moral competence' of Parliament to legislate for disestablishment, 'without an appeal to the nation – You cannot come, on a sudden, and without the country being the least informed of your intention, to a decision that will alter the character of England and her institutions – Technically, no doubt, Parliament has power to do so. But, Sir, there is a moral exercise of power as well as a technical, and when you touch the principles on which the most ancient and influential institutions are founded, it is most wise that you should hold your hand unless you have assured yourselves of such an amount of popular sympathy and support as will make your legislation permanent and beneficial'.[14] Disestablishment was, so Disraeli told the Queen, 'too grave a question to be decided upon without

---

[11] R. M. MacIver, *The Modern State* (Oxford: Clarendon Press, 1926), pp. 204–205; Peter G. J. Pulzer, *Political Representation and Elections in Britain* (London: Allen and Unwin, 1967), pp. 131–137; Birch, *The British System of Government*, 3rd ed. (London: Allen and Unwin, 1973), pp. 96–99; Ivor Jennings, *The Law and the Constitution*, 5th ed. (London: University of London Press, 1959), p. 176; Jennings, *Cabinet Government*, 3rd ed. (Cambridge: Cambridge University Press, 1964), p. 505.

[12] Cecil S. Emden, *The People and the Constitution*, 2nd ed. [1956] (Oxford: Oxford University Press, 1962), p. 315.

[13] Benjamin Disraeli, *Vindication of the English Constitution* (London: Saunders and Otley, 1835), p. 65.

[14] House of Commons Debates, 16 Mar. 1868, vol. 190, cols. 1785–1786, 1788.

the opinion of the nation being taken'.[15] Gladstone countered that this doctrine was 'most extraordinary', if not also 'ultra-democratic – anarchical'.[16] Nevertheless the general election of 1868 did, so it was believed, give Gladstone's Liberals authority to legislate, and Lord Salisbury, the future Conservative Prime Minister urged the peers to accept it since 'when the House of Commons is at one with the nation', the Lords should give way.[17] In 1886, during the debate on Irish Home Rule, Lord Hartington, the Whig leader, complained that the electorate had not been consulted. 'Although no principle of a "mandate" may exist, I maintain there are certain limits which parliament is morally bound to observe, and beyond which Parliament has morally not the right to go in its relations with the constituents'.[18] This speech elicited, according to Lord Curzon, a great shout of approval with its emphasis on the 'moral incompetence of parliament, with no mandate from the constituencies'.[19] A mandate, so it appeared, was required before a government had the right to *initiate* legislation. But Lord Salisbury also argued that a specific mandate in the form of a general election was required before a government could *enact* legislation. The implication was of course that the elected Commons was not a trustworthy expression of the popular will and that, where a measure had *not* been put before the electorate, the Lords had the right to reject it; and this was indeed Salisbury's view. 'We are agreed', the Conservative, Lord Selborne, Salisbury's son-in-law, declared in the debates on the Parliament bill in 1911, 'that the sovereign power of government in this country resides in the Crown and in the people'. He was corrected by Lord Morley, speaking for the Liberal government, who interjected, 'Crown and Parliament'. But Selborne reiterated 'In the Crown and the people', while Morley reiterated in his turn, 'Crown and Parliament'.[20] The implication of the doctrine was that the Lords could force a dissolution, something which would have placed the elected Commons in an inferior constitutional position to the non-elected Lords. And, given that the almost wholly hereditary house had a large and permanent Conservative majority, Salisbury's mandate theory was one that would in practice apply

---

[15] G. E. Buckle, ed., *Letters of Queen Victoria*, 2nd series (London: John Murray, 1926), vol. I, p. 516.
[16] House of Commons Debates, 3 Apr. 1868, vol. 191, col. 931.
[17] House of Lords Debates, 17 June 1869, vol. 197, col. 84.
[18] House of Commons Debates, 9 April 1886, vol. 304, col. 1244.
[19] Corinne Comstock Weston, *The House of Lords and Ideological Politics: Lord Salisbury's Referendal Theory and the Conservative Party, 1846–1922* (Philadelphia, PA: American Philosophical Society, 1995), p. 115.
[20] House of Lords Debates, 5 July 1911, vol. 9, cols. 274–275.

only when Liberal governments were in office. It meant, in the words of the radical, Sir Charles Dilke, 'a claim for annual Parliaments when we are in office, and septennial parliaments when they are in office' – before the 1911 Parliament Act, the maximum length of a Parliament was seven years rather than five.[21] 'If, said the Radical, Henry Labouchere, MP for Northampton, 'there were a House of 500 shoemakers of Northampton and the Conservatives when in power had to submit everything to these excellent Radicals, honourable Gentlemen would say the system was monstrous'.[22] But it was the Salisbury doctrine that led to the Conservatives rejecting the 1909 'People's Budget.' Lord Lansdowne, leader of the Conservatives in the Lords, moved *not* that the budget be rejected. but rather that it be referred to the people via a general election. His motion declared that the Lords would not be 'justified in giving its consent to this Bill, which contains provisions of a dangerous and unrepresentative character, until it has been submitted to the judgment of the country'.

The doctrine of the mandate was intended as a barrier to radical change. When, in 1903, Joseph Chamberlain proposed tariff reform, he accepted that so radical an alteration in the fiscal system could not be introduced without the sanction of the people, but he advocated a referendum rather than a general election to secure this sanction.[23] Salisbury himself had come to be sympathetic in the 1890s to the referendum and his successor as Conservative leader and Prime Minister, his nephew, Arthur Balfour, sceptical of the Chamberlain programme, nevertheless agreed with Chamberlain that it would indeed be beyond 'the limits of constitutional propriety' to introduce so major a change without the sanction of the voters.[24] The Liberals too regarded the 1906 election as a referendum on the tariff, and were happy to accept the verdict of the voters as a mandate to preserve free trade. The two general elections of 1910 were also alleged to be on specific issues, the first on whether the Lords should pass the 1909 budget, the second on whether the Parliament bill, curtailing the powers of the Lords, should be enacted. Significantly, George V had pressed Prime Minister Asquith to agree that the bill and the alternative Conservative scheme for Lords reform be introduced into the Lords before the December 1910 election so that voters could

---

[21] S. Gwynn and G. Tuckwell, *Life of the Right Hon. Charles Dilke* (London: John Murray, 1917), vol. 1, p. 371.
[22] House of Commons Debates, 21 Nov. 1884, vol. 294, col. 142.
[23] Joseph Chamberlain, *Imperial Union and Tariff Reform* (London: Grant Richards, 1903), pp. x–xi.
[24] House of Commons Debates, 9 Mar. 1904, vol. 131, col. 679.

know exactly on what issues their opinion was being sought.[25] The outcome of the election gave the Liberals a mandate for the Parliament bill. But the Liberal government then proceeded to introduce a bill providing for Irish Home Rule. Conservatives objected that this had not been the prime issue before the voters in December 1910 and that the government had no right to legislate for so major a change in the constitution without securing another mandate from the voters. But by that time the power of the Lords to force a dissolution had gone, having been replaced by a delaying power for two sessions.

In 1923, tariff reform was again to become an issue, Prime Minister, Stanley Baldwin, having come to believe that a tariff was needed to reduce unemployment. But his predecessor, Bonar Law, had promised in the election campaign of 1922 that no tariff would be introduced without the consent of the voters.[26] Baldwin felt bound by this pledge and dissolved a parliament just one year old to secure a mandate for this new policy.

These instances, however, may be regarded as exceptional rather than typical, and indeed the doctrine of the mandate was often used for tactical purposes, so giving credibility to Ivor Jennings's view that 'it was part of the political cant'. When governments found it expedient to introduce radical changes, they generally did so regardless of whether they had received a mandate from the voters. Examples might include the Conservative government's Education Act of 1902, the National Government's departure from the Gold Standard in 1931 and its policy of Imperial Preference in 1932, the Labour government's Parliament Act of 1949, further curtailing the delaying powers of the House of Lords, the Conservative government's application under Harold Macmillan to join the European Communities in 1961, the Conservative government's introduction of a statutory incomes policy under Edward Heath in 1972, the Conservative government's withdrawal from the European Monetary System under John Major in 1992 and the Conservative government's enactment of the Same Sex (Couples) Act under David Cameron in 2013. Indeed, many radical policy changes occur in the middle of the term of a government, rather than after a general election – for example the post-war Labour government's move to a less regulated economy with the bonfire of controls in 1949, the Conservative government's move to planning

---

[25] Harold Nicolson, *King George V* [1952] (London: Pan Books, 1967), pp. 208–209.
[26] Robert Blake, *The Unknown Prime Minister: The Life and Times of Andrew Bonar Law 1858–1923* (London: Eyre and Spottiswoode, 1955), p. 468.

policies and entry to the European Communities in 1961, and the Conservative government's move to a statutory incomes policy in 1972.

It is in any case hardly possible to apply the doctrine of the popular mandate to general elections. For it presupposes that voters have a precise understanding of the dominant issue at general elections, and vote on the basis of that issue. These presuppositions have been undermined by the findings of modern electoral research. Voters, so it seems, often have only a rather hazy idea of what is in manifestoes; and, with the increasing length of manifestoes, few electors bother to read them through. Further, it has been long established that few electors agree with all of the policy proposals of their favoured party. Voters, so it appears, often choose a party on the basis of its general orientation, its image or the record of a government in office. They tend to support the broad direction of policy of their chosen party rather than specific policies. It is, therefore, hardly possible to determine from the outcome of a general election what the voters believe in relation to particular policies. An X on the ballot paper legitimises the authority of the party which wins the election, but it does not give specific directions as to policy.

Nevertheless, the doctrine of the mandate appeared more plausible in the years before 1914 when the final shape of the representative system was still unclear, even if it did not attain the status of a convention of the constitution; and, as we have seen, it led political leaders such as Joseph Chamberlain to toy with the idea of the referendum as an alternative to a general election. For a referendum, unlike a general election, can yield a specific mandate. It was because he appreciated that a general election could not yield a reliable indication of the views of voters on a specific policy that Dicey, the first in Britain to advocate it, had asked in an article published in the *Contemporary Review* in April 1890. 'Ought the Referendum to be Introduced into England?' In the abortive Constitutional Conference of 1910, the referendum was the main Conservative alternative to the Parliament bill as a means of resolving conflicts between the Commons and Lords.[27] And, shortly before the December 1910 election, Arthur Balfour, the Conservative leader, proposed a referendum on tariff reform in an effort to heal divisions in his party. In 1910, Dicey could write, that 'the name of the referendum is now on the lips of every person interested in political theory'.[28] But the doctrine of the

---

[27] John Fair, *British Interparty Conferences: A Study of the Procedure of Conciliation in British Politics, 1867–1921* (Oxford: Clarendon Press, 1980), chapter IV.
[28] A. V. Dicey, 'The Referendum and Its Critics', *Quarterly Review* 1910, p. 538.

specific mandate and with it support for the referendum became dormant after the First World War, although there was a renewed flurry of interest in 1930 when the Conservatives in opposition temporarily agreed to a referendum on the principle of Empire Free Trade.

Loss of interest in the mandate and the referendum coincided with the advent of universal suffrage in 1918 and 1928, the development of a disciplined two-party system, and the reduction in the powers of the House of Lords. In their seminal work on party systems, the political scientists, Seymour Martin Lipset and Stein Rokkan put forward a 'freezing hypothesis'; according to which there had been a 'freezing of the major party alternatives in the wake of the extension of the suffrage and the mobilisation of major sections of the new reservoirs of political supporters'. That mobilisation occurred with the advent of universal suffrage in 1918 and 1928. The British party system became frozen when what had seemed an incipient multi-party system came to be replaced in the 1920s by a two-party system. Writing in 1967, Lipset and Rokkan concluded that in Europe 'the party system of the 1960s reflect with few significant exceptions the cleavage structure of the 1920s'.[29] With this freezing of the major party alternatives, there was also a freezing of institutions, and, with the rise of unemployment, constitutional questions came to be replaced by socioeconomic issues. British politics came to be a politics of the democratic class struggle. The Labour Party, which replaced the Liberals as the main party of the left, was committed to policies of redistribution rather than constitutional reconstruction. The referendum, moreover, would have threatened the very interests of the parties themselves, since it might prevent them from passing measures which they believed desirable – as was to occur with the devolution referendums of 1979 which rejected the policies of the then government. And the reduction of the powers of the Lords in the Parliament Act meant that the peers could no longer refer issues to the people; while in 1918, the Bryce report rejected the referendum as a means to end deadlocks between the two houses.[30]

With the growth of strong and disciplined parties, the doctrine of the sovereignty of the people, of which the referendum was an emanation, faded away. Before 1914, Switzerland, the country which appeared to have carried the principle of the sovereignty of the people to its logical extreme, had seemed a paradigm of democratic government, a model worthy of some

---

[29] Seymour Martin Lipset and Stein Rokkan, eds., *Party Systems and Voter Alignments: Cross-National Perspectives* (Glencoe, IL: Free Press, 1967), p. 50.
[30] Cd. 9038, 1918.

imitation, and perhaps the direction in which other democracies were moving, After 1918, however, the Swiss model tended to be forgotten, and when it was remembered, it was seen as a quaint anomaly rather than a model. The experience on the Continent of Fascist and Nazi regimes, which misused the referendum, further discredited ideas of popular sovereignty. There was some fear of the plebiscitary techniques which had supposedly assisted these regimes to retain power. When Churchill in 1945 proposed a referendum on continuation of the wartime coalition, Attlee rebuffed him, saying 'I could not consent to the introduction into our national life of a device so alien to all our traditions as the referendum, which has only too often been the instrument of Nazism and fascism. Hitler's practices in the field of referenda and plebiscites can hardly have endeared these expedients to the British heart'.[31] The sovereignty of the people was seen not only as perhaps unattainable, but also as undesirable.

But the doctrine of the mandate, and with it, support for the referendum, came to be revived in the 1970s. Lipset and Rokkan published *Party Systems and Voter Alignments* in 1967. But from the 1970s, there appeared signs of a glacially slow but nonetheless perceptible unfreezing of the British party system and a decline in the dominance of the two major parties. This can be graphically illustrated in the table below. In 1951, there were just nine MPs, who did not belong to the Labour or Conservative parties. By February 1974, there were thirty-seven, but by 2017 there were seventy – and in 2019, there were eighty-two.

MPs elected from parties other than the Conservatives or Labour

1945	34
1950	11
1951	9
1955	8
1959	7
1964	9
1966	14
1970	12
February 1974	37
October 1974	39
1979	27
1983	40
1987	45

---

[31] *The Times*, 22 May 1945, 'July Election Nearer'.

1992	44
1997	76
2001	81
2005	92
2010	85
2015	85
2017	70
2019	82

In addition, wider social changes in Britain as in other western societies – the spread of ownership of property, shares and other assets – helped to diffuse power and to undermine the culture of deference. There was a greater emphasis on consumerism and choice in the public services. It would be unrealistic to expect that these changes would not have their consequences in the political sphere. They led to some distrust of political parties and other mediating institutions that had come to dominate Britain and other representative democracies. This distrust led to a renewed interest in measures of popular participation such as the referendum. As Dicey had written in 1915, 'no man who is really satisfied with the working of our party system will ever look with favour on an institution which aims at correcting the vices of party government'.[32]

There were also three specific reasons for the introduction of the referendum in the 1970s. The first was the return of the Irish Question into British politics, a result of the troubles at the end of the 1960s. The second was Europe. The third was devolution. All of these issues involved questions of identity, questions which the party system, based as it was on a socioeconomic cleavage, found it difficult to handle. Indeed, on none of these issues was the party system working effectively. The politics of the democratic class struggle was coming to seem less important; and with the growth of the politics of identity, there was a return of constitutional issues to the forefront of politics. But the main issue now was not the House of Commons versus the House of Lords, as had been the case before 1914, but the conflict between Britain and the EU and between Westminster and the non-English parts of the United Kingdom.

In Northern Ireland, the Westminster Model of alternating party majorities could not work, since there was a permanent Unionist majority, composed primarily of Protestants and a permanent Nationalist minority, primarily

---

[32] A. V. Dicey, 'Introduction' to 8th edition of *Law of the Constitution* (London: Macmillan, 1915), p. c.

Catholic, which had been discriminated against under the system of devolution from 1921 to 1972, dominated as it had been by the Unionists. In the early 1970s, the Heath government proposed a border poll, hoping that it could 'take the border out of politics' and so contribute to a cessation of violence. If the issue of the border could be settled once and for all, then, so it was hoped, sectarian animosity might be lessened. The border poll yielded a 98.6 per cent vote for maintaining the Union, but this landslide majority occurred because the parties representing the Nationalist minority advised their supporters to boycott the poll. The poll in fact did little to reduce violence, and the reasoning behind it was perhaps somewhat simplistic. For the Nationalists could argue that the outcome of the poll had been predetermined when the British government had legislated for partition in the Government of Ireland Act of 1920. Northern Ireland had been established on the basis of the six counties precisely because it was the largest area with a permanent Protestant majority that could comfortably be carved out of the island of Ireland. The referendum can only be used to resolve a political problem when there is agreement on the unit within which it is to be held. As Sir Henry Maine had noticed, 'Democracies are quite paralysed by the plea of Nationality. There is no more effective way of attacking them than by admitting the right of the majority to govern, but denying that the majority so entitled is the particular majority which claims the right'.[33] A referendum cannot resolve the problems of a divided society. For that to occur, it would not be sufficient to display the obvious fact that there is a Unionist majority in the North. What was needed was a settlement that could accommodate the needs of both the Unionist and Nationalist communities. That was not to be achieved until the Belfast or Good Friday Agreement of 1998.

An even more fundamental issue on which the party system seemed not to be working was Britain's relationship with the European Community. Whether Britain should or should not enter the Community was clearly a matter of major importance. But voters had not been given the opportunity of giving their view on that vital issue. In the 1970 general election – the last before Britain entered the Community in 1973 – all three major parties had been in favour of entry. So there was no way in which an elector could indicate by her vote that she was opposed to entry. The government that took Britain into the Community could not, therefore, claim a mandate for entry. The party system was not providing a democratic choice on this fundamental question.

---

[33] Henry Maine, *Popular Government*, 5th ed. (London: John Murray, 1897), p. 28.

But there was a further and even more important rationale for a referendum on the issue. For, even if the party system **had** been working effectively, many felt that a decision made by Parliament alone on so momentous an issue would lack legitimacy. The, Leader of the House of Commons, Edward Short, told the Commons in March 1975, that 'The issue continues to divide the country. The decision to go in has not been accepted. That is the essence of the case for having a referendum'.[34]

That 1975 referendum yielded a two to one majority for remaining in the Community. It was intended as a unique and unrepeatable event. The preface to the 1975 White Paper, *Referendum on UK Membership of the European Community*, declared 'The referendum is to be held because of the *unique* nature of the issue'.[35] After the referendum, a Conservative backbencher, asked Prime Minister, Harold Wilson,

> Will he keep to his determination not to repeat the constitutional experiment of the Referendum?

The Prime Minister replied, 'I certainly give the Right Honourable member – the assurance he seeks'.[36]

A junior minister had explained before the referendum why the European issue was unique:

> I have made it absolutely clear that in my view and that of the Government, the constitutional significance of our membership of the EEC is of a quite different order from any other issue. It is not just that it is more important; it is of a different order. There is, and there can be, no issue that is on all fours with it. That is why we say that this issue is the sole exception to the principle that we normally operate through parliamentary democracy.[37]

But Roy Jenkins, who had resigned, in 1972, from Labour's Shadow Cabinet, because he was opposed in principle to the referendum, exposed the weakness of this argument:

> Who can possibly say that? Once the principle of the referendum has been introduced into British politics it will not rest with one party to put a convenient limit to its use.[38]

---

[34] House of Commons, 11 Mar. 1975, vol. 888, col. 292.
[35] Cmnd. 5925, 1975, p. 2. Emphasis added.
[36] House of Commons Debates, vol. 893, col. 37, 9 June 1975.
[37] House of Commons Debates, vol. 881, cols. 1742–1743, 22 Nov. 1974.
[38] *The Times*, 11 Apr. 1972, cited in Bogdanor, *The People and the Party System*, p. 48.

Within just 18 months of the European Community referendum, the Labour government found itself committed, as a result of back-bench pressure, to concede referendums on devolution to Scotland and Wales. As Dicey had predicted in 1894, 'Once established the Referendum would never be got rid of short of a revolution'.[39] There were, admittedly, to be no further national referendums in the twentieth century but the twenty-first century has so far seen two national referendums, the first in 2011 on the alternative vote electoral system, and the second in 2016 on Britain's continued membership of the European Union. There have also, since 1997, been a number of referendums at sub-national level on devolution in the non-English parts of the United Kingdom, Scottish independence in 2014, and on directly elected mayors in England. A list is provided in the appendix to this chapter.

Referendums in Local Government

But it is perhaps at local level that the scope for the people to have a role in government is greatest and most educative. In his review of Tocqueville's *Democracy in America*, John Stuart Mill remarks that 'as we do not learn to read or write, to ride or swim, by being merely told how to do it, but by doing it, so it is only by practising popular government on a limited scale that the people will ever learn how to exercise it on a larger'.[40] There have been numerous local referendums, some on ad hoc issues. The issue of temperance led to local areas in Scotland and Wales being given the right to hold referendums. In Scotland, provision was made in the Temperance (Scotland) Act of 1913 for referendums on prohibition. Between 1913 and 1965, 1,131 of these were held.[41] The provision was abolished by the Licensing (Scotland) Act 1976. In Wales, the Licensing Act of 1961 provided that referendums on it could be held at seven-year intervals in local government areas on Sunday closing on the initiative of 500 local government electors. This provision was removed by the Sunday Licensing Act of 2003.

Since the late 1990s referendums have become a more regular feature of local government, due primarily to the provision in the Local Government Act, 2000, which required a referendum to be held before a local authority

---

[39] Letter to Leo Maxse, 2 Feb. 1894, cited in Richard A. Cosgrove, *The Rule of Law: Albert Venn Dicey, Victorian Jurist* (London: Macmillan, 1980), p. 107.
[40] In Mill's review of 'De Tocqueville on Democracy in America', in John M. Robson (ed.), *Collected Works*, vol. XVIII, *Essays on Politics and Society*, part 1 (Toronto: University of Toronto Press, 1977), p. 63.
[41] House of Commons Debates, 15 Dec. 1965, vol. 722, col. 283w.

can have a directly elected mayor. There had already been a referendum in 1998 on establishing a mayor in London, the first directly elected local government leader in British history. In the Local Government and Public Involvement in Health Act of 2007, the *requirement* for a referendum before a local authority could establish a directly elected mayor was abolished for English local authorities. But they still have the *power* to hold referendums, not only on whether to have an elected mayor, but on any alteration in governance. Fifty-two referendums have so far been held on directly elected mayors, of which sixteen have been successful. Six have been held on abolishing the post, three of which have been successful. In addition, Stoke-on-Trent held a successful referendum in 2008 on the council leader system while Fylde Borough Council in July 2014 held a referendum on reintroducing a committee system following a petition. In Wales, a referendum is still required, under the Local Government (Wales) Measure of 2011, to establish or abolish an elected mayor. There has, however, been just one such referendum, following a successful initiative, in 2004, in Ceredigion, in which the mayoral model was rejected.

In 2012 the coalition government declared that it would introduce directly elected mayors in the twelve largest English cities, subject to referendum. But only three of the twelve – Bristol, Leicester and Liverpool – voted to have a mayor. The new metro mayors introduced in combined authorities under the provisions of the Cities and Local Government Devolution Act in 2016 were introduced without referendums.

In addition to providing for referendums, the 2000 Local Government provided, for the first time in Britain, with the exception of Welsh Sunday closing referendums and parish council referendums, for use of the initiative in local government by means of which 5 per cent of local government electors could require their local authority to hold a referendum on an elected mayor. Two referendums have been held in response to petitions on moving from a mayoral system to a committee system – in the borough of Fylde and in West Dorset. Both were successful. The purpose of introducing the device of the initiative was to overcome the opposition of local councillors, a vested interest, to the introduction of directly elected mayors. For the first time in local government, therefore, electors were given the power to override the wishes of their local authority. The referendum allows voters to repair sins of *commission* committed by a governmental authority. The initiative allows them to repair sins of *omission*.

The Labour government elected in 1997 was anxious to encourage local participation and in its 1998 White Paper, *Modern Local Government in Touch with the People*, declared. 'The Government believes that councils should use referendums as an important tool to give local people a bigger say. The Government will therefore introduce legislation to confirm the power of councils to hold referendums. However, they would be neither obligatory nor binding –. Councils might wish to use referendums to consult their local people on such issues as major local developments or matters of particular local controversy.'[42] This commitment was given statutory form in section 16 of the Local Government Act, 2003.

Under the Coalition government which came to power in 2010, local authorities were required, under the provisions of the Localism Act of 2011 to hold a referendum if they were proposing an excessive increase in council tax, as defined in terms of principles defined by the Secretary of State and approved by the House of Commons. The provision does not apply to combined authorities, nor to Wales, where the National Assembly enjoys the power to cap excessive rises in council tax. There has been just one referendum under this provision so far when in 2015 the Bedfordshire Police and Crime Commissioner proposed a 15.8 per cent increase in council tax, a proposal rejected in the referendum. Warwick District Council proposed to hold in May 2020 a referendum, to offer residents the choice of whether to pay 3 per cent extra in council tax to fund a ring-fenced climate action fund. Due to the coronavirus crisis, however, the referendum was postponed. At the time of writing, it is not clear when or whether it will be held. The 2011 Act also provided for binding local referendums in England on neighbourhood development plans on which there have been around 1,000 to date.

There is also provision for non-binding referendums in parish councils, sometimes called town councils in urban areas, and community councils in Wales. Such councils currently cover around 37 per cent of England and Wales. The 1972 Local Government Act, section 12, provided for referendums in such councils on parish affairs. These could be triggered by one of two methods. Either six parishioners could trigger it with the support of the chairman of the parish council; or, alternatively, ten parishioners or one-third of those present at a parish meeting whichever was the smaller, could trigger it. Draft regulations prepared in 2017 propose increasing the trigger needed to call a poll; but at the time of writing, they have not been implemented. In Wales, the Local Government (Wales) Measure of 2011 provided for non-binding referendums to be held if demanded by a majority of community

---

[42] Cm 4014. Para. 4.8.

council electors present at a meeting comprising no fewer than 10 per cent of local government electors for the community or 150 of the electors – whichever is the fewer.

Parish Meetings

In the late nineteenth century, it was thought by some, mainly but not exclusively in the Liberal Party, that the people could govern themselves locally, enacting measures for themselves through parish meetings. The parish as a unit of government in addition to its ecclesiastical role can trace its history to medieval times, and there seems to have been a long tradition of direct democracy at parish or village level. Under Elizabeth I, the parish was given functions in relation to vagrancy and poor relief. There seems to have been a long tradition of direct democracy at parish or village level. In the seventeenth and eighteenth centuries, there were around 9,000 parish vestries which were generally assemblies of male ratepayers, with labourers excluded. But in some vestries, only landowners or the more influential ratepayers could participate, while in some other places meetings were open to everyone in the parish. In a few, unmarried women otherwise qualified could vote and hold office, long before they had the vote for local government or House of Commons elections. These vestries, presided over by the local vicar or rector, were responsible for welfare services – poor relief, provision for orphans, housing for the elderly or homeless, and medical attention. It has even been suggested that 'To the people of a village in the eighteenth century the real government was not the Cabinet or Parliament but the parish vestry. It mattered much more who was the overseer of the poor or the surveyor of highways in the parish than whether the Duke of Newcastle, the Duke of Grafton, or the Marquis of Rockingham was Prime Minister in far-away Westminster'.[43] But this picture must be qualified by the fact that officers such as the overseer of the poor or the surveyor of highways were, like other local officials, not elected but 'nominated by and technically responsible only to the Crown'.[44] And the decisions of the parish could always be over-ridden by Justices of the Peace, again appointed by central government. In 1831, an Act was passed providing for elected vestries, but

---

[43] K. P. Poole and Bryan Keith-Lucas, *Parish Government 1894–1994* (London: National Association of Local Councils, 1994), p. 17.

[44] Basil Williams, *The Whig Supremacy 1714–1760*, 2nd ed. (Oxford: Clarendon Press, 1962), pp. 46–47.

their functions came to be attenuated in the 1834 century with passage of the Poor Law. Then, in 1868, Gladstone abolished compulsory church rates. So, in 1834, the parish had 'lost its most important administrative function' while after 1868, 'the parish as a unit of government fell into decay'.[45]

Parish government was revived in the 1894 Local Government Act, sometimes called the Parish Councils Act. This Act separated the civic parish from the ecclesiastical parish and provided for parish councils and parish meetings. It put the coping stone on a structure of local government which was not altered in any fundamental respect until the 1970s. Radicals in 1894 hoped that parish meetings would become genuine village parliaments, so proving the virtues of direct democracy as village parliaments. A Continental lawyer, Josef Redlich, observed of the 1894 Act that by it, 'England has created for herself "Self Government" in the true sense of the word. – And this is the root of the incomparable strength and health of the English body politic'.[46] But such hopes, inevitably no doubt, remained unfulfilled. In its written evidence to the 1966–1969 Royal Commission on Local Government, the Redcliffe-Maud Commission, the National Association of Local Councils declared that 'these 3,300 independent parish meetings are not effective bodies and that, with notable exceptions, despite the statutory requirement of half-yearly meetings, they seldom meet at all.' In Northumberland, none of the forty parishes without councils held any meetings at all. By 1988, only five out of forty-six parish meetings in the county actually met, and where meetings were held, attendance was very sparse.[47] The main role of parish meetings seems to have been to act as lobbyists to district and county councils. They have not become active local authorities in their own right. Even so, Lord Redcliffe-Maud, chair of the Royal Commission on Local Government, declared in a House of Lords debate on the 1972 Act that 'We in the Royal Commission thought, and I still think, that the parish provides some of the best examples of genuine British self-government that one could find anywhere in this country, and as fine an example of local self-government as one would find anywhere in the world. In the parish community there are people who at least know each other by sight. It is that grass-roots community which I think should continue to be

---

[45] Sir Llewellyn Woodward, *The Age of Reform 1815–1970*, 2nd ed. (Oxford: Clarendon Press, 1962), p. 459.
[46] Josef Redlich and F. W. Hirst, *The History of Local Government in England*, [1903] (London: Macmillan, 1958), p. 221.
[47] Quoted in Poole and Keith-Lucas, *Parish Government*, p. 240, 243.

the basis of the whole structure of local self-government.'[48] The Commission received evidence that in rural areas, around 85 per cent thought of their home area as the civil parish or an even smaller area, and only 2 per cent their rural district council. 'Of all types of local authority, parishes are seen as natural communities by the overwhelming majority of their inhabitants.' The Commission declared that, since they were recommending larger units of local government, parishes would become more important than in the past.[49] Even so the 1972 Act removed many of the powers of parish meetings.

The provision for parishes is now largely determined by the Local Government Act of 1972, as amended by the Local Government Finance Act of 1992, the Local Government and Rating Act of 1997, and the Local Government and Public Involvement in Health Act of 2007. Provision depends upon the size of the parish. Where there are more than 1,000 electors, the principal council – either the district council or, in unitary authorities, the county council – is required to create a parish council, and the parish meeting there functions perhaps as an electoral college for a system of representative democracy. Where there are between 150 and 1,000 electors, the principal council may recommend either a parish council or a parish meeting detached from a parish council. But the parish can, if it so wishes, apply to the district or unitary council for the parish council to be abolished. With under 150 electors, there cannot be a parish council and so, if the parish seeks self-government, it must establish a parish meeting. It is the parish meeting detached from a parish council which constitutes direct democracy. In these circumstances, the parish meeting assumes the role of a parish council and enjoys certain statutory powers, though powers more restricted than those of a parish council. However, under section 109 of the 1972 Local Government Act, a parish meeting may request that its principal council confers the powers of a parish council on it. A parish meeting detached from a parish council must assemble annually between 1 March and 1 June and on at least one other occasion during the year. A meeting may be convened by the Chair, the district councillor – or county councillor where there is a unitary authority – or any six electors. A parish meeting has no councillors, but officers are elected at the annual general meeting to carry out its decisions. There are currently over 13,000 parish meetings in England, though over 700 have no financial transactions, Their powers are either

---

[48] Ibid, pp. 204–205.
[49] Report of Royal Commission on Local Government (Redcliffe-Maud Report), Cmnd 4040 1969, paras. 233, 236, 235.

statutory or acquired by inheritance from pre-1894 authorities over such matters as allotments, burials, bus shelters, the appointment of trustees to parochial charities, churchyards, lighting, public open spaces, and war memorials.[50] They have no revenue raising powers but section 39 of the Local Government Finance Act of 1992 provides for a power to precept on their principal council for funds.

But the sad truth is that, contrary to the hopes of Liberals in 1894, while there may be enthusiasm for public participation in the abstract, there is comparatively little willingness to take advantage of such possibilities of local participation as are actually available. And indeed participation in local government elections remains the lowest in western Europe. By 2007, one authority could declare that 'Local government is no longer, in any meaningful sense, a part of the British constitution.'[51]

Recent Experiments

There have been some recent experiments with other instruments designed to increase public participation – primary elections, the recall of MPs and the e-petition system.

Between 2006 and 2009, the Conservative party, traditionally a party deferential to its elites, experimented, as part of the modernisation agenda of David Cameron, the party leader, with open primaries to select parliamentary candidates. Such primaries provide for the selection of parliamentary candidates, not just by party members, a small minority of the electorate, but by the voters as a whole. In Britain, by contrast with the United States, there has been no tradition of open primaries, candidates having been generally selected by party members or by party committees. One hundred and eighteen open primaries have been held by the Conservatives to choose parliamentary candidates from a short list drawn up by local committees. In two of these, there has been provision for postal votes. There have also been open primary elections in London to choose Conservative candidates for mayor of London. Some feared that primaries would be open to tactical manipulation by supporters of the other parties who would deliberately support the Conservative candidate least likely to win. But there has been no evidence of this. The first London primary

---

[50] In Wales, however, community councils have no executive powers at all.
[51] Anthony King, 'The Ghost of Local Government', in Vernon Bogdanor (ed.), *The British Constitution* (Oxford: Oxford University Press, 2007), p. 177.

resulted in a victory for Boris Johnson, the most popular of the candidates on offer, and the one most likely to win the election for the Conservatives as he was in fact to do in 2008. But the experiment with primary elections came to an end after 2015 largely because of its high costs. Some supporters of primaries have argued that they should be financed by the state, but this proposal raises the thorny issue of the public funding of political parties, something unlikely to be popular especially after the parliamentary expenses scandal of 2009.

One response to the expenses scandal was the Recall of MPs Act 2015, in which provision was made for recall by constituents in three cases – first, when an MP was convicted of an offence or sentence which did not already lead to automatic disqualification – MPs receiving a custodial sentence of over a year automatically lose their seats under the provisions of the Representation of the People Act of 1981; second, when an MP has been suspended from the Commons for at least ten sitting days; and third when an MP has been convicted of an offence under section 10 of the Parliamentary Standards Act of 2009 of making false or misleading parliamentary allowances claims. Petitions are to be available for signature for six weeks and have to be signed by at least 10 per cent of eligible registered voters. If a petition is successful, the seat becomes vacant, but the recalled ex-MP is allowed to stand again as a candidate in the ensuing by-election. By August 2019, there had been three such recall petitions, two of which succeeded in attracting the required number of signatures. The first, in July 2018, concerning the MP for North Antrim who had been suspended for thirty parliamentary sitting days for offences against Commons rules, failed to attract the required number of signatures. The second, concerning the MP for Peterborough, who had been sentenced to a three-month custodial sentence for perverting the course of justice, in May 2019, was successful and the MP did not contest the ensuing by-election. The third, concerning the MP for Brecon and Radnor, who had offended against section 10 of the Parliamentary Standards Act, in June 2019, was also successful. In this case the recalled ex-MP, a Conservative, stood in the by-election, but lost the seat to the Liberal Democrats. He did not stand again in the 2019 general election. One local council, Kingston upon Thames, has introduced a non-statutory system of recall of councillors. But, at the time of writing, no such petition has yet been triggered. Some have argued for wider use of the recall, an instrument designed to provide for accountability between elections. Voters, it is argued, should not have to wait until a general election to remove an unrepresentative or otherwise unsatisfactory MP. But governments have resisted wider use of the recall since they believe that it would make MPs vulnerable to attack on grounds of policy disagreement, or subject to excessive pressure from local interest groups, so undermining the representative function of MPs.

A further response to the parliamentary expenses crisis was the relaunching of an e-petition website, introduced by Tony Blair in November 2006. There has been a long tradition of parliamentary petitions in Britain. Indeed it appears that there were around a million such petitions between 1780 and 1918. One such petition in 1783 called for the abolition of slavery, but this did not have effect until 1833. In August 2011, the government relaunched the website. Any e-petition securing over 100,000 signatures would be eligible for parliamentary debate, either in Westminster Hall or the floor of the Commons, while e-petitions gaining more than 10,000 signatures receive a government response. During the 2015–2017 parliament, 10,950 such petitions were submitted and in the 2017–2019 parliament, 28,102. In the 2017–2019 parliament, 456 petitions received a response from the government and 74 were debated. An early petition, in 2011, calling for a referendum on the EU proved a source of considerable embarrassment to the government which was at that time opposed to a referendum. In a debate in the Commons in October 2011, eighty-one Conservative MPs defied a three line whip to support a referendum. This revolt may well have played a factor in Prime Minister, David Cameron's decision, in January 2013, to reverse Conservative policy by proposing a referendum. Further embarrassment followed an e-petition on fuel prices in November 2011, which persuaded the government in its Autumn Statement to cancel a scheduled increase in fuel duty, and postpone a further planned rise in June 2012. In March 2019, over 6 million signed a petition calling on Britain to remain in the EU, in effect reversing the outcome of the 2016 referendum. This was the largest petition in the website's history. Four million signed a petition calling for a second EU referendum. These petitions were, of course, unsuccessful. Later in 2019, 1.7 million signed a petition urging the Prime Minister not to suspend Parliament; while in 2017 1.8 million had signed a petition urging Parliament to stop President Trump from making a state visit to the UK. These petitions too were unsuccessful. The only other petition to attract over a million signatures was one in 2007 opposing government plans to introduce national road pricing. Charges were not in fact introduced. But, amongst successful e-petitions have been one in 2015 to abolish the tampon tax on female sanitary products, organised by a student, which attracted around 64,000 signatures. But the tax could not be abolished until after Brexit in 2020, since the government claimed that it was required by EU regulations. There were also successful e-petitions on matters such as funding for brain tumour research, giving police dogs and horses greater legal protection if they are attacked on duty, and one launched by the restaurateur, Jamie Oliver, calling for the taxing of sugary drinks, launched in 2013, which led to legislation in 2018. But there have also been many frivolous e-petitions, all unsuccessful, including petitions to flood the Channel Tunnel, to ban cats from going outdoors, and to restore fish and chips wrapped in newspaper!

It is, of course, too early to come to any definite conclusions concerning the extent to which these three recently introduced devices have genuinely increased public participation in politics and brought the people closer to government.

The Referendum and the Constitution

It is the referendum which, of all the instruments of direct participation, has the greatest constitutional significance. It has indeed now become an accepted part of the British constitution. This was recognised in the Political Parties. Elections and Referendum Act of the year 2000, which in Part VII provided a legislative framework for the conduct of referendums. Since 1997, a huge number of referendum promises have come to be made by the three main political parties in their election manifestoes.

1997.
Conservative Party. Referendum on single currency.
Labour Party. Referendum on the voting system.
        Referendums on devolution in Scotland and Wales.
        Referendum on establishment of London mayor.
        Referendums on regional devolution.
        Referendum on single currency.
Liberal Democrat Party. Referendum on constitutional issues.
        Referendum on 'any transfer of power to European institutions'.
        Referendum on single currency.

2001.
Conservative Party.   Referendum on 'surrender' of 'any more of Parliament's rights and powers to Brussels'.
Labour Party.   Referendum on voting system.
        Referendum on single currency.

Liberal Democrat Party. Referendum on the voting system.
Referendum on single currency.
Referendums on regional devolution.

2005.
Conservative Party. Referendum on the Welsh Assembly.
Referendum on the EU Constitutional Treaty.
Labour Party. Referendum on the voting system.
Referendum on the EU Constitutional Treaty.
Referendum on the single currency.
Liberal Democrat Party. Referendum on the EU Constitutional Treaty.
Referendum on single currency.

2010.
Conservative Party. Referendum lock on 'any proposed future treaty that transferred areas of power or competences'.
Referendum on any use of a 'major' ratchet clause in the Lisbon Treaty,
Labour Party. Referendum on the voting system.
Referendum on reform of the House of Lords.
Referendum on single currency.
Liberal Democrat Party. Referendum on national constitution.
Referendum on membership of the European Union 'the next time a British government signs up for fundamental change in the relationship between the UK and the EU'.

2015.
Conservative Party. Referendum on a negotiated 'New Settlement for Britain in Europe', before the end of 2017.
Labour Party. Referendum lock on any 'transfer of powers from Britain to the European Union'.
Liberal Democrat Party. In-out referendum on 'any Treaty change involving a material transfer of sovereignty from the UK to the EU'.[52]

Before the 1970s, however, the referendum had come to be seen as unconstitutional. Indeed, in 1964, the author of a standard work on British government remarked, 'It has occasionally been proposed that a referendum might

---

[52] Martin Westlake, *Slipping Loose: The UK's Long Drift Away from the European Union* (Newcastle: Agenda Publishing, 2020), pp. 35–36.

be held on a particular issue, but the proposals do not ever appear to have been taken seriously'.[53] A main reason for this is that the referendum was seen to contradict the principle of the sovereignty of Parliament. But, of course, if Parliament can enact any law that it chooses, it can enact a statute providing for a referendum. What it cannot do, according to this principle, is to enact a referendum that is binding on Parliament, although that too may now be in question. In 2011, the legislation providing for the alternative vote referendum – the Parliamentary Voting System and Constituencies Act of 2011 – imposed upon the government, in the event of a vote in favour of the change, a legal duty to bring the new system into force; if the vote was against change, the government was required to repeal the Act. The Scotland and Wales Acts of 1978 providing for devolution referendums in Scotland and Wales, had required the minister to bring the Act into force in the event of a 'Yes' vote, comprising at least 40 per cent of the electorate – the referendums held under the Acts have been the only ones so far held with a threshold over and above a bare majority of voters – and if the threshold was not achieved, he was required to lay an order repealing the Act. The Northern Ireland Act of 1998, section 1, provides that if a referendum in the province were to yield a majority in favour of joining the rest of the island of Ireland, the Secretary of State must lay the appropriate provision before Parliament. But this legislation does not – and perhaps cannot – impose legal duties upon Parliament which could, presumably in each case, vote against the provisions laid down by the government. And, indeed, in March 1979, there was some talk by ministers in the Labour government of asking Parliament to reject repeal of the Scotland Act, since the devolution referendum in Scotland had yielded a Yes vote of 33 per cent of the electorate and a No vote of 31 per cent of the electorate, a majority but insufficient to meet the threshold. In the event, however, the Scotland Act was in fact repealed by the Conservative government elected later in 1979. A referendum can legally bind the government, but there must, nevertheless, remain some doubt as to whether a referendum could legally bind Parliament.

The 1975 referendum, however, had been explicitly advisory, as was the 2016 Brexit referendum. But, on both occasions, the government agreed to be bound by the result. The constitutional status of an advisory referendum was well summarised by Edward Short, Leader of the House, in 1975, when he said, 'The Government will be bound by its result, but Parliament, of course, cannot be bound by it'. He then added, however, that, 'one would not expect

---

[53] Birch, *Representative and Responsible Government*, p. 227.

honourable members to go against the wishes of the people'.[54] So far MPs have not done so. In practical terms, indeed the advisory referendums have been binding since it was widely, though not universally, accepted that a further mandate in the form of another referendum would be required to avoid implementing the outcome. Most of those who argued against Brexit accepted that a second referendum would be needed to avoid it. From a practical point of view, it would be difficult to imagine a referendum outcome that would not be perceived as binding, unless perhaps there was a very small turnout and a very small majority. If, for example, the alternative vote referendum had yielded a 1 per cent vote for change on a 25 per cent turnout, some MPs might well have sought to ignore it.

Some believed in 1975 that the referendum would cause an upheaval in the constitution. It did not. Its main effects have been on the party system. The 1975 referendum prefigured the breakaway of pro-Europeans in the Labour Party into the SDP in 1981, where they worked in alliance with the Liberals as they had done in the referendum. The 2011 alternative vote referendum undermined the bonds of confidence between the Conservatives and their Liberal Democrat coalition partners. The 2014 Scottish independence referendum, in which 45 per cent voted for independence gave a boost to the SNP which in the 2015 general election won fifty-six of the fifty-nine seats in Scotland; while the 2016 referendum transformed the Conservative Party into a Brexit party and destroyed UKIP as a protest party.

The referendum seeks to separate the issue of which policy voters favour from the issue of which government they favour. But it does not always succeed in achieving this aim. Particularly when holding a referendum is discretionary, the rejection of a government proposal seems inevitably to involve the standing of the government, and a defeat is seen as a humiliation. Voters opposed to the government may, therefore, be encouraged to reject a proposal not so much because they dislike it but because they dislike the government putting it forward. Instead of answering the question, 'Do you support the proposal?' they might in effect be answering a quite different question, 'Do you support the government?' That was part of the reason why Scottish devolution failed to achieve a 40 per cent Yes vote in the referendum in March 1979, which occurred shortly after the 'winter of discontent' of public sector strikes had rendered the Labour government deeply unpopular. Defeat in the referendum did indeed lead to the end of that government, which was in a minority in the Commons, after the SNP withdrew its

---

[54] House of Commons, 11 Mar. 1975. vol. 888, col. 293.

support in the vote of confidence held on 28 March 1979, four weeks after the referendums, and the government was defeated by one vote. In 2016, following the referendum vote to leave the European Union, Prime Minister David Cameron immediately resigned. The referendum had thus become a form of recall, used to oust an unpopular government or Prime Minister.

A further constitutional difficulty is that the referendum has so far been triggered primarily for reasons of convenience of the political class, to avoid a party split or a backbench rebellion. It has been used only when the political class found itself unable to resolve a problem. Precisely for this reason it, is unlikely to be used very frequently; and when it is used it is likely to be as a tactical weapon. It is political leaders, not the people, who make the decision to commit to a referendum. The people, although they can put pressure upon the political class, cannot, as they can in Italy and Switzerland, *require* a referendum to be called. It is, therefore, somewhat misleading to speak of 'direct democracy' when the use of the referendum is controlled by political elites.[55] The referendum is a weapon for the political class, not the people.

Even so, the referendum has created a new method of validating laws. It provides that some laws can be demarcated from others as being so fundamental that they require validation from the people acting as a third chamber of Parliament. To this extent there is entrenchment against change, and the referendum provides a form of constitutional protection. But, because Britain lacks a codified constitution, there seemed no clear method of demarcating those laws that *are* fundamental and require the special protection of a referendum from laws that are not fundamental. Dicey's friend, James Bryce, asked him in 1915,

(1) What is to be the authority to decide when a Bill should be referred?
(2) How can 'constitutional changes' be defined in a country that has no [rigid] constitution?[56]

Since Britain has an elastic constitution, so also, it appeared, use of the referendum must be elastic.

---

[55] Matthew Mendlessohn and Andrew Parkin, 'Introduction: Referendum Democracy' in Mendlessohn and Parkin (eds.), *Referendum Democracy: Citizens, Elites and Deliberation in Referendum Campaigns* (London: Palgrave, 2001), p. 4.
[56] Bryce to Dicey, 6 Apr. 1915, Bryce papers, Bodleian Library, MS 4 fo.84.

The People and the Constitution

But it seems that in an unplanned and ad hoc way, it may be said to have become a convention of the constitution that decisions involving the transfer of the legislative powers of Parliament – whether upwards to a European body or downwards through devolution – require endorsement by the people. So also does a decision to join or leave the European Union and a decision by one part of the United Kingdom – for example, Scotland or Northern Ireland – to secede. The Northern Ireland Constitution Act 1973 established the principle that the province would remain in the United Kingdom only for as long as the majority consented to it, consent now to be established by a referendum. While there is no equivalent legislation in the case of Scotland, it has come to be accepted that Scottish independence requires validation in a referendum. In addition, the introduction of a radically new constitutional mechanism such as a new electoral system is held to require a referendum. The referendum has so far been used only to validate legislative proposals providing for a fundamental alteration in the status of Parliament, the machinery by which the law is made, or the methods by which those who make the law are chosen. There is a strong rationale for this requirement in liberal thought. In his *Second Treatise of Government*, Locke argues that, 'The Legislative cannot transfer the power of making laws to any other hands. For it being but a delegated power from the People, they who have it cannot pass it to others'.[57] Voters, it might be said, entrust MPs as agents with legislative powers, but they give them no authority to transfer those powers, to make radical alterations in the legislature, in the machinery by which the laws are to be made, or in the method by which representatives are elected. Such authority, it may be suggested, can be obtained only through a specific mandate, that is, a referendum. The referendum, therefore, could be argued to be in accordance with, rather than in opposition to, basic principles of liberal constitutionalism.

Referendums, even when advisory, pose the political principle of the sovereignty of the people against the legal principle of the sovereignty of Parliament. The 2016 referendum has been called the most significant constitutional event in Britain since the Restoration of the monarchy in 1660.[58] For it showed, or perhaps confirmed, that, on the issue of Europe, the sovereignty of the people trumped the sovereignty of Parliament. Even though the

---

[57] Para. 141.
[58] By my colleague, Takis Tridimas, Professor of European Law at King's College, London, in a seminar at King's shortly after the referendum.

majority for Brexit was narrow, it was regarded by nearly all MPs as decisive. And in 2017, MPs accepted it when they passed the EU Notification of Withdrawal Bill on second reading by a majority of 384 votes. Nevertheless, Brexit has come about, not because government or Parliament favoured it, but because the people favoured it. Government and Parliament felt themselves constrained to do something that they did not wish to do. That was a situation quite without precedent in Britain's long constitutional history. The majority of the Cabinet which legislated for Brexit were Remainers; so were the majority in the Commons, and even the majority of Conservative MPs; and the majority in the Lords for Remain was even larger than that in the Commons. In the conflict between a supposedly sovereign Parliament and a sovereign people, the sovereign people triumphed. Europe, therefore, has been responsible for the introduction of a new principle into the British constitution – the principle of the sovereignty of the people. The people had become, on the European issue, in effect, a third chamber of Parliament, issuing legislative instructions to the other two. The sovereignty of Parliament was now to be constrained not by Brussels, as it had been while Britain remained in the European Union, but by the people, since the decisions of MPs on major constitutional issues could be overcome by those of the people.

The principle of the sovereignty of the people which the referendum exemplifies has proved by no means uncontroversial. Indeed, some of the arguments used against holding a referendum in 2016 echoed those used by conservatives in the nineteenth century against the extension of the franchise. Some even feared mob rule. After the French revolution, the French reactionary, Joseph de Maistre, went so far as to declare that 'The principle of the sovereignty of the people is so dangerous that, even if it were true, it would be necessary to conceal it'.[59] But the referendum, far from leading to mob rule, has proved an instrument of constitutional protection, providing a safeguard against major constitutional changes which the people do not want. It prevented, for example, devolution to the North-East in 2004, a policy favoured by the government, but rejected by the people by a four to one majority. It may also have prevented Britain from joining the euro, since that too was a policy favoured by the Blair government. But the government had promised that Britain would not join without endorsement in a referendum. The referendum on the euro, however, never occurred, since not a

---

[59] Joseph de Maistre, *Oeuvres Completes*, various editions, vol. 9, Paris.

single opinion poll showed a majority of voters in favour of it. The referendum, therefore, has become the people's veto. It was, Dicey believed, 'the only check on the predominance of party which is at the same time democratic and conservative'.[60] Had it not been for the European issue, however, it is perfectly possible that the referendum and the principle of the sovereignty of the people would not have become part of the twenty-first century constitution. And it is just possible that the twenty-first century constitution will prove more hospitable to the doctrine of popular sovereignty than the twentieth century constitution has been.

---

[60] Dicey, 'Ought the referendum to be introduced into England?' [sic], *Contemporary Review* 1890, p. 507.

Appendix: The Referendum in Britain

A Referendums Held

1. **1973. Northern Ireland Border poll.** Turnout 59%.
   591,820 (57.5%) for Northern Ireland to remain part of United Kingdom.
   6,463 (0.6%) for Northern Ireland to be joined with the Republic of Ireland.

2. **1975. Referendum on EEC membership: 'Do you think that the United Kingdom should stay in the European Community (the Common Market)?'**
   Turnout 65%
   65% Yes
   35% No

3. **1979. Should the Scotland Act, 1978 be implemented?** Turnout 63%.
   52% Yes (33% of electorate)
   48% No

4. **1979. Should the Wales Act, 1978 be implemented?** Turnout 58%.
   20% Yes
   80% No

5. **1997. Scottish Devolution.** Turnout 61%.
   Establishment of Scottish Parliament.
   Yes 74%
   No 26%
   Limited taxing powers.
   Yes 64%
   No 36%

6. **1997. Welsh Assembly.** Turnout 50%.
   Yes 50.3%
   No 49.7%

7 **Government proposals for Greater London Authority with a directly elected mayor and council.** Turnout 34%.
   Yes to government 72%.
   No 28%

8 **1998. Northern Ireland. Belfast Agreement.** 80% turnout.
   Yes 71%
   No 29%

9 **2004. Regional Assembly in North-East.** 48% turnout.
   Yes 22%
   No 78%.

10 **2011. Referendum on Extending Powers of the Welsh Assembly.** Turnout 36%.
   Yes 64%
   No 36%

11 **2011. Referendum on the Alternative Vote Electoral System.** Turnout 42%.
   Yes 32%
   No 68%

12 **2014. Referendum Should Scotland be an independent country.** Turnout 85%.
   Yes. 45%
   No 55%

13 **2016. Referendum on Membership of the European Union.** Turnout 72%.
   Remain 48%
   Leave 52%.

10

Constitutional Theory and Thought*

JEFFREY GOLDSWORTHY

The Medieval Period

Origins

The main questions concerning English governance addressed by medieval theorists were: (a) the division of authority between the Church, headed by the Pope, and the king; (b) the extent to which the king was bound by law and custom; (c) whether he was bound to act with the counsel and consent of his magnates; and (d) whether he could legitimately be resisted or even deposed for violating moral, religious, customary or legal constraints.

Underlying these questions was a tension between the need for effective royal power to achieve the principal responsibilities of kingship – defending the realm, while maintaining peace and dispensing justice within it – and prevention of misuse or under-use of that power, which threatened the same goals. Attempts to constrain royal authority might undermine the supreme, unitary power required for successful governance.[1]

To answer these questions various sources were consulted:

(1) Scripture and theology, including teachings of Church Fathers such as Augustine.[2]
(2) Long-standing laws and customary norms, real or supposed, mentioned in royal charters, purported compilations such as *The Laws of Edward the Confessor* (twelfth century) and legal treatises such as 'Bracton'.[3] These were

---

* I thank Johann Sommerville, Wilf Prest, Michael Lobban and the editors for helpful comments on earlier drafts.
[1] C. Carpenter, 'Resisting and Deposing Kings in England in the Thirteenth, Fourteenth and Fifteenth Centuries', in R. von Friedeburg, ed., *Murder and Monarchy: Regicide in European History, 1300–1800* (Palgrave Macmillan, 2004), 99.
[2] J. Kilcullen and J. Robinson, 'Medieval Political Philosophy' (2017), *Stanford Encyclopedia of Philosophy* at https://plato.stanford.edu/entries/medieval-political/ sections 2, 3 and 4 (viewed 16 May 2019).
[3] D. Carpenter, *Magna Carta* (Penguin Classics, 2015), 253–254.

woven together into what modern historians describe as a largely fictional 'ancient constitution' supposedly created by the Anglo-Saxons or Britons.[4]
(3) Roman law and canon law, which helped the formation of the 'ius commune', a European common law developed by medieval jurists,[5] from which English lawyers borrowed useful concepts, terminology and norms.[6]
(4) Classical philosophy, including writings of Cicero, the Stoics, and Aristotle, and especially their theories of natural law.[7]

Each source could be enlisted to support two competing kinds of theories.[8] 'Descending' theories held that kings derived their authority from, and were accountable only to, God, were the source of all other secular authority in the kingdom, and apart from God's law, were subject only to self-imposed constraints that could be overridden in circumstances of necessity. 'Ascending' theories held that royal authority, and the secular norms constraining it, both derived ultimately from the community, which could legitimately resist egregious violations of them.[9] From the fourteenth century, 'inconsistent legacies and uneasy compromises' between these two kinds of theories created

> a constant tension between the elements of the polity – king, magnates, churchmen, commons – which could at times lurch into crisis … The political system of late medieval England, because it was a historical amalgam, was essentially unstable, its tensions exposed by conflict and fuelled by precedents. So it would remain until the seventeenth century.[10]

King and Church

The king was the foundation and centre of the apparatus that wielded public power.[11] He was a quasi-sacred figure – anointed with holy oil at his

---

[4] See M. Goldie, 'Retrospect: The Ancient Constitution and the Languages of Political Thought' (2019) 62 *The Historical Journal* 3–34.

[5] K. Pennington, 'Politics in Western Jurisprudence', in A. Padovani and P. G. Stein, eds., *The Jurists' Philosophy of Law from Rome to the Seventeenth Century* (Springer, 2007), 157, especially 172–173.

[6] R. H. Helmholz, 'Magna Carta and the *ius commune*' (1999) 66 *University of Chicago Law Review* 297; H. Berman, *Law and Revolution: The Formation of the Western Legal Tradition* (Harvard University Press, 1983), 123.

[7] Kilcullen and Robinson, 'Medieval Political Philosophy', section 7.

[8] J. Greenberg and M. J. Sechler, 'Constitutionalism Ancient and Early Modern: The Contributions of Roman Law, Canon Law and English Common Law' (2013) 34 *Cardozo Law Review* 1021, 1026–1043.

[9] See G. Harriss, *Shaping the Nation: England 1360–1461* (Clarendon Press, 2005), 3–6.

[10] Ibid, 5.

[11] C. Carpenter, *The Wars of the Roses: Politics and the Constitution in England, c. 1437–1509* (Cambridge University Press, 1997), 27.

coronation, and reputed to have healing powers – and the overlord of a feudal system structured by the reciprocal rights and obligations of lords and their vassals.[12] Kingship was originally personal, but gradually the idea developed that the Crown was a continuing public office, with intrinsic possessions, powers and rights, distinct from the individuals who from time to time held it.[13]

Throughout Europe, the temporal power of secular rulers co-existed with the power of the Church, headed by the Pope, in spiritual affairs. It was accepted that the Church possessed liberties, powers and jurisdictions that kings could not encroach upon. Despite continual disagreements about details, 'the doctrine of the two powers as such was never questioned' and 'provided the framework for debate'.[14] Most disagreements concerned which of the two powers was in principle superior, the appointment of churchmen, their immunity from prosecution in secular courts, and liability of the Church to taxation. Some Popes claimed authority to superintend the conduct of temporal affairs, by appointing secular rulers, instructing them on their moral duties, and chastising, excommunicating or even deposing them for their failings.[15] Papal claims of supremacy were supported by scholars such as Thomas Aquinas and Giles of Rome,[16] but opposed by others, including John of Paris, Marsiglio of Padua, and William of Ockham.[17] But expansive Papal claims never prevailed in England, where the king was always the dominant partner in 'a close and symbiotic relationship between church and state',[18] with disagreements usually resolved in his favour.[19]

England's best-known twelfth century political philosopher, the cleric John of Salisbury, defended the supremacy of the Church over the temporal power. He was influenced by classical writings available to him, particularly of Cicero, and the teachings of Augustine and the Church.[20] His book on

---

[12] R. Bartlett, *England under the Norman and Angevin Kings 1075–1225* (Clarendon Press, 2000), 121–130.
[13] J. Allison, *The English Historical Constitution* (Cambridge University Press, 2007), ch. 3.
[14] S. L. Jenkinson, 'Church and State', in D. Miller, ed., *The Blackwell Encyclopaedia of Political Thought* (Blackwell Reference, 1987), 69.
[15] Kilcullen and Robinson, *'Medieval Political Philosophy'*, sections 8 and 10.
[16] Ibid, sections 9.1 and 10.   [17] Ibid, sections 11, 12 and 13.
[18] G. W. Bernard, *The Late Medieval English Church: Vitality and Vulnerability before the Break with Rome* (Yale University Press, 2012), 20 and ch. 2 passim.
[19] Bernard, *Late Medieval English Church*, 18, 23, 27, 34, 37, 39, 41, 47–48.
[20] See K. Bollermann and C. Nederman, 'John of Salisbury' (2016), in the *Stanford Encyclopedia of Philosophy* at https://plato.stanford.edu/entries/john-salisbury/ (viewed 16 Mar., 2019), sections 2 and 3.

statecraft, *Policraticus* (c 1159), analogised the body politic to a natural organic body, in which the ruler is the head, the Church the soul, the ruler's counsellors the heart, the peasants the feet, and so on.[21] All parts of this body had to perform their roles in a spirit of cooperative reciprocity for the community to enjoy peace, justice and prosperity.[22] A prince should comply with both positive and natural law, but there was no legal remedy for royal misconduct: he 'ought to be one who cultivates equity from love of justice rather than from fear of punishment.'[23] However, rulers whose flagrant crimes endangered the body politic could be deposed or even killed, because tyrants were not genuine kings.[24]

Legal Constraints

John of Salisbury influenced the thirteenth century legal treatise known as 'Bracton',[25] which declared that the king is 'under God and under the law, because the law makes the king'.[26] That law presumably included, as well as the law of royal succession, divine and natural law, and customary laws protecting the rights of subjects which were thought to bind the king, even though he could change them by making new laws after consulting his magnates.[27]

The belief that the king should uphold the customs and laws of the realm was 'part of the very fabric of English society'.[28] Kings swore a solemn coronation oath to do so, which was taken very seriously, and has been described as 'one of the two most fundamental documents of the [medieval] constitution'.[29] The other, Magna Carta, was one of many charters of liberties that kings throughout Europe promised to uphold, often at the time of their coronation, in order to bolster support.[30]

---

[21] Bollermann and Nederman 'John', section 8.   [22] Ibid.
[23] John of Salisbury, *Policraticus*, Book IV, chs. 1, 2 and 7.
[24] Ibid, discussed in Bollermann and Nederman, 'John', section 8.
[25] C. Nederman, 'Bracton on Kingship Revisited' (1984) 5 *History of Political Thought* 61, 72–74. On the authorship of 'Bracton', see C. Nederman, 'The Royal Will and the Baronial Bridle, the Place of the *Addicio de Cartis* in Bractonian Political Thought' (1988) 9 *History of Political Thought* 415, 416.
[26] H. Bracton, *De Legibus et Consuetunidibus Angliae*, G. E. Woodbine, ed., S. E. Thorne, trans., (Belknap Press, 1968–1977), vol. II, 33; see also 110, and 305–306 generally.
[27] M. Lobban, *A History of the Philosophy of Law in the Common Law World, 1600–1900* (Springer, 2007), 3–5.
[28] D. Carpenter, *Magna Carta*, 265.   [29] Carpenter, 'Resisting and Deposing Kings', 108.
[30] A. Spencer, 'The Coronation Oath in English Politics, c1272–1399', in B. Thompson and J. Watts, eds., *Political Society in Later Medieval England; A Festschrift for Christine Carpenter* (Boydell Press, 2015), 42.

But there were no legal mechanisms to compel the king to keep these promises; 'Bracton' relied mainly on the virtue of the properly educated king.[31] The king was the apex of the legal system, the source of all temporal jurisdictions including those of his judges.[32] No writ could run against him; he could be beseeched by petition to correct an injustice, but if he refused, the only remedies were divine punishment and rebellion.[33] The judges were essentially bureaucrats appointed by and subordinate to him; they could not decide against him, as the barons sometimes complained.[34] Moreover, the common law rarely dealt with matters of high politics of the kind involved in disputes between kings and their magnates.[35]

Political Constraints

'Bracton' mentioned a political rather than legal method of controlling kings. It described the earls as the king's companions or partners, whose counsel and perhaps even consent was necessary for law-making.[36] A passage inserted later, called the *addicio*, states that if the king 'is without a bridle, that is without law', the earls and barons 'ought to put a bridle on him ... [since] he who has a partner has a master'.[37] This is presumably because a partner can refuse to give the necessary consent.[38] Of course, if the earls were themselves unbridled, there was no remedy other than divine retribution.[39]

But the author of the *addicio* may also have had in mind the unprecedented 'security clause' in Magna Carta, authorising a committee of twenty-five barons to review the king's compliance with it, and if necessary remedy non-compliance by seizing his property.[40] This inspired later proposals for councils of earls or barons empowered to compel kings to amend egregious misconduct.[41]

---

[31] J. Baker, *The Reinvention of Magna Carta 1216–1616* (Cambridge University Press, 2017), ch. 1; Bracton, *De Legibus*, vol. II, 33; Nederman, 'Bracton on Kingship', 69–77.
[32] Bracton, *De Legibus*, vol. IV, 281.
[33] Bracton, *De Legibus*, vol. II, 33; see also vol. III, 43.
[34] D. A. Harding, *The Law Courts of Medieval England* (George Allan & Unwin, 1973), 80; W. Hanson, *From Kingdom to Commonwealth: The Development of Civic Consciousness in English Political Thought* (Harvard University Press, 1970), 159, 188–190 and 214.
[35] Hanson, *From Kingdom to Commonwealth*, 131–132 and 180; J. Goldsworthy, *Parliamentary Sovereignty, Contemporary Debates* (Cambridge University Press, 2010), 25–27.
[36] Bracton, *De Legibus*, vol. II, 19, 22, 32 and 305.   [37] Ibid, 110; see also vol. III, 43.
[38] Nederman, 'The Royal Will', 426.   [39] Bracton, *De Legibus*, vol. II, 110.
[40] D. Carpenter, *Magna Carta*, 325–331, esp 330–331.
[41] Maurice Keen, *England in the Later Middle Ages*, 2nd ed. (Routledge, 2003), 69–70.

The provision of proper counsel to the king was regarded as almost as important to good governance as his moral virtue.[42] By the fifteenth century 'the main endeavour of English political society was not to restrain, or to divide, its executive, but to direct it'.[43] But imposing a council on the king was impractical.[44] Everyone knew that kings received conflicting counsel from different sectional interests. The peace of the realm required a single, ultimate authority able to take them all into account, before reaching even-handed decisions binding on everyone.[45] Limiting the king's freedom to choose his counsellors would disable him from fulfilling that function, and risk substituting one partisan faction for another.[46]

The idea of subjecting the king to political control by the nobility lost ground by the fifteenth century.[47] It came to seem too feudal and aristocratic, as Parliament grew into the preferred institution for settling grievances.[48] In the meantime, '[r]oyal virtue was the best – in a sense, the only – constitutional safeguard'.[49] If that proved unreliable, 'laws and councils would not work. Nothing short of ... civil war was sufficient to reform a king who would not reform himself'.[50]

Some kings governed so abysmally that aggrieved magnates turned to armed resistance and deposition, albeit reluctantly.[51] In 1308, a parliamentary indictment of Edward II's closest adviser declared that, given the lack of legal remedies,

> in order to save the [coronation] oath ... when the King will not redress a matter ... damaging to the Crown and hurtful to the people, it is adjudged that the error be removed by violence ...[52]

Attempts to justify deposition usually appealed to every available argument, no matter how uneasy, contrived and legally unpersuasive.[53] These

---

[42] J. L. Watts, *Henry VI and the Politics of Kingship* (Cambridge University Press, 1996), 28–29.
[43] Ibid, 21; also 25, 29–30, 54 and 57.   [44] Keen, *England in the Later Middle Ages*, 71.
[45] Watts, *Henry VI*, 77–78; see also, 27, 31, 38 and 62–63.
[46] Carpenter, 'Resisting and Deposing Kings', 104–106; Carpenter, *Wars of the Roses*, 28, 39.
[47] Watts, *Henry VI*, 20; for examples of the recognition of royal sovereignty, see 60.
[48] Keen, *England in the Later Middle Ages*, 70 and 72–79, esp 78–79.
[49] Watts, *Henry VI*, 28; see also, 23, 25, 45 and 61.   [50] Ibid, 80.
[51] John, Henry III, Edward II, Richard II and Henry VI faced rebellions, and the last three were deposed.
[52] B. Wilkinson, *Constitutional History of Medieval England 1216–1399* (Longmans, 1952), vol. II, 111.
[53] Carpenter, 'Resisting and Deposing Kings', 108–117.

included claims that a tyrant was not a true king; that rebels kept faith with the Crown as an office that was endangered by the king as an individual; and that the king had voluntarily abdicated, and not been deposed.[54] But baronial rebellions 'almost always ended badly', which 'would only have confirmed the belief that the king's authority had to be absolute'.[55]

Fortescue

Sir John Fortescue, England's most influential constitutional theorist of the fifteenth century, sought to reform English governance to rebuild royal authority after the Wars of the Roses.[56] An eminent judge and parliamentarian, he was influenced by the Bible, classical philosophers and medieval scholastics, English historical (or pseudo-historical) works, and legal texts such as 'Bracton'.[57]

Fortescue regarded kingship as originally established by the consent of the community, to secure its well-being.[58] He famously depicted England as having a 'mixed monarchy', which he called *'dominium politicum et regale'* (rule political and regal). A purely regal king was an absolute ruler, as in France. England's king was regal; he could, for example, use his prerogative to override the law in an emergency.[59] But the political element required him to make laws and impose taxes only with the consent of his subjects in Parliament; generally to obey those laws; and to be guided in administering the realm by good counsel.[60] Fortescue recommended that counsel be provided by salaried, expert and representative advisers, rather than self-interested nobles.[61] But that was too radical to be achievable.[62]

The Reformation

Constitutional thought developed in the sixteenth century largely in response to the religious disputes that fractured European communities due to the Reformation. In England, some Catholics, Anglicans (or 'conformists') and Puritans found it difficult to accept the legitimacy of governments controlled

---

[54] Ibid; E. Powell, *Kingship, Law, and Society; Criminal Justice in the Reign of Henry V* (Clarendon Press, 1989), 33f.
[55] Carpenter, *Wars of the Roses*, 39–40.
[56] S. Lockwood, 'Introduction', to Sir John Fortescue, *On the Laws and Governance of England*, S. Lockwood, ed. (Cambridge University Press, 1997), xv; Watts, *Henry VI*, 50–51.
[57] Lockwood, 'Introduction', xix–xx, xxiii.   [58] Ibid, xxvi–xxviii, xxx.
[59] Lobban, *History of the Philosophy of Law*, 14.   [60] Lockwood, 'Introduction', xxx–xxxii
[61] Ibid, xxxvi.   [62] Watts, *Henry VI*, 47–50.

by their religious antagonists. Political theorists examined the propriety of disobedience, resistance or rebellion, which were opposed by emerging theories of absolute sovereignty expounded by thinkers such as Jean Bodin in France.[63] Remembering the Wars of the Roses, the English feared the possible consequences of conflicting religious loyalties, especially since invasion by Catholic powers was a constant threat. It was widely agreed that the anarchy which rebellion could unleash might be worse than tyranny.[64]

The English Reformation was legally established in the 1530s by statutes that made Henry VIII the supreme head of the Church, abolished all forms of papal authority, and even prescribed religious doctrine. Many traditionalists agreed with Thomas More that these statutes were void for being 'directly repugnant to the laws of God and His Holy Church'.[65] Indeed, some Catholics continued to avow that the Pope could authorise the deposition of monarchs who violated those laws.[66] But More's trial and execution 'finally and terribly demonstrated the legal omnipotence of the king in Parliament'.[67] Tudor statutes also altered other matters of fundamental importance, including the succession to the throne and rights to property. All statutes were treated as law until formally repealed, even by those who regarded them as contrary to fundamental or divine law.[68]

The omnicompetent and legally unchallengeable authority of the 'King in Parliament' was frequently acknowledged, but there were two different kinds of theories of its nature and source.[69] According to descending ('royalist') theories, statutes were made by the king alone, exercising law-making power conferred on him directly by God, with the advice and consent of the Houses of Parliament.[70] Similarly, his supremacy over the Church was not conferred but merely confirmed by statute, so that it could be enforced in the

---

[63] For Bodin's influence in England, see D. Lee, *Popular Sovereignty in Early Modern Constitutional Thought* (Oxford University Press, 2016), ch. 9.
[64] E.g., W. Tyndale, *The Obedience of a Christian Man*, in H. Walter, ed., *Doctrinal Treatises and Introductions to Different Portions of the Holy Scriptures* (Cambridge University Press, 1848), 180.
[65] W. Roper, *The Life of Sir Thomas Moore, Knight*, E. V. Hitchcock, ed., (Oxford University Press, 1935), 92.
[66] See, e.g., G. Burgess, *British Political Thought 1500–1660; The Politics of the Post-Reformation* (Palgrave Macmillan, 2009), 104–107.
[67] J. H. Baker, ed., *The Reports of John Spelman* (Selden Society, 1978), vol. II, 'Introduction', 44.
[68] See J. Goldsworthy, *The Sovereignty of Parliament, History and Philosophy* (Clarendon Press, 1999), 54.
[69] F. Le V. Baumer, *The Early Tudor Theory of Kingship* (Yale University Press, 1940), 57–62.
[70] Goldsworthy, *Sovereignty of Parliament*, 65–67.

secular courts, for example, in cases of treason.[71] His authority was limited by divine law, but no human agency could enforce it against him; he was accountable only to God. According to ascending ('parliamentarian') theories, statutes were made by the king, Lords and Commons in Parliament as, in effect, three partners sharing the legislative power, whose absolute authority was due to their collectively representing the entire community, which God had made the original source of all authority.[72]

While Henry VIII and some of his leading clerics endorsed royalist theories, other key supporters, including Thomas Cromwell and Christopher St German, supported parliamentarian ones.[73] There was an 'ideological ambiguity in the core of Henricianism', and 'the crux of English politics' was to satisfy the proponents of both.[74] The 'little-understood mythic accommodation that the English called "King-in-Parliament" . . . was a fused bomb waiting to be ignited.'[75]

Cromwell, the Henrician Reformation's principal architect, was influenced by the fourteenth-century political philosopher Marsiglio of Padua.[76] Marsiglio had argued that the authority of the Church was subordinate to that of the secular state, which derived from its citizenry, who constituted the Church within their community and therefore had ultimate authority in spiritual as well as temporal matters.[77] When Cromwell financed the publication of an English translation of Marsiglio's *Defensor Pacis* in 1535, it was adjusted to attribute ultimate authority to the community's representatives in Parliament rather than the populace at large.[78]

Even in the fifteenth century, it had often been said that all members of the community were present in Parliament, by proxy if not in person, and

---

[71] G. R. Elton, '*Lex Terrae Victrix*: The Triumph of Parliamentary Law in the Sixteenth Century', in his *Studies in Tudor and Stuart Government and Politics* (Cambridge University Press, 1974–1992), vol. iv, 37, 44–45.
[72] Ibid, 46–57.
[73] Ibid, 43–56; J. A. Guy, *Tudor England* (Oxford University Press, 1988), 133–134, 233 and 370–375.
[74] J. J. Scarisbrick, *Henry VIII* (Eyre & Spottiswoode, 1968), 393–394 and 397.
[75] G. J. Schochet, 'The English Revolution in the History of Political Thought', in B. Y. Kunze and D. D. Brautigam, eds., *Court, Country and Culture; Essays on Early Modern British History in Honour of Perez Zagorin* (University of Rochester Press, 1992), 10.
[76] G. R. Elton, 'The Political Creed of Thomas Cromwell', in Elton, *Studies in Tudor and Stuart Government*, vol. ii, 215, 228–230.
[77] J. A. Watt, 'Spiritual and Temporal Powers', in J. H. Burns, ed., *The Cambridge History of Medieval Political Thought c 350–c1450* (Cambridge University Press, 1988), 416–421.
[78] S. Lockwood, 'Marsilius of Padua and the Case for the Royal Ecclesiastical Supremacy' (1991) *Transactions of the Royal Historical Society, Sixth Series*, 89, 89–90 and 95–96; Burgess, *British Political Thought*, 50.

were therefore 'privy and parties' to its decisions.[79] That idea became a commonplace during the sixteenth century.[80] Parliament's decisions were often said therefore to reflect the collective wisdom of the community, which made them virtually infallible.[81]

St German's *Doctor and Student*[82] was arguably 'the most famous legal treatise composed between the time of Fortescue and that of Sir Edward Coke'.[83] Probably influenced by Marsiglio as well as Fortescue, in more polemical works he provided the Henrician Reformation with its most legally persuasive defence, based on an ascending theory of the royal supremacy.[84] Because the king in Parliament represented 'the estate of all the people within this realm, that is to say of the whole catholic church thereof', it was able to legislate with respect to spiritual as well as temporal matters.[85] It was inconceivable that those representing the collective wisdom of the entire realm and church would violate God's laws.[86] Anyway, a statute was legally unchallengeable; it could not be judged void by a court, but had to be repealed by a later Parliament.[87]

St German anticipated the more famous parliamentarian theory expounded in Richard Hooker's *Of the Laws of Ecclesiastical Polity*. Hooker maintained that in any legal system, jurisdiction 'must have necessarily a fountain that derives it to all others, and receives it not from any; because otherwise the course of justice should go infinitely in a circle, every superior having his superior without end, which cannot be'; so 'there is required an universal power' which

---

[79] G. R. Elton, *The Tudor Constitution; Documents and Commentary*, 2nd ed. (Cambridge: Cambridge University Press, 1982), 236.
[80] P. Williams, *The Later Tudors: England 1547–1603* (Clarendon Press, 1995), 135.
[81] R. Eccleshall, *Order and Reason in Politics: Theories of Absolute and Limited Monarchy in Early Modern England* (Oxford University Press, 1978), ch. iv, *passim*.
[82] St German, *Doctor and Student* (1523), T. F. T. Plucknett and J. L. Barton, eds. (Selden Society, 1974).
[83] J. A. Guy, 'Thomas Moore and Christopher St German: The Battle of the Books', in A. Fox and J. A. Guy, eds., *Reassessing the Henrician Age: Humanism, Politics and Reform 1500–1550* (Basil Blackwell, 1986), 99–100.
[84] J. A. Guy, *Christopher St German on Chancery and Statute* (Selden Society, 1985), 40; J. A. Guy, 'The Later Career of Christopher St German (1534–1541)', in John Guy, Ralph Keen, Clarence Miller and Ruth McGugan, eds., *The Complete Works of St Thomas More* (Yale University Press, 1987), vol. x, *The Debellation of Salem and Bizance*, 395–398 and 402.
[85] St. German, *An Answer to a Letter* (1535), quoted by Guy, 'The Later Career', 402–403. But St German later changed his mind on this last point: ibid, 413.
[86] St German, *Treatise Concerning the Power of the Clergy and the Laws of the Realm* (1534/1535), quoted in Guy, 41 and 41–44.
[87] St German, *A Little Treatise Concerning Writs of Subpoena*, in Guy, 116, discussed in ibid, 87. For nuances, see Lobban, *History of the Philosophy of Law*, 14–25.

is accountable only to a heavenly tribunal.[88] In England, this power was Parliament, which represented the community as a whole – the source of all governmental authority.[89] It comprised the king and all his subjects, who were 'there present, either in person or by such as they voluntarily have derived their very personal right unto'.[90] Being equivalent to the Church of England, which consisted of the king, the clergy, and all lay believers, Parliament could make 'even laws concerning the most spiritual affairs of the Church'.[91] Since it spoke for everyone, expressing a collective wisdom superior to that of any other body, not even religious dissidents could legitimately disobey its statutes.[92]

The king, Lords and Commons were sometimes said to make different, but equally valuable, contributions to good government. England enjoyed a felicitous combination of all three kinds of government – monarchy, aristocracy and democracy – the virtues of each compensating for the vices of the others. The monarchical element suppressed the vices of faction and anarchy, the democratic element that of tyranny, and so on.[93] This theory of 'mixed government' would become more commonplace in the next two centuries.[94]

Arguably eclipsed by parliamentarian theories after Henry VIII died, royalist theories made a comeback in the 1590s, especially among the higher clergy who sought a more powerful defence of the Elizabethan Church against Catholic and Puritan attacks.[95] The fusion of Church and State made it impossible to separate constitutional and religious issues.[96] Influential bishops, determined to defend the episcopacy against Puritan demands for its abolition, were supported by the Queen. Strongly royalist theories held that the Church was governed by the Queen alone, acting through her bishops, rather than the Queen in Parliament.[97] In 1592, the Queen's

---

[88] J. Keble, ed., *The Works of Mr Richard Hooker* (7th ed., Georg Olms Verlag, 1977), vol. III, 445–446, bk. VIII, ch. ix, 2, and vol. III, 433, bk. VIII, ch. viii, 4.
[89] P. Lake, *Anglicans and Puritans? Presbyterianism and English Conformist Thought from Whitgift to Hooker* (Unwin Hyman, 1988), 201–202, 209–211 and 224.
[90] Keble, *Works of Mr Richard Hooker*, vol. III, 408–409, bk. VIII, ch. vi, 11.
[91] Ibid, vol. III, 340, bk. VIII, ch. i, 7; vol. III, 412, bk. VIII, ch. vi, 11. See Lake, *Anglicans and Puritans?* 207–208.
[92] Keble, *Works of Mr Richard Hooker*, vol. III, 412, bk. VIII, ch. vi; and vol. I, 164, 'Preface'.
[93] C. C. Weston, *English Constitutional Theory and the House of Lords 1556–1832* (Routledge & Kegan Paul, 1965), ch. I, esp 15–23.
[94] See notes 149 and 185–186 below.
[95] Guy, *Tudor England*, 233; J. A. Guy, *The Reign of Elizabeth I: Court and Culture in the Last Decade* (Cambridge University Press, 1995), 11–13.
[96] C. W. A. Prior, *A Confusion of Tongues; Britain's Wars of Reformation 1625–1642* (Oxford University Press, 2012), 18 and passim.
[97] C. Cross, 'Churchmen and the Royal Supremacy', in F. Heal and R. O'Day, eds., *Church and Society in England: Henry VIII to James I* (Macmillan, 1977), 15, 28–30.

Printer published an influential defence of divine right kingship by the theologian Hadrian Saravia, who argued that the Queen alone made laws, with the Houses of Parliament acting in a merely advisory capacity.[98] Disputes over religion, not finance, were the initial stimulus for the reassertion of royal absolutism, which continued into the next century.[99]

Rebellion and Revolution

Introduction

Constitutional disputes in early Stuart England over religion, fiscal imposts and parliamentary privileges brought to the surface the long latent disagreement between royalist and parliamentarian theories. Hoping to resolve those disputes, common law theories proposed that both the king and the Houses of Parliament derived their respective powers from the ancient common law, which held both in balance.[100] These competing theories drew (often tendentiously) on the familiar sources – scripture, theology, common law and custom, Roman and civil law, classical philosophy and natural law – as well as more recent writings on sovereignty and social contract.[101] Their debates produced a flood of pamphlets and books that include many of the greatest works of British legal and political theory.

There was widespread agreement about many principles, but disagreement about their application. It was generally agreed that God was the ultimate source of all authority; that everyone under God had superiors and inferiors, the latter being bound to respect and obey the former;[102] that every community needed a supreme decision-maker, even in matters of religion, or disagreements would never be resolved because appeals would be infinite or circular;[103] that the supreme decision-maker, while accountable to God, had to be trusted to exercise the powers of government for the

---

[98] J. P. Sommerville, 'Richard Hooker, Hadrian Saravia, and the Advent of the Divine Right of Kings' (1983) 4 *History of Political Thought* 229, 239–242.
[99] Guy, *The Reign of Elizabeth I*, 149; Lake, *Anglicans and Puritans?* 64–65, 131 and 212.
[100] J. P. Sommerville, *Royalists and Patriots, Politics and Ideology in England 1603–1640*, 2nd ed. (Routledge, 1999), 91–96.
[101] For the tendentious use of 'Bracton', see C. J. Nederman, 'Bracton on Kingship First Visited: The Idea of Sovereignty and Bractonian Political Thought in the Seventeenth Century' (1988) 40 *Political Science* 49.
[102] J. Daly, 'Cosmic Harmony and Political Thinking in Early Stuart England' (1979) 69 Part 7 *Transactions of the American Philosophical Society* 1; Eccleshall, *Order and Reason*, 9, 18, 22, 33, 47–49, 56–59.
[103] Keble, *Works of Mr Richard Hooker*; Goldsworthy, *Sovereignty of Parliament*, 87–88 and 101–102, n. 178.

common good;[104] that of these powers, that of law-making was the most 'absolute' (meaning legally unchallengeable);[105] and that the supreme decision-maker necessarily had authority to override the law to protect the vital interests of the community in an emergency.[106]

The main question that remained in dispute was whether God had conferred this supreme authority on kings directly, who had then established laws and representative advisory bodies, or on the community as a whole, which acting through representative bodies had established kingship and law.

Royalist Theories

Royalist theories, some more extreme than others, were defended on various grounds. One was the practical argument that, given human nature, there would be anarchy without an undisputed ruler maintaining order.[107] This was considered a basic principle of natural law, confirmed by scripture.[108] Thomas Hobbes later became the most famous proponent of this argument, but combined it with a voluntarism about moral and legal standards and a social contract theory that were distasteful to most royalists.[109] Another argument was that England had been conquered in 1066, and kingship acquired by conquest rather than consent was absolute and unconditional, albeit subject to God's laws.[110] A third argument likened the king to the father of the community, entitled to exercise the same absolute authority, and be accorded the same love and respect, as God had ordained for the father of any family.[111] According to Robert Filmer among others, kings possessed the same patriarchal authority that Adam had received from God, a claim later ridiculed by John Locke.[112]

Because the king was unaccountable to his inferiors, his actions could not be questioned by his judges without his permission.[113] Kings swore solemn

---

[104] Goldsworthy, *Sovereignty of Parliament*, 87, 104 and 107.   [105] Ibid, 89–91 and 95.
[106] Ibid, 83, 104–106, 119–120 and 129.
[107] Sommerville, *Royalists and Patriots*, 9, 39, 42, 52, 69.   [108] Ibid, 51,
[109] M. Goldie, 'The Reception of Hobbes', in J. H. Burns and M. Goldie, eds., *The Cambridge History of Political Thought 1450–1700* (Cambridge University Press, 1991), 579.
[110] Sommerville, *Royalists and Patriots*, 65–68.
[111] J. P. Sommerville, ed., *Filmer; Patriarcha and Other Writings* (Cambridge University Press, 1991).
[112] Ibid, 34; J. Locke, *Two Treatises of Government* (1689), P. Laslett ed. (Cambridge University Press, 1988).
[113] James I, *Speech to Parliament* (21 March 1610), in J. P. Kenyon, *The Stuart Constitution 1603–1688*, 2nd ed. (Cambridge University Press, 1986), 12–13.

oaths to abide by the law, but they were bound only by their own promises rather than the law as such. They entrusted their judges to help them keep their oaths, through the accepted judicial practice of declaring unlawful royal commands to be void and penalising the advisors held responsible for them.[114] But this did not apply to the exercise of their 'absolute' prerogatives, which were discretionary powers only they possessed.[115] Their paramount duty in exercising these powers was to defend the realm from both external and internal threats, which in an emergency might require them to act outside or even contrary to law.[116]

To the objection that they offered no practical means of restraining tyrants, royalists replied that kings were imbued with special wisdom and virtue.[117] Furthermore, it was necessary to trust a supreme decision-maker, and it was better to trust one man than many, because many men might disagree among themselves, sparking violence and anarchy that might be worse than tyranny.[118] Finally, the king was subject to divine punishment in this world or the next.[119]

Royalists agreed that the highest of the king's 'absolute' powers was that of law-making, even if he could exercise it only with the assent of the two Houses.[120] But they denied that it was completely unlimited. Because God conferred kingship directly on kings and their natural heirs in perpetuity, not even the king, in Parliament, could control the royal succession or limit various powers that constituted and were therefore 'inseparable' from kingship.[121] These included the powers to make laws, conduct foreign affairs, make war or peace, appoint judges, and grant pardons.[122]

---

[114] Sommerville, *Royalists and Patriots*, 97.
[115] See G. Burgess, *Absolute Monarchy and the Stuart Constitution* (Yale University Press, 1996), 31–34; Sommerville, *Royalists and Patriots*, 12–13 and 35–36. For examples, see page 267, main text accompanying n. 122.
[116] Sommerville, *Royalists and Patriots*, 41, 120, 138–139, 155, 161–162, 232, 234 and 243.
[117] Eccleshall, *Order and Reason*, 93–96.
[118] R. Filmer, *The Anarchy of a Limited or Mixed Monarchy*, in Sommerville, *Filmer; Patriarcha*, 131–171; Sommerville, *Royalists and Patriots*, 42
[119] Goldsworthy, *Sovereignty of Parliament*, 88.
[120] See page 266, main text accompanying n. 105.
[121] Goldsworthy, *Sovereignty of Parliament*, 91–94, discussing inter alia Filmer in Sommerville, *Filmer; Patriarcha*, 35 and 40. Royalists denied that statute could control the succession partly because James I had succeeded Elizabeth contrary to a statute enacted under Henry VIII.
[122] J. P. Sommerville, *Thomas Hobbes: Political Ideas in Historical Context* (Houndmills: Macmillan, 1992), 83 and 85.

Parliamentarian Theories

Parliamentarian theories maintained that God had originally conferred the highest powers of government on the community as a whole, which had delegated them to kings, subject to the conditions that they make laws and impose taxes only with their subjects' consent, and that they exercise their other powers subject to law. Those conditions, reiterated in every coronation oath, had the force of contractual obligations, which many regarded as enforceable through active resistance organised by the community's representative institutions.[123] This understanding of the origins of government was held by many, including John Selden and Sir Matthew Hale.[124]

The notion that Parliament spoke for the whole community was a commonplace.[125] It was depicted as the community in miniature, encapsulating its collective wisdom.[126] Moreover, it acted only with painstaking deliberation; because new laws had to be read three times in both Houses and approved by the king, they were 'like gold seven times purified'.[127] It was often said to be virtually infallible.[128] But even if it could err, its decisions were final and unappealable; to appeal from the kingdom's highest court to an inferior one would 'invert the course of nature.'[129] Ultimately guided by *salus populi* – the welfare of the community – Parliament was not bound by the common law as inferior courts were.[130] It necessarily possessed a paramount and overriding power to take extraordinary measures to avert disaster.[131] An attempt to limit that power would be more dangerous than its possible abuse, by preventing it being used in the public interest. Parliamentarian theorists condemned rebellion against Parliament as vehemently as royalist theorists condemned resistance to the king.[132]

---

[123] Sommerville, *Royalists and Patriots*, ch. 2, Burgess, *British Political Thought*, 195.
[124] Sommerville, *Royalists and Patriots*, ch. 2 esp 61–65; Goldsworthy, *Parliamentary Sovereignty*, 37–41.
[125] Goldsworthy, *Sovereignty of Parliament*, 96–98 and 114.   [126] Ibid, 97–100.
[127] Edmund Waller in Parliament following the *Ship-Money* case: T. B. Howell, ed., *A Complete Collection of State Trials* (Longman, 1816–1828), vol. 3, 1302–1303.
[128] Goldsworthy, *Sovereignty of Parliament*, 97–100, 113 and 118.
[129] H. Parker, *Observations upon Some of His Majesties Late Answers and Expresses* (1642), 43, reprinted in W. Haller, ed., *Tracts on Liberty in the Puritan Revolution 1638–1647* (Octagon Books, 1979).
[130] Goldsworthy, *Sovereignty of Parliament*, 102–103, 105, 110 and 119.
[131] Sommerville, *Royalists and Patriots*, 73–74, 76; Goldsworthy, *Sovereignty of Parliament*, 104–106.
[132] Goldsworthy, *Sovereignty of Parliament*, 97–98.

Common Law Theories

The historical origins of government and law were considered important because a derived authority was deemed inferior to an original one.[133] But all disputants could claim to be vindicated by history, by arguing that either kings, representative bodies or customary law came first in time. Royalists, for example, held all law to have been established by kings; statutes were their Acts, and the common law had been made by their judges.[134] Some lawyers, including Sir Matthew Hale, thought that the common law had originated in ancient statutes passed by representative institutions from which Parliament evolved.[135] Henry Parker, the most influential defender of the parliamentary cause, described Parliament as 'that court which gave life and birth to all laws'.[136]

What modern historians call 'ancient constitutionalism' is a persistent English tendency to seek the origins of their governing institutions and liberties in the laws and customs of the Anglo-Saxons or even ancient Britons.[137] Many lawyers held the common law to be the original source and continuing measure of the authority of both king and Parliament.[138] But this was not in itself inconsistent with either royalist or parliamentarian theories, because the common law might have conferred sovereign power on the king either alone or in Parliament.[139] Some lawyers held that the authority of the common law and that of Parliament were one and the same: the common law embodied the wisdom of the community, as expressed in immemorial customs, and that wisdom, as Charles Herle put it, 'lives still in that which the law calls the "reason of the kingdom", the votes and ordinances of Parliament'.[140]

It has been argued that a kind of 'common law constitutionalism' developed from 1528 until 1628, as common lawyers came to regard their

---

[133] C. C. Weston, 'England: Ancient Constitution and Common Law', in J. H. Burns, ed., *The Cambridge History of Political Thought 1450–1700* (Cambridge University Press, 1991), 374, 377.

[134] Goldsworthy, *Parliamentary Sovereignty*, 36–37.   [135] Ibid, 380–389.

[136] Ibid, 38, n.137.

[137] For an overview, see M. Goldie, 'Retrospect: The Ancient Constitution'.

[138] E.g., H. Finch, *Law, or a Discourse Thereof, in Four Books* (Richard & Edward Atkins, 1678, 1st ed., 1627), 85.

[139] This depends on sovereign power being conferred by law, rather than as a power standing above, and creating, all law: see Goldsworthy, *Sovereignty of Parliament*, 109–110, esp n. 231, and 236–238.

[140] C. Herle, *A Fuller Answer to a Treatise Written by Doctor Ferne* (John Bartlet, 1642), 6; Goldsworthy, *Sovereignty of Parliament*, 109.

law as a 'master science' that determined the respective rights of the king and his subjects.[141] The belief that the common law was the source of all royal prerogatives was certainly popular, although not universal even among common lawyers let alone civilians.[142] But Sir Edward Coke, who exemplifies that view, held that the king's title to the throne came directly from God, and also denied that the common law was the source of 'the law and custom of Parliament' (which we now call parliamentary privilege).[143]

Several notorious judicial decisions upholding contested exercises of royal prerogatives caused a crisis of confidence in the common law's ability to protect traditional liberties.[144] Consequently, many turned away from the common law and sought new statutes to remedy its deficiencies.[145] Common law theories became subservient to the parliamentarian cause during the 1640s, their primary role being to prove that a sovereign parliament had existed from time immemorial.[146] That the king in Parliament in effect possessed sovereign power was affirmed by many lawyers and polemicists, and expressed most forcefully by Henry Parker.[147]

The eve of the Civil War brought new claims that only the Houses of Parliament rather than the King in Parliament – and later, that the House of Commons alone – truly represented the community, and were therefore entitled to exercise supreme power if necessary to protect public safety.[148] These claims purported to justify actions taken without the king's assent, such as the seizure of armaments in preparation for war. Moderate royalists persuaded Charles I to claim the middle ground, accusing the two Houses of subverting the ancient constitution of mixed government, with legislative power shared by the king, Lords and Commons, to which he remained faithful.[149]

---

[141] A. Cromartie, *The Constitutionalist Revolution: An Essay on the History of England, 1450–1642* (Cambridge University Press, 2006).
[142] E.g., Sir John Davies, Francis Bacon and others: see Goldsworthy, *Parliamentary Sovereignty*, 35.
[143] Goldsworthy, *Parliamentary Sovereignty*, 32–33.
[144] G. Burgess, *The Politics of the Ancient Constitution: An Introduction to English Political Thought 1603–1642* (Macmillan, 1992), ch. 8.
[145] D. Wootton, ed., *Divine Right and Democracy* (Penguin, 1986), 34.
[146] Weston, *England: Ancient Constitution*, 397–398.
[147] Parker, *Observations*; Goldsworthy, *Sovereignty of Parliament*, 96–135. See also Lee, *Popular Sovereignty*, 290–294.
[148] Goldsworthy, *Sovereignty of Parliament*, 120, 129–132.
[149] Ibid, 131; Burgess, *British Political Thought*, 196–197 and 205–206.

The Interregnum

After Charles I's execution, various experiments in republican government were tried, and failed. Neither the Army leadership nor the Levellers among its rank-and-file had consistent opinions about whether the powers of Parliament were, could or should be limited. But in general they tried to improve governance through frequent, free and fair elections of a popular assembly.[150] The Levellers proposed a radical program of constitutional reform, based on popular rather than parliamentary sovereignty, that anticipated many features of modern constitutionalism. This included a higher law protecting rights from all branches of government, although these were not judicially enforceable, universal manhood suffrage, a separation of powers and judicial independence.[151] James Harrington's *The Commonwealth of Oceana* (1656) was published in the hope that Oliver Cromwell would establish the republican model it recommended.[152] He condemned the Leveller proposal to restrict legislative sovereignty by an 'Agreement of the People', enforceable through popular resistance, as a recipe for anarchy.[153] In his ideal commonwealth, laws would be made by a sovereign parliament, consisting of a senate and a popular assembly, so carefully structured and balanced that it would never abuse its power.[154] John Milton and Marchamont Nedham both wrote influential republican tracts that also advocated a popularly elected assembly exercising unlimited legislative power.[155]

The failure of the various regimes of the 1650s led to the monarchy being restored in 1660, along with an abiding preference for pragmatic, incremental adaptation of established institutions rather than radical constitutional innovation.[156]

The Restoration

After the Restoration, some royalists insisted that the succession and 'inseparable' prerogatives of the Crown were guaranteed by immutable fundamental

---

[150] Goldsworthy, *Sovereignty of Parliament*, 135–139.
[151] M. Loughlin, 'The Constitutional Thought of the Levellers' (2007) 60 *Current Legal Problems* 1.
[152] J. G. A. Pocock, *The Political Works of James Harrington* (Cambridge University Press, 1977), 9–14.
[153] Ibid, 657–658.
[154] Ibid, 145; Burgess, *British Political Thought*, 346–363, esp 348–349 and 355–356.
[155] For Milton, Goldsworthy, *Sovereignty of Parliament*, 138 and 140; for Nedham, Burgess, *British Political Thought*, 337–346.
[156] D. L. Smith, 'The Struggle for New Constitutional and Institutional Forms', in J. Morrill, ed., *Revolution and Restoration: England in the 1650s* (Collins and Brown, 1992), 15, 33–34.

laws.[157] But most royalists drew a different conclusion from the destruction of the civil war: the people had to be more thoroughly instructed that supreme decision-making power was vested by God in a single, undivided and unchallengeable authority.[158]

These different views emerged during the Exclusion Crisis of 1680–1681, when several attempts were made to enact a statute excluding the future James II from inheriting the throne. Some royalists objected that this would be legally void for contradicting fundamental law. But others were divine right absolutists; because God conferred sovereign authority on kings, even they could not alienate or limit it, or alter the right of their rightful heirs to succeed them.[159] Yet others opposed exclusion for being politically imprudent, although legally valid.[160]

The proponents of exclusion, who became known as Whigs, had no doubt that Parliament's unlimited legislative power could be used to alter the royal succession. This was strenuously affirmed by their leaders, including the Earl of Shaftesbury (John Locke's patron), the historian William Petyt, and eminent lawyers John (later Lord) Somers and Sir Robert Atkyns.[161] It was also the view of many eminent non-partisan figures, such as Lord Halifax, Sir Matthew Hale, and Sir Heneage Finch.[162]

Locke in his *Second Treatise of Government* argued that government is established by the people and authorised to exercise only limited powers. Nevertheless, in any commonwealth, the legislative power must be supreme while the system of government subsists, all others including the executive power (which included what we now call the judicial power) being subordinate.[163] No earthly tribunal was authorised to oppose a tyrannical legislature; the people could only 'appeal to heaven' by resorting to armed rebellion.[164] The radical Whig authors Algernon Sidney and William Disney agreed that as a matter of law, the legislative power is necessarily unlimited.[165]

---

[157] Goldsworthy, *Sovereignty of Parliament*, 145.
[158] H. P. Dickinson, *Liberty and Property, Political Ideology in Eighteenth Century Britain* (Weidenfeld & Nicolson, 1977), 13–14.
[159] Goldsworthy, *Sovereignty of Parliament*, 146–147. [160] Ibid, 147. [161] Ibid, 149–155.
[162] Ibid, 156–158.
[163] Locke, *Two Treatises*, 366–368. See A. Tuckness, 'Locke's Political Philosophy' (2016), *Stanford Encyclopedia of Philosophy*, at https://plato.stanford.edu/entries/locke-political/, section 6 (viewed 6 July 2020).
[164] Locke, *Two Treatises*, 356, 379–380. [165] Ibid, 154.

The Eighteenth Century

After the Revolution of 1688, statutes controlled the royal succession and limited the important Crown prerogatives of suspending and dispensing with statutes.[166] The sovereignty of Parliament became 'one of the supreme touchstones of the ideology and language of Whiggism'.[167] It was also accepted by most Tories, when it became undeniable that the royal succession could in fact be altered by statute. Anxious to preserve a hierarchical society in which their rank and property were secure, they transferred their unconditional loyalty from the king alone to the king in Parliament.[168]

The major division of political sentiment in the early part of the century is usually described as pitting the 'Court' against the 'Country'. 'Court' refers to the Crown, its Ministers and their political supporters, whether Whig or Tory, while 'Country' refers to the Court's critics, who abhorred the manipulative and often corrupt methods by which it attempted to maintain majority support in Parliament. The Country opposition included both Tories, such as Viscount Bolingbroke, who suspected Court Whigs of favouring financiers and business entrepreneurs at the expense of the landed gentry, and 'old' or 'radical' Whigs, who championed the rights and liberties of 'the people'. Both groups demanded that Members of Parliament be financially independent of the Crown and defer to their electors' wishes.

Members of the Country opposition occasionally queried Parliament's sovereignty, but never suggested that it was subject to judicially enforceable limits.[169] Instead, they insisted that it was limited by its duty to act in the interests of 'the people', meaning the men of property who constituted the electorate. For example, Bolingbroke denied that Parliament possessed 'arbitrary power' to impair subjects' liberties or 'annul the constitution.'[170] But if it did, the only possible remedies lay in the hands of the people: dismissal of wrongdoers at the next election, or failing that, rebellion.[171] Although a Tory, he twice quoted Locke in discussing the right of the people to take up arms and 'appeal to heaven' if the Constitution provided no adequate remedy.[172]

---

[166] Goldsworthy, *Sovereignty of Parliament*, 159.
[167] M. Schonhorn, *Defoe's Politics, Parliament, Power, Kingship, and Robinson Crusoe* (Cambridge University Press, 1991), 61.
[168] Dickinson, *Liberty and Property*, 43 and 28–29, and also 33–34 and 46–47.
[169] P. Langford, *Public Life and the Propertied Englishman 1689–1798* (Oxford: Clarendon Press, 1991), 150–153.
[170] H. St John (Viscount Bolingbroke), *A Dissertation upon Parties, In Several Letters to Caleb D'Anvers* (H. Haines, 1735), Letter XVII, 210.
[171] Langford, *Public Life*, 154; Dickinson, *Liberty and Property*, 287–290.
[172] St John, *A Dissertation upon Parties*, Letter XI, 129 and Letter XVII, 210.

Court Whigs and Tories agreed that 'the people' could not be trusted with more power than the indirect and limited role of electing Members of Parliament. As Edmund Burke famously maintained, Members were not delegates of their electors, obligated to follow their instructions or wishes; Members should exercise an independent judgment as to the best interests of the nation, after being fully informed by discussion in Parliament.[173] The Court party regarded the Lockean theory of popular rebellion as a dangerous doctrine that threatened to promote civil discord and make government precarious.[174] While accepting the legitimacy of the Revolution, it sought to discourage future acts of rebellion against the regime it had established.

One method was to assert that the people's right to resist the Crown was exercisable only by their representatives in Parliament; there could be no right to resist Parliament itself.[175] A more subtle position was to concede that there was a moral right of resistance, but deny that it could ever be recognised as lawful, because it was limited to extraordinary emergencies justifying dissolution of the constitution itself.[176] There was solid support for this position in Locke's writings, which denied that any power could 'have the force and obligation of a *law*, which has not its *sanction from* that *legislative.*'[177] The law did not give the people a power superior to the legislature's; their right of revolution derived from a law 'antecedent and paramount to all positive laws of men', enforceable not by legal methods but by rebellion against the positive law.[178]

Court Whigs and Tories followed suit, arguing that the law neither could nor should recognise any limits to the authority of either Crown or Parliament that were enforceable by popular resistance. Such limits could never be enumerated with sufficient clarity or comprehensiveness, and in the vast majority of cases likely to arise, any attempt to do so was more likely to provoke unjustified resistance than prevent tyranny.[179] Many statesmen, lawyers and political theorists endorsed this thesis.[180] As Blackstone put it, any adequate remedy for abuses of sovereign power 'must necessarily be out

---

[173] See Dickinson, *Liberty and Property*, 157–159.   [174] Ibid, 71–78, 125–126 and 130.
[175] Goldsworthy, *Sovereignty of Parliament*, 178.   [176] Dickinson, *Liberty and Property*, 132.
[177] Locke, *Two Treatises*, 356.   [178] Ibid, 379–380; see also nn 163–164 above.
[179] Goldsworthy, *Sovereignty of Parliament*, 179.
[180] Including Sir Robert Walpole, Charles Yorke, Adam Smith, George Chalmers, William Paley, Henry Dundas and William Blackstone: see Goldsworthy, *Sovereignty of Parliament*, 178–184.

of the reach of any *stated rule*'.[181] But as the Revolution had shown, when 'the *ordinary* course of law' fails to prevent 'unconstitutional oppressions', the people naturally turn to 'those *extraordinary* recourses to first principles, which are necessary when the contracts of society are in danger of dissolution'.[182]

Blackstone's reference to 'unconstitutional oppressions' was not unusual: it was common to distinguish between unconstitutional acts and illegal ones. Everyone agreed that while Parliament's authority was subject to both natural law and 'constitutional principles', its Acts were legally valid even if unjust or unconstitutional. There had to be an ultimate tribunal with authority conclusively to resolve disagreements of principle, even if it erred. Moreover, Parliament's ultimate responsibility was to safeguard public welfare, which in emergencies might justify violations of constitutional principles.[183] The notion that something could be unconstitutional despite being legal survives today in the terminology of 'constitutional convention'.[184]

It was widely believed that any risk of tyranny was minimised by checks and balances within Parliament itself. The Constitution was frequently praised as a well-balanced combination of the best aspects of the monarchical, aristocratic and democratic forms of government, each of which checked the worst aspects of the others and thereby protected the rights of all sections of the community.[185] This was 'a fundamental assumption of eighteenth-century England', which 'pervaded English political life in the years from the Restoration to the passing of the Great Reform Bill'.[186] David Hume defended the Crown's methods of exerting influence within the House of Commons, which the Country opposition condemned as corrupt, as exemplifying the desirable balance achieved by this mixed constitution; they were a counter-weight to the Commons' power of the purse, which might otherwise overwhelm the deliberations of the Crown.[187]

---

[181] W. Blackstone, *Commentaries on the Laws of England, Book the First: The Rights of Persons* (Clarendon Press, 1765), 237–238; emphasis in original.
[182] Ibid, 237–238 and 243; emphases in original.
[183] Goldsworthy, *Sovereignty of Parliament*, 188–192.
[184] See page 279, main text accompanying n. 228.
[185] D. Lieberman, 'The Mixed Constitution and the Common Law', in M. Goldie and R. Wokler, eds., *The Cambridge History of Eighteenth-Century Political Thought* (Cambridge University Press, 2008), 317 at 318–319, 324–325; see also Weston, *English Constitutional Theory*, 3, 123–178.
[186] Lieberman, *The Mixed Constitution*, 317 at 318–319.   [187] Ibid, 328–330.

Most theorists treated the judicial power as a branch of the executive power, vested in the Crown and subordinate to the legislature.[188] Montesquieu, discussing the British Constitution, emphasised the executive and the two branches of the legislature as checks on one another, and dismissed the judicial power as 'in some measure next to nothing'.[189] The judges were merely the mouthpieces of the law, who could 'moderate neither its force nor its rigour'; the legislative power would not 'bow before the tribunals of law, which are lower than it'.[190] When he did mention 'the power of judging' as an independent check on injustice, he was referring to the power of common law juries, representing local communities.[191]

But Montesquieu's English translator used the term 'judicial power', and later writers including Jean-Louis de Lolme and Blackstone developed this into a defence of a tripartite separation of powers and offices, with the judiciary joining the legislature and executive as a vital component of the overall system of checks and balances. The idea of separating these three powers gradually replaced the older idea of a mixture and balance of powers within Parliament itself.[192]

The idea that the people rather than Parliament were sovereign became increasingly popular towards the end of the century, until being discredited by the excesses of the French Revolution. Radicals advocated constitutional reforms to enhance the people's power, including universal male suffrage and annual Parliaments. They rarely looked to the judiciary to control Parliament's power, and usually appealed to natural rights, ascertained by reason, rather than legal rights established by precedent.[193] Democrats such as Thomas Paine did not regard any law as immutable; that would have been inconsistent with the equal right of every generation to govern its own affairs, as well as impossible to enforce.[194] Jeremy Bentham later attacked

---

[188] See S. Jay, 'Servants of Monarchs and Lords: The Advisory Role of Early English Judges' (1994) 38 *The American Journal of Legal History* 117, 160–165, and references cited therein.

[189] Weston, *English Constitutional Theory*, 125.

[190] C. Montesquieu, *The Spirit of Laws* (1748), A. M. Cohler, B. C. Miller and H. S. Stone, eds. (Cambridge University Press, 1989), 163.

[191] Ibid, 157–158.

[192] Lieberman, *The Mixed Constitution*, 331–336; see page 279, main text accompanying n. 216.

[193] Dickinson, *Liberty and Property*, 240–244.

[194] T. Paine, *Rights of Man, Part One*, in H. H. Clark, ed., *Thomas Paine: Representative Selections* (rev'd ed., Hill & Yang, 1961), 61, 64 and 65.

what he called 'the fallacy of irrevocable laws';[195] unless deceived by it, the living could not be compelled to obey the dead.[196]

Most reformers sought not to limit Parliament's powers, but to make it more accountable to the general public.[197] Joseph Priestley expressed confidence that if the House of Commons became a truly representative body, 'every other reform could be made without any difficulty whatever.'[198] Richard Price agreed: provided that the Commons truly represented the people, government by king, Lords, and Commons 'is the perfection of government'.[199]

The Nineteenth Century

The Constitution stood at the centre of British political thought throughout the nineteenth century. A profusion of books and essays examined it from a historical and practical, rather than theoretical, perspective. The trend was set by members of the Scottish Enlightenment, including David Hume, who promoted empirical enquiry into the historical developments and practical effects of particular constitutions, rather than the theoretical elaboration of universal, a priori principles.[200] The horrors of the French Revolution had revived the British distrust of radical change motivated by abstract ideals.[201] Edmund Burke had persuaded many of the wisdom of preferring cautious, organic development of customary practices and traditional institutions.[202]

Historical accounts of the Constitution in the nineteenth century were typically Whiggish and self-congratulatory.[203] A 'rallying point for popular patriotism', its superiority to those of other European nations was triumphantly proclaimed, for helping to avoid both revolution and despotism by

---

[195] H. A. Larrabee, ed., *Bentham's Handbook of Political Fallacies* (Thomas Y Cromwell Co, 1952), ch. III.
[196] Ibid, 57.
[197] P. Langford, *Public Life and the Propertied Englishman 1689–1798* (Clarendon Press, 1991), 154.
[198] J. Priestley, *A Political Dialogue on the General Principles of Government*, in J. T. Rutt, ed., *The Theological and Miscellaneous Works of Joseph Priestley* (Klaus Reprint Co, 1972), vol. xxv, 81, 107.
[199] R. Price, *Observations on the Nature of Civil Liberty: The Principles of Government and the Justice and Policy of the War with America* (6th ed., E & C Dilly, 1776), 20.
[200] A. Hawkins, *Victorian Political Culture, 'Habits of Hearts and Minds'* (Oxford University Press, 2015), 42–43, 54, 55, 57.
[201] Ibid, 36, 38.   [202] Ibid, 39–40, 59, 61.   [203] Ibid, 53–55.

providing stability together with progressive reforms.[204] Even proponents of radical change, such as the Chartists in the 1840s, proclaimed fidelity to the supposed traditional Constitution, founded on ancient liberties, Magna Carta and so on, and demanded its restoration.[205] It was acknowledged that the Constitution would continue to evolve, but within a narrower range of possibilities considered practicable, compared with elsewhere in Europe where more sweeping transformations were still advocated.[206]

Leading Chartists claimed that natural law and common law limited the powers of the Crown and even Parliament.[207] They relied heavily on Blackstone's ruminations about natural law, while ignoring his clear affirmation of parliamentary sovereignty.[208] But Parliament's gradual reforms of the political system 'slowly blunted their grievances', and marginalised appeals to 'natural rights'.[209] Progressive thought shifted from speculations about natural law, social contract and individual rights, to more utilitarian considerations, aimed at expanding commerce, increasing prosperity and fostering a law-abiding and well-educated middle-class.[210]

As the consequences of the Reform Acts of 1832, 1867 and 1884 unfolded in stages, the Crown lost its ability to control the Commons through patronage, and was eventually compelled to accept the judgment of the Commons in appointing a Ministry.[211] The House of Lords also grew increasingly reluctant to resist the popular will.[212] The Commons became dominated by political parties, elected on the basis of widely publicised platforms implemented through strict party discipline.[213] After 1867, the judgment of the electorate was recognised as determining which party would form a Ministry.[214]

The jurist J. J. Park, in *Dogmas of the Constitution* (1832) argued that 'parliamentary government' had replaced 'prerogative government'.[215] As the power of the monarchy and the Lords declined, it also displaced the

---

[204] Ibid, 75, 30 and 217; R. Saunders, 'Parliament and People: The British Constitution in the Long Nineteenth Century' (2008) 6 *Journal of Modern European History* 72, 72–73, 81.
[205] Saunders, 'Parliament and People', 75; J. Gibson, 'The Chartists and the Constitution: Revisiting British Popular Constitutionalism' (2017) 56 *Journal of British Studies* 70, 70–72, Hawkins, *Victorian Political Culture*, 53–54.
[206] Hawkins, *Victorian Political Culture*, 55, 57–58, 268. Saunders, 'Parliament and People', 76.
[207] Gibson, 'The Chartists and the Constitution', 73–74, 76–78, 80, 82, 87, 89.
[208] Ibid, 88.   [209] Hawkins, *Victorian Political Culture*, 151–152, quotes at 151 and 153.
[210] Ibid, 44, 47–48, 51.   [211] Ibid, 122–124, 127–128.
[212] Saunders, 'Parliament and People', 83–84, AH 313–314.
[213] Hawkins, *Victorian Political Culture*, 72–73, 86, 100.
[214] Saunders, 'Parliament and People', 82, but cf Hawkins, *Victorian Political Culture*, 173–174.
[215] Hawkins, *Victorian Political Culture*, 97–98.

traditional model of 'mixed government' which was eventually discarded as an out-dated fiction.[216] In 1858, the third Earl Grey – arguably 'the leading Whig theorist of his generation'[217] – declared parliamentary government to be 'government by party'.[218] His essay *Parliamentary Government* (1858) attempted to explain how this new system actually worked, to describe both its advantages and deficiencies, and to show that the former outweighed the latter. Erskine May's *Constitutional History of England* (1861–1863) and Bagehot's *The English Constitution* (1867) followed suit. Neither Grey nor Bagehot found much to say about law or the judiciary.[219]

Bagehot's emphasis on current realities rather than outdated ideals included his famous distinction between the 'dignified' and 'efficient' components of the Constitution. He announced that a republic had insinuated itself under the folds of a monarchy,[220] which retained an important role as a symbol of national unity and a focus of loyalty.[221] He attributed the allegiance of the populace to the Constitution largely to habitual deference to its 'dignified' components along with ignorance of how its 'efficient' components made it actually work.[222]

Some conservatives professed distaste for the rise of political parties,[223] but their views were soon rejected as anachronistic even by fellow conservatives.[224] 'The Whig view of the constitution, or at least of its main features, was accepted by the great majority of people in political life down to the 1880s ... even [by] the Conservatives after 1846.'[225]

Parliament's sovereignty in law-making was firmly established,[226] although regarded as constrained in practice by 'a framework of customs, conventions and principles of which the most important was public opinion'.[227] 'It was a commonplace that a practice might be legal and yet also be unconstitutional.'[228] These orthodoxies were given canonical expression in A. V. Dicey's *Introduction to the Study of the Law of the Constitution* (1885), which also emphasised and expounded on Britain's long-standing commitment to the

---

[216] Ibid, 65, 86, 97–98, 173, 227; Saunders, 'Parliament and People', 83, n. 52.
[217] H. J. Hanham, *The Nineteenth-Century Constitution 1815–1914, Documents and Commentary* (Cambridge University Press, 1969), 3.
[218] Hawkins, *Victorian Political Culture*, 101.   [219] Ibid, 239.   [220] Ibid, 124.
[221] Ibid, 124–125, 238–241, 378.   [222] Ibid, 240–241.
[223] Hawkins, *Victorian Political Culture*, 134–136, 170.   [224] Ibid, 137.
[225] Hanham, *The Nineteenth-Century Constitution*, 4.
[226] Hawkins, *Victorian Political Culture*, 31–33, 34–35; Goldsworthy, *Sovereignty of Parliament*, ch. 8.
[227] Saunders, 'Parliament and People', 76.   [228] Ibid, 76–77.

Rule of Law.[229] Dicey, and the legal philosopher John Austin who held all law to be founded on sovereign power, emphasised that abuse of Parliament's power might provoke popular disobedience or resistance.[230]

Because Parliament was the fulcrum of the Constitution, in legislative and executive affairs, 'all the major political parties of the nineteenth century acted within the context of a constitutionalism focusing their aspirations upon Westminster'.[231] This was equally true of most radical advocates of reform outside Parliament, such as the Chartists; despite claiming that Parliament was bound by fundamental laws, they aimed to persuade it to adopt their proposals so as to enable their own participation within it.[232] '[T]he key problem was ... how to secure a good parliament through a good electoral system.'[233] The focus of constitutional reformers throughout the century was the franchise, the constituencies, and electoral procedures.

In the early nineteenth century Parliament came to be regarded as representing the diverse 'interests' of the nation, in property, commerce, the professions and industry, rather than individuals.[234] These interests had to be represented by men sufficiently independent of others for their livelihoods, and well-educated, to be capable of autonomous and informed decisions.[235] Property ownership was long considered the best proxy for these qualities.[236] But radicals demanded broader popular participation.[237]

It became increasingly accepted that the franchise must be expanded to accommodate the educated and 'respectable' middle classes.[238] Moral character and education, rather than property, became the touchstone for representation, which invited claims on behalf of the 'respectable' working-classes as well.[239] The Reform Act of 1867 enfranchised three out of five adult males in England and Wales.[240] This further propelled the political competition between parties appealing to popular opinion, and made full democracy appear more acceptable.[241] The further reforms of 1884 were recognised as

---

[229] Recently republished as A. V. Dicey, *The Law of the Constitution*, J. W. F. Allison, ed. (Oxford University Press, 2013).
[230] Goldsworthy, *Sovereignty of Parliament*, 19.
[231] Hawkins, *Victorian Political Culture*, 64.
[232] Ibid, 216, 372, 376–377; also Saunders, 'Parliament and People', 78; Gibson, 'The Chartists and the Constitution', 88.
[233] Hanham, *The Nineteenth-Century Constitution*, 3.
[234] Hawkins, *Victorian Political Culture*, 40–41, 52, 86, 90, 93, 156, 158, 173, 217,
[235] Ibid, 61, 157, 173.
[236] Ibid, 62–63, 87, quote at 63; also Saunders, 'Parliament and People', 79.
[237] Hawkins, *Victorian Political Culture*, 150.   [238] Ibid, 91.   [239] Ibid, 248–250.
[240] Ibid, 268.   [241] Ibid, 269–271, 274, 319, 329.

making the system more truly democratic,[242] with universal male suffrage following in 1918 and universal female suffrage in 1928.

From the 1870s the Conservative Party attempted to reinvigorate the House of Lords by proclaiming its right to veto any measure that lacked an electoral 'mandate'.[243] That battle was lost in 1911, when the Lords was stripped of its veto power.[244] But the Conservatives had joined the other major parties in accepting the political sovereignty of the people.[245] Electoral reforms had reconciled the legal sovereignty of Parliament and the political sovereignty of the people, and thus the constitutional theories of eighteenth- and nineteenth-century conservatives and radicals.[246]

The Twentieth and Twenty-First Centuries

Sufficient space remains only to mention subsequent developments. The first half of the twentieth century saw few notable developments in constitutional theory. From the 1950s, scholars began to debate whether or not Parliament could bind its own legislative power, if not substantively, then at least procedurally.[247] The importance of that question increased when the *European Communities Act* (UK) 1972 required that statutes incompatible with relevant European laws should be disapplied by British courts: the question was whether this was consistent with parliamentary sovereignty. From the 1970s, there were growing demands for other major constitutional reforms, especially the adoption of a Bill of Rights entrenched against amendment or repeal by ordinary legislation. Parliamentary sovereignty was increasingly challenged by those who argued that the Rule of Law requires judicially enforceable checks on all forms of government power. Some scholars claimed that Parliament's power was already limited by a 'common law constitution', which generated considerable theoretical debate.[248] So did efforts to provide a theoretical justification, consistent with parliamentary sovereignty, of the enormous expansion of the grounds of judicial review of executive decision-making that began in the 1960s.[249] The Blair Labour government eventually achieved a number of important constitutional

---

[242] Ibid, 273, 374, 382.
[243] Saunders, 'Parliament and People', 82, 85; Hawkins, *Victorian Political Culture*, 313–314.
[244] Saunders, 'Parliament and People', 85–86.   [245] Ibid, 85–86.   [246] Ibid, 82.
[247] See M. Gordon, *Parliamentary Sovereignty in the UK Constitution; Process, Politics and Democracy* (Hart Publishing, 2015), ch. 2.
[248] E.g., T. R. S. Alan, *The Sovereignty of Law; Freedom, Constitution, and Common Law* (Oxford University Press, 2013); J. Goldsworthy, *Sovereignty of Parliament*, ch. 10.
[249] See C. Forsyth, ed., *Judicial Review and the Constitution* (Hart Publishing, 2000).

reforms, which are discussed elsewhere in these volumes, as is Britain's withdrawal from the European Union in 2020. The ramifications of these changes, and judicial responses to them, continue to stimulate an enormous output of jurisprudential commentary.

PART II

★

ACTORS AND INSTITUTION

II

Monarchy

EDWARD CAVANAGH

By the second quarter of the fourteenth century, England had developed many attributes of a 'constitutional monarchy': one that would later expand and contract, in cycles, across the British Isles. This constitutional monarchy has been subject to many minor recalibrations; more major recalibrations have occurred between 1640 and 1690, and also between 1820 and 1870. To focus on the *function* and *form* of this hereditary institution of governance, it can be seen operating in accordance to rules and conventions within three separate if overlapping spheres: that is, the parliamentary, the personal and conciliar, and the judicial. Over time, there may have developed different understandings about the instrumentality and enforceability of these rules and conventions. But these rules and conventions could never be disregarded outright.

The adoption here of a broad English perspective upon the constitutional history of monarchy in the United Kingdom over the *longue durée* is a regrettable but necessary expedient. The Crown, as it survives today, is a thoroughly English institution. No amount of symbolism or ornateness in the Queen's royal styles and titles can change that, even if this will annoy certain pedants and nationalists. It is true, but not for this chapter to explore, that medieval statecraft took many forms in the deeds and words of kings and queens, princes and princesses, noblemen and sometimes even churchmen across the British Isles. It is also true, however, that key holders of the office of English monarch proved more effective than their neighbours in rehearsing expressions of 'overkingship'. This expression captures something of the arrogance of English presumptions of superiority over inferior monarchies: the ability, in plainer words, to lord it over a king, in relationships that were contractual and often coerced in contexts of violence.[1] In reality, as the

---

[1] R. R. Davies, *Domination and Conquest: The Experience of Ireland, Scotland, and Wales, 1100–1300* (Cambridge: Cambridge University Press, 1990).

Middle Ages played out, dynasties competed and overlapped with each other. Sometimes they interbred. And on those rare, constitutionally important, and often just as arrogant occasions when multiple claims were grafted onto a single consolidated crown, it was almost always intended to be worn at the seat of English power. Admittedly this does *not* require any unthinking acceptance of a 'common law-perspective on the constitution'.[2] It does, however, appeal to a *statutory* perspective, for all of these relationships took on their early modern forms with constitutional ratification, instrumentally, through parliamentary enactments: Wales in 1535,[3] Ireland in 1542, 1719, and 1800,[4] and Scotland in 1603 and 1706.[5]

Many aspects of monarchy have indeed come to be defined by parliament, including its relationship with the *church*, its main institutional competitor – and that is another story playing in the background of this chapter. Before the Reformation, English monarchs and Roman Popes often fell into disagreement over the appointments of high church offices and, as well, the coexistence of ecclesiastical jurisdiction with English secular jurisdictions. The statutory enhancement of the powers of the Crown against ecclesiastical authority was the breakthrough of Tudor parliaments.[6] The monarch became the head of established churches in Ireland and England, but never managed to do so in Scotland. The church remained central to united Stuart conceptions of kingship, which carried over into an uncompromisingly Protestant eighteenth century. An ecumenical age slow to follow may have been rife, at first, with disharmony, but Victoria was wise not to attempt any exertion of constitutional influence over crises of disruption, doctrine, and disestablishment. This was an example followed by George V. Into the twenty-first century, the monarch of the United Kingdom enjoys only a symbolic standing in relation to the established church in England, with no constitutional standing at all beyond. All of this, again, is largely the work of statutes.[7]

Any constitutional history of monarchy as an office will demand sensitivity towards the word 'crown', a term of art that changed its meaning from epoch to epoch. The Saxon king's headpiece – whether *galea* (helmet) or *corona*

---

[2] N. MacCormick, 'The English Constitution, the British State, and the Scottish Anomaly', *Proceedings of the British Academy* 101 (1999), 300.
[3] 27 Hen. VIII, c. 24 and c. 26.
[4] 33 Hen. VIII, c. 1 (Ireland), 6 Geo. I, c. 5, and 39 & 40 Geo. III, c. 67.
[5] 1 Jac. I, c. 1; 6 Ann., c. 11.
[6] 24 Hen. VIII, c. 12; 25 Hen. VIII, c. 19, 21, and 22; 26 Hen. VIII, c. 1; 1 Eli. c. 1 and 2.
[7] Act 1707 (Scotland), c. 6; 32 & 33 Vic. c. 42; 4 & 5 Geo. V, c. 91; 11 & 12 Geo. V, c. 29.

(crown) – was regarded with solemnity but it was revered less, overall, than his *sceptrum* (sceptre). As the aesthetics of English regalia became more French during the first half-century of Norman rule, the *corona* was abstracted into an incorporeal symbol of the king's tenure in England. From the late thirteenth century, the Crown became suspended in a kind of timelessness above the realm and king alike, to be deployed as legal shorthand for three distinct meanings: the bundle of powers enjoyed by the monarch, the source of all privileges and liberties claimed from the monarch, and the adjudicator to whom pleas were addressed.[8]

For the rest of the medieval period up to the commencement of the modern period, equal regard must be shown for how monarchy was *described* (as a corporation sole or in the form of two bodies, noting two memorable examples from Tudor-Stuart legal thought) and how monarchy was *operated* (by office-holders). We see that the Crown is invoked today in a way very different from the constitutional registers of the past: either now as the source and shorthand for executive action, a synonym for the state, or a metaphor for public authority, good and bad. The purpose of this chapter will be to reveal what happened in the background to take us from the fourteenth century to the twenty-first.

The Parliamentary Monarch

The word *parlement* might have been used in political registers within England from the 1160s or even earlier, but a more consistent constitutional appropriation of the term for the kingly consultation of noblemen, clergymen, and commune-men is a feature of the Plantagenet period. In the reign of Edward II, the Ordinances of 1311 provide one of the earliest renditions of the corporate character of parliament as distinct from the king or any of his councils. The barons used this instrument, which they issued on their own authority, to denounce an administration carried on mostly within the confines of the royal household. It declared that all of the king's gifts, official appointments, and military campaigns had to receive 'the common assent of his baronage, and that in parliament', for them to have any effect.[9] Although these ordinances were 'repealed' in 1322, and were never again reissued, their

---

[8] G. Garnett, 'The Origins of the Crown', *Proceedings of the British Academy* 89 (1996), 171–214.
[9] *Statutes of the Realm*, 11 vols. (London, 1810–1822), I: 157–167.

importance as an expression of the need to consult baronial advice within the institution of *parliament* cannot be understated.

The deposition of the king followed shortly afterwards. This was the collaborative endeavour of knights and barons, which was important as a constitutional event for bringing on the more popular reign of Edward III (1327–1377). The first of many kings after him to master the role of king-in-parliament, Edward III showed few signs of disobedience towards a simple and now very important rule: namely, that as king he should never introduce direct taxation without summoning the nobility and commonalty to parliament for their consent.

By the fourteenth century, it becomes possible to identify a number of procedural and functional consistencies in relation to the role of English monarch in parliament.[10] Indirectly, the king enjoyed some control over its composition. Lords spiritual were comprised of clerical office-holders who owed their positions and status to the church *and* the Crown in precarious tandem. Lords temporal were comprised of earls, barons, and other peerages, all of whom were dependent, to varying degrees, on the king's graces for their status. Commons were comprised of knights in service, as well as citizens and burgesses from towns and boroughs whose privileges to send representatives could be determined in royal charters at the king's pleasure. As segmented blocs, the Lords (spiritual and temporal) on the one hand, and the Commons on the other, were only ever able to meet in parliament once the king had issued a writ of summons. By his writs, the king was also empowered to prorogue, suspend, and dissolve parliament as he saw fit. His motivation to call parliament was plain enough: without their consent, he could not implement schemes of direct taxation. Dependent, therefore, on its supply, the king came to adopt other important roles in parliament's legislative and judicial work. Petitions came into the king from individuals and communities across the realm, and these could either take the form of a complaint (usually about some defect in the common law) or a request (usually for some office, pardon, or favour). Petitions were also addressed to the king by the corporate Commons whenever members were united in concern for a public rather than a specific good, before consistency in procedure and form coincided with the adoption of the term 'bill' for this

---

[10] R. G. Davies and J. H. Denton, eds., *The English Parliament in the Middle Ages* (Manchester: Manchester University Press, 1981); G. Dodd, *Justice and Grace: Private Petitioning and the English Parliament in the Late Middle Ages* (Oxford: Oxford University Press, 2007).

kind of instrument. For a bill to become statute, Lords and Commons had to endorse it, and then ask for the king's assent, which could always be withheld. Legislation of this kind was designed to endure, ideally facing repeal only by subsequent acts of parliament. Usually, the momentum behind most legislative activity came from the Commons. On the other hand, it was the Lords who enjoyed responsibility for the judicial business of parliament. The jurisdiction of the king-in-parliament, which involved the king, his prelates, and peers, did not include a role for the commonalty; it normally covered exceptional felonies, treasons and attainders, errors or defects in the law, and disputes among peers. One might infer something of the priorities of English kings by noting that it was always the Lords, and not the Commons, who kept a throne, and always the Lords, and not the Commons, whom the king addressed in parliamentary speeches.

Bedevilled as the constitutional history of England is, between 1398 and 1487, with mixed-up allegiances and competitiveness among dynasties, it is remarkable that so many of these conventions about the role of king-in-parliament were established to remain fixed and observed for subsequent centuries. Another noteworthy development is to be identified over the same period with regard to the relationship of monarchy and parliament. From the elective kings of Anglo-Saxon mythology through to the deposition of Edward II, English laws of succession comprised a vague combination of theories about custom, consent, conquest, and divine right. These 'laws', such as they were, became statutory over the course of the fifteenth and sixteenth centuries.[11] In 1399, Henry Bolingbroke moved on Richard II with the support of Lords and Commons to claim a 'vacant' crown and all the attachments affixed to it.[12] Before the great age of crown-swapping got underway, parliament established the succession of Henry IV's children in 1405 for the first time by statute.[13] Only a couple of generations later, in 1461, parliament was conditionally agreeing to recognise the Yorkist claim to the throne on the eve of the death of Henry VI. In 1484, the line of kingly succession (*titulus regius*) was amended again in parliament to provide for the inheritance of the Crown of Edward V by Richard III, only to be repealed in the first sitting of Henry VII's parliament in 1485.[14] This king's genius was to infuse the Yorkist and Lancastrian claims into a single Tudor line and to insist

---

[11] S. B. Chrimes, *English Constitutional Ideas in the Fifteenth Century* (Cambridge: Cambridge University Press, 1936), pp. 22–33.
[12] G. T. Lapsley, 'The Parliamentary Title of Henry IV', *English Historical Review*, 49, 195 (1934), 423–449.
[13] 7 Hen. IV, c. 2.   [14] PROME, Ric. III (January, 1484), 240–242; 1 Hen. VII.

thereby upon his right to the throne as the work of God and nature. But Henry VII's certainty in respect of his claim was not enjoyed by subsequent Tudors, largely as a result of the promiscuity of Henry VIII and the politics of Reformation. Acts of succession were to be passed again and again through parliaments in the decade following 1533.[15] For all that legislation, only during the reign of Elizabeth would it become entrenched constitutional practice in England that the amendment of the laws of succession required the agreement of monarch, Lords, and Commons in parliament. Elizabeth's own accession had followed a series of short and disappointing reigns, heavily scrutinised wills, and 'devices' drafted and redrafted anew.[16] By 1560, the hereditary aspect of monarchy had definitively become a statutory concern.

The reign of Henry VII is not commonly remembered as one in which the institution of parliament had much eminence. Seven times it was called before 1509, though its members were entrusted with little. This was instead an age of 'personal monarchy', which saw the government of the country managed as though its affairs were like that of any private estate, by the king himself and a handful of men he trusted, confined to the chamber.[17] His successor, Henry VIII, made use of the chamber too, but preferred a government in council. In addition, he managed to secure for himself an extraordinary degree of parliamentary support for acts of his royal will, statutory or otherwise.[18] Compared to others, Henry VIII's parliaments were pushovers.

An indication of this can be gleaned from the Proclamations Act 1539, which provided the king with the power to make proclamations away from parliament with all the force of statutes.[19] It speaks volumes for Henry's unimpeachability while alive that, in the very first year of the minority regency of the less fearsome Edward VI, this law was repealed and thereafter never renewed. Moreover, 'its enactment and repeal', F. W. Maitland lectured to his students in 1888, '... seem distinctly to confirm the doctrine that the king is not supreme, king and parliament are supreme; statute is

---

[15] 25 Hen. VIII, c. 22; 26 Hen. VIII, c. 2; 28 Hen. VIII, c. 7; 32 Hen. VIII, c. 25; 35 Hen. VIII, c. 1.

[16] D. Loades, *The Mid-Tudor Crisis, 1545–1565* (Basingstoke: Palgrave Macmillan, 1992), 9–41.

[17] A. P. Newton, 'The King's Chamber under the Early Tudors', *English Historical Review*, 32, 127 (1917), 348–372; P. Tucker, 'Reaction to Henry VII's Style of Kingship and Its Contribution to the Emergence of Constitutional Monarchy in England', *Historical Research* 82, 217 (2009), 511–525.

[18] G. R. Elton, *The Tudor Revolution in Government: Administrative Changes in the Reign of Henry VIII* (Cambridge: Cambridge University Press, 1969).

[19] 31 Hen. VIII, c. 8.

distinctly above ordinance or proclamation; statute may give to the king a subordinate legislative power, and what one statute has given another statute may take away'.[20]

Elizabeth I was less capable than her father had been of relying upon unanimous parliamentary support for expressions of her royal will. Still, she was the inheritor of great power in parliament. While Elizabeth preferred, as her father had, to govern by council instead of through parliament, she, unlike her father, had to deal with growing dissatisfaction about her dependency upon a few selected ministers and secretaries.[21]

The accession of James I/VI provided the best opportunity in generations for the Lords and Commons to rebalance the institution of monarch-in-parliament. But the Stuart king had other ideas, most of which had stemmed from experience. Winning for his young brow the Scottish crown on the back of a fractious civil war, James VI's kingship had taken on a form of personal rule that veered very close to absolutism during the 1580s and 1590s. Accustomed to a much less deliberative, if overwhelmingly more *productive*, legislature in Scotland, James I/VI harboured conflicting ideas about his constitutional supremacy over the English parliament.[22] In 1610, before parliament was dissolved, the Commons debated the prerogative more openly than ever before. The King's refusal to summon parliament for seven years was disquieting, but in this abeyance, James proved no real tyrant. Relative, anyway, to some of his Tudor predecessors, he proved respectful of the need to consult Lords and Commons on matters of national importance, as he would in 1621 – 'for what is here done', said the member for York in that year, 'is done but by the King himself'.[23] What remained to be seen, upon his death in 1625, was how far a monarch could diverge from parliamentary expectations of the royal office before the onset of constitutional crisis.

Charles I was an absolutist king with a contempt for parliament that brought him undone. In the Commons, petitions and 'protestations' indicting the king's rule were ineffectually made before parliament was dissolved and

---

[20] F. W. Maitland, *The Constitutional History of England* (Cambridge: Cambridge University Press, 1908), p. 253.
[21] G. R. Elton, 'Parliament', in C. Hague (ed.), *The Reign of Elizabeth I* (London: Macmillan, 1981), pp. 79–100.
[22] A. M. Godfrey, 'Parliament and the Law', in K. M. Brown and A. R. Macdonald (eds.), *Parliament in Context, 1235–1707* (Edinburgh: Edinburgh University Press, 2010), pp. 174–182.
[23] *Proceedings and Debates of the House of Commons in 1620 and 1621*, 2 vols. (Oxford: Clarendon Press, 1766), I: 318–319.

uncalled again for over a decade.[24] New 'protestations' and 'propositions' were entered when it returned, before the 'remonstrances' of both Houses in 1641 and 1642, and finally the presentation of parliament's 'nineteen propositions'.[25] Although Charles was not the first king in English history to face demands of this kind, he was surely more confounded than any other before him by the paradox that an assembly which derived its authority entirely from the Crown appeared hopeful of using this power to dispossess him of it.

Civil war waxed and waned before the astonishing developments of January 4th–February 7th, 1649. The Commons, resolving that support from the Lords was no longer necessary for its enactments, empowered itself to establish a special court staffed by parliamentary appointees to try the King for treason.[26] Less than two weeks later, the King was examined by this court; another week later, he received a death sentence; the following day, he was beheaded by axe. A week later, the Commons voted to abolish the Lords; the following day, the monarchy.[27]

The most extraordinary decade in constitutional history to follow was, therefore, one entirely without a monarch and with parliaments hardly qualifying of the name. This was a period of personal rule, coalescing around Protector Oliver Cromwell, whose government developed a reliance upon an assortment of unwilling and insolent members of the army. When Scotland was incorporated into the kingless Commonwealth of England and Ireland, a surprising union of parliaments was achieved. How this arrangement was meant to work, however, remained unclear. An 'instrument of government' was designed, debated, but never properly implemented, before the unfinished Commonwealth died with Cromwell. When his moderately capable son, Richard, was proposed to succeed in his dead father's place in 1659, an assembly met to propose, instead, the restoration of the Stuart monarchy. This is known as the 'Convention Parliament' because it met without a writ of summons and therefore enjoyed no authority to invite Charles II to emerge from exile and take up the throne of his father. To address this defect, Charles II accepted the Crown, restored the parliament in Westminster, and then used its authority to provide retroactive endorsement

---

[24] J. P. Kenyon (ed.), *The Stuart Constitution, 1603–1688: Documents and Commentary*, 2nd ed. (Cambridge: Cambridge University Press, 1986), pp. 68–71.
[25] Kenyon, *Stuart Constitution*, pp. 200–204, 207–217, 222–227.
[26] Act for Erecting of a High Court of Justice (1649), in C. H. Firth and R. S. Rait (eds.), *Acts and Ordinances of the Interregnum, 1642–1660*, 3 vols. (London: HMSO, 1911) I: 1253–1255.
[27] B. Worden, *The Rump Parliament, 1648–53* (Cambridge: Cambridge University Press, 1977), pp. 1–160.

of the Convention Parliament while backdating the regnal period.[28] All acts passed between 1642 and 1659 were now void in the absence of the king's assent. Parliaments in the king's name were then convened in Scotland and Ireland. It was as if the throne had never been vacated at all.

The statutory restoration of monarchy was followed by the imposition of further statutory limitations on monarchy, although this was hardly an inevitable outcome in 1661. Charles II may have cherished his prerogatives, even facing criticism at times for reputedly 'unconstitutional' expressions of his royal will. But his rule was conservative, even popular, owing in part to the sitting of the long 'Cavalier' parliament. His judicial supremacy over both Lords and Commons would not be challenged, either; indeed, his interventions were required to bring their major jurisdictional conflicts to a close, first in *East India Company* v. *Skinner* (1666), then in *Shirley* v. *Fagg* (1675).[29]

It was the reign of his successor that saw things fall apart. James II/VII looked to protect nominated subjects from the effects of statutes while meddling enthusiastically with the boroughs, actions which were irritating, but not technically unlawful, expressions of his royal will. More problematic was the apparent inspiration behind such expressions: namely, the sympathy he, as an open devotee of the faith himself, showed towards Catholics. Even the most loyal of parliamentarians who, at the outset of 1685 comprised the majority of both houses, could not keep up their support for the King as so many Church of Englanders came to fear that their state religion might soon revert to Catholicism. This lack of parliamentary support, in turn, enticed the King towards a Tudor kind of personal and conciliar rule. In 1688, an unusual assembly was convened, not by the King, but by a foreign prince, William of Orange. On 26 December, this admixture of former parliamentarians from Charles II's reign, along with a few London aldermen, advised the prince to invite representatives of the counties and boroughs to another Convention Parliament. Summoned on 22 January 1689, this was the assembly which declared the English throne to be vacant. Members of the Scottish parliament had to make their own overtures to the Dutch prince. This was dissimilar to Ireland, where a 'Patriot Parliament' rejected the claim to the throne of the Prince of Orange, who later had to be installed by force (and by statute).[30]

---

[28] 12 Car. II, c. 1.
[29] *Skinner* v. *East India Company* (1666) 6 St. Tr. 710–770; *Cobbett's Parliamentary History*, 36 vols. (London, 1806–1820), IV: 444; *Shirley* v. *Fagg* (1675) 6 St. Tr. 1122.
[30] *Cobbett's Parliamentary History*, V: 19–111; *Records of the Parliaments of Scotland* 1689/3/16, 108, and 1689/6/11; J. Bergin and Andrew Lyall (eds.), *The Acts of James II's Irish Parliament of 1689* (Dublin: Irish Manuscripts Commission, 2016), 3–6, 54–57.

Finally in the possession of all three crowns, William III ruled with his wife, Mary, until 1694, and then on his own, to 1702.

This reign saw the passage of extraordinary legislation in relation to monarchy and parliament. In Westminster, the Bill of Rights 1689 rendered 'illegal' all attempts by *future* monarchs – including the current pair, confirmed by the same instrument – to suspend law, hold 'commission' (i.e. prerogative) courts, levy money, refuse petitions, keep standing armies, and allow inequitable judicial procedures and convictions. It also affirmed elections in the future to be free, permitted 'freedom of speech' in parliament, and demanded parliaments to be 'held frequently'.[31] Similar provisions are carried in the Scottish parliament's Claim of Right 1689, even if the subsequent passage of the Act of Security 1704 presented a short-lived prospect for Scotland to diverge from English laws of succession and provide a new footing to the prerogatives of the Scottish crown.[32] But, in the end, Westminster's installation of the foreign House of Hanover, as heralded by the Act of Settlement 1701, was eventually accepted across Britain. This Act also imposed a series of new conditions on the monarch pertaining to certain acts of state (now subject to parliamentary discussion), office-holders (now banned from parliament), and the established religion (now enforced upon the monarch and all office-holders).[33] Even if most of the meat in these measures was pared back in repeals between 1705 and 1715 – a Georgian parliament without office-holders is impossible to imagine – the Act of Settlement offered the best indication yet that a new age of parliamentary control of monarchy was underway.[34]

Key to this achievement was the security of a more regular parliamentary timetable and a reduction in monarchical discretion over summons and dissolution. These preferences were sounded out in the Bill of Rights but were achieved only with the culmination of the Parliament Acts 1694, 1695, the Succession to the Crown Act 1707, and the Septennial Act 1716. These laws empowered parliament to last, initially, for three years, and to endure the death of the monarch, and ultimately inaugurated the convention that parliaments ought to sit for seven years, not three, before re-election.[35]

For their part, Hanoverians saw that greater parliamentary vibrancy in the newly united Anglo-Scottish legislature was in their interests. Visits became

---

[31] 1 Wil. & Mar., s. 2, c. 2.   [32] 1689 (Scotland), c. 28.   [33] 12 & 13 Wil. III, c. 2.
[34] 4 & 5 Ann., c. 20; 1 Geo. I, st. 2, c. 51.
[35] 6 & 7 Wil. & Mar., c. 2; 7 & 8 Wil. III, c. xv; 6 Ann., c. 41; 1 Geo. I, st. 2, c. 38. See B. Kemp, *King and Commons, 1660–1832* (London: Macmillan, 1968).

rare. Opening speeches became less personal and less responsive to principles and practices. Responsibility for their preparation was eventually given over to partisans, transforming the monarch's speech into a statement of government policy. More covertly, the Hanoverian monarchs were able to steer policy through strategic official appointments, none more important than ministers, a few of whom were allowed into the 'inner cabinet'.[36] Members of parliament, now speaking for 'the public', tendered demands to make the king's ministry accountable as a group, rather than as individual ministers, to the legislature.[37] Concerns of this kind only grew when the eagerness of George III to participate in a kind of politics by proxy, through the use of strategic appointments, became apparent. 'The power of the Crown, almost dead and rotten as Prerogative, has grown up anew, with much more strength, and far less odium, under the name of Influence', wrote Edmund Burke in 1770. 'The discretionary power of the Crown in the formation of Ministry, abused by bad or weak men, has given rise to a system, which, without directly violating the letter of any law, operates against the spirit of the whole constitution'.[38]

Not until the King was enfeebled with insanity and replaced by his son, as prince regent, were the conditions provided for the introduction of new measures of 'responsibility' to govern the indirect relationship between monarch and parliament. Cabinet began to exercise the prerogatives of the Crown, which was a degree worse than what Burke had decried earlier of the king exercising his prerogative through ministers. One result of this reversal of power was the development of a growing distance between ministers of the Crown (who appeared less accountable than ever before) and regular members in parliament (who grumbled while enquiring into public finances and sinecures). When George IV was finally crowned in 1820, much of the influence he might have wielded in this capacity had been surrendered to the cabinet and a few ministers, while a number of his other powers faced challenge in a reforming parliament.[39]

The Whigs then busied themselves with fleshing out a plan to transform the ministry into an institution accountable to a more representative

---

[36] R. R. Sedgwick, 'The Inner Cabinet from 1739 to 1741', *English Historical Review* 34, 135 (1919), 290–302.
[37] C. Roberts, *The Growth of Responsible Government in Stuart England* (Cambridge: Cambridge University Press, 1966).
[38] E. Burke, *Thoughts on the Cause of the Present Discontents* (London: J. Dodsley, 1770), pp. 12, 41.
[39] A. S. Foord, 'The Waning of the Influence of the Crown', *English Historical Review* 62, 245 (1947), 484–507.

parliament. After 1834, and more especially after the Bedchamber Crisis of 1839, it became a principle of British government, which found no expression in statute, that while the ministry enjoyed the *confidence* of the monarch, the same ministry was more importantly *responsible* to the House of Commons.[40] Changing expectations of the role of monarch followed. Shorn first by convention, and then by statutes, of many personal prerogatives, Victoria withdrew from public political view and adopted a consultative, occasionally critical, but overwhelmingly ceremonial role within government. Definitively by the age of Gladstone and Disraeli, the queen-in-parliament had finally become a behind-the-scenes affair. The monarch existed to be consulted, to encourage, and to warn, as Bagehot first summated in 1867. Monarchs after Victoria, and indeed sometimes even Victoria herself, only occasionally had to be reminded of the expectation that their partisanship should also be discreet.[41]

The firm contemporary convention is that all prerogative powers, whether 'personal' or not, will be exercised only on, and in accordance with, the advice of the Prime Minister. This was demonstrated by the 2019 Brexit prorogation affair, in which it was widely assumed on all sides that Queen Elizabeth II had no choice but to accept the Prime Minister's advice to prorogue Parliament for an unusually long period. Apparently, the prerogative of dissolution was abolished by the Fixed-Term Parliaments Act 2011, but experts remain unable to agree upon the consequences to this. It is noteworthy that the use of personal prerogatives by the monarch in the UK has atrophied to a significantly greater extent than deployment of so-called 'reserve powers' by heads of state in systems of responsible government derived from the same crown. This might be a sign of things to come.[42]

The Personal and Conciliar Monarch

By following the rise and decline of personal and conciliar government, a different constitutional perspective becomes apparent. The starting point here is to acknowledge that the taproot of all the monarch's personal authority was

---

[40] N. Gash, *Reaction and Reconstruction in English Politics, 1832–1852* (Oxford: Clarendon Press, 1965).

[41] F. Hardie, *The Political Influence of the British Monarchy, 1868–1952* (New York: Harper & Row, 1970).

[42] H. Kumarasingham, 'The Role and Powers of the Queen in the 2019 Brexit Political Crises: Reflections from British and Commonwealth History' (2020) 48 *Journal of Imperial and Commonwealth History* 1; A. Twomey, *The Veiled Sceptre: Reserve Powers of Heads of State in Westminster Systems* (Sydney: The Federation Press, 2019).

the power of appointment: a right that went unchallenged throughout the Middle Ages and was mostly uncontroversial until outbreaks of anti-Catholic unrest during the seventeenth century and later when there were concerns over Hanoverian royal 'influence'. The highest officers of state and the judiciary all owed their appointments to the monarch, as did individual members of the nobility; many church office-holders did too, bound though they were to canons, archbishops, and popes, before break with Rome and the establishment of the Church of England entrusted the Tudor monarchs (and all who succeeded them) with a supreme power of appointment in the religious sphere. To the extent, then, that office-holders did the bidding of the government, they did so under the spell of the monarch.

Tracking the early evolution of the king's council is an uncertain task. The important consistency to recognise concerns the means of its creation. Very gradually, some office-holders may have expected to receive an invitation into the council as a matter of convention, but always their invitation lay with the king's personal discretion as an extension of his power of appointment. Assuming legislative as well as judicial functions within the English constitution, the king-in-council sounded out the clearest expressions of his will as ruler. A number of instruments lay at his disposal to that end. Every writ necessary to summon parliament was prepared in council. Charters and letters patent tended to originate in council, before passing the seal in chancery. Ordinances and proclamations were promulgated in order to hurry along or add procedural details to the execution of a variety of administrative, financial, and mercantile policies across the realm. There was much inconsistency within central and local courts between the thirteenth and seventeenth centuries over the enforcement and interpretation of ordinances and proclamations, but most kings accepted that these were not the instruments to promulgate or repeal general laws for the entire realm; this was better the job for statutes issued in parliament. Like parliament, councils received petitions. The king-in-council was also a judicial institution, accepting many bills of action, and assuming original jurisdiction over special criminal or civil matters. It could also correct errors in the ordinary courts. Disputes concerning foreign merchants and maritime matters were not uncommon here. All of this judicial work in council was fairly uncontroversial, except when it was seen to be augmenting the king's power (as it was, for example, during James III's reign in Scotland, and during Charles I's in Britain).[43]

---

[43] J. F. Baldwin, *The King's Council in England during the Middle Ages* (Oxford: Clarendon Press, 1913), pp. 262–306, 419–458.

Over the same later medieval period, 'prerogative' became the word to capture any number of recognisably superior or inalienable powers, whether legal or political, inherent to the monarchy away from parliament. Its precise meaning is difficult to pin down from century to century, however. The word 'prerogative' is not altogether helpfully kept in mind as the sum of its Latin parts. It is more conventional to attribute its meaningful expression to an unusual document from the later part of Edward I's reign, the *Praerogativa Regis*, which was probably a kind of statute and subject later to commentary and amendment. Many of its provisions are feudal in nature, concerning restrictions upon alienation, escheats, and knight's service. Other provisions concern marriage, widows, heiresses, and the king's right to sturgeon, whales, and wreck.[44] Gradually, 'prerogative' became less feudal and developed its more recognisable association with royal statecraft. By the fifteenth century, according to Stanley Chrimes, there developed a distinction between *the* prerogative and *a* prerogative in English constitutional language: the prerogative in the singular referring to 'that reserve of undefined power necessary to any government to enable it to deal with emergencies' but in the plural, to those specific 'exercises of the Prerogative which have received definition and therefore restriction, by litigation and the process of law'.[45] Some of these prerogatives, such as that of waging war, were subject to less restriction than others. The most important parts of the royal prerogative remained its *realpolitik* aspects. The maturity of Tudor constitutionalism saw a hardening in distinction between 'separable' and 'inseparable' prerogatives, in relation to the beginnings of the idea that royal power was accountable to parliamentary surveillance, amid ongoing enquiries about the office of monarch, what it entailed, and how it should be held.[46]

Personal and conciliar government surged with the Tudors but crashed with the Stuarts. Heady matters of state were discussed and often decided in council during this period. If these were mostly the political concerns of a new modern age, still there were many throwbacks in council to medieval statecraft too. Plantagenet-era writs were reprised *en masse* to demand that holders of certain privileges and liberties prove them, pay for them again, or surrender them. These writs may have been unpopular, even though, for

---

[44] *Statutes of the Realm*, 1: 226–227. See also F. W. Maitland, 'Praerogativa Regis', in *Collected Papers*, 2 vols. (Cambridge: Cambridge University Press, 1911), II: 183–189.
[45] Chrimes, English Constitutional Ideas, pp. 42–43.
[46] W. S. Holdsworth, 'The Prerogative in the Sixteenth Century', *Columbia Law Review* 21, 6 (1921), 558–560.

subjects wanting confirmation, they could be desirable; but nobody for the moment would dare question this part of the prerogative until it contravened the statute books.[47] Rather, it was the *judicial* business of the king-in-council that led parliament to impose restraints upon the institution, when the jurisdiction of Star Chamber was extinguished in 1641.[48] Most other features of the institution of king-in-council were preserved in a mostly benign form of 'privy' council, which endured into the Restoration period, and testified to the preference of Charles II and James II for advice from a small number of office-holders, experts, confidants, and committees.

During the Hanoverian period, privy council and cabinet became two distinct consultative and deliberative mechanisms for the monarch in the United Kingdom. Cabinet was the more political of the two. There developed among some office-holders new expectations as to which should be admitted into cabinet as a matter of custom, if not of right, notwithstanding Anne's efforts to discourage these expectations.[49] Georges I, II, and III were less able and occasionally less willing to dominate the deliberations of cabinet, which tended to concern the operation of executive government more than it did the king himself.[50] By degrees, as cabinet became subject to greater parliamentary scrutiny, it lost exposure to royal control, and so the monarch stopped attending by the nineteenth century. Privy Council was the safer home for the prerogative, though its work became increasingly formal. Letters and instructions were drawn up here. The Georges only went to meetings of the privy council to provide their assent or authorisation to all actions associated with their residual power. Charters and the like were granted to a great number of entities in this way. Over the nineteenth century, statutory legislation reduced the remit of prerogative instruments of this kind, relegating their applications to matters (for example, the founding of individual charities) which parliament had not traditionally prioritised. For the advertisement and clarification of matters of state, ordinances and royal proclamations were gradually replaced by acts of parliament over the same century.

---

[47] E. Jenks, 'Prerogative Writs in English Law', *Yale Law Journal* 32, 6 (1923), 523–534; C. Patterson, '*Quo Warranto* and Borough Corporations in Early Stuart England: Royal Prerogative and Local Privileges in the Central Courts', *English Historical Review* 120, 488 (2005), 879–906.

[48] 16 Car. I, c. 10.

[49] J. H. Plumb, 'The Organization of Cabinet in the Reign of Queen Anne', *Transactions of the Royal Historical Society* 5, 7 (1957), 137–157.

[50] It remains difficult to generalise on this contested topic any more than this here. Start with T. Williams, 'Cabinet in the Eighteenth Century', *History* 22, 87 (1937), 240–252.

By contrast, from the end of the eighteenth century, through to the Napoleonic Wars, and more especially during the regency, there can be noticed a rise in prerogative legislation through orders-in-council. As a means of passing fast law, the technique was generally reserved for colonies, and was manipulated not by the monarch personally but by the executive in his or her name. Around the 1830s, it came to be thought that the monarch's power to legislate through orders-in-council actually derived from parliament.[51] This idea would have been a hard sell to monarchs ruling in the seventeenth and eighteenth centuries. But that is the direction things were heading at Victoria's accession. By the end of her reign, not only had the royal instruments of legislation become statutorily conditioned, but most of the personal prerogatives of the Crown more generally – concerning the army and navy, ports and havens, aliens, wartime appropriations, weights, measures, coinage, and the like – had become subsumed within or superseded by statute.

Office-holding within the administrative system took on new forms. The indirect influence, wieldable by a monarch through exercising his or her personal power of appointment, became scandalous during the age of George III but dropped away in the years between 1830 and 1860. In this window, the civil service became a more professionalised bureaucracy, answerable to ministers who were, in turn, responsible to parliament. This development coincided with inevitable changes in the function and performance of servants of the Crown, salaried under contracts and subject to expectations of conduct with greater consistency than before. Holder of the highest office in the United Kingdom, Queen Victoria may not have been subjected to precisely the same kind of transformation in regard to her own position, but the power she was seen to enjoy through appointments diminished, as the discretion of the monarch over a rule-bound office-holding class eventually became unnecessary. For this reason, it was mostly uncontroversial that, throughout the twentieth century, the exercise of just about every aspect of the royal prerogative would be apportioned, by statute if not by convention, to individuals holding office under the Crown.

Counselled or self-willed, the monarch is left with little constitutional role in the meting out of law and policy in the United Kingdom today. The King is a consultative entity away from parliament. In regular audiences with the prime minister he is able to express his opinions and, if necessary, provide

---

[51] 6 and 7 Vict., c. 94.

advice when it comes to policy, which the prime minister is obliged to hear but not to heed. The Privy Council, on the other hand, has swollen to several hundred life appointees, comprising now an eccentric combination of nobles, partisans, experts, and others mostly from a parliamentary background. A portion of this large number may congregate with him to carry out some of the mostly unexciting business of the Crown over which the King himself no longer enjoys any direct agency - that is, if the reign of his predecessor, Elizabeth II, is anything to go by. Prorogation is an example of this business. As noted earlier, in the context of the Brexit prorogation affair in 2019, it was assumed by all involved, including the UK Supreme Court,[52] that the Queen had no choice but to accept the advice of the Prime Minister to exercise the power to prorogue Parliament as he requested.

The Judicial Monarch

To explore the constitutional history of the monarch and the courts is to confront a paradox.[53] In the Middle Ages, all secular judicial power resided in the king under God, although such power might be exercised by delegates of the king.[54] Amongst such delegates were the judicial officials who exercised jurisdiction on the monarch's behalf. These holders of judicial office were subject to varying degrees of royal influence and control. However, at the same time as monarchs were the source of judicial power they were also 'under the law'. Herein lies the paradox. It did not follow from subjection to law that the monarch could be personally sued in the monarch's own courts. However, as a sort of *quid pro quo* for crown immunity, it was recognised that servants of the Crown could be sued in respect of things said or done on the monarch's behalf. Nor did the famous phrase 'the King can do no wrong' refer to the monarch's moral standing but rather to the fact that royal breaches of the law were only cognisable in a royal court with the monarch's consent, given in response to what came to be called a 'petition of right' (the very name of which implies that there was a wrong that needed to be righted). In the early seventeenth century, the amenability of officials, such as sheriffs and constables, to personal liability for wrongs attributable to performance of their official duties, came to be seen potentially as unduly

---

[52] In R *(Miller)* v. *Prime Minister* [2019] UKSC 41.
[53] This section was jointly written by Edward Cavanagh and Peter Cane, and Peter takes full joint responsibility for it.
[54] *Bracton on the Laws and Customs of England*, trans. S. E. Thorne (Cambridge, MA: Harvard University Press, 1968), II: 167.

onerous. The Court of King's Bench adapted existing administrative writs (notably *certiorari* and *mandamus*) for use, in the name of the monarch, to quash illegal decisions made in the King's name or prohibit breaches of the law, as well as to order royal officials to perform duties imposed on them by law. These writs came to be called 'prerogative' to indicate that they were issued centrally, formally in the name of the King, to control servants and agents of the Crown.[55] Here we find the origins of modern 'judicial review of administration'.

One effect of Crown immunity from suit was that complaints and grievances against the monarch, senior crown servants, and local officials were often made directly to parliament or the council. This typically suited monarchs, both Scottish and English. On the one hand, it gave monarchs the opportunity to supervise administration of local justice to minimise the risk of damage it might cause to the interests of favourite delegates or by detracting in other ways from royal prestige. On the other hand, it enabled monarchs to earn popular favour by providing avenues of justice that were typically less clogged, less expensive, and less slow than those available in the judicial system. In Scotland, Stewart monarchs installed and maintained lordly and heritable jurisdictions for this purpose,[56] whereas in England, Tudor monarchs established prerogative (or 'conciliar') courts that were identifiably separate manifestations of the council. In England, in the sixteenth century in particular, the Courts of Star Chamber and Requests, as well as the Councils of the North, and of Wales and the Marches, provided large numbers of poorer people with relatively informal, inexpensive, and timely legal redress.

The Court of Chancery also grew out of the practice of petitioning the monarch more directly (through the office of the Chancellor) when other available avenues of redress had failed to provide satisfaction.[57] At first, Chancellors developed the practice of issuing 'writs' giving access to royal justice for those dissatisfied with exercises of local and seigneurial jurisdiction. In due course, administration of royal justice was institutionalised in the Courts of Common Pleas, King's Bench, and the Exchequer. Early flexibility and creativity in the formulation of writs gave way to ossification

---

[55] E. G. Henderson, *The Foundations of English Administrative Law: Certiorari and Mandamus in the Seventeenth Century* (Cambridge, MA: Harvard University Press, 1963).

[56] Many such jurisdictions endured in Scotland until the mid eighteenth century, when it was only their association with Highland Jacobitism that led to their extinguishment by Westminster. 20 Geo. II, c. 43.

[57] See generally J. Baker, *An Introduction to English Legal History*, 5th ed. (Oxford: Oxford University Press, 2019), ch 6.

of the 'forms of action' for which writs would issue. At the same time, the royal courts adopted a policy of preferring certainty and the rigid application of established rules to discretion and flexibility in administration of the law. As a result, and as social circumstances changed, the 'common law' became less-and-less adequate to litigants' needs and desires, and more-and-more technically complex; and suing in the common-law courts became progressively slower, and more complicated and expensive. In response, Chancellors began supplementing the work of the common-law courts by providing remedies that were not available 'at law', and introducing flexibility (for instance, by creating exceptions to or qualifying rules) to ameliorate the rigidity of the common law. For various reasons, by the sixteenth century, the legal processes of the chancellor's court were well on the way to becoming as complex, expensive, and dilatory as those of the common-law courts; and the law administered by the chancellor's court had become as rigid as the common law which it supplemented. It was not until the nineteenth century that radical reforms were adopted to deal with the deficiencies of the English legal system that were clear by the end of the Tudor period.

By and large, the common-law courts, the conciliar courts, and Chancery co-existed peacefully, each making a distinct and significant contribution to the dispensing of royal justice. However, there could be trouble when a monarch was seen to be using conciliar jurisdiction to provide a glove of law for the fist of power. Most notoriously, perhaps, this happened in the case of the Court of Star Chamber in the reign of Charles I. As a forum allowing the Tudor monarchs to exercise closer control over proceedings of particular interest and concern to the Crown, which inevitably included complaints against crown servants and officials, the Star Chamber has come to be viewed (benignly and nostalgically) as the prototypical specialist administrative court. However, its jurisdiction attracted controversy and courted unpopularity when Charles I became deeply imbricated in its operations. Sometimes Charles attended its sessions, but when absent, his royal power was seen in the image of mace, purse, and grand chair left empty in the room, if heard more unmistakably in the judgements themselves: for whereas before the king-in-council had only ever proclaimed law at the pleasure of the monarch, now Star Chamber took pains to enforce that law. Exorbitant financial penalties were sometimes imposed. Cruel and arbitrary punishments were sometimes exacted. In the 1630s, some common lawyers attempted to undermine Star Chamber through innovative use, among other things, of habeas corpus; but only the Long Parliament had the boldness to abolish it and the other conciliar courts.[58] Statute put an end to the centuries-long personal participation of the monarch in the administration of justice; this paved the way for justice to be administered, as it is to this day, in the name and on behalf of the monarch but entirely without the monarch's personal involvement in judicial processes.

Judges of the common-law courts were typically careful not to appear too eager to down-size the prerogatives of the early Stuart kings. James VI of Scotland, whose declared belief it had been, in 1598, 'that Kings were the authors and makers of the lawes, and not the lawes of the Kings', was often outspoken in his dislike for common lawyers who dissected and anatomised his royal prerogative within his newly inherited English courts.[59] Over the course of his reign, and that of his successor Charles, the prerogative became 'captured' in the Common Pleas and the King's Bench where, for various reasons, it was often divided into 'absolute' and 'ordinary' components.[60] Nevertheless, most important judicial decisions of this period touching the king and his royal power were in fact expansive, and not restrictive, of his prerogatives.[61] Of course, lawyers could always be found around the Inns to profess reservations about overly generous descriptions of the constitutional attributes of the monarch (usually when it came to a king's unfettered discretion to exercise them, or otherwise when a conciliar jurisdiction offered unwanted competition with common-law courts). Yet, for the most part, loyalty to a crown by whose graces they enjoyed office remained an important expectation of judicial appointees.

On the eve of the Glorious Revolution, it came to be thought by some lawyers and legal commentators that the king enjoyed his prerogatives *because* of the common law, and that, by extension, the task of 'expounding' upon these prerogatives fell to nobody but the lawyers.[62] The position of the

---

[58] E. Jenks, 'The Story of Habeas Corpus', *Law Quarterly Review* 18 (1908), 64–79.
[59] J. Stewart, *The True Lawe of Free Monarchies* (Edinburgh: Robert Waldegrave, 1598). For Scottish traditions of thinking about the powers of the Crown, see J. Goodare, *Government of Scotland, 1500–1625* (Oxford: Oxford University Press, 2004), pp. 87–112; J. Goodare, *State and Society in Early Modern Scotland* (Oxford: Clarendon Press, 1999), pp. 38–100.
[60] P. Halliday, *Habeas Corpus: From England to Empire* (Cambridge, MA: Harvard University Press, 2010), 39–95; D. Chan Smith, *Sir Edward Coke and the Reformation of the Laws: Religion, Politics, and Jurisprudence, 1578–1616* (Cambridge: Cambridge University Press, 2014), 249–277.
[61] *Case of Impositions* (1606) 2 St. Tr. 371; *Five Knights' Case* (1627) 3 St. Tr. 1.; *R v. John Hampden* (1637) 3 St. Tr. 826; *R v. City of London* 8 St. Tr. 1039; *Godden v. Hales* (1686) 89 E. R. 1050.
[62] W. Petty, 'The Powers of the King of England' (1685), in C. H. Hull (ed.), *The Economic Writings of Sir William Petty* (Cambridge: Cambridge University Press, 1899), II: 631.

judges vis-à-vis the monarch was then strengthened by the Revolution Settlement. Hitherto they, like justices of the peace and other officers of justice, had been dismissible at the monarch's pleasure, and they were used to losing their offices when the Crown changed heads. However, by an important clause of the Act of Settlement, one that was not immediately subject to repeal, judicial office was guaranteed to all appointees who met standards of 'good behaviour' in their duties; subsequent to this, a statute of 1760 provided for judicial office to continue irrespective of any demise of the Crown.[63] Although these changes significantly altered the position of the senior judiciary vis-à-vis the monarch, they did not affect the institutional character or role of the senior courts in relation to the Crown. Their legitimacy continued to flow from the royal fount of justice: they continued to administer justice in the name, and on behalf of, the Crown. Crown immunity from suit remained the rule. King's Bench further developed its judicial review jurisdiction over local administration, but central administration remained beyond its reach. After the abolition of the conciliar courts, scrutiny of central government fell to parliament.

Various developments over the next 150 years were needed to embolden the courts to extend their judicial review jurisdiction to the centre. Perhaps the most significant was the gradual shift of the ministry's answerability and responsibility from the monarch to the House of Commons and the associated transfer of most of the Crown's prerogative powers from the monarch personally to the government. As already noted, by the end of the nineteenth century, the understanding was that the monarch would exercise the prerogative only on, and in accordance with, the advice of the Prime Minister. The distance thus created between the Crown and the Crown's ministers enabled the law to contemplate the possibility that prerogative writs, issued in the name of the Crown, might go against ministers of the Crown.

The assertion of judicial review jurisdiction over ministers of the Crown was a long and slow process. Having started to flex their muscles in the nineteenth century, in the first half of the twentieth the courts fell into what Stephen Sedley calls a 'long sleep'[64] encouraged, no doubt, by the need for and public tolerance of large doses of unencumbered executive discretion needed to deal with a succession of national emergencies and disasters. After WWII, the senior judiciary, led by figures such as Lord Denning and Lord

---

[63] 12 & 13 Will. III, c. 2; 1 Geo III, c 23.
[64] S. Sedley, 'The Long Sleep' in M. Andenas and D. Fairgrieve (eds.), *Tom Bingham and the Transformation of the Law: A Liber Amicorum* (Oxford: Oxford University Press, 2009).

Reid, started to wake up. Judicial tools forged in the nineteenth century were dusted off, sharpened, and applied with renewed vigour to central government in the 1960s, 1970s, and 1980s. A landmark decision in 1984[65] established a basic rule that exercises of prerogative power by the government were reviewable by the courts except to the extent that they raised 'non-justiciable' issues – that is, issues (considered by the courts to be) unsuitable for judicial resolution. In 1994, the House of Lords held, for the first time, that the coercive remedy of an injunction could be (and was in that case) issued against a minister of the Crown acting officially (in that case, the Home Secretary in relation to a deportation) to prevent illegal action.[66] Further new ground was broken in 2019 when the Supreme Court held illegal an exercise of the prerogative power to prorogue Parliament.[67] It was widely accepted that the Queen was obliged to receive and act upon the advice of the Prime Minister. Judicial control of government now penetrates into even the most political of corners, subject only to contrary statutory provision or self-imposed judicial abstinence.

For the purposes of crown immunity from legal liability (as opposed to judicial review of exercises of government – including prerogative – power), courts in the nineteenth century drew a distinction between organs of central government that were, and those that were not, parts of the Crown. Immunity extended only to the monarch personally and those central government organs and officials that fell within a narrow concept of 'the Crown'. The procedure for making petitions of right was simplified by statute. But major reform had to wait until the Crown Proceedings Act 1946. The Act does not define 'the Crown'. It abolished the petition of right procedure, enabling claimants to instigate litigation against the Crown without the consent of the Attorney General. However, it did not straightforwardly abolish Crown immunity. Rather, it selectively extended to the Crown the substantive law of liability including, very importantly, the principle of 'vicarious liability' according to which an employer is liable for wrong committed by employees in the course of their employment. Although Crown immunity remains the law's technical starting point, in practice the basic rule is Crown liability. Importantly, too, the Act does not create a special regime of liability law applicable to the Crown but rather extends the 'ordinary law' to the Crown.

---

[65] *Council of Civil Service Unions* v. *Minister for the Civil Service* (the 'GCHQ case') [1984] AC 374.
[66] *M v. Home Office* [1994] 1 AC 377.   [67] *R (Miller)* v. *The Prime Minister* [2019] UKSC 41.

That government and citizen alike should be subject to the same law, not different laws, was a major plank of A. V. Dicey's 'rule of law'.[68] On the other hand, in Westminster-derived systems (such as Australia) where Crown immunity was abolished outright (in that case, in the middle of the nineteenth century), the statutory formula typically subjects the Crown to the ordinary law with some sort of 'other things equal' qualification allowing modification of liability law in its application to the government to take account of its special powers and responsibilities. De facto, English courts have gone down a similar path although, in recent years, the UK Supreme Court has pulled back and declared that there is only one law of liability, not two – a private law applicable to citizens and a public law applicable to the government.

Senior judicial posts remain, technically, royal appointments; and the power of senior courts continues to be based on the medieval idea of the monarch as the fount of justice. At its base, the UK judicial system (unlike the US Supreme Court and the Australian High Court, for instance) is the creature neither of a written constitution nor of a statute. In practice, of course, the prerogative of appointment shifted to the government in the nineteenth century. This did not put an end to patronage but merely changed its source as more and more judges came into their offices as reward for their services to political parties. Politically motivated judicial appointments became controversial by the late nineteenth century.[69] It would take another century for the door from politics onto the bench to close. The concept of the independence of the judiciary, enshrined in the Constitutional Reform Act 2005 (and then by its amendment in 2007), underpinned the creation of the Judicial Appointments Commission to advise the government in the exercise of the power to staff the bench, and the transfer of the final appellate jurisdiction of the House of Lords (exercised by an appellate committee for most of the twentieth century) to a freestanding United Kingdom Supreme Court. The Lord Chancellor is no longer head of the judiciary. The ironic outcome is that, in a meaningful way, things have come full circle for the senior judiciary. The high degree of independence and insulation from the rest of government enjoyed by the senior judiciary, coupled with gold-plated security in office, has encouraged those dissatisfied

---

[68] J. W. F. Allison (ed.), *AV Dicey, The Law of the Constitution* (Oxford: Oxford University Press, 2013).

[69] H. T. Hanham (ed.), *The Nineteenth-Century Constitution, 1815–1914* (Cambridge: Cambridge University Press, 1969), pp. 402–403.

with the political process increasingly to have recourse to the courts and has loosened inhibitions that, for much of the twentieth century, protected the senior courts from popular and political scrutiny and assessment.

The Future of Monarchy?

Over a near-millennium of English/British/United Kingdom constitutional history, from being the repository of all governmental power, the monarch has, it seems, been reduced to a mere symbolic figurehead – a focus of feelings of national identity, perhaps, but not much else. Legislative, executive, and judicial powers have technically or effectively devolved from the Crown to other governmental actors who operate independently of royal control or even influence. However, the constitution constantly evolves. A modest recrudescence of the personal power of the monarch is not impossible to conceive. The 2019 prorogation affair has led some to question the near-universal assumption that the Queen had 'to do what she was told' in exercising powers that affect the very ways in which the institutions of government operate and interact. One effect of the settlement after the Glorious Revolution, which has proved to be of very long-term structural significance, was the gradual separation of the offices of Head of State (the monarch) and the Head of Government (the Prime Minister). In practice, those two roles have become effectively fused by the conventions about receiving and following advice that developed by the late nineteenth century. The monarch apparently has less power in the UK constitutional system than heads of state in at least some former British colonies. Whether this position is sustainable remains to be seen. Ironically, perhaps, proposals to abolish the monarchy raise, in acute and unavoidable form, questions about the need for and the appropriate role of a head of state in the governmental and political system of the UK.

12

Legislatures

MICHAEL GORDON

The legislature has been one of the central institutions in the UK's constitutional history, a forum in which major political events occurred and decisions were taken. The legislature projects constitutional values: its practice is based on the significance of representation, accountability, transparency, deliberation, contestation, and collective action. Moreover, the UK Parliament is the focus of the fundamental norm around which the constitution is structured. It possesses legislative sovereignty, the constitutional authority to make law on any topic. The UK's political constitution is therefore crucially a parliamentary constitution, organised around the doctrine of parliamentary sovereignty. The UK Parliament's role, composition and functions have changed significantly over time – as indeed have the number of legislatures within the UK. Yet in many ways the institution also provides a notable example of continuity in the constitution.

This chapter first identifies the basic functions of legislatures, and discusses how those functions have evolved in the UK's history. It then explores three key themes: first, the development of parliamentary sovereignty; second, the democratisation of the UK Parliament; and third, the dispersal of power from the UK Parliament, in particular to other legislatures within the state. While this is not suggested to be a simple (or comprehensive) chronological narrative, in broad terms we see the UK Parliament becoming sovereign in the sixteenth and seventeenth centuries, then becoming democratic in the nineteenth and twentieth centuries, and in the twenty-first century the UK's legislature remains central, but within a constellation of legislatures.

In exploring these themes, the focus of this chapter will be the UK Parliament, given its overarching constitutional authority over all institutions of government in the UK, not just other legislatures. But while the Parliament based in Westminster has been the predominant legislature during the history of the UK (and remains so), its composition and reach have not been constant: it has variously been the English Parliament, the

Parliament of England and Wales, the British Parliament, the Imperial Parliament and the UK Parliament. Moreover, other legislatures have existed within the UK throughout its history, most notably in Scotland until the union founding Great Britain in 1707, in Ireland until the union founding the UK in 1800 and then again from 1919 until the independent Irish Free State was established in 1922, and in Northern Ireland from 1920 to 1972 when direct rule was re-imposed (subject to sporadic attempts to restore an assembly in 1973–1974 and 1982–1986).[1] Despite the dominance of the English Crown since the conquest of Wales in the late thirteenth century, this territory was not routinely represented in English parliaments until the formal Acts of Union in 1536.[2] The advent of the modern devolution system in 1998 has seen the (re-)emergence of legislatures in Scotland, Northern Ireland and Wales, and an important new dynamic emerging between them and the UK Parliament.

The Legislature's Functions

The legislature is a complex, multi-faceted institution. In essence, it is a political assembly which contributes to the governing of the state. Yet the precise contribution made to governing can vary, for a legislature has the potential to perform a range of connected functions in a political system. These functions have changed considerably over time – the Parliament of Simon de Montfort, identified as the first recognisable Parliament judged against modern standards,[3] was very different to the UK Parliament, or the devolved legislatures, in the present-day constitution. That a legislature performs multiple functions makes the development of these institutions over time especially interesting from a constitutional perspective. As Jennings suggests, '[t]here was not, and there has never been, conscious planning of

---

[1] The Government of Ireland Act 1920 sought to establish Parliaments for both 'Northern' Ireland and 'Southern' Ireland following the formation of an independent Dail Eireann in 1919. The Irish Free State Constitution Act 1922 provided British recognition to the Constitution passed by the Third Dail Eireann acting as an Irish constituent assembly in 1922.

[2] T. Glyn Watkin, *The Legal History of Wales*, 2nd ed. (University of Wales Press, 2012) 112, 126–128. Act for Law and Justice to be Ministered in Wales in like Form as it is in this Realm of 1535/6; Act for Certain Ordinances in the King's Dominion and Principality of Wales of 1542/3.

[3] As claimed on the UK Parliament's website: www.parliament.uk/about/living-heritage/evolutionofparliament/originsofparliament/birthofparliament/overview/simondemontfort/.

the common law or of political institutions'.[4] Yet we can identify a core set of functions performed by a legislature, even if they have developed at different points in the UK's history. These core functions are: (i) representation; (ii) legislating; (iii) scrutiny; (iv) debating; (v) producing, sustaining, and holding a government to account; and (vi) legitimisation of the wider constitutional system. The process of development of these functions was not an inevitable or smooth evolution – rather, the various functions had disparate, historical roots.

The first of a legislature's functions is representation. This has been clear since the very earliest Parliaments in England. The legislature provides a forum in which a range of interests can be represented to attempt to influence political decision-making. In the earliest manifestations of legislatures, we see the representation of the interests of the aristocracy to the monarch. Simon de Montfort's Parliament between January and March 1265 is generally regarded as the first assembly which exhibited characteristics of a modern legislature. It followed attempts to impose limits on the power of King Henry III, to provide a means through which the consent of barons could be required for raising revenue through taxes. The principle that taxation required representation had emerged in Magna Carta in 1215, which leading barons created to impose constraints on King John.[5] The de Montfort Parliament took this idea further, with wider representation and scope: it included representatives from cities, boroughs, knights from counties, and considered issues beyond taxation.[6] In this way, the de Montfort Parliament could be viewed as a potential precursor to the House of Commons – it established representation of interests beyond the Anglo-Saxon Witan of the eleventh century, or the King in Council, which were intended to advise the Crown and solidify royal power. Representation was further regularised in the 'Model Parliament' of Edward I, which was composed of two knights per county and two burgesses per town, driven by the need for representation to gain consent for taxation in support of war.[7] The pattern of representation for the modern tripartite legislature combining Crown, Lords, and an increasingly independent Commons developed under Edward II, and even if the

---

[4] See H. Kumarasingham, 'Sir Ivor Jennings' "The Conversion of History into Law"' (2016) 56 *American Journal of Legal History* 113–127, 124 (making available the text of a lecture given by Jennings in March 1960).
[5] See E. Jenks, 'The Myth of Magna Carta' (1904) 4 *Independent Review* 260.
[6] See M. W. Labarge, 'Simon de Monfort's Parliament' (1964) *Parliamentary Affairs* 13–19.
[7] Stubbs, *Constitutional History*, 134; see generally H. G. Richardson and G. O. Sayles, *The English Parliament in the Middle Ages* (Hambledon Press, 1981) 31–32.

Commons were not then formally 'members' of Parliament, the basic existence of this framework seemed broadly established by the end of his reign in 1327.[8] The representative function has been a central parliamentary function throughout the UK's history. For Maddicott, Parliament in the Middle Ages had 'long been' a 'national occasion unique in providing a political focus for the whole community'.[9] And we can see a similar sentiment in Elton's observation on the Tudor period: 'Parliament, after all, was thought of as the image of the nation in common political action'.[10]

The second function of the legislature is to enact legislation. Based on its representative character, Parliament was an assembly which was needed to endorse decisions taken by the Crown, thereby strengthening royal authority. The requirement that the Commons provided its assent to Bills, in addition to that of Crown and Lords, is commonly thought to have been established by 1414 under Henry V, when the Commons petitioned the King for full rights of assent to legislation. However, the king did not consistently seek the Commons' positive assent throughout the fifteenth century, although would not enact law contrary to their substantive petitions.[11] The reliance of the Crown on Parliament when legislating was most vividly demonstrated during the Reformation. This Parliament, sitting under Henry VIII from 1529 to 1536, enacted a range of legislation altering religious doctrine and practice in fundamental ways, and challenging the established power of the Catholic church. The authority of Parliament was essential to make such fundamental changes to the relationship between the state and the church. For, as Henry VIII would claim in 1543: 'We be informed by our judges that we at no time stand so highly in our estate royal as in the time of parliament, wherein we as head and you as members are conjoined and knit together into one body politic.'[12] As Elton argued, following this parliamentary Reformation, the 'basis of Tudor government' was '[f]ull legislative supremacy vested in the image of the nation and politically active there'.[13] This does not mean we should imagine all legislation from that point onwards was concerned with general matters of considerable public

---

[8] See J. Maddicott, *The Origins of the English Parliament, 924–1327* (Oxford, 2010).
[9] Ibid, 305–306.
[10] G. R. Elton, 'Presidential Address: Tudor Government: The Points of Contact: I. Parliament' (1974) 24 *Transactions of the Royal Historical Society* 183–200, 185.
[11] See S. B. Chrimes, *English Constitutional Ideas in the Fifteenth Century* (Cambridge, 1936) 161–164.
[12] See G. R. Elton, *Studies in Tudor and Stuart Politics and Government, Paper and Reviews 1946–1972: Volume 2, Parliament/Political Thought* (Cambridge University Press, 1974) 32.
[13] Elton, *Studies in Tudor and Stuart Politics*, 186.

significance. Instead, private legislation dealing with highly specific issues was a key aspect of Parliament's legislative business. For example, as Lemmings notes in a study of the massive increase in primary legislation enacted in the eighteenth century, 'parliament was increasingly open to the influence of public opinion, but the overwhelming majority of its acts were initiated by local combinations of private propertied interests'.[14]

The third function of a legislature is to scrutinise decisions made by those exercising governmental authority. Parliamentary scrutiny of the exercise of public power allows ministers to be challenged for specific decisions and the general governance of the state. This practice pre-dates the existence of the more recent constitutional idea that the government must sustain the confidence of the House of Commons to retain office. Even in the period when monarchs ruled with the support of their Councils, the legislature could be involved in challenging the decisions of those royal advisors, who remained responsible to the sovereign, rather than Parliament itself. For example, in the famous 'named Parliaments' of the fourteenth century,[15] we see examples of the king's counsellors and Ministers criticised to the point where they were removed from office. In the 'Good Parliament' of 1376, key advisors of Edward III were the subject of serious criticism for corruption and extortion, leading to the first impeachments, including of Lord Latimer, the King's chamberlain.[16] But this critical atmosphere was not sustained, and was followed by the 'Bad Parliament' of 1377 (so-named by more modern historians), in which a more pliant Speaker of the House of Commons was appointed in place of the imprisoned Sir Peter de la Mare, who had been a leading actor against the King's ministers during the previous 'Good Parliament'. Then, under Richard II, in the 'Wonderful Parliament' of 1386, the Commons again impeached key ministers, most notably the chancellor, Michael de la Pole, in a challenge to excessive royal spending on extravagant patronage and war with France.[17] This Parliament also created a commission

---

[14] D. Lemmings, *Law and Government in England during the Long Eighteenth Century: From Consent to Command* (Palgrave Macmillan, 2011) 171.

[15] See H. Kleineke, 'The Good, the Bad and the Wonderful: The dramatic Parliaments of the late 14th century (Part One)', *The History of Parliament Blog* (18 June 2019): https://thehistoryofparliament.wordpress.com/2019/06/18/the-good-the-bad-and-the-wonderful-the-dramatic-parliaments-of-the-late-14th-century-part-one/.

[16] See T. F. T. Plucknett, 'The Origin of Impeachment' (1942) *Transactions of the Royal Historical Society* 47–71; J. G. Bellamy, 'Appeal and Impeachment in the Good Parliament' (1966) 39 *Historical Reach* 35–46; G. Holmes, *The Good Parliament* (Oxford University Press, 1975).

[17] See J. G. Palmer, 'The Parliament of 1385 and the Constitutional Crisis of 1386' (1971) 46 *Speculum* 477–490.

of peers to restrain royal power and manage the implementation of reform to financial governance, which Richard II was forced to accept but worked to circumvent. Division between the King and this group of influential barons, who became known as the 'Lords Appellant', culminated in extreme fashion in the 'Merciless Parliament' of 1388, when many royal advisors were accused of treason and executed.[18] Scrutiny was therefore irregular, dictated by the wider political climate alongside factors such as the frequency and length of each parliamentary session.[19] The 'Good Parliament', for example, lasted ten weeks, longer than any previous Parliament at that point,[20] but this was far from the regular, institutionalised scrutiny and accountability expected from the nearly ever-present modern legislature. These challenges to royal authority could also be short-lived – following the 'Merciless Parliament', many of the Lords Appellant who confronted Richard II were exiled or killed as the King regained power.[21]

The fourth function of a legislature is to provide a forum for debate. While related to representation, legislation and scrutiny, facilitating debate is a distinct function. As Elton argues, the 'practical needs of cash and laws do not fully explain the attitude of Tudor governments to Parliament, at least not after 1529 when all possibility ceased of ruling without the meetings of the estates. Parliaments were wanted because there the great affairs of the nation could be considered, debated and advertised: Parliament was a part of the machinery of government available to active rulers.'[22] The extent to which Parliament has provided a hostile environment for the monarch and their ministers has varied considerably from time to time. In relation to the Tudor period, for example, there is disagreement about the development of the idea of parliamentary opposition, with the traditional view that this emerged under Elizabeth I, with figures like Peter Wentworth famously speaking in Parliament in 1576 in favour of freedom of speech for members of the legislature, which he used to criticise the Queen (resulting in his detention in the Tower of London).[23] However, this is contested by revisionists,

---

[18] See A. K. McHardy, *The Reign of Richard II: from Minority to Tyranny, 1377–97* (Manchester University Press, 2012) ch 3.
[19] See A. L. Brown, 'Parliament, c. 1377–1422' in R. G. Davies and J. H. Denton (eds.), *The English Parliament in the Middle Ages* (Manchester University Press, 1981) 112–113.
[20] Ibid.
[21] See A. Tuck, 'The Cambridge Parliament 1388' (1969) 84 *English Historical Review* 225–243.
[22] Elton, *Studies in Tudor and Stuart Politics*, 188.
[23] See J. Loach, *Parliament under the Tudors* (Clarendon, 1991) 105–108.

who argue that Parliament at the time was 'not a political arena'[24] – instead 'co-operation' with the Crown was the norm.[25] Whether in a hostile manner or not, debate within a legislature allows issues to be explored and decisions to be analysed, which requires the representation of different political views and perspectives. This is reflected in the emergence of political parties in the late seventeenth century to early eighteenth century,[26] representing alternative values and policy priorities within the legislature. While the various political parties in the ascendency have changed over time they have also become the primary means of organising parliamentary business, to the point where it is difficult to imagine how the legislature could function in practice in the absence of political parties to structure its activity.

The fifth function of a legislature is to produce, sustain and hold a government to account. The importance of the Cabinet as the decision-making body of the government was established in the early eighteenth century under George I, who did not speak English well and rarely attended Cabinet meetings. This left much greater political power to his appointed ministers and initiated a separation between Crown and Cabinet which would become the norm under future monarchs.[27] Under George II, Sir Robert Walpole became the first modern Prime Minister (although that terminology would not become common until later). The close connection between the authority of the government and the confidence of Parliament in the Cabinet also emerged in this period, when the Regency Act 1705 made it possible for Members of Parliament to be appointed as ministers.[28] The idea of parliamentary government therefore extended beyond the scrutiny of government in Parliament, to establish the principle of government within Parliament, with responsibility to the Commons. Walpole's individual resignation in 1742 was prompted not by the monarch whom he served, but followed defeat on a vote in the Commons: it was 'the first time that a Prime Minister had resigned solely on account of having lost the support of the Commons majority'.[29] Subsequently, under the ministry of Lord North in

---

[24] D. Dean, 'Revising the History of the Tudor Parliaments' (1989) *The Historical Journal* 401, 402.
[25] M. Graves, *The Tudor Parliaments: Crown, Lords and Commons, 1485–1603* (Longman, 1985) ch.1.
[26] W. C. Abbott, 'The Origin of English Political Parties' (1919) 24 *American Historical Review*, 578–602, 582.
[27] See W. F. Wyndham Brown, 'The Evolution of the Cabinet System in England' (1910) 36 *Law Mag & Rev Quart Rev Juris* 49, 57.
[28] P. Langford, 'Prime Ministers and Parliaments: The Long View. Walpole to Blair' (2006) 25 *Parliamentary History* 382–394, 382–383.
[29] Wyndham Brown, 'The Evolution of the Cabinet System', 59.

1782, the entire government would resign for the first time having lost the Commons' confidence.[30] These are the origins of the crucial idea which underpins the formation and termination of governments. A government must be drawn from and operate within the legislature to retain office, but an administration which no longer commands a majority in the Commons must be replaced.

The sixth function of the legislature is the legitimation of the wider political system. As Elton argues, Parliament was 'the premier point of contact between rulers and ruled, between the Crown and the political nation, in the sixteenth century' and 'fulfilled its function as a stabilizing mechanism because it was usable and used to satisfy legitimate and potentially powerful aspirations'.[31] Parliament provided a forum which connected those with authority and those subject to it. Even prior to the advent of democracy in the UK, when this connection was theoretical rather than actual, governing with and through a legislature offered a greater justification for the exercise of power than could be claimed by a hereditary monarch acting on their own judgement. That Parliament performed some legitimising function does not mean that Parliament has been a benevolent institution throughout the history of the UK. Indeed, Parliament played a central role in enabling the worst atrocities of the British state, including slavery, colonialism and other oppressions of Empire.[32] However, we must recognise that Parliament played a significant role in legitimising the constitutional system in which these decisions were taken. Following the slow democratisation of the House of Commons between 1832 and 1928, the UK's legislature gained a clearer claim to legitimacy, and is better positioned to perform its legitimating role (without this guaranteeing the legitimacy of every substantive decision it makes).

Other functions were exercised by the legislature at different points in the UK's history, but have fallen away. The most important example is the idea of Parliament operating as a High Court receiving individual pleas for justice. This was far from a trivial function; Pollard argues it was key to the development of Parliament as an institution: 'It was to a high court of law and justice that the taxing and representative factors of parliament were wedded; and it was this union that gave the English parliament its strength.'[33] In the late fourteenth century, panels of peers were still set up to receive

---

[30] Ibid, 62. [31] Elton, *Studies in Tudor and Stuart Politics*, 200.
[32] See R. Gott, *Britain's Empire: Resistance, Repression and Revolt* (Verso, 2011).
[33] A. F. Pollard, *The Evolution of Parliament*, 2nd ed. (1926) 43.

private petitions in Parliament, yet by this point it had become 'an ancient but now relatively unimportant part of parliament' because 'petitions could be presented to the king, the council or the chancellor at any time'.[34] Members of the House of Lords with legal expertise continued to act as a final court of appeal, and after a radical decline in cases in the sixteenth century, this work expanded again from the seventeenth century onwards. The professionalisation of the judicial element of the Lords was confirmed by the Appellate Jurisdiction Act 1876, which allowed the appointment of salaried judges as Law Lords. The Appellate Committee of the House of Lords continued to function as the highest court of appeal in the UK until 2009 when it was replaced by a Supreme Court, suggesting that the residual judicial role was a function which occurred within the legislature rather than a function of the legislature more generally.[35]

Parliamentary Sovereignty

The first theme which illustrates the key position of the legislature in the UK's constitutional history is parliamentary sovereignty. Parliamentary sovereignty is the foundational principle of the UK's constitution. It is a legal principle that confers unlimited law-making power on 'the Crown-in-Parliament': the House of Commons and the House of Lords, acting with the assent of the monarch. In Dicey's famous phrase, it means that Parliament has 'the right to make or unmake any law whatever; and, further, that no person or body is recognised by the law of England as having a right to override or set aside the legislation of Parliament'.[36]

Yet it is not simply a principle distributing legal power. Parliamentary sovereignty is also a legal doctrine with crucial constitutional implications. It shapes and structures the constitution, and the institutional relationships and interactions which occur within it. It acts as a 'central organising principle', establishing the hierarchy of constitutional sources in the UK, as well as structuring the interactions between the legislature and the other constitutional actors who exercise their power in a framework which is premised on Parliament's sovereignty.[37] And it functions as 'constitutional focal point',

---

[34] See A. L. Brown, 'Parliament, c. 1377–1422' in R. G. Davies and J. H. Denton (eds.), *The English Parliament in the Middle Ages* (Manchester University Press, 1981) 122.
[35] Constitutional Reform Act 2005, s.40 & Schedule 9.
[36] A. V. Dicey, *Introduction to the Study of the Law of the Constitution*. 8th ed. (1915) 39–40.
[37] M. Gordon, *Parliamentary Sovereignty in the UK Constitution: Process, Politics and Democracy* (Hart, 2015) ch 1.

offering citizens and official actors a means by which to begin to access constitutional knowledge, while sending a signal about the potential normative basis of the constitutional order. This in turn creates space for necessary debate about the legitimacy of the system.[38]

The 'doctrine' of parliamentary sovereignty does not derive its force from being formally enacted in any legal or constitutional instrument or document or by having been announced by courts. In other words, its authority does not derive from the legal system because it constitutes the legal system, creating the very criteria by which the validity of law can be established. For Jennings, parliamentary sovereignty was crucially a product of the seventeeth-century clashes between supporters of the Crown and of the legislature. While Jennings was clear that parliamentary sovereignty was a legal rule, he argued that it 'was not established by judicial decisions, however; it was settled by armed conflict and the Bill of Rights and the Act of Settlement. The judges did no more than acquiesce in a simple fact of political authority, though they have never been called upon precisely to say so.'[39] The legal doctrine, said Jennings, illustrates 'the conversion of history into law'.[40] The pivotal events included the parliamentary trial and execution of Charles I in 1649, the subsequent failure of Cromwell's Instrument of Government and the Restoration of the monarchy in the form of Charles II by the Convention Parliament in 1660, the replacement of James II with William and Mary in 1688, their subjection to the statutory constraints on royal prerogative power enacted by Parliament in the Bill of Rights 1689,[41] and the definitive shift in the line of succession to the Protestant House of Hannover made by Parliament through the Act of Settlement 1701.[42] In the course of this seventeenth-century 'revolution',[43] we see on one level the reconciliation of monarchy with Parliament's assertions of legislative power and, at another level, the use of that power to select and control the monarch. The constitutional doctrine of Parliamentary sovereignty emerges to capture and explain the power exercised by the legislature in response to political events.

---

[38] Ibid.
[39] W. I. Jennings, *Law and the Constitution*, 5th ed (University of London Press, 1959), 39.
[40] H. Kumarasingham, 'Sir Ivor Jennings'.
[41] Including limits on suspending or dispensing with laws, levying money, or establishing a standing army without parliamentary consent.
[42] Act of Settlement 1701, s.1.
[43] See e.g., C. Hill, *Intellectual Origins of the English Revolution* (Clarendon, 1965).

This historical period remains crucial to our understanding of parliamentary sovereignty. The authority of parliamentary sovereignty has been most influentially demonstrated by Goldsworthy's exhaustive study. Goldsworthy charts the evolution of parliamentary sovereignty from that held by medieval kings.[44] He shows that the Reformation Parliament in the 1530s was the point at which the legislature asserted its power over religious (or 'spiritual') matters, previously held by the Pope. When added to its already established power to make law on all other matters of concern within the nation ('temporal' matters), this marked the point at which the king in Parliament could be considered 'in practice, fully sovereign'.[45] Yet Goldsworthy shows that while the full legally unlimited scope of legislative sovereignty was widely recognised from this point, the identity of the institution which possessed it remained disputed: was the authority of the king in Parliament 'that of the King alone, which he chose to exercise only in Parliament, or that of a composite institution, the "king-in-Parliament"?'[46] This was the question resolved in the seventeenth century, in the events of the Civil War and its aftermath, with abundant examples demonstrating that the authority of the Crown had been subordinated to the authority of the Crown-in-Parliament. This reorganisation of sovereignty produced (and perhaps to some extent masked) by institutional fusion became dominant: 'even by the beginning of the nineteenth century, parliamentary sovereignty had become a rarely questioned assumption of British constitutional thought, an apparently necessary truth'.[47] And over time, the Crown became a more and more peripheral element of this combination, to the point where 'the Queen's part in legislation is now formal only', with royal assent having not been refused since Queen Anne rejected the Scottish Militia Bill in 1708.[48]

That there is no single constitutional source or statute which establishes a legal basis for Parliament's legislative authority, and its unlimited sovereign character, is not evidence of uncertainty about the existence of the doctrine. Indeed, in contrast, the fact that parliamentary sovereignty is rooted in a complex mixture of the beliefs of key constitutional actors, the outcome of decisive political events at crucial historical moments, and enduring practice recognising the absence of any legal limitations on Parliament's law-making, is all evidence of the strength of this doctrine. It is of such a fundamental nature

---

[44] J. Goldsworthy, *The Sovereignty of Parliament: History and Philosophy* (Oxford University Press, 1999) ch 2.
[45] Ibid, 230.   [46] Ibid, 53.   [47] Ibid, 233.
[48] Jennings, *Law and the Constitution*, 143.

that formal enactment of the doctrine is unnecessary. Nevertheless, as a legal doctrine with legal implications for the authority and the interpretation of statute law, the existence of parliamentary sovereignty has been unambiguously recognised in judicial precedents extending back at least 170 years.[49]

The historic character of parliamentary sovereignty has been crucial in sustaining the authority of the doctrine in the courts. A classic example is *Pickin v. British Railways Board*,[50] decided in the House of Lords in 1974, which until recently was regarded as the leading precedent on parliamentary sovereignty. As in *Edinburgh & Dalkeith Railways* before it, the House of Lords rejected a challenge to the validity of a private Act of Parliament in stark language, relying on the judgment of Lord Campbell in 1842 among other nineteenth-century precedents. For Lord Reid:

> The idea that a court is entitled to disregard a provision in an Act of Parliament on any ground must seem strange and startling to anyone with any knowledge of the history and law of our constitution, but a detailed argument has been submitted to your Lordships and I must deal with it.[51]

Crucial here is the explicit connection made between history and law by Lord Reid in establishing the constitutional authority of parliamentary sovereignty. And this connection is used to reinforce the fundamental character of the doctrine, which is presented as long accepted and therefore (at this point) utterly unquestionable. Indeed, Lord Reid expressly identifies the seventeenth-century conflicts as being the context in which 'the supremacy of Parliament was finally demonstrated by the Revolution of 1688', which had therefore rendered 'obsolete' any prior idea that an Act of Parliament could be unlawful if contrary to the law of God or nature.[52] The longevity of parliamentary sovereignty therefore contributed directly to its contemporary authority because 'so far as I am aware, no one since 1842 has doubted that it is a correct statement of the constitutional position'.[53]

The historical approach taken by the courts to parliamentary sovereignty is a minimalist one – the doctrine is presented as a constitutional norm which has been long accepted and is, therefore, far beyond the authority of the judges to change or question. Yet this approach is now in decline and is in the process of being replaced by a judicial approach which may be considered maximalist and overtly normative. This has led the courts to adopt a

---

[49] See e.g., *Edinburgh & Dalkeith Railways v. Wauchope* (1842) 8 Cl. & F. 710.
[50] [1974] AC 765.   [51] Ibid, 782.   [52] Ibid, 782.
[53] Ibid, 787. See also Lord Morris, 789–792; Lord Simon, 798.

contradictory modern attitude to parliamentary sovereignty. On one hand, some senior judges have expressed doubts about the continuing existence of parliamentary sovereignty. In the watershed case of *Jackson* in 2005, Lords Steyn, Hope and Lady Hale (albeit obiter, and only as a minority of the judges hearing the case in the House of Lords) explicitly questioned whether Parliament's legislative power was now, or could become, limited by the common law.[54] This judicial speculation about the potential for judicial limitation of legislative power has been controversial, and challenged by some judges,[55] but it has also intensified and been reinforced in successive cases, including *Axa*,[56] *Moohan*,[57] *Public Law Project*,[58] and *Privacy International*.[59] On the other hand, however, the contemporary doubts which have been expressed by some judges – but not yet acted upon – sit very uneasily with a number of decisions relating to the process of Brexit, which placed the Supreme Court at the centre of a heated public debate about whether it had strayed into the political realm. In the cases of *Miller*,[60] the *Reference on the Scottish Continuity Bill*,[61] and *Cherry/Miller (No.2)*,[62] the Supreme Court explicitly reaffirmed the importance of parliamentary sovereignty, paradoxically relying on the doctrine to bolster the judges' authority in contentious constitutional circumstances.

This is a remarkable shift in substance and approach from the minimalist historicism of *Pickin*. Whether the judges are hypothesising limits on parliamentary sovereignty or declaring its constitutional fundamentality, they are positioning themselves as active agents of constitutional principle, rather than the legal and institutional subordinates of the legislature. Whether the normative balance in any particular case tips for or against parliamentary sovereignty, the courts are explicitly conducting that normative balancing exercise. And in that sense, we see the common law is becoming disconnected from the history of parliamentary sovereignty and is being shaped instead by abstract – and often controversial – normative principles determined a priori by the judiciary.

---

[54] [2006] UKHL 56, [102], [104], [159]. For critique see Gordon, *Parliamentary Sovereignty*, ch.5.
[55] Lord Bingham, 'The Rule of Law and the Sovereignty of Parliament', *King's College London Commemoration Oration 2007* (31 Oct. 2007) 22.
[56] [2011] UKSC 46, [2012] 1 AC 868, [50]–[51].   [57] [2014] UKSC 67, [2015] AC 901, [35].
[58] [2016] UKSC 39, [2016] AC 1531, [20].   [59] [2019] UKSC 22, [144].
[60] [2017] UKSC 5, [2018] AC 61, [43].   [61] [2018] UKSC 64, [63], [54].
[62] [2019] UKSC 41, [40].

The a-historical, normative approach now being taken by the courts to parliamentary sovereignty represents a significant change of attitude to legislative authority in the constitution which empowers the courts to become more active interpreters of parliamentary sovereignty. This may be the ultimate legacy of Dicey's legal chauvinism, based on his view that constitutional law is autonomous and untethered from historical context (history being 'simple antiquarianism' on his account).[63] For if so, the law relating to parliamentary sovereignty might then be made and re-made by the judiciary, who are self-empowered in the process.

Democratisation

The democratic character of Parliament is central to its institutional and constitutional legitimacy – it has developed in tandem with the evolution of Parliament as an institution, but not in a precise way. The representative character of Parliament was key in the seventeenth-century English civil war in distinguishing rule by a legislature from that of a singular, hereditary monarch acting by divine right, and to Parliament's forceful acquisition of legislative sovereignty. But Parliament was certainly not, at this point, a democratic institution in the modern sense. Consequently, we can see that changes in Parliament's constitutional position, legal authority and institutional functions are shaped by parallel, if uneven, shifts in our understanding of political ideas. While a pre-democratic Parliament could obtain sovereignty in the sixteenth and seventeenth centuries, the justification for that power could not be static, if the legislature was to sustain its claim to legitimate authority. Consequently, while the legal sovereignty held by the English, then British, then UK Parliament has endured as a relatively constant constitutional norm for in excess of 300 years, the nature and location of what Dicey described as 'political sovereignty' has changed considerably.[64]

This is primarily due to the slow process of parliamentary democratisation, which has aligned Parliament's legally unlimited legislative authority with democratic principle after the fact. While Dicey argued that political sovereignty was vested in the electorate, with those in the legislature exercising their legal sovereignty in accordance with the 'will of the electors', the electorate of Dicey's era was not based on an equal franchise. Voting rights were only extended to women (over thirty years old, who satisfied a property

---

[63] Dicey, *Introduction to the Study of the Law*, 14–15.   [64] Ibid, 71.

qualification) for the first time by the Representation of the People Act 1918, enacted just four years before Dicey's death in 1922. And it was not until six years later, under the Representation of the People (Equal Franchise) Act 1928, that men and women over the age of twenty-one could vote on equal terms, regardless of whether they occupied land or premises of a minimum value.

The democratisation of Parliament has also, in institutional terms, only been partial. A clear division exists between the two Houses, the Commons and the Lords, which is rooted in their historic origins. The House of Commons developed as a supplement to the House of Lords, allowing a broader representation of (still wealthy, elite) interests than the chamber composed of aristocrats. In the late fourteenth century, the Lords, as the 'original members' of Parliament, remained 'the most important', and 'it was their advice that counted most'.[65] It was in the mid-fifteenth century that an equivalence between the two Houses can be clearly seen: 'By the 1450s references to a lower and a higher House of Parliament were so casual as to show them to be commonplace; and Edward IV, who deliberately wooed non-aristocratic opinion, from the first treated the House of Commons as effectively comparable to the Lords in constitutional standing.'[66]

The Commons' modern primacy over the Lords – in terms of law-making, and as the source of confidence and supply for the government – is ultimately a consequence of its growing democratic composition, and the more authentic breadth of representation that provides. But in addition to providing a basis for rebalancing power between the two Houses of Parliament, it is also important to recognise that democratisation has contributed to the subordination of the Crown within the Crown-in-Parliament. The legislative role of the unelected hereditary monarch has also been eroded to a mere technicality as the House of Commons has become a genuine (if far from perfect) democratic entity. The royal assent is now a formality to signal the end of the legislative process, can be given by Lords Commissioners on behalf of the monarch,[67] and, most importantly, by constitutional convention cannot be refused.

Following the English Civil War, the inadequacy of representation in Parliament was challenged by the Levellers, a group of democratic radicals

---

[65] See A. L. Brown, 'Parliament, c. 1377–1422' in R. G. Davies and J. H. Denton (eds.), *The English Parliament in the Middle Ages* (Manchester University Press, 1981) 131–132.
[66] G. R. Elton, *Studies in Tudor and Stuart Politics and Government, Paper and Reviews 1946–1972: Volume 2, Parliamentary/Political Thought* (Cambridge University Press, 1974) 25, citing Chrimes, *Constitutional Ideas*, 128–129.
[67] Royal Assent by Commission Act 1541; replaced by Royal Assent Act 1967, s.1(a).

in Cromwell's New Model Army, who (among other things) called in the Putney Debates in 1647 for universal male suffrage.[68] These calls for reform were resisted by Cromwell, and the link between representation and property rights remained strong throughout the seventeenth and eighteenth centuries. John Locke, for example, argued in 1690, that 'there can be but one supreme power, which is the legislative', yet this being 'only a fiduciary power to act for certain ends, there remains still in the people a supreme power to remove or alter the legislative, when they find the legislative act contrary to the trust reposed in them'.[69] Since '[t]he reason why men enter into society, is the preservation of their property', legislative power could be challenged as illegitimate 'whenever the legislators endeavour to take away, and destroy the property of the people'.[70] Locke's views were criticised by William Blackstone, who argued in his *Commentaries* in 1765 that '[s]o long therefore as the English constitution lasts ... the power of parliament is absolute and without control'.[71] Yet for Blackstone, any 'devolution of power, to the people at large, includes in it a dissolution of the whole form of government established by that people, reduces all the members to their original state of equality, and by annihilating the sovereign power repeals all positive laws whatsoever before enacted'.[72] Even the most timid, and only loosely popular, restraints on the use of legislative power were therefore to be understood as inconsistent with the entire constitutional system which, as a result of the partial and manipulable nature of the electoral process, in reality represented only wealthy property owning classes.

The 'Great' Reform Act 1832 was the beginning of the actual process of democratisation. Campaigning for parliamentary reform was strongly resisted by the political establishment during the age of the American and French revolutions at the end of the eighteenth century. Thomas Paine was successfully prosecuted (in his absence) for seditious libel following the publication of Part 2 of his republican pamphlet, the *Rights of Man*, in 1792[73] and a new Treasonable and Seditious Practices Act was enacted in 1795, which was concerned to prevent discussion of 'the overthrow of the

---

[68] M. Loughlin, 'The Constitutional Thought of the Levellers' (2007) 60 *Current Legal Problems* 1–39.
[69] J. Locke, *Second Treatise of Government*, C. B. Macpherson (ed.) (Hackett Publishing Company, 1980) para 149.
[70] Ibid, para 222.
[71] W. Blackstone, *Commentaries on the Laws of England* (Oxford: Clarendon Press, 1765) 157.
[72] Ibid, 157.
[73] *The Trial of Thomas Paine* (C. and G. Kearsley Fleet Street, London, 1792), online at: https://quod.lib.umich.edu/e/ecco/004809446.0001.000/1:1?rgn=div1;view=fulltext.

laws, government and happy constitution of these realms'.[74] The Peterloo Massacre in Manchester in 1818, at which cavalry charged on a large crowd of protestors at a rally in support of parliamentary representation, killing 11 and injuring up to 500, provided a vivid example of establishment opposition to reform. In 1830, following revolutions in France and Belgium, legislation to emancipate wealthy Catholics in Ireland, and against a backdrop of famine and growing insurrection, the Tory government was replaced by a Whig administration led by Lord Grey. More radical calls for universal male suffrage and a secret ballot were disregarded, but the Reform Act 1832 was eventually enacted, in the face of substantial opposition in the House of Lords (and only following threats to create new peers to force through the legislation).

The 1832 Act abolished many rotten boroughs but retained a property qualification which limited the size of the (exclusively male) electorate dramatically: on Foot's calculation, '[o]nly a fortieth of men over twenty-one (and no women at all) were entitled to vote'.[75] During the course of the nineteenth century, two further Reform Acts were required – each decades apart – to further democratise elections in the UK. Much of the pressure for additional parliamentary reform was organised around the Chartist Movement, and focused on the six demands contained in 'the People's Charter' published in 1838, including universal male suffrage, constituencies of equal size, annual parliaments and secret ballots.[76] Yet the Reform Act 1867 still based the franchise on a property qualification,[77] as did the Reform Act 1884, which made the 1867 reforms – expanding the electorate in urban boroughs – universally applicable, extending them to rural constituencies. The Third Reform Act was preceded by the Ballot Act 1872, which introduced secret ballots in parliamentary elections, and the 1884 reforms were accompanied by a separate Redistribution Act 1885, to equalise the size of constituencies and therefore the weight of each vote. Yet, although the electorate had increased from around 350,000 in 1831 to some 8 million in 1885, Foot concludes that, '[f]or all the gains made in 1867 and 1884, at least two-thirds of the population – all the women and more than a third of the

---

[74] Renamed the Treason Act 1795 by the Short Titles Act 1896.
[75] P. Foot, *The Vote: How It Was Won and How It Was Undermined* (Bookmarks Publications, 2012) 91; see generally 45–88.
[76] Ibid, 92. See D. Thompson, *The Chartists* (Temple Smith, 1984).
[77] See R. Saunders, 'The Politics of Reform and the Making of the Second Reform Act, 1848–1867' (2007) 50 *The Historical Journal* 571–591.

men – still had no votes'.[78] Only in the twentieth century, from 1928 onwards, were members of the House of Commons able to truly claim the democratic legitimacy of having been elected to represent their constituency on a universal and equal franchise.[79] And it was not until 1948 that plurality votes attaching to business premises and universities were abolished,[80] and only in 1969 that voting was extended to adults from the age of 18.[81]

The story of the House of Lords, in contrast, is one of a failure to democratise. The most far-reaching changes to its composition have been largely modern, occurring in the second half of the twentieth century, and arguably incomplete. The House of Lords Act 1999 was not intended to be a final settlement for the Lords, but the first stage of reform. Yet, currently it seems likely that this status quo could endure for some time, in the absence of clear ideas or strong motivation to replace it. Moreover, the reform which has occurred has made the Lords less aristocratic but no more democratic. The life peerages created in the Life Peerages Act 1958 gave the right to membership of the Lords by appointment, but with a title which cannot be inherited by the children of a life peer. Hereditary peers were almost all excluded from membership of the House of Lords by the 1999 Act, subject to the exception that ninety-two may remain, with 'by-elections' introduced among all previously eligible hereditary peers to select ninety of those retaining their seats.

The House of Lords has historically consisted of a combination of the Lords Temporal and Lords Spiritual, the former being the hereditary aristocracy and the latter members of the church, who sit in the upper chamber by virtue of their religious office. The eligibility of bishops, archbishops and other clergy to sit in the Lords (as Lords of Parliament, rather than peers[82]) stems from 'ancient usage'.[83] But the number of office-holders, now exclusively from the Church of England, entitled to attend the Lords has been limited by statute to twenty-six since the Bishopric of Manchester Act 1847 – the Archbishops of Canterbury and York, and Bishops of London, Durham and Winchester,[84] with the remaining positions filled in accordance with seniority (subject, until 2025, to a preference for female bishops). So, while

---

[78] Foot, *The Vote*, 170.   [79] Representation of the People Act 1928.
[80] Representation of the People Act 1948.   [81] Ibid, 1969.
[82] House of Lords Standing Order No.6 (first recorded 1621).
[83] A. Harlow, N. Doe and F. Cranmer, 'Bishops in the House of Lords: A Critical Analysis' [2008] *Public Law* 490–509, 490.
[84] Bishoprics Act 1878.

the religious component of the House of Lords has been diminished, it has also remained relatively stable since the nineteenth century.

Alongside the hereditary and religious elements of the House of Lords, the judicial element has also diminished, albeit much more recently. Under the Appellate Jurisdiction Act 1876, the monarch was empowered to appoint experienced judges or lawyers as Lords of Appeal in Ordinary, 'for the purpose of aiding the House of Lords in the hearing and determination of appeals'.[85] Although these judges did not receive a hereditary title, they could continue to sit in the Lords after their retirement from judicial work. With the creation of a Supreme Court in 2005 to replace the Appellate Committee of the House of Lords as the highest appeal court in the UK,[86] no further Lords of Appeal in Ordinary have been appointed since 2009, although the remainder can sit in the Lords after retirement from the Supreme Court.[87] New Supreme Court Justices use the courtesy title 'Lord' or 'Lady' by royal warrant, although it confers no eligibility to sit in the House of Lords.[88]

The democratisation of the House of Commons and the resilience of the House of Lords to such reform have a number of important implications. Most significantly, the relationship between the two Houses of Parliament has been defined by their respective characters. The shifting balance of power between the elected Commons and the unelected Lords has been a key strand of the UK legislature's constitutional history. The notion of the House of Lords as possessing a veto which allowed it to check or obstruct constitutional change came under growing pressure as the Commons became increasingly democratic and representative. The doctrine of the mandate was popularised by the third Marquess of Salisbury between 1868 and 1900. Salisbury, who was Prime Minister on three occasions during this period, argued that the Lords had a right to refer constitutionally controversial legislation proposed by the Commons back to the electorate, to ensure the government possessed a mandate for such change.[89] However, this approach was inverted in the twentieth century, on the election of a majority Labour government in 1945. The Leader of the House of Lords, Viscount Addison, and the Leader of the Opposition in the Lords, the fifth Marquess of Salisbury, announced an understanding that the Conservative dominated upper chamber would not seek to obstruct manifesto legislation,

---

[85] Appellate Jurisdiction Act 1876, s.6.   [86] Constitutional Reform Act 2005, s.23.
[87] Ibid, s.137.
[88] However, on becoming President of the UK Supreme Court in 2019, Lord Reed was appointed to a Life Peerage.
[89] House of Lords Library Note, *The Salisbury Doctrine* (LLN 2006/006, 30 June 2006).

on the basis that a pre-existing mandate for any such change could be inferred from the Labour government's election victory. This 'Salisbury-Addison' convention is a clear manifestation of the wider subordination of the Lords to the elected Commons.

The primacy of the Commons and the constrained right of the Lords to veto the choices of the democratic chamber have also been reflected in law. The Parliament Act 1911 was enacted to reduce the House of Lords' absolute veto over legislation to a delaying power of two years, over three successive sessions of Parliament in relation to any public Bill (excluding a Bill to extend the life of Parliament beyond five years, and with a delaying power of only one month in relation to a money Bill).[90] This followed the budget crisis of 1909, when the Lords refused to approve a Finance Bill of the Liberal Chancellor David Lloyd George, including taxes on high incomes and capital gains from land, which had been passed in the Commons. Following general elections in January and December 1910 focused on the constraint of the upper chamber's veto, and the threat of the King to create some 500 new peers, the House of Lords eventually assented to the Parliament Act, which curtailed its power.[91]

A further constraint on the Lords' legislative authority was imposed in 1949, without its consent, using the procedure established in the Parliament Act 1911. The Parliament Act 1949 reduced the Lords' delaying power over public Bills to one year, over two successive sessions, but was subject to a legal challenge over fifty years later, on the basis that it had been unlawful for the Commons to use the Parliament Acts process to expand its own power without the Lords' consent. This argument was rejected in the Appellate Committee of the House of Lords in *R. (Jackson) v. Attorney General*.[92] For Lord Bingham, the historical context in which the 1911 Act was enacted was a significant factor: 'The suggestion that Parliament intended the conditions laid down in section 2(1) to be incapable of amendment by use of the Act is in my opinion contradicted both by the language of the section and by the historical record.'[93] Moreover, the longstanding acceptance by political actors of the validity of the 1949 Act over half a century was noted by Lord Bingham,[94] and for Lord Hope, this fact was definitive 'political reality' which it was 'not ... open to a court of law to ignore'.[95]

---

[90] Parliament Act 1991, s.2(1); s.1(1).
[91] See C. Ballinger, *The House of Lords 1911–2011: A Century of Non-Reform* (Hart Publishing, 2012) ch.1.
[92] [2005] UKHL 56; [2006] 1 AC 262.   [93] Ibid, [30]. See also Baroness Hale, [156]–[158].
[94] Ibid, [36].   [95] Ibid, [124].

The long process of the democratisation of the Commons has led to its primacy within the legislature being recognised in constitutional convention and constitutional law. And the historical context in which the partial democratisation of the legislature occurred continues to shape the constitutional relationship between the Commons and the Lords today. Yet while the democratic character of the UK Parliament changed considerably during the nineteenth and twentieth centuries, this change has occurred essentially within an enduring institutional framework. We can therefore also see the UK Parliament as a source of relative institutional continuity, especially when compared to the other branches of the state: a government which has seen the dramatic expansion of welfare state and, more recently, extensive contracting out of the provision of public services to the private sector; the courts, which have gone from the fragmentation prior to the Judicature Act 1873 to a uniform system headed by an institutionally independent Supreme Court; and the Crown which has experienced the radical change from an active Head of State to a ceremonial figurehead with few remaining powers.

Dispersal of Legislative Power

The third theme illustrating the changing role of the legislature in the UK's constitutional history is the distribution and dispersal of legislative power within the UK. But first, it is also important to note that a key strand of British constitutional history saw Parliament claim legislative power over territories beyond the UK, consolidating a colonising process driven by the Crown using the royal prerogative, and providing legal legitimation of the creation of the British Empire. An important aspect of decolonisation has been the dispersal of Parliament's legislative power to legislative institutions in former colonies. This process of unravelling the Empire has been complex, and has taken various paths. Some colonies simply declared their independence from Britain during revolution, such as the United States of America in 1776. Some obtained independence after protests and resistance to British rule, such as India in 1947.[96] Some became largely self-governing Dominions under the Colonial Laws Validity Act 1865, gaining effective independence while joining the Commonwealth following the Statute of Westminster 1931 (initially Canada, Australia, New Zealand, South Africa, Newfoundland and

---

[96] Indian Independence Act 1947.

the Irish Free State).[97] In a number of instances, the UK Parliament held a residual legislative responsibility in relation to the constitutions of former colonies which were long independent (such as Canada – a link only severed by the Canada Act 1982). There are continuing exceptions, in particular the UK's fourteen Overseas Territories, which have their own constitutions and systems of government, but in relation to which the UK Parliament retains its unlimited legislative authority in principle.[98] That such imperial legislative power has now been largely dispersed does not in any way negate the illegitimacy of the initial colonial appropriations, nor the fact that the UK Parliament's authority was a central instrument by which the legal architecture of Empire was constructed, as well as deconstructed.

Within the UK, we have already seen that a number of different legislatures existed in the four constituent nations and provinces at various points in the constitutional history of the state. In general, the development of the UK's legislative institutions was based on the absorption of law-making powers and functions into the English, then British, and then UK Parliament following the Acts of Union with Scotland in 1707 and Ireland in 1800. Inversely, as the Republic of Ireland became independent from the UK (initially, from 1922 to 1937, as the Irish Free State), a new legislature, the Oireachtas, was established to reclaim powers and functions from the Westminster Parliament. This does not mean all differences in constitutional ideas about legislative authority have been eliminated across the different nations and provinces of the UK. The best example relates to conceptions of sovereignty, with a strong tradition of Scottish popular sovereignty which is presented as a distinct alternative to the 'English' doctrine of parliamentary sovereignty. Whether the acceptance of Scottish popular sovereignty amounts to a rejection of the legislative sovereignty of the UK Parliament is open to debate. According to Goldsworthy, those provisions of the Acts of Union that were expressed to be unalterable 'had little noticeable impact on the English doctrine of parliamentary sovereignty, which eventually came to be accepted by Scottish lawyers as well'.[99] Moreover, there is arguably no

---

[97] The Colonial Laws Validity Act 1865 provided legislative autonomy for colonies, subject to the constraint that their laws could not contradict the legislation of the Westminster Parliament (s.2). The Statute of Westminster 1931 eliminated the power of the UK Parliament to legislate for 'Dominions' other than with express consent (s.4).

[98] Foreign and Commonwealth Office, *The Overseas Territories: Security, Success and Sustainability* (Cm 8374, 2012) 14. The OTs are former colonies, and distinct from three internally self-governing dependencies of the Crown – Jersey, Guernsey and the Isle of Man – which were never colonies.

[99] Goldsworthy, *The Sovereignty of Parliament*, 232.

conceptual incompatibility between popular and parliamentary sovereignty, with the former an extra-constitutional democratic ideal which can be institutionalised in many ways, including through a doctrine of legislative sovereignty.[100] And even if this conception of popular sovereignty were incompatible with parliamentary sovereignty, there are significant legal barriers to giving it tangible constitutional effect. For example, in *MacCormick* v. *Lord Advocate* the Scottish Court of Session held that even if parliamentary sovereignty was 'a distinctively English principle which has no counterpart in Scottish constitutional law', there was no jurisdiction for the courts to enforce any constraints on the UK Parliament which might be identified in the Acts of Union.[101]

If much of the UK's constitutional history has seen the central Westminster Parliament operate as the dominant legislature – and the only legislature with primary law-making authority – this has changed in the twentieth century. After the intermittent existence of a legislature in Northern Ireland since 1920, and failed attempts in the 1970s to establish Parliaments in Scotland and Wales, a devolution settlement was established in 1998. Following approval at referendums held in 1997 in Scotland and Wales, and in Northern Ireland in 1998, the UK Parliament enacted legislation creating a Scottish Parliament,[102] a National Assembly for Wales,[103] and a Northern Ireland Assembly.[104] These devolution settlements have diffused legislative power among legislatures in the UK. They are based on a relatively complex, asymmetrical and dynamic model[105] – for example, while the Scottish Parliament and Northern Ireland Assembly were allocated primary legislative power in relation to all substantive matters other than those explicitly reserved (or excepted) to Westminster, the Welsh Assembly initially possessed only secondary legislative power, until a further referendum in 2011,[106] and only in 2017 was the reserved powers model also extended to Wales.[107]

There are still some differences in the topics which have been devolved to the legislatures in these three nations, especially in relation to taxation powers, which are most extensively devolved in Scotland. The scope of

---

[100] Gordon, *Parliamentary Sovereignty*, 48–49.
[101] *MacCormick* v. *Lord Advocate* 1953 SC 396, 411. See also *Lord Gray's Motion* [2002] 1 AC 124.
[102] Scotland Act 1998.   [103] Government of Wales Act 1998.
[104] Northern Ireland Act 1998.
[105] P. Leyland, 'The Multifaceted Constitutional Dynamics of UK Devolution' (2011) 9 *ICON* 251.
[106] Government of Wales Act 2006, ss.103–104.   [107] Wales Act 2017.

devolved power has also been expanded over time through successive legislative interventions by the UK Parliament.[108] There are still disputes about what is or should be a devolved matter, most notably in relation to the power of the Scottish Parliament to hold a referendum on independence from the UK[109] and, in the aftermath of the UK's exit from the European Union, in relation to the distribution of legislative competence repatriated from the EU.[110] Moreover, the devolution settlement has not operated without interruption, in particular in Northern Ireland, where the Assembly has been suspended on multiple occasions, including for three years between January 2017 and January 2020, when a political scandal led to the collapse of its power-sharing executive.[111]

The modern devolution settlement therefore creates a new paradigm for legislative activity in the UK. The Scottish Parliament, the Northern Ireland Assembly, and the Welsh Parliament or Senedd Cymru (as renamed by its own legislation[112]) have been created in recognition of the distinct histories of these nations within the UK. Yet their legislative authority is derived from positive law, which presents a clear contrast with the UK Parliament. Moreover, while primary legislative power has been devolved in a range of important substantive areas, including healthcare, education, transport, and the environment, this statutory settlement still exists subject to the sovereignty of the UK Parliament which, from a legal perspective, retains the power to redraw the boundaries of devolution, or intervene in devolved areas.[113] And while there is a constitutional convention which indicates that the UK Parliament will not normally legislate on devolved matters without the consent of the relevant devolved legislature, the 'Sewel convention' has come under considerable strain during the Brexit process, to the point where the EU (Withdrawal) Act 2018 was imposed without the consent of the

---

[108] See e.g., Scotland Act 2012; Scotland Act 2016; Corporation Tax (Northern Ireland) Act 2015.

[109] A temporary power to hold an independence referendum in 2014 was granted to the Scottish Parliament by Order in Council following negotiations with the UK government; The Scotland Act 1998 (Modification of Schedule 5) Order 2013.

[110] See e.g., *The UK Withdrawal from the European Union (Legal Continuity) (Scotland) Bill Reference* [2018] UKSC 64.

[111] Direct rule by the UK government was not reimposed, but the Westminster Parliament was required to legislate to provide for the Northern Ireland civil service to exercise administrative functions, and to repeatedly extend the statutory window for a new executive to be formed: Northern Ireland (Executive Formation and Exercise of Functions) Act 2018; Northern Ireland (Executive Formation etc.) Act 2019.

[112] Senedd and Elections (Wales) Act 2020.

[113] Scotland Act 1998 s 28(7); Northern Ireland Act 1998 s 5(6); Government of Wales Act 2006 s 107(5).

Scottish Parliament.[114] The UK Supreme Court held, in the case of *Miller*, that the recognition of the Sewel convention in the Scotland Act 2016 and Wales Act 2017 did not mean that it had been converted into a legal rule which was enforceable in the courts.[115] Other legislation relating to Brexit has also subsequently been enacted by the UK Parliament without the consent of all of the devolved legislatures, including the EU (Withdrawal Agreement) Act 2020 and the UK Internal Market Act 2020.

Devolution has therefore been a dispersal of primary legislative power by the UK Parliament, but not a transfer of its legal sovereignty to the institutions in Scotland, Wales or Northern Ireland. It has established new sites of national law-making authority and democratic representation and, consequently, has created internal competition between legislatures within the UK. The devolved legislatures occupy a slightly ambiguous position – from a functional perspective they are in many ways politically equivalent to the UK Parliament, possess a clear (perhaps even arguably superior) democratic weight, and tangible constitutional influence. Yet while they possess primary legislative power, in legal terms their law-making authority is also subordinate and constrained. While this is in contrast with the break-up of the British Empire, which did eventually see 'sovereignty' transferred, often through the law,[116] devolution has also only been partial in another sense. Some parts of the UK are devoid of that additional layer of representation: within England, after the rejection of a regional assembly at a referendum in the North East in 2004,[117] only London has an elected assembly,[118] but one which does not possess anything like the primary legislative power devolved to Scotland, Wales and Northern Ireland.

Devolution has been a momentous development in the modern history of legislatures in the UK, yet its trajectory remains somewhat uncertain. Despite recent declarations in legislation enacted by the UK Parliament, it cannot be guaranteed that the devolved legislatures will be a 'permanent part of the United Kingdom's constitutional arrangements'.[119] Instead, the devolution of legislative power, combined with the UK government's lack of respect, during the Brexit process, for the competences and expectations which are

---

[114] Consent was (eventually) obtained from the Welsh Assembly, and there was no Northern Ireland Assembly in operation at the time.
[115] [2017] UKSC 5, [2018] AC 61, [136]–[151].
[116] See P. Oliver, *The Constitution of Independence* (Oxford University Press, 2005).
[117] Regional Assemblies (Preparations) Act 2003.
[118] Greater London Authority Act 1999.   [119] Scotland Act 2016, s.1; Wales Act 2017, s.1.

central to the devolved arrangements,[120] could lead to the fragmentation of the UK. One independence referendum has already been held in Scotland since devolution was established in 1998, a second seems a realistic prospect in the aftermath of Brexit, despite the fact it is being resisted by the UK government.[121] A referendum on the reunification of Northern Ireland with the Republic of Ireland is also impossible to rule out in the future, given that a mechanism for this already exists in devolution legislation,[122] and since the UK's exit from the EU has established regulatory barriers between Northern Ireland and the rest of the UK.[123] In that sense, even if the devolved legislatures have quickly become an embedded part of the UK's constitutional architecture, the stability and longevity of that architecture cannot be taken for granted.

Conclusion

The legislature is a multidimensional institution which exercises a broad range of functions, reflecting its constitutional role as the central political forum of the nation. Its constitutional history is complex. Overall, we can see the historical development of the legislature in the UK first, in terms of its increasing constitutional authority; second, its democratic legitimation; and, third, the creation of other legislatures to which it has dispersed (some of) its law-making power. The risk in this narrative is that it tempts us to believe there is a natural next step, which is the creation of a federal UK in a codified constitution. Yet this is not the inevitable end of the UK's constitutional history, but a political choice which must be approached as such. Further change to the relationships between the UK's legislatures may be ahead, but constitutional history suggests that reform will continue to occur within our enduring parliamentary framework.

---

[120] See House of Lords EU Select Committee, *Brexit: Devolution* (HL Paper 9, 19 July 2017).
[121] See A. McHarg and J. Mitchell, 'Brexit and Scotland' (2017) 19 *British Journal of Politics and International Relations* 512–526.
[122] Northern Ireland Act 1998, s.1.
[123] See S. de Mars, C. Murray, A. O'Donoghue and B. Warwick, *Bordering Two Unions: Northern Ireland and Brexit* (Bristol: Policy Press, 2018).

13

The Executive and the Administration

JANET MCLEAN

Introduction

The history of the relationship between the executive and the administration has been largely invisible to lawyers and constitutional law. The provision of the Magna Carta 1215 in which King John promises to '[ ] *appoint as justices, constables, sheriffs, or other officials, only men that know the law of the realm and are minded to keep it well*' is not well known. The organisation of the administration has been missing from or has been given scant treatment over time in the iconic *constitutional* texts and legal commentaries to which we still refer. The common-law cases concerning governmental powers, liabilities and duties, tend to emphasise continuities and to avoid confronting directly the sometimes-fundamental changes in how public power has been organised and distributed and from whence it has drawn its authority over time. If historicism is 'engaged in rescuing the past from the distortions of the present-minded and emphasising the embeddedness of legal forms in the peculiarities of context',[1] then the common-law method often tends to be engaged in a version of counter-historicism – particularly in the realm of public law where there is an imperative to preserve, stabilise and legitimate the status quo and to conserve authority if at all possible. If administration appears at all in constitutional histories, it is often in the crevices, peripheries or silences of such narratives.

The work of historians on the history of administration and institutions is rich by comparison. There is a wealth of institutional histories. There are

---

[1] Faculty of Law, University of Auckland. Thanks to John Hudson, Michael Lobban, Josh Getzler, John Allison and other members of the audience of The British Legal History Conference July 2019, and to Arie Rosen, Nicole Roughan, David Dyzenhaus and Liz Fisher. All errors remain my own.
R. W. Gordon, "Critical Legal Histories Revisited': A Response', *Law and Social Inquiry* 37 (2012), pp. 200–215, 200.

letters, diaries and biographical accounts of particular office-holders and of the patronage systems which attached to them. There are histories of particular periods or subjects (the navy, the church) which tell a story of administration in a highly contextual way. Despite what Ed Rubin calls our 'social nostalgia' for the pre-administrative state ruled personally by kings and queens, there is much that we would recognise as impersonal administration (the collection of taxes, the organisation of charity) from at least the medieval period.[2] The sheer volume of such material creates a different set of problems. If constitutional lawyers have said too little about this kind of administration, administrative histories are usually too granular to establish a coherent 'long term' narrative – commonly describing administration in terms of a complex mosaic, a patchwork, the new engrafted onto the old, or changing with every king and office-holder. Administrative histories also present an additional, more theoretical question: what, if any, of this history, could one properly describe as *constitutional*?

There is a major challenge, then, to establish what it is that transforms administrative histories into *constitutional* history. John Griffith famously argued that 'the constitution is no more and no less than what happens. Everything that happens is constitutional. And if nothing happened that would be constitutional also'.[3] That statement may serve as an important antidote to the romanticisation and insularity to which British constitutional history has often been prone, but Griffith's approach would also render constitutional history of the kind contemplated by this volume well-nigh impossible.

For a *constitutional* history to be possible it needs to be approached as a special kind of history of ideas. It cannot be focused exclusively on the materiality of history but also needs to extend to how people have thought about, analysed and categorised legal and political events and institutions (even when they may have misunderstood or even overlooked how things actually were). There is something necessarily normative in rendering the materiality of history into legal categories for the purposes of telling a constitutional history.[4] Constitutional history tends to give either the best account of our constitutional selves, or uses past events to serve as a moral tale which demonstrates how tyranny should be avoided in the future. This

---

[2] E. L. Rubin, *Beyond Camelot: Rethinking Politics and Law for the Modern State* (Princeton University Press, 2005), pp.1–6. See J. Sabapathy *Officers and Accountability in Medieval England* (Oxford University Press, 2014).
[3] J. A. G. Griffith, 'The Political Constitution', *Modern Law Review* 42 (1979), pp. 1–21, 19.
[4] G. Samuels, *Epistemology and Method in Law* (Ashgate, 2003), pp. 125–148, 125–48, 173–191.

inevitably selective treatment is informed by undoubtedly contestable notions of what we mean by a "constitutional" concept or question.[5]

This is powerfully illustrated by Blackstone's eighteenth-century omission of the Prime Minister and Cabinet from his account of constitutional law and executive power. This omission is not aberrant and neither is it uninteresting. It was perfectly consistent with the pre-modern approach which viewed administration and government through the lens of 'office' with which Blackstone and his readers would have been familiar, and it can be explained by reference to his wider normative constitutional framework. Cabinet only came to be conflated with the executive in the nineteenth century. Up until that time, executive power was usually understood to refer to the execution of the laws rather than advisory or deliberative functions. It was the judiciary and certain other officials who were its principal agents. While all officials were titularly appointed by the king, many enjoyed a certain degree of independence – especially in the localities. Conferral of office in earlier times was often likened to the enjoyment of jurisdiction over lands and estates understood as the exercise of a defined mandate (which should not interfere with the mandates of others), a certain degree of discretion, and obligations such as the duty to account.

The focus of this chapter will be on how the *relationships between* the political centre and the official were understood – both prior to and post the advent of democratic government. Understood in this way, the history of the executive and administration is not exclusively or even centrally the history of the development of Cabinet Government.

It is the 'official' which will serve as the organising concept. The idea of the 'official' has a provenance going back to Roman law. It serves both as a locus for executive power (the power of *imperium* in Roman parlance) *and* as a concept which can be used to *limit* sovereign power. Its meanings and implications have radically changed over time. So, for example, in the medieval period the Crown was itself considered to be a species of office. By the coronation oath, kings accepted their office which was both separate from and embodied in their natural person. The administration too was 'bodified' and was imagined in organic terms as a part of the king's person.[6] During the constitutional turbulence of the seventeenth century the

---

[5] B. Straumann, 'The Energy of Concepts: The Role of Concepts in Long Term History and Social Reality', *Journal of Philosophy of History* (2019), pp. 1–36.
[6] E. H. Kantorowicz, *The King's Two Bodies: A Study in Medieval Political Theology* (Princeton University Press, 1957).

accusation that the king had somehow failed in his office featured as a rhetorical trope. In the Scottish Claim of Right 1689, James II was said to have forfeited the Crown (an office) and in the Bill of Rights 1689 the Crown (an office) is offered to William and Mary on the basis of a new set of conditions. Office understood in this way both empowers and limits the king.

Jean Bodin is responsible for translating elements of these ideas and giving them an early modern turn.[7] Office is central to his thought, but crucially, unlike his predecessors, he imagines officials as separate from the sovereign. Officials instead have an important role in mediating between the sovereign and the citizen while sharing the characteristics of both. For this to be the case, the sovereign must itself be imagined as something other than an official. Under such a schema, the official limits the sovereign because the official, unlike the sovereign, is defined and limited by law and it is the official under the law, rather than the sovereign personally or through a cypher, who should act. Importantly, the official, understood in this way, protects against the tyrannies associated with direct and personal rule.

In the nineteenth century, Dicey reimagines the official in yet another way. For him, the official does not necessarily share characteristics with the sovereign but rather with the citizen. Office-holders (political or administrative) should be treated as far as possible as ordinary persons. For Dicey, this has two advantages: it requires positive authorisation for official action; and in the absence of such positive authorisation it keeps the powers of the administrative state small. This reimagining of the official for the democratic era is explicable as an adaptation to the fact that officials no longer derive their legal authority largely from custom and their political authority from their social standing, but it leaves something wanting in that it fails to acknowledge the extent to which official power had inevitably increased in order to meet the new challenges associated with industrialisation and urbanisation and the new expectations associated with democratisation. The authority in office would now for the most part be derived from the statute enacted by the elected Parliament which delegated power to the official.

These theoretical perspectives can be used to frame a metanarrative of the distinct ways in which the concept of office has been used to define and limit sovereign power. Of course none of 'what actually happened' fits neatly into

---

[7] J. Bodin, *Six Livres de la Republique* (1575). J. Bodin, *Six Books of the Commonwealth* (abridged, translated M. J. Tooley) (Oxford: Basil Blackwell, 1967) at 79 [hereafter Bodin, *Six Books* (trans Tooley)].

these theories or epochs. There are numerous ways in which the theory did not fit the facts at any given time, and this chronology was not strictly followed. The embodiment of the administration with the Crown would from time to time be revisited – even in the twentieth century.[8] Nevertheless the theoretical metanarrative offers a general frame. For present purposes I begin, as the given title 'The Executive and Administration' seems to assume, in the early modern period during which the sovereign power is beginning to be imagined as something separate from administration. I trace the separation of the sovereign from office – a separation which was never wholly completed, the pre-democratic position of the office-holder and his (or sometimes her) relative independence from the sovereign, and the radical reforms to the civil service in the nineteenth century.

Separating the Sovereign from the Official

Theoretical Influences

There is a strong tradition in English thought which 'bodifies' the king together with his officials. We can see this even today in the way in which 'the Crown' is sometimes used to describe the central administration as a whole (incorporating the sovereign, Ministers and civil servants). In this section we will look at the ways in which the law *distinguished* between the king and his officials and the normative consequences of this distinction.

Roman thought figured prominently in Tudor education and legal thinking. Indeed, the renaissance humanists to a large extent treated classical sources much as if they were contemporary documents.[9] Office and office-holder (in the Roman nomenclature 'magistracy' and 'magistrate'), were originally used to refer to a range of roles including political, (deliberative, advisory, decision-making) administrative and judicial. Jean Bodin, the sixteenth-century French political theorist, took up these shared Roman concepts together with their medieval understandings and gave them an early modern turn which began to differentiate between making and administering the law. There was, he says, 'never a council in any well-ordered commonwealth with a power to command. It should advise and not execute policies.'[10]

Famously, Bodin is a theorist of absolute sovereignty. His sovereign is not bound by his own law but only by the laws of God and nature. What makes

---

[8] See e.g., *Town Investments v. Secretary of State for Environment* [1978] AC 359.
[9] Q. Skinner, *Forensic Shakespeare* (Oxford: Oxford University Press, 2014), p. 26.
[10] Bodin, *Six Books* (trans Tooley), p.79.

that palatable is that 'office' –separate from the sovereign – militates against the potential tyrannies associated with the direct or personal rule of an absolute sovereign (be he the one or the many). Bodin allows instead for the possibility of indirect rule by officials appointed according to and constrained by law. He considers there to be a natural evolution from personal rule or rule by 'commissioners'[11] (defined as persons who temporarily perform the will of the sovereign and whose role does not survive their tenure) to indirect rule by officials who have responsibilities to law as well as to the sovereign. By carefully distinguishing between the *right* of sovereignty and its *exercise*, he explicitly creates a place for administration in constitutional thought.

Describing himself as the first political thinker to define the concept of office, Bodin conceives of an official, as being neither sovereign nor subject, and thus as occupying a crucial interstitial space between the citizen and the state.[12] Officers 'resembled the sovereign because they, like the sovereign, could exercise public powers', and yet 'in other respects, officers ... shared the subordinate position of subject ... occupied positions carved out by law and must remain, in theory, the inferiors of sovereign authority'.[13] The idea that officials share characteristics of both the sovereign and citizens, and mediate between them, is a powerful one. Importantly Bodin likens the relationship between sovereign and office-holder to that of a commercial transaction between a lender and a borrower rather than to that of master and slave. An office continues after the person appointed to it has left it. Offices belong to the Commonwealth and are 'a thing put in trust'.[14]

Bodin was providing a theoretical framework in advance of the materiality of history. The separation of office from the sovereign in British thinking and practice was in fact never completed. There are, however, clear indications that British constitutional lawyers and actors recognised the *normative* force of Bodin's work and in particular the proposition that the making and execution of the law should not be performed by one and the same person or body, and that officials should have a certain degree of legal independence from the sovereign.

Materiality of History

What *'actually happened'*, to distinguish between the sovereign and his officials institutionally and to separate the making from the execution of the law,

---

[11] D. Lee 'Office is a Thing Borrowed' Political Theory 41(3) 409–440, 420. [12] Ibid.
[13] Ibid, 410.   [14] Ibid, 427.

was much more messy. The monarch had originally governed through ministers using an intricate writ and seal system rather than by way of a permanent council of officials or by reference to representatives of the barons. Gradually, Tout tells us, institutions 'that had arisen out of the primitive household' (such as the Exchequer and Chancery) began to go 'out of court' 'and to think as much of the traditions and rules of the office as of the immediate interests of their master'.[15] By the end of Edward III's reign, the exercise of power under the privy seal had gone entirely 'out of court'. Personnel were paid out of the Exchequer rather than out of the Wardrobe and hence were more capable of giving the king independent advice.[16] By the same process, the king's private secretary ('confidant and custodian of the king's correspondence') evolved into the offices of the Secretaries of State as we now know them.[17] Over time "the king's personal household merged imperceptibly into the general government so that ... the Master of the Horse or the Lord Chamberlain were regarded as equivalent positions to the Lord High Chancellor or the Secretary of State'."[18] A more unified administrative system eventually emerged, with personnel moving between household offices and offices out of court.

Concerns about the monarch's potential influence over such officers came to a head in the seventeenth century. A perceived lack of independence from the king of those office-holders sitting in the Commons was already viewed as a serious political issue by 1625. Office-holders increasingly found they were required to support royal policies which they also felt bound to criticise. Unsurprisingly given these experiences, issues relating to the tenure and independence of officials from the Crown became a central preoccupation of the Rump Parliament.[19] There were Leveller proposals for a Place Bill which would have excluded all officials from the Commons. A self-denying ordinance compelled members to withdraw from holding certain offices in

---

[15] T. F. Tout, 'Some Conflicting Tendencies in English Administrative History during the Fourteenth Century', *Bulletin of the John Rylands Library* (1923), p. 83, 84.
[16] Ibid, 94.
[17] A closer reading of Tout suggests that control in fact fluctuated and was the site of political conflict. Under Edward III, for example, the receivers of the royal household rendered accounts to the King personally, refusing to account to the Exchequer and destroying records (at 88). It was the more responsive Royal household which grew in power as it expanded its activities in support of Edward III's military ambitions in Scotland and France.
[18] Rubin, *Beyond Camelot*, p. 26.
[19] See generally G. E. Aylmer, *The State's Servants: The Civil Service of the English Republic 1649–1660* (London: Routledge, 1973).

the absence of an indemnity ordinance[20] and a more systematic approach to determining the length of appointments and their conditions of tenure (whether at pleasure or for cause) was introduced.[21] For a time, it was Parliament which made the most important appointments, albeit in the name of the Protector.[22]

After the Restoration, there were renewed concerns about the king's influence – with a particular focus on those office-holders who also held seats in the Commons. According to the original terms of the Act of Settlement intended to take effect when the Hanoverians came to the throne, no person who held an office or place of profit under the Crown was able to serve as a member of the Commons. Had this come into force, it would not only have effectively reduced Crown influence in the House but also forestalled the development of the Westminster system of king and government in Parliament. Before the provision came into effect, however, it was amended to disqualify from the House of Commons only those persons holding an office or a place for profit created after 25 October 1705.[23]

This is a graphic illustration (to embellish upon Griffith) of an instance when what 'nearly happened' has strong claims to be included in a work of constitutional history. It is significant in a number of ways. The present Westminster system of government originates in an obscure and apparently arbitrary provision: holders of high office (tending to be older offices) can sit in the Commons, while holders of subordinate offices are generally disqualified from sitting. The distinction between high political and subordinate administrative offices (the civil service) was originally a thin and an arbitrary one. Clarity about the distinction took a long time to emerge. Throughout the eighteenth century the 'King's Friends' who held offices and sat in the Commons continued to use their votes in support of the king's policies and considered themselves the king's servants rather than having a primary loyalty to Party.[24] And even until 1830 the line between a political minister and a permanent official was a blurred one.[25] The under-secretaries of the Admiralty and Treasury, exempted from the subsequent Place Acts and

---

[20] Ibid, p. 96.   [21] Ibid, pp. 82–86.   [22] Ibid, p. 59.
[23] See 4 Anne c 8 (1705) and 6 Anne c 41 (1707). Accepting such an office voided election to the House, though a person was capable of standing for re-election. F. M. Maitland, *The Constitutional History of England* (1961 paperback edition Cambridge University Press 1908), pp.326, 368–369.
[24] F. B. Wickwire, 'King's Friends, Civil Servants, or Politicians' *American Historical Review* 71 (1965), pp. 18–44, 34.
[25] G. Kitson Clark, "Statesmen in Disguise': Reflexions on the History of the Neutrality of the Civil Service' *The Historical Journal* 2(1) (1959), pp. 19–39, 34.

allowed to sit in the Commons, for example, served more as expert civil servants (permanent secretaries) than as politicians.[26]

The main point for now is that the failure to disqualify all office-holders of the king from the Commons created a category of officials who could both advise the king and contribute to the making of law. This offends a number of Bodin's central tenets. It means that there is never a complete separation of the sovereign from the official. It also appears to be the case, at least prima facie, that there is no necessary separation between those who make and those who execute the law.

Blackstone's Reception of Bodin

There is evidence that the normative force of Bodin's principle that the same body or person should not both make and execute the law appears to have been accepted by William Blackstone in his *Commentaries*. Indeed, it is rather remarkable the lengths to which Blackstone is prepared to go in his attempt to square the fact of the presence of the king's senior officials in the Houses of Parliament with this principle. Blackstone's attempt to suggest that the principle was nevertheless accepted and applied within the framework of the eighteenth-century British constitution is illuminating not because it is necessarily successful or coherent, but for what it tells us about how executive power was thought about at the time. Blackstone presents the British constitution as maintaining a separation between law-making and administration by denying that the members of the Houses of Parliament who make law also execute the law. It is the king who executes the law through his officers. His role in Parliament is not a law-making one but amounts only to a right of veto.

Blackstone, like Bodin, incorporates the Roman law language and concepts of magistracy throughout his treatise, and like Bodin, his central concern is to avoid tyranny. In Britain, he says, there are two *supreme* magistrates: the legislative branch consisting of the king, Lords and Commons (in whom the 'supreme and absolute authority of the state is vested, by our constitution');[27] and the executive consisting of the king alone in 'whom the sovereign power of the state resides' who is the 'the sole *executive* magistrate'.[28] Thus, he claims, supreme power is divided.[29] It is important that these be separate, Blackstone

---

[26] Ibid, 27.
[27] Sir William Blackstone, *Commentaries on the Laws of England* (Dublin: Exshaw, 1766) 142. (1992 edition Hein-on-line) [hereafter Blackstone, *Commentaries*].
[28] Ibid, p. 151.   [29] Ibid, pp. 141–142.

emphasises, because if the 'making and the execution of the laws were vested in one man (or the same body of men)' . . . 'there can be no public liberty'.[30] 'A total union of [legislative and executive functions] would be productive of tyranny', a 'total disjunction of them' would produce the same result given that 'the legislature would gradually assume to itself the rights of executive power'.[31]

According to Blackstone's account, the sense in which legislative and executive powers are functionally distinct is that power can only be used coercively if the different parts act in concert. The king has power of veto only – power of rejection rather than proposal – not the power of doing wrong but only of preventing wrong from being done. On the other hand, the king's consent is required for legislation that would abridge his executive power. So far all is in balance.

The way that Blackstone squares this with the inconvenient fact that the king's high officials sit in Parliament (including law officers such as himself) is to maintain that the king's officials in Parliament do not in fact qualify as subordinate magistrates or as exercising executive power as that concept was understood in the eighteenth century. Of the great officers of state such as the Lord Treasurer, Lord Chamberlain and the principal secretaries he says 'I do not know that they are in that capacity in any considerable degree the objects of our laws, or have any very important share of magistracy conferred upon them: except that Secretaries of State are allowed the power of commitment, in order to bring offenders to trial.' Secretaries of State would certainly have been surprised by this description of the paucity of their power, though admittedly Blackstone was writing before *statute* had begun to confer broad powers on the Secretaries of State.[32]

Blackstone's approach reflects the fact that up until the seventeenth century, executive power meant either the function of administering justice under the law or the machinery of justice under which the law was put into effect. The term 'executive' was used almost exclusively to describe judicial functions – literally to refer to executing the laws or putting laws into effect at the behest of the king. The executive necessarily included the judges. This made sense at a time when the most significant impact of government upon

---

[30] Ibid, p. 142.   [31] Ibid, pp. 149–150.
[32] Ibid. Notably this statement was probably written before the famous case of *Entick v. Carrington* 19 Howell's State Trials 1029 which considered whether Secretaries of State were authorised to issue search warrants. Privy Counsellors who *advised* the king, had not enjoyed significant *judicial* (executive) power since the abolition of the Star Chamber.

its subjects was through the courts or law enforcement officers.[33] The idea of an executive function, separate from the judicial function, only emerged sometime in the seventeenth century and did not fully develop until the end of the eighteenth.[34]

This can be seen even more clearly when we consider which officials Blackstone *does* include in the category of subordinate magistrates who '[derive] all their authority from the supreme magistrate, [are] accountable to him for their conduct and [act] in an inferior secondary sphere.'[35] In a short separate chapter, Blackstone confines himself to discussing a somewhat perplexing list of those who 'execute the laws' such as 'sheriffs; coroners, justices of the peace; constables; surveyors of highways; and overseers of the poor'.[36] His focus is on those officials concerned in matters [affecting] 'the liberty of the subject'. In terms reminiscent of Bodin, Blackstone describes the coroner acting as verderer of the forest as a person *'whose business is to stand between the prerogative and the subject in the execution of the [ ] laws'* (my emphasis).[37] He leaves out both the great officers of state and, with the exception of the justices of the peace, the many officials involved in the administration of local government.[38] A large part of administration and government more broadly construed is consequently denied a place in constitutional theory, in order to maintain a normative distinction between the making and the execution of the laws.

In other parts of the *Commentaries*, by contrast, Blackstone describes a number of prerogative powers which go well beyond the function of executing the law in this narrow sense and which '[constitute] the executive power of government'.[39] These include powers in relation to foreign affairs,[40] the military, coinage, ports and harbours, and maintaining borders. He does not consider the officers associated with these activities to be worthy of special treatment.

---

[33] Lord Reed casts the courts in the role of administrators and executors of the laws in the recent case of *R (Unison)* v. *Lord Chancellor* [2017] UKSC 51 [68]: 'Courts exist in order to ensure that the laws made by Parliament, and the common law created by the courts themselves are applied and enforced'.
[34] M. J. C. Vile, *Constitutionalism and the Separation of Powers* (Indianapolis: Liberty Fund, 1998), p. 31.
[35] Blackstone, *Commentaries*, p. 142.
[36] Ibid at 339. Even at the time, however, the role of the highest of these ancient officers, the sheriff, had become increasingly ceremonial in England – though not so in Scotland.
[37] Ibid at 335.
[38] Such as mayors, aldermen or officials of corporations and local franchises who administer local government.
[39] Blackstone, *Commentaries*, p. 269   [40] Ibid, Book I, chapter 7.

Blackstone also largely ignores the actual workings of Parliament. By the late eighteenth and early nineteenth centuries the legislature had taken upon itself a large administrative role through the extensive use of private and local acts (thus unifying executive and legislative power). Maitland reckons that only after the Reform Act 1832 did Parliament cease to attempt to 'govern' the country with legislation effecting specific enclosures, widening of roads, allocating paid constables and so on, and begin to make more general rules or entrust matters to Commissioners and Secretaries of State.[41]

Theoretical Difficulties with Blackstone's View, and Their (Partial) Solution

Blackstone's omission of the development of Cabinet government is unlikely to be inadvertent. A Cabinet in the Commons caused difficulties for Blackstone's theory. Blackstone's central concern, in attempting to maintain a separation of executive and law-making power, was to effect liberty and prevent tyranny. Like Bodin, he contended that the king was above the law but that the focus should be on holding *officials* to account. He quotes John Locke to the effect that while the king could do no wrong, the king seldom acted personally and hence was not in a position to do significant harm: 'harm which the sovereign can do in his own person not being likely to happen often, nor to extend itself far, nor being able by his single strength to subvert the laws, nor oppress the body of his people'[42] This works relatively well when the sovereign is one person rather than a collective body of the many, but it is not as easy to square with cabinet government. The incomplete separation of the executive (sovereign) and administration (official) at the very highest political levels, potentially causes difficulties for the integrity of Blackstone's theory and its potential to control tyranny. Blackstone presumes the existence of officials who act for the king and who are answerable in various ways including through the High Court of Parliament.[43]

At least in that respect, Blackstone also prefigured what would eventually emerge as the political solution to the incomplete separation of law-making from executive power. This was gradually to reverse the political practice of attempting to exclude Ministers from the Commons. Instead, Ministers would be part of and answerable to the Commons and it would become an institution which could oversee the work of the executive.

---

[41] Maitland, *The Constitutional History*, p. 384. My own reading is that practice did not really change until mid-century with reforms to the way in which legislation was made.
[42] Blackstone, *Commentaries*, p. 243.   [43] Ibid, p. 243.

The practice of using Parliament to scrutinise the actions of officials has historical antecedents. The impeachment power in the Commons was used to draw attention to officials' bad administration and counsel, and poor judgment.[44] The Commons viewed this power expansively and would seek to hold officials responsible for errors of judgment and the misuse of discretion as well as breaches of the law. The Lords took a more restrictive view and allowed only breaches of the law to be punished.[45] The seeds of ministerial responsibility can be found here.

There were other historical antecedents which Blackstone does not mention. Complex laws relating to the different seals of office had long served as a means to verify that an official was acting under valid authority. There had been attempts in the Act of Settlement to refine the law further by imposing an obligation on the king's counsellors individually to give advice 'under his hand, so that his responsibility for the advice might be brought home to him'.[46] The clause itself did not survive. The law relating to the seals fell into disuse. But the practice of the advisor countersigning after the king has survived in certain instances. According to Maitland, it is in these *forms* we can see the foundation for the modern doctrine of ministerial accountability.[47] For every exercise of royal authority some Minister could be made answerable to Parliament and the minister and ministry as a whole could be held accountable. This, too, took a long time fully to emerge. Well into the nineteenth century, significant bodies, such as the Poor Law Commissioners, enjoyed independence and a power to make regulations and yet had no one to speak or answer for them in the Commons.[48]

Even though a *political* solution was found to the incomplete separation of law-making from executive functions, the absence of a complete separation would continue to create legal doctrinal difficulties in the allocation of and responsibility for executive power. It would make it difficult, for example, to determine whether and when the Crown's immunities should extend to the king's Ministers[49], whether a mandamus action was available which could force an official to act[50] or alternatively was not available because the official

---

[44] C. Roberts, 'The Law of Impeachment in Stuart England: A Reply to Raoul Berger', Yale LJ 84(7) (1975), 1419–1439. Blackstone *Commentaries*, p. 243.
[45] Roberts, *The Law of Impeachment*. [46] Maitland, *The Constitutional History*, p. 390.
[47] Ibid, p. 203. [48] Kitson Clark, *Statesmen in Disguise*, p. 29.
[49] *Town Investments v. Secretary of State for the Environment* [1978] AC 359.
[50] See e.g., *R v. Lords Commissioners of the Treasury* (1851) 16 Q B 358; 117 Eng Rep 916; cf *R v. Commissioners of Inland Revenue, in re Nathan* (1884) 12 Q B 461 (availability of mandamus against an officer as opposed to a servant of the Crown).

was acting for or on behalf of the Crown and was thus exempt from coercive orders,[51] and to distinguish the exercise of ministerial power from the exercise of the Crown's prerogative power.[52]

The Persistence of the Blackstone's "Narrow" View of Executive Power

Blackstone's view that the institutions for the making and execution of the law should be kept separate retained some normative influence on the broader constitution of the Empire, as well as on the United States Constitution. In the British self-governing colonies the approach of the United Kingdom government was to grant local legislatures law-making powers but to repose executive power in Governors answerable to London. This resulted in numerous conflicts including, most dramatically, in British North America. In response to the 1839 report of Lord Durham, the Governor-General of British North America, the United Kingdom government eventually accepted that a system of government by those holding a majority in the Houses of Parliament and responsible to it, such as was by then beginning to be recognised at the metropole, should also be allowed in the colonies.[53]

And the old narrow understanding of executive power as the execution of the laws, together with the close association of the judges with that role, also survived well into the twentieth century in the tests for the availability of judicial review. Decisions would not be subject to judicial supervision unless the decision-maker was under a 'duty to act judicially'. It is striking that even those early twentieth-century UK administrative lawyers who generally thought that courts should not supervise the administration or the growing public service functions of the state, made an exception for the supervision of the exercise of such executive powers which potentially interfered with an individual's liberty.[54]

Notwithstanding that Blackstone's account of the executive and administration did not fully reflect the practices of his own time, its significance long outlasted the eighteenth century.

---

[51] Ibid.   [52] *Council of Civil Service Unions* v. *Minister for the Civil Service* [1985] AC 374.

[53] A. Quentin-Baxter and J. McLean, *This Realm of New Zealand: The Queen, The Governor-General, The Crown* (Auckland: Auckland University Press, 2017), pp. 12–14.

[54] In the twentieth century William Robson conceded that police powers should be susceptible to judicial oversight even if other executive action ('service functions') should be left to administrators: J. McLean, *Searching for the State in British Legal Thought* (Cambridge University Press, 2012), p. 180.

Subordinate Officers Involved in Government Administration

So much for the highest political officers. Most office-holders – whether of a narrow 'executive' kind or otherwise – did not hold seats in the Commons or Lords. A huge range of administrative activities took place at central and local level and it is these kinds of offices which would gradually evolve into the civil service. This story too tends to be left out of British constitutional history.

Many of its officials were volunteers who, while formally appointed by and deriving their authority from the king, de facto governed on the authority of their personal standing in the social hierarchy. The primary institutions governing ordinary people after 1750 – the vestry or kirk session, the individual Justice of the Peace and the courts of requests – were oligarchical or patrician centres of authority. It is not a complete exaggeration to say that, at least as far as the centre was concerned, the issues of administration in the localities were as much to do with officials not being responsive enough to the centre, as they were about officials not enjoying sufficient independence from the king's influence. Much of the constitutional effort and political contest in relation to such officials was devoted to *ex ante* issues concerning appointment, term of office and tenure.

Appointment

While all public offices were formally in the grant of the king, the processes for appointment varied greatly according to the office. In the fourteenth century the king had successfully rejected demands for the *election* of sheriffs in the shire courts and of justices of the peace in the Commons. By the fifteenth century, a compromise seems to have been reached. The king's counsellors, Lords spiritual and temporal, the justices, barons of the exchequer, clerk of the rolls and certain other officers nominated three names of suitable persons to be put before the king for selection as sheriff for the following year.[55] In many other cases, even though the grant of an office appears to be in the name of the king, in practice the position was in another person's patronage.[56] Offices were openly bought, sold, deposed, used in marriage settlements, borrowed against and were generally treated as a form of property.

---

[55] Sir John Fortescue, (Chrimes trans) *De Laudibus Legum Anglie* (Cambridge University Press, 1949), p. 55.
[56] See J. C. Sainty, 'The Tenure of Offices in the Exchequer', *English Historical Review* 316 (1975), pp. 449–475.

Terms of office were a matter of custom and varied dramatically. The preoccupation with the length of an official's term may have begun as an overhang of the medieval position under which certain officers, such as city magistrates, were held to account at the end of their term, at which time they offered redress for wrongs done.[57] In contrast to a sheriff's one-year term, during the first half of the seventeenth century most middle-ranking officers in the courts, departments and regions were held for life.[58] The use of reversions could effectively make such offices hereditary in certain families. This was a system of bureaucratic subinfeudation which limited the Crown's future freedom of appointment and effectively created a queue of people to whom the office would pass. No doubt this made for stability and a certain independence. It also significantly limited the monarch's ability to reward and control grantees as James I (VI) and Charles I found to their frustration.

Tenure varied as between fixed-term offices, offices held at the king's pleasure, offices held for life and offices held on good behaviour. The travails to establish the independence of the judges in the seventeenth century which resulted in their special protection from removal in the Bill of Rights 1689 are well known[59]. We can detect a more general normative shift in expectations about the degree of independence which should be enjoyed by various offices and how this should be reflected in tenure arrangements during the same period. It had earlier been assumed, for example, that judges should be easily removable to make them especially answerable for their role. In contrast 'ministerial' officers being the Crown's executive agents, should be less responsible for what they did and were thought properly to hold their offices for life – in other words a reversal of modern expectations.[60] By 1640, these ideas were clearly being challenged. A Judge ruled invalid a grant of the Marshalship of the King's Bench for a fixed term on the basis that it was an office of great trust and should therefore attract greater security of tenure.[61]

Aside from the common-law judges who also acted as advisors, there is little evidence that officials were regularly removed from office. Office-holders such as Lords Lieutenants, sheriffs, Justices of the Peace, and Judges of the Assize had long been critical to the working out of the relationships between the centre and the localities. Their very function was to mediate between central government and the locality and often local

---

[57] J. Sabapathy, *Officers and Accountability*.
[58] G. E. Alymer, *The King's Servants: The Civil Service of Charles I, 1625–1642* (Boston, Routledge, 1974), p. 96. Reversions were not available in relation to the great offices of state.
[59] Discussed in Vol 1, Ch 18, Getzler Judiciaries. [60] Ibid, p. 109. [61] Ibid, p. 122.

loyalties prevailed. Why remove a Justice of the Peace when the king was just as likely to be unable to control his replacement?[62]

Administrators, for their part, often sought to distance themselves from parliamentary politics. The Whig purges of Jacobite officials (1694–1695) and, later, of Tory officials alleged to be disloyal to the Hanoverian Crown (1715–1717), were widely condemned as 'extremely obstructive of good government'.[63] According to a contemporary account, excessive politicking was regarded as leading to 'administrative confusion, low morale, and uncertain prospects for employment' ... 'emboldening the bad and terrifying the good' and 'limiting security of tenure'.[64] The same excise officers collected taxes for Jacobite and Hanoverian kings alike.

Controls on Independence

There was a variegated set of rules, having their source in statute and the common law,[65] which regulated the independence of offices.[66] Statutes prohibited specified offices from being sold, deposed, and the like, and from being held together in the same person. Specified officers were prohibited by a series of statutes from sitting in the Commons or as magistrates. Most offices could be performed by a deputy – but there were common-law exceptions for those offices which were considered to be of great trust, or which required particular skill or diligence. Together these rules regulated the property in office and the independence of the office-holder.

---

[62] Under Wolsey, Justices of the Peace would be summoned to meetings of the Royal council sitting as the Star Chamber as a control on misconduct. They would also be ordered annually to renew their oaths of loyalty, and the impression was given that the King was personally following their activities, see D. Maccullogh, *Thomas Cromwell: A Life* (London: Penguin, 2018), pp. 546–547.

[63] J. Brewer, *The Sinews of Power: War, Money and the English State 1688–1783* (Harvard: University Press, 1990), p. 74.

[64] Ibid.

[65] See e.g. *Garforth v. Fearon* 126 Eng Rep 193 (1787). See also *Law v. Law* 3 P. WMS 390 (1735). A contract entered into to pay for the recommendation of a place in the excise was unenforceable and equity would relieve against it. It was argued 'that it could be no objection that the whole salary or profits belonging to an office ought to be received by him who executed it, for this was frequently otherwise, and yet tolerated in law and equity'. But the Lord Chancellor's objection was that 'merit, industry and fidelity ought to recommend persons to these places and not interest with the commissioners, who, it is presumed, had they known from what motive the plaintiff at law applied to them on behalf of his brother, would have rejected him' ... 'It is a fraud on the public, and would open the door for the sale of offices relating to the revenue'.

[66] For a sense in which tenure waxed and waned see e.g. J. C. Sainty, 'The Tenure of Offices', who suggests that life tenure was introduced after laity were appointed in the stead of clergy (p. 456).

Offices which did not carry a stipend or attract fees appeared to carry the greatest degree of independence. For such officials 'voluntarism produced plurality'.[67] In the seventeenth century, at least Justices of the Peace regularly 'appraised and interpreted' kingly authority rather than simply obeying it.[68] Despite a significant expansion of their jurisdiction into the eighteenth century, they were subject to very little judicial or other supervision short of situations of financial corruption.[69] As for criminal law controls, the common-law criminal offences of 'misconduct in public office' and 'wilful neglect of public office' (i.e. offences of both misfeasance and nonfeasance) were rarely allowed to be brought by the citizen 'informer'. Hay sums it up: 'It is absolutely clear from the case law that the need to support justices of the peace, and not to discourage a magistracy that acted (at least nominally) without compensation, and the identification of a free service with gentlemanly integrity, all made the granting of criminal informations an extremely rare occurrence, particularly outside London.'[70] Such magistrates were by no means in a master and servant relationship with central government.

Money

There were more avenues for supervision in respect of offices to which stipends, fees and perquisites attached, or who held revenue on behalf of the king. Indeed the history of administration could be told entirely through the elaborate institutions, including the Court of Exchequer, which enforced duties to account upon officials, and which had existed in various forms since medieval times.[71] Unfortunately I cannot undertake a full treatment here.

In the eighteenth century, the stipend attaching to an office often bore little relationship to how onerous the office was. Indeed, there are reports of people paying *not* to have an office imposed on them,[72] as well as of the more notorious instances of sinecures (which often provided the equivalent of a pension to the office-holder or his family). Until the nineteenth century reforms to the banking system and systems of payment into Treasury, those

---

[67] M. J. Braddick, *God's Fury, England's Fire: A New History of the English Civil Wars* (London: Penguin, 2009), p. 70.
[68] Ibid, p.74.   [69] For the earlier position see Brewer, *The Sinews of Power,*.
[70] D. Hay, 'Legislation, Magistrates and Judges: High Law and Low Law in England and the Empire' in D. Lemmings, *The British and Their Laws in the Eighteenth Century* (Boydell Press, 2005), p. 67.
[71] See J. Sabapathy, *Offices and Accountability*; J. Brewer, *The Sinews of Power*.
[72] Fines could also be imposed on elected officials who failed to take office which was particularly hard on dissenters, see A. Page, 'Rational Dissent and Blackstone's Commentaries' in A. Page and W. Prest (eds.) *Blackstone and His Critics* (Hart, 2018), pp. 83–83.

officials who took revenue on behalf of the king appeared to be able to use it on their own account before it was due to the Exchequer. Offices to which perquisites and fees attached could be extremely lucrative and an important source of patronage. Holders of such offices commonly employed their own servants who were often required (by statute or practice) to take an oath and to pay a bond upon appointment against any misconduct (including excessive fee taking). Principals could be liable for such employees (depending once again on the rules attaching to the particular office). There was also an extensive case law which finely distinguished between extortion and bribery (which were criminal offences), and the fees, perquisites and gifts properly given and taken according to 'ancient customs of the office'.[73]

Radical Reform: From Office to Contract

By the late eighteenth century, Edmund Burke would lament the paucity of political oversight of executive power by the House of Commons, which would, in turn lead to a series of high-profile inquiries into the misuse of patronage, corruption, fee-charging and sinecures.[74] These would include the impeachment proceeding against William Hastings, and an inquiry into the actions of the Duke of York's mistress in securing military commissions and promotions. John Wade's *Red* and *Black* books detailing the sinecures, pensions and corruption of named members of the clergy and aristocracy added fuel to the campaigns for both parliamentary and administrative reform.[75] There was a concerted Whig campaign to expose the aristocratic, indolent, infirm and the dissolute among office-holders. Property in office, formerly considered to be a token of independence and authority, increasingly came to be associated with old Toryism and to be viewed as carrying the same taint as the rotten boroughs.

The move to a permanent, neutral, unified, salaried civil service appointed on merit was both radical and gradual. There were a number of drivers, the most important being the extension of the franchise and new expectations surrounding executive government which *gradually* followed upon an

---

[73] Quantum meruit actions by officials for unpaid fees were used to control the other side of the ledger. The judges had a potentially large role in monitoring 'decentralised negotiations' about fee taking and consequently profit-making in office.
[74] See e.g., J. Torrance, 'Social Class and Bureaucratic Innovation: The Commissioners for Examining the Public Accounts 1780–87' (1978) 78 *Past and Present* 56–81.
[75] J. Wade, *Extraordinary Red Book* 1816; J. Wade, *The Black Book or Corruption Unmasked* (London: Fairburn, 1819).

increasingly democratic system of government. It came to be established that members of cabinet and the Prime Minister would be drawn from the party or parties commanding a majority in the Commons.[76] Ministries would newly stand and fall together. Ministers would increasingly become answerable for the conduct of their officials and, although attempts at centralisation remained controversial, there was a new need for more responsive officials capable of meeting the challenges posed by industrialisation and urbanisation. This was all amid public dismay and frequent scandal about the existing calibre of officials.

The nature of legislation also changed.[77] By mid-nineteenth century, legislation began to take the form of general rules and increasingly included the delegation of general powers to central officials such as Secretaries of State. It no longer took the predominant form of local legislation focused on administrative minutiae, or of model Acts to which local government could voluntarily adhere. This would become hugely significant for the twentieth century developments in judicial review of administrative action in which judges came to treat officials as 'conveyor belts'[78] for the will of the legislature. This is a very long way from the broad, largely customary, mandates enjoyed by officials in the eighteenth century.

Fiscal matters, always central to administration, were significant drivers for civil service reforms and the consequential changes to audit and accounting practices brought about by the Exchequer and Audit Departments Act of 1866[79] were critical. Office was decoupled from property. Compensation was paid for those offices, including sinecures, which were abolished. Salaries replaced fee-taking.

Officials, though they continued to be appointed and regulated under the prerogative orders and were by such orders subject to distinct public rules of employment, were increasingly regarded in contractual terms. Officers, who

---

[76] Queen Victoria and Sir Robert Peel clashed over whether members of the royal household should change with the advent of a new Prime Minister (the Bedchamber crisis).

[77] R. MacLeod, *Government and Expertise: Specialists, Administrators and Professionals, 1860–1919* (Cambridge University Press, 1988); O. MacDonagh, 'The Nineteenth Century Revolution in Government: A Reappraisal', I(1) *Historical Journal* (1958), pp. 52–67. The move to a 'merit-based' system of appointment upon examination also met with a significance resistance – in part because of the associated centralising tendencies of such a policy, and also because it was an attack on patronage. E. Hughes, 'Civil Service Reform 1853–5' *History New Series* 27 (105) (1942), pp. 55–83.

[78] The term belongs to R. Stewart, 'The Reformation of American Administrative Law' 88(8) *Harvard Law Review* (1975), pp. 1667–1813.

[79] 29 & 30 Vict cap 39.

had formerly been understood as quasi-independent sources of authority with special public law duties, became a residual category. Special rules would continue for the police, the defence forces, the judiciary and for others holding high office. For everyone else, the relationship between the state and the official would become increasingly *contractual*.

The civil service reforms have commonly been attributed to the Gladstone commissioned Northcote-Trevelyan report 1854 which proposed a competitive public examination for entry to the civil service and removal of the patronage system (or rather, as some commentators observed, relocating patronage in examiners).[80] In fact, many of their recommendations had already been adopted by various departments after earlier, more specialised, inquiries.[81] Moreover, the Report's focus on entrance examinations ignored bigger issues such as whether *promotion* too should be on merit rather than seniority, and whether and how the political neutrality of the civil service was to be maintained.[82] The latter took much longer to crystallise.

The reluctance of experienced and senior permanent officials to kowtow to temporary elected Ministers is not surprising. One striking element of continuity is that formerly, a great number of officials held places for life and for them the move to a *permanent* cadre of officials was thus not a big one. A much bigger shift in thinking was required in relation to issues of relative authority and expertise between elected and other officials. Some members of the Commons (for example officers in Admiralty) had traditionally behaved more like civil servants than politicians and stood on equal footing with them: they were relied on for their dispassionate expert advice to the Commons. Equally, heads of departments, were used to a fair degree of discretion, independence and personal authority. In the 1830s and 1840s, for example, James Stephen, who was officially the Undersecretary of the Colonial Office, was still *publicly* identified with the Colonial Office's policies. Edward Gibbon Wakefield referred to him derisively as 'Mr Over-Secretary Stephen' and 'King Stephen'.[83] In the first half of the nineteenth century there were several important boards – the Poor Law Commissioners, the factory inspectorate, and the Tithe Commissioners – who were pretty much autonomous of

---

[80] Reproduced in Appendix 3, *Fulton Report 1968: The Civil Service 1: Report of the Committee 1966–1968* (1968), pp. 108–131.
[81] Kitson Clark, *Statesmen in Disguise*.   [82] Ibid.
[83] N. Fletcher, *A Praiseworthy Device for Pacifying Savages? What the Framers Meant by the English Text of the Treaty of Waitangi*, 2013 PhD Thesis at the University of Auckland, p. 179.

Parliament and could make their own regulations.[84] The same Trevelyan of the report fame notably offended expectations of neutrality in 1843.[85] Even later in the century, Ministers holding a seat in Parliament would sometimes become commissioners of Boards together with non-Parliamentary officials, but were 'never held accountable as a minister might be'.[86] Each Commissioner, civil servant or Minister, would be answerable publicly.

Only very gradually after the Parliamentary reforms of the 1830s, were the permanent, experienced officials, often with significant expertise, expected to accept a *subordinate* position to temporary politicians who often had little or no knowledge of, or sometimes even interest in, the subject matter of their portfolios. Even then, however, officials were not expected merely to obey but also to advise and influence. This was later to crystallise into the convention that civil servants should supply Ministers with free and frank advice. A new convention developed that officials would become the invisible 'guardians of [constitutional] continuity' in the unwritten constitution.[87] Their own status and special character would be defined by culture and convention but without much more in the way of other constitutional or legal scaffolding.

Dicey's famous formulation of the rule of law in 1885 needs to be read in light of these dramatic changes. He says that:

> With us every official, from the Prime Minister down to a constable or a collector of taxes is under the same responsibility for every act done without legal justification as any other citizen. . . . The official has the same duties as an ordinary citizen.[88]

When Dicey uses the word 'official' here and throughout his constitutional treatise, it is stripped of all the public law understandings that had defined and constrained an official qua official in the eighteenth and early nineteenth centuries. Indeed, the central thrust of Dicey's invocation of the rule of law is that there should be no special category of law for officials. Officials should be treated more like citizens than sovereigns, and are not considered to have any mediating role.

---

[84] S. Anderson, 'Public Law' in W. Cornish et al. (eds.), *The Oxford History of the Law of England XI 1820–1914 English Legal System* (Oxford University Press, 2010), pp. 354–355.
[85] Kitson Clark, *Statesmen in Disguise*, pp. 29–30.   [86] S. Anderson, 'Public Law', p. 355.
[87] To paraphrase P. Hennessy, "Harvesting the Cupboards: Why Britain Has Produced No Administrative Theory or Ideology in the Twentieth Century" *Transactions of the Royal Historical Society* 4 (1994), pp. 203–219, 206.
[88] A. V. Dicey, *An Introduction to the Study of the Law of the Constitution*, 10th ed. (London: MacMillan, 1959).

It is unsurprising that a Whig, such as Dicey, would be loath to defend the concept of office qua office, given the connotations of corruption and old Toryism that it carried by his time. But Dicey goes further. He ignores history. In his introduction he says that he is looking at the constitution strictly through the lens of his own time – 'not to criticise or venerate but to understand'. He accuses other more historically minded constitutional lawyers such as Freeman of 'antiquarianism'.[89] Dicey says that he is not interested in origins.[90] '[It] is not the role of a trained lawyer to know what the law of England was yesterday, still less what it was centuries ago, or what it ought to be tomorrow, but to know and be able to state what are the principles of law which actually and at the present day exist in England'.[91]

His associated disavowal of political theory[92] is almost certainly disingenuous. Like Bodin, he is trying to limit sovereignty. Unlike Bodin, who would do so by elevating the distinct constitutional role of the official, Dicey considers the best way to limit sovereignty is to treat the agents of sovereigns as ordinary individuals subject to ordinary law. But this seems like a vain hope in the face of what he himself recognised as the new collectivism, the new burgeoning administrative state,[93] and the increasingly large conferrals of power on the executive by Parliament.

It is not Dicey, but his acolyte Lord Hewart, who better captures the historical changes to the role of the official in his polemic *The New Despotism* 1929.[94] He draws implicit comparisons between present and past systems of administration. Gains by way of the new 'scientific and benevolent'[95] expertise in the civil service may have been made, he grudgingly admits,[96] but some of the merits of the old system have also been lost and replaced by 'anonymous' and 'unascertainable' civil servants,[97] who 'lack independence',[98] 'further the instructions of superiors'[99] under a 'secrecy which is inveterate',[100] lack personal responsibility[101] and operate under a 'cloak of obscurity'.[102] Whatever the gains on former centuries in terms of efficiency and responsiveness to social need, administration had undoubtedly become less local, less personal, and less participatory.

Lord Hewart's attacks both signalled and sustained a crisis in legitimacy for the administrative state. A new narrative was needed as the basis for its legitimacy. And in the 1960s the courts would begin to provide such a

---

[89] Ibid, p.15. [90] Ibid. [91] Ibid, pp. 14–15. [92] Ibid, p. 19.
[93] A. V. Dicey, 'The Development of Administrative Law in England', 31 (1915) *Law Quarterly Review*, 148–153.
[94] (London: Ernest Benn, 1929). [95] Ibid. p. 14. [96] Ibid. p. 14. [97] Ibid. p. 43.
[98] Ibid. p. 46. [99] Ibid. p. 46. [100] Ibid. p. 48. [101] Ibid. p. 43. [102] Ibid. p. 12.

narrative through iconic cases such as *Ridge v. Baldwin*,[103] *Anisminic Ltd v. Foreign Compensation Commission*[104] and *Padfield v. Minister of Agriculture and Food*[105] through which the courts undertook greater supervision of administration and simultaneously offered a new rationale for the administration of democratic responsiveness.[106]

Concluding Remarks

Administration has long been with us – but the core understandings of executive power have changed and so have the relationships between politicians and administrators. Key British constitutional writers marginalised the executive, and the administration. Blackstone overlooked Cabinet and Dicey overlooked the institutions and law relating to administration. Blackstone deliberately took a narrow view of executive power in order to satisfy his normative expectations of the separation of powers and to subdue tyranny. Dicey deliberately took a narrow view of administrators' powers – viewing officials as far as possible as ordinary persons – as a means for the protection of the citizen's liberty against a burgeoning administrative state. Meanwhile, almost as if in a different kingdom, actual administration subsisted and in the nineteenth century radically changed. The twentieth century common-law adjustments, as ever, occurred a long time after changes to authority and practice.

---

[103] [1964] AC 40 [HL].   [104] [1968] 2 AC 147 [HL].   [105] [1968] AC 997 [HL].
[106] See J. McLean, 'The Authority of the Administration' In E. Fisher, J. King, A. Young (eds.), *The Foundations and Future of Public Law* Oxford University Press 2020 (in press).

14
Judiciaries

JOSHUA GETZLER

Sources of the Judiciary

Judiciaries in England emerged from four interacting historical sources. At the foundation lay the authority of monarchs empowered to judge their subjects' rights, duties and status by virtue of the regal office. The second form of judiciary arose by royal delegation of decisional power to dedicated judges sitting in permanent courts of common law, or to executive courts with a more political mandate. A third source of judicial power was local and widely distributed, whereby groups or associations or sub-units of government solved disputes and allocated rights and duties as a process of self-direction, taking place for example in manors, boroughs, guilds, and church assemblies. The fourth source emerged from the great national tribunal of Parliament, which issued legislation, conducted trials, and reviewed and settled points of law from all other jurisdictions. The overlaps, seams, and frictions between royal, common-law, local, and parliamentary justice drove the constitutional development of the nation, as principles had to be devised to distribute the wielding of power in the various law-making and law-enforcing institutions. The common-law judiciary was constantly involved in deciding jurisdictional competencies: judges not only identified the primary rights and duties of parties, but also secondary sources of power to enforce, change and adapt rights and duties – authority to decide law.

It can be helpful to take a long view of the constitutional history of judiciaries, searching for origins and showing how contingent events could shape the system. We next turn to some key episodes in what is now a thousand years of continuous judicial practice in the English and British legal-constitutional order.

Norman Origins

Anglo-Saxon kings intervened sporadically in the local system of lordly and communal courts as supreme or guiding judge, but their main judicial role lay in the trying and punishment of crime.[1] William the Conqueror, reigning 1066–1087, claimed legitimate succession from Edward the Confessor and accordingly adopted the Coronation Oath of the Anglo-Saxon kings, promising to keep the peace, govern by law through honest servants, and give due judgments to all in the realm.[2] These duties took on fresh resonance in the context of the centralising Norman monarchy. William headed a reconstituted and integrated feudal order, where all other lords and tenants in the hierarchy of estates owed him fealty directly, having been confirmed in or admitted to their fees at the time of conquest. The mutual bond of loyalty and protection between king and subjects was affirmed in the Salisbury Oath of 1086.[3] By the reign of Henry I (1100–1135), the idea had taken root that all tenants could petition the king as of right to correct any failures of protection or adjudication by the local lord. The king might offer justice in person, or via the royal court, which 'preserves the use and custom of its law at all times and in all places with constant uniformity'.[4] This court dealt mainly with affairs of the royal demesne and the higher lords in direct tenurial relations with the Crown. However, subjects outside immediate tenurial relations could (for a fee) seek justice in this authoritative court, and many litigants chose the royal jurisdiction as superior to local tribunals.

Henry I also enlarged the Anglo-Saxon practice of inserting royal justices into the local shire, county, and borough courts to try crime and thereby strengthen the authority of local jurisdictions. In 1130 officials described as 'justiciars' were sent to ten counties and also to London to try wrongdoers. This experiment in governance seeded the growth of a national judiciary and a unified system of laws. The justiciars were originally regents empowered to rule when the king was absent, and were freely appointed both by William and his son and successor William Rufus (reigning 1087–1100), each of whom spent much time in Normandy. Regents with plenary power were typically trusted family members, such as Bishop Odo, brother of William I, or

---

[1] J. Hudson, *The Oxford History of the Laws of England, Volume II 871–1216* (Oxford: Oxford University Press, 2012) 66–92.
[2] D. Pratt, 'The Making of the Second English Coronation Ordo' (2018) 46 *Anglo-Saxon England* 147.
[3] J. C. Holt, '1086', in Holt (ed.), *Domesday Studies* (Woodbridge: Boydell, 1987) 41–64.
[4] L. J. Downer (ed. and trans), *Leges Henrici Primi* (1118) (Oxford: Clarendon Press, 1972) 97, 109.

Matilda of Scotland, wife of Henry I; both are recorded as sitting as judges. The king also appointed regents with limited mandates even when he was present in the realm, to extend the reach of his power and achieve specific goals. William I is recorded charging a group of 'leading men of the realm of England' (including lords and bishops) to make inquests of sheriffs and correct wrongful appropriations of church lands. Under William Rufus, the chief administrator of royal justice and finance was Ranulf Flambard, who adjudicated causes in the presence of the King. Henry I described Bishop Roger of Salisbury as his 'justiciar of the whole of England', and Ralph Basset was identified in 1129 as 'having the dignity of justice in all the realm of England'. The king still reserved important cases for his personal attention, particularly when they concerned land tenures and lordships emanating immediately from the Crown. But routine adjudications were increasingly delegated to permanent officials with specialised juridical and administrative roles, drawn from all estates, churchmen, lords and commoners, chosen for their skills and loyalty.

Another stream of regular and independent court justice emerged from administration of royal finance. The Norman kings by tradition used a chequered table to set out tallies recording fiscal debts and quittances, and they imported this system of 'exchequer' accounting to the realm of England. By the 1170s, barons of the Exchequer were appointed to run what was, in effect, a permanent Crown tax accounting office, and part of the work was to try land and contract claims bearing on fiscal liabilities.[5] By the 1190s, adjudication was separated from tax collection, and the panel making decisions was described as the Exchequer of Pleas. Early on, this specialist tribunal followed the king as a department of his prerogative council, but then convened independently at Westminster without the king. By the later twelfth century, the court had a legal power to decide practically any case involving property or contract, using inquisitorial procedures alongside the more formal forensics of witnesses, juries, and written evidence. The Exchequer of Pleas set the pattern for much judicial development that followed.

The Angevin Judiciary

On Henry I's death, there was protracted civil war as rival family members battled for the Crown and, in the ensuing anarchy, justice broke down and

---

[5] E. Ant and S. D. Church (eds.), *The Dialogue of the Exchequer* (1180) (Oxford: Oxford University Press, 2017).

tenures were disrupted. On the accession in 1154 of Henry II, grandson of Henry I, peace was restored and major steps taken to return the country to orderly rule. The new King was vigorous in dispensing personal justice, most commonly in the setting of a large assembly of senior prelates and lords being tenants in chief.[6] This was the great court *coram rege* ('in the presence of the king'), and it followed Henry as he moved around the kingdom, deciding important cases of land, status and crime. The major mischief to be corrected was the breakdown of protection of tenures in the manorial courts of the lords. The Crown began to insist that lords' courts do justice in 'real' or property matters on the initiation of a royal writ *de recto* ('of right') issuing from the king's chancery. In default of satisfactory lord's justice, the case would be removed from feudal jurisdiction to the sheriff's county court or to a royal court, there to be decided definitively.

Around a decade into his long reign (1154–1189), Henry II introduced fresh property actions, using a speedy form of jury trial conducted by a royal judge, to put right recent dispossessions and also to correct nuisances or interferences in land use between neighbours. These were the 'petty assizes' of *novel dissesin* (recent dispossession) and nuisance. The aim was to restore tenants to secure possession and quiet enjoyment by reversing recent disruptions – a juridical technique borrowed from Roman classical law – thereby enabling and inducing the local manorial courts to sort out the long-term stability of titles. The assizes soon expanded to embrace matters of inheritance, marriage rights, and church patronage. From 1176, judges were appointed to go on circuit ('in eyre') taking the new king's justice to every corner of the realm.[7] The justices in eyre sat with local juries charged to collect and assess evidence and so integrated elements of local peer justice. Important cases could be removed to the court *coram rege*, or the Exchequer of Pleas, or (by the time of Henry's successor Richard I, reigning 1189–1199) a new court of general jurisdiction at Westminster, known as the Court of Common Bench (or Common Pleas). This began as a group of seven or eight professional judges meeting in four regular terms, and attending purely to judicial business, divorced from politics and finance.

---

[6] Constitutions of Clarendon 1164, c 11.
[7] P. A. Brand, '"*Multis Vigiliis Excogitatam et Inventam*": Henry II and the Creation of the English Common Law', in Brand, *The Making of the Common Law* (London: Hambledon Press, 1992) 77–102; Hudson, *History* (n 1), 574–626.

The High Medieval Judiciary

The system of royal courts remained in flux in the thirteenth century, balanced between the political jurisdiction of the king's personal and conciliar power, and partnership with local justice. Richard I was often absent from the kingdom during the decade of his reign, giving the lawyers space to work and experiment with their writs of action. The reign of John (1199–1216) put the nascent system under strain. John took the Common Bench of professional judges with him on his journeys across the kingdom, and blended it into his court *coram rege* as a re-assertion of personalised royal judicial power. In 1209, he suspended the regular sittings of the Bench as an independent tribunal at Westminster. The lords thought that John was adding too much of his personal prerogative to the running of law and government, and they sought a restoration of arms-length justice at Westminster. This can be seen in the text of Magna Carta, a declaration of constitutional principles imposed on the king by the chief barons and prelates in 1215.[8] Magna Carta amounted to a package of measures for the protection of lords' estates, inheritance, and jurisdiction, and restraint of unilateral royal takings and taxes, underpinned by guarantees of fair and neutral procedures of adjudication. Common Bench was to sit permanently at Westminster, so that 'ordinary lawsuits shall not follow the royal court around'. Juries (that is, local peer groups drawn from the membership of manors, vills, and towns) and not judges should decide guilt in the assizes, and local judges should join royal judges there to decide fair remedies. Nobles were to be tried by their peers, not commoners. Confession alone without witnesses would be insufficient to prove guilt.[9] Chapter 39 elaborated the core idea of due process:

> No free man shall be seized or imprisoned, or stripped of his rights or possessions, or outlawed or exiled, or deprived of his standing in any other way, nor will we proceed with force against him, or send others to do so, except by the lawful judgment of his equals or by the law of the land.[10]

By chapter 40 the king promised 'To no one will we sell, to no one deny or delay right or justice', and chapter 45 added, 'We will appoint as justices, constables, sheriffs, or other officials, only men that know the law of the realm and are minded to keep it well', which purported to take bribery and political favouritism out of royal adjudication and administration. These

---

[8] J. C. Holt, *Magna Carta*, 2nd ed. (Cambridge: Cambridge University Press, 1992).
[9] Magna Carta 1215, Chapters 17–22, 38.
[10] Reiterated in Liberty of Subject Act 1354 (28 Edw III).

legal-constitutional elements informing Magna Carta suggest that the political elites had accepted a large dose of the common lawyers' own ideology. This is especially striking considering that the practice of common law was only about sixty years old in 1215, albeit resting on older Anglo-Saxon roots.

John died the next year and Henry III, then a minor just turned nine, was crowned. Perhaps because of the consequent gap in personal rule, the court *coram rege* ceased to involve the king presiding in person surrounded by justices and courtiers. Instead, the judges of this court came to sit mainly at Westminster alongside Exchequer and Common Bench, known as the Court of King's Bench, with the king's presence in that court now only notional. King's Bench dealt with two broad areas closely associated with the Crown's prerogative justice, namely the repression of wrongdoing – crimes, trespasses – and the control of royal servants and delegates. King's Bench jurisdiction thus reflected the Crown's role as a public actor charged with government. Common Bench remained the senior court, since Magna Carta gave it a constitutionally protected control of the great business of land titles and associated private transactions, and moreover guaranteed it a permanent seat in Westminster Hall. In the high medieval period, Common Bench had some ten times the volume of judicial business of King's Bench, and its judges prospered proportionately from the flow of fees into their court, so that a justiceship in Common Bench was the more desirable appointment for ambitious lawyers. This imbalance changed with time. The King's Bench developed the trespass jurisdiction creatively to become a court of general competence, pulling in land title cases by allowing feigned pleading of fence breaking, forcible invasion, wilful damage and assault. Similar ploys were used to compete for business from Exchequer; trespass writs could be adapted to cover merchant law, where sales could be enforced and debts collected in the guise of repression of frauds. King's Bench also had the advantage of enhanced arrest powers associated with tort and crime, allowing litigants an easier route to enforcement than the more limited mesne procedures of the rival common-law courts.

Both Common Bench and King's Bench joined in extending common-law jurisdiction throughout the realm by new modes of itinerant justice. By the 1270s, the eyre circuits were superseded by assizes, whereby delegated royal judges, including serjeants on commission, would try cases of property, trespass and crime on circuit, either in pairs, or as sole judges joined by a local knight, empanelling local juries to return verdicts triggering common-law remedies. These came to be known as '*nisi prius*' hearings, the judge being authorised to run a trial 'unless before' there had been a full formal hearing initiated in Westminster. The judge on circuit would give a conditional order on verdict, upon which the legal decision would be returned to Westminster to be reviewed by the royal justices, who thereby kept a close control of the juristic content of decision-making, without having to be involved in the forensics of the trial. Exchequer soon joined the system, which allowed every subject of the king to turn to the expert common-law courts for legal redress without having to trudge to the capital.[11]

Common-law trials revolved around the writs of action, being terse stereotyped commands in the name of the king, issued from his chancery, requiring a sheriff or other official to summon litigants to answer for a particular claim or render a duty before a court. At trial, counsel would argue before the judge whether the court should admit certain sworn evidence or valid documentation, and whether the evidence could activate the particular claim as pleaded. The substance of the argument was concealed within formal analysis of forensics, claim and remedy, with judges debating counsel over the most fine-grained legal points and constantly manoeuvring the onus of proof of particular points. The nascent system of common-law pleading and argumentation was restated using the revived vocabulary of Roman jurisprudence in the great treatise *On the Laws and Customs of England*, probably written by a group of judges around 1230 and completed under the name of the royal justice Henry de Bracton around 1260.[12] This codification of early common-law practice showed a fierce commitment to legality, the supposition that power must operate according to established rules as interpreted by independent courts. Bracton's rule-of-law ethos extended to the actions of the sovereign Crown:

> The king must not be under man but under God and under the law, because the law makes the king ... for there is no *rex* where will rules rather than *lex*. ... The king has a superior ... the law by which he was made king. Also his curia, namely, the earls and barons, because if he is without a bridle, that is without law, they ought to put the bridle on him.[13]

This idea was refined by later judges and jurists into the principle that the courts would presume the king wished to do right by law and avoid evil, and the courts would act on that presumption. 'We understand that he [the king] wishes to be guided, in his own Court, by right and reason, as the others

---

[11] W. R. Riddell, 'New Trial at the Common Law' (1916) 26 *Yale Law Journal* 49.
[12] S. E. Thorne (trans), Cambridge, MA: Belknap/Harvard University Press 1968–1977, 4 vols.
[13] Ibid, vol. 2, 33, 110.

will', argued Serjeant Herle in a case of 1312 that was much reported and circulated.[14] The idea that the king was presumed to do right was the corollary of the idea that the king could do no wrong, and the courts, by interpretation of law, would help him avoid wrongdoing that would diminish his rulership.[15]

The High Court of Parliament and the Hierarchy of Review

The three common-law courts were formed before Parliament as permanent organs of the constitution; but that latter institution must also be counted as a great court of the realm, wielding a powerful original, reviewing and appellate jurisdiction alongside its conciliar and legislative functions. It was early known as the 'High Court of Parliament', and still bears that ancient title.[16] It grew out of assemblies of barons and magnates in the 1260s that advised the Crown, debated national and local policies, and voted supply and support to the Crown for its ventures at home and abroad. The assembly came to be divided into the two houses of lords and commons, with bishops sitting in the lords. Many judges sat in one or the other house, for example in the lords as barons or clerics (some half of the early medieval judiciary fitted one of those two categories), or as members of the commons elected by boroughs or shires. Judges were also regularly summoned to the bar of one or other house to advise the members on points of law. Parliament under Edward I (reigning 1272–1307) became a major partner in government, legislating with great detail and precision to codify and develop matters of jurisdiction, procedure and curial remedies, with topics covered including the accountability of guardians, stewards, bailiffs, and merchants, the restraint of grants of wealth to the church, and the regulation of land title, inheritance, debt, escheat and forfeiture. This great programme of statutes was regarded at the time as a series of general judgments as to how the common law of the realm should best be applied, and much of this legislation was drafted by the judges themselves, to solve problems that escaped solution in the case-driven business of the ordinary courts. In 1305, Chief

---

[14] *R v. Prior of St James and Walda* (1312) 6 Edw II; 34 *Selden Society* 73, 74.
[15] Sir John Fortescue, *De Laudibus Legum Angliae* (c 1470 published c 1543) c 13, 14.
[16] Sir Henry Finch, *Nomotechnia: A Description of the Common Laws of England* (London: Society of Stationers, 1613) ff 21v–22; Sir Matthew Hale, *The Jurisdiction of the Lords House, or Parliament, Considered according to Antient Records* (F. Hargrave (ed.), London: Cadell, 1796) 17, 84–86, 205–208.

Justice Hengham in Common Bench interrupted a serjeant-at-law (a senior counsel), who was expounding how the court should apply distraint for debt as set out in the 1285 Statute of Westminster. Hengham snapped at counsel: 'Do not gloss the statute, for we understand it better than you; we made it'.[17] Hengham was an interesting judicial figure: a cleric as well as judge, he had been penalised in a purge of the higher judiciary in 1290, but readmitted to favour and high office after paying an enormous fine. He seemed to embody the confidence and independence of the common-law judge, confronting Edward I in Parliament when the King summoned a duchess before the bar of Parliament to face an attainder of eight serious charges with no notice given. Protesting the lack of fair warning, Hengham spoke for all the judges assembled in Parliament, asserting that –

> 'the law wills that no one be taken by surprise in the king's court; but if you had your way, this lady would answer in court for what she has not been warned to answer by writ; therefore she should be warned by writ of the article of which she is to answer, and this is the law of the land'; then the king, who was very wise, arose and said: 'I have nothing to do with your disputations, but, God's blood!, you will give me a good writ before you arise hence'.[18]

The point of the story is not only that the King was dismayed by the challenge thrown at him in Parliament by a senior judge, covered by his jesting complaint (which was remarkable enough), but that the King publicly submitted to the judicial officer's arguments that Parliament must uphold natural justice and prospective rule-making as embedded constitutional principle.

Parliament's authority was at its highest when it legislated with the consent of the king, though either or both houses could pass resolutions and make judgments without him. Conversely, the Crown had once freely made decrees changing the law of the land, but it was gradually accepted that the king must only legislate in Parliament. Parliament also acted – without the king – as a judicature, with original power to attaint or impeach powerful subjects.[19] The House of Lords led as judicial body within Parliament, though after 1681, the Commons joined in bills of attainder, and claimed its

---

[17] *Aumeye's Case* (1305) YB Mich 33 Edw I (RS) pl 40 f 79–83.
[18] Reported by Bereford C. J. in *Goldrington's Case* (1310) YB Mich 3 Edw II pl [16], Vulgate 81, 82.
[19] F. W. Maitland, 'Introduction to *Memoranda de Parliamento, 1305*' (1893), in H. Cam (ed.), *Selected Historical Essays of F. W. Maitland* (Cambridge: Cambridge University Press, 1957) 52–96; F. W. Maitland, *The Constitutional History of England* (Cambridge: Cambridge University Press, 1931) 64–96.

own impeachment jurisdiction applicable to commoners in public office. The Lords might also empanel a committee of legally minded members to guide its jurisdiction as a review court, and when resolutions of technical law were needed the committee could call before it the judges and serjeants to argue and advise. Review here might effortlessly merge into fresh law-making.

Common Bench and (especially) King's Bench could also review inferior jurisdictions for error on the face of the record, so ensuring due application of extant law; but the fact findings of the lower court could not be appealed, as determination of fact was the province of the jury involving face-to-face assessment of witnesses. There could be an order of a new trial by the reviewing court if errors of law infected the fact-finding process. Much legal argumentation concerned where decisional authority within a court lay, for example, was determination of libel a matter of fact for the jury or law for the judge? The judges of King's Bench could convene with judges drawn from Common Bench to review decisions of Exchequer, or they could join with Exchequer barons to review Common Bench. That superior court of review, up and running as early as 1347, was known as the Court of Exchequer Chamber (named from the room where it habitually met). It was less common for King's Bench to be reviewed by judges of the other two courts because of its closeness to prerogative power. Review lay from Exchequer Chamber, and also directly from King's Bench, to the House of Lords sitting as a judicial committee. Decisions of Exchequer Chamber were supposed to settle the law by majority ruling of the superior justices, but strategic voting could undermine the sense of reasoned collegiate decision-making. In 1610, Chief Justice of Common Pleas Coke in an Exchequer Chamber of seven judges protested that a majority of four reviewing judges could there overturn a unanimous judgment of five King's Bench justices, resulting in four superior judges prevailing over eight.[20] When Justice Walmsley proposed to do just that, the Chief Baron of Exchequer Tanfield rejoined on the meta-point of procedure: 'That is your opinion, but you stand alone and our opinion is to the contrary.' Coke added waspishly that his Common Pleas colleague Walmsley was prone to re-open settled points of law simply because an influential opposing justice (such as Coke himself) was not on the bench that day. Arguably such squabbles and power plays ended up strengthening the law, as unsatisfactory points could be scrutinised,

---

[20] *Maine v. Peacher* (1610) in J. H. Baker and S. F. C. Milsom (eds.), *Sources of English Legal History: Private Law to 1750*, 2nd ed. (Oxford: Oxford University Press, 2010) 490–491.

destabilised, and gotten rid of by a persistent judge building a coalition against a former vulnerable consensus.

From the late thirteenth century, the strong partnership of Parliament and the courts in developing the common law only added to the prestige and importance of the royal courts as places of adjudication. The siting of the three common-law courts, together with the Court of Chancery, in adjacent corners of the great Westminster Hall of the Angevin kings, adjoining and even dominating the Houses of Parliament, emphasised the overlapping roles of these two branches of government. Serjeants and judges in the courts parsed the growing body of statutory provisions, writ collections, and former judgments and curial debates, exploring how the rules fitted together and how actions should be pursued with an eye on the best practice of former court cases, as well as the latest policies initiated by Parliament. The debates in court were watched by student barristers and the most interesting recorded in elaborate reports, intended for teaching as well as professional consultation, known as Year Books. Another important source of legal ideas and interpretations were the 'readings' in the Inns of Court, where senior lawyers lectured on the meaning of important statutes and showed their juniors how to read and apply legislation within the framework of the common law. Lawyers compiled registers of writs with glosses explaining the practicalities of pleading, and edited collections of interesting judicial decisions.[21] By the mid fifteenth century, epitomes of the leading cases ranging over the main subjects of the law (such as land title) became essential tools for lawyers constructing court arguments, and this added to the sense of judges as oracles of the law.

The voluminous and difficult technical literatures of the law, and the long years of arduous training required to master these, added to the self-regard and elitism of the profession, with judges at the apex of esteem. Large professional incomes for counsel prior to their elevation to the bench helped cultivate independence, and avoiding political intrigue and patronage once appointed was usually a prudential strategy. The judges remembered the fate of Chief Justice Tresilian of King's Bench who, in 1386, sided with Richard II and gave an advisory opinion upholding the king's objections to a commission of barons seeking to curb royal power. For this Tresilian was attainted in Parliament and executed. Judges were members of the ruling class concerned to maintain order, and they contributed substantially to social policy and

---

[21] E. Shanks and S. F. C. Milsom (eds.), *Novae Narrationes* (1963) 80 *Selden Society*; J. H. Baker (ed.), *Spelman's Reports Vol 2* (1978) 94 *Selden Society*.

discipline through their work in court, for example during turbulent periods such as the aftermath of the Black Death in the late fourteenth century when the economic order shook,[22] or again in the Wars of the Roses in the fifteenth which undermined the lines of feudal fealty. Judges, however, set limits for the law in deciding fraught political questions. In 1461, the House of Lords summoned the judges to take their advice on the legality of the Duke of York's claim to the throne as Edward IV. The judges declined to answer, stating that this was a policy question to be decided by peers of the king's blood and not by the king's judges.[23]

The Prerogative Courts

The common-law system had reached maturity by 1400, but it never attained a monopoly over the provision of justice at the national level. Both original causes and appeals lay directly to the king's court of close advisers, his 'Privy Council', operating as an informal executive court echoing the form and function of the original *curia coram rege*. As England launched colonial ventures in the 1500s, the Privy Council sitting as a judicial committee provided a plenary court of justice for the empire. In the later 1400s, the Privy Council delegated authority to a further specialist executive court of high prestige and power, regularly trying matters of crime, public order, market abuse, and good morals, and comprising Crown councillors, prelates, and judges who met in the Star Chamber in the Palace of Westminster. Yet another executive court had emerged in the prior century, certainly operating by the 1320s, run by the king's Lord Chancellor, later assisted by the Master of Rolls, the Lord Keeper and other deputies. This Court of Chancery was distinct from the Chancery as the justice office issuing common-law writs. The Chancellor held this court 'in camera', hearing actions initiated by suitors by petition informally stating their case. In Chancery suits the judge sat without a jury, and took evidence directly from witnesses including the parties, and also from widely admissible paper records, using subpoenas, interrogatories and oaths to extract the truth. Where necessary, cases were sent to King's Bench to decide legal issues needing strict-form legal evidence before a jury (as per Magna Carta, ruling that serious legal matters such as

---

[22] R. C. Palmer, *English Law in the Age of the Black Death 1348–1381: A Transformation of Governance and Law* (Chapel Hill: University of North Carolina Press, 1993).

[23] *Rot Parl* v. 376 (39 Hen VI no 12); G. Sayles, 'Medieval Judges as Legal Consultants' (1940) 56 *Law Quarterly Review* 247.

land titles and crimes could not be decided on confession of the parties themselves). In addition to wide inquisitorial powers, the Chancellor had an array of remedies unavailable to the common-law courts, including declaration of rights and supervised personal orders constraining the parties' formal contract and property rights and preventing harsh or abusive exercise of those rights. Chancery jurisdiction rested on a delegation of the prerogative of the Crown as *parens patriae* or father-confessor of the nation; the Chancellor by uncovering and assessing the detailed facts driving transactions could claim to be enforcing men's conscience or self-knowledge. The equity judges freely drew ideas from civil and canon law and theology, and were usually high-ranking prelates up until Thomas More's appointment in 1529. Mary I briefly restored bishops to the role to help her push back against Protestantism, and this experience delegitimated the participation of clerics in the secular court system thereafter.

Other prerogative courts deploying civilian doctrine and procedure included High Court of Admiralty, which dealt with cases on the high seas from the late fourteenth century, and Court of Requests for debt (known before 1529 as the Court of Poor Man's causes). There was, in addition, the extensive and ancient system of church courts based on the bishops' sees, dealing with family, personal inheritance, charities, reputation and morals using Romano-canonical procedure. Henry VIII established an equitable Court of Wards in 1540, dealing with real inheritance and the enforcement of mortmain and tax policies; and the courts of Augmentation, First Fruits, and High Commission, controlling church wealth and policing religious practice in the wake of the Reformation.

Common lawyers, including royal justices, might help run these executive courts as part of conciliar government. There was an analogue with the justices of the peace who wielded wide powers over the local population as a kind of prerogative justice on a local scale. But there was also hostility towards the national-level prerogative tribunals as too discretionary and political in approach, undermining the formal justice and jury trials of the ordinary courts. The common-law judges refused to extend comity (recognition) to prerogative remedies and doctrines in common-law proceedings, and even issued prohibitions against resort to prerogative courts.[24]

---

[24] J. H. Baker, *The Oxford History of the Laws of England, Volume VI: 1483–1558* (Oxford: Oxford University Press, 2003) 117–319.

The Tudor Judiciary

The royal courts took on much new business during the tumultuous period of religious and political upheaval and agrarian reorganisation under the Tudor dynasty. Indeed, the common law may have contributed to the rapid pace of change by ratifying concentrations of private property in land, freeing factor and credit markets from medieval controls, and weakening guilds. At the same time, common-law business in basic contract and debt leaked away to merchant tribunals and prerogative and church courts, perhaps encouraged by royal policy. Yet the king also needed the help of able common lawyers to represent him in courts and Parliament, pen his statutes, and promote his fiscal claims. In 1533 and 1535 respectively, the Court of Chancery and the Parliament were pressured by the Crown's law officers to weaken the trusts and wills that protected estates from the king's feudal taxes. The consequences were severe: the estates system was thrown into disarray, and the independence of the entire judiciary and the stability of the constitution was brought into doubt.[25] Henry VIII soon learned that his power had its limits; he found his legitimacy weakened by these aggressions against settled laws and institutions and, by 1540, was forced to concede ground to the landed and mercantile classes, permitting a restoration of wide trust and succession powers in return for a negotiated tax settlement.

In Elizabeth I's reign (1558–1603), judicial prestige and independence was afforced by the appointment to the bench of many capable and confident lawyers. Increased commercial activity enlarged business for all the courts, prerogative and common law. The courts competed for lucrative work regulating novel transaction forms including leases and secured debts. King's Bench expanded its jurisdiction using its basic trespass writs based on wrongdoing and its prerogative writs to control public power; its actions could now encompass almost any claim. Common Pleas and Exchequer slipped back, but Chancery business continued to expand in the fields of trusts and agency.

Intra-court competition over jurisdiction raised a further constitutional question of the basis for common-law creativity and change. Could judges in effect legislate, recognising new interests and actions by freely adapting existing concepts and procedures to meet the needs of present-day litigants?

---

[25] *Re Lord Dacre of the South* (1533) YB Pasch 27 Hen. VIII, f 7, pl 22 (arguments in the Exchequer Chamber); *Spelman's Reports Vol 2*, 228–23c (coercion of the judges); Statute of Uses 1535; generally Baker, *History* (n 24), 661–683.

Or ought the judges be conservative, and defer to Parliament and the Crown to devise solutions to novel problems? An artful solution was evolved by the great common lawyer Edward Coke (1552–1634), successively Attorney General under Elizabeth and Chief Justice of Common Pleas and King's Bench under her successor James I. In a series of learned judgments and writings, Coke portrayed the law as a form of public reason, resting on timeless principles, but mediated by the customs of the courts and the skill of the lawyers in adapting those customs to new situations. Coke's work was widely studied and was seen to embody the deep traditions of the common law in the thinking of a single jurist. In the time of James (reigning 1603–1625), Coke's career took a new turn as he assumed judicial office and applied his common-law theories to the challenges of constitutional power.

The Stuart Judiciary

Coke presaged his legal-constitutional ideology in his report of the 1603 King's Bench case of *Semayne*, three years before his elevation to head the Common Pleas in 1606. In that case a Crown sheriff had broken into a house to collect assets in acquittance of debt by a lodger, without pre-announcement or request for permission from the householder. Coke's report acknowledged the sheriff's power as having a sound royal basis, but hedged it with constitutional requirements:

> That the house of every one is to him as his castle and fortress, as well for his defence against injury and violence as for his repose. ... In all cases when the King is party, the sheriff ... may break the party's house, either to arrest him, or to do other execution of the K[ing]'s process, if otherwise he cannot enter. But before he breaks it, he ought to signify the cause of his coming, and to make request to open doors.[26]

In 1607, Chief Justice Coke affirmed the importance of due process and protection of property, denying James the power to try in person a case involving common-law rights to land. Coke argued that the royal delegation of adjudicative power to his professional judges was final, and no personal dispensation of royal justice interfering in common-law jurisdiction was possible. Common-law causes were 'not to be decided by natural reason but by artificial reason and judgment of law, which law is an art which requires long study and experience'.[27] In 1610, Coke ruled that the king could

---

[26] (1604) 5 Coke's Reports 91.   [27] *Case of Prohibitions* (1607) 12 Coke's Reports 63.

not issue prerogative decrees changing the laws, voiding an order of James that purported to regulate building in London. According to Coke, 'the King cannot change any part of the common law, nor create any offence, by his proclamation, which was not an offence before, without parliament'. The judiciary, not the king, should decide the boundaries of royal power, for 'The King has no prerogative but that which the law of the land allows him.'[28] This was to abstract the Crown as a corporate office held by the king as defined by law; he did not have an absolute power in his person to define his own command.[29]

In *Dr Bonham's Case*, also decided in 1610, Coke extended the power of common-law review to the actions of the Parliament itself. He held void a statute empowering a physicians' college to try disputes over admission to the college; the power was bad as any adjudication of interests required an independent judge, and here the college was an interested party.[30]

> One cannot be Judge and attorney for any of the parties ... [T]he common law will control Acts of Parliament, and sometimes adjudge them to be utterly void; for when an act of Parliament is against common right and reason, or repugnant, or impossible to be performed, the common law will control it, and adjudge such an Act to be void.

By subjecting statutes to a test of 'common right and reason' Coke may have meant nothing more than a power to identify irrational, contradictory or illogical laws, justified on the basis that the sovereign legislator could not have intended to make incoherent or impossible rules.[31] But Coke's rivals, including Lord Chancellor Ellesmere and the Attorney General Francis Bacon, attacked the presumption that judges could review and suspend both statute and prerogative. Coke was demoted, and then dismissed for refusing to discuss with the king how he might decide an upcoming controversial case.

The weakening of the judiciary by James was exacerbated by his son Charles I (reigning 1625–1649). Coke's attempts to constrain the prerogative to 'what the law allows' were swept away in the *Case of Ship Money* in 1637, when Exchequer Chamber held by seven judges against five that Charles could validly interpret the extent of his own military and fiscal prerogatives without challenge in court or pre-authorisation by parliament. This judicial

---

[28] *Case of Proclamations* (1611) 12 Coke's Reports 74.
[29] E. Kantorowicz, *The King's Two Bodies: A Study in Medieval Political Theology* (Princeton NJ: Princeton University Press, 1957).
[30] (1610) 8 Coke's Reports 107. See also 3 *Blackstone's Commentaries* 25.
[31] I. Williams, 'Dr Bonham's Case and "void" statutes' (2006) 27 *Journal of Legal History* 111.

deference, in effect, voided the *Case of Proclamations* and rendered the prerogative non-justiciable. Charles gaoled resisters of the Ship Money tax, including members of Parliament. In a pushback in 1640, Parliament passed the Habeas Corpus Act, banning imprisonment without precise legal cause. Then in 1641, on the brink of civil war, the majority judges legalising the expansion of Ship Money were impeached by Parliament for subverting the constitution. That parliament also abolished most of the prerogative courts, saving the useful Chancery. The conduct of the courts was clearly a core issue in the run-up to civil war. It is a tantalising question whether the cataclysm of war, regicide and dictatorship that followed would have played out differently had just two judges of Exchequer Chamber in 1637 found against the King in court and required that Parliament authorise the new tax of ship money.

The battle over prerogative resumed under the restored Stuarts. Chief Justice Hale in King's Bench (who had helped broker the Restoration of the monarchy in 1660) and Lord Chancellor Nottingham brought high standards of probity, skill and political neutrality to the courts in the 1670s, but other parts of the constitution frayed. A fresh Habeas Corpus Act was passed in 1679 to protect members of Parliament from pre-emptive imprisonment, as the Whig lords waged a bitter campaign to exclude James, the King's Catholic brother, from accession to the Crown. On Charles II's death in 1685, a rebellion against James II was defeated. James's new Chief Justice of King's Bench George Jeffreys then organised extraordinary assizes in lieu of parliamentary treason trials, and executed 300 Whig rebels, including the leader James Scott, natural son of Charles II, who had claimed the throne in the Whig Protestant cause. Jeffreys ordered the transportation of over a thousand more rebels to penal settlements abroad. Jeffreys was accused of launching an arbitrary judicial terror far worse than anything that had passed in old Star Chamber. His rule established, King James then claimed a prerogative power to dispense with the Test Acts and admit non-Anglicans loyal to him (notably, Catholics) to high office, so acting against the express will of Parliament. Late in 1685 James prorogued Parliament. He then expanded the military under a purged leadership, and he replaced local justices of the peace who controlled elections, in an attempt to sway the next election to Parliament and pack it with his supporters. He appointed an Ecclesiastical Commission as an executive court under Jeffreys to root out Protestant opposition in church and universities. He dismissed many judges, relying on Jeffreys, now Lord Chancellor, to pack the courts with his partisans, many of them legally unqualified.

The King's attempt to enlarge the prerogative and supplant the elites with his followers led to rebellion in the summer of 1688. James was abandoned by his military and fled the country. A Convention Parliament met to install William of Orange and his wife Mary, daughter of James, as dual rulers. The coup came to be known as the Glorious Revolution, with constitutional principles restated and buttressed in the Bill of Rights passed by the Convention Parliament, with assent of the newly installed Crown, in 1689–1690. This constitutional document made clear that Crown prerogative was always to be subordinate to statute, and could not be used to levy taxes or flout the will of Parliament; it also affirmed the privileges of Parliament as a deliberative body and condemned the use of judicial courts for political trials that ought to be reserved to Parliament. At the close of William's reign the Act of Settlement 1701 was passed enforcing a Protestant succession, and a measure was tacked on protecting judicial tenure during good behaviour (*quamdiu se bene gesserint*) rather than service at the monarch's pleasure.[32] This constitutional sweep-up may have reflected lingering anxieties at how the judiciary had been attacked and subverted at the turning of the last reign. After 1701 new monarchs retained the privilege of reappointing all judges, who lost their commissions on the death of the prior ruler; but it became the custom that the king should reappoint all capable judges on accession, and in 1760 that position was entrenched by legislation.[33]

The Eighteenth-Century Judiciary

England made political and constitutional union with Scotland in 1707 to form the kingdom of Great Britain. Wales as a principality had been integrated into England since medieval times, and Ireland formed a separate monarchy, largely ruled from England, and formally folded into a new United Kingdom in 1801. Scotland and Ireland maintained separate judiciaries, with appeal avenues to the Lords at Westminster. The formation of the 1707 union made the modern British state and was also associated with vast extensions of empire in North America, India, China and Australasia, and new assertiveness against European rivals. It was also a period of intense partisanship as Whigs confronted Tories in a scrabble for power and profit in

---

[32] R. Stevens, *The English Judges: Their Role in the Constitution* (Oxford: Hart Publishing, 2002) 1–13.
[33] 1 Geo III c 23; D. Lemmings, 'The Independence of the Judiciary in Eighteenth Century England' in P. Birks (ed.), *The Life of the Law* (London: Hambledon Press, 1993) 125–149.

a rapidly expanding polity. In 1714 Lord Chief Justice Thomas Parker convened a group of regents to ensure that the Stuarts were kept out after Queen Anne's death (sister of Mary), and the Hanoverian George I was made king. In 1725, pro-Stuart Tories took their revenge on Parker, now Lord Chancellor Macclesfield, and had him impeached for misappropriation of funds in court. This led to an anti-corruption drive in the courts led by the succeeding chancellor Peter King, who inaugurated a newly professionalised career structure including improved salary and pension rights, and insisted that officials eschew conflicts of interest. Strong judges were recruited from the bar, most having garnered prior political experience serving as Solicitor General or Attorney General. The Lord Chancellors Hardwicke, Bathurst, Thurlow, Wedderburn, and Eldon all fitted this model, as did Chief Justices of King's Bench Mansfield, Kenyon and Ellenborough. The Lord Chancellor served *ex officio* as a powerful minister in Cabinet and was speaker of the House of Lords; this anomaly of a politically active judge was accepted, perhaps on the basis that chancellors were readily replaced if they crossed lines of proper judicial conduct. It was also common for the chief justices of King's Bench, notably Mansfield and Ellenborough, to serve in Cabinet whilst holding judicial office. Yet despite this mixing of powers and functions, judges might oppose government policies when applying the law in court; and perhaps they might warn the administration from within when it drifted into illegal or unconstitutional acts.[34]

Judicial discipline of government took many forms. The courts could try agents of the Crown in normal litigation for wrongdoing (e.g. tort, crime), and also curb executive conduct via special actions known as prerogative writs and petitions of right and grace.[35] The core of judicial review lay in King's Bench, where servants of the Crown acting outside authority or abusing their authority could be disciplined by writs of certiorari, prohibition and mandamus, at the motion of any subject whose rights or liberties were thereby injured.[36] The Crown or other interested parties could also bring action or suits against officials who had breached their duties, including actions for misfeasance in public office or breach of trust.[37] Perhaps the most

---

[34] D. Lemmings, *Law and Government in England During the Long Eighteenth Century: From Consent to Command* (London: Palgrave Macmillan, 2011) 17–80.
[35] *R v. Windham* (Case of *Wadham College, Oxford*) (1776) 1 Cowper 377 (per Mansfield LCJKB).
[36] 3 *Blackstone's Commentaries* 42.
[37] *Charitable Corporation v. Sutton* (1742) 2 Atkin 400 (Hardwicke LC); *R v. Bembridge* (1783) 3 Douglas 327 (per Mansfield LCJKB).

constitutionally important area here was the use of trespass actions to discipline Crown agents who intruded on the property or privacy of a person without authority, recalling the 1603 precedent of *Semayne's Case*. In *Entick v. Carrington* in 1765, Crown agents were sued in trespass after entering a house looking for incriminating evidence with no warrant, under a claimed prerogative authority to protect the public. Lord Camden held that no general assertion of state interest could be used to justify intrusion on property rights, and nominal damages were charged against the aberrant Crown servants to uphold those rights.[38] In this period, the judiciary also elaborated protections of personal liberty based on the writ of *habeas corpus* as re-founded in 1679, requiring a show of legal authority for any intrusions on personal liberty.[39]

Suing the Crown directly to make it fulfil its positive obligations, or to pay out for vicarious liability of its agents, was more difficult. The first point was addressed in the great *Bankers Case* of 1691–1700, where the Court of Exchequer Chamber, backed by the House of Lords, ruled that the courts could bind the Crown to pay its bond debt obligations, overcoming a plea of prerogative immunity, and utilising the legal powers of the Barons of the Exchequer to order the Treasurer to pay as contracted. The deeper principle at stake was that the Crown could not use its prerogative position to evade the legal supervision of public finance. Petitions of Right were used liberally to enforce a wide range of Crown contracts or other obligations, but an array of immunities undermined enforcement and the law was unpredictable. Not until 1947 did Parliament finally vote to make the Crown regularly liable on obligations as if it were a private actor.[40]

The leading judge in the *Bankers' Case* was Sir John Holt (1642–1710), Chief Justice of King's Bench. In 1703, he gave a dissenting judgment in the case of *Ashby v. White*,[41] this time turning the power of common-law claims against an abuse of privilege by the sovereign Parliament itself. In that case, an elector in Aylesbury had been denied his right to vote by corrupt local officials. Holt held that even if the registering of the vote would not have made any difference to the election, the right to vote was in itself 'a most

---

[38] 19 Howell's State Trials 1029 (Camden LCJCP).
[39] P. Halliday, *Habeas Corpus: From England to Empire* (Cambridge, MA: Harvard University Press, 2012); A. L. Tyler, *Habeas Corpus in Wartime* (Oxford: Oxford University Press, 2017) 13–61.
[40] Crown Proceedings Act 1947; J. McLean, *Searching for the State in British Legal Thought: Competing Conceptions of the Public Sphere* (Cambridge: Cambridge University Press, 2012) 204–240, 278–308.
[41] *Ashby v. White* (1703) 2 Lord Raymond 938, 954–957 (Holt LCJKB).

transcendent thing, and of an high nature', a species of both personal and proprietary right distinct from the underlying franchise, such that its obstruction was an indirect trespass demanding the payment of nominal damages. Holt further argued that such judicial discipline would push officials to observe the law most scrupulously, whilst formally respecting the Parliament's privilege to control its own procedures; the courts' actions were designed to perfect the work of other jurisdictions when they strayed. Holt's dissent was upheld in the Lords,[42] but then overturned by the members of the House of Commons who resented outside intervention in the electoral process that had put them there. Despite this reversal, Holt's high statement of legal principle was taken to have captured, in its essence, the role of the judiciary as maintaining a due balance of jurisdictions under the common-law constitution. His arguments were amplified in William Blackstone's popular *Commentaries on the Laws of England* (1765–1770), and were to have enormous influence, not just in Britain but across the common-law world, notably in America.[43]

The eighteenth-century judiciary were also called upon to make decisions concerning status, often invoking wider constitutional questions of jurisdiction and the power of superiors over inferiors. The courts had long struggled with the law of alienage and nationality, for example, whether persons subject to the sovereignty of the monarch in right of one territory had claims to protection of the laws and membership of the polity in a separate jurisdiction ruled by the same monarch. Was the Crown in right of Ireland or Massachusetts divisible from the English Crown?[44] Were the subjects of a colony able to maintain their own laws and customs in their own courts, and how far could they resort to the courts of the imperial state to work out their disputes? Was the appropriate forum an overseas court, a gubernatorial prerogative tribunal, an imperial court (e.g. Privy Council) or the domestic legal order (e.g. Chancery of King's Bench)?[45] The 1763 Royal Proclamation in the wake of the Seven Years' War had tried to settle these questions in the American empire, but the courts could not settle the principles of colonial or native rights and titles, and the imperial legal-constitutional system broke down in 1776 with the Americans declaring independence.

---

[42] (1703) 1 Brown 62 (HL).
[43] W. E. Nelson, *Marbury v. Madison: The Origins and Legacy of Judicial Review*, 2nd ed. (Lawrence: University Press of Kansas, 2018).
[44] This problem was adumbrated in *Calvin's Case* (1608) Coke's Reports 1a.
[45] *Case of Tanistry* (1608) Davis 28; *Campbell v. Hall* (1774) 1 Cowper 204, 208 ff; Lofft 655, 741 ff, per Lord Mansfield LCJKB.

The courts also had to address troubling questions of religion and race, cutting across domestic and imperial jurisdiction. Some judges regarded adherence to non-Anglican religious community as a civic disability, barring the individual from public office, denying access to the professions and higher education, and refusing legal protection of disfavoured religions.[46] Other judges were more liberal, allowing contractual associations underpinned by trust holdings to underpin faith communities, and showing latitude in admittance to public office.[47] The law was increasingly pluralistic and tolerant, but was still informed by assumptions of hierarchy and privilege between different communities – a jurisprudence typical of empire. Racial laws showed a similar ambivalence. In 1772, in *Somerset's* Case, Lord Mansfield held that the status of chattel slavery was not known to the English domestic legal order and no slave under a foreign or colonial law could be coerced as such using English law on English soil.[48] The decision attracted both applause and condemnation, and may have helped induce the slave-holding American colonies to break free of the empire. Yet the English legal system did not move against slave trading abroad nor the structure of commerce built upon it, from which domestic British traders and industry continued to benefit. In 1783, Mansfield himself held that slaves could be treated as disposable property for the purposes of marine insurance.[49] A generation later, Lord Eldon could sneer at the idea that a beneficial fund to free slaves could count as a valid public charitable purpose. Meanwhile the subordinate position of women and servants was preserved in the common law, though the Chancery made inroads with some paternalistic barriers to exploitation, notably protecting wealthy women from their husbands (and creditors). Greater equality would have to wait for legislation at least a century later. The criminal law system was also harsh: rule-of-law constraints on prosecution and conviction only partly mitigated an enormous apparatus of legislative criminalisation (with the penal statutes often promoted by the judges in Parliament). In criminal courts, strong levels of discretion in punishment ritualised the power of the judiciary as agents of mercy, pain,

---

[46] See e.g. *Da Costa* v. *De Paz* (1754) Ambler 228 per Hardwicke LC.
[47] *Chamberlain of London* v. *Evans* (1767) per Lord Mansfield, affirmed in *Harrison* v. *Evans* (1767) Brown 465 (HL).
[48] *Somerset* v. *Stewart* (1772) 20 State Trials 1 (1772) Lofft 1.
[49] *The Zong, Gregson* v. *Gilbert* (1783) 3 Douglas 232; (2007) 28 *Journal of Legal History* 283–370.

exile, and death, and under William Pitt's administration many judges avidly promoted the prosecution of oppositional radicals.[50]

The Modern Judiciary

By the early nineteenth century Parliament became ever more active, codifying and reforming many branches of the old common law, notably property and commercial law, and developing modern areas such as copyright, taxation, banking, and company law. New welfare and environmental laws were developed to replace outdated Tudor systems. With increased industrialisation, urbanisation and demographic growth, the political elites faced a double challenge: to regulate and stabilise the economic order, and to legitimate the state by broadening political participation and so blunting calls for more radical change. The 1832 Reform Act expanded the franchise and started a long march to universal suffrage, completed nearly a century later. The 1846 repeal of the Corn Laws cheapened food and enhanced the incomes of 90 per cent of the population, at landowners' expense. Both Liberals and Tories competed for working class votes by instituting and supervising welfare measures, for example legislation to protect from workplace and environmental harms, or to ensure safe sea passage for emigrants to the colonies.[51]

Judges accepted the will of Parliament as popular sovereign, and deferred to executive government ruling with parliamentary support, but there was still room to allow challenges to government action by ensuring compliance with the terms of authorising legislation. Many of the new regulating and inspecting boards were further armed with a rule-making power expressed in delegated or subordinate legislation. Courts could test whether rule-making had been duly authorised by the empowering primary statute, and prevent egregious ultra vires conduct. Where tribunals had quasi-adjudicative powers over property rights, as with tithe and enclosure commissioners, or exercise of eminent domain, the judges were more comfortable exercising judicial review and permitting appeals, as if controlling a subordinate court. In 1848, Sir John Jervis passed legislation protecting magistrates in summary courts from personal liability for wrongful imprisonment, fines, or levying of

---

[50] P. King, *Crime, Justice, and Discretion in England 1740–1820* (Oxford: Oxford University Press, 2000).
[51] O. Macdonagh, *A Pattern of Government Growth 1800–1860: The Passenger Acts and Their Enforcement* (London: MacGibbon & Kee, 1961).

distress, instead strengthening rights to seek review of jurisdiction by mandamus or to bring appeal on both law and fact; legislation in 1857 opened up a path by writ of certiorari to quash tribunal decisions for legal error. These were important waystations in subjecting government action to more penetrating judicial review, whereby the manner of decision-making could affect jurisdiction. In a seminal Common Bench decision of 1863[52] the court held that a householder who breached administrative rulings dealing with housebuilding and sanitation had a natural right not to have his property affected by a government agency without a right of hearing. Further judicial scrutiny of executive action was squarely oriented to decisions touching property interests, including collection and spending on rates to pay for poor relief, education and health expenditures in local government. Some judges were also concerned to regulate corporations licenced by the state, and to control business monopoly and market competition; some class bias could be shown in the keen application of anti-trade union laws passed by Parliament.[53] When confronted with imperial cases of executive wrongdoing, judges were particularly loath to intervene: a stark example was given in the 1868 trial of Governor Eyre who had ordered the summary killing of rebels in Jamaica. The jury was instructed by Justice Blackburn to respect prerogative decisions taken by the governor in an emergency, over the objections of Chief Justice Cockburn; the case thrust imperial violence into public attention and caused furore in liberal circles.[54]

The higher judiciary remained compact into the nineteenth century, mainly drawn from the ranks of the professional bourgeoisie, and with only four or five judges in each major division (Exchequer, Common Bench, King's Bench, Chancery), plus the ad hoc judicial committee of the House of Lords, now staffed mainly by ex-lord chancellors. The year 1851 saw the creation of a Chancery appellate jurisdiction to assist the Lord Chancellor, and in 1854 the Common Law Procedure Act attempted to streamline proceedings and cross-vest jurisdictions and remedies. Legislation re-established the county courts in 1846, and recruited better-paid and professionally skilled lawyers to run these tribunals. In 1857, Courts of Probate and Divorce replaced the older

---

[52] *Cooper* v. *Wandsworth Board of Works* (1863) 14 CB(NS) 180.
[53] S. Anderson, 'Judicial Review' in W. R. Cornish et al., *The Oxford History of the Laws of England, vol. XI: 1820–1914* (Oxford: Oxford University Press, 2010) 486–522.
[54] *The Queen* v. *Edward John Eyre* (London: Finlason, Stevens, 1868), Charge of Mr. Justice Blackburn, 53–102, rebuttal by Cockburn LCJ, 103–107; R. Kostal, *A Jurisprudence of Power: Victorian Empire and the Rule of Law* (Oxford: Oxford University Press, 2008) 370–431.

ecclesiastical jurisdictions. Yet, despite these modernisations, the entire judicial system remained slow and expensive, and was increasingly seen as archaic and unable to deal with the litigation needs of a burgeoning industrial, commercial and imperial state. When the courts were reorganised in 1875, it was at first envisaged that an enlarged review and appeal court would replace the ad hoc judicial committee of the House of Lords, as part of a professionalised hierarchy of courts avoiding wasteful jurisdictional overlaps and conflicts. The Lords rebelled, and a statutory appendix was rushed through to preserve the judicial committee of the Lords as the supreme court of appeal. At the same time, the association of that court with high politics was loosened by the creation of life peerages for lawyers who staffed the judicial committee. By convention, the 'lords of appeal in ordinary', as these peers were described, were not supposed to participate in the ordinary political life of the House, though this norm was ignored when convenient.

The 1875 Judicature reforms amalgamated the three great courts of common law, together with the courts of Chancery, admiralty, and probate and matrimonial causes, as divisions of a new High Court, with the number of judges greatly increased, and jurisdictional limits on each division removed. Above the High Court sat a separate Court of Appeal able freely to re-assess facts as well as law, on the model of the prior Court of Appeal in Chancery rather than the archaic Court of Exchequer Chamber. A mirrored hierarchy of criminal courts was created. The members of the judiciary were given stable pensions to encourage retirement and turnover, and were also granted generous salaries. The judges vied to produce meticulous judgments and dealt with heavy workloads. The greater prestige lay in mastering the rules of private law rather than public or criminal law. In consequence, there was an efflorescence of jurisprudence in the spheres of partnership, insurance, shipping, banking and companies, and the traditional areas of contract, tort, agency, property and trusts.

At the turn of the century, public law was largely confined to control of local governments and boards spending public money, which could attract sometimes hostile supervision from anti-socialist judges.[55] The central executive attracted little judicial control. It took the experience of massive government penetration of society and economy in two world wars and then post-war reconstruction for the courts to enter the field of judicial review of government more surely. A galvanising ideological moment was the

---

[55] See e.g., *Roberts v. Hopwood* [1925] AC 578.

notorious decision by the House of Lords in 1941 allowing the Home Secretary to detain any person he deemed to be 'hostile', based on his own unreviewable opinion. The sharp dissent by Lord Atkin warned of the threat to liberty posed by such measures and his speech helped foster a more liberal climate of opinion after the war.[56] An intricate set of judicial tests for the propriety of government executive action was developed from around 1960, expanding to embrace powers based on prerogative as well as statute.[57] The rise of a large public sector meant that principles for state contracting and delivery of services had to be hammered out; from 1947, full liability of the Crown in private-law proceedings promoted this regulatory project.[58]

Large steps in judicial constitutional authority came with accession to the European Community in 1972, vesting power in the courts to interpret or suspend domestic legislation so as to eliminate inconsistencies with the European legal order. Human rights commitments were legislated in stages, initially with protections of traditional liberties such as rights of free movement and assembly, followed by protection from race discrimination. Broader human rights entitlements had earlier been accepted under the European Convention on Human Rights, largely drafted by British lawyers post-war[59] and binding state signatories from 1953. The Blair Labour government legislated direct domestic enforcement of Convention rights in 1998, and concomitantly revived the project of taking appellate jurisdiction from the House of Lords and so distancing adjudication from the legislative process.[60] In 2009, the law lords were transferred to a new United Kingdom Supreme Court and removed from Parliament. The Lord Chancellor ceased to be a judicial officer in 2003, and now serves as a justice minister with no special role to represent the judiciary in the constitution and defend the rule of law, but rather acting as a manager concerned to curb the costs of the judicial system. In 2017 the Supreme Court decried such budgetary policies as throttling general access to the courts and misconceiving litigation as a user-pays service.[61] Conflict between government and the new Supreme Court took on new intensity when the Court insisted on parliamentary control over the executive in the Brexit negotiations.[62] Following sharp political attacks,

---

[56] *Liversidge* v. *Anderson* [1942] AC 206.
[57] *GCHQ Case* [1985] AC 374; Stevens, *English Judges*, 14–29.
[58] Above, text accompanying n 40.
[59] A. W. B. Simpson, *Human Rights and the End of Empire: Britain and the Genesis of the European Convention* (Oxford: Oxford University Press. 2001).
[60] Constitutional Reform Act 2005. [61] *UNISON Case* [2017] UKSC 51.
[62] *Miller (No 1)* [2018] AC 61; *Miller (No 2)* [2020] AC 373.

the Court has signalled greater deference to the executive, notably in national security policy.[63] It remains to be seen whether the current uneasy position of the United Kingdom judiciary – the formal elevation of its review and appellate jurisdiction, its rigid institutional separation from government and politics, and its position as an arbiter of constitutional powers – will be practicable or enduring in the mid twenty-first century.

[63] See *Begum v. Home Secretary* [2021] AC 765.

15

Coercive Institutions

BRICE DICKSON

It is almost the definition of a State that it has control over territory, control which has to be exercised through the application, or the threat of application, of physical force. The United Kingdom is no different from other States where, over time, the institutionalisation of this physical force has taken the form of an everyday service – the police – and a service which can be called in aid at times when unusual dangers have to be confronted – the armed forces. As the principle of the rule of law has evolved, so has the way in which the police and army have come to be regulated. Rather than being the enforcers of the law they are now viewed as its servants. The history of Britain's coercive institutions is the history of how legal principles have gradually usurped the responsibility for ensuring that people are kept safe and that right wins over might. Whether the optimal position has yet been reached is another question. Because what we now call the armed forces were active long before the police became so, we will begin our exploration of the subject by looking at the former. The murky area of 'secret services' – espionage and counter-espionage – is not addressed because, while often coercive in practice, their methods are primarily investigative.

The Armed Forces

The history of the organisation of groups of people into cohesive collectivities is basically the history of the use of physical force. An area became ruled by whoever was in command of the physical forces able to exert control over the area. In the area we now refer to as England and Wales it was the Romans who first exerted such widespread control as to be able to designate the country as a combination of *Britannia Superior* and *Britannia Inferior*. Once they departed the area fragmented into a number of 'kingdoms', again as a result of armed conflict. After the Norman conquest in 1066 the army became increasingly identified as King William's personal force, regulated by his prerogative powers as the monarch. To encourage soldiers to fight for them rich warlords began to promise a reward, be that money or something more tangible. As elsewhere in Europe a system of 'knight service' developed whereby men provided their military services to their overlord in exchange for the right to occupy and farm areas of land. This feudal system gradually became more systematised so that, rather than personally providing the military services, tenants could instead pay money to the overlord, a tax which was called 'scutage', from the Latin word for a shield. Inevitably the focus of attention of those who bore arms was on maintaining the security of their own overlord in a particular locality but as the power of the highest overlords – the monarchs – developed it became necessary to develop a national army.

The Statute of Winchester in 1285 was an important landmark in the development of peace-keeping since it regularised the keeping of the peace more generally throughout the country. The practice of using 'watchmen' to keep the peace had already been in use for some time, but the 1285 Statute commanded every man to keep arms in his house, the nature of which depended on his wealth. Every two years two constables were required to inspect the domestic arms and report any deficiencies to the local justices, who in turn had to report to the king. It is perhaps from this point that the distinction between armed forces and the police can first be meaningfully dated. Around the same time monarchs began to appoint commissioners to visit parts of the country to bring together ('array') able-bodied men who could help the monarch deal with some emergency, such as an invasion or uprising. This early form of conscription reflected the reality that there was no 'standing army' in Britain until much later, in the seventeenth century. The common-law power to array was eventually replaced by a statutory right given to the monarch to 'impress' both soldiers and sailors, including for service in wars taking place abroad. At times of severe civil unrest within the country it was possible under the common law for 'martial law' to be declared. This authorised the setting aside of certain basic freedoms, but not, usually, the right to seek liberty under a writ of habeas corpus. The term military law was coined to designate the specific legal rules which were binding on the members of the armed forces alone. They were not usually subject to the jurisdiction of civilian courts for their actions as soldiers or sailors but instead to 'courts martial' set up and staffed by senior members of the forces.

The Civil War of the 1640s highlighted how important it had become to regulate the armed forces and to discourage the formation of private armies.

In 1628 the Petition of Right outlawed, amongst other things, the quartering of soldiers in citizens' homes as well as the use of martial law during peacetime. It added that civilians, and soldiers in England during peacetime, had to be judged by common law and equity courts, not by military courts. It was partly the refusal by Parliament to grant King Charles I the money he claimed was needed to pay for military campaigns he wanted to wage in France, Spain and Scotland that triggered the Civil War. His attempt to levy a 'ship money' tax in every county was also a contributing factor.

After its victory in the Civil War, Parliament obviously remained suspicious of the army. It was therefore disbanded, except for some special groups of guards and garrisons.[1] Several nobles were impeached for trying to raise an army and in 1685 martial law had to be introduced to help quell a rebellion led by the Duke of Monmouth. At the end of the so-called Glorious Revolution, which followed a three-year period of civil upheaval sometimes referred to as the Second Civil War, steps were taken by Parliament to place more curbs on the military's power. In 1689 the Bill of Rights focused on definitively restricting the powers of the monarch, including the raising of an army during peacetime, and also guaranteed the right of people to bear arms in self-defence. Later the same year the first Mutiny Act was passed, making mutiny an offence punishable in a court-martial and limiting the monarch's power to resort to the use of martial law.[2] Similar Mutiny Acts were enacted almost every year until 1879. In the nineteenth century detailed provision was made by Parliament for a reserve 'militia', effectively, in Maitland's eyes, a second standing army, but when and how to deploy the armed forces remained a matter for the royal prerogative, exercised on the Crown's behalf by the government of the day.[3]

In 1904, as a result of the report of a commission chaired by Viscount Esher, an attempt was made to improve the governance of the army by establishing an Army Council. Britain's army had not performed well during the Second Boer War in South Africa and politicians were therefore keen to reduce the power of the army's Commander-in-Chief and re-distribute it amongst a group of experts. The Army Council mirrored to some extent the

---

[1] Henry Reece, *The Army in Cromwellian England, 1649–1660* (Oxford: Oxford University Press, 2013); John Childs, *The Army of Charles II* (London: Routledge and Kegan Paul, 1976).

[2] G. A. Steppler, 'British Military Law, Discipline, and the Conduct of Rregimental Courts Martial in the Later Eighteenth Century' (1987) *English Historical Review*, Vol CII, 859–886.

[3] F. W. Maitland, *The Constitutional History of England* ed. Hal Fisher (Cambridge: Cambridge University Press, 1908), 459.

Board of Admiralty, which was responsible for the navy and had been in existence since 1628 and before that, in the guise of the Navy Board, since 1546. The Army Council, chaired by the Secretary of State for War, comprised a mixture of senior politicians and generals, but the overall effect was to greatly increase the democratic accountability of the army to Parliament.[4] It was renamed as the Army Board in 1967. The chair today is the Secretary of State for Defence but the Board's Executive Committee is chaired by the Chief of the General Staff, the title given to the head of the British army.

The main legislation governing all of the UK's armed forces is now the Armed Forces Act 2006, which replaced the Army Act 1955, the Air Force Act 1955 and the Naval Discipline Act 1957. It endures for periods of five years until renewed, as it was by Armed Forces Acts passed in 2016 and 2021, but it must also be endorsed annually through an Order in Council approved by a resolution of both houses of parliament.[5] In 2018 the 2006 Act was amended to allow members of the armed forces to engage in flexible working, a reform which goes some way towards recognising the preferences of female members of the forces. The early 2000s also saw the development of the idea of an 'Armed Forces Covenant', whereby members of the armed forces community would be supported in areas such as education, housing, healthcare and starting a new career. The Covenant was first given statutory recognition by the Armed Forces Act 2011[6] and the Armed Forces Act 2021 strengthened its legal status.

Martial Law

Martial law is a term usually applied to a situation where a territory is governed by military officials rather than by elected politicians.[7] It is a common-law concept but, as already noted, the Petition of Right of 1628, which is still in force, restricted its use in Great Britain to times when the country was not at peace. Although never expressly abolished by Parliament, the concept of martial law has now been effectively replaced by the concept of a declaration of emergency made by the government under the authority

---

[4] See, generally, Paul Smith (ed.), *Government and Armed Forces in Britain, 1856–1990* (London: Bloomsbury, 1996).
[5] See e.g., the Armed Forces Act (Continuation) Order 2021, SI 289. The Armed Forces Act 2021 received Royal Assent on 15 December 2021.
[6] s 2 inserted ss 343A and 343B into the 2006 Act.
[7] Harold M. Bowman, 'Martial Law and the English Constitution' (1916) 15 *Michigan Law Review* 93.

of the Civil Contingencies Act 2004.[8] Once an emergency has been declared the government may require a range of people and bodies to take steps to deal with the effects of the emergency.[9] Chief Constables of police forces, who otherwise have operational independence (see below), are included within this list of people and bodies, but the armed forces are not. Deployment of the armed forces within the UK is a matter within the prerogative powers of the government,[10] so members of the army are frequently deployed to assist with preventative or clear-up operations when there are severe weather events, terrorist threats, pandemics or finds of unexploded munitions.

The most significant deployment of armed forces within the UK in the past 100 years was Operation Banner, whereby the army was sent to Northern Ireland to assist the Royal Ulster Constabulary in maintaining law and order. The operation endured for thirty-eight years, from 1969 to 2007, and involved a total of some 300,000 soldiers, the highest number at any one time being around 21,000 during the most dangerous years of the troubles, 1971 to 1975. Having at first been welcomed into the province by Catholic nationalists, who saw the soldiers as people who would protect them against violent Protestant unionists, the relationship soon soured. The first member of the armed forces to be killed in action died on 6 February 1971, and a further 721 were to follow, including 204 members of the Ulster Defence Regiment, which was recruited only from within Northern Ireland. According to *Lost Lives*, which records all deaths occurring during the Northern Ireland troubles, 309 people were killed by the British armed forces.[11] A handful of soldiers were convicted of murder and occasional prosecutions were still taking place in 2022.

The Ministry of Defence also employed many agents and informers in Northern Ireland, people whose full story will probably never be told. The army's intelligence gathering department was named the Force Research Unit. In his final report on his inquiry into alleged collusion between the security forces and loyalist paramilitaries Sir John Stevens, by then the Commissioner of the Metropolitan Police Service, found that there had been

---

[8] Clive Walker and James Broderick, *The Civil Contingencies Act 2004: Risk, Resilience and the Law in the United Kingdom* (Oxford: Oxford University Press, 2006).
[9] Civil Contingencies Act 2004, s 5.
[10] Ministry of Justice, *The Governance of Britain: Review of the Executive Royal Prerogative Powers: Final Report* (London, 2009).
[11] David McKittrick, Seamus Kelters, Brian Feeney, Chris Thornton, and David McVea, *Lost Lives* (Edinburgh and London: Mainstream Publishing) 1527 (301 'Army' + 8 'UDR/RIR' killings). See too Fionnuala Ní Aoláin, *The Politics of Force: Conflict Management and State Violence in Northern Ireland* (Belfast: Blackstaff Press, 2000).

security force collusion even in murders.[12] He indicated that his inquiry had so far led to 144 arrests, with 94 persons convicted. But no senior official or politician has ever been prosecuted in relation to their role in authorising or tolerating such collusion.

Military Law

As the UK has long had a permanent army, navy and air force, as well as part-time reserve forces, it is only very rarely that it will provide for compulsory conscription. It did so in 1916 during World War One and again in 1939 on the outbreak of World War Two.[13] In this latter period the system initially applied to all men aged between eighteen and forty-one but in 1942 the upper age limit was extended to fifty-one. The system of compelling young men aged between seventeen and twenty-one to undertake short-term 'national service' continued from 1949 until the end of 1960.[14] In both World Wars those who had a conscientious objection to combat were permitted to apply for exemption from conscription. In the First War they had to persuade a Military Service Tribunal that their objection was genuine and they could still be assigned to non-combatant service rather than granted an outright exemption.[15] A similar system was set up during the Second War, this time with Conscientious Objection Tribunals.[16] Currently the extent of the right to conscientious objection for those who are already serving in the armed forces is unclear. It is not provided for in any legislation nor, except for the army, in any of the regulations governing the armed forces.[17] Opportunities to insert such provisions into the Armed Forces Acts 2011, 2016 and 2021 were not taken. The European Court of Human Rights, meanwhile, has stated that the right to conscientious objection against military service is a fundamental right guaranteed by Article 9 of the ECHR.[18]

---

[12] See *Stevens Enquiry: Overview and Recommendations* (2003), available at http://news.bbc.co.uk/1/shared/spl/hi/northern_ireland/03/stephens_inquiry/pdf/stephens_inquiry.pdf.

[13] Military Service Act 1916; National Service (Armed Forces) Act 1939. See, generally, Roger Broad, *Conscription in Britain, 1939–1964: The Militarisation of a Generation* (London: Routledge, 2006).

[14] National Service Act 1948.   [15] Military Service Act 1916, ss 2(1)(d) and 2(3).

[16] National Service (Armed Forces) Act 1939, s 5 and Sch, para 1; National Service Act 1941, s 7. See too the National Service (Release of Conscientious Objectors) Act 1946.

[17] See the briefing paper prepared for Parliament by ForcesWatch in 2011, available at www.parliament.uk/documents/joint-committees/human-rights/Briefing_from_Forces_Watch_Conscientious_objection.pdf.

[18] *Bayatyan v. Armenia* (2012) 54 EHRR 15.

It is the Armed Forces Act 2006, as continued in force by the 2016 and 2021 Acts, which provides the legal basis for the application of military law and the operation of courts martial. The Act sets out the various offences for which members of the armed forces can be prosecuted, the powers of the service police officers when investigating offences, the system for testing for alcohol and drugs, the powers to hold suspects in custody, the procedures to be followed at summary hearings and courts martial, and the punishments that can be imposed on those found guilty of offences. There are comparable provisions for offences allegedly committed by civilians while working for the armed forces. The current legislation incorporates changes which had to be made as a result of several judgments by the European Court of Human Rights holding that the previous procedures violated provisions in the European Convention on Human Rights (ECHR).[19] Some doubts remain over whether servicemen or women who play a role in the sentencing process receive enough training to ensure that the process is entirely fair as required by Article 6 of the ECHR.[20] The trend in the UK has been to make the military courts as independent as the civilian courts. However, Frederic Lederer has argued, albeit from a US standpoint, that the trend towards civilianisation of military justice systems can only go so far: the specific needs of the military as regards the maintenance of discipline must always be borne in mind.[21]

The Deployment of Armed Forces Abroad[22]

There is now a practice that deployment of British armed forces abroad – at any rate if their role relates to an armed conflict rather than to a natural disaster – requires the consent of Parliament. That was what occurred in 2003 in relation to the sending of British forces to Iraq[23] and also in 2013 when consideration was given to posting British troops to Syria.[24] On account of

---

[19] See e.g., *Findlay v. UK* (1997) 24 EHRR 221; *Morris v. UK* (2002) 34 EHRR 1253; *Cooper v. UK* (2004) 39 EHRR 8.

[20] Jo Morris and Fiona McAddy, 'The Court Martial and the HRA [Human Rights Act]', *The Barrister*, 21 Sept. 2016, available at www.barristermagazine.com/the-court-martial-and-the-hra.

[21] 'From Rome to the Military Justice Acts of 2016 and beyond: Continuing Civilianization of the Military Criminal Legal System' (2017) *Military Law Review* 512.

[22] See, generally, David French, *Army, Empire and the Cold War: The British Army and Military Policy, 1945–1971* (Oxford: Oxford University Press, 2012).

[23] On 18 March 2003 the House of Commons decided by 412 votes to 149 in favour of the deployment.

[24] On 30 August 2013 Parliament voted by 285 votes to 272 not to send British armed forces to assist with US-led strikes in Syria.

the political fall-out which is likely to result from engaging troops abroad without first seeking Parliament's consent, it is reasonable to state that the practice is now already a constitutional convention. That, however, does not make it legally enforceable, since UK courts maintain that constitutional conventions have only political, not legal, authority.[25] The consent of Parliament is not required for the transfer or arms to another country, as is clear from the arming of Ukraine in 2022.

A significant step towards increasing executive accountability for the deployment of armed forces abroad was taken with the establishment of the Iraq Inquiry by Prime Minister Gordon Brown in 2009. Conducted by a committee of privy counsellors led by Sir John Chilcot, the Inquiry's report was eventually published in 2016.[26] Over the course of twelve volumes it painted a damning picture of the decision-making processes that led up to the invasion of Iraq and was highly critical of the tactics used during the invasion and the lack of post-invasion planning. Whether lessons will be learned from this monumental study of military deployment it is still too early to say.

If UK armed forces cause damage to property abroad, even if it belongs to British subjects or companies, the government is not obliged to pay compensation to the owners of the property. This was affirmed by Parliament in the War Damages Act 1965, which is still in force. It was enacted after the Law Lords had held, in *Burmah Oil* v. *Lord Advocate*, that compensation *should* be paid in such circumstances.[27] In addition the UK adheres to the 'foreign act of state doctrine'. This means that it does not allow the actions taken by state authorities in other countries to be the subject of litigation in UK courts. The reason underlying the doctrine is that such litigation would impede good relations between nation states. But the Supreme Court has recently confirmed that there is an exception to the doctrine if what was done by the foreign state amounts to a grave violation of human rights, such as the long-term internment and mistreatment of a suspected dissident or terrorist, and if this was facilitated by actions of UK armed forces.[28] Strangely, it remains the

---

[25] *R (Miller)* v. *Secretary of State for Exiting the EU* [2017] UKSC 5, [2018] AC 61, where the Supreme Court held that the Sewel Convention, relating to whether Westminster could enact legislation on matters devolved to the legislatures in Wales, Scotland and Northern Ireland, could not be enforced through the courts.

[26] Chilcot, Sir John, *The Report of the Iraq Inquiry*, HC 265, available at www.gov.uk/government/publications/the-report-of-the-iraq-inquiry.

[27] [1965] AC 75. The case involved the destruction of British oil installations in Burma in order to stop them falling into the hands of the Japanese during the Second World War.

[28] *Belhaj* v. *Straw* [2017] UKSC 3, [2017] AC 964.

position both of the UK Supreme Court and of the European Court of Human Rights that victims of torture have no right to sue in UK courts the foreign state which was responsible for the torture.[29]

In recent years two important questions have been raised concerning the position of armed forces deployed abroad. First, are those forces bound to comply with the European Convention on Human Rights and, second, are members of the forces entitled to claim the protection of that Convention for themselves if they are injured or killed while abroad?

The answer to the first question is still unclear because the case law of the UK Supreme Court and of the European Court of Human Rights is open to different interpretations. They turn on what is meant by the ECHR's requirement that states which are parties to it must secure the Convention's rights 'to everyone within their jurisdiction'. What seems settled is that if armed forces from a Council of Europe state engage in an aerial attack over territory which is not part of such a state, the jurisdictional requirement is not satisfied.[30] But in later cases the European Court of Human Rights has accepted that in exceptional circumstances the actions of armed forces operating outside their home state or causing harm there (e.g. through the use of drones) might indeed constitute the exercise of jurisdiction,[31] especially if the Council of Europe state is exercising public powers in the foreign territory at the time[32] or if its forces are in physical control of alleged victims of human rights.[33] The underlying principle was said to be that extra-territorial jurisdiction exists whenever a state through its agents exercises authority and control over an individual. It also indicated that a state's extra-territorial jurisdiction over local inhabitants exists because of the authority and control that is exercised over them as a result of the authority and

---

[29] *Jones v. Ministry of the Interior of Saudi Arabia* [2006] UKHL 26, [2007] 1 AC 270, confirmed in *Jones v. UK* (2014) 59 EHRR 1.
[30] *Banković v. Belgium* (2007) 44 EHRR SE5, decision of the Grand Chamber, 19 December 2001, where seventeen Council of Europe states, including the UK, were accused of violating the right to life of people killed in an air attack on Serbian Radio-Television headquarters in Belgrade in 1999.
[31] *Issa v. Turkey* (2005) 41 EHRR 27, where Turkish soldiers were accused of killing shepherds in an area of Northern Iraq near the Turkish border, but on the facts no direct causation could be proved. In a later case involving a helicopter incursion by Turkish forces into Iran Turkey paid compensation to Iranian victims and the ECtHR confirmed that jurisdiction did exist on the facts: *Pad v. Turkey*, decision of 28 June 2007.
[32] *Al-Skeini v. UK* (2011) 53 EHRR 18 (Grand Chamber), where in 2003 six men died at the hands of British soldiers in Basrah, Iraq.
[33] *Hassan v. UK*, judgment of the Grand Chamber, 16 September 2014.

control which the state has over its own armed forces. They are all brought within the state's jurisdiction by the application of the same general principle.

If victims bring their case in the home state of the armed forces, jurisdiction might then be established.[34] However, if the armed forces are functioning as part of a UN, or presumably NATO, military operation Council of Europe states may escape accountability under the ECHR.[35] The European Court of Human Rights has also accepted that if Council of Europe states have jurisdiction, it may apply to only some of the rights guaranteed by the ECHR: those rights can be 'divided and tailored' to meet the particular circumstances of the conduct in question.[36] In the UK, the Overseas Operations (Service Personnel and Veterans) Act 2021 creates a presumption against prosecution of a member of the armed forces for actions taken outside the UK more than five years earlier. It also makes it more difficult to extend the limitation periods for civil claims.

As regards the second question, there remains some doubt as to whether members of the armed forces serving abroad are as entitled to the protection of the Human Rights Act 1998 as they are when serving at home. In the leading case decided by the Law Lords in 2008, which involved the deaths of two British soldiers in Iraq, the majority of the court held that the soldiers were not 'within the jurisdiction' of the UK when they died.[37] Even if they were within that jurisdiction, the court added, the duties to protect life and to investigate loss of life imposed by Article 2 of the ECHR did not apply when a country decides to send its troops to war, whether or not that step was mandated by the UN Charter's provisions on the use of force. A similar position was adopted by the UK Supreme Court two years later when a mother of a soldier who died of heatstroke while serving at a military base in Iraq was denied an Article 2-compliant investigation of her son's death

---

[34] *Markovic v. Italy* (2007) 44 EHRR 52 (Grand Chamber), where the ECtHR accepted that victims of the aerial bombing in Belgrade (see n 30) who opened civil proceedings in Italy did fall 'indisputably' (para 54) within Italy's jurisdiction.

[35] *Behrami v. France* (2007) 45 EHRR SE10 (Grand Chamber), where a brigade led by France as part of the international security force in Kosovo was held not to be exercising jurisdiction over particular children who were harmed in the process. But in *Al-Jedda v. UK* (2011) 53 EHRR 23 (Grand Chamber), the ECtHR found that the UK, not the UN, had jurisdiction over an area of Iraq at the time of the internment of an Iraqi civilian for more than three years, and in *Jaloud v. The Netherlands* (2015) 60 EHRR 29 (Grand Chamber) it was the Netherlands, not the UK or Iraq, which was held to have had jurisdiction over a civilian at the time he was shot dead in 2004.

[36] *Al-Skeini v. UK*, n 32, para 137.

[37] *R (Gentle) v. Prime Minister* [2008] UKHL 20, [2008] AC 1356; Lady Hale dissented on this point.

because he was not within the jurisdiction of the UK at the time.[38] However, in a remarkable turnaround just three years further on, a unanimous seven-judge Supreme Court held that two soldiers killed in Iraq by an improvised explosive device which blew up the Land Rover in which they were travelling *were* within the jurisdiction of the UK at the time.[39] The judges departed from the earlier decision because of the stance taken by the European Court of Human Rights in the *Al-Skeini* case, mentioned above in relation to Iraqi victims of British army brutality.[40] If home state authority and control exists in relation to such victims one might have supposed that *ex hypothesi* it exists in relation to the state's own soldiers who are fighting for the state. To date, however, the European Court of Human Rights has not expressly endorsed the conclusion that when a Council of Europe's armed forces are serving abroad they enjoy the protection of ECHR rights vis-à-vis their home state.

Moreover, it remains the case that states enjoy a wide margin of appreciation as regards the obligations they owe under Article 2 of the ECHR in this context. The Supreme Court has said that high level policy decisions as well as steps taken on the battlefield cannot be scrutinised for compliance with Article 2, but claims which are 'in the middle ground' can be. What Article 2 requires in those cases will depend on the facts of each case.[41]

The Police

The significance of the Statute of Winchester in 1285 has already been highlighted as far as keeping the peace is concerned. The inspecting constables appointed under that legislation are the forerunner of today's police officers, though it is also possible to go back still further to Ordinances of 1233 and 1252. The former provided for 'night-watchmen' to be appointed to patrol the streets during hours of darkness, enforcing the curfews that were often in place and removing the weapons from people who were armed. The latter specified that in every city there should be twelve men at every gate in a borough, six at every gate in a city and four at every gate in a town. 'Strangers' were to be detained until the next morning.

Gradually towns and parishes began to systematise their approach to watchmen. Instead of able-bodied males being required to undertake the role in turn, for perhaps a year at a time, local authorities began to pay

---

[38] *R (Smith)* v. *Oxfordshire Assistant Deputy Coroner* [2010] UKSC 29, [2011] 1 AC 1.
[39] *Smith* v. *Ministry of Defence* [2013] UKSC 41, [2014] AC 52.   [40] See n 32.
[41] *Smith*, n 39, [76], per Lord Hope.

experienced men to do the job. The individual who did most to professionalise the role was Robert Peel. While he was serving as the Chief Secretary for Ireland he created a Peace Preservation Force in 1814. This built on reforms which had already been introduced for Dublin in 1786. Later, during his second period as Home Secretary for the United Kingdom, Peel established London's Metropolitan Police Service in 1829 and within the next thirty years every city in the country had a similar police force. In acknowledgment of Peel's influence the officers became known as 'bobbies' or 'peelers'.[42] Peel's great insight was that police officers were ordinary members of the public – but in uniform. In his famous 'Peel Principles' he set out nine key ideas that should underpin policing. The first two were that the police should prevent crime and that their position was always dependent on public approval and respect. The fifth was that the police should demonstrate 'impartial service to law, in complete independence of policy' and readily offer 'individual service and friendship to all members of the public without regard to their wealth or social standing, by ready exercise of courtesy and friendly good humour'.

The role and organisation of the police have been the subject of several reviews since the days of Peel. The template for policing the boroughs of Great Britain was set by the Municipal Corporations Act 1835 and for the counties by the County Police Act 1839. There was little or no appetite for nationalising the police service, nor for making the police susceptible to political interference. When an attempt was made to make Oldham Corporation responsible for the actions of the local Chief Constable in 1930, the High Court robustly rejected the idea.[43]

By 1960 there were 158 police forces in Great Britain and one in Northern Ireland, with almost 100,000 officers in total. In reaction to disputes over who should exercise control over these forces – the Chief Constables, the local government authorities or central government – a Royal Commission was established, reporting in 1962.[44] It led to the Police Act 1964, which, amongst other things, greatly reduced the number of police forces, created new Police Authorities for each force comprising a mixture of magistrates and elected councillors, required the chief constables to report annually to the Authorities and conferred new powers on the Home Secretary to exercise some central supervision over the various forces. Further re-shaping of the

---

[42] Douglas Hay and Francis Snyder (eds.), *Policing and Prosecution in Britain 1750–1850* (Oxford: Clarendon Press, 1989); Clive Emsley, *The Great British Bobby: A History of British Policing from the 18th Century to the Present* (London: Quercus, 2010).
[43] *Fisher v. Oldham Corporation* [1930] 2 KB 384.   [44] Cmnd 1728 (1962).

police forces took place under the Local Government Act 1972 and the powers of Police Authorities were altered by the Police and Magistrates' Courts Act 1994 and the Police Act 1996: 'independent' members became appointable to the Authorities for the first time.

Many of the Peelian principles are just as relevant today as they were nearly 200 years ago. In particular, the principle that the police should operate independently, free from any direction by the government, remains a fundamental aspect of the UK constitution. Whether the police and government have always fully adhered to that principle is a matter for debate. Lustgarten states that '[t]he single most important feature of the constitutional position of the police is that they have the status of constable', but he maintains that police independence from democratic reform is a heresy and he is very critical of the degree of discretion allowed to police officers in Britain compared with the position in other European democracies.[45] It remains the case today that police officers are not, in law, employees and therefore do not automatically qualify for all the rights which employees enjoy. In many respects separate regulations have extended similar rights to police officers, but they still cannot claim unfair dismissal or go on strike.

Malpractice by police officers when investigating the murder of Maxwell Confait in 1972 eventually led to the establishment of a Royal Commission on Criminal Procedure,[46] which in turn resulted in the Police and Criminal Evidence Act 1984 (see below) and the creation of the Crown Prosecution Service.[47] During the miners' strike in 1984 it appeared to many that the police were too enthusiastic in their efforts to implement the Conservative government's policies on strike action.[48] But the police were also more likely to be violently attacked: in 1985 Keith Blakelock was killed during a riot in Tottenham, London, the first police officer to die in a riot in Britain for 150 years. After the death of a black teenager, Stephen Lawrence, in 1993 the Metropolitan Police were found to have been institutionally racist.[49] There have also been suggestions that the police sometimes engaged in unacceptable duplicity, as when they embedded undercover agents in protest groups and even allowed them to have enduring sexual relationships with

---

[45] Laurence Lustgarten, *The Governance of Police* (London: Sweet & Maxwell, 1986). The quote is from p. 25.
[46] Cmnd 8092 (1981); Harlow, Carol, 'The Royal Commission on Criminal Procedure' (1981) 52 *Political Quarterly* 239.
[47] By the Prosecution of Offences Act 1995.
[48] Bob Fine and Robert Millar (eds.), *Policing the Miners' Strike* (London: Lawrence & Wishart Ltd, 1985).
[49] *The Stephen Lawrence Inquiry*, Cm 4262-I (1999), para 6 45.

protestors.[50] In 2015 an inquiry into undercover policing activities in England and Wales since 1968 was established and is still on-going, currently led by a retired judge, Sir John Mitting.[51] It has already revealed that during the years in question undercover police spied on more than 1,000 political groups in the United Kingdom.[52] In 2011 the killing by police officers of Mark Duggan, again in Tottenham, sparked the infamous London riots of that year, arguably because of local resentment at the frequent use of stop and search powers against young black males.[53] In more recent years the police have also been criticised for aspects of their investigations into alleged sexual misconduct by celebrities such as Paul Gambaccini and Cliff Richard, which were part of Operation Yewtree, the investigation of abuse allegations made against the entertainer Jimmy Savile. In 2019 there was publication of further criticism by another retired judge, Sir Richard Henriques, of the botched police investigation into allegations made by Carl Beech, which had led to the searching of the homes, and prolonged questioning, of several prominent individuals who in due course turned out to be entirely innocent.[54] In 2020 there was some criticism of the way in which police in Britain dealt with Black Lives Matter protests[55] and further revelations about serious police misconduct in 2021, including the murder of Sarah Everard by a serving constable, led to the resignation of the Metropolitan Commissioner, Cressida Dick, in 2022.

The United Kingdom has continued to resist the temptation to create a nationwide police force, except in relation to certain functions. There are currently forty-three separate police forces in England and Wales, with about 123,000 officers.[56] Scotland used to have eight separate forces but in 2013 they were merged into just one, Police Scotland.[57] Northern Ireland's police force, formerly part of the Royal Irish Constabulary, became the Royal Ulster Constabulary in 1922 and then, after reforms proposed by an Independent

---

[50] *The Guardian*, 28 August 2019, available at www.theguardian.com/uk-news/2019/aug/28/police-investigate-officer-who-infiltrated-environmental-groups.
[51] See www.ucpi.org.uk. The Inquiry is due to report in 2023.
[52] *The Guardian*, 27 July 2017, available at www.theguardian.com/uk-news/2017/jul/27/undercover-police-spied-on-more-than-1000-political-groups-in-uk.
[53] Michael Matthews, *The Riots: The Police Fight for the Streets during the UK's Deadly 2011 Riots* (London: Silvertail Books, 2016).
[54] Available at www.met.police.uk/henriques. This police investigation was codenamed Operation Midland.
[55] Nadine White, *Huffington Post*, 12 November 2020, available at www.huffingtonpost.co.uk/entry/black-lives-matter-protests-policing_uk_5facfe86c5b6d647a39c05de.
[56] *Police Workforce, England and Wales, 31 March 2019 (2nd ed.)*, Home Office, Statistical Bulletin 11/19 (18 July 2019), p. 6.
[57] Police and Fire Reform (Scotland) Act 2012.

Commission on Policing led by Chris Patten,[58] the Police Service of Northern Ireland in 2001. The specialist nationwide police services include the National Crime Agency (which focuses on serious and organised crime, but not terrorism), the British Transport Police, the Civil Nuclear Constabulary and the Ministry of Defence Police. The Border Force, which enforces the rules on immigration and customs, is not a police force but its officials do have some powers to detain people for short periods. The heads of all of the police forces, except for Police Scotland and the National Crime Agency, are members of the National Police Chiefs' Council, a body which replaced the Association of Chief Police Officers in 2015.

In England and Wales, under the Police Reform Act 2002 and the Policing and Crime Act 2017, there are some 10,000 Police and Community Safety Officers, uniformed police staff who carry out some of the more community-based work of fully warranted police officers. Neither Scotland nor Northern Ireland has equivalent officers. In addition, there are approximately 12,000 'Special Constables' and a further 12,000 Police Cadets in England and Wales. Each of these is a volunteer service, even though the former are fully warranted police officers. There is a Citizens in Policing National Board which provides strategic oversight for volunteer policing.

Police Powers

The powers and duties of the police are extensive and are now clearly laid down in legislation, although until comparatively recently many of the powers were regulated only by the common law. In England and Wales the Police and Criminal Evidence Act 1984 significantly clarified the law and it has since been complemented by a series of codes of practice to help guide the police in how they should exercise their powers. In Northern Ireland a similar Police and Criminal Evidence (NI) Order was introduced in 1989, but in Scotland reform had to await the Criminal Procedure (Scotland) Act 1995, now largely superseded by the Criminal Justice (Scotland) Act 2016, an Act of the Scottish Parliament.

In general,[59] the police can arrest a person without a warrant only if they reasonably suspect that person of having committed an offence and they

---

[58] Chris Patten et al., *A New Beginning: Policing in Northern Ireland* (1999), available at https://cain.ulster.ac.uk/issues/police/patten/patten99.pdf.

[59] For England and Wales the details on powers of arrest and detention are set out in the Police and Criminal Evidence Act 1984, ss 24-52.

reasonably believe that the arrest is necessary to ensure, for example, that the person can be identified or that further injury or loss can be avoided. The police can also summarily arrest someone for the rather vague concept of 'a breach of the peace'. Arrests with a warrant can take place if the police have first obtained the approval of a magistrate for the issue of the warrant. Once arrested a person can be detained for up to thirty-six hours, so long as a police superintendent authorises the last twelve hours of that period. To detain the person for a longer period the police need the approval of a District Judge sitting in open court, but such further detentions can last only until ninety-six hours after the person's arrest. At that point the person must either be charged and brought before a court or released without charge. When brought before a court the person can apply for bail and must be granted it unless the police can show good cause for why it should be refused. The rules for terrorist suspects are more restrictive: they can be initially detained by the police for up to forty-eight hours and magistrates can extend that period to a total of fourteen days.[60]

Police questioning of detained persons is highly regulated and is video-recorded with sound.[61] The person is entitled not to answer questions and nothing must be done to oppress the person into making a confession or to make a confession unreliable. In a court case a confession is not admissible as evidence unless the prosecution proves beyond reasonable doubt that it was properly obtained. As well, a court can refuse to admit any evidence if it thinks that, 'having regard to all the circumstances, including the circumstances in which the evidence was obtained', its admission would have such an adverse effect as to render the trial unfair.

The police have significant powers to stop and search people and vehicles and to enter and search premises. They can also take photographs, fingerprints and DNA samples from detained persons. There are restrictions on how long such personal data can be retained, especially if the person involved is not later convicted of any offence. The police also have power to limit people's freedom of movement, especially at times when there is a risk of public disorder. The relatively new tactic of 'kettling' protestors into confined areas for quite lengthy periods has been held by the European Court of Human Rights not to be a breach of the right to liberty.[62]

---

[60] Terrorism Act 2000, 41(3) and Sch 8, paras 29 and 36.
[61] For the detail regarding England and Wales see the 1984 Act, n 59, ss 53-65B, 76 and 78.
[62] *Austin v. UK* (2012) 55 EHRR 14.

Police Accountability

To ensure that the police keep within the limits of their legal powers, and that they operate effectively and efficiently, various accountability mechanisms have been established. What is now called Her Majesty's Inspectorate of Constabulary and Fire and Rescue Services conducts annual inspections of the police services in England and Wales and Northern Ireland; in Scotland this function is performed by Her Majesty's Inspectorate of Constabulary in Scotland. Each police force is also accountable to a local body. In England and Wales, with some exceptions, these are now individual Police and Crime Commissioners, elected to office for periods of four years. The main exceptions are London's Metropolitan Police and the Greater Manchester Police, each of which is accountable to the office of an elected mayor. It was in 2012 that Police and Crime Commissioners replaced local Police Authorities, which by then comprised a mixture of elected councillors and independent members. That older model still persists in Northern Ireland, where there is one Policing Board as well as eleven Police and Community Safety Partnerships in the district council areas. In Scotland there is a Scottish Police Authority, but it does not comprise any members who are elected. Throughout the United Kingdom police performance can also be examined by committees of legislatures and by official auditors such as the National Audit Office.

Accountability has also been strengthened through the establishment of specialised bodies to handle complaints against the police. Police services have their own internal disciplinary systems, but if a member of the public makes a complaint against a police officer it is important that it is examined by people who are not themselves members of the police service in question. In England and Wales the responsibility for ensuring lack of bias in handling complaints against the police is now the Independent Office for Police Conduct, established under the Policing and Crime Act 2017.[63] It is the latest in a list of bodies which have struggled with the challenges of providing an impartial yet effective system for processing complaints.[64] Even today the new body attracts criticism from time to time, such as

---

[63] See www.policeconduct.gov.uk. Usually between 30,000 and 35,000 complaints are recorded each year.
[64] The prior bodies were the Independent Police Complaints Commission (2004–2018), the Police Complaints Authority (1985–2004) and the Police Complaints Board (1977–1985).

when it seemed to adopt an overly tolerant attitude towards the Metropolitan Police's handling of Operation Midland, the investigation into allegations of physical abuse made by the fantasist Carl Beech. Similarly, a predecessor body, the Independent Police Complaints Commission, was heavily criticised for concluding that no disciplinary proceedings should be taken against any of the frontline and surveillance officers implicated in the shooting of Jean Charles de Menezes at Stockwell tube station on 22 July 2005. On account of the number of complaints in England and Wales it is impossible for all of them to be investigated by non-police officers, so only the more serious complaints are investigated directly by the Independent Office for Police Conduct. Some police investigations are supervised by the Office. In Scotland complaints against the police are investigated by Police Scotland but complainants who are unhappy with the way their case has been handled can ask for a review by the independent Police Investigations and Review Commissioner.

Since 2000 Northern Ireland has had a Police Ombudsman, who alone can investigate any complaint against the Police Service of Northern Ireland. The work done by the Police Ombudsman – especially the initial office-holder Nuala (now Baroness) O'Loan – has helped to ensure that levels of public confidence in the Police Service of Northern Ireland have remained high. In so-called 'historical cases' the Ombudsman has been able to unearth serious malpractice on the part of officers in the now disbanded Royal Ulster Constabulary, including what appears to be tantamount to collusion in murder. Examples include the investigations into how Loyalist informers were allegedly allowed by their RUC handlers to commit very serious crimes in the late 1980s and early 1990s, how the RUC seems to have neglected to intervene in the transportation of illegally obtained weapons prior to a mass murder at Loughinisland, County Down, in 1994, and how the RUC and later the PSNI handled the detection of those who planted the bomb in Omagh in 1998.

The police in the United Kingdom also benefit from the work of volunteer 'independent custody visitors', people who in pairs make unannounced visits to police stations at any time of the day or night to check on the conditions of detainees who are in custody there. The reports they compile are examined by the Police and Crime Commissioner or other accountability body. The Independent Custody Visitors Association is part of the UK's National Preventive Mechanism, which seeks to ensure that the UN Convention against Torture and other Cruel, Inhuman or Degrading Treatment or Punishment is fully complied with in places of detention.

The Effect of the Human Rights Act on Policing

The Human Rights Act 1998 obliges all public authorities, including the police and army, to protect the rights of individuals and companies conferred on them by the European Convention on Human Rights, a treaty which the UK government was centrally involved in drafting in 1949–1950 and was the first to ratify in 1951. The Act's impact on policing in the United Kingdom has been considerable. Policies and codes of practice have had to be altered to take account of the human rights of everyone in society, not just those suspected of committing a crime. The Act imposes neither criminal nor civil liability directly on police officers who violate human rights, but the courts have a discretion to award monetary compensation if it believes that a mere declaration that a right has been violated is not by itself 'just satisfaction'.[65]

Initially there was some judicial reluctance to allow the Act to influence police operational independence, the argument being that if police officers always have to be looking over their shoulder at some hypothetical judge who is assessing their compliance with human rights standards those officers could not carry out their policing functions effectively. It would lead, so the argument went, to defensive policing, just as some medically qualified people may be reluctant to voluntarily intervene in emergencies just in case something goes wrong with the treatment given and they are sued by the people they were trying to help. For a while the UK courts adhered to the precedent set in Hill v. Chief Constable of West Yorkshire,[66] where the mother of one of the last murder victims of Peter Sutcliffe, the so-called 'Yorkshire ripper', failed in her bid to sue the local police for negligence on account of the way they had conducted their investigation into the series of murders. The House of Lords, Britain's top court at the time, ruled that the police did not owe any duty of care to members of the public when investigating crime.

The Hill case was followed in several subsequent cases and after the Human Rights Act came into force the Appellate Committee of the House of Lords remained reluctant to expand the police's duties in a way which went beyond what was required by the common law on negligence.[67] But in 2018, in a case concerning alleged police failures in the investigation of sexual crimes committed by a London taxi driver, John Warboys, the Supreme Court (which replaced in 2009) held, by a majority, that duties under the

---

[65] Human Rights Act 1998, s 8(1)–(3).   [66] [1989] AC 53.
[67] See Van Colle v. Chief Constable of the Hertfordshire Police [2008] UKHL 50, [2009] 1 AC 225.

Human Rights Act *could* go beyond the common law's requirements.[68] Claims under the common law and the Human Rights Act involve different bases of liability and policy. This decision should ensure that in future cases the police are more careful than before in following up all leads when investigating crimes. As for other professionals, more is expected of them too than in the pre-Human Rights Act era.

In Northern Ireland the Police Service is now recognised as having sincerely embraced a human rights approach to policing. Chief Constables there now say that the purpose of policing is to protect human rights. As a result of the recommendations of the Patten Commission, referred to earlier, the performance of the PSNI is measured against a human rights monitoring framework which has been drawn up and applied by the Northern Ireland Policing Board, with the assistance of an independent human rights adviser. A substantial annual report is issued detailing what steps the PSNI has taken to comply with human rights standards. All PSNI officers are also obliged to comply with a Code of Ethics which is heavily imprinted with references to human rights. A breach of the Code of Ethics is itself a breach of the police's disciplinary regulations.

---

[68] *Commissioner of Police of the Metropolis* v. *DSD* [2018] UKSC 11, [2019] AC 196.

16

Locality, Regionality and Centrality[*]

LUKE BLAXILL

No account of the 'rise of the modern British state' would be complete without an appreciation of the ways in which *local* institutions, constitutional principles and precedents, laws – and ultimately governance – evolved. Prior to the twentieth century, locality defined the overwhelming majority of British subjects' lived constitutional experience: the shire rule of Anglo-Saxon ealdormen, medieval corporations and county corporates, fourteenth-century Quarter Sessions, the empowered Elizabethan parish, and then the explosion of 'ratepayer democracy' in the nineteenth century featuring municipal corporations and county councils, Poor Law unions, and ad hoc statutory bodies (including school boards, public health authorities, and improvement committees) of all kinds. This whole level of governance – concerning such matters as local infrastructure, legal disputes, care of the poor, and the vast majority of taxation and expenditure in the locality – was conducted by local constitutional officers: sheriffs, county magistrates, councillors, Poor Law guardians, and others. They were often overseen (and sometimes led) by local members of parliament. In practice, this constitutional matrix meant that landowners, employers, important families, local clergy – what contemporaries might have described as the 'fit and proper persons' of the locale – were frequently of much greater visibility and practical importance to people's lives than the king, Prime Minister, and cabinet far away.[1]

This chapter provides a broad commentary of the evolving constitutional relationship between local government, parliament, and 'the centre'.[2] This

---

[*] I am grateful to the editors, and Taym Saleh, for supplying comments on earlier drafts.
[1] E. P. Hennock, *Fit and Proper Persons: Ideal and Reality in Nineteenth-Century Urban Government* (London: Edward Arnold, 1973).
[2] To precisely define 'the centre' in a temporally robust sense in British history is impossible, so I am taking it to mean (at various points) the named or de facto Prime Minister and his immediate governing inner circle, the monarch and his or her inner circle (and occasionally both).

tripartite structure can be said to have materialised from approximately the 1370s, where the Parliament of England clearly emerged to 'represent the body of all the realm'.[3] By the Tudor period, the House of Commons had assumed its place as the premier point-of-contact between central government and the localities. The bulk of this chapter's analysis, however, concerns the 300 years since the Hanoverian succession, where the constitutional role of locality has been an explicit and enduring subject of political argument and introspection. In the eighteenth century this debate centred on the ambiguous role of the MP as a simultaneously local and national representative, the function of parliamentary constituencies as units of representation, the employment of acts of parliament as instruments of local law-making, and the emergence of the office of Prime Minister. The debate in the nineteenth century centred on local government itself, where the emergent 'ratepayer democracy' was discussed in strikingly utopian terms – as a tool for efficient administration, representative morality, and civic education – and where even ambitious national legislation was frequently framed explicitly as expanding and enabling the permissive powers of local authorities. The twentieth century, with its two world wars, saw the debate turned on its head, with the quintessentially Victorian aversion to central statism swept away in a scramble to centralise, featuring powerful and frequently 'presidential' Prime Ministers, disciplined MPs loyal to party above locality, and local government increasingly viewed largely as a delivery instrument for nationally financed and directed policies designed to accomplish national outcomes. Finally, the twenty-first century has featured the curious combination of almost continuous central political advocacy for re-empowering local government accompanied by the almost complete unwillingness to actually surrender any power to it.

This chapter contains three sections. The first is largely chronological, focusing on local government itself, paying particular attention to its wholesale reform and reinvention in the Victorian period, and then its twentieth-century decline in the face of the seemingly irresistible force of centralisation. The second takes a step back from historical events, and introduces and explores the analytical concept of 'constitutional

---

[3] David Dean, 'Introduction: Parliaments and Locality from the Middle Ages to the Twentieth Century' in David Dean and Clyve Jones (eds.) *Parliament and Locality, 1660–1939* (Edinburgh: Edinburgh University Press, 1998), pp. 1–2.

communities'. The final section focuses on the relationship between parliament and the localities, especially focusing on the role of the MP as a bridge between them, and how this role has been affected by the evolution of national political parties.

Local Government: From Civic Dream to Centralisation?

After the end of Roman rule, Britain's villages and townships were largely self-governing until the emergence of defined shires in the kingdom of Wessex during the ninth century, with the term 'boroughs' (fortified places) emerging in the eleventh. By the time of the Norman Conquest, the position of landowners as de facto heads of communities, who could appoint local court leets, was established. Importantly, the feudalism which accompanied the Conquest – where all land was forfeited to the king to distribute amongst his barons – cemented the concept that the aristocracy held the Crown's land as de facto leaseholders, and wielded authority over it by royal consent. At the same time, however, these lords were free to draw revenue from the lands and bequeath them to heirs. This effective co-option of great landowners as local royal servants had the effect of tying the aristocracy in the localities more strongly to the Crown at the centre, without making them mere employees of the king. This binding of the local and the central served simultaneously to avoid both the extreme fragmentation of central authority in the Middle Ages, and the rapid advance of royal authority at the direct expense of the local aristocracy in the early modern age (both trends exemplified by the changing fortunes of the French monarchy in the centuries preceding their Revolution). By the Tudor period, the basic structure of local government that lasted until the late nineteenth century was complete: in the counties, sheriffs or Lord Lieutenants represented the Crown's local officer in the shire, working in concert with local aristocrats by appointing justices of the peace to administer Quarter Sessions to deal with legal disputes. Boroughs were recognised through charters of incorporation (which gave them the right to self-government and return MPs to parliament) and these 'corporations' soon became dominated by smaller landowners, royal servants, and increasingly by merchants and men of commerce. The most fundamental tier of local government, however, (and the most basic constitutional community) was the parish, usually run from the local church vestry. Parishes became extremely important under Elizabeth I, where they were charged with maintaining local roads, distributing poor relief, and given delegated authority to raise the necessary funding through the rates (a tax on property or land).[4] In the seventeenth century, the victory of parliament in the civil war served to protect Britain's highly varied system of boroughs, counties and parishes from the Crown's centralising ambitions. After the Glorious Revolution of 1688, Britain was governed by a curious combination of ancient bodies, crown power (in practice limited, although theoretically unlimited), monitored and mediated by a parliament which had not fully decided whether its role was primarily as a representative chamber of localities or as an embodied synthesis of the nation's general will that could sponsor an executive to lead.

These idiosyncrasies make it all but impossible to write a general history of local government prior to the early nineteenth century because, as Bryan Keith-Lucas has pointed out, there was no system: only localised examples which can be inadequately caricatured by discerning general patterns.[5] The noble ambition to write a history of local government from 1688 to 1835 consumed the energies of Sidney and Beatrice Webb (and dozens of researchers in their employment) for three decades, producing an unfinished study spanning nine volumes.[6] Even given the extent of local nuances explored in this mammoth study (featuring many pages consisting almost entirely of footnotes) Beatrice was still minded to describe the period between the turn of the nineteenth century and the 1830s as 'but the tag-end of a period opening with the Revolution of 1688'.[7] In this key decade, Britain saw the Great Reform Act and its far-reaching redistribution of parliamentary constituencies in 1832, the New Poor Law Amendment Act in 1834 which created unions of parishes to administer the Poor Law on the 'less eligibility' principle, and the Municipal Corporations Act of 1835 which established a uniform system of municipal boroughs governed by town councils elected by ratepayers. These reforms, in effect, gave rise to the age of 'ratepayer democracy' where local authorities acted within the limits of delegated statutory powers. This underpinned the (often romantically stereotyped) story of the growth of Victorian towns and cities as centres of civic pride,

---

[4] Hannis Taylor, *The Origin and Growth of the English Constitution* (Massachusetts: Houghton, 1892), vol. 2, pp. 183–188; J. A. Chandler, *Explaining Local Government* (Manchester: Manchester University Press, 2007), pp. 1–2.
[5] Bryan Keith-Lucas, *The Unreformed Local Government System* (London: Croom Helm, 1980), pp. 11–14.
[6] Sidney and Beatrice Webb, *English Local Government*, 9 vols. (London: Longmans, Green and Co., 1906–1929).
[7] Beatrice Webb, *Our Partnership* (Cambridge: Cambridge University Press, 1975), p. 151.

featuring magnificent and ostentatious public buildings. The raft of permissive legislation passed throughout the nineteenth century gave municipal corporations (and from 1888 counties and county boroughs) wide-ranging powers to build schools, demolish and rebuild slum housing, set up police forces, and construct hospitals, tramways, and sewers. Some, perhaps most famously Joseph Chamberlain's Birmingham, were highly innovative, practicing what became known as 'gas and water socialism' by taking control of utilities and reinvesting the profits in city facilities. Sidney Webb, a keen subscriber to the romantic vision of progress powered by municipal socialism, poked fun at the 'Individualist Town Councillor' (a thinly disguised caricature of his penny-pinching 'economist' political opponents on the London County Council), writing in 1890 that he:

> will walk along the municipal pavement, lit by municipal gas and cleansed by municipal brooms with municipal water, and seeing by the municipal clock in the municipal market that he is too early to meet his children coming from the municipal school hard by the county lunatic asylum and the municipal hospital, will use the national telegraph system to tell them not to walk through the municipal park, but to come by the municipal tramway to meet him in the municipal reading room, by the municipal art gallery, museum, and library, where he intends to consult some of the national publications in order to prepare his next speech in the municipal town-hall, in favour of the nationalization of canals and the increase of government control over the railway system. 'Socialism, sir,' he will say, 'don't waste the time of a practical man by your fantastic absurdities. Self-help, sir, individual self-help, that's what's made our city what it is.[8]

While this rose-tinted progressive's view of ratepayer democracy had many adherents, there were many corporations which were less like Birmingham, and much more like Norwich, where the *laissez-faire* economisers associated with figures such as George Goschen – concerned principally with keeping the rates low and avoiding lavish spending – held the upper hand. While the powers vested in Victorian local government were considerable, they were almost entirely permissive. Even in areas such as public health central government had little power to interfere, with its powers (especially following the creation of the Local Government Board in 1871) relegated to oversight from inspectors who would assess such matters as factory safety,

---

[8] Sidney Webb, *Socialism in England* (London: S. Sonnenschein & Co, 1890), pp. 116–117. Cited in John Davis, 'Central government and the towns' in *The Cambridge Urban History of Britain* (Cambridge: Cambridge University Press, 2001), p. 261.

sanitation, and Poor Law provision before reporting to the Board, which could then fine errant local authorities. It was also the case that neither of the major reforms of 1835 and 1888 had a revolutionary effect in changing the men who ran local government: in both cases magistrates, justices of the peace, and former corporation members made up a substantial proportion of the new corporations and councils (either because they succeeded at the ballot box or were appointed as aldermen).[9] Overall, nineteenth-century local government reformers were motivated by an overriding distaste for central interference in local affairs through ad hoc interventions, or as a consequence of sweeping national legislation. They were fully prepared to accept that different authorities would manage matters differently: some would experiment and others would not; some would elect new men and others stick with the old; some would embody Chamberlainite municipal socialism and others Goschenite economisation. Implicitly, such a system would never deliver uniform national standards or be counted on to march to the centre's tune.

The twentieth century saw the gradual but comprehensive dismantling of this system and a steady march of centralisation. The 'new liberal' welfare reforms from 1906 to 1914 – inspired in part by the legacy of the national efficiency movement – included old age pensions, national insurance, workmen's compensation, and were notable for almost entirely bypassing local government. Other important reforms – for example the 1902 Education Act and the 1919 Housing Act – featured substantial exchequer grants to incentivise local authorities to build, supplemented by fairly explicit central 'encouragement'. The watershed moment was the Local Government Act of 1929. Motivated by the centre's desire to rationalise the unwieldy and highly variegated Victorian system, the Act altered the basis of the (by now rapidly escalating) central funding of local authorities, switching away from Goschen's traditional system of assigned revenues (where grants were made in proportion to local authority tax take) and towards block grants calculated on the basis of a local authority's population and its numbers of unemployed and children. The old Poor Law was abolished and placed under centralised oversight, and powerful regional quangos were established over domains such as transport, electricity, and unemployment.[10] Abetted by the de-rating of farmland and industrial premises, the financial footing of local government

---

[9] J. P. D. Dunbabin, 'British Local Government Reform: The Nineteenth Century and after', *English Historical Review*, 365 (1977), pp. 775, 794.
[10] Davis, 'Central government', pp. 279–280.

had been transformed: Ben Weinstein estimates that in 1880, it raised ten times the revenue from the rates as it received from central grants, but by 1931 these proportions were about 1:1.[11] Simply put, local government was now much more dependent on central funding, which would not be supplied without central instructions. Opponents of centralisation like the outspoken academic W. A. Robson described the 1929 Act as 'a subordination of local autonomy to the dictates of central power which, if pursued, will be the virtual end of local government' and described 'the complete abdication by the local authorities of the right to think for themselves; their transformation into mere receptacles for Government policy'.[12] While Robson placed too much emphasis on the 1929 Act as an instigator of change in itself, there was no doubt that zeitgeist was rapidly transforming as the twentieth century political mentality of national standards began to take hold.

Another area where the forces of 'nationalisation' were in evidence was in the changing character of post-1918 local elections. While there had been occasional periods of hotly contested partisanship since 1835, many localities – including Guildford and Wolverhampton, which have been the subject of detailed local political studies – had lapsed into one-party rule, featuring numerous uncontested elections and (in most places) the exchange of traditional party labels for monikers such as 'progressive', 'moderate', and 'independent'. After the First World War, the escalating electoral ambition of the avowedly socialist Labour party – who roundly refused to fight under such labels – had the effect of uniting Conservatives and Liberals around the common cause of anti-socialism.[13] As the Liberals became weaker throughout the 1920s they increasingly chose to form up behind the Conservatives and local elections more and more became two-party affairs in which central party managers began to take a keen interest. By the later twentieth century, the nationalisation of electoral culture was so complete that results of national parties in local elections began to be widely interpreted as public verdicts on the performances of Prime Ministers and Leaders of the Opposition.

---

[11] Ben Weinstein, 'Local Government', in David Brown et al., *The Oxford Handbook of Modern British Political History, 1800–2000* (Oxford: Oxford University Press, 2018), p. 200.
[12] W. A. Robson, 'The Central Domination of Local Government', *Political Quarterly*, 4 (1933), pp. 85–104.
[13] Roger Ottewill, 'The Changing Character of Municipal Elections 1835–1974', *The Local Historian*, 34:3 (2004), pp. 170–174.; G. W. Jones, *Borough Politics: A Study of the Wolverhampton Town Council, 1888–1964* (London: Macmillan, 1969), pp. 37–48.

After 1945, local government was the subject of a royal commission enquiry chaired by Richard Crossman, designed to thoroughly review the system's functionality. This was, of course, in the context of widescale nationalisations taking place across the economy, and a desire to use local authorities to deliver central government's plans to rebuild a nation stricken by war. From the commission's perspective, local government did not appear ready to co-operate: according to Jon Davis they were 'consumed by particularistic squabbles over boundaries, hostile to new powers, increasingly parsimonious in the exercise of the powers they did possess'.[14] In the later years of the twentieth century, the public also began to lose interest in local government: turnout in local elections fell further and further behind that of general elections, and an enquiry of 1967 found 'ignorance and indifference to local government on behalf of the public ... it is not uncommon to hear contempt expressed'.[15] The 1972 Local Government Act, which followed shortly after, uprooted the old municipal corporations, and amalgamated boroughs, urban districts, and rural districts into larger unitary units covering both town and country. With their links to ancient communities broken, their range of powers dwindling, their ability to independently fundraise diminished, and national parties dominating local elections, it is unsurprising that the final decades of the twentieth century saw local government become a political backwater mainly run by technocrats. While the Labour party – with its core commitment to nationalisation and centralised management – was never likely to be amenable to returning power and autonomy to the localities, local government found few Conservative friends either, with the Tories increasingly viewing it as inefficient and providing potential boltholes for the militant 'loony' left to assemble fiefdoms and grandstand against central government in the style of the Poplar Rates Rebellion of 1921. Subsequent years have seen the centre asphyxiate local government still further, with the Coalition of 2010–2015 reducing local authorities' central budget by more than 30 per cent while making it illegal to raise council tax by more than 2 per cent without approval through local referendums. Today, lip service is paid, ad nauseum, to the re-empowerment of local government by politicians of all stripes, but few would disagree with the Institute for Public

---

[14] Davis, 'Central government', p. 285.
[15] Bryan Keith-Lucas, *English Local Government in the Nineteenth and Twentieth Centuries* (London: Historical Association, 1977), p. 37.

Policy Research's judgement of July 2019: that 'the UK is one of the most politically centralised countries in the developed world'.[16]

Constitutional Communities

Because the lived constitutional experience of British subjects has been so heterogeneous and localised, this section introduces and explores an analytical concept I have coined: the 'constitutional community'. Operationally, constitutional communities were simply groups of the population who, at different times, were governed by different agencies with demarcated administrative geographies: parliamentary constituencies, municipal corporations, county boroughs, parishes, boards of Poor Law guardians, improvement committees, unitary authorities, and so on. How and where their administrative boundaries were drawn on maps could determine the elective basis, revenue collecting powers, and even official constitutional status of a locality. Constitutional communities were usually also exclusive, with rights and obligations conferred on various groups who lived or owned property within their boundaries: for example, ratepayers who funded local services and wielded the franchise, and paupers and women who were sometimes formally excluded.

Perhaps the most historically enduring constitutional community is that of the parliamentary constituency: a defined geographical area which sent one or more members to the House of Commons to represent it. Before 1832, constituencies were founded on the ancient principle that each county should be permitted two MPs and, with special dispensation – via the granting of royal charters – for this to be extended to boroughs which merited independent representation. Within these constituencies, the franchise was usually bestowed through property qualifications or other residency criteria, but qualification could often be determined by miscellaneous systems such as access to a fireplace suitable for a cooking pot (so-called 'potwolloper' boroughs). Even as late as the Regency period, constituencies remained exceptionally variegated, featuring numerous 'rotten' or 'pocket' boroughs (such as Old Sarum, a ploughed field, and Dunwich, where the majority of the borough had fallen into the sea) which possessed few – if any – resident

---

[16] Romain Esteve et al., 'Decentralising Britain: The "Big Push" towards Inclusive Prosperity', *Institute for Public Policy Research Report* (2019), p. 36. See: www.ippr.org/files/2019-07/decentralising-britain-july19.pdf.

electors, alongside 'scot and lot' boroughs such as Coventry and Westminster where the majority of resident men qualified for the franchise.[17] One of the principal functions of the Great Reform Act (regarded by many contemporaries as more important than enfranchisement) was the redistribution of constituencies to remove the majority of rotten boroughs and grant booming metropolises like Manchester their own dedicated representation. It is important to note that the Whig architects of redistribution were largely unconcerned with the actual population of constituencies, and were primarily interested in updating the psephological map to strengthen representation of important emerging interests (principally commerce and industry) at the expense of the landed interest. While the redrawing of some constituencies could be justified in such principled terms, there were also numerous instances – such as the revision of Woodstock from 0.1 to 33.7 square miles – where gerrymandering electoral boundaries for party advantage clearly trumped any desire to preserve the constitutional integrity of age-old localities.[18] The desire to tinker with boundaries for party advantage likewise informed Disraeli's 1867 redistribution, which sought to reassign swelling suburbs back into the (often radical) boroughs to prevent them eating into the Tory counties.[19] The most dramatic break from the past was the Redistribution of Seats Act of 1885, which saw the triumph of the modern principle of parliamentary constituencies as population units. It was not for nothing that Lord Acton described the newly elected Commons of 1885 – explicitly designed to represent 'the people' with 'one vote one value' rather than an amalgam of sanctioned interest groups wielding variable franchises – as the 'first of our democratic constitution'.[20] This transformation also represented the end, to most intents and purposes, of the guiding principle of ancient communities warranting their own independent representation, with mathematically constructed constituencies with utilitarian titles as 'Leicestershire North East' or 'Birmingham Bordesley' becoming the norm outside of a remaining handful of provincial boroughs. By the twenty-first century, the 'one vote one value' redistributive principle has achieved hegemonic status, with periodic boundary commissions seeking to equalise

---

[17] Edward Porritt, *The Unreformed House of Commons*, vol. 1 (Cambridge: Cambridge University Press, 1903), pp. 35–36, 64.
[18] Eastwood, p. 80.
[19] Charles Seymour, *Electoral Reform in England and Wales* (London: Humfrey Milford, 1915), pp. 338–345.
[20] Lord Acton cited in T. A. Jenkins, *The Liberal Ascendancy 1830–86* (Basingstoke: Macmillan, 1994), p. 208.

constituency populations, birthing such inelegant amalgamations as 'Suffolk Central and Ipswich North' and 'York Outer' (a doughnut-shaped seat around York). In 2013 the commission even proposed the historically unthinkable in the name of psephological equality: the merger of parts of Devon and Cornwall to create a 'Devonwall' constituency. While the proposal was withdrawn following a West-Country backlash, it perhaps underscored that constitutional locality (in parliamentary terms) is now almost entirely a function of population arithmetic.

Moving onto constitutional communities for first-tier local government administration, it may be observed that these, for the period prior to 1832, often remained the same as for parliamentary constituencies at corporation and county level. This naturally helps explain the frequently very close relationship (that we shall later explore) that existed between borough corporations and borough MPs, and between Lord Lieutenants and county MPs: they could both be viewed as local constitutional representatives for the same geographical area, but with separate functions and roles. Interestingly, the Great Reform Act's attack on the voting power of non-resident 'out-voters' (whom Lord Russell branded as the cause of 'manifold and manifest evils') actually tightened the link between MPs and corporations because it weakened the former's capacity to draw upon an elective power base outside of local influence.[21] After the 1885 redistribution, the link between first tier local government and MPs was weakened because, while counties were sliced into multiple single-member divisions, local government continued to be conducted on a pan-county basis (underscored by the creation of County Councils in 1888). This break between the areas of parliamentary and local government psephology was continued by the 1972 Local Government Act – which controversially eliminated ancient English and Welsh counties, county boroughs, and municipal corporations – and replaced them with huge regional conglomerates (unitary authorities, and metropolitan and non-metropolitan district councils) with invented names such as 'Avon', 'Humberside', 'Salop', and 'Dyfed'.

The most basic constitutional community, the parish vestry, proved more historically enduring, with even the unifying of multiple parishes for administrative purposes (as was increasingly seen in the early nineteenth century for improvement commissions and the Poor Law) having little dilutive effect on the traditional principle of government at the 'neighbourhood' level. Indeed,

---

[21] David Eastwood, 'Parliament and Locality: Representation and Responsibility in Late-Hanoverian England' in Dean and Jones (eds.) *Parliament and Locality*, p. 79.

the enduring centrality of the ancient parish even to late-Victorian reformers was underscored by the Liberals' 1894 Parish Councils Act, which boldly attempted to re-energise the parish as the basic unit of government by requiring them to be elected. While the abolition of the Poor Law in 1929 removed their principal historic role, parish councils maintained a number of their original functions (such as footpath and verge maintenance, vermin control, and administration of local charities) in around a third of English and Welsh postcodes. Apathy began to take its toll after 1945, however, and today the declining relevance of the parish as a constitutional community is symbolised by the fact that many struggle even to fill councillor vacancies unopposed, let alone entertain contested elections for them.[22]

The observation that historic constitutional experiences have varied significantly by locality also stems from the fact that, prior to their formal assimilation in 1948, local and parliamentary franchises were different. The right to vote in local elections of any kind was by historic principle simply vested in ratepayers who funded the services being delivered, without the property valuations which (prior to 1884) could determine parliamentary franchise qualification. It was thus perfectly possible for a man to qualify for the local but not parliamentary franchise. Equally, the reverse could also be the case because qualification for the former required residency as ratepayer for three years, whereas the latter required occupation of a qualifying property for just one year.[23] Substantial discrepancies thus emerged: for example, in mid-Victorian Liverpool 22 per cent of adult males enjoyed the parliamentary franchise but just 10 per cent the municipal, whereas in Stockport there were nearly triple the number of municipal electors as parliamentary.[24] Different constitutional communities could thus be said to exist simultaneously even inside identically mapped areas: people who could vote in both parliamentary and local elections, in one or the other, or in neither.[25] Interestingly, the link between property and voting, formally abolished in 1928 for parliamentary elections, survived for another two decades locally, which resulted in the maintenance of considerable franchise discrepancies in the twentieth century also: for example, the 1929 local

---

[22] See, for example, *Knutsford Guardian*, 6 Feb. 2017; *Pevensey Bay Life*, 12 Apr. 2019; *Wharfdale Observer*, 19 Apr. 2007.
[23] Philip Salmon, *Electoral Reform at Work* (Woodbridge: Boydell & Brewer, 2002), p. 219.
[24] Weinstein, 'Local Government', p. 194; Bryan Keith-Lucas, *The English Local Government Franchise: Short History* (Oxford: Oxford University Press, 1952), p. 61.
[25] Salmon, *Electoral Reform*, p. 221.

electorate was around 40 per cent smaller than its parliamentary equivalent.[26] Indeed, in Northern Ireland, the constitutional enshrinement of the ancient link between paying tax and voting enjoyed a still more protracted swansong, surviving in local government elections into the late 1960s, with the old cry of 'one man one vote' still finding expression as a campaigning slogan (through the Northern Ireland Civil Rights Association).[27]

Another longstanding constitutional distinction has been between boroughs and counties. This dates to the thirteenth century, when the distinction between 'knights of the shire' (county MPs) and 'burgesses' (borough MPs) clearly emerged. Operationally, county MPs before the 1880s were invariably aristocrats and landed gentry whose election to the Commons was largely a formalisation of power and influence held locally. Borough MPs, meanwhile, were often more heterogenous: while they could be minor gentry, they were also often merchants, tradesman, or royal servants for whom a local link to the town was a lesser pre-requisite than a long purse for distributing bribes. Unsurprisingly, contested elections were generally more of a recurring feature in borough than county political life, and limited public space and easier communications were likelier to create a more competitive hothouse featuring rival speechmaking campaigns, handbills and posters, and mass consumption of local newspapers.[28] The belief that boroughs and counties were, *sui generis*, different, was central to the thinking of electoral reformers: in 1832, they set quite different franchise qualification criteria for boroughs and counties; in 1867 they granted household suffrage to boroughs but denied it to counties until 1884; in 1835 they established elected municipal corporations for boroughs but denied equivalent reform to counties until 1888.[29] In part, borough democratisation was expedited and county democratisation delayed on account of *Realpolitik*: Whigs and Liberals generally believed they would retain dominance of radical urban centres by enlarging their franchises, while Tories and Conservatives took the view that the aristocracy's pre-eminence in the shires could be best defended by excluding

---

[26] This figure is based on my own collaborative analysis (with Taym Saleh) of a sample of 169 constituencies (exclusively London and county boroughs) where comparison between local and parliamentary electorates was possible at the time of writing. In 1929, the total parliamentary electorate in these consistencies was 7,392,651 but the county borough/London County Council electorate of only 4,477,534.

[27] Dunbabin, 'British Local Government Reform', pp. 801–802.

[28] For a general summary of borough and county political traditions, see Frank O'Gorman, *Voters, Patrons, and Parties: The Unreformed Electoral System of Hanoverian England 1734–1832* (Oxford: Oxford University Press, 1989), pp. 334–359.

[29] For full borough and county franchise qualification criteria in 1832, see Salmon, *Electoral Reform*, pp. 253–255.

social classes below the tenant farmer. It may also have stemmed from the enduring belief that the urban working classes were more literate, more amenable to political education, and better able to cope with the disruptive experience of election campaigns, than agricultural labourers who might be debilitated by 'slow mental digestion' and poor literacy.[30] The twentieth century generally saw the constitutional distinction between boroughs and counties effectively disappear, in large part on account of the fact that the populations of the latter increasingly lived in small or medium-sized towns rather than villages and hamlets.[31] Since the millennium, policy-maker's interest in rural (or county) local government has been largely non-existent, but there has been considerably more focus on cities since the establishment of the high-profile London Mayor and Greater London Authority, including local referendums to set up directly elected town and city mayors.

It is also revealing to dwell upon those formally excluded from voting. Property qualifications – be they payment of rates, property valuation, or even the potwolloper principle – were designed to ensure that only those with a more material stake in government, be it in terms of property or taxation, should be permitted to stand for, and participate in, elections of any kind. This also meant that the franchise would be wielded by those who had the education, literacy and leisure time to consider local or national political questions (as John Bright put it) 'without an absolute stupidity'.[32] Mid-Victorian opponents of working-class enfranchisement might well have sympathised with Robert Lowe's acerbic assessment of 1866:

> If you want venality, if you want ignorance, if you want drunkenness and the facility for being intimidated ... if you want impulsive, unreflecting and violent people, where do you look for them in the constituencies ... to the top or to the bottom?[33]

The question of the *suitability* of electors for inclusion in the national constitutional community was of such paramount importance that Lowe and other opponents of reform made a sharp distinction between a £10

---

[30] J. Seymour Lloyd, *Elections and How to Fight Them* (London: Vacher & sons, 1905), p. 39.
[31] The fact that, even in the late nineteenth century, county divisions could be mainly urban is easy to overlook. One of the three case-study constituencies in a recent study of rural Liberalism was Holmfirth in Yorkshire, where – as Paul Readman has pointed out – 92 per cent of the population in fact lived in towns of over 1,000 inhabitants. See Patricia Lynch, *The Liberal Party in Rural England 1885–1910* (Oxford: Oxford University Press, 2003).
[32] *Hansard*, 30 May 1866, vol. 183, col. 1515.
[33] Robert Lowe, *Speeches and Letters on Reform* (London: R.J. Bush, 1867), p. 25.

borough franchise qualification and Gladstone's modest bill in 1866 to reduce this to £7. Simply put, even though Disraeli's Second Reform Act one year later brought household suffrage almost by accident, it was widely believed – even amidst a background of democratisation – that parliamentary franchise property qualifications should be sufficiently restrictive to exclude less suitable electors even if they otherwise paid rates and enjoyed the local franchise.[34]

Perhaps a still more notable exclusion from the franchise was women, who had been formally prevented from voting in municipal corporations in 1835 but continued – as they had since the eighteenth century and possibly before that – to enjoy the franchise (as ratepayers) for various improvement commissions and in elections to the parish vestry even though, in practice, their participation was likely limited.[35] The Municipal Franchise Act of 1869 formally gave women ratepayers the vote in local elections and allowed them to serve as Poor Law Guardians, and they were permitted to become fully fledged councillors in 1907. The noteworthy point here is that the practical (and from 1832 formal) exclusion of women from the parliamentary franchise until 1918 meant that, for half a century, women were deliberately included in the local constitutional community but deliberately excluded from the national. The contemporary justification for this fascinating inconsistency, which is explored in detail in Patricia Hollis' *Ladies Elect*, ultimately stemmed from women's perceived aptitude for local government's 'caring' and 'nurturing' functions such as oversight and management of education, health, and looking after the poor and the insane: what contemporaries regarded as 'family management writ large', 'the domestic work of the nation', and 'municipal housekeeping'.[36] Indeed, Weinstein cites a telling example from 1889 where anti-suffragists Mary Ward and Elizabeth Burgwin, founders of the Local Government Advancement Committee, explicitly advocated the advance of women's involvement in the more parochial domain of local politics precisely because it contrasted with 'questions of foreign and colonial policy ... or of grave constitutional changes ... that the necessary and normal experience of women ... does not and can never provide them with

---

[34] This point was indeed acknowledged by Gladstone himself who remarked that 'Municipal franchises are in a predominant degree working men's franchises'. See *Hansard*, 12 Apr. 1866, vol. 182, col. 1136.

[35] The extent to which qualifying early- and mid-Victorian (and indeed pre-Victorian) women wielded the franchise is somewhat debatable. See Sarah Richardson, 'The Victorian Female Franchise', *The Victorian Commons* (18 Mar. 2013) published online at: https://victoriancommons.wordpress.com/2013/03/18/the-victorian-female-franchise/.

[36] Patricia Hollis, *Ladies Elect: Women in English Local Government 1865–1914* (Oxford: Oxford University Press, 1987), p. 6.

such materials for sound judgement as are open to men'.[37] While such contemporary attitudes were by no means universal, they remind us that inclusion or exclusion from local and national electorates reflected contemporary judgements on the relative suitability of electors from the separate (although often overlapping) local and national constitutional spheres.

A final major dimension to consider is the simple fact that the United Kingdom has always constituted four nations rather than one. Variations in the nature and timing of the evolution of local government itself between Scotland and Ireland (compared to England and Wales) have been notable but not fundamental.[38] By far the most significant constitutional change was the establishment of a devolved Scottish Parliament and Welsh Assembly from 1999. As well as their devolved powers (in the case of Holyrood, generally over all domains barring defence, foreign policy, taxation, and some welfare) both bodies use the Additional Members System whereby two-thirds of MSPs and AMs are elected via First-Past-the-Post constituencies (using a different psephological map to Westminster) with the remaining third being allocated through an adjusted system of proportional representation using a central party list. This has had the effect of creating two classes of representatives occupying the same chambers: MSPs and AMs with constituencies and party list MSPs and AMs without them. The 'list' members are a significant landmark in the sense that they represent the first occasion (outside of European elections) where electors have cast votes for *parties themselves* rather than for individuals, thus building political parties formally into the constitution. Another notable constitutional dilemma has been the so-called West Lothian Question where Scottish MPs were able to vote on English legislation but not the reverse, which has been addressed by the adoption of the 'English votes for English Laws' convention since 2016, thus in a sense creating a fractured concept of a 'government majority': on the one hand over England, and on the other, over the whole of the UK. In Northern Ireland, the Stormont Parliament enjoyed considerable

---

[37] Weinstein, 'Local Government', p. 199.

[38] In Scotland, the Commissioners of Supply took on most of the equivalent responsibilities of the sheriffs and Lord Lieutenants from 1667 and 1889, and the operation of the amended Poor Law (from 1845) was in some respects different. In Ireland, the Local Government Act of 1898 created county councils in a similar vein to England, but the effect was much more dramatic in ending Protestant landlord control of local government and placing most Irish local government in the hands of nationalists. For further reading, see George Pryde, *Central and Local Government in Scotland Since 1707* (London: Routledge and K. Paul, 1960); Mark Callanan and Justin Keogan (eds.), *Local Government in Ireland: Inside out* (Dublin: IPA, 2003).

autonomy (roughly equivalent to that of the Holyrood Parliament) between 1921 until its suspension in 1972 during the troubles. Following the Good Friday Agreement in 1999, Stormont was revived, but with two very unique constitutional conditions: the first being mandatory power sharing between nationalists and unionists, and the second the facility (exercised on several occasions) for Westminster to suspend Stormont's operations and reimpose direct rule. Notably, these unique constitutional arrangements and devolutions of power in Northern Ireland and Scotland have not affected these nations' ability to return MPs to Westminster (aside from a reduction in the number of seats allocated per-head of population). They have, however, led to their domination by unique Northern Irish and Scottish political parties, which has in practice partially disconnected them from the political body clock of England and Wales.

Parliament, MPs and Parties

Parliament's historic role has always been to sit between the centre and the peripheries: representing neither centrality nor locality exclusively. Prior to the Glorious Revolution, the monarch could summon it as required, principally to approve taxes. It was also possible for the Crown to impose central reforms directly upon the localities through its network of appointed royal officials, principally Lord Lieutenants and sheriffs. In 1555 for example, the maintenance of highways was made the responsibility of a town's sheriff and leet, and in 1601, Elizabeth I co-opted parish vestries as state agents for the supervision of poor relief, and legally required church-wardens to raise funds through collecting rates on suitable lands and houses.[39] Constitutionally, parliament had very limited formal capacity to check monarchical power, highlighted most starkly when Charles I attempted to govern without it throughout the 1630s, imposing his own system of generating revenue by co-opting local officials in ports to collect the 'ship money'. The tumultuous events of the civil war, the interregnum, and Glorious Revolution heralded the effective permanent supremacy of parliament which moved from 'irregular assemblies, dependant on Royal authority ... to emerge as the most important place in which the British state's authority and jurisdiction would be debated'.[40] Fairly obviously, the resounding checks to the absolutist ambitions of Charles I and James II delivered a vast de facto decentralisation

---

[39] Taylor, *English Constitution*, vol. 2, pp. 190–191. [40] Dean, 'Introduction', p. 4.

of power, which was exaggerated when it eventually fell to the commons – a heterogenous assembly of the kingdom – to fill the vacuum. This new supremacy of parliament had important implications for local government because it drastically weakened the Crown's ability simply to delegate power to Lord Lieutenants or other local networks of appointed officials.[41] Thus, especially from the Hanoverian succession in 1714, local MPs had an important role to play in local governance in their constituencies, and parliament had become the chief intermediary where central-local government relations were worked out.[42]

A key practical reason MPs became directly involved in local government was the importance of an often-overlooked, branch of law-making: the private local act of parliament. Members frequently presented local bills to the commons (as petitions) and then steered them through parliamentary scrutiny to the statute book. Even in the late nineteenth century, it is often forgotten that local – rather than public (national) – acts represented the vast majority of parliament's legislative output, and the latter only actually overtook the former after the Second World War.[43] Local bills might relate to collection of local rates, land disputes, poor relief, or the building of improvements such as highways, railways, canals, or gaols. In the seventeenth and eighteenth centuries, local acts were necessary not just because local authorities lacked a full range of delegated statutory powers, but also because local magistrates often doubted the legal basis of those which were theoretically at their disposal, many of which were ancient or observed only by tradition. A new proposal, especially one which might prove controversial amongst persons of influence in the locale, or require the levying of rates, was potentially vulnerable to legal challenge, especially since the decline of *quo warranto* writs (a formal order issued by authority of the king) and other archaic crown enforcement mechanisms. The most obvious instrument for resolving local disputes, or indeed for local government to simply establish (or re-establish) the operational scope of its statutory powers, was thus the local act, and by the 1740s these had been accepted as an important part of an

---

[41] Joanna Innes, 'The Local Acts of a National Parliament: Parliament's Role in Sanctioning Local Action in Eighteenth-Century Britain' in Dean and Jones (eds.) *Parliament and Locality*, p. 47.

[42] John Prest, *Liberty and Locality: Parliament, Permissive Legislation, and Ratepayers' Democracies in the Nineteenth Century* (Oxford: Oxford University Press, 1990), p. 1.

[43] Philip Salmon, 'Parliament' in David Brown, Robert Crowcroft and Gordon Pentland, *The Oxford Handbook of Modern British Political History, 1800–2000* (Oxford: Oxford University Press, 2018), pp. 89–90.

MP's parliamentary work.[44] Of course, local circumstances that produced a successful local act might well apply elsewhere, and a diligent MP would pay close attention to the passage of other local bills which might (suitably re-purposed) also be suitable for his own constituency.[45] This resulted in, for example, a rush of applications to establish small debt collection courts in the mid eighteenth century when parliament established the precedent that it would approve such acts.[46] This growing tradition of localities taking inspiration from each other's successfully carried acts was facilitated first by the adoption of standing orders from the 1770s (which specified procedures to be followed in the assessment of turnpike, river, canal and enclosure bills) and second by a marked increase in the number of 'clauses acts' which supplied approved sets of rules and wording which could be copied to speed up the drafting and scrutiny of new similar acts. By the nineteenth century, local measures were even sometimes used as templates for national acts, as occurred with the Metropolitan Police Act of 1829 for London (which eventually culminated in the national County and Borough Police Act of 1856) and the Improvement Act of 1844 for Manchester (which formed a template for the Public Health Act of 1848).

An MP's claim to 'represent' his constituency has also invariably been based on his own biography and local activity. Prior to 1885, his position as the dominant political force in the locality – at the centre of established networks of deference and plutocracy – would simply be confirmed by the absence of opposing candidates attempting to create a disruption by contesting his seat at elections.[47] Pocket boroughs, on the other hand, were not always controlled by the MPs that sat for them, but often by patrons some of whom, like the Duke of Newcastle in the early to mid eighteenth century, might have several under their thumb.[48] Boroughs which were not irredeemably rotten naturally still featured large corrupt elements in their electorates even after 1832, and incoming candidates – even with the longest purses – were usually not able to bring all local interests under their personal financial

---

[44] Innes, 'Local Acts', p. 26.
[45] See Paul Langford, 'Property and "Virtual Representation" in Eighteenth-Century England', *Historical Journal*, 31:1 (1988), pp. 83–115.
[46] Innes, 'Local Acts', p. 38.
[47] D. C. Moore, *The Politics of Deference* (Hassocks: Harvester Press, 1976), pp. 295–297.
[48] Frank O'Gorman, *Voters, Patrons, and Parties: The Unreformed Electoral System of Hanoverian England 1734–1832* (Oxford: Oxford University Press, 1989), pp. 27–67.

control.[49] They were thus often obliged to toe the line of the powerful borough corporations which were invariably composed of important local employers, aristocrats, and magistrates, and these often wielded such decisive electoral influence that they became de facto electoral colleges for parliament and effectively simply picked the local MPs.[50] Such corporations – roundly condemned by the Whigs' 1835 *Inquiry into the Municipal Corporations of England and Wales* as 'political engines' – often took it to be axiomatic that they had the right to advise their sitting members, and for such advice to be heeded.[51] Perry Gauci demonstrates the considerable influence wielded, in the seventeenth century, by the Yarmouth corporation over the parliamentary behaviour of the borough MPs, especially relating to their involvement in maritime legislation in which the town had an obvious interest.[52] J. V. Beckett gives a telling example from Nottingham around the turn of the nineteenth century: a sitting member Daniel Parker Coke (who had previously been awarded freedom of the city for 'zealous assiduity in parliament') provoked the ire of the corporation for proposing a jurisdiction bill of which it disapproved and for failing to oppose war with France to its satisfaction.[53] The corporation not only withdrew support from Coke at the election of 1802, but financed their own last-minute candidate and successfully unseated their disobedient member, only for the election to be declared void on petition. While the Great Reform Act and Municipal Corporations Act in the 1830s undid much of the direct power that local government could wield over local MPs, a much weaker informal link came to exist in the later nineteenth century through the not-uncommon practice of a person serving simultaneously as an MP and county councillor. This was true for eighty-seven members in 1899, but died out in the closing decades of the twentieth century on account of the physical impossibility of juggling escalating dual workloads.[54]

---

[49] Two examples of comprehensive bribery of virtually all the political power bases in the Beverley and Kinsale consistencies as late as the 1850s (by Henry Edwards and Sir John Arnott respectively) are given in K. Theodore Hoppen, 'Roads to Democracy: Electioneering and Corruption in Nineteenth-Century England and Ireland', *History*, 81:264 (1996), pp. 563–564.

[50] Keith-Lucas, *English Local Government*, pp. 9–10.

[51] Cited in Chandler, *Explaining Local Government*, p. 6.

[52] Perry Gauci, '"For Want of Smooth Language": Parliament as a Point of Contact in the Augustan Age' in Dean and Jones (eds.) *Parliament and Locality*, pp. 12–22.

[53] J. V. Beckett, 'Parliament and the Localities: The Borough of Nottingham' in Dean and Jones (eds.) *Parliament and Locality*, pp. 63–64.

[54] Bryan Keith-Lucas and Peter Richards, *A History of Local Government in the Twentieth Century* (London: Allen & Unwin, 1978), p. 99; J. A. Chandler, *Local Government Today* (Manchester: Manchester University Press, 2001), pp. 84–85.

Even in the absence of a formal link to local government, the obligations a nineteenth- or twentieth-century MP had to his (or her) constituency electors were still considerable. In the mid nineteenth century, these could include requests for patronage, jobs, sinecures, and pensions.[55] By the end of the century, the practice known as 'nursing', where MPs would spend large sums on local subscriptions to charities, chapels, and sports clubs, was often simply an expected part of elected service, despite claims in some quarters that it should be considered a form of electoral corruption.[56] After the 1885 redistribution had broken the link between ancient community and parliamentary constituency, there is considerable debate on how far local credentials continued to matter, especially given Edwardian commentators' estimations that around half of election contests were fought by 'carpetbaggers' from outside the constituency.[57] Carpetbaggers' comparative ignorance of their chosen constituency often gave them little choice but to campaign largely on national political questions, although their lack of local credentials were frequently criticised by opponents.[58] The argument that electoral culture saw increasing 'nationalisation' after 1885 – and thus that MPs were increasingly seen as representatives of national parties rather than local champions – also rests on the increasing external influence of national electioneering bodies such as the National Liberal Federation and Conservative National Union, and on the marked increase in local newspapers' reporting of speeches from front-bench politicians. However, other historians, while acknowledging the new strength of the nationalising tensions at play in this period, have, however, tended to stress the enduring 'centrality of locality' in electoral politics until after the Great War and the dawn of universal suffrage.[59]

However, there is a distinction to be drawn between candidates and MPs. Analyses by J. P. Cornford and G. L. Bernstein suggest that the majority of elected members between 1885 and 1914 forged strong business or property

---

[55] Michael Rush, *The Role of the Member of Parliament since 1868* (Oxford: Oxford University Press, 2001), p. 203.

[56] Kathryn Rix, *Parties, Agents and Electoral Culture in England, 1880–1910* (Woodbridge: Boydell & Brewer, 2016), pp. 177–178. See also J. J. Davis, 'Electoral Blackmailing', *National Review*, xvi (1890), pp. 50–54.

[57] Moisei Ostrogorski, *Democracy and the Organisation of Political Parties* (New York (State): Macmillan, 1902), vol. 1, p. 451; A. Lawrence-Lowell, *Government of England* (New York (State): Macmillan, 1908), vol. 2, p. 5.

[58] Luke Blaxill, 'Electioneering, the Third Reform Act, and Political Change in the 1880s', *Parliamentary History*, 30:3 (2011), p. 350; Rix, *Electoral Culture*, pp. 179–183.

[59] See esp. Jon Lawrence, *Speaking for the People: Party, Language and Popular Politics in England, 1867–1914* (Cambridge: Cambridge University Press, 1997).

interests in their constituencies, even if they were carpetbaggers at the point they were elected.[60] Indeed, the degree to which an MP with a large constituency electorate was bound to do what would now be called 'constituency work' to maintain rapport with voters, and to be seen to be a good local member between elections, has been analysed by Michael Rush. He cites a number of late nineteenth century members who, while they might have featured prominently in local subscription lists and been diligent at answering letters, visited their constituents just a handful of times a year.[61] However, such members – including, in the twentieth century, Roy Jenkins who only travelled to his constituencies of Birmingham Stechford (1950–1977) and Glasgow Hillhead (1982–1987) monthly – did appear, however, to be the exception rather than the rule: H. C. G. Matthew suggests that by the 1890s 'regular tours of autumn speeches – mini-Midlothians – had become the rule' and Kathryn Rix gives several examples of onerous 'local political education' campaigns by more diligent MPs.[62] Recent research has also focused on political promises (which can be conceptualised as informal 'contracts' candidates made with voters at election). Here, quantitative textual analyses suggest a marked increase after the Great War in politicians' tendency to make promises, abetted by national party manifestos becoming an established part of political culture from the 1920s.[63] While the later twentieth and twenty-first centuries have seen the continuation of many of these nineteenth century trends (especially that of carpetbagging) there has been something of a swing back to locality in the very recent past on account of the fact that more MPs are ex-councillors, and also that MPs ask more parliamentary questions specifically related to their constituencies.[64]

For their own part, MPs from at least the late eighteenth century were consistently mindful of shifting conceptions of what it meant to 'represent' a constituency, and they spent no little time debating the question. Here, it is impossible to ignore Edmund Burke, or to avoid quoting his celebrated 1774 speech to the electors of Bristol, where he argued that:

[60] J. P. Cornford, 'Parliamentary Foundations of the Hotel Cecil', in *Ideas and Institutions in Victorian Britain*, ed. Robert Robson (Cambridge: Cambridge University Press, 1967), p. 284; G. L. Bernstein, *Liberalism and Liberal Politics in Edwardian England* (London: Allen & Unwin, 1986), p. 16.
[61] Rush, *Member of Parliament*, pp. 200–201.
[62] H. C. G. Matthew, 'Rhetoric and Politics' in P. Waller (ed.), in *Politics and Social Change in Modern Britain* (Brighton: Harvester Press, 1987), p. 41; Rix, *Electoral Culture*, p. 144.
[63] Luke Blaxill, 'Election Promises and Anti-promises After the Great War' in Richard Toye and David Thackeray, *Electoral Pledges in Britain Since 1918* (Cham: Palgrave Macmillan, 2020), pp. 22–26.
[64] Rush, *Member of Parliament*, pp. 204–206.

> Parliament is not a congress of ambassadors from different and hostile interests; which interests must each maintain, as an agent and advocate, against other agents and advocates; but Parliament is a deliberative assembly of one nation, with one interest, that of the whole; where not local prejudice ought to guide, but the general good, resulting from the general reason of the whole. You choose a member, indeed; but when you have chosen him, he is not a member for Bristol ... he is a member of parliament[65]

Burke's advocacy of what modern politicians might call 'the national interest' counselled an MP to eschew selfish advocacy of his constituency's material wishes – what would later be called 'pork barrel' politics – but also refuse to act as a delegate for local interest groups, including local government officers looking to 'instruct' their members. As well as asking an MP to consider the 'general good' and be guided by it, Burke's maxim also granted a member considerable liberty to exercise his own judgement and follow his conscience. The wide-ranging influence of these high-minded principles inspired a diverse range of early nineteenth century politicians of all stripes: Lord Eldon, Robert Peel, and even reformers actively seeking to remedy representative defects in the system such as Lord Russell, James Mackintosh, and Thomas Macaulay.[66]

The principal challenge to Burkean maxims arrived after 1867 with the rise of mass competitive elections and recognisably modern political parties. This was graphically illustrated by the eye-catching electoral success of the radical Birmingham caucus which, through adopting highly organised machine politics, enabled the Liberals to win dazzling victories in the city's parliamentary and municipal elections. This in turn made it difficult for Liberal candidates to dissent from policies approved on the caucus floor. While this conception of an MP as a local party delegate – who owed his office to an electioneering instrument – was naturally the antithesis of the Burkean ideal, its effect was not in fact to put constituencies back in charge of their members, but rather to put levers of control into the hands of central party managers. Birmingham's caucus became affiliated with the new National Liberal Federation founded in 1877 led by chief organiser Francis Schnadhorst, and the Conservatives also soon developed their own centralised party organisation. While the power of central party leadership was increasing (also on account of more effective whipping) perhaps the apogee

---

[65] Edmund Burke, 'Speech to Electors of Bristol', in *The Works of the Right Hon. Edmund Burke*, vol.1 (London: Holdsworth & Ball, 1842), p. 180.
[66] Eastwood, 'Representation and Responsibility', pp. 70–73.

was reached in 1886 when Gladstone, as Prime Minister, attempted to force the policy of Irish Home Rule on Liberal MPs. One of the many critics of such seemingly overbearing leadership was MP for Mid-Norfolk Robert Gurdon, who complained that:

> a member of parliament was not to have any opinions ... but simply to act as a machine to register the decrees of the minister and of the party whips. Is it wise to even have a man at all? Would it not be better to have a machine which could be wound up?[67]

While Gladstone's actions – which split the Liberal Party – clearly exceeded the contemporary power of the Prime Minister to control constituency MPs, it was a clear portent of things to come. The twentieth century (and the dawning of the radio and TV age) saw growing party organisation, professionalism, centralisation of election-fighting resources, and nationalised election campaigns featuring 'presidential' leaders advancing national manifestos. In the 1950s, most electors voted on national party lines regardless of their MP, delivering exceptionally uniform swings across England and Wales, and (as we have seen) were also increasingly likely to vote in local elections on national party lines.[68] Nationalisation has, unsurprisingly, led to power gathering in the hands of Prime Ministers and coteries of advisers, with perhaps Tony Blair's 'sofa government' representing the zenith of oligarchic centralised leadership in Britain. That being said, the extent to which small parliamentary majorities (and hung parliaments) can clip the wings of Prime Ministers has been memorably demonstrated since 2016, and several MPs have returned to Burke to justify their parliamentary actions over the Brexit schism. More broadly, such hitherto ubiquitous political staples as national election swing, safe seats, and fixed and stable party labels, have suddenly begun to look rather dated. As such, the constitutional role of the constituency MP remains (arguably both by accident and design) ambiguous.

Conclusion

It would not be an inaccurate caricature – in terms of local government, autonomous constitutional communities, and independent constituency MPs – to argue that Britain has, in the course of the last three centuries,

---

[67] See Luke Blaxill, *The War of Words: The Language of British Elections, 1880–1914* (Woodbridge: Boydell & Bewer, 2020), p. 118.

[68] Martin Rosenbaum, *From Soapbox to Soundbite: Party Political Campaigning in Britain since 1945* (Basingstoke: Macmillan, 1997), pp. 224–253.

seen the slow rise, brief apogee, and rapid decline of the constitutional ideal of locality (broadly defined). Gone is the municipal romance of the Webbs and Chamberlain, symbolised by the magnificent town halls whose optimistic grandeur today strikes a melancholy chord amidst the decayed cityscapes of Bradford, Rochdale, Huddersfield and other declining post-industrial towns. Gone is the ideal of the local constitutional community *esprit de corps*, symbolised by the almost-forgotten parish councils and miniscule turnouts in local elections. Gone also is the independent Burkean member, pushed aside by the escalating domination of central parties and the birth of the 'career politician'. That being said, the twenty-first century has witnessed the emergence of powerful new forces: for example, the rediscovered salience of questions of sovereignty, the unresolved status of devolution, the renewed relevance of parliament, and the potential for technology to reshape how people even conceive of locality. While it seems unlikely that future decades will see an unwinding of the seemingly inexorable march towards centralisation, it would be unwise indeed to believe that any final word has yet been had on the constitutional role of locality in Britain.

17
Political Parties

ROBERT CROWCROFT

'Societies, all societies, are constituted in a certain way, and this way is their constitution.'[1] So observed Philip Bobbitt in 2003, and the connection between the life of a society and its constitution has only become more pronounced during the years since. Constitutions frame and regulate the political; and this in turn both reflects, and makes possible, the social. The constitutional order – a nexus of institutions, laws, values, and practices – is an integral component of the self-image of a people. In February 1792, William Pitt told the House of Commons that 'love of the constitution' was a 'natural instinct' of Britons, for it 'provides, beyond any other frame of government which has ever existed, for the real and useful ends which form at once the only true foundation and only rational object of all political societies'.[2]

Events during the second decade of the twenty-first century – the 2014 referendum on Scottish independence from the Union, the Nationalists' rejection of the result as settling the matter, the 2016 referendum on Britain's membership of the European Union, and the subsequent struggle to implement or overturn the decision of the latter – electrified the United Kingdom's public affairs, not least its political parties. The independence question turbocharged a secessionist Scottish National party which perhaps specialised more in grievance than governing. 'Brexit', as it instantly became known, heightened and then forced the resolution of a decades-long civil war within the Conservative party and led to the Labour party's worst electoral performance since 1935. This was a period of tumult unlike any in living memory.

---

[*] I am grateful to the two editors, as well as Will Hawkins, Francesca Morphakis, and Gordon Pentland for helpful comments on an earlier draft of this essay. Geoffrey Fry, Owen Hartley, and Richard Whiting offered valuable ideas in conversation.
[1] Philip Bobbitt, *The Shield of Achilles: War, Peace, and the Course of History* (London: Penguin, 2003), p. 206.
[2] Quoted in John Derry, 'Governing Temperament under Pitt and Liverpool', in John Cannon (ed.), *The Whig Ascendancy: Colloquies on Hanoverian England* (London: Edward Arnold, 1981), pp. 125–145, at 127.

This essay examines the relationship between the constitutional order and political parties. It argues that parties have been a primary vehicle for constitutional contestation and innovation. The importance of party in constitutional history was a major theme in David Hume's eighteenth-century masterwork *The History of England*.[3] Parties are, as Edmund Burke grasped, integral to the practical operation of the constitution and the parameters within which peaceful politics are carried out.[4] They reinforce, or contest, the very legitimacy of the existing order. Meanwhile the constitutional system has created parties, torn them apart, and yielded both irresistible opportunities and cosmic dangers for the individuals who lead them. Parties have been ubiquitous, even if they have not always enjoyed a good press.[5] It is true that there are ambiguities in defining what constitutes a 'party', as distinct from a faction, a group, or a 'connexion' of individuals; and depending on these definitions one could cast our net very widely. Jennings and Keith Feiling plausibly argue that the roots of party can be located in the wedding of Henry VIII and Anne Boleyn.[6] The bitter division of political elites during the reign of Charles I also has a good claim.[7] For the sake of coherence, however, it seems sensible to restrict our attention to the period since the late seventeenth century. The first section examines the highly interactive relationship between parties and the constitution. From there, the second section asserts the primacy of high-political manoeuvre in constitutional conflict. The third section ponders the impact of individual leaders on the constitution-party linkage. A conclusion then draws things together. Given that other pieces in the volume provide chronological coverage as well as accounts of the major bodies of doctrine, this essay will move back and forth in time, identifying a series of recurrent themes and problems. That selection is arbitrary, but not accidental.

First things first. Political parties were, from the very beginning, inextricably intertwined with the constitutional order. Indeed, it was a deep crisis in that order which first summoned the Whig and Tory parties into existence during the Exclusion Crisis of 1679–1681. The question of whether the Duke of York, later James II, should be barred from ascending to the throne due to his Roman Catholicism provoked acute constitutional strain as the Earl of

---

[3] David Hume, *The History of England*, 6 vols. (1754–1761).
[4] Edmund Burke, *Thoughts on the Cause of the Present Discontents* (1770).
[5] Harvey Mansfield Jr., *Statesmanship and Party Government: A Study of Burke and Bolingbroke* (Chicago: University of Chicago Press, 1965).
[6] Ivor Jennings, *Party Politics, Volume II: The Growth of Parties* (Cambridge, 1961), p. 4; Keith Feiling, *A History of the Tory Party, 1640–1714* (Oxford, 1924), p. 13.
[7] John Adamson, *The Noble Revolt: The Overthrow of Charles I* (London: Orion, 2007).

Shaftsbury and his 'Whig' supporters endeavoured to preserve the Protestant succession, even at the price of departing from hereditary principles and laying down the law to the Crown. The 'Tories' were King Charles II's personal followers who resisted this. Importantly, however, both sides saw themselves as standing for traditional 'English liberties'.[8] The existential constitutional struggles which wracked the English polity during the seventeenth century thus provided the spark that created political parties. Decades of successive crises and intrigue running through the reign of Charles I, Civil War, the Commonwealth, the Restoration, and the Glorious Revolution meant that organised division developed into a habit. Polarisation became normalised. Parties, however loose they may have been at times, were a crucial facet of British politics thereafter. From their inception, then, political parties were based at least in part around important constitutional questions of who should rule, how, and by what authority. Those questions often furnished parties with their very identity. And, as Isaiah Berlin grasped, conflict between identities – which define who we are – cannot be easily adjudicated and will remain a source of intractable dispute.

This pattern persisted into the eighteenth century. While the cohesion of parties fluctuated dramatically, and most governments were coalitions of some kind, for several decades opposition to the king's ministers was considered to be synonymous with repudiation of the Hanoverian settlement and the possibility of political violence in order to affect a restoration of the Stuarts. The prospect of a fundamental challenge to the constitution hung over politics in the era of Viscount Bolingbroke and Sir Robert Walpole. This climate favoured the Whig successors of those who had backed the revolution of 1688 and penalised the Tories. Party allegiance, even if it was only a label, impacted where one stood on matters that affected the stability of the polity – and by extension on one's career prospects. This began to recede in the aftermath of the failed 1745 Jacobite rising, but it was a slow process. Until the Seven Years War, Britain lived with the spectre of invasion and revolution. And throughout the century, 'the routes to power ran through the courts, both the king and his heir, more than through Parliament'.[9] In this world, the basis of political loyalties was constitutional in the form of dynastic commitment.[10] Parliamentary opposition thus generally consisted

---

[8] J. C. D. Clark, *English Society, 1660–1832*, 2nd ed. (Cambridge, 2000), p. 83.
[9] Jeremy Black, *Pitt the Elder: The Great Commoner* (Stroud: Sutton, 1999), p. 33.
[10] J. C. D. Clark, *The Dynamics of Change: The Crisis of the 1750s and English Party Systems* (Cambridge, 1982), p. 4.

of Whig factions opposed to the personnel who made up the executive, rather than a rival party per se. Still, a seasoned 'wirepuller' like the Duke of Newcastle knew that the constitution 'would not work without parties', and these needed to attend to the self-interest of politicians.[11] As the century progressed, the furore over the self-assertion of George III, and later his illness, sent shockwaves through the political system and sparked a realignment of parties and relations between senior politicians. It is important not to impose an ahistorical purposiveness onto the politics of this period, for that competition was largely about getting power, but the 'issues' that animated individuals were often constitutional.[12]

During the nineteenth century, many of the problems that shaped party politics continued to revolve around the constitution. This ranged from the rights of non-Anglicans to, repeatedly, the extension of the franchise and management of the Union with Ireland. These questions destabilised the body politic and were interwoven with party advantage and doctrine. After the Reform Act of 1832 it became necessary for parliamentarians to seek support from a wider electorate, and extra-parliamentary organisation was necessary in order to mobilise it. Parties thus played an important role in registering citizens to vote. One way or another, political parties and the constitution could not be untangled. This pattern persisted through the end of the century and into the early twentieth century, with Ireland and the relationship between the House of Commons and the House of Lords at the forefront of national politics. Ireland, particularly, was always primed to provoke party-political responses: 'Liberal support for Home Rule and Conservative opposition did more to define party political identity in late Victorian and Edwardian Britain than any other single issue'.[13] Indeed, 'Home Rule' combined Irish nationalism with a parliamentary political strategy. The Irish Nationalist leadership made the case that party politics was a more efficacious route to constitutional reform than agitation and disturbance. And the fact that the Conservatives became known, until the end of the First World War, as the 'Unionists' underlined the persistent primacy of constitutional issues to party-political identity. Meanwhile the enactment of universal adult suffrage, particularly votes for women, signified another major change in the conceptualisation of the constitution.

---

[11] Jennings, *Party Politics*, pp. 33–34. [12] Clark, *The Dynamics of Change*, p. 4.
[13] Matthew Kelly, 'Home Rule and Its Enemies', in A. Jackson (ed.), *The Oxford Handbook of Modern Irish History* (Oxford, 2014), p. 582.

Yet once these issues were settled, for several decades there was an unusual lull. A workable constitutional settlement for a democratic age had been achieved, and politics became primarily about economic and social questions. The Labour party proved as constitutionally unadventurous as the Conservatives. It was in this safe and reassuring socio-political context that the teaching of constitutional history went into steep decline.[14] Even so, the flammability of constitutional matters remained undiminished, as the Troubles in Northern Ireland affirmed. And leaders such as Stanley Baldwin and Margaret Thatcher appealed to 'constitutionalism' to justify contentious policies, not least when it came to the trade unions. Constitutional problems were reawakened by Britain's immersion in European federal integration from 1973 and then the reforms of the Labour government of 1997–2010. These had long-term effects that were often unforeseen and would eventually return constitutional issues to the fore of public life. In fact, the period from the 1970s onwards represented one of the most rapid episodes of constitutional change since the Norman Conquest. The passage of the European Communities Act and subsequent European treaties, the Human Rights Act, devolution, Lords reform, and the introduction of referenda essentially created a new, quasi-federal, constitutional order and diluted the sovereignty of both the Westminster Parliament and the United Kingdom as a whole. Meanwhile the referendum of 2016 sparked the most serious party-political crisis for at least a century.

What can we glean from this necessarily breathless sketch? Most fundamentally, it is clear that the constitutional order and the political parties were bound together in a mutually affecting relationship. There were a number of dimensions to this. Nowhere was it more apparent than in the gradual development of party government. From the nineteenth century onwards, governments were increasingly elected and defeated *as parties*. Parliamentary opposition was as integral to this system as the government of the day: the rival party constituted an alternative government, a minority in Parliament but ready to appeal to the electorate and take office. The two warred for the support of voters. From the 1830s, party was 'an all-embracing modality from which there was no escape'.[15] It amounted to a foundational shift in the

---

[14] See the related discussion in Michael Bentley, *Modernizing England's Past: English Historiography in the Age of Modernism, 1870–1970* (Cambridge, 2005), pp. 19–44.
[15] Peter Ghosh, 'Gladstone and Peel', in Peter Ghosh and Lawrence Goldman (eds.), *Politics and Culture in Victorian Britain: Essays in Honour of Colin Matthew* (Oxford, 2006), pp. 46–73, at 54.

constitution. The parties alternated in office depending on the outcome of general elections. Parties became the vehicle through which the electorate selected, evaluated, and dismissed ministries. They formed and sustained governments, and engaged the citizenry. They generally embodied different sentiments and priorities. Party thus became the basis of executive authority. In this environment the old ideal of supra-party government, embodied by both Pitts, lost its practicability. As early as 1813, Lord Grenville declared that 'party connexion ... on its true foundation of public principle' was indispensable 'to the benefit of a parliamentary constitution'.[16] Walter Bagehot wrote in 1867 that party was of the system's 'essence': 'bone of its bone, breath of its breath'.[17] Benjamin Disraeli argued in April 1872 that 'without party, parliamentary government is impossible'.[18] By 1902, Arthur Balfour told a public audience at Fulham that 'In English domestic politics ... we are never at peace. ... Our whole political organisation is arranged in order that we may quarrel; and we always do...'[19] This 'quarrel' was facilitated by the interaction between the constitutional order and the political parties. Rule by party therefore generated crucial constitutional norms and habits.

A second dimension was the impact that the constitution-party nexus had on the government machine. Let us begin with the Cabinet. It was during the long premiership of Lord Liverpool between 1812 and 1827 that the principle of Cabinet 'collective responsibility' came into being for the first time. This was both a crucial step in the cohesion of the executive and an essential basis for party government. The Cabinet acted as the link which fused the executive and legislative powers together. It was, as Bagehot put it, a 'hyphen which joins, a buckle which fastens'.[20] It was a committee, chosen of and by the legislature, to form the executive body. Instead of ministries being loose collections of individuals, they would increasingly act together in a common enterprise. This practice of collective responsibility had a transformational effect on the British polity. Moreover – and crucially – party allegiance would be the basis of identifying who might, and might not, participate in a government. In the judgement of Jennings, Cabinet government 'could not function' without parties, and 'Party warfare is thus essential

---

[16] Cited in W. H. Greenleaf, *The British Political Tradition, Volume Three, A Much-Governed Nation Part 2* (London: Methuen, 1987), p. 879.
[17] Walter Bagehot, *The English Constitution*, ed. Paul Smith (Cambridge, 2001), p. 101.
[18] *The Times*, 4 Apr. 1872.   [19] *The Times*, 21 July 1902.
[20] Bagehot, *The English Constitution*, p. 68.

to the working of the democratic system'.[21] In such an environment, the Cabinet came to enjoy 'a life and authority of its own', emerging as 'the core' of the whole constitution, 'the supreme directing authority'.[22] Party made this possible.

No less dramatic was the effect on the premiership itself. The post of Prime Minister began to assume something recognisable to a modern audience under Pitt the Younger and, still more so, Liverpool. The individual at the centre of the day-to-day functioning of the constitution was increasingly able to wield huge influence. Party acted as a crucial force multiplier in the legislature, permitting the will of one person to hold sway in a manner that had not previously been the case. And as electioneering and bureaucracy became ever-more complex, parties required a recognised leader who would direct a ministry, organise its policy priorities, and shape the appeal to the electorate. All these tasks were essential in a liberal constitutional state and, increasingly, a democratic one. Sir Robert Peel's Tamworth Manifesto of 1834 was a landmark moment in placing directly before the electorate details of the measures a leader intended to pursue. In this respect Peel was the first modern Prime Minister (though he was also distinctly old-fashioned in his supra-party ideals that harked back to an era before party government). A need for a pre-eminent leader stemmed from the party system, and, once again, altered the practical operation of the constitution. Prime Ministers set policy, appointed and removed ministers, and dominated the business of the Commons. They were able to do this because their power was underpinned by political parties.

Finally, the interaction between party and constitution accelerated the growth of the Whitehall apparatus. The wars of the seventeenth and eighteenth century came at vast cost, and paying for them necessitated a larger executive and bureaucracy than the country had ever known. The executive needed to be able to reliably control the legislature in order to extract money from it and use it as an instrument for passing laws. Managing Parliament to this end was another spur to the formation of parties. Whereas the Commons had long been impossible to consistently control – Charles I just ruled without it for eleven years – party now became an essential aid to doing so. The embedding of the executive in the legislature was critical to this. And the growth in the boundaries, duties, and capacities of the state

---

[21] Ivor Jennings, *The Law and the Constitution*, 5th ed. (London, 1959), p. 86; Ivor Jennings, *Cabinet Government*, 3rd ed. (Cambridge, 1959), p. 16.

[22] Jennings, *The Law and the Constitution*, p. 89, and Jennings, *Cabinet Government*, p. 1.

gradually altered what it was possible for parties to promise to do, and the posts that Prime Ministers were able to offer to supporters. The policies of successive governments and the need to finance these through a legislature shaped, at least in part, by parties transformed the state itself.

The empirical record is clear. During the last four centuries, the constitutional order was often at the forefront of British politics, and the party system has both shaped, and been shaped, by it. Indeed, the constitution proved to be one of the three major political battlegrounds that have preoccupied parties and the British state. The others were war, grand strategy, and foreign policy on one hand, and economic and social policy on the other. The constitutional order was consistently a major theme in public strife and a subject that fixated the parties. One might plausibly argue that the most consistent initiators of political conflict were constitutional matters. There is, of course, a certain attraction in enmity; and politicians have understood this better than most. Enmity provides clarification, and in a realm as ambiguous as the political, a shortcut is always welcome. The nature of party politics is defined at least as much by whom, and what, people are *against*, as by whom, and what, they are *for*. The very existence of parties presupposes disagreement and conflict. Enmity thus serves critical definitional purposes within the party system. The primacy of enmity as a political lubricant was one of the great insights of Carl Schmitt, captured in his friend/enemy distinction.[23] And few things are as likely to provoke enmity as the constitutional order.

The British constitution is the child of conflict. What Bagehot described as its 'Gothic grandeur' obscures the reality that its form and practices are the result of an accretion of contingencies, played out over centuries.[24] It owes much to violence – real, feared, and rhetorical. Upheaval, turmoil, and plot was the norm throughout much of British history and shaped the rules under which these islands were governed. The course of political struggles, and consequences both intended and unintended, left behind rich alluvial deposits of constitutional sediment. Think of the crisis in relations between the Crown and the barons that prompted, and followed, the signing of the Magna Carta by King John in 1215 as one powerful exemplar of this. Thomas Cromwell's innovative conceptualisation and use of parliamentary statutes as a means of abolishing papal jurisdiction and enabling Henry VIII to have his

---

[23] Carl Schmitt, *The Concept of the Political*, trans. George Schwab (Chicago: University of Chicago Press, 2007).
[24] Bagehot, *The English Constitution*, p. 8.

way is another. And David Cameron conceded a referendum on membership of the European Union in order to shore up his position in the Conservative party. These and many other tactical devices, employed for instrumental purposes, crafted a series of constitutional norms and precedents, encompassing the parameters of Opposition, the relationship between Commons and Lords, the powers of the monarch, the contract between the state and citizen, the legal status of parliamentary legislation, and innumerable additional issues. The constitution is at least as much the product of conflict, and the resolution of conflict, as it is of reasoned reflection.[25]

In this, high politics counts. The history of British public affairs since the seventeenth century, and long before, demonstrates that constitutional controversies have been a site of intense high-political manoeuvres between talented and ambitious politicians engaged in a ruthless quest for office. The character of politics necessitates a capacity for intrigue and imagination in selecting issues that can be used to enhance one's influence and that of one's party. Politicians take advantage of, and at times invent, disagreements in order that they might provide the basis of tactical gambits. Acquiring power, pursuing advantage, and destroying opponents is the coin of political life, and to seek out other purposes is often to falsely rationalise events and to refuse to take *politics* seriously as an activity. The nature of political behaviour is 'semi-autonomous' from the policy issues with which it interacts.[26] Far from being above this kind of conduct, the constitutional order has provided rich pickings. As J. C. D. Clark put it, 'constitutional precedents are generated and used in the business of political manoeuvre'.[27] Such is the sublunary nature of the human world.

So far as the political parties were concerned, constitutional controversies proved very dangerous indeed. Few subjects were as certain to provoke the politics of conflict, even hatred. Not only did they create parties, but they consistently tore them apart and triggered radical realignments in the party system. To play the constitutional game was to run grave, potentially terminal, risks. Indeed, the lineage of British parties is 'fragmented and discontinuous'; and breaks in it are a product of high-political competition frequently centred on the constitution.[28] The Tory party called into being during the Exclusion Crisis was destroyed just a few years later when the

---

[25] A wonderful account of the centrality of the constitutional order can be found in Robert Tombs, *The English and Their History* (London: Penguin, 2014).
[26] Clark, *The Dynamics of Change*, p. 6.   [27] Ibid, p. 20.
[28] J. C. D. Clark, 'A General Theory of Party, Opposition and Government, 1688–1832', *Historical Journal* (1980), pp. 295–325, at 295.

Tories consented to the dethronement of James II and the revolution of 1688. The manoeuvres of 1714–1717, which centred on the accession of the House of Hanover, created a new order in which the Whigs were the party of government for most of the eighteenth century and into the nineteenth century, with political competition largely conducted between a kaleidoscopic array of Whig factions. Those who succeeded in politics did so having 'fought their way to the top of the Whig party'.[29] The Tories were sidelined for most of the rest of the century, and one could argue that it was their exile from high office that turned some of them into Jacobites.[30] Their only viable option for getting into government was a revolution. After the 1760s, the Tories essentially ceased to exist in Parliament; the later 'Tory' or Conservative party of the 1820s and 1830s was Whig, not Tory, in its genealogy. Governments were coalitions of Whig factions, bolted together by personal loyalty, administrative competence, and support for the status quo – exemplified by dominant individuals such as Newcastle, Pitt the Younger, and Liverpool.

Then there was the importance of the Crown as a high-political actor. Monarchs remained central political figures and active executive authorities until the late eighteenth century, playing parties and factions off against one another in the contest for royal favour. The Stuarts were at the hub of politics, and their positions and preferences were a source of crisis. William III and later, with declining success, Anne, sought composite ministries that would draw upon men from both parties. The Crown held the balance at a time when the clash between Hanoverian and Jacobite 'permeated all public action'.[31] Moreover the tendency for heirs to the throne to develop antagonistic relations with their fathers opened up opportunities for attentive politicians. Later, George III was determined to be the prisoner of no one. The attempt by Charles James Fox and Lord North to establish a ministry in defiance of the king's wishes saw 'a party in command of a majority in the House of Commons ... pitted against a monarch employing every weapon in the still formidable arsenal of prerogative', leading to 'the most acute political convulsion' since 1688.[32] Now remembered as a preliminary to the rise of Pitt, the episode underlined the surviving prerogatives of the monarch.

This system endured, with some important shifts, until it was demolished during the crises over the Anglican supremacy and the extension of the

---

[29] Ibid, p. 307.   [30] Ibid, p. 316.   [31] Ibid, p. 303.
[32] John Cannon, *The Fox-North Coalition: Crisis of the Constitution, 1782–4* (Cambridge, 1969), ix–xi.

franchise in 1827–1832. Importantly, the ethos underpinning the constitutional order remained robust until the moment of its obliteration; to contemporaries it did not seem primed for collapse.[33] Its destruction was instead a product of high-political intrigue. At first, the issues of reform and emancipation 'cut across party lines'; yet 'when they ceased to do so ... the parties were torn apart'.[34] The two-party polarity that resulted from constitutional innovation was almost instantly cemented by party rule, rotation in office, the selection of leaders, and policy platforms to capture public support. As we have discussed, this had enormous effects. Meanwhile the reform debates of 1832, 1867, and 1884 saw party politics marked by what Richard Shannon termed a 'game of menaces and counter-menaces', with a relentless series of constitutional spectres being raised to intimidate both adversaries and allies alike.[35] The outcome of 1884 saw the Conservatives under the Marquess of Salisbury outfox the Liberals on the redrawing of constituency boundaries in ways that cemented suburbia as the demographic foundation of the Conservative party. Thus did the interactive relationship between constitutional reform and party advantage retain its potency. The party system was again blown apart shortly afterwards, as important elements of the Liberal party walked out over Gladstone's enthusiasms for constitutional reform in the form of Home Rule, forging the 'Unionist' alliance with the Conservatives that reconfigured the political landscape once more.

The struggle between the Liberal government and the Unionist opposition between 1909 and 1914 was constitutional conflict for party advantage in its purest form. When the House of Lords, dominated by Unionists, broke a convention of 150 years' standing and rejected the Budget in November 1909 this was an ideal situation for an actor with the fertility of mind and political ambition of David Lloyd George. Balfour, meanwhile, spotted an opportunity to hold the Unionist party together – cripplingly divided as it was over trade policy – and wreck the Liberals' Commons majority at the same time.[36] The result was a quite remarkable shift in the practice of party conflict, one that brought about a terminal blow to the independent power of the Lords. Nor was that the end. By 1912, in what was undoubtedly one of

---

[33] John Derry, 'Governing Temperament under Pitt and Liverpool', in Cannon (ed.), *The Whig Ascendancy*, pp. 124–145, at 125.
[34] Clark, 'A General Theory of Party, Opposition, and Government', p. 310.
[35] Richard Shannon, *The Age of Salisbury, 1881–1902: Unionism and Empire* (London: Longman, 1996), p. 83.
[36] Bruce K. Murray, *The People's Budget 1909/10: Lloyd George and Liberal Politics* (Oxford, 1980), pp. 209–221.

the most remarkable episodes in British political history, the Unionists were giving rhetorical support to the paramilitary Ulster Volunteers and pondering inciting a revolt by the army in a bid to raise the spectre of civil war in Ireland.[37] Their hope was that this might coerce the fragile Liberal government – its majority successfully destroyed in the two general elections of 1910 – into another election over Home Rule that would, the new Unionist leader Andrew Bonar Law calculated, see his party returned to office. The Unionists ratcheted up the pressure in order to break the government. They hoped to present it with a choice – abandon Home Rule and lose the support of the Irish Nationalist MPs who kept it in office, or implement Home Rule, ignite civil war, and use the armed forces to suppress British citizens in Ulster for the crime of wishing to remain British – that it dare not face. The Prime Minister, Herbert Asquith, accused Bonar Law of a 'declaration of war against constitutional government'.[38]

Of course, the Liberals were far from innocent. They submitted to pressure from the Irish to introduce Home Rule as the price of retaining office, pursuing radical constitutional change with no obvious sanction from the electorate and in the likelihood of unleashing civil war in the British Isles. Having lost a quarter of their seats and their Commons majority at the January 1910 general election – something which can be read as a public rebuttal of their Budget that had prompted the crisis – the Liberals placed themselves in the hands of the Irish in return for support in curtailing the Lords. The second election of that year, in December, saw the Unionists win the popular vote and the same number of seats as the Liberals; by-elections soon established the Unionists as the largest party in the Commons. In this environment, the Liberals collaborated with the Irish and Labour to pass the Parliament Act. F. E. Smith declared Liberal behaviour 'an outrage on democracy', and Lansdowne stated that the Commons was in the grip 'of a vast and organised conspiracy against the public welfare', with minority parties engaging in a series of blatantly corrupt bargains.[39] Home Rule was placed on the statute book, only to be immediately suspended due to the difficulties of implementing it. Conservative propaganda posters stressed that

---

[37] Robert Saunders, 'Tory Rebels and Tory Democracy: The Ulster Crisis, 1900–14', in Richard Carr and Bradley W. Hart, *The Foundations of the British Conservative Party; Essays on Conservatism from Lord Salisbury to David Cameron* (London: Bloomsbury, 2015), pp. 65–83; Jeremy Smith, *The Tories and Ireland, 1910–1914: Conservative Party Politics and the Home Rule Crisis* (Dublin: Irish Academic Press, 2000).
[38] H.C. Debs., 31 July 1912, 41, col. 2137.   [39] *NUCA Annual Conference Report*, 1911, p. 13.

'Every Vote for the Liberal is a Vote for Civil War'.[40] Smith warned that 'Ministers who try to use the army [to suppress the Ulster Volunteers] will end up swinging from the lamp-posts of London'.[41] This was truly audacious stuff. We will never know whether the public would have backed the Unionists or the Liberals at a general election to break the deadlock; both were extricated from the situation by the outbreak of war in Europe.

No crisis in the age of mass democracy matched the constitutional turmoil unleashed by the EU referendum of 2016. This episode too had party-political origins: it represented the climax of a long struggle within the Conservative party over the constitutional dimension to the European question that had impacted every leader since Edward Heath and destroyed or wounded four successive Conservative Prime Ministers. This conflict brought about the referendum in the first place, as the spectre of the insurgent Nigel Farage and his United Kingdom Independence Party loomed over the Conservatives and spooked Cameron into conceding an 'In or Out' national poll. And then, in the aftermath of the referendum, it ensured that the question of how to deliver Brexit would prove contentious. But the other parties soon got in on the act. The spectacle that followed was extraordinary. The referendum constituted the largest political exercise in British history; and more people, 17.4 million, voted to leave the EU than had ever voted for anything in these islands. However, the Conservative and Labour parties were trapped in a crisis of their own making, with many leading figures privately reluctant to break with the EU despite the verdict of the electorate. A subsequent general election in 2017 saw 83 per cent of votes cast for parties that still publicly promised to honour the referendum result; yet, thereafter, important elements within those parties – including at the apex of government – displayed even less enthusiasm for doing so. The result was chaos and paralysis. Indeed, it is almost certain that opponents of Brexit manoeuvred to bring about precisely this state of affairs. To function effectively the British constitution depends on the broad consent of the governing class, but between 2016–2019 it was clear that this was being withheld. This was a situation ripe for high-political manoeuvre of the type that amused the historian Maurice Cowling.

It was a predicament unlike any in living memory, and few politicians possessed the constitutional temperament to effectively respond. Parties risked destruction as they navigated a constitutional and electoral minefield.

---

[40] Saunders, p. 79. [41] Ibid.

The Cabinet haemorrhaged members throughout 2018 as Theresa May's 'deal' for exiting the EU took shape. When that deal was put to Parliament, it sustained the worst Commons defeat on record, leaving May on the brink of being toppled. In 2019 a new entity led by Farage, the Brexit party, was formed and within a matter of weeks comfortably won a national poll, the elections to the European Parliament; that same contest saw the Conservative share of the vote slump to 8.8 per cent. Meanwhile the Labour party discerned opportunities in the crisis engulfing the Conservatives but came to realise that the dangers to its own electoral base were every bit as profound. Neither major party had uniform or clear views on Brexit, and their voters were even more divided. Many politicians flirted with the idea of asking the public to simply vote again on whether they really wanted to exit the EU after all. And the Liberal Democrats calculated that pledging to cancel the referendum result outright might play to their electoral advantage. Nor did it end there. The Crown was dragged in. The Supreme Court intervened in matters of executive prerogative. There was the remarkable sight – absent since the eighteenth century – of political factions plotting in concert with the emissaries of foreign powers – individual EU member states and the institutions of the EU itself – on questions of constitutional orientation. Most importantly, the House of Commons took on some of the functions of the executive, as splits in the Conservatives enabled anti-Brexit elements from that party to join with other parties to temporarily seize control of parliamentary business and foist a foreign policy on the government to which it was opposed. The Speaker of the Commons, an opponent of Brexit, reinterpreted procedure in order to facilitate the Commons acting as a quasi-executive. Party-political manoeuvre and schism thus raised fundamental questions of legitimacy and authority.

This was a contest to make up the rules under which the country was governed. By 2019, British politics had arguably lapsed into something resembling a Schmittian state of exception, with many of the conventions of public life in abeyance and constitutional formalism little more than a fig-leaf employed by politicians seeking to assert themselves relative to adversaries. The stock phrases which structure the day-to-day practice of politics were turned into 'empty and ghostlike abstractions' as norms broke down.[42] Separate elements of the polity were brought into a relational position of radical conflict. And 'exceptional circumstances' were used to provide a

---

[42] Schmitt, *The Concept of the Political*, p. 30.

blanket justification for behaviour – indeed many actors deployed adjectives like 'exceptional' and 'unprecedented' repeatedly. This situation underlined the stark reality that all political norms are ultimately situational, and liable to be amended as expediency necessitates. If, from a certain perspective, the essence of politics is the power to decide, the deadlock of 2019 underlined what follows when the power to decide is stripped away or otherwise hobbled. There seemed no way out of this jam. The result was a conflict of wills, in the truest sense. Potent myths, in the way conceived by Plato and Georges Sorel, as forms of collective expression, were brought into collision, and galvanised action. A seemingly endless contest was only resolved through yet another general election which saw a new Prime Minister, Boris Johnson, secure an unexpectedly decisive Commons majority and a mandate to exit the EU in January 2020. Labour won fewer seats than at any point since 1935. It was a sudden climax to a dramatic period of recrimination, one that had taxed the resources of liberal democracy. Throughout the strife of 2019, actors had asserted claims to make decisions in the public interest, attempting to legitimate their own roles and preferences in doing so. The ensuing contest transfixed, then exhausted, millions. Its resolution reflected both public anger and fatigue. To mischievously rework Schmitt's most famous maxim, perhaps sovereign is he who can get away with it.[43]

What we can detect, then, is a close connection between the fortunes of parties and their interaction with the constitutional order. Parties have proven notably resilient institutions, successfully navigating the vicissitudes of a perpetually adversarial system until shattered in high-political episodes. These episodes often centred on the constitution. Constitutional questions repeatedly recast the party system; to engage with them was an activity that was high risk and high reward. Parties were torn asunder, and new policy choices made feasible. High-political manoeuvre as it touched on delicate constitutional questions accelerated the centrifugal forces present in all parties. And the constitution was routinely used to unsettle matters and open up opportunities. In summary, if constitutional history is to be written once more – and it must – an important component of that history should be the primacy of high-political calculation.

The impact of specific individuals on the relationship between the constitutional order and political parties is also worth pondering. William Gladstone

---

[43] 'Sovereign is he who decides on the exception': Carl Schmitt, *Political Theology: Four Chapters on the Concept of Sovereignty*, trans. George Schwab (Chicago: University of Chicago Press, 2005), p. 5.

was the dominant political figure of Victorian Britain, and a Peelite who believed that the Conservatives had let down their chief over the Corn Laws; the job of parties was to retain discipline and show loyalty to the leader. Gladstone learned from Peel 'that the highest exigencies of the state might well require heroic sacrifice of the interests of party'.[44] The attraction of his adopted home, the Liberal party, for Gladstone was it offered 'the only plausible prospect of Peelite government'; his Liberalism was thus 'essentially adaptive'.[45] His deep religious faith and conviction of the role of Providence in the world was integral to his self-understanding as an 'instrument of God' and a 'Christian statesman'.[46] Statecraft was about 'heroic' measures undertaken by individuals such as Peel and Gladstone, and the responsibility of parties was to obey. Like Peel, Gladstone had only disdain for his followers and an imperious manner of leadership that left the Liberal party deeply resentful. He looked to public opinion outside Parliament as a tool through which his party might be intimidated into obedience. He aimed at 'active and coercive manipulating and directing of noisy popular energies', of demagogic 'agitation and even intimidation'.[47]

Yet Gladstone's imperious manner of leadership meant that he often failed to read his party correctly, not least over the constitutional issues which continually tempted him into action. This enabled Disraeli to successfully divide the Liberals over reform in 1866–1867. And it led to the implosion of the Liberal party in the Home Rule crisis of 1886. Constitutional reform in Ireland offered an enticing stage for Gladstonian providential statesmanship, the results of which would, he wrote in his diary, be 'offered before the Eternal Throne'.[48] When he had decided upon Home Rule as the way forward, Gladstone plumped for what Richard Shannon describes as 'shock tactics' in order to 'coerce the Liberal party'.[49] And on details he played his cards close to his chest, repeatedly refusing to inform his colleagues of his plans. Given that this entailed massive disruption in the constitutional order, for nervous Liberals it was all simply bewildering. As a despairing Lord Hartington enquired of Granville: 'Did any leader ever treat a party in such a way as he has done?'[50] Unable to think like a party politician, Gladstone's reckless leadership on Home Rule saw the Liberals partially buried 'under the volcanic ashes of a fierce racial and sectarian controversy'.[51] A style of

---

[44] Richard Shannon, *Gladstone: Heroic Minister, 1867–1898* (London: Allen Lane, 1999), xiii.
[45] Ibid, xv, p. 3.   [46] Ibid, xii.   [47] Ibid, xiv.   [48] Ibid, p. 50.
[49] Ibid, pp. 365–366.   [50] Ibid, p. 405.
[51] Sidney Low, *The Governance of England* (London: T. F. Unwin, 1914), p. 134.

leadership that 'turned politics into combat' showed little regard for the centrality of party to the constitutional order.[52]

Equally, however, parties also furnished the resources for constitutional stability and social equilibrium. This was one of their most important benefits. Nowhere was this clearer than in the person of Walpole, one of the central politicians in British history. By 1714, it seemed likely that political instability would continue to be the norm. Yet, within a decade, all was changed. A 'politician of genius' was able to 'create what had eluded kings and ministers since the days of Elizabeth I – a government and a policy acceptable to the Court, to the Commons, and to the majority of the political establishment at large'.[53] This was an extraordinary achievement that is now mostly forgotten. On his watch, the state became nothing less than 'a Whig enterprise'.[54] As Harry Dickinson put it, Walpole was in power for more than twenty years 'because he had an unrivalled ability to manage men and a profound understanding of how the political system ... actually worked'.[55] Taking full advantage of Whig domination, Walpole was able to craft a constitutional order which anaesthetised many of the conflicts of the preceding decades by investing the larger part of the political nation in the status quo. This commanded broad and deep support, and relatively few people had an interest in challenging it. Through an intricate system for the distribution of spoils in the form of lucrative posts and sinecures, the executive was able to render many MPs dependent on, or beholden to, the ministry. The sheer cost of electioneering – bribing voters in a borough to vote a certain way – had to be recouped; the prize had to be worth the expense. Cooperation with the government brought jobs, influence, and profit.

Moreover, 'no one understood the value of Jacobitism better' than Walpole.[56] The great majority of the Tory party 'had never been and never was to be Jacobite'.[57] They were backbenchers, suspicious of the Court and executive, and anxious to curtail government spending and retain traditional liberties. Jacobitism was the folly of Bolingbroke and a few others. Yet there were several armed Jacobite risings, and even more scares. This presented

---

[52] Jonathan Parry, *The Rise and Fall of Liberal Government in Victorian Britain* (New Haven: Yale University Press, 1993), p. 247.
[53] J. H. Plumb, *The Growth of Political Stability in England, 1675–1725* (London: Macmillan, 1967), p. 158.
[54] Clark, 'A General Theory of Party, Opposition and Government', p. 305.
[55] H. T. Dickinson, *Walpole and the Whig Supremacy* (London: English Universities Press, 1973), p. 68.
[56] Plumb, *The Growth of Political Stability*, p. 168.   [57] Ibid, p. 169.

ideal propaganda fare for the Whigs. 'Walpole realised the immense potential in a political situation that might permit him to smear his opponents with treason'.[58] Once he was in power after 1720, he used this to the full, drawing to him the support of much of the gentry and the Crown. The result was the effective destruction of the Tory party and the establishment of a single-party state under a Whig oligarchy. The Tories were outcasts, consigned to the frontiers of the political system. Ostracism paid long-term dividends. There was, it must be noted, a close connection between the achievement of constitutional stability and the erection of single-party government via the virtual proscription of political opposition.[59]

Walpole's Septennial Act strengthened the drift towards control of Parliament by the executive. He was a dominant leader who exercised authority over the Commons, the Lords, and the Court. The full Cabinet rarely met; instead, he preferred to work through small informal meetings of the chief officers of state – Walpole himself, the Chancellor, the Lord President, the Lord Privy Seal, and the two Secretaries. His financial policies were to lower taxes, be generous towards the Court and the gentry, and incentivise commerce. He thus 'welded' the 'nodules of power' into a system of 'formidable strength'.[60] It gave the ruling class a stake in the system: concrete objects in the form of jobs (money) and posts (status) to fight for; and raised the costs of challenging the system when those who did so stood to lose a great deal ('last ditches' became 'unattractive', as Sir John Plumb put it).[61] Walpole knew that 'Men love the smell of power', and principle 'tended to wilt in its resplendent ambience'.[62] This system of patronage – a means of collectively investing the ruling class in the existing Whig settlement – 'cemented the political system, held it together, and made it an almost impregnable citadel, impervious to defeat'.[63] Regarding the political structure that he crafted, we can see that 'it possesses an almost monolithic stability, a political system more secure than any England had ever known or was to know'.[64] The manoeuvring of Walpole, underpinned as it was by a dominant party, thus helped to stabilise the entire constitutional system for decades.[65] What is perhaps most telling, however, is that once political actors were content with the system, and confident that they could secure their spoils via competition *within* it, there was a marked diminution in constitutional crisis and instability. There can be few better illustrations of the primacy of high

---

[58] Ibid, p. 170. [59] Ibid, p. 172. [60] Ibid, p. 186. [61] Ibid. [62] Ibid.
[63] Ibid, p. 189. [64] Ibid.
[65] See Jeremy Black, *Walpole in Power* (Stroud: Sutton, 2001).

politics in public life. When the system needed to change in order for the spoils to be acquired, policy issues were invented and weaponised. But, when that was no longer the case, such issues simply did not rear their head.

Some individual leaders have been demonstrable enthusiasts for constitutional innovation, eager to set sail across the vast ocean of laws, statutes, and precedents that is the British constitution. Gladstone is the outstanding example, but there are others, such as Lloyd George; and Blair stands out from the vantage point of the twenty-first century. Blair's Labour government shifted towards a constitutional order predicated on a separation of powers between Parliament, new devolved assemblies, reformed courts, and the expanding European supranational bureaucracy. The resultant dispersal of authority meant that, often, elected officials lacked the power to take effective decisions. Labour's reforms limited the rights of Westminster as a sovereign parliament. When policy problems arose, Westminster blamed the devolved governments or Brussels, and vice versa. Devolution is particularly interesting. Blair's bid to strengthen Labour's position in Scotland prior to the 1997 election through the inducement of constitutional reform not only empowered the SNP within a few years of devolution, but quickly threatened the territorial integrity and very existence of the United Kingdom. He was also an enthusiast for European integration, supporting the development of an EU settlement that would arouse growing resistance and eventually pave the way for Brexit. Under Blair, a dominant party achieved the remarkable feat of driving fundamental constitutional reform without provoking immediate public controversy – another indication of how far constitutional thinking had ossified. Many barely noticed, much less understood the seismic changes that had taken place. It was only once this new system was put to the test, and promptly broke down, in the years following Blair's retirement that the full implications became apparent. The consequences for the Labour party's own electoral position were stark.

Individual leaders whose influence was underpinned and multiplied by political parties thus had transformative effects on the constitutional order. Some were devotees of this kind of activity. Others were far less keen on constitutional tinkering, but still calculated that they had little choice but to accede to it: this was true of Asquith from 1910, and later of Cameron in agreeing to referenda on both electoral reform and the European Union. Many politicians have been deeply wary of constitutional disruption, seeking to avoid such questions whenever and wherever possible. These individuals recognised that when one seeks to reprogram the operating system of the constitutional machine, one is liable to provoke a major crisis. The genuine enthusiasts for constitutional 'improvement' were rarer, but it was their decisions which tended to produce upheaval and tear political parties asunder. Britain's wisest living expert on its constitution, Vernon Bogdanor, remarked that 'constitutions are concerned with the grandest and most important of issues – the relationship between the individual and the state, the conditions of political order, and the methods by which men and women ruled'.[66] This touches on something important. After all, so much of the history, philosophy, law, and political science of antiquity boiled down to the mechanics of constitutions, for that is how power is distributed and wielded. Meanwhile Angus Hawkins noted that the British constitution is 'a thin soil overlaying the bedrock of historical experience'.[67] It is difficult to disagree with this, too. The constitution is not a document but a series of laws, statutes, and precedents. In other words, it is a product of both history, and interpretation of that history.

Yet several generations of historians have displayed a curious aversion to taking the constitutional order seriously. To be sure, a huge volume of scholarship has been produced on the politics of constitutional issues, from electoral reform to Ireland, European integration to the erosion of the Anglican supremacy.[68] Some of this work is very good. For example, a recent study by Hawkins is not only the best and richest book on British political history written for many years but is suffused with constitutional perspectives.[69] Alvin Jackson has conducted important work on the Unions with Scotland and Ireland.[70] What is perhaps missing from the field as a whole, however, is routine analysis of constitutional problems in the broadest sense, and, crucially, in their own right rather than as windows into other issues. There is no longer a strong disciplinary tradition of attending to the British constitution *as a machine*. Few political historians are experts in the operating system of British politics as were, say, a Sir Geoffrey Elton or Frederic William Maitland.[71] It is probable that many

---

[66] Vernon Bogdanor, *The New British Constitution* (London: Hart, 2009), xi.
[67] Angus Hawkins, *Victorian Political Culture: 'Habits of Heart and Mind'* (Oxford, 2015), p. 57.
[68] For example, Ross Cotton and Cary Fontana, 'Political Parties at Critical Junctures: Explaining the Decisions to Offer Referendums on Constitutional Change in the United Kingdom', *Contemporary British History*, 33, 1 (2019), pp. 1–27.
[69] Hawkins, *Victorian Political Culture*.
[70] Alvin Jackson, *The Two Unions: Ireland, Scotland, and the Survival of the United Kingdom, 1707–2007* (Oxford, 2012), p. 280.
[71] F. W. Maitland, *The Constitutional History of England: A Series of Lectures* (Cambridge, 1909).

simply never read Sir Ivor Jennings and Sir Sidney Low; much less Sir William Blackstone and Sir Edward Coke.[72]

If historians had been attentive to that operating system, it is quite possible that they would have had more useful commentary to offer in the aftermath of the 2016 referendum. It was striking that most scholars had less to say on the constitutional dimension to what was, pre-eminently, a constitutional question than they did on such contemporary liberal tropes as imperial nostalgia, pretensions to international power, and xenophobia.[73] Compared to those themes, there was little serious engagement with the fact that EU integration had always been a problem for an island state with a distinctive constitutional tradition and which did not share many of the problems the EU had been created to address. It is even possible that a better-equipped community of historians might have educated a governing class in its responsibilities to think more seriously about the machinery they operated. Either way, the reconstitution of these habits of mind is plainly an urgent matter. In the *Edinburgh Review* in 1809, Sydney Smith wrote that those who were preparing to enter politics should study the history of how the British constitution had 'grown into its present state, – the perils that threatened it, – the malignity that had attacked it, – the courage that had fought for it, and the wisdom that made it great'.[74] Smith's advice is unlikely to be rendered redundant any time soon. Constitutional history is imperative to those who wish to take up John Robert Seeley's famous conception of History as a 'school of statesmanship', a discipline of genuine public utility.[75]

The theme of the great Burkean scholar William Stubbs – like Seeley, a Regius Professor at one of the ancient universities – was the organic evolution of the English constitution towards perfection.[76] Both the English and then British constitution have consistently been in a state of flux. If it is anything at all, the constitutional order is a product of contingency and strife. Those 'grandest ... of issues' identified by Bogdanor proved a natural hunting ground for politicians and, as we have seen, both summoned

---

[72] William Blackstone, *Commentaries on the Laws of England*, four volumes (London, 1765–1770). Coke is best approached through Edward Coke, *The Selected Writings of Sir Edward Coke*, ed. Steve Sheppard (Indianapolis: Liberty Fund, 2005).
[73] For an important exception, examine Helen Thompson, 'Inevitability and Contingency: The Political Economy of Brexit', *The British Journal of Politics and International Relations*, 19, 3 (2017), pp. 434–449.
[74] *Edinburgh Review*, 15 (Oct. 1809), p. 52.
[75] J. R. Seeley, *Lectures and Essays* (London: Macmillan, 1870), p. 296.
[76] William Stubbs, *The Constitutional History of England in Its Origin and Development*, 3 vols. (Oxford, 1874–1878).

political parties into existence and tore them asunder. Iain McLean goes so far as to describe the constitution as the product of a series of contingent 'train crashes'.[77] At the same time, however, political parties were essential to its operation and resilience. One of the secrets of the British constitution was its malleability; and parties were often the instruments through which that was taken advantage of. Frequently, parties derived their very identity from constitutional questions.

A. V. Dicey argued that the party system 'involves a waste of capacity' and by dividing political talent into opposed camps it weakens the quality of governance available to the country.[78] Similar anxieties were expressed by H. G. Wells.[79] This plea for a culture of permanent non-party rule by the best and brightest is romantically appealing but, ultimately, wrongheaded. Burke correctly discerned that party represented a means of binding together like-minded individuals. Thomas Erskine May concluded that parties underpinned the freedoms of the polity.[80] Deep antagonisms could be fought to a resolution – and a legitimate one at that – through the mechanism of party conflict. While the conduct of representative politics is founded on a misleading pursuit of certainty, nevertheless parties carved out, and safeguarded, vital space for a practical pluralism and multiplicity of views. The division into parties offered clear choices to the electorate and cohesion to the executive. Party provided the numerical strength in the Commons for governments to act with vigour; they compelled ambitious politicians to appeal to a large section of the electorate, imperative to success in the First-Past-the-Post system; and they offered a straightforward instrument through which the voters might judge success and failure. Moreover, the very existence of parties served to focus elite minds: leaders were usually vulnerable to pressure from followers, and their position was dependent on merit. Party thus acted as a crucial check on the executive. Last, but very far from least, the presence of an opposition in the Commons always meant there was a credible alternative government. Those who lost the confidence of Parliament or the public would quickly be replaced. Britain was never stuck with just one set of possible leaders.

---

[77] Iain McLean, *What's Wrong with the British Constitution?* (Oxford, 2009), p. 45.
[78] A. V. Dicey, *Lectures on Comparative Constitutionalism*, ed. J. W. F. Allison (Oxford, 2013), p. 127.
[79] H. G. Wells, *Mankind in the Making* (London: Macmillan, 1914 ed.), pp. 28–31.
[80] Thomas Erskine May, *The Constitutional History of England since the Accession of George III, 1760–1860*, 3 vols. (London: Longmans, Green, 1875 ed.).

There is something else, as well. In all of this, party-political competition immensely strengthened Parliament as a national institution. The key to the success of the English political system, and then its British successor, over centuries was that Parliament was widely 'considered the representative of the whole community'.[81] Its responsiveness to public problems served to reaffirm the authority and legitimacy of Westminster. One reason why politicians and parties largely accepted the prevailing order was that, at its heart, lay the concept of sovereign authority. In Parliament, the executive, legislature, and judiciary were merged. Britain possessed a 'unitary, absolutist doctrine of sovereignty' which was 'inviolab[le]'.[82] And due to the achievements of Thomas Cromwell, parliamentary statutes stood 'omnicompetently sovereign'.[83] Indeed, an important component of British national identity was constitutional: for many citizens, Parliament represented the epicentre of the lawful social order. The prospect of being able to exercise control over a system with such a high degree of inbuilt legitimacy proved irresistible. Britain's lack of a written constitution meant that, in practice, there were few legal limits to the legislative power of Parliament. Far better to reconcile oneself to that system and seek to capture it than campaign to overturn it. Walpole discerned the possibilities of such a settlement, and his successors rarely felt an inclination to demur. This contributed in real and fundamental ways to the stability of British life and the possibilities of political change. As the turmoil of the twenty-first century underlines, that is a record not to be taken lightly. And parties were integral to its organisation, practice, and resilience. Political parties have been far from a straightforward solution to the problems of conducting peaceful conflict in human associational life; but they are, perhaps, the best we have yet discovered.[84]

---

[81] Tombs, *The English and Their History*, p. 235.
[82] J. C. D. Clark, *The Language of Liberty, 1660–1832: Political Discourse and Social Dynamics in the Anglo-American World* (Cambridge, 1994), p. 66.
[83] G. R. Elton, *Reform and Renewal: Thomas Cromwell and the Common Weal* (Cambridge, 1973), p. 67.
[84] On which, see Alexis de Tocqueville, *Democracy in America*, trans. James T. Schleifer (Indianapolis, IN: Liberty Fund, 2012) Volume I, Part II, chapter x.

PART III
★
POLITICS

18
Conservatism

ASANGA WELIKALA

Introduction

The British constitution is typically seen as not only a unique, but a uniquely conservative, set of political arrangements among the constitutions of the world. This characterisation stems from the constitution's pre-modern origins and continuity over time, and its unwritten, traditional, and organic nature. This historical experience has been far from free of crises, fundamental changes (and reversals), or violent conflict. But the distinguishing feature of British constitutional history is the absence of a modern moment of revolutionary rupture, marking the shift of the state's foundations from traditional rule to constitutional modernity and documentary constitutionalism.[1] Until recently, therefore, because of this unusual longevity of the institutional complex of Crown-in-Parliament at its core, the descriptive features that lent themselves to the constitution's conservative appearance were generally accepted as stable facts. More recently, however, with long-gestating internal tensions coming to the fore as constitutional conflicts, not only the constitution, but also the conservative defence of the constitution and mode of constitutional practice, are under major interrogation.

This chapter seeks to provide an account of British constitutionalism as understood from a conservative perspective. It does not offer a narrative history of the constitution and the evolution of Crown, Parliament, and the courts in the British Isles, or an analysis of the Tory and Conservative party's constitutional policies over time. Nor does it focus on theoretical debates about the general nature of conservatism as a political, cultural, and aesthetic

---

[1] Thanks to Peter Cane, Alan Convery, H. Kumarasingham, Paikiasothy Saravanamuttu, and Stephen Tierney for comments which improved previous drafts of this chapter. All remaining deficiencies are my responsibility alone.
Martin Loughlin (2010) *Foundations of Public Law* (Oxford University Press): ch.10.

phenomenon.[2] It is also not a legal history of how constitutional doctrines and principles have developed in common law and statute.[3] Instead, it adopts a 'history of ideas' approach to explaining how conservatism has provided the intellectually dominant conception of constitutional self-understanding in British constitutional history so far. Following this approach, the chapter is concerned with both substance and process, that is, the substantive themes associated with conservative constitutional ideology, and the conservative disposition with regard to constitutional change.

The chapter establishes some working definitions of the three key concepts of 'conservatism', 'constitution', and 'constitutionalism'. It outlines a history of British conservative ideas about self, state, and society as they were shaped by the crucial debates of the European Enlightenment, and how those ideas formed the basis of a constitutional ideology that evolved through successive stages of constitutional development from absolutism to constitutional government and mass democracy. It also looks closely at normatively conservative theories of both the substance of the ideal-type constitution and the mode of constitutional change. Its conclusion is that the ideational resources internal to conservatism remain relevant and serviceable in meeting the challenges facing conservative constitutional orthodoxies today.

The central thesis of the chapter is this. British constitutional conservatism is defined more by its incrementalist theory of constitutional evolution than by its commitments to any particular institutions. The normative conception of the good that it represents is immanent in the processes and practices of its constitutionalism. Non-dogmatism *is* its ideology. British conservatism is an ideological broad church circumscribed by its philosophical and temperamental moderation. The political party that represents conservative values and policies has generally been more interested in the pursuit of power than the purity of principles. This may make them seem expedient and devious – their

---

[2] Jerry Z. Muller (ed.) (1997) *Conservatism: An Anthology of Social and Political Thought from David Hume to the Present* (Princeton University Press); Edmund Fawcett (2020) *Conservatism: The Fight for a Tradition* (Princeton University Press); Jan-Werner Mueller, 'Comprehending Conservatism: A New Framework for Analysis' (2006) *Journal of Political Ideologies* 11(3): 359–365; Paul Wetherly (2017) *Political Ideologies* (Oxford University Press): ch.3.

[3] Martin Loughlin (2013) *The British Constitution: A Very Short Introduction* (Oxford University Press); Anthony King (2007) *The British Constitution* (Oxford University Press): ch.3; F. W. Maitland (1919) *The Constitutional History of England* (Cambridge University Press); J. G. A. Pocock (1987) *The Ancient Constitution and the Feudal Law* (Cambridge University Press).

'brutal pragmatism'[4] – but it is also what has kept British conservatism consistently in the centre-ground of politics. The ancient provenance of the British constitution gives the appearance of a formal continuity of institutions, but yet their underlying foundations of legitimacy have profoundly changed. Across the space and time of centuries, there have been many substantive visions, not entirely consistent with each other, subsisting under the conservative label. In such a milieu, any attempt to provide an account of constitutional conservatism by focusing on a particular set of institutions cannot go very far. But what does arguably unite most conservatives across space and time is the attitude to constitutional change, of which the essential elements are a starting presumption against change for the sake of change, and the placing of the burden of justification on those who seek change.

The commitment to incrementalism in turn is based on sceptical assumptions about human nature and intellect, and the relative weight to be given to tradition and modernity. These themes pervade conservative views in relation to both the institutions and the operational culture of the constitution, including its change. But in the absence of a documentary constitution, the practice of constitutionalism is primarily focused on the dynamic relationship between preservation and reform. This does not mean that British conservatism lacks substantive commitments. It is the ideology that is most closely associated with the defence of inherited institutions like the monarchy, the territorial union, the established church, and, at least since the mid eighteenth century, the legislative supremacy of the Crown-in-Parliament.[5] It is also the ideology that is most likely to commend the rituals and traditions of the constitution against the claims of modernisation, and to celebrate its unwritten nature as a unique national achievement and organic representation of collective identity. And there is a well-established Tory rival to the Whig tradition of historiography that upholds this constitutional settlement according to conservative values. Nevertheless, British constitutional conservatism is primarily distinguished from rival ideologies and dispositions, as well as from other comparable conservative national constitutional traditions such as those of France, Germany, and the United States, by the manner in which it purports to manage change.[6]

---

[4] Nevil Johnson (2004) *Reshaping the British Constitution: Essays in Political Interpretation* (Basingstoke: Palgrave Macmillan): 10.

[5] Robert Saunders, 'Parliament and People: The British Constitution in the Long Nineteenth Century' (2008) *Journal of Modern European History* 6(1): 72–87.

[6] See also Graham Gee and Grégoire Webber, 'A Conservative Disposition and Constitutional Change' (2019) *Oxford Journal of Legal Studies* 39(3): 526–552. These authors define the three core elements of the conservative disposition to constitutional change as traditionalism, scepticism, and organicism.

Conservatism, Constitution, Constitutionalism

It is notoriously difficult to articulate a general doctrine of conservatism, for, as J. G. A. Pocock observed, 'too many minds have been trying to "conserve" too many things for too many reasons.'[7] This is not surprising given that the ideological distinctiveness of conservatism derives from its ideas about human imperfection, its epistemological modesty and scepticism of abstract rationality, its reliance on evolved customs and habits, and its focus on the historicised particularism of place (what Scruton called 'oikophilia'[8]).[9] Our task, however, is marginally easier in that the aim here is not to provide a general account of conservatism. It is simply to outline the recurrent themes that together comprise an identifiable body of thought in the United Kingdom that might be understood as the conservative view of the constitution and constitutionalism.

Different strands of Western conservative thinking on constitutionalism can be more or less reactionary or liberal, radical or moderate, romantic or empiricist. They may stem from theological or secular philosophical principles as from cultural and aesthetic sensibilities or theories of economic organisation.[10] While this diversity is reflected within British conservatism, the dominant tradition is a moderate conservatism marked by prudence and accommodation in practice, and public virtue in aspiration.[11] It is a broad social ethic that was made possible in a polity that had, at the ripening of the Enlightenment moment, already experienced its religious Reformation and political Glorious Revolution.[12] British conservatism responded to, and its modern tradition emerged from, the European Enlightenment in two complementary ways. It rejected the more extreme versions of rationalist and

---

[7] From his introduction to the Hackett edition of Burke's Reflections on the Revolution in France, cited in Muller (1997): 22–23.

[8] Roger Scruton (2017a) *Where We Are: The State of Britain Now* (London: Bloomsbury Continuum): 86.

[9] Muller (1997): 9–14.

[10] Noël O'Sullivan, 'Conservatism' in Michael Freeden and Marc Stears (eds.) (2013) *The Oxford Handbook of Political Ideologies* (Oxford University Press): 293–312; Samuel P. Huntington, 'Conservatism as an Ideology' (1957) *American Political Science Review* 51: 454.

[11] For discussions of shades of conservatism ranging from reaction to social democracy, see Fawcett, *Conservatism: The Fight for a Tradition*; Berhard Dietz (2020) *Neo-Tories: The Revolt of British Conservatives against Democracy and Political Modernity (1929–1939)* (London: Bloomsbury); Mark Garnett and Kevin Hickson (2009) *Conservative Thinkers: The Key Contributors to the Political Thought of the Modern Conservative Party* (Manchester University Press).

[12] Gertrude Himmelfarb (2008) *The Roads to Modernity: The British, French and American Enlightenments* (New York: Vintage Books): 3–22.

revolutionary thinking, while at the same time it made empirically grounded pragmatic compromises with the intellectual implications and the political consequences of the Enlightenment.[13]

What unites the heterogeneity of conservative views on the British constitution, therefore, is not an irreducible core of substantive constitutional ideas and institutions, but a spontaneous consensus about the process of constitutional change and evolution. Constitutional monarchy and parliamentary sovereignty can, of course, lay claim to the loyalties of most constitutional conservatives. But since British constitutional conservatism is not confined to members of the Conservative party, or those more or less on the political right, it is not explained by a necessary commitment to an American-style fixed and romanticised constitutional object on either historical or ideological grounds.[14] Put another way, the unity of constitutional conservatism is explained neither by nostalgia nor exceptionalism, but a deep commitment, concomitantly with aversion to revolutionary upheaval, to incrementalism as the preferred mode of necessary change within a narrative of continuity.

George Custance got to the gravamen when he wrote in 1808, 'Not that perfection attaches to our Constitution, or that it is free from abuse; but that there is a constant tendency in it to correct the latter and promote the former.'[15] Two centuries later, in the context of the knowledge economy of 2011, O'Hara defended conservatism as the theory of change that was justified by public reason. He used this conceptualisation to distinguish conservatism from ideologies that either oppose all change or want everything changed: 'conservatism is an ideology concerned with change. Those unconcerned with, or actively supportive of, change, whatever else they are, are not conservative. In particular, "conservative" is not simply interchangeable with "right wing".'[16]

Whether or not the incrementalist narrative is more national myth than constitutional reality need not detain us at this stage.[17] What is important to emphasise here is the belief conservatives hold that incremental development

---

[13] Roger Scruton (2017) *Conservatism* (Profile Books): ch.2.
[14] Thus, for example, the constitutional dispositions of the last 'Old Labour' Prime Minister, James Callaghan, can be described as conservative in the sense argued in this chapter. See Kevin Hickson and Jasper Miles (eds.) (2020) *James Callaghan: An Underrated Prime Minister?* (London: Biteback).
[15] Cited in J. W. F Allison (2007) *The English Historical Constitution: Continuity, Change and European Effects* (Cambridge University Press): 16.
[16] Kieron O'Hara (2011) *Conservatism* (London: Reaktion Books): 20.
[17] Christine Bell, 'Constitutional Transitions: The Peculiarities of the British Constitution and the Politics of Comparison' (2014) *Public Law*: 446–471; Neil Walker, 'Our Constitutional Unsettlement' (2014) *Public Law*: 529–548.

is the defining feature of their constitutional ideology. More specifically, the modesty of substantive expectations, and the preference for procedural incrementalism, mark out the distinguishing feature of British constitutional conservatism as in essence a theory of limits.[18] In the creation, structuring, and exercise of political power and legal authority, the conservative idea of limits pervades the internal strands of the ideology, and distinguishes it from theories of limits in liberalism and other political ideologies. Understood this way, constitutional conservatism is a latitudinarian framework that can subsume cultural traditionalists, civic nationalists, economic socialists, social liberals, or even normative republicans.[19] The relative formalism of its unity enables a multitude of substantive conceptions of the good to flourish under its umbrella.[20]

Bolingbroke's definition of 'constitution' can still be regarded as encapsulating the British conservative perspective: 'By constitution we mean ... that assemblage of laws, institutions, and customs, derived from certain fixed principles of reason, directed to certain fixed objects of public good, that compose the general system, according to which the community hath agreed to be governed.'[21] It is a descriptive and empiricist definition of constitution that acknowledges the descent of constitutional arrangements from time immemorial, but also, crucially, the function of principles derived from reason and the common good. The presence of a role for reason as opposed to solely religious faith or other such ascriptive cultural demand is a key characteristic of the dominant tradition's separation from reactionary conservatism and ethnic nationalism. There is also an underlying concept of social consent to constitutional arrangements; but this is organic rather than rationalist. The longevity of the constitution and its deep social acceptance are symbiotic. Its historicity and organicism invest the constitution with legitimacy. The constitution is the whole body of legal and political rules and moral principles that authorise the institutions of government and regulate the relationship between government and society. No sharp distinctions are drawn in this conception between the political, social, and cultural spheres of life. In this understanding, written constitutions are seen as

---

[18] Noël O'Sullivan (1976) *Conservatism* (London: J.M. Dent & Sons): ch.1.
[19] Roger Scruton (2001) *The Meaning of Conservatism* (3rd ed.) (Basingstoke: Palgrave-Macmillan): ch.1.
[20] Neil Walker, 'Beyond the Unitary Conception of the United Kingdom Constitution' (2000) *Public Law*: 384–404 at 389–394.
[21] *Craftsman* 395, 26 January 1734, in David Armitage (ed.) (1997) *Bolingbroke: Political Writings* (Cambridge University Press): 88.

artificial and legalistic, and if not exactly undesirable, then certainly unnecessary to a well-governed and ordered society.

Within this framework of rules and institutions, 'constitutionalism' can be said to have two meanings. In the first, it identifies the body of normative principles through which the specifically conservative theory of limited politics and limited government is legitimated through appeals to reason as well as to sentiment and experience. In the other sense, it denotes constitutionalism as a category of political practice which, in the conservative worldview, encompasses statecraft at the highest reaches of the state as well as the life of rooted freedom lived in Burke's 'little platoons'.[22] The constitution and constitutionalism understood in this way are a reflection of a deeper idea of commonwealth or *res publica* undergirded by what de Tocqueville called '*moeurs*': the 'habits of the mind' and the 'habits of the heart' that make up 'the whole moral and intellectual state of a people.'[23]

The Conservative Enlightenment

Constitutional government as a form of collective human organisation has been central to Western philosophy from ancient times. Aristotle's defence of constitutionally constrained government finds consideration even today among conservative thinkers.[24] But, as Scruton bluntly put it, 'Modern conservatism is a product of the Enlightenment.'[25] There are both 'accommodationist' and 'revisionist' approaches to historicising British conservative constitutional ideas, centring around alternative theorisations of the conservative encounter with the European Enlightenment. The former presents the encounter as the way in which conservatism modernised through adaptive incorporation of some of the principal insights of Enlightenment thought into a pre-existing worldview. The latter makes the more ambitious claim that the material and ideational circumstances of Britain in the eighteenth century created not only a distinctive 'British Enlightenment' but also that this was, notwithstanding radical dissenters, normatively conservative in character.

---

[22] Scruton, *Conservatism*: 40–47.
[23] Himmelfarb, *The Roads to Modernity*: 5. See also, Bill Schwarz, 'Philosophes of the Conservative Nation: Burke, Macaulay, Disraeli' (1999) *Journal of Historical Sociology* 12 (3): 183–217.
[24] Christopher Fear, 'The "Dialectical" Theory of Conservatism' (2020) *Journal of Political Ideologies* 25(2): 197–211.
[25] Scruton, *Conservatism*: 3.

In the accommodationist account, the Enlightenment overturned the medieval conception of divine authority of kings in favour of the modern conception of legitimate authority based on popular consent. But two debates that began in the medieval period were the precursors of this dramatic watershed: around the relationship between church and state, and the limits to both embodied in a law of nature. The idea of natural law as providing an immutable standard of assessment and constraint on earthly authority was propounded by St Thomas Aquinas in the thirteenth century. In the sixteenth century, Richard Hooker deployed the concept of natural law to constrain the power of both church and state in the interests of peace and liberty in a recognisably conservative sense.[26]

According to Scruton, the work that did the most to influence later conceptions of authority and legitimacy in British conservatism was the version of social contract theory advanced by Thomas Hobbes in the seventeenth century. This monistic and even authoritarian conception of political sovereignty arguably assisted conservatism's accommodation, in the following century, with the unitary conception of legal sovereignty embodied in the post–Glorious Revolution institutional set up of the Crown-in-Parliament. Unlike that in the work of other major founders of social contract theory such as Locke or Rousseau, life in Hobbes's state of nature was 'solitary, poor, nasty, brutish, and short.' It is to escape this predicament that in Hobbes's theory, individuals agreed a social contract to bring into being a sovereign who would provide security and order. The sovereign, although created by the contract, was neither a party to nor bound by the contract, and in order to serve the purposes of the contract, would enjoy absolute power. However, some conservatives' embrace of Hobbes creates a significant unresolved tension on the question of sovereignty within conservatism, given the anti-contractualism that stamps the work of other conservative thinkers such as Hume and Burke.[27] For some conservatives at least, their acceptance of Hobbes seems to derive from a shared anxiety about the consequences of disorder, and the consequent insistence that liberty is grounded in order, and not the other way around. But neither Hume nor Burke saw consent to authority in terms of voluntary consent, and Oakeshott's twentieth-century enunciation of 'civil association' demonstrates that Hobbesian contractualism is inessential to conservative constitutionalism (discussed below). Moreover,

---

[26] Ibid, ch.1. [27] Muller (1997): 12–13.

these thinkers clearly countenanced customary or natural constraints on political sovereignty contrary to Hobbes's theory.

James Harrington followed Hobbes in affirming consent as the basis of legitimate authority. But he went further in articulating in detail the institutional features of a constitutional system that would lay the basis of both a 'commonwealth for increase' and an 'empire of laws, not of men.' Hooker, Hobbes and Harrington all had an influence on John Locke's major contribution at the end of the seventeenth century. Locke's version of social contract theory drew from Hooker on natural law and from Harrington on the separation of powers, but disagreed with Hobbes on the nature of sovereignty and the form of the sovereign. In the early eighteenth century, all these ideas coupled with his observation of the English constitutional settlement of 1688, enabled Montesquieu to formulate a systematic theory of the separation of powers, which came to be the indispensable basis of constitutional government in the future.[28]

Thus, even before Continental Enlightenment thought had culminated in the French Revolution and given Burke the opportunity to lay down the foundations of modern British conservatism, conservatism had begun an engagement with modernist political thought. Conservatives came to accept the idea of legitimate authority as being based on consent in some form, rather than religious obedience or kinship ties. But they did not jettison the importance of communal 'we-feeling', and the shared institutions that express that sentiment, for the coherence and stability of polities.[29] Many conservatives, although not all, accepted at some level the idea that the individual liberties of natural law constituted limits on the reach of government, but they did not extend natural rights to mean either absolute rights or rights to revolution. They also foregrounded custom and common law as an organic expression of social rules, which both enabled liberty and constrained government. And they accepted that good government required institutional checks and balances, even where they held, with Hobbes, that legal sovereignty was ultimately illimitable.

The revisionist argument developed by Himmelfarb shares this view of the conservative position but gives it the much more developed character of a distinctively British Enlightenment. One of her purposes is also to controvert the view that Burke's seminal contribution was to champion a

---

[28] Scruton, *Conservatism* : ch.1.
[29] Scruton, *Where We Are*: ch.3; Linda Colley (1992) *Britons: Forging the Nation, 1707–1837* (Yale University Press).

reactionary counter-Enlightenment. In Himmelfarb's argument, the British Enlightenment, seen as the embodiment of *moeurs* in Tocqueville's sense, was a 'sociology of virtue' (counter-posed in particular to the French Enlightenment as the 'ideology of reason'):

> In the usual litany of traits associated with the Enlightenment – reason, rights, nature, liberty, equality, tolerance, science, progress – reason invariably heads the list. What is conspicuously absent is virtue. Yet it was virtue, rather than reason, that took precedence for the British, not personal virtue but the 'social virtues' – compassion, benevolence, sympathy – which, the British philosophers believed, naturally, instinctively, habitually bound people to each other. They did not deny reason, they were by no means irrationalists. But they gave reason a secondary, instrumental role, rather than the primary, determinant one that the *philosophes* gave it.[30]

Himmelfarb marshals the thinking of a wide range of eighteenth-century thinkers in sustaining the argument that the Enlightenment she describes was sociological and historical in its approach. It was normatively concerned with social virtue and political morality. It was sociologically Scottish, Irish and Welsh, as well as English, in its Britishness. And because the relation between church and state and between Monarch and Parliament had more or less been resolved at previous junctures, it was without a driving animus towards religion or monarchy. In all these ways, the British Enlightenment was able to take the fact of a settled constitutional order for granted. To be sure, how that constitutional order was conceptualised revealed rich nuance among the thinkers of a conservative bent in the British Enlightenment. But what was common was the foregrounding of the innate human sense and capacity for moral conduct as the basis of a constitutionalism, and a statecraft, of prudence and accommodation. Concomitantly, the British philosophers treated human reason as only one within a basket of constitutional virtues, and crucially, that the constitution related not only to space but also to time as an intergenerational compact.

The 'sociology of virtue' is historically important in one last respect, and that is how it, and Burke in particular, treated the peoples of the burgeoning Empire. This is a conservative legacy of significant relevance and value to contemporary concerns of constitutionalism. Its basis lies in the conservative critique of rationalism and its defence of tradition in the European context. Burke got to the crux of the matter in his speech on Fox's India Bill in 1783,

---

[30] Himmelfarb, *The Roads to Modernity*: 5–6.

when he said, 'I am certain that every means, effectual to preserve India from oppression, is a guard to preserve the British constitution from its worst corruption.'[31] If it is striking how tightly intertwined were Britain and India in Burke's worldview, it is even more so when it is recalled that for him, colonial peoples fully enjoyed 'the rights of men – that is to say, the natural rights of mankind.'[32] The equal – and not merely the decent – treatment of colonial peoples in imperial policy, a matter that deeply divided nineteenth-century liberalism, presented no difficulty for Burke in the preceding century.[33]

Burke's concern with how British imperial relations with India dialectically affected both nations gave rise to a rich body of moral and political principles as a legacy for conservative constitutionalism.[34] This ideational legacy addresses major themes of contemporary constitutionalism such as compassion, collective identity, the individual self, and incrementalism. As Mehta has pointed out, Burke's work on India represents, 'the most sophisticated and moving elaboration on the idea of sympathy – the means through which one develops in oneself a feeling for another person or collectivity of persons' and which moreover was clearly influenced by Hume's moral philosophy.[35] Against the Lockean and Rousseauan rationalist conceptions of order, Burke's view posited individual identity as rooted in a collective identity, which in turn is inextricably linked with social experience and attachment to a place.[36] These insights prefigure twenty-first-century Western liberal democratic constitutionalism's normative debates over mass immigration and multiculturalism.[37] Finally, Burke's approach, for reasons further elaborated below, favours incremental change and opposes revolutionary change: the hallmark of conservative constitutionalism.

Conservatism and Constitutional Modernity

Edmund Burke's robust response to the French Revolution is the point in history at which it is widely held that modern British conservatism emerged as

---

[31] Uday Singh Mehta (1999) *Liberalism and Empire* (University of Chicago Press): 171.
[32] Himmelfarb, *The Roads to Modernity*: 78.
[33] C. A. Bayly (1989) *Imperial Meridian: The British Empire and the World, 1780–1830* (Harlow: Longman): ch.5; Karuna Mantena (2010) *Alibis of Empire: Henry Maine and the Ends of Liberal Imperialism* (Princeton University Press): ch.1.
[34] Mehta, *Liberalism and Empire*: 170–171. Cf. Himmelfarb, *The Roads to Modernity*: 78–79.
[35] Mehta, *Liberalism and Empire*: 170. [36] Ibid, 175–178.
[37] Stephen Tierney (2006) *Constitutional Law and National Pluralism* (Oxford University Press): 9–12.

a distinctive ideology in terms recognisable today. The genealogy of conservative thought goes back to Aristotle, as we have seen. Literary politicians like the first Marquess of Halifax and Viscount Bolingbroke, in the seventeenth and early eighteenth centuries, had already laid down some of the foundations of modern conservative constitutionalism. But it was the French Revolution that forced conservatives to answer questions like: why do we oppose revolution? What, in particular, are we opposed to? What was it about the old order that was worth preserving? What alternative do we have to offer? The revolution in France alarmed British conservatives, who feared its repercussions within their own country. Faced with the prospect of revolutionary upheaval, conservatism had to urgently make explicit the principles and values of constitutional order that it had hitherto mainly taken for granted. And the articulation of second order constitutional principles, of course, demanded reflection about the first order assumptions on which they were grounded.

The French Revolution was the culmination of the work of the *philosophes* of the Continental Enlightenment, which held that human society was the source of human misery. By the application of human reason and human will, therefore, society and indeed human nature could be radically reconstructed so as to ensure liberty, equality, and fraternity for all. The revolution provided the practical demonstration that humans indeed possessed the vast power to destroy and recreate society on a total scale. If revolutionary thought was based on the power of reason and will, then conservatives had to show why rationality and intent divorced from experience and tradition were unreliable or inadequate vectors in understanding human nature, and in refashioning human society. The conservative response, therefore, had two closely intertwined elements. The first was to show that society was not as comprehensible and malleable as Enlightenment rationalism projected and, in particular, that human suffering was not simply a temporal and temporary problem. The second was the assertion that revolutionary replacement of the constituted hierarchical order with a new egalitarian social order based on popular will would come at a cost. That cost was stable order, the loss of which would, paradoxically, destroy the very individual liberty that the revolution was seeking to instantiate. In advancing these arguments, modern conservatism emerged, as O'Sullivan observes, 'as a philosophy of imperfection, committed to the idea of limits, and directed towards the defence of a limited style of politics.'[38]

---

[38] O'Sullivan, *Conservatism*: 12.

British conservatives, able by the late eighteenth century to rely on the stability of the balanced constitution provided by the 1688–1689 settlement, did not approach this task by foregrounding the defence of a particular form of ideal government.[39] They focused instead on the defence of a style of constitutionalism which is marked simultaneously by an opposition to radical change based on abstract rationality, and a commitment to reform, based on concrete experience and limited by practical necessity. Radical change, according to Burke, 'alters the substance of the objects themselves, and gets rid of all their essential good as well as of all the accidental evil annexed to them', whereas conservative reform, 'is not a change in the substance or in the primary modification of the objects, but a direct application of a remedy to the grievance complained of'.[40]

The notion of reform defined by imperfection and limits gives conservative constitutionalism a wider freedom of action in practice than might at first be thought. Sometimes it may demand the defence of the constituted order, as Burke provided against the French Revolution. But at others it may require the defence of liberty against misdirected or overweening authority, as Burke offered in relation to the American Revolution and in prosecuting the impeachment of Warren Hastings for abuse of power in India. And in yet others, it may require actively taking the initiative in change in order to achieve deeper goals of constitutional preservation, as seen, for example, in Peel's repeal of the Corn Laws in 1841 and Disraeli's expansion of the franchise in 1867. But this fluidity exposes conservatism to three lines of criticism, namely, inconsistency, negativity, and duplication.

Conservatives may see their idea of reform as based on a prudential framework of sound judgement for a well-governed society; but from different normative perspectives, choices made within that framework may not always seem consistent. Without substantive first principles, literally any change might be justified on grounds of expediency unconstrained by principle. Yet, conservatives see this as a strength. As O'Sullivan notes, 'the meaning of reform cannot be specified in advance, and ... the content of a limited style of politics must inevitably vary with changing circumstances ...'.[41] Oakeshott's concept of 'intimations' (discussed below), and the relation between what he characterised as the 'politics of faith and the politics of scepticism', drive at the same point.[42] Oakeshott in turn was

---

[39] Armitage, *Bolingbroke*: xv.   [40] O'Sullivan, *Conservatism*: 12.   [41] Ibid, 12–13.
[42] Timothy Fuller (ed.) (1996) *Michael Oakeshott: The Politics of Faith and the Politics of Scepticism* (Yale University Press).

reformulating Halifax's idea of the politics of 'trimming'. The 'trimmer', according to Halifax, was the practitioner of moderation in any given situation including the constitutional conundrums of his day:

> ... if Men are together in a Boat, and one part of the Company would weigh it down to one side, another would make it lean as much to the contrary; it happeneth there is a third Opinion of those, who conceive it would do as well, if the Boat went even, without endangering the Passengers; now 'tis hard to imagin by what Figure in Language, or by what Rule in Sense this cometh to be a fault, and it is much more a wonder it should be thought a Heresy.[43]

Second, the argument that imperfection and limits make for a negative style of politics that legitimises established hierarchies and disregards the condition of the masses is often made by left-wing critics. But according to conservatives, their motivation is neither complacent nor sinister. The underlying moral principle is concerned with protecting society as a whole from the domination of unlimited power, and from grand social experiments driven by powerful elites motivated by abstract principles. Again, as O'Sullivan points out, 'radical ideologies have generally done more to strengthen the chains which bind the masses than to improve their condition' and 'it is worth pondering a little before dismissing the conservative preference for reform as nothing more than a desire to perpetuate inequality and social injustice'.[44]

The criticism of conservative constitutionalism that has the strongest purchase is the one of duplication. What distinguishes the conservative conception of limited politics from liberalism, the ideology that is more often associated with the principle of constrained government? Conservatives usually give a two-step response to this question. The first is to acknowledge the historical fact that modern conservatism is a product of an accommodation with Enlightenment liberalism. This enabled the moderate tradition of British constitutional conservatism to embrace both popular sovereignty and individual autonomy (albeit with some important qualifications, discussed below). In this sense, then, moderate conservatism is part and parcel of the European grand liberal tradition.

This was, of course, an accommodation with classical liberalism, and conservatives argue, secondly, that since the nineteenth century, liberalism

---

[43] Walter Raleigh (ed.) (1912) *The Complete Works of George Savile, First Marquess of Halifax* (The Clarendon Press at Oxford): 48.
[44] O'Sullivan, *Conservatism*: 13.

has gradually adopted the causes of human progress and improvement which have necessitated an increasingly interventionist rather than limited style of liberal politics. Moderate constitutional conservatism, by contrast, is not concerned with 'the regeneration of human nature through the imposition of new creeds which politicise the inner, spiritual life of man'.[45] Unlike modern and postmodern liberalisms, therefore, conservativism is concerned to ensure that the constitution is not instrumentalised in favour of this or that substantive conception of the good drawn from abstract rationalism. The constitution, rather, must remain fundamentally a procedural framework that enables the peaceful coexistence of multiple and competing conceptions of the good, albeit within the *moeurs* of the particular society in which it is founded.

This commitment to political pluralism within the overall framework of the conservative constitution is one way in which modern moderate conservatism reconciled itself with democracy. But its precise – and qualified – relationship with popular sovereignty needs further explication. Here the crucial theoretical issue is the moral basis of political obligation. Their different responses to this question sharply distinguish conservatism and liberalism. Today, every version of democracy is underpinned in some way by the idea of democratic self-government or popular sovereignty. In other words, social contract theory, and in particular Rousseau's account of human nature and the nature of authority and obedience, now pervades all respectable models of democratic constitutionalism and international human rights law.[46] In Rousseau's work, the first premise is that human beings are innately good; the second, that reason exercised by naturally good people is the sole basis of thought and action; and the third, that the human will exercised in this way can bring every aspect of human life under its control. The important corollary of this view of human nature and behaviour is that the only legitimate basis of any restraint that can be placed on human will must be that the restraint is self-imposed.

Rousseauan thought has two crucial implications for constitutional theory. The first is that constituted authority is legitimate only to the extent that it is based on the general will of (good) people. Second, the moral basis of any obligation of obedience to authority (which necessarily involves some

---

[45] Ibid.
[46] Anthony J. Langlois, 'Normative and Theoretical Foundations of Human Rights' in Michael Goodhart (ed.) (2013) *Human Rights: Politics and Practice* (2nd ed.) (Oxford University Press): ch.1.

restriction on individual freedom) is that it is self-imposed. It also follows from the ideal of human perfection that only the individual can decide what these self-imposed limits are, based on the individual's own exercise of reason. Any other restraint emanating from existing legal, political, and social structures of the community in which the individual lives, must be presumed to be potentially if not actually illegitimate.

From even the moderate conservative perspective, there are a number of important philosophical objections to this – now commonplace – view of democratic constitutional order. To start with, it represents a stark rejection of the conservative view of human nature that human beings are imperfect, fallible, limited, and capable of evil as well as of good. It is also contrary to the conservative view on the nature of social life and of political obligation, where the legitimacy and acceptance of existing arrangements are not solely dependent on an individual's reason and will. Conservative objections to the idea of popular sovereignty alight upon three undesirable consequences. In O'Sullivan's terms, these are: anarchism, populism, and fanaticism.[47]

First, if individuals' own reason and will are the only basis on which they have an obligation to respect political institutions, then it follows that an individual or group of individuals have no bar to withdrawing from that obligation, at any time, for their own reasons. Moreover, since there will be various groups with different reasons for withdrawing their political obligation at will, this leaves the polity constantly exposed to the prospect of anarchy.[48] Second, by shifting the focus away from the exercise of governmental power to the source of governmental power, the principle of popular sovereignty provides populist governments with a ready justification to do anything whatsoever, including the destruction of individual liberty and the rule of law, in the name of the general will of the people.[49] Third, the notion that only self-imposed limits are legitimate logically means that all established institutions and rules can in principle be rejected because they impose restraints that are not self-imposed. This provides validation for subjective, atomistic, selfish, and intransigent forms of political behaviour inimical to the common good and to the stability of the established constitutional order.[50]

---

[47] O'Sullivan, *Conservatism*: 18–22.
[48] Margaret Moore (ed.) (1998) *National Self-Determination and Secession* (Oxford University Press).
[49] Samuel Issacharoff, 'Populism versus Democratic Governance' in Mark A. Graber, Sanford Levinson and Mark Tushnet (eds.) (2018) *Constitutional Democracy in Crisis?* (Oxford University Press): ch.25.
[50] Francis Fukuyama (2018) *Identity: The Demand for Dignity and the Politics of Resentment* (New York: Macmillan).

Conservatism and the Democratic State

Conservatism, in terms both of values and interests, has been the fearful enemy of democratisation in many countries. In the United Kingdom, Tories and Conservatives have also often opposed democratising reforms, and sometimes to the point of constitutional crisis (e.g., 1830–1832, and especially 1909–1911). But on a longer historical view, the consistent tendency to accommodate rather than reject or reverse reform is the noteworthy feature of early modern British conservatism, compared to other European conservative traditions such as those of Germany and France. This is true even, or especially, of reforms championed or implemented by its ideological opponents, provided the reforms meet the conservative virtues of good sense and prudence, as well as strategic expediency and class interests.

Bolingbroke, shunned by Burke but described by Disraeli as the 'Founder of Modern Toryism',[51] became a canonical figure in early Tory constitutional thought 'by adopting the formerly Whig theory of the Ancient Constitution and giving it new life as an anti-Walpole Tory principle'.[52] This is a conservative constitutional technique that has been liberally emulated since, and it is a key to understanding its capaciousness, and thereby its resilience. The modern Conservative party from its inception has made general, rather than ideologically particularistic, appeals to the public. Thus, in the Tamworth Manifesto of 1834, Peel appealed to 'that great and intelligent class of society ... which is far less interested in the contentions of party, than in the maintenance of order and the cause of good government'.[53] This propensity to appeal to general sentiments rather than goods based on convictions is a key factor in the explanation of the role of conservatism in British democratisation. In the longer view of history, Whig, Liberal and Labour constitutional reforms have been met, not with reaction, but with accommodation by the dominant conservative tradition.

The accommodationist tendency of British conservatism played a central or even the decisive role in the democratisation of the state. Democratisation is assessed by developments in three key institutional domains: the expansion of the franchise, civil liberties and the accountability of the executive.[54] In European democratisation, Britain was a case of 'settled democratisation'

---

[51] Benjamin Disraeli (1914) *Whigs and Whiggism: Political Writings* (New York: Macmillan): 218–220.
[52] Ruth Mack (2009) *Literary Historicity: Literature and Historical Experience in Eighteenth-century Britain* (Stanford University Press): 8.
[53] Cited in Scruton, *The Meaning of Conservatism*: 4.
[54] Charles Tilly (2007) *Democracy* (Cambridge University Press); Robert Dahl (1971) *Polyarchy: Participation and Opposition* (Yale University Press).

whereby '... democracy ... was gradually constructed via a relatively direct path, [and] absent high-profile moments of backsliding, authoritarian detours, or disruptive coups'.[55] The Tory acceptance of the post-1688 settlement has long been thought to have been the key explanatory factor in providing the preconditions for the gradual but settled democratisation that came in the nineteenth and early twentieth centuries.[56] Through the balance of power between the Crown and the nobility, this settlement established two key preconditions. The first was the establishment of a constrained (as opposed to an absolutist and extractive) state tradition. The second was the time it provided landed elites – otherwise the conservative opponents of democracy – to assimilate the practices of competitive politics before the introduction and expansion of the franchise.

British democratisation came in four major waves: the Reform Acts of 1832, 1867, 1884, and 1918. Several other reforms were also important: anti-electoral corruption reform (1868), the secret ballot (1872), limits of vote-buying (1883), the reform of the House of Lords in 1911, and full female enfranchisement in 1928.[57] Throughout these changes, not only did the organised vehicle of British constitutional conservatism, the Conservative party, learn to adapt, survive, and compete in an expanding electorate, but its acceptance of electoral reform was decisive for the settled and irreversible nature of democratisation. As Ziblatt argues,

> ... the development of these organisational resources meant that in the major constitutional crises that might have sent Britain off its path, the Conservative Party, *democracy's main potential saboteur in Britain, actually was pivotal in keeping democracy intact*. The organisational development of the British Conservative Party made democracy safe for landed elites into the twentieth century.[58]

The Normative Nature of Conservative Constitutionalism

The two outstanding twentieth-century British philosophers of moderate conservatism were Anthony Quinton and Michael Oakeshott. Quinton was

---

[55] Daniel Ziblatt (2017) *Conservative Parties and the Birth of Democracy* (Cambridge University Press): 10.
[56] Dahl, *Polyarchy*: 36–38.   [57] Ziblatt, *Conservative Parties*: 55.
[58] Ibid, 56, emphasis added. For the full elaboration of this argument, see Ziblatt, *Conservative Parties*: chs.3, 4.

moderate conservatism's historian of ideas, drawing on the metaphysical thought of Hooker, Burke, Coleridge, and Newman and the political thought of Halifax, Bolingbroke, Hume, and Disraeli.[59] However, it was Oakeshott who offered the most systematic and sophisticated theory of the constitutional state from a conservative perspective. His work built qualifiedly on the thought of Aristotle, Hobbes, Halifax, and Hegel – and more ambiguously – of Burke.[60] In his survey of the structures and styles of contemporary British public law thought, Loughlin rightly identified Oakeshott as the emblematic theorist of 'conservative normativism'.[61] Oakeshott's work is not only substantial and subtle, but constantly re-evaluated.[62] What follows is a very selective snapshot of his views to enable us to apprehend the contours of the ideal type of the conservative constitutional state, in the light of the ideational history of conservatism discussed above.

For Oakeshott, politics is the pursuit, not of grand visions or general principles, but of 'intimations'. Intimations in politics are discovered by experience in the form of traditions. It is when traditional societies end that politics becomes a rationalist activity. Without the guidance of experience and tradition, new societies require a new framework for their government and organisation. Various rationalist ideologies then step in to fill the vacuum left by experience. Rationalist ideologies believe that experience can be substituted by technical rules, and traditional rule with administration. But Oakeshott does not agree that experience and 'know-how' can be replaced with technical rules and technique. In the conservative way of thinking, rationalism is generally undesirable because it is politically monistic, invasive, and intolerant of human imperfection. When the rigidity of rationalist models inevitably rubs up against the fluidity of human life, rationalism can become both dangerous and expensive.[63]

The politics of intimations based on the authority of tradition is not, as it may seem to some, a naïve or ominous defence of pre-modern hierarchy.[64] In Oakeshott's view, it is a procedural politics both of liberty and pluralism

---

[59] Anthony Quinton (1978) *The Politics of Imperfection: The Religious and Secular Traditions of Conservative Thought from Hooker to Oakeshott* (London and Boston: Faber & Faber).
[60] Jesse Norman (ed.) (1993) *The Achievement of Michael Oakeshott* (Richmond upon Thames: Duckworth).
[61] Martin Loughlin (1992) *Public Law and Political Theory* (Oxford: Clarendon Press): 63–83.
[62] Edmund Neill, 'The Nature of Oakeshott's Conservatism' in Noël O'Sullivan (ed.) (2017) *The Place of Michael Oakeshott in Contemporary Western and Non-Western Thought* (Exeter: Imprint Academic): ch.6.
[63] Loughlin, *Public Law*: 68–70.
[64] Paul Franco (1990) *The Political Philosophy of Michael Oakeshott* (Yale University Press): 7.

and of coherence and order. As a tradition of behaviour, the politics of intimations 'is neither fixed nor finished; it has no changeless centre to which understanding can anchor itself; there is no sovereign purpose to be perceived or invariable direction to be detected; there is no model to be copied, idea to be realised, or rule to be followed'. Such an open-textured conception of politics, however, is given coherence through Oakeshott's 'principle of continuity' whereby, 'authority is diffused between past, present and future ... It is steady because, though it moves, it is never wholly in motion; and though it is tranquil, it is never wholly at rest ... Everything is temporary, but nothing is arbitrary'.[65]

Oakeshott's conception of the modern state is embodied in the idea of 'civil association'. All human associations are either 'enterprise associations' or 'moral associations'. Enterprise associations are formed by prudential practices for the achievement of some substantive purpose. Commercial companies or sports clubs are examples. Moral associations are based on moral practices and are not bound by a common purpose but by the authority of common practices and the obligations that flow from those rules. An example is a speech community; the speakers of the language use it as 'an instrument of understanding and a medium of intercourse, in having a vocabulary and syntax of its own, and in being spoken well or ill'. Civil association is also a type of moral association. In Loughlin's summary,

> Civil association is comprehensive, compulsory, and exclusive since citizens are subject to one sovereign who has authority over all within that jurisdiction and whose laws are obligatory. It is a rule-articulated association which leaves its citizens free to pursue their own interests; civil association is not constituted for any common purpose. The key to civil association as a moral association is to be found in the office of rule and the nature of the rule of law.[66]

Oakeshott's anti-rationalist theory can thus be regarded as articulating the ideal type of modern conservative constitutional state due to the presence of the following elements. In form, the constitutional state is fundamentally a procedural framework that facilitates liberty and political pluralism. This is predicated on an open-ended yet limited style of politics based on an acceptance of the imperfection of human nature and behaviour. The constitution eschews the instrumentalisation, let alone reification, of any substantive (rationalist) conception of the good life. Political obligation is based on the compulsory authority of the existing order of rules and institutions, not

---

[65] Loughlin, *Public Law*: 70–71.   [66] Ibid, 74–75.

on individual reason. The source of collective consent to the order of authority is organic and historic. But authority is ameliorated by depersonalised office and a rule of law based on laws of general application, which stand guard against arbitrariness, excess, and zeal. Due to the value placed on tradition, based on concrete experience, against universal claims based on metaphysical abstractions, and on the intergenerational principle of continuity, there is a presumption against precipitate constitutional change. However, this is balanced by the politics of intimations, which presupposes a dynamic culture of continuous but prudent change. Oakeshott's approach is also specifically modern, because of the departures it marks from the classical conservative luminaries. It is Burkean in many obvious respects; but it is conspicuously irreligious and does not enthrone the wisdom of tradition. It is Hobbesian in its conception of constituted authority and obligations of obedience, but it rejects any notion of social contract. It is empiricist and has a concept of morality, but not in the moralistic sense of Hume and Smith. Conservative constitutionalism defined in this way is not beyond critique. But it does demonstrate the capacities of conservatism to offer a coherent theoretical construct of the constitutional state to compete with any more rationalist ideology in the contemporary world.[67]

Conclusion: Conservative Constitutionalism in Crisis?

In a recent book advocating the adoption of a written constitution, along the lines of the 'Westminster model' that decolonising Britain bequeathed to the Commonwealth, Bulmer offers an interesting periodisation of constitutional development. The seven stages he identifies are: (1) 1660–1689: English Restoration; (2) 1689–1746: Hanoverian Settlement; (3) 1746–1832: Parliamentary Oligarchy; (4) 1832–1928: Struggle for Democracy; (5) 1928–1997: Majoritarian Heyday; 1997–2016: Incoherent Reform; and (7) 2016: Decline and Fall.[68] In the preceding discussion, we have seen how the substance of conservative constitutionalism evolved to meet the realities of the 'Hanoverian Settlement' and through the 'Struggle for Democracy'. While it was New Labour that enacted most of the 'Incoherent Reforms', these reforms were a direct response to the conservative operation of the

---

[67] Ibid, 76–83.
[68] W. Elliot Bulmer (2020) *Westminster and the World: Commonwealth and Comparative Insights for Constitutional Reform* (Bristol University Press): 2.

constitution when Conservatives were the party of government for much of the 'Majoritarian Heyday'. The statutory recognition of justiciable human rights, the freedom of information, the greater institutionalisation of the judiciary and the expansion of its constitutional role, and the devolution of power, were all long-incubating responses to disaffection with conservative constitutionalism and statecraft. Customarily, conservatives accepted the altered arrangements after the fact, albeit without much thought to their implications, either for the constitution itself, or for their style of constitutionalism.[69] For the model of conservative constitutionalism that we defined at the beginning of this chapter, the consequence has been, to use Gee and Webber's metaphor, its 'eclipse': 'its significance has receded, but its influence is not altogether absent'.[70]

There are multiple interpretations of the causes of this eclipse. For Bulmer, it is the failure of conservative incrementalism to modernise the Hanoverian Settlement through the codification of an entrenched constitution of superior legal status.[71] For Fawcett, the collapse of conservatism's radical embrace of economic liberalism has enabled a new 'hard right' of populists and libertarians to supplant moderate constitutional conservatism.[72] For Bell, the tendency to gloss all constitutional change in a narrative of seamless continuity serves either to conceal or deny what are in fact fundamental revisions, and even ruptures.[73] For Walker, incrementalism is a method of change that was appropriate to a 'settled constitution', but not to a state of 'constitutional unsettlement'.[74] For the academics and public intellectuals joining the New Putney Debates in 2017, the transformation of constitutional politics from a state of general social and political consensus to a state of persistent flux and serious crisis, implies that the stability presumed by 'constitutional maintenance'[75] no longer exists.[76]

But against all these cogent critiques, it can yet be maintained that constitutional conservatism, properly understood, has plausible answers.[77] In this chapter we have seen that the core ideas of conservative constitutionalism, as

---

[69] Kevin Hickson (2020) *Britain's Conservative Rights since 1945: Traditional Toryism in a Cold Climate* (Basingstoke: Palgrave Macmillan): chs.4, 5, 6.
[70] Gee and Webber, 'A Conservative Disposition': 543.   [71] Bulmer, *Westminster*: 34–35.
[72] Fawcett, *Conservatism: The Fight for a Tradition*: 416.
[73] Bell, 'Constitutional Transitions'.   [74] Walker, 'Our Constitutional Unsettlement'.
[75] Brian Christopher Jones (2020) *Constitutional Idolatry and Democracy: Challenging the Infatuation with Writtenness* (Cheltenham: Edward Elgar): 28.
[76] D. J. Galligan (ed.) (2017) *Constitution in Crisis: The New Putney Debates* (London: IB Tauris).
[77] Gee and Webber, 'A Conservative Disposition': 542–552.

primarily a mode of change, have been put forward by conservative thinkers as concrete responses to situations of deeply unsettling constitutional crisis throughout a long span of history. It is not in times of peace and placidity but at moments of conflict and revolution that conservatives have historically defended the virtues of traditionalism, scepticism, and organicism.

19
Liberalism

EMILY JONES

Introduction

The Liberal Democrats, at the time of writing, have only fourteen MPs. Yet the significance of Liberalism in the history of the Constitutional History of the United Kingdom does not lie in the immediate present: this is a story that stretches deep into the past; covering not merely the giants of the historic Liberal Party in the nineteenth century, but the Whig inheritance from seventeenth- and eighteenth-century constitutional disputes. Hence, while this chapter will conclude with reference to the modern Liberal Party – an alliance, from 1981, between historic Liberalism and the Social Democratic Party; fusing formally in 1988 – it will primarily consider the longer history of Liberalism and the British Constitution.[1] But this is not to say that a 'historic' reading is of antiquarian interest only; based, as it is, on an understanding of national and political identities that reached forwards, far into the twentieth century, and which has had important consequences for current debates on sovereignty and the relationship between Britain, Northern Ireland, and Europe.

Definitions

Before we begin, however, we must define what the terms 'Liberal' and 'Liberalism' mean in the context of British constitutionalism. This is particularly important given the scholarly impetus to describe the nineteenth century – and Victorian Britain in particular – as the apex of 'liberalism' in the modern 'West'. Until the early nineteenth century, and specifically in Britain, to be liberal was linked, first and foremost, to notions of liberality in the sense of 'generosity of spirit', rather than any specific political, economic, religious,

---

[1] For much of the period discussed the common terminology has been the 'English' or more recently 'British' Constitution.

or constitutional approach.[2] It was therefore from the early nineteenth century that the idea of 'liberalism' took a more familiar, though still distinct, shape; focused especially on notions of constitutional development.[3] In a (continental) European context, a fixed point of reference in the years following the French Revolution has been the belief in 'liberal' fixed, or written, constitutions.[4] The term 'liberal' may also, at this time, be found in reference to non-protectionist, free trade economic policies surrounding tariffs and trade,[5] as well as broad church Christian conceptions of inclusive religious 'liberalism' that was opposed to a more stringent insistence on principle and practice, or 'dogma' in its more derogatory guise.[6] Most importantly for our purposes, in the British context Liberalism in its constitutional and political sense worked rather specifically. This was thanks in large part to, first of all, the Whig and Tory inheritance of the seventeenth and eighteenth centuries, and second, the distinct role the British Constitution held in the national consciousness. Both of these points will be discussed in detail below.

As with like descriptors such as 'conservative' and 'socialist', 'liberal' arrived in Britain as an import from the continent, in this case Spain – *liberales* – in the 1820s.[7] In the years that followed the term was given a distinctly British flavour as it was linked to Whiggism and presented with a capital 'L'. The Liberal Party proper was formed in 1859, following a pact between Whigs, Radicals, and Peelites (those Conservatives who had supported the Prime Minister Sir Robert Peel in his repeal of the Corn Laws in 1846), though the term became popular as a political label in the years following the 1832 Reform Act.[8] In the years after the death of Lord Palmerston in 1865, a much clearer two-party politics resumed and the Liberal Party enjoyed considerable electoral success under the leadership of W. E. Gladstone. By 1886, however, Gladstone's

---

[2] D. Craig, 'The Origins of "Liberalism" in Britain: The Case of the Liberal', *Historical Research*, 85 (2012), pp. 469–487; D. Craig, 'The Language of Liberality in Britain, c.1760–c.1815', *Modern Intellectual History*, 12 (2019), pp. 771–801.

[3] L. Colley, 'Empires of Writing: Britain, America and Constitutions, 1776–1848', *Law and History Review*, 32 (2014), pp. 237–266.

[4] This continued into the twentieth century: see, for example, G. de Ruggiero, *The History of European Liberalism*, trans. R. G. Collingwood (Oxford: Oxford University Press, 1927).

[5] Hence the label 'Liberal Tory': see, for example, 'Table of Ministerial Characters', *The Examiner*, 28 Nov. 1830, p. 754. The classic study of a coherent form of Liberal Toryism is B. Hilton, 'Peel: A Reappraisal', *Historical Journal*, 22 (1979), pp. 585–614; idem, *The Age of Atonement* (Oxford: Oxford University Press, 1988), esp. pp. 203–208, 220–231.

[6] J. H. Newman, *Apologia Pro Vita Sua* (London: Longman, 1864), s.v. 'Liberalism'.

[7] J. P. Parry, *The Rise and Fall of Liberal Government in Victorian Britain* (New Haven: Yale University Press, 1993).

[8] I. Newbould, 'Whiggery and the Growth of Party 1830–1841: Organization and the Challenge of Reform', *Parliamentary History*, 4 (1985), pp. 137–156.

support of Irish Home Rule, or devolution, caused irreparable damage; resulting in the creation of a separate Liberal Unionist Party. The Liberal Unionists, who interpreted Liberal constitutional principles rather differently than the Liberal Home Rulers, formed an alliance with the Conservatives in 1895, eventually leading to formal union as the Conservative and Unionist Party in 1912 – the name which has endured ever since. The remaining Liberals carried on, bolstered by the support of Irish Nationalists and Home Rulers, as well as the nascent Labour Party. Later in the twentieth century, following the longstanding decline of Liberal electoral fortunes and another significant political divorce – this time between Labour and what became the Social Democratic Party – the much-depleted Liberals merged with the Social Democrats in 1988 to found the Liberal Democrats. At the core of the decline in Liberal success was not merely the rise of a new party with a vastly expanded, increasingly working-class electorate, but a new, shifting landscape for national politics; one which moved away from the historic constitutional agenda that had consumed Whigs, Tories, Liberals, and Conservatives alike for much of the previous two centuries.

The Whig Heritage

To understand the relationship of Liberalism and the British Constitution, we must look to two distinct though connected themes: first, the history of the Whig party and, second, what is now called 'Whig history' – that is, a distinct approach to writing the history of the (specifically) English past that became part of a national, 'British' story.

'The first Whig', the Tory essayist, Samuel Johnson, famously quipped, 'was the Devil'. Refining our definition somewhat, the Whig inheritance of Liberal constitutionalism lay in the parliamentary and Protestant constitutional settlement following the Glorious Revolution of 1688 – in which the Catholic James II was replaced with the Protestant William and Mary, who signed the Declaration of Right in 1689. Following a long period of Whig monopoly under Sir Robert Walpole, more recognisably distinct cleavages based on constitutional principles of parliamentary government and the place of the 'Crown-in-Parliament' emerge from the 1760s – at least in wider literature if not in strictly parliamentary terms.[9] The most famous statement of Whig principles down to the mid-Victorian period was that of Edmund

---

[9] J. J. Sack, *From Jacobite to Conservative: Reaction and Orthodoxy in Britain, 1760–1832* (Cambridge: Cambridge University Press, 1993). For more on parliamentarism in the

Burke's (1730–1797), *Thoughts on the Cause of the Present Discontents* (1770). Here, Burke attacked royal prerogative and defended party government as an essential of good, constitutional government. It was a concerted effort to defend liberty from an imperious executive and thus promoted the value of political parties; defined as 'a body of men united for promoting by their joint endeavours the national interest upon some particular principle in which they are all agreed'.[10]

'Civil and religious liberty' stood, therefore, as the Whig, and later Liberal, motto. In 1815, for instance, the jurist and historian James Mackintosh stated that 'a Tory is more influenced by loyalty, and a Whig by the love of liberty – that a Tory considers liberty as the second interest of society, while a Whig regards it as the first'.[11] So although liberty was cherished as a national inheritance, secured by the constitution, it was also seen to be treasured more by a particular political party. Hence reforms which were seen to remove restrictions, including the 'Great' Reform Act of 1832 and the removal of religious tests for qualifying offices of state and admittance to the ancient universities of Oxford and Cambridge, were often justified as the continuation of the unfolding history of British liberties. Thus, as the 1832 Reform Act shifted the focus of parliamentary government towards the House of Commons in particular, Liberal constitutionalism moved away from concerns of improper royal prerogative and towards perceived grievances elsewhere: to political and religious reform in its nineteenth-century guise.

Liberal constitutionalism also stood as a negation of an alternative stance: the Tory (and later, Conservative) interpretation of the constitution, which upheld the principle of 'the Constitution in Church and State'. Johnson once more provided a definition in his *Dictionary* (1755): a Tory was 'one who adheres to the ancient constitution in the State, and an apostolic hierarchy of the church of England'.[12] This constitutional principle had the flexibility to unite Conservative Prime Ministers as diverse as Sir Robert Peel (1788–1850), Benjamin Disraeli (1804–1881), and Lord Salisbury (1830–1903) – though ways

---

later period, see W. Selinger, *Parliamentarism: From Burke to Weber* (Cambridge: Cambridge University Press, 2019).

[10] *Writings and Speeches of Edmund Burke, Vol. 2: Party, Parliament, and the American War: 1766–1774*, eds. P. Langford and W. B. Todd (Oxford: Oxford University Press, 1981), p. 317.

[11] A. D. Kriegel, 'Liberty and Whiggery in Early Nineteenth-Century England', *Journal of Modern History*, 52 (1980), pp. 253–278.

[12] S. Johnson, *A Dictionary of the English Language*, 2 vols. (London: Longman, 1755), s.v. 'Tory'.

and means could vary substantially in the process of interpretation.[13] It was a principle that offered space for intra- as well as inter-party understandings, which naturally changed over time, as contexts and priorities shifted. Tories of all classes were committed to the maintenance of the formal relationship between the State and the established Church of England, which still includes privileges such as bishops in the House of Lords, and were generally hostile to expansive changes to the political constitution.[14] Indeed, the position of the established Church, as a constitutional question, was central to some of the most explosive political issues both between and within the two parties: the political rights of Irish Catholics after Britain and Ireland were united in 1801; the exclusion of non-Anglican Christians, such as Protestant Nonconformists, Jews, and other non-Christians from public office and university education; and the funding of denominational primary and secondary education.

This political history was then linked to a vision of British – and specifically English – historical development which favoured Whig developments and Whig priorities – also known as the 'Whig interpretation of history'. Commonly, the term 'Whig history' is used in a broad sense to describe historical writing or broadcasting that presents historical processes as teleological or inevitable – towards 'progress' or enlightenment – and that views historical persons and events only through the eyes of the present. The original use of the term, however, referred to a party-political interpretation of constitutional history: a Whig, as opposed to a Tory or Conservative, interpretation of history. Whig historians wrote a particular view of British and/or English constitutional development that was a story about political continuity: it was a story of the country's slow progress and gradual reform, focusing in particular on the development of Britain's mixed constitution – Commons, Lords, Monarch – which was viewed as a continuously evolving organism, through which the growth of individual freedoms, such as habeas corpus and freedom of speech, could be traced from Magna Carta through to the Glorious Revolution of 1688. In this account, British, but especially English, history was the history of human progress and liberty, embedded in the constitution, gradually triumphing over prejudiced authorities until we reach the glorious present. Mackintosh, for instance, offered an interpretation

---

[13] E. Jones; 'Constructive Conservatism in Conservative and Unionist Political Thought, c.1885–1914', *English Historical Review*, 134 (Apr. 2019), pp. 334–357.

[14] J. Neuheiser, *Crown, Church and Constitution: Popular Conservatism in England 1815–1867*, trans. J. W. Neuheiser (New York and Oxford: Berghahn Books, 2016).

of constitutional history as the source of moral guidance in politics, in which the growth of Parliament stood as the essence of the nation itself.[15]

The Whig historian *par excellence* in the nineteenth century – and therefore the classic exposition of Victorian constitutional exuberance – however, was Thomas Babington Macaulay (1800–1859), a Whig politician and literary critic. His *History of England*, published between 1848 and 1861, began in 1685 with the accession of James II and finished with the death of William III in 1702. It was the most popular historical work of the century, selling hundreds of thousands of copies in the years following its publication. In Macaulay's hands, British history was again a story of gradually expanded liberties, based on a flexible balanced constitution which could enact conservative reforms reflective of specific historical circumstances. In doing so, radical, violent social and political upheaval like that of the French Revolution was prevented.[16] The idea of an adaptable mixed constitution – made up of Commons (democracy), Lords (aristocracy) and Crown (monarchy), with executive ministers in the legislature – provided the British with a national history of liberty which was viewed as being vastly superior to Continental despotism and even American pure democracy, with its more rigorous separation of powers – a sentiment reaffirmed following the European revolutions of 1848 and the American Civil War (1861–1865).[17] A mixed constitution ensured balance, and this was seen as the best way to secure personal liberty and national stability.

And it was liberty – ordered 'rational' liberty[18] – that was seen as the true and most beneficial consequence of the British constitutional tradition. A unique degree of political freedom and religious toleration, combined with a stability that ensured its continuity. As the Poet Laureate, Alfred Tennyson, famously wrote:

---

[15] M. Francis and J. Morrow, *A History of English Political Thought in the Nineteenth Century* (London: Duckworth, 1994), pp. 83, 86. See also H. Hallam, *The Constitutional History of England from the Accession of Henry VII to the Death of George II*, 2 vols. (London: John Murray, 1827).

[16] T. B. Macaulay, *The History of England from the Accession of James the Second*, 5 vols. (London: Longman, 1848–1861), ii. s.v. 'On the peculiar character of the English Revolution'.

[17] J. P. Parry, 'The Impact of Napoleon III on British Politics, 1851–1880', *Transactions of the Royal Historical Society*, 11 (2001), pp. 147–175. See also J. P. Parry, *The Politics of Patriotism: English Liberty, National Identity, and Europe, 1830–1886* (Cambridge: Cambridge University Press, 2006), esp. ch. 1.

[18] E. Burke, *Reflections on the Revolution in France*, ed. J. G. A. Pocock (Cambridge: Cambridge University Press, 1987), p. 7.

> This is the land that freemen till,
> That sober-suited Freedom chose,
> The land, where girt with friends or foes
> A man may speak the thing he will;
> A land of settled government,
> A land of just and old renown,
> Where Freedom slowly broadens down
> From precedent to precedent ...[19]

Macaulay had claimed that this was no mere accident: England's (and by extension Britain's) unique national history was no mere accident, but divinely ordained. 'The weather had served the Protestant cause so well,' Macaulay explained, 'that some men of more piety than judgement fully believed the ordinary laws of nature to have been suspended for the preservation of the liberty and religion of England'.[20] The great success of Macaulay's work, and 'Whig' or English constitutionalist history in general, however, was that this became a national history of considerable longevity with a reach beyond Whigs and Liberals, and beyond England. The historian John Burrow describes how Macaulay's *History* was felt to embody a sense of the privileged possession by all Englishmen (and, by extension, women) of their history, as well as of the epic dignity of government by free discussion.[21] Macaulay's history was so popular that it became more reflective of English respectability than of either Whig or Tory political views on history: Tennyson's words were happily cited by the Oxford Regius Professor of History and Tory, William Stubbs.[22] Indeed, by the mid nineteenth century a great majority of Tories and High Churchmen, as well as subjects from around all four nations of the British Isles, agreed that the Glorious Revolution had been a positive development in British history and the development of national liberties, though emphases could vary. This became part of a national story that believed, with Macaulay, that, 'It is because we had a preserving revolution in the seventeenth century that we have not had

---

[19] A. Tennyson, 'You Ask Me, Why, Tho' Ill at Ease', *Poems*, 2 vols. (London: Edward Moxon, 1842).
[20] Macaulay, *History of England*, ii. 378.
[21] J. W. Burrow, *A Liberal Descent: Victorian Historians and the English Past* (Cambridge: Cambridge University Press, 1981). See also H. Trevor-Roper, 'Whig History', in his Penguin ed. of Macaulay, *History of England* (London: Penguin, 1986). On Scotland, see C. Kidd, *Subverting Scotland's Past: Scottish Whig Historians and the Creation of an Anglo-British Identity* (Cambridge: Cambridge University Press, 1993).
[22] W. Stubbs, *Lectures on Early English History* (London: Longmans, Green and Co., 1906), pp. 352–353.

a destroying revolution in the nineteenth.'[23] Thanks to Macaulay's immense popularity, English constitutional history became *the* popular national story, providing a consensual narrative of not only English, but British history. It provided both a logic for and a rationale of British domestic government and global imperial rule.

Yet this was still distinctly 'Whig' in content. Macaulay's partisanship is infamous: he viciously attacked those historical figures, such as the Catholic James II, whom he disapproved of, while fervently eulogising his idols, such as the Protestant William III. He made strong historical judgements on those he wrote about, according to his own values and views. Moreover, the constitutional reforms of the nineteenth century were often presented as the continuation of this history, particularly by Whigs and Liberals who fought for the continued extension of civil and religious liberty to excluded groups such as Roman Catholics and non-Anglican Protestant dissenters. Constitutional history also provided a means of working the Whig and Liberal desire for political and religious reform, such as the 1832 Reform Act, into an authoritative narrative of the English or British constitutional tradition. Hence Macaulay wrote:

> Those who compare the age in which their lot has fallen with a golden age which exists only in imagination, may talk of degeneracy and decay; but no man who is correctly informed as to the past, will be disposed to take a morose or desponding view of the present[24]

The constitution was, to use a metaphor popular at the time, a living, developing organism; growing ever stronger. Whig constitutional history was 'Whig' in the sense that the bountiful progress of English constitutional history was, according to Macaulay's account, largely thanks to the actions of the Protestant Whigs.

Despite Macaulay's critics, his *History* conveys the reverence for the constitution that provided the bedrock of British, and particularly English, political thought and party politics. In telling a powerful, eloquent national story – 'bad' historical myth-making though it is – the Whig interpretation of constitutional history provided the backbone of British national identity, and of intellectual and political life, too. His was a history written to be consumed: around the fireplace, the public library, or the school room. It

---

[23] Macaulay, *History of England*, ii. s.v. 'On the peculiar character of the English Revolution'.
[24] Macaulay, *History of England*, i. 14. For more on Macaulay, see P. Ghosh, 'Macaulay and the Heritage of the Enlightenment', *English Historical Review*, 112 (1997).

centred on the supposed excellence and exceptionalism of 'English' institutions, and on the importance of continuing a tradition of gradually unfolding liberties whose interpretation was as appealing to High Church Tories, Chartists and Suffragettes, as well as to its Whig and Liberal progenitors. Macaulay's *History* and its popular success therefore demonstrates the importance of recognising the cultural and mythical aspect of the constitutional history of the UK.

Liberal Constitutionalism

To be Liberal in nineteenth-century Britain therefore held strong connotations of a distinctive interpretation of the British Constitution. It was deeply indebted to the Whig vision of constitutional development, as well as the Whig emphasis on the 'popular' element of the constitution (i.e. the House of Commons) and the related motto of 'civil and religious liberty'. Liberal constitutionalism was thus distinctive both from Tory constitutionalism in Britain, and liberal constitutionalism in Continental Europe: Liberals in Britain were not fighting against royalist absolutism or republican revolutionaries clamouring for a codified constitutional document. What this entailed, in terms of practical policy, was therefore the expansion not only of political privileges such as public office and suffrage to those deemed fit to exercise such duties, but the expansion of religious freedoms to non-Anglican subjects. But 'toleration', 'freedom', and 'sovereignty' can be slippery concepts, and thus remained the subject of heated debates both between Liberals and with their Conservative opponents. Of primary concern were the limits of inclusion on topics such as education, disestablishment, parliamentary reform, and devolution within the British Isles.

This did not, however, mean that all Liberals thought or acted alike, and agreed 'ends' did not necessarily produce agreement on 'means'. Comprehending this important point is key for understanding the nuances and differences within higher Liberal political and constitutional thought, as well as Liberal political action and reform inside and outside of Parliament. Before exploring the latter in more detail, it will therefore be useful to outline some of the main strands in Liberal constitutional thinking. For it is constitutionalism that provides the most convincing argument for the necessity of ideas to nineteenth-century politics; that political life was not merely a struggle for power or electoral success, but an arena for the discussion and enactment of more or less sincerely held political principles. To Liberals, this lay in the expansion of 'civil and religious liberty', variously interpreted.

Walter Bagehot's *The English Constitution* (1867) stands as one of the most well-known commentaries on the 'real workings' of the constitution, in comparison to the mythologised constitutional history outlined above. Yet this is, in many ways, a 'Liberal' reading. Bagehot, now most frequently remembered as a principal editor of *The Economist*, was one of the last Whig-Liberals, a tradition which he described in 1855 as rooted in two key principles: 'The first wish of the Whig is to retain the constitution; the second – and it is of almost equal strength – is to improve it'.[25] *The English Constitution*, first serialised in the advanced Liberal *Fortnightly Review*, reflected a Liberal bias in some of its most central conceptual terms. Hence while the 'distinguished' sections of the constitution, such as the monarchy and the House of Lords, had a crucial role in the story, it was to the House of Commons that one must look towards to discover the 'efficient' part of the constitution.

A more critical eye was taken by those who stood in a clearer line of descent from the Philosophic Radicalism of Jeremy Bentham and, in modified form, John Stuart Mill. For 'advanced Liberals' such as John Morley, editor of the *Fortnightly Review* and later Liberal Chief Secretary of State to Ireland and India, the constitution was not something to be revered, but a machine that must be adapted to suit the people it is meant to serve – hence his support for Home Rule for Ireland. Morley and his friends were happy to denounce the mystical reverence held by eighteenth-century Whigs such as Edmund Burke, although they saw much else that was admirable in his writings.[26] Even in 1917, following the turn towards social and economic questions as well as the outbreak of war, Morley could still happily stress Liberal intellectual continuity via the constitution; describing men like himself as 'root-and-branch men' – seventeenth-century reformers – who had opposed the modern (Conservative) upholders of the creed of 'Church and Queen'.[27]

This sits in contrast to the more radical form of constitutional thinking (and polemical argument), of the ancient constitution. This was far less prevalent in Whig-Liberal traditions as compared to strictly Radical ones: an appeal to the ancient constitution was to make an argument about the need to restore liberties that had once been held, but had been 'lost' due to

---

[25] W. Bagehot, 'The First Edinburgh Reviewers' [1855], *Literary Studies: Volume One* (London: J.M. Dent, 1920), p. 15.
[26] J. Morley, *Burke* (London: Macmillan, 1879).
[27] J. Morley, *Recollections* (London: Macmillan, 1917), i. 107.

interventions in the more recent past.[28] Such an argument did not fit easily into Whig narratives with regards to either the slow growth of freedoms – or privileges – alongside the development of Parliament and 1688 as a 'Glorious Revolution', founding a uniquely 'free' and stable political order based on parliamentary government. Hence it was an argument more popular with Radicals than Dukes of Omnium. During the debates over women's suffrage, however, ancient constitutionalist arguments were used by female historians – many of them Liberals – who claimed that lost rights of women could be located in the distant past, and that this provided precedent for their 'restoration'.[29] This was a highly significant mode of reforming argument that was at one time radical, reformist and constitutionalist; restorative rather than 'revolutionary'.

A significant portion of Liberal constitutional thinking, then, was dedicated to the forms and workings of constitutional institutions themselves. Yet this was not simply a task of increasing the 'democratic' element of the constitution, and most Liberals were equally concerned with the character of those tasked with upholding the constitution. The questions of, first, who were the groups and individuals most in need of representation, and, second, who could be trusted to enact and uphold representative institutions, did not necessarily produce similar answers. Responses to such questions in Britain, Ireland and the Empire were undoubtedly informed by hierarchical notions of class and status, gender, civilisation, and race.[30] Liberal constitutionalism in this context was not simply about a set of positions on the legislative and institutional framework of Parliament, the Church, or the Empire, but the political actors responsible for its maintenance.

Religion

On questions of religious constitutional politics, Liberals held strong views. While many Liberals – especially the Whigs – were sincere Anglicans who believed in the maintenance of the established Church, Whig, and later Liberal, policy ensured that Britain was no longer a 'consecrated state'. Religious dissenters, particularly Protestant nonconformists, also formed a significant Liberal political cleavage, demanding relief from the grievances

---

[28] J. Barnes, 'The British Women's Suffrage Movement and the Ancient Constitution, 1867–1909', *Historical Research*, 91 (2018), pp. 505–527.
[29] C. C. Stopes, *British Freewomen: Their Historical Privilege* (London: S. Sonnenschein, 1894).
[30] A. Clark, 'Changing Concepts of Citizenship: Gender, Empire, and Class', *Journal of British Studies*, 42 (2003), pp. 263–270.

which branded them second-class citizens: access to public office; suffrage; the registering of births, marriages, and deaths; burial sites; admission to – and fellowship of – Oxbridge colleges; and the endowment of non-Anglican colleges and seminaries, such as Maynooth College in Ireland. Indeed, many of the advanced Liberals, Morley included, had grown up in nonconformist households, critical of the Anglican constitutional establishment. However, as the Test and Corporation Acts and Catholic Emancipation also show, reforming legislation could equally find support among Tory ministries split on the question of how best to maintain the status of the Church. 'Reform to conserve' was thus a constitutional principle that could be sincerely invoked across the political spectrum.

This did not mean that religious pluralism and tolerance abounded: this is not a teleological narrative of inevitable progress towards enlightenment. Anti-Catholicism was prevalent among all classes in British society; including Protestant dissenters who – despite coming from a similarly 'excluded' background, for religious reasons despised Catholic worship. Nor did it solve the intractable problem of education in Britain and Ireland, which invariably produced frenetic debates right down to the 1902 Education Act which – though passed without any cabinet resignations – produced a response among Nonconformists which rallied support for the Liberals in the 1906 General Election; that is, the last time the Liberal Party obtained a parliamentary majority.[31]

Parliamentary Reform

Parliamentary reform served as another key indicator of Liberal constitutional credentials, but this did not mean that all Liberals agreed on ways and means – not to mention the end product. This was as true for older Whigs and Liberals such as Lord John Russell and Lord Palmerston, as for later Liberals: on women's suffrage, for example, the views of leading advocates such as John Stuart and Harriet Taylor Mill were not shared by notorious 'antis' such as Gladstone and Asquith. As with religious reform, it is also possible to find Conservative reformers of all stripes – men as well as women. It was, after all, the government of Benjamin Disraeli which passed the 1867 Reform Act. Again, this rests on differing interpretations of constitutional maintenance and preservation both within and between the mainstream political parties. Despite this, however, it was the Whigs who

---

[31] Simon Skinner, 'Religion', in David Craig and James Thompson, eds., *Languages of Politics in Nineteenth-Century Britain* (London: Palgrave Macmillan, 2013).

championed the 'people' as the lesser danger to the constitution (as compared to unchecked royal power) and, likewise, it was their Liberal successors who desired the expansion of the 'pale of the constitution' to those then excluded. While the notion that Disraeli's actions in passing the 1867 Act was mere political manoeuvring to 'dish the Whigs' has fallen out of favour with historians, the comment itself indicates how, whatever Disraeli's actual motivation may have been, mainstream opinion connected the cause of parliamentary reform with the Whig-Liberal Party. From the Foxite Whigs advocating for reform in the late eighteenth century to later Whigs and Liberals in the 1830s, the nascent Liberal Party was associated with the cause of parliamentary reform. It was the Liberals, too, who had taken the active role in shaping and promoting arguments for further reform for twenty years prior to 1867.[32]

Whig-Liberal parliamentary reform was not, however, a simple narrative of democratic suffrage. It also took in the reform of constituency size, location and representation – including the representation of excluded 'interests' in the bid to extirpate 'old corruption'. There were also arguments – from Chartists but also by other figures, including Conservatives – for the payment of MPs, the adoption of a proportional voting system, annual elections, the equalisation of constituencies, and second chamber reform. This is all suggestive of the centrality of constitutional politics to conceptions of effective social and political change; and the vitality of constitutional discussion this produced – although the form this discussion took remained quite different when compared to the more philosophical constitutional writing undertaken in other European countries.

Home Rule

The debates over Irish Home Rule in Britain laid bare significant divisions between Liberal conceptions of sovereignty and the constitutional integrity of the imperial parliament at Westminster. The Home Rule Bill introduced to parliament by Gladstone on 8 April 1886 proposed a single chamber assembly in Dublin, which would legislate for Ireland within well-defined limits. Gladstone's Bill proposed retaining specific powers of taxation, defence, and foreign policy at Westminster and, in Gladstone's eyes, served the primary purpose of maintaining the 1801 Act of Union. Yet the classic

---

[32] R. Saunders, *Democracy and the Vote in British Politics, 1848–1867* (Farnham: Ashgate, 2011). See also R. Saunders, 'Parliament and People: The British Constitution in the Long Nineteenth Century', *Journal of Modern European History*, 6 (2008), pp. 72–87.

formulation of Victorian Liberal accounts of sovereignty was that of the legal scholars John Austin (1790–1859) and A. V. Dicey (1835–1922).[33] Here, the unitary sovereignty of Parliament at Westminster was paramount, and that sovereignty was rigid and theoretical. Apart from distant colonies such as Canada, the idea of devolving power from the Westminster parliament was unheard of, and to critics such as Dicey the bill was an attempt to overturn the inviolable principle of 'parliamentary sovereignty'. For Dicey, devolution was the first stepping stone to the dissolution of the Union and perhaps the Empire as a whole. In contrast, to Gladstone and his supporters including the constitutional writer and historian James Bryce, sovereignty was historically defined and therefore malleable and responsive.[34] Home Rule was therefore not just an Irish issue but a constitutional argument about parliamentary sovereignty within the UK.

Here, as in other constitutional disputes such as women's suffrage and the privileges of the established Church, the 'Liberal' constitutional position was again contested. To Liberal Unionists – who broke away from Gladstonian Liberals on this issue – this was a question of interpretation, and how one read the old Liberal motto of 'Civil and Religious Liberty'.[35] To Gladstone, Home Rule would give justice to Ireland; create a 'union of hearts and minds' through timely conciliation; and avoid further coercion. To most Liberal Unionists, however, Gladstone's plan was nothing less than a constitutional revolution which, rather than restoring liberty in Ireland, would put the liberty of the Protestant minority in Ireland in grave danger and damage irreparably the centre of imperial government – unitary sovereignty at Westminster. This, in turn, would begin a longer process of dissolution taking in the entire British Empire. On a pragmatic note, Liberal Unionists also argued that a constitutional measure was unnecessary for solving Irish grievances with regards to land and education. Such arguments were made by politicians inside and outside of Parliament, as well as by Liberal and Liberal Unionist intellectuals – many of whom were Anglican or agnostic. But Home Rule also cut across Liberal Nonconformity: for those associated with the voluntaryist strand of Nonconformity and who identified with Roman Catholics as the fellow oppressed in need of constitutional liberation were as able (though generally less willing) to make anti-Home Rule

---

[33] E. Jones, *Edmund Burke and the Invention of Modern Conservatism, 1830–1914: An Intellectual History* (Oxford: Oxford University Press, 2017), ch. 5.
[34] J. Bryce, *Studies in History and Jurisprudence*, 2 vols (Oxford: Oxford University Press, 1901), p. 524.
[35] A. Jackson, *Ireland, 1798–2008* (Oxford: Oxford University Press, 2010), 130.

arguments as compared to more theologically anti-Catholic strands of Protestant dissent: the Quakers, for example, were generally opposed to Home Rule.[36]

By the turn of the twentieth century, Liberal scholars and commentators interested in the role of the state and its relation to both individuals and communities were also challenging unitary conceptions of sovereignty. While Victorian Liberal thinking such as that expressed by Dicey and Austin stressed the importance of fixed 'ultimate' sovereignty based unitarily at Westminster, later critics began to emphasise the importance of a more pluralistic form of sovereignty. Pluralism, such as that formulated by the lawyer and Cambridge historian F. W. Maitland, focused especially on the history and role of group communities that had developed since the medieval period, and, as such, had developed their own legal identities.[37] Such an approach stood in sharp contrast to the conception of sovereignty as it had been laid down in earlier Liberal legal and constitutional thought, and also with the account of constitutional history focused essentially on the growth and development of Parliament from the thirteenth Century or the Glorious Revolution as laid down by Whigs and Liberals such as Macaulay and E. A. Freeman.

To be Liberal, therefore, was to hold specific interpretations of broad constitutional principles that were determined by a variety of contexts, including, but not limited to, region, status, and religious denomination. In an election address of December 1910, the Liberal Herbert Samuel proclaimed:

> When the Parliament Bill is passed then at last the principles of social reform, of religious equality and of self-government, which the Nation desires to see established as the guides of our policy, will have a prospect of the equal treatment at the hands of the Constitution which has been denied them too long.[38]

Samuel demonstrates how constitutional principles intertwined with other political considerations: welfare, political economy, foreign policy, empire,

---

[36] T. C. Kennedy, 'Quakers', in T. Larson and M. Ledger-Lomas, eds., *The Oxford History of the Dissenting Traditions, Vol. III: The Nineteenth Century* (Oxford: Oxford University Press, 2017), p. 93.

[37] J. Kirby, 'History, Law, Freedom: F. W. Maitland in Context', *Modern Intellectual History*, 16 (2019), pp. 127–154; idem., 'A. V. Dicey and English constitutionalism', *History of European Ideas*, 45 (2019), pp. 33–46.

[38] Quoted in *The Campaign Guide: A Handbook for Unionist Speakers* (London and Edinburgh: D. Douglas, 1914), pp. 340–341.

and more. The power of constitutional party-political principles lay in their interconnection with a particular story of British history and national exceptionalism. The extent to which such principles could survive in the twentieth century, however, is another matter entirely.

Liberalism in Contemporary Britain

Liberal (as well as Conservative and Radical) constitutionalism was no less than the basis of the party system in nineteenth-century Britain and thus central not only to British political and constitutional history but also in explaining the ways in which Britons saw themselves in the world. Yet the relationship between Liberalism and the history of the British Constitution significantly alters in the twentieth century following the two World Wars of 1914–1918 and 1939–1945. The impact of the Second World War, the dissolution of the British Empire and the decolonisation that followed, and the devolution of powers within the UK, had a profound impact on the constitution as it had hitherto existed. The British *Sonderweg* of political stability and national exceptionalism which had stood at the heart of a triumphant national, imperial and global identity became increasingly difficult to sustain, especially in the aftermath of the 1956 Suez Crisis. The Whig narrative of evolutionary constitutional development and its gift of ordered liberty lost its place in an expanding and diversifying historical profession, and in the broader 'national story', as Parliament was replaced by the NHS as the nation's favourite national institution.[39]

A shifting political landscape, in which the political agenda moved away from constitutional issues and towards questions of economic management, welfare, and the role of state had devastating consequences for the Liberal Party proper – the so-called 'death of Liberal England' and the rise of Labour as the socialist – yet still *parliamentary*, non-republican, constitutionalist – opposition. The constitution no longer acted as the master-key to British party politics, and by the 1924 General Election, Liberal voters generally voted for the Conservative Party by about three to two.[40] Yet George Dangerfield's 'death of Liberal England' thesis, which posited that the Liberal political battles of the Edwardian period – suffrage, Lords reform,

---

[39] 'NHS Tops the Pride of Britain List', *Opinium* (2016): www.opinium.co.uk/nhs-tops-the-pride-of-britain-list/ Accessed 2/8/2019.
[40] R. McKibbin, 'Class and Conventional Wisdom: The Conservative Party and the "Public" in Inter-War Britain', in *Ideologies of Class: Social Relations in Britain* (Oxford: Oxford University Press, 1990), pp. 260–261.

Irish Home Rule, and trade union regulation – effectively tolled the bell for the post-war Liberal Party, has been challenged by historians, and there are other arenas in which the Liberal constitutionalism of the nineteenth century was not so easily forgotten. On issues such as House of Lords reform, the voting system, devolution, decolonisation, and Europe (and the related question of the European Convention on Human Rights), it is possible to identify continuities and legacies.

Certainly, Liberals and Liberal Democrats have appealed consistently to the need for a programme of constitutional reform. On the House of Lords, serious questions about its role and composition began to be addressed by the major parties: first, by Liberals and, second, by Conservatives desirous of 'reforming to conserve'. The Liberal historian E. A. Freeman argued that the composition of the Lords could easily be reformed, as this was not an essential part of its character: the hereditary element only became the majority once the Henrician Reformation ensured the exclusion of the abbots.[41] This line of argument – that the Lords need not be exclusively hereditary – was subsequently taken up by the Liberal leader Lord Rosebery in a number of reports and proposals which soon followed. What resulted was not compositional reform but the subordination of the Lords to the Commons by the 1911 Parliament Act passed by the last Liberal government during another period of constitutional crisis. The Parliament Act would, the preamble claimed, serve as the basis for significant reconstruction of the second chamber. The failure to act on this statement beyond compositional reform is clear enough: Liberals – and now Liberal Democrats – have been notably committed to significant second chamber reform down to Paddy Ashdown and Nick Clegg. Indeed, while Clegg's distance from the social democratic element within the party may be clear enough, the same cannot be said for the interest in constitutional reform ubiquitous with the Liberal tradition.[42]

While the 2010 Liberal Democrat-Conservative coalition was unsuccessful in achieving Lords reform, they secured the (failed) referendum on the Alternative Vote (AV) as well as legislation securing fixed-term parliaments

---

[41] H. S. Jones, 'Historical Mindedness and the World at Large: E. A. Freeman as Public Intellectual', in G. A. Bremner and J. Conlin, eds., *Making History: Edward Augustus Freeman and Victorian Cultural Politics* (Oxford: Oxford University Press, 2015), pp. 304–305.

[42] '"Rewiring power", Nick Clegg's Constitutional Vision', *Open Democracy* (19 Nov. 2010): www.opendemocracy.net/en/opendemocracyuk/rewiring-power-nick-cleggs-constitutional-vision/ Accessed 2/8/2019.

and further devolution of powers to Scotland. Indeed, though AV is by no means a proportional system, Liberals and Lib Dems have been consistently critical of the First-Past-the-Post voting system.[43] The manifesto proposals for proportional representation (PR) proper began in 1922 with those independent Liberals in contention with David Lloyd George's Coalition Liberal Party, and commentators have often divined a relationship between the uptake of PR and a growing realisation that the Liberals were becoming a minor party.[44] Thus while Liberal policy on PR is situated within a broader programme of constitutional reform concerned with fair representation, it is often read as a Lib Dem fixation grounded in self-interest.

A more contentious theme is Britain's relationship with Europe. In the years preceding the 1975 European referendum, Jeremy Thorpe's Liberals were fully committed to joining the European Community. Much the same was demonstrated by the Liberal Democrats during the 2019 General Election campaign and beyond. Yet it is worth noting here that we have moved quite a long way from the Diceyean Liberal conception of unitary sovereignty at Westminster, as well as from the 'Whig' narrative of British historical and constitutional exceptionalism that would prove its potency in the Brexit debates. Similarly, the growth of universal human rights based in international law is another significant development, far removed from the civil and religious liberty beloved by Liberals in Victorian Britain, based as it was on a set of legal privileges bequeathed by the state, rather than any conception of innate abstract rights.[45] This is not to say that one or the other is 'true' Liberal constitutionalism; more to stress that what it means to be a Liberal with constitutional principles (or to identify oneself as constitutionally liberal) means something quite different today than it did 150, or even 50, years ago. Such a transformation is due in large part to the staggering challenges to the concept of a nation state posed by international forms of political and economic governance, but also due to the inevitable need for thinkers and political actors situated in specific contexts to reposition as new issues and opponents arise.

---

[43] 'Blair and Ashdown Join Forces', Guardian (11 Nov. 1998): www.theguardian.com/politics/1998/nov/11/libdemleadership.liberaldemocrats1 Access 2/8/2019.
[44] Liberal Party 1922 General Election Manifesto: www.libdemmanifesto.com/1922/1922-liberal-manifesto.shtml Access 2/8/2019.
[45] S. Moyn, *The Last Utopia: Human Rights in History* (Cambridge, MA: Harvard University Press, 2010).

Conclusion: Liberalism beyond Liberals?

As the relationship between Liberalism and the constitution altered alongside the shifting party-political landscape, it may also be said that 'liberal values' such as liberty, rationality, tolerance, 'liberal internationalism', and the rule of law, as well as the ideas and policies of individual Liberals such as William Beveridge and John Maynard Keynes, have been divorced from the Liberal Party proper and now permeate both 'left' and 'right'.[46] In this context, liberalism has also been reduced to economic ideas surrounding free trade, marketisation or 'neoliberalism', while others have added equality, social justice, and human rights.[47] Today, 'liberalism' may be used and abused by figures across the political spectrum; 'liberal values' – all of which have constitutional ramifications – are by no means the sole property of capital-L Liberalism.[48]

This chapter has demonstrated that Liberalism and liberalism are not clear-cut analytical tools to assess the history of the UK Constitution – political and intellectual traditions adapt and evolve. Following the 1688 Revolution, the constitution was 'liberal' in contrast to continental absolutism; in the twentieth century its liberality was relative to continental fascism and Cold War communism. Likewise, prominent figures such as A. V. Dicey, a Benthamite democrat who argued for the referendum and unitary parliamentary sovereignty, but against women's suffrage and Irish Home Rule, was rather unlike a modern Liberal Democrat committed to European integration, devolved national assemblies, and human rights as based in international law. Nevertheless, this does not lead to the conclusion that discernible histories and traditions cannot be found. In fact, it has been shown that a loose tradition of Liberal constitutionalism had significant impact not only in relation to the history of the UK Constitution itself, but in developing a powerful, pervasive mythical narrative of British (and sometimes Irish) history rooted in the growth of Parliament.

---

[46] I. Bradley, *The Strange Rebirth of Liberal Britain* (London: Chatto & Windus, 1985), p. 3.
[47] See, for example, E. Green and D. Tanner, eds., *The Strange Survival of Liberal England* (Cambridge: Cambridge University Press, 2007).
[48] E. Robinson, 'Defining Progressive Politics: Municipal Socialism and Anti-Socialism in Contestation, 1889–1938', *Journal of the History of Ideas*, 76 (2015), pp. 609–631, p. 630.

20

Socialism

STEPHEN SEDLEY

Matters goeth not well to pass in England, nor shall do till everything be common.[1]

*We're going to take a good sharp axe
Shining steel tempered in the fire
Knock you down like an old dead tree
Dirty old town, dirty old town.*[2]

The Peasants' Revolt

The desire to end privilege and exploitation and to reconstitute society as a community of equals runs through Britain's history, from the Peasants' Revolt (and with little doubt from earlier than that) to modern times. The uprising which for a few weeks in the summer of 1381 set the south-east of England ablaze was a direct challenge to a system which was now piling upon feudal rents the taxes – above all the poll tax – demanded by an increasingly centralised state. The rebels' immediate political objectives were limited,[3] but their demand for the abolition of villeinage was a revolutionary demand.

The English civil war

Egalitarianism resurfaced in the English civil war, not in the programme of the Levellers but in the beliefs and practices of smaller sects like the Diggers and the Ranters. Although opponents accused them of wanting to level all social differences (hence the name), the Levellers' *Agreement of the People* – the first modern political manifesto – shows them to have been, at least by modern standards, moderate in their demands. Socialist historiography has fastened upon the intervention of Thomas Rainborough (who had returned

---

[1] Attributed to John Ball, 1381. [2] Ewan MacColl, c. 1950.
[3] The confession attributed to Jack Straw included the rebels' aim of setting up a king in each county.

499

from the American colonies to fight for Parliament) in the three-day debate in Putney parish church in the winter of 1647 between the Army grandees and the spokesmen of the Leveller regiments:

> The poorest he that is in England hath a life to live as the greatest he ... [E]very man that is to live under a government ought first by his own consent to put himself under that government.[4]

The Leveller programme, though confined to a limited male franchise, was radical not only in its advocacy of annual parliaments, reform and codification of the law, abolition of feudal tenures and extended religious toleration, but in its premise that ultimate state power lay not in monarchs or even in elected parliaments but in those who elected them. Natural law, the Levellers contended, set limits to what even a parliament could do – for example, deny equality before the law or enact statutes 'destructive to the safety and well-being of the people'.[5]

The historian Frances Dow summarises:

> Perhaps not surprisingly, the Levellers do not always score highly in terms of logic and intellectual coherence. But as political activists and innovators, they pushed forward the frontiers of political debate, expressed the aspirations and grievances of sections of the population who had been ignored by many parliamentarian writers, and prefigured the radical agitators of the later eighteenth century.[6]

And it is in the Leveller pamphlet literature of the Civil War that the phrase 'people's rights' first appears, a century and a half ahead of its time.[7]

The abolition in 1649 not only of the monarchy[8] but of the hereditary House of Lords as 'useless and dangerous to the people of England'[9] set a constitutional precedent to which modern socialists still look back. But to regard the Commonwealth, much less the Protectorate which succeeded it,

---

[4] The Putney Debates, 28 October 1647: see A. S. P.Woodhouse (ed.), *Puritanism and Liberty (the Clarke MSS)* (London: Dent, 1938), p. 53; Adrian Tinniswood, *The Rainborowes* (London: Vintage Books, 2013), p. 139. A resourceful commander, Rainborough had reached the rank of lieutenant-colonel when he was killed at Doncaster in 1648.

[5] See Donald Veall, *The Popular Movement for Law Reform, 1640–1660* (Oxford: Clarendon Press, 1970), passim; S. Sedley, *Lions under the Throne* (Cambridge: Cambridge University Press, 2015), ch. 4.

[6] F. D. Dow, *Radicalism in the English Revolution 1640–1660* (Blackwell, Oxford, 1985), p. 38.

[7] John Warr, *The Corruption and Deficiency of the Laws of England*, Giles Calvert (London, 1649), ch. 1: '... the proper fountain of good and righteous laws, a spirit of understanding big with freedom and having a single respect to people's rights'.

[8] An Act for abolishing the Kingly Office in England and Ireland, 17 March 1648/9 (*Acts and Ordinances of the Interegnum*, ed. Firth and Rait, vol. 2, p.18).

[9] An Act for the Abolishing the House of Peers, 19 March 1648/9 (ibid., vol. 2, p.24).

as a prefigurative socialist regime is to allow the present to colonise the past.[10] What the Interregnum did accomplish in constitutional terms, notwithstanding the reversal after 1660 of almost everything it had achieved, was the establishment of an elective legislature free of hereditary entitlement and, in the short-lived Instrument of Government 1653, the United Kingdom's first and only written constitution, a perceptible source of elements of the 1689 Bill of Rights and a matrix of presidential systems of government.[11]

The Historic Compromise of 1689

The establishment at the end of the seventeenth century of a constitutional monarchy, its terms of tenure settled by Parliament and its throne now in Parliament's gift, was to have profound implications for the socialist movements of modern Britain. For a majority it signalled that the commanding heights of power, now elective rather than monarchical, were constitutionally accessible. For a minority it signalled only that the battleground of revolution had shifted, for history had taught them that a ruling class, whether monarchical, aristocratic or mercantile, would violate its own constitutional norms in order to hold on to power. If this has been an enduring cleft between legitimist and revolutionary socialism in the United Kingdom, it is because a Labour Party committed until the late twentieth century to the public ownership of key sectors of the economy has more than once won power by constitutional means, and at its post-war apogee carried through a series of measures arguably capable of forming the foundation of a socialist society. Whether such an enterprise, if carried through, would have been unconstitutional or, simply by happening, would have reformed the UK's constitution is one of the great counterfactual questions of modern history. In the event, as will be seen, the onward march of Labour was halted by a Conservative counter-revolution.

***

Revolution and Constitutionalism

The word socialism first makes its appearance in the 1820s, more or less contemporaneously with the word conservatism.[12] Initially it had no

---

[10] See F. D. Dow, n.5 ante, ch. 3.
[11] See S. Sedley, *Ashes and sparks* (2011), ch. 8; *Lions under the Throne* (2015), ch.4.
[12] Raymond Williams, *Keywords* (Oxford: Oxford University Press, 1976), p.238–243.

programmatic or methodological content: it signified rejection of individualism as the foundation of a morally worthwhile society. But the early utopian socialist communities which tried to make it a reality – Robert Owen's are the best known – all failed, and it became apparent that it was not by opting out of the industrial societies of Europe and the Americas that socialism might be achieved, but by gaining political power and transforming them. The question for socialists, from that day to this, has been how to do it.

The answer has flowed broadly down two channels, separated by considerable mutual antipathy. One socialist tradition has been insurrectionary, looking back to Britain's revolutionary past and anticipating a fresh crisis provoked by the internal contradictions of capitalism, from which would follow the possibility of a popular seizure of power. Its principal European theoreticians, Marx and Engels, developed a following in the United Kingdom, chiefly within the Social Democratic Federation but also in thinkers and writers like William Morris. And for a brief moment following the collapse of France's civil government in the face of military defeat by Prussia, revolutionary socialists during the spring of 1871 saw their predictions vindicated both in the spontaneous establishment of popular power by the Paris Commune and in the bloody vengeance of the ruling class which followed. But in spite of occasional revivals of revolutionary hopes, for example in the General Strike of 1926 and even in the dockers' strikes of 1967 and 1972, an insurrectionary – and therefore unconstitutional – path to socialism in Britain has remained a sectarian pipe dream.[13]

What has come arguably closer to realisation in Britain since the nineteenth century is legitimist, or constitutional, socialism – the capture by lawful electoral means of the political and economic power of the state, and through it the transformation of society. Its critics on the left have argued that this is a contradiction in terms: a state-managed capitalist society will still be an unjust and exploitative society. Moreover, it is one thing for a socialist party to win an electoral victory and to set about making radical social and economic changes and another for it then to alter the rules – the constitution – to forestall a reversion to the former system. While the Labour Party between 1945 and 1951 accomplished much in the former category, its leaders (though not necessarily all of its rank and file) would have considered it

---

[13] As early as 1947 the Communist Party of Great Britain, encouraged by developments in Italy and France and almost certainly on the prompting of Moscow, abandoned its insurrectionary policy in favour of electoral politics. Since then revolutionary socialism in Britain has been confined effectively to Trotskyist and anarchist organisations outside and inside the Labour Party.

impermissible to attempt to change the constitutional rules, for instance by banning pro-capitalist parties as had happened in eastern Europe. Comparable scruples did not inhibit the Attlee government's participation in the US-led Cold War, using prerogative powers to dismiss civil and public servants suspected of communist or radical sympathies.

The Franchise

Britain's leadership of the world in industrial development had thrown up a vast, discontented and almost wholly unenfranchised working class. When the pressure for enfranchisement became too great, the Reform Acts of 1867 and 1884[14] grudgingly gave adult men the vote, and in doing so raised the spectre of revolution through the ballot box. The minimal changes made by the 1832 Reform Act had prompted a huge movement in support of a People's Charter whose central demands, many of them variants of the Levellers' programme two centuries earlier, were annual parliaments, universal male suffrage, equal electoral districts, secret ballots, salaries for MPs and abolition of property qualifications for their office. The agitation for reform reached its height in 1842. In 1848, with popular anger at the Peterloo massacre of 1819 still alive, the outbreak of revolutions in continental Europe prompted the government to call out the Duke of Wellington to contain a further Chartist demonstration. Although the combination of military opposition and rain was enough to dispel the physical threat, two million signatures (ignoring the obviously fake ones) could not be indefinitely ignored, and politicians of both parties came to accept that adult men, at least, had to be accorded the vote if (as Thomas Rainborough had urged two centuries before) they were to put themselves under any government.

The eventual achievement of votes for women, despite its social and political importance (both Owenite socialists and Chartists had supported it), and despite the active presence of both male and female suffragists in the Labour Party, was not part of the labour movement's prospectus until after the First World War. For as long as the right to vote was subject to a property qualification there was a not wholly unreal fear that if the franchise was enlarged to include female householders most of them would vote Conservative. There was also a well-organised Women's National Anti-Suffrage League, while the trade union movement, whose Labour Representation Committee had become the

---

[14] The 1832 Reform Act redistributed parliamentary seats but actually reduced the franchise.

Labour Party, was in many sectors uneasy about women taking what it regarded as men's jobs. It was left to the women's movement itself, most prominently through Sylvia Pankhurst, to campaign for female suffrage to become part of the socialist agenda. Her Women's Social and Political Union, founded in 1903, had by 1912 succeeded in moving the Labour Party into a position in which it would not support any electoral reform that did not include women equally with men. Although the Labour agenda by 1918 included a non-discriminatory franchise, it was probably the suffragist movement rather than (with honourable exceptions) the traditional labour movement which had brought this about. The suffragist movement itself has, however, been largely hidden from history: the contribution of thousands of working-class women who campaigned not only for the vote but for better conditions of life[15] has been eclipsed by the attention sought and obtained by the Pankhursts' campaigning, both legitimist and activist, for the vote as an end in itself.

> To the radical suffragists, such an attitude was little short of ridiculous. What was the point of a vote without any idea of how it could be used? Without exception, they were all involved in wider campaigns for working women.[16]

The Civil Service

It was partly in response to the widening of the male franchise[17], as well as because of the intrinsic need of an ever-expanding state for a solid body of dependable administrators, that the ground-breaking Northcote-Trevelyan report of 1854 made the case for a competent and educated civil service, recruited by open competition from Britain's public schools[18] and universities and rewarded by generous salaries, good pensions and the prospect of civic honours, anticipating that this would place the governance of country beyond the reach of transient parliamentary majorities, including any set on radical change.[19]

---

[15] See Jill Liddington and Jill Norris, *One Hand Tied behind Us* (London: Virago Press, 1978), passim.
[16] Ibid., p.20.
[17] Sir Charles Trevelyan had noted that 'The irresistible tendency of the times is to bring into activity the political power of the lower classes...' Gladstone accordingly supported Trevelyan's and Northcote's reforms 'to strengthen and multiply the ties between the higher classes and the possession of administrative power'. (Asa Briggs, *Victorian People*, pp. 169, 117, cited by Peter Hennessy, *Whitehall* (London: Secker and Warburg, 1989), pp. 33, 31).
[18] I.e. private fee-paying schools.
[19] See Hennessy, *Whitehall*, ch. 1, esp. pp. 31–51; Sedley, *Lions under the Throne*, ch. 2, esp. p.55.

The civil service which in consequence was in post by the turn of the century[20] had a dual set of loyalties: a political loyalty to the body of ministers for the time being in office, and an institutional loyalty to the system of government of which the executive now formed the central pillar. Its defining mindset, embodied in the barely fictional Sir Humphrey Appleby,[21] was a reluctance to recognise that the two things were not necessarily the same.

It is generally accepted that it was between the two world wars that the power of the civil service reached its zenith. The senior judges, who by the end of the nineteenth century had developed a sophisticated system of judicial oversight of public administration, now stepped back and left governance to a mandarin class whose members came, by and large, from the same schools and universities, and belonged to the same London clubs, as themselves,[22] forming an élite which was able to provide stability and continuity in government as prime ministers, cabinets and parliaments came and went. In this way the destabilising effect between the two world wars of a succession of ministers with little or no experience of government and few thought-out policies was in large part compensated for by a now entrenched and experienced civil service, accustomed to taking responsibility for policy implementation (and as often as not, policy formation).

But what was going to happen when in July 1945, at the conclusion of another close-run and debilitating conflict, the victorious war leader, Winston Churchill, was voted out of office and a Labour government swept in by a decisive electoral majority?[23] Would the executive remain loyal to its political masters and carry through radical, possibly even revolutionary, policies? And if it did, would the senior judges, with their long history of hostility towards the labour movement, continue to stand by or begin to prime their weapons?

---

[20] The Foreign Office was the last major department to make the transition, since it was considered that in diplomacy character was more important than brains. Separate attention, beyond the remit of this chapter, is needed to SpAds (special advisers) now brought in as 'temporary civil servants' under the Civil Service Order in Council 1995 with the role of providing ministers with political advice which permanent civil servants are in principle debarred from giving. Their piecemeal introduction in the latter part of the twentieth century was considered by some to be a reversion to the 'placemen' who accompanied Victorian ministers, albeit now based on intellectual merit rather than personal connection. See further T. Daintith [2002] Public Law 13.

[21] Sir Humphrey Appleby, GCB, KBE, MVO, MA (Oxon), permanent secretary, later cabinet secretary, still later Master of Baillie College, Oxford: see the British television series *Yes Minister* and *Yes Prime Minister*.

[22] See Sedley, *Lions under the Throne*, ch. 2, esp. p.53–56.

[23] 394 seats, to the Conservatives' 210.

Poplar 1919–1925

There had been at least one principled attempt in the aftermath of the First World War to put the conduct of local administration on an egalitarian footing.[24] The Labour Party in the borough of Poplar, which included most of the London docks and a quarter of whose population fell below the poverty line,[25] in 1919 won thirty-nine of the forty-two seats on the borough council. Four of the thirty-nine new councillors and one of the new aldermen were women.[26] Most of the men elected were skilled or manual workers. As mayor they elected the veteran Christian socialist and pacifist George Lansbury, who was by then the editor of the Daily Herald.

The eventual imprisonment in 1921 of thirty-one councillors, five of them women, for contempt of court in refusing to collect precepts on behalf of wealthier boroughs and resolving to pay equal wages, well above the market rate, to both men and women, is a heroic episode in Labour history. When other Labour councils threatened to do likewise, the government began to negotiate with the still imprisoned councillors, who were released after six weeks. Although denounced by Labour leaders such as Herbert Morrison as revolutionary and unconstitutional, their objectives all eventually became law. The ironic reality was that it had taken a historic rupture of constitutional norms to bring about a modest, and in the end barely contentious, reform of local government finance.

Both the achievement and the eventual nemesis of the Poplar councillors was, in the historian Noreen Branson's view, that, 'as one of the first groups of socialists to achieve a working majority, they were also among the few who refused to remain confined within the limits of the system'.[27] Yet what the Times had denounced as a 'revolutionary movement for the equalisation of wealth'[28] – the equalisation of London rates, rate support grants for the poorer boroughs and proper benefits for the unemployed – was by mid century a constitutional norm. 'Convinced of the need for fundamental changes in the system,' wrote Branson, 'such people have believed that if elected they will be in a position to make a major impact on the lives of those they represent. But once elected, whether in local or national government,

---

[24] See generally Noreen Branson, *Poplarism* (London: Lawrence & Wishart, 1979).
[25] *New Survey of London Life and Labour* (1932), vol. III, using Booth's definition, which in 1889 had classified over a third of the population of Poplar as 'in poverty'.
[26] They included Susan Lawrence, who went on to become a distinguished parliamentarian.
[27] Branson, *Poplarism*, p. 26–27.   [28] 3 Sept. 1921.

they have found that their opportunities are smaller than expected ... The existing framework is too strong for them.'[29]

The 1945–1951 Labour Government

The Labour Party's principal objective in its early years had been the containment of repeated legislative and judicial assaults on trade unions' freedoms and funds. It had not been until the outburst of militancy among unskilled workers in 1888–1889, including the match-girls' strike, the seamen's strikes and the achievement of the 'docker's tanner' (a basic wage of sixpence an hour), that socialist leaders, notably Ben Tillett, John Burns and Tom Mann, emerged, arguing that society did not have to be a site of unending social immiseration and class conflict. Their position was reinforced by the minority report of the Royal Commission on Labour which reported in 1894, contending that legislative provision was required for an eight-hour working day, the extension and enforcement of the Factories Acts, decent housing for workers and social security in their old age, payment of union rates by all governmental bodies, the institutionalisation of collective agreements – and the substitution wherever feasible of public enterprise for private capital.[30] The minority report was intellectually indebted to the Fabian Society;[31] but more than this, it looked forward to something recognisably like the political programme of the Attlee government half a century later. By then – in fact in 1918 – the Labour Party had amended its constitution to include Clause 4, calling for the common ownership of the means of production, distribution and exchange. Its 1945 manifesto did not mention the word socialism. But although Clause 4, regarded by leaders from Gaitskell to Blair as a blight on the party's electability, was dropped in 1995, it had arguably done its work in the years of Clement Attlee's administration.

---

[29] It was not over. The district auditor decided to impose a £5,000 surcharge – in effect a fine – on the councillors to recoup some of what they had overspent by paying wages above the market rate. Their challenge to the decision succeeded in the High Court but was overset by the House of Lords in a famously political judgment: see n. 65.

[30] See W. Cornish and G. Clark, *Law and Society in England 1750–1950* (London: Sweet & Maxwell, 1989), p. 309–336.

[31] The Fabian Society, founded in 1884 and named after the Roman general Quintus Fabius Maximus whose principal tactic was the avoidance of confrontation, argued consistently against revolution as a path to socialism. Its influential *Fabian Essays* (1889), written by a number of celebrated socialist intellectuals, set out the case for a non-violent, gradual and constitutional transition.

Peter Hennessy catches the post-war mood that swept Labour unexpectedly into office:

> Never again would there be war; never again would the British people be housed in slums, living off a meagre diet thanks to low wages or no wages at all; never again would mass unemployment blight the lives of millions; never again would natural abilities remain dormant in the absence of educational stimulus. Of course there were setbacks. The economy was a near-constant disappointment. The bundle of social and economic problems the welfare state was designed to break open proved tough to crack. But real progress there was; progress on a scale and a duration never surpassed in the nation's history.[32]

The sheer extent of the Attlee government's assumption of central economic power is worth listing: civil aviation,[33] the Bank of England,[34] coalmining,[35] cable and wireless,[36] public transport,[37] town and country planning,[38] electricity,[39] gas,[40] nuclear power,[41] iron and steel,[42] dock labour,[43] rent controls,[44] fisheries,[45] and guaranteed agricultural prices in return for good husbandry,[46] Labour's first eighteen months in office, Kenneth O. Morgan wrote, saw Britain 'undergo a massive transformation unique in her history. Over 20 per cent of the economy was taken into public ownership or was well on course for it.'[47]

Also on Labour's list, but not reached by 1951 when the party lost office, were the chemical industry, insurance, shipbuilding, engineering and textiles. The list itself dated from 1934; in the intervening decade new public authorities – the Central Electricity Generating Board, the British Overseas Airways Corporation and the London Passenger Transport Board – had been set up. Moreover, in the course of the war the population had become accustomed, in particular through the rationing of food, clothing and fuel and the requisitioning of buildings for official use, to state regulation of most aspects of life. It was becoming accepted that the state might be required to take

---

[32] P. Hennessy, *Never Again: Britain 1945–1951* (London: Penguin, 1992), p.2.
[33] Civil Aviation Act 1946. [34] Bank of England Act 1946.
[35] Coal Industry Nationalisation Act 1946. Coal deposits, but not the mine-owning companies, had in fact been taken into public ownership by the Coal Mines Act 1938.
[36] Cable and Wireless Act 1946; Wireless Telegraphy Act 1949.
[37] Trunk Roads Act 1946; Transport Act 1947 (vesting the canals and railways in the newly constituted British Transport Commission).
[38] New Towns Act 1946; Town and Country Planning Act 1947; National Parks and Access to the Countryside Act 1949; see also the Building Materials and Housing Act 1945.
[39] Electricity Act 1947. [40] Gas Act 1948. [41] Atomic Energy Act 1946.
[42] Iron and Steel Act 1949. [43] Dock Workers (Regulation of Employment) Act 1946.
[44] Furnished Houses (Rent Control) Act 1946. [45] Sea Fish Industry Act 1951.
[46] Agriculture Act 1947; Agricultural Holdings Act 1948. [47] Morgan (1990), p. 29.

responsibility for functions that private enterprise could not efficiently supply and that its proper role might be as the individual's support and protector.

For these reasons the post-war impact of the state's assumption of control of Britain's major industries and services was not as seismic as it would have been earlier or later in the century. Opposition was largely silenced by the colossal compensation paid to the owners of the mines and railways, both of them industries in chronic need of capitalisation which now became the state's burden.[48] It was also not as radical in its mode of operation as it could have been – and, its critics on the left argued, should have been: in no instance were workers given even partial control of their own industries or services.[49]

The major unions were not unduly exercised by this situation. So long as they could preserve their bargaining status, they were for the most part satisfied with a change to a putatively more benign employer and the opportunity to bargain nationally on wages and conditions. It was among the rank and file that the case for workers' control began to gain traction.[50]

In addition to the establishment of state control of key economic activities, three major public welfare systems were instituted: social security, healthcare and legal aid.

Social Security

It was the Liberal administration which was swept into power in 1906 with the support of thirty MPs of the newly founded Labour Party (set up in 1900 as the Labour Representation Committee of the Trade Union Congress) that set the social security ball rolling and brought about both the

---

[48] D. N. Pritt QC, MP, *The Labour Government 1945–1951* (1963), p. 40–43; 97–98. Pritt a fierce left-wing critic of the Attlee government, pointed out that the mine-owners had been paid £164,660,000 in compensation, and that on the railways 769 locomotives and 85,000 wagons had had to be scrapped.

[49] There is a well-known scene in Alan Plater's play *Close the Coalhouse Door* where a veteran miner recalls New Year's Day 1947 (when the National Coal Board's flag was run up at the pitheads and colliery bands played the morning shifts in): 'Utopia, they telled me, bloody Utopia, and I comes in, first day after nationalisation – and what do I see? ... The same gaffers': A. Plater, *Close the Coalhouse Door* (London: Methuen & Co, 1968), Act 3. See generally *Alternatives to State Socialism in Britain*, ed. Peter Ackers and Alastair Reid (Cham, Switzerland: Palgrave Macmillan, 2016).

[50] Workers' control, both as a theory and in practice, has been revived, often in association with guild socialism, at intervals since it was first attempted by the Diggers during the English Civil War. It is explored in G. D. H. Cole, *The World of Labour* (London: G. Bell, 1913). See further Ackers and Reid, *Alternatives to State Socialism*, chs. 1 and 12.

introduction of means-tested old age pensions[51] and social insurance against ill-health and unemployment.[52] These benefits, adopting Bismarck's scheme of social welfare (which Lloyd-George had seen for himself) and more recent developments in Sweden and New Zealand,[53] were funded not by taxation but by obligatory contributions from a restricted range of workers and from the state.

The post-war social security system[54] was a logical extension of this. The case for a universal safety-net based on entitlement, not charity or discretion, was made by the 1942 Beveridge Report and adopted by Churchill in a cabinet paper in 1943 as 'an essential part of any post-war scheme of national betterment'.[55] It was Churchill's caretaker government which initiated the five-part legislative scheme that introduced a modern system of social security, putting an eventual end to the centuries of the Poor Law and the workhouse.

The National Health Service

In addition to its assumption of control of major industrial and financial enterprises and the extension and entrenchment of social security, the post-war Labour government created one enduringly popular institution: a National Health Service (NHS). Such a scheme, funded out of general taxation and free at the point of use, was first adumbrated by the minority report of the Fabian socialists Sidney and Beatrice Webb for the Royal Commission on the Poor Law in 1909 and was endorsed as essential by the 1942 Beveridge Report.[56]

By the end of the twentieth century, it had become strongly arguable, notwithstanding repeated political, structural and economic buffetings, derogations and defalcations, that the principle of taxation-funded, free healthcare has come to form part of the United Kingdom's constitutional arrangements. The creation of the NHS in July 1948 was nevertheless bitterly opposed by

---

[51] Old Age Pensions Act 1908.   [52] National Insurance Act 1911.
[53] See Hennessy, *Never Again*, p. 121–131.
[54] National Insurance Act 1946; National Assistance Act 1948, the latter terminating the Poor Law; Family Allowance Act 1945.
[55] Cited by Hennessy, *Never Again*, p. 124.
[56] National Health Service Act 1946 (s.1: '(1) It shall be the duty of the Minister ... to promote the establishment in England and Wales of a comprehensive health service designed to secure improvement in the physical and mental health of the people ... and the prevention, diagnosis and treatment of illness ... (2) The services so provided shall be free of charge ...'); reproduced in the National Health Service (Scotland) Act 1947. See also the Civic Restaurants Act 1947.

the doctors' principal organisation, the British Medical Association. It was also fiercely resisted by Britain's Conservatives. A free national health service, they contended in Parliament,

> discourages voluntary effort and association; mutilates the structure of local government; dangerously increases ministerial power and patronage; appropriates trust funds and benefactions ... and undermines the freedom and independence of the medical profession to the detriment of the nation.[57]

'The State medical service,' said the Daily Sketch, 'is part of the Socialist plot to convert Great Britain into a National Socialist economy. The doctors' stand is the first effective revolt of the professional classes against Socialist tyranny. There is nothing that Bevan or any other Socialist can do about it in the shape of Hitlerian coercion.'[58]

Such invective was not simply gutter journalism: as we shall see, in characterising socialist measures as a form of tyranny it formed part of the ideological undertow carrying the movement for what was, paradoxically, to become the European Convention on Human Rights.

Legal Aid and Advice

Perhaps the most commonly overlooked of the Attlee government's constitutional measures was the system introduced by the Legal Aid and Advice Act 1949 for assuring professional advice and access to justice for people otherwise unable to afford a lawyer. In common with many of Labour's postwar social innovations, the case for a comprehensive legal aid system had been developed in the war years, in this instance by the Rushcliffe Committee.[59] Until it was eviscerated by the coalition government and its successors in the wake of the 2008–2009 economic crisis,[60] the legal aid system was an integral part of a constitution which as long ago as 1215 had undertaken – an undertaking enduringly honoured in the breach[61] – that nobody would be denied justice.[62]

---

[57] Conservative amendment moved on the third reading of the National Health Service Bill 1946.
[58] Daily Sketch, 13 February 1948.
[59] (1944–1945) Cmnd. 6641. In the event defamation was the only area of law excluded.
[60] An attenuation of legal aid had in fact begun some time before this.
[61] 'In England, justice is open to all, like the Ritz': Mathew J, quoted in Megarry, Miscellany-at-Law (London: Stevens, 1955), p.254.
[62] Magna Carta, 1225 version, ch. 29.

By the 1940s there was still little provision beyond the degrading dock brief procedure in criminal cases (which was not substantially reformed until 1960) and the parsimonious Poor Persons Procedure in civil matters. Eschewing the National Health Service model of alternative employment, Labour's legislation left the practising profession intact and instead provided means-tested public funding of its fees, filtered through a merits system run by the solicitors' own body, the Law Society. Even so, it was not until the 1960s that a suspicious profession realised that legal aid brought in new clients and a respectable income, and legal aid practices began to develop.

In principle, anyone who could demonstrate an arguable case but lacked the money for a lawyer could now have their fees paid in part or in full by the state. In practice the test of financial eligibility gradually became so stringent that only the poorest (and occasionally the more dishonest) clients could obtain legal aid. The middling sort – millions of citizens – could neither obtain legal aid nor afford legal fees. This calculated shortfall, like much else that has come to distort the administration of justice in the United Kingdom, was the doing principally of the Treasury, which saw justice not as a public good but as a hole into which public money was constantly poured. It was also the doing of ministers, whose reaction to undoubted abuses of the system was not to stop the abuses but to abolish the system. By the beginning of the twenty-first century the Treasury had not only secured the effective replacement of civil legal aid by insurance-backed conditional fees but had raised court fees to a level which, while prohibitive to many individuals and smaller enterprises, made the justice system a source of net profit. Criminal legal aid, meanwhile, had become subject to increasingly stringent means-testing and to attenuation of fees to a point where practice was barely remunerative.

Access to justice is both the least contentious and the most elusive of the United Kingdom's constitutional rights. The introduction of a publicly funded legal aid system, both civil and criminal, was a principled attempt to close a chronic affordability gap in the system of justice, and to the extent that it worked, it was the closest the United Kingdom had come in eight centuries to fulfilling the monarchical undertaking given at Runnymede in 1215.

Crown Proceedings

Suing the state had always been problematical. Since the monarch was believed to be above the law, and since almost all of the state's business, from waging war to delivering letters, was conducted in the monarch's name, either an official had to be personally sued or the Crown's own fiat had to be obtained. In 1947 the Crown Proceedings Act did away with the Crown's, and hence the state's, immunity from suit and allowed it to be sued as if it were an individual. Here too was a shift into constitutional modernity.[63]

The Empire

This is not the place to do more than note the Labour government's near-catastrophic colonial record. Labour had never been a party of empire. While the majority of socialists, including leading Labour figures like Keir Hardie and George Lansbury, had consistently opposed colonialism, other Labour leaders were well aware that their working-class base had benefited, however unjustly, from the long-term exploitation of colonial labour and resources. Labour's imperial conscience, the Movement for Colonial Freedom, was consequently kept in a marginal political role; such policies as the party had came from the Fabian Colonial Research Bureau.

There was a longstanding Labour commitment to Indian independence, but general decolonisation (on which both the Soviet Union and the United States were becoming extremely keen) remained otherwise off Labour's agenda. In this political limbo, Attlee's Britain became involved in a vicious colonial war in Malaya; crudely and hastily partitioned India in 1947, plunging the subcontinent into intercommunal bloodshed; and abandoned Palestine[64] to a Zionist-Arab territorial war the moment Britain's international peace-keeping mandate expired in May 1948, with consequences the world is still living with. Almost alone in these years, Ceylon (now Sri Lanka) achieved independence peacefully in 1948; its prolonged intercommunal strife was to come later.

The Counter-Revolution That Wasn't

Anybody familiar with the record of the higher judiciary in dealing with the trade union and labour movement would have expected an immediate

---

[63] See further Sedley, *Ashes and Sparks*, p. 83–84; (2015), p. 217–218.
[64] Palestine Act 1948, passed less than 3 weeks before the mandate was due to expire.

outbreak of judicial interference with the post-war Labour government's domestic measures. They would have recalled the Taff Vale decision,[65] which exposed union funds to sequestration for damages at the suit of an employer, and Lord Atkinson's judicial fulmination against the 'eccentric principles of socialistic philanthropy and feminist ambition' of the Poplar councillors who had resolved to pay a living wage to both men and women.[66] Looking across the Atlantic, they would have recalled not only the threatened sabotaging by the United States Supreme Court of Roosevelt's New Deal legislation but the contemporaneous obstruction by the Privy Council's judicial committee, populated by the same judges as the appellate committee of the House of Lords, of Canada's parallel efforts to recover from the great depression.[67]

Yet, in spite of opportunities, it did not happen.[68] What happened was, in its essentials, a continuation of the judicial abstentionism from which cases like that of the Poplar councillors had represented a temporary arousal – the passivity excoriated in Lord Atkin's assault on 'judges who are more executive-minded than the executive'.[69] Sir Raymond Evershed MR was able to tell an Australian audience in the early 1950s:

> It was believed by many when the Attlee government was elected in 1945 that, based on past performance, the courts would emasculate any social welfare or other collectivist legislation ... I am pleased to say that that did not happen. The judges did not sabotage the social welfare state.[70]

So it was that the Attlee government found itself unexpectedly untroubled either by restrictive judicial interpretation of its enactments or by public law challenges to what ministers and permanent secretaries were doing in pursuance of its more radical policies.

---

[65] *Taff Vale Railway* v. *Amalgamated Society of Railway Servants* [1901] AC 426 (in which one law lord described unions as 'irresponsible bodies with ... wide capacities for evil').
[66] *Roberts* v. *Hopwood* [1925] AC 578.
[67] *A–G for Canada* v. *A–G for Ontario* [1937] AC 326; *A–G for British Columbia* v. *A–G for Canada* [1937] AC 105.
[68] What eventually happened, in and after the 1960s, was a steady regrowth of judicial review, at least partly motivated by a determination not to allow government in the future as free a rein as it had had in the 1940s and 1950s: see Lord Diplock's remarks in *R* v. *IRC, ex p. National Federation of the Self-Employed* [1982] AC 617, at 639–640. See further Sedley, *Lions under the Throne*, ch. 1, esp. p. 37–44.
[69] *Liversidge* v. *Anderson* [1942] AC 206, 244–245. See also Sedley, *Lions under the Throne*, p. 31–32.
[70] Zines, Leslie, *Constitutional Change in the Commonwealth* (1991), p.36–37.

The Co-operative Critique

Radical criticism of the Labour government's programme came, however, not only from the political right but from what should have been Labour's natural ally, the Co-operative movement. The reason, in short, was that the top-down command socialism both preached and practised by the Labour Party was antithetical to the egalitarian co-operative ethos of mutual help. While both were legitimist – in fact the co-operative movement was heavily regulated by legislation[71] – they represented incompatible social philosophies and sharply divergent paths to socialism.

From its brave beginnings in 1844 in Rochdale, the co-operative movement had by 1945 grown into a major player in the UK's economy and, through the Co-operative Party, a participant in its political system. The collective purchase, supply and sale of unadulterated foodstuffs, and the distribution of available profits to members (men and women were equally eligible) by way of a dividend on their purchases, was in some ways a revival of the utopian flame which in the past had guttered out. The £28 subscribed by Rochdale workers as their co-operative's initial capital became the catalyst of a self-help movement which by 1900 included an insurance society (founded in 1867) and a bank (founded in 1863), forming part of the Co-operative Wholesale Society (also founded in 1863). The latter was to become the world's largest association of co-operatively run farms and factories, commanding over 6 per cent of the entire UK retail trade, while the Co-operative Union brought together more than 1,400 consumer societies with over 1,700,000 members.

Although the regional co-operative congresses in 1900 voted heavily against seeking political representation, the sense that the movement needed its own political clout brought into eventual being, in 1917, the Co-operative Party.[72] This was in part the co-operative movement's reaction to its near-exclusion, despite its size and efficiency, from the many government contracts handed out, frequently to profiteers, in the course of the First World War.[73] The bias reflected the open hostility of private enterprise, backed by

---

[71] The Industrial and Provident Societies Acts 1852, 1854 and 1856 replaced the Friendly Societies Act 1846, which had afforded limited protection to members' capital. The 1852 Act was in part the result of Disraeli's decision that, as well as being a vote-earner for the Tory party, legitimation of working-class enterprise was a desirable social aim. The Act steered a middle course by permitting distribution of one third of profits as dividends, the remainder to be ploughed back into the business.

[72] Initially named the National Co-operative Representation Committee.

[73] Among the most notorious was Ticklers, whose factory in Grimsby appears to have secured the entire War Office contract to supply the troops with marmalade and plum-and-apple jam – a constant butt of soldiers' songs and jokes.

newspapers such as the Daily Mail, to social enterprises which prioritised quality and returned profits to their members rather than distribute them to shareholders (in whose hands they were marketable but also taxable).[74]

The Co-operative party was not, however, a straightforward voluntary organisation. With the initial affiliation of fewer than half of the country's co-operative societies, it was nonetheless bound by decisions of the movement's annual congress and so had little freedom to develop its own platform or policies. It ran candidates only where Labour did not, and, although unable to agree on a durable strategy for electoral collaboration, found itself with six MPs in the 1923 Parliament and twenty-three in the 1945 Parliament. By then, however, the opportunity for an electoral pact had passed, because Labour had grown from a marginal party capable of benefiting from an electoral truce to a party of government with a colossal majority. What remained was an agreement reached in 1927 (with great reluctance on the Co-operative side), and still in force in the twenty-first century, to allow mutual affiliation of Labour and Co-operative party branches without any forfeiture of identity. Because many co-operative societies were prosperous, the arrangement, which allowed them to choose their political partners, was from the start a source of friction; and beyond it lay the consistent policy of the Co-operative Party not to affiliate to the Labour Party. But its 1931 pamphlet campaign, 'Britain Reborn', set out a programme differing little from Labour's apart from its emphasis on the relevance of co-operation, and the movement greeted Labour's victory in 1945 with optimism.

Disillusion came when Labour's programme for a second term was published in 1949, proposing among other things the nationalisation of areas of enterprise in which the co-operative movement was engaged, including sugar, cement, meat wholesaling and industrial assurance. The experience of pre-war Europe had not been forgotten, when the German, Austrian and Italian co-operative movements had been taken over by fascist states for their own purposes. The UK's co-operative movement had no interest in abandoning the voluntarist principle and becoming a set of state-sanctioned monopolies, and the Conservative party capitalised on this by warning voters that Labour was getting ready to nationalise their co-op. Labour, bruised by near-defeat in the 1950 general election, responded by seeking a formal rapprochement with the trade union and co-operative movements; but the return of a Conservative government the following year relegated such plans

---

[74] The wartime government eventually extended its excess profits tax to co-operative-dividends.

to the realm of theory. Thereafter the economic strength of the co-ops began to decline, and the report in 1958 of a powerful Labour party commission, characterising the co-operative method as inefficient and dated, did nothing to repair the breach. The uneasy liaison has continued into the twenty-first century.

Vorberg-Rugh and Whitecross summarise:

> Although it was the weaker voice, the co-operative movement's ongoing effort to push for change through voluntary, civil society action represented a distinct alternative to the increasingly statist tendency of Labour Party thinking in the twentieth century.[75]

The Counter-Revolution That Was

This was by no means the totality of resistance to Labour's programme. The country's war leader, Winston Churchill, might be out of office, but he and his allies were not out of energy or ideas. It may seem counter-intuitive, even counterfactual, in an era which has seen widespread Conservative denunciation and rejection of European institutions in the United Kingdom, that the adoption of a binding Europe-wide human rights code was the work not of liberals or socialists but of a Conservative movement committed to reversing the tide of socialism and statism which, with Britain in its vanguard, seemed about to engulf much of post-war Europe. One has only to read the European Convention on Human Rights to see how single-mindedly it treats the state as the natural enemy of the individual – the antithesis of the kind of society the Labour government was trying to bring into being.

The European Federalist Movement was founded in December 1946. Its Secretary-General was Alexandre Marc, a Catholic social conservative, and it counted a number of prominent British Conservative politicians among its members. Its first congress, held in Montreux in August 1947, was attended by Churchill's son-in-law, the right-wing politician Duncan Sandys, as joint secretary of the British United Europe Movement, of which Churchill was chairman. The Parliamentary Labour Party's Europe Group, about eighty strong, had to devote energy to putting clear water between itself and what

---

[75] See 'The Co-operative Party: An Alternative Vision of Social Ownership', in Peter Ackers and Alastair Reid (eds.), *Alternatives to State Socialism in Britain* (2016), ch. 3, p. 83.

became, in 1949, the European Movement. In parallel the Labour government, on the advice of its Foreign Secretary Ernest Bevin and of the party's general secretary Morgan Phillips, kept the United Kingdom clear of the European integrationist movement. The consequence was that when in May 1949 the United Kingdom became a founding member of the Council of Europe, the European Movement was waiting to present the new intergovernmental body with the draft European Convention on Human Rights. By November 1950 it had been adopted and was open for signature, with the United Kingdom among its first signatories.[76]

Although the draft had required some amendment (the omission of gender from the grounds of discrimination proscribed by Article 14 was cured on the insistence of Denmark, but the omission of any social or economic rights was not), the eventual Convention included not only a series of (mostly qualified) guarantees of individual rights – to life and to bodily integrity, to personal liberty and a fair trial, to respect for private and family life including marriage, and to freedom of thought, conscience, religion, expression, assembly and association – but a supranational court, the European Court of Human Rights,[77] with power to determine its own jurisdiction[78] and whose judgments were to be binding on respondent states.[79]

The Labour government had played a bystander's role in this process, not because it was necessarily opposed to what the Convention contained but because it had a different agenda: the realisation in practice of economic and social justice rather than the tabulation of broadly stated rights. Attlee's chancellor of the exchequer, Stafford Cripps, had in August 1950 warned Cabinet that 'a government committed to the policy of a planned economy could not ratify the covenant on human rights', instancing 'powers of entry into private premises, which were inconsistent with the powers of economic control'.[80] But while this would have confirmed the accusations levelled at Labour by the convention's promoters, it did not in the event stand in the

---

[76] See A. W. B. Simpson, *Human Rights and the End of Empire* (Oxford: Oxford University Press, 2001), passim; Marco Duranti, *The Conservative Human Rights Revolution* (New York: Oxford University Press, 2017), chs. 3 and 4.
[77] Article 19.   [78] Article 32(2).
[79] Article 46. The European Movement's joint international committee, chaired by Duncan Sandys, had proposed in 1948 that the court's judgments should be implemented where necessary by the use of force, and had recruited General Sir Frederick Morgan (planner of Operation Overlord) as a consultant: Duranti, *The Conservative Human Rights*, p. 169. This was dropped when Churchill opposed it.
[80] Duranti, *The Conservative Human Rights*, p. 248–249.

way of British signature and ratification. Bevin agreed to it, albeit resignedly, in the belief that Strasbourg would only be a talking shop.

So it was that the United Kingdom under a Labour government entered into a constitutional commitment, albeit by treaty and not until 1998 by statute,[81] to a European bill of rights which prioritised the individual vis-à-vis the state. Two years later, with Churchill back in office, the Council of Europe added a protocol enshrining private property rights and an entitlement to state education according to parents' religious and philosophical convictions. The conservative counter-revolution to roll back socialism and statism seemed destined to succeed. That, like other revolutions, it went on to consume its own children is another story.

---

[81] Human Rights Act 1998.

21
Unionism

JAMES MITCHELL AND ALAN CONVERY

Introduction: Unionism in a *State of Unions*

The UK is an 'evolved' state[1] that has become a devolved state. It was created by a series of bilateral arrangements to become a 'state of unions'.[2] The centre is key to how any state develops, extending its authority over a wider geography, whether by enforcing uniformity or permitting diversity. The rationale for each union has changed over time, reflecting the changing views on how the UK should stay together as a multi-national state.

Unionism is a form of nationalism. Every state requires a degree of loyalty from its citizens unless it makes crude use of the state's 'monopoly of legitimate use of physical force' to impose its authority. A transcendent loyalty, a sense of belonging, is more effective in ensuring compliance. Unionism is the loyalty and sense of belonging within each component to the wider state.

Richard Rose, an American political scientist, noted that trying to name the nation associated with the UK 'displays the confusion about national identity. One thing is certain: No one speaks of the "Ukes" as a nation.'[3] But this does not mean that there is no state ideology or that it is weak. On the contrary, the absence of a state ideology or even a name for UK national identity has been a sign of its strength. It is notable that state nationalism in the UK has been strongest when and where national identity and loyalty to the state is (or was) taken for granted, unquestioned, uncontested and required no name. Unionism, as the ideology of UK state nationalism, was first given this name in Ireland, that part of the United Kingdom which proved least susceptible to UK state nationalism.

---

[1] Neil MacCormick. *Questioning Sovereignty* (Oxford: Oxford University Press, 1999), 49.
[2] James Mitchell, *Devolution in the UK* (Manchester: Manchester University Press, 2009).
[3] Richard Rose, *Understanding the United Kingdom* (Harlow Essex Longman, 1982), p. 11.

Each union involved in creating the UK began in pre-democratic times. Unionism was initially an 'elite creed before it was a popular one'.[4] Security and trade were key considerations in forging these unions but unionism required a more popular element especially following the processes of modernisation and democratisation. Popular unionism, much like other nationalisms, has been thin-centred.[5] As such, it is an ideology with a central core – maintaining the integrity of the UK – but otherwise with little ideological agreement amongst its adherents. This has allowed it to be a diverse and flexible ideology. There may also be different motivations behind the core belief. Alvin Jackson has referred to the 'spiritual union', referring to its practice 'bound with a range of more earthy, material, and pragmatic concerns' and the 'material union' 'self-interest – national, sectional, and individual'.[6] Similarly, McLean and McMillan distinguish between primordial and instrumental unionisms: the former would defend the integrity of the state at all costs while the latter required evidence of the union's value.[7] McLean and McMillan have argued that there are 'no primordial unionists left in Great Britain' and no instrumental reason for holding onto Northern Ireland though there are instrumental reasons for holding on to Scotland.[8]

Unionism's core belief may be supported by the right or left of the political spectrum and by parties that believe in more or less decentralisation of power from Westminster. Left-wing unionists in Britain included many who supported republicanism though this political position has never attained significance and would, at the very least, require a new name for the state should a UK republic ever exist given the oxymoron of a *United Kingdom republic*. Unionism might also entail a commitment to a more assimilationist UK or support a formally federal UK, though some federalists deny being unionists and instead see federation as a distinct constitutional form.

Loyalism and Domestic Security

While there was an absence of a state ideology, a doctrine of sovereignty did exist. The Crown was the institution to which people would be expected to

---

[4] Iain McLean and Alastair McMillan, *State of Union* (Oxford: Oxford University Press, 2005), p. 239.
[5] Michael Freeden (2002), 'Is Nationalism a Distinct Ideology?', *Political Studies*, vol.46, pp. 748–765.
[6] Alvin Jackson, 'The Two Unions' in Michael Keating (ed.) *The Oxford Handbook of Scottish Politics* (Oxford: Oxford University Press, 2020), pp. 337, 343.
[7] McLean and McMillan, *State of Union*. [8] Ibid, p. 249.

show loyalty. When called upon to make the ultimate sacrifice, people were asked to fight for 'King and country'. There would be many instances when disloyalty to the Crown would be stamped upon, whether Jacobite rebellions or Irish republicanism, while sympathy for sub-state national identities was not only accepted by the Crown but embraced. Hence Rose's observation that no one speaks of Ukes. It is the Crown that has 'no territorial adjective to describe it.'[9] The 'country' in 'King and country' was nameless and the army was organised into regiments with territorial names. Burke understood the value of the 'subdivision, to love the little platoon we belong to in society, is the first principle (the germ as it were) of public affections'[10] and so, it appears, did the Crown.

The process of 'nation building' that followed 'state building' usually involves 'nation destroying'. As Walker Connor argued, 'Since most of the less developed states contain a number of nations, and since the transfer of primary allegiance from these nations to the state is generally considered the *sine qua non* of successful integration, the true goal is not "nation-building" but "nation-destroying".'[11] This did not apply in quite the same way to nation-building in the UK. What had to be *destroyed* was not so much pre-union national sentiment but disloyalty to the Crown. Unionism permitted sub-state nations to continue to exist so long as loyalty to the Crown was confirmed. Hence, the 1747 Disarming Act permitted the king's servants to wear highland dress. Highland families were able to redeem estates and titles by raising regiments loyal to the Hanoverians, while draconian powers were used to eradicate emblems of disloyalty amongst opponents of the Hanovers. Scottish clan loyalties were 'exploited' by the state to 'form regiments while simultaneously destroying the clans themselves'.[12] Jacobitism was 'by its very nature a British political ideology, shared with Englishmen and many Scots, and concerned with restoring a Scottish dynasty to the combined thrones of England, Scotland and Ireland'.[13] Loyalism (to the Hanoverians and successors) and unionism might be related but were not the same in all parts of the

---

[9] Rose 1982, p. 10.
[10] Edmund Burke, *Reflections on the Revolution in France* (London: Hackett, 1987), p. 41.
[11] Walker Connor, 'Nation-Building or Nation-Destroying', *World Politics*, vol.24, 1972, p. 336.
[12] Huw Strachan, 'Scotland's Military Identity', *Scottish Historical Review*, vol.85, 2008, p. 323.
[13] S. J. Connolly, 'Varieties of Britishness: Ireland, Scotland and Wales in the Hanoverian state' in Alexander Grant and Keith Stringer (eds.), *Uniting the Kingdom? The Making of British History* (London: Routledge, 1995), p. 197.

UK.[14] In Ireland, loyalism and unionism would become fused to an extent unseen elsewhere. Loyalist Irish unionism was challenged by republicanism rather than a pretender.

Novelist Walter Scott assisted in the monarch's embrace of Scotland in preparation for George IV's 1822 visit to Scotland during which the King appeared in a kilt. Queen Victoria developed a fondness for Scotland, even to the point of feigning a Scottish accent on visits, and travelling to Balmoral each Autumn, though she paid only four visits to Ireland during her long reign.[15] The Prince of Wales title was bestowed on the heir apparent from 1301. Investitures were abandoned until reinstated in 1911 for the future King Edward VIII. Lloyd George organised the investiture at Caernarfon Castle, in the heart of his constituency, despite the original 1301 investiture being a celebration of the conquest of Wales. Unionism has had a capacity, as other nationalisms, to manipulate symbols in its own interests. Lloyd George was able to 'gratify Welsh national pride and, at the same time, to reassure traditionalists in every part of the Kingdom'.[16]

In 1958, the Queen announced that Prince Charles would be made Prince of Wales at the Empire Games in Cardiff. His investiture in 1969 came three years after Plaid Cymru won its first seat in Parliament. Charles spent a term at Aberystwyth University where he was taught the Welsh language (by a leading figure in Plaid Cymru). Plaid Cymru boycotted the investiture and two radical Welsh nationalists were killed preparing explosives in an attempt to cause disruption on the morning of the ceremony. The Palace's plan had been to 'use the Prince of Wales to remind people of their British loyalties'. In the event, it did that and provoked hostility from a radical strand of Welsh nationalism.[17] When banal unionism becomes hot unionism to meet a challenge it not only becomes an assertive ideology but raises the profile of the challenging ideology.

---

[14] As Allan McInness stated, 'Literary history of Scottish Jacobitism, while strong on the discourse of patriotism, cultural networking and political symbolism, is currently in danger of confusing nationalist aspirations of the eighteenth century with the present day.' 'Jacobitism in Scotland: Episodic Cause of National Movement?', *The Scottish Historical* Review, vol.86, 2007, p. 228.

[15] James Mitchell 'Sovereigns, Sovereignties and the Scottish Question: Identities and Constitutional Change' in Harshan Kumarasingham (ed.), *Viceregalism: The Crown as Head of State in Political Crises in the Postwar Commonwealth* (Palgrave Macmillan, 2020).

[16] John Grigg, *Lloyd George: The People's Champion, 1902–1911* (London: Penguin, 1997), p.303.

[17] Martin Johnes, *Wales since 1939* (Manchester: Manchester University Press, 2012), kindle edition, loc.5544.

Unionism in England

In his account of territory and power in the UK, Bulpitt noted that the development of the early English state is of 'crucial importance for an understanding of the making of the United Kingdom'.[18] A degree of autonomy was permitted to the periphery before the centre's authority could develop firm control throughout its territory. 'If we want a birth date for an English kingdom', Robert Tombs suggests, then King Alfred's seizure of London in 886 is 'as good as any' after which the King pursued a 'policy of what today we might term nation-building'.[19] It was a monocephalic centre where military-administrative, economic and cultural, as much as political, resources are concentrated.[20] Religion and ecclesiastical institutions played prime roles in constitutional politics and legitimacy. The Church played an 'important part in the administrative and psychological unification of England' though the separate province of York would create a barrier to unification.[21] Language too played a significant part and would be a factor as in other polities.

According to Bulpitt, a distinction between 'high' and 'low' politics developed with the former being the prerogative of the centre while the latter offered scope for local autonomy. While Bulpitt saw defence, foreign affairs, and taxation as constituting 'high politics', the distinction broke down with the growth in state intervention as central government penetration of the periphery increased. Ultimately, almost anything could become 'high politics' and the centre could extend its rule with impunity. Attempts to 'locate the tradition of local self-government on some ancient constitution which interposes local institutions as the key institutions of government' proved 'highly implausible'.[22] Unionism was a central state ideology with little to say about local self-government. This did not mean that a system of local government did not exist or that all local loyalties were eradicated. Local loyalties, James Campbell noted, did 'not so much contradict as reinforce' central authority and contributed to the 'long success of the

---

[18] Jim Bulpitt, *Territory and Power in the United Kingdom, Manchester* (Colchester: ECPR Press edition, 2008), p. 78.
[19] Robert Tombs, *The English and Their History* (London: Penguin, 2015), p. 29.
[20] Stein Rokkan and Derek Urwin, *Territory, Identity, Economy* (London: Sage, 1983), p. 7.
[21] James Campbell, 'The United Kingdom of England: The Anglo-Saxon Achievement' in Alexander Grant and Keith Stringer (eds.), *Uniting the Kingdom? The Making of British History* (London: Routledge, 1995), p. 39.
[22] Martin Loughlin, *Legality and Locality* (Oxford: Clarendon Press, 1996), p. 17.

English state'.[23] Occasional popular references have been made to the seventh century Heptarchy, even occasionally the need to 'return to the Heptarchy',[24] in the search for historic legitimacy for a federated England[25] but these have always been on the fringe of English unionism.

The development of an English state nationalism became the prototype for unionism. Units of local government were 'creatures of statute' and could only operate within their powers which were determined by primary legislation that was, in turn, regularly subject to change. The doctrine of parliamentary sovereignty meant that reforms and major overhauls could be instituted without the agreement of local authorities themselves. This ideology of the English state would transfer and operate largely unchallenged into each subsequent union. England was one and indivisible and this notion would carry over in the minds of central governing elites as far as each successive union was concerned.

Wales

In his study of modern Welsh history, Johnes included a chapter entitled, 'Nationalists of many varieties'.[26] Unionists in Wales mirrored nationalists in variety, as elsewhere. Union with Wales was by conquest and largely assimilationist though significant vestiges of Welsh identity persisted, most notably Welsh language and associated culture. The legal codes of England and Wales were integrated and the Wales and Berwick Act, 1746 provided that any legislative references to England applied to Wales. Assimilation would become associated with the Anglican Church in Wales and the Conservative Party.[27] The Welsh Nonconformist movement in the late eighteenth and early nineteenth century assisted the transmission of Welsh national identity through into the twentieth century.

The incomplete nature of assimilation and assertion of Welsh identity sometimes assisted by the centre, including the 1588 Privy Council Order that

---

[23] James Campbell, 'The United Kingdom of England', p. 35.
[24] Tom Shakespeare, 'A Point of View: Takin England back to the Dark Ages', BBC 6 June 2014, www.bbc.co.uk/news/magazine-27731725;
[25] Neil Evans, '"A World Empire, Sea-Girt": The British Empire, State and Nations, 1780–1914' in Stefan Berger and Alexei Miller (eds.), *Nationalizing Empires* (Budapest: Central European Press, 2015), p. 83.
[26] Martin Johnes, *Wales since 1939* (Manchester: Manchester University Press, 2012), ch.8.
[27] Ian C. Thomas, 'The Creation of the Welsh Office: Conflicting Purposes in Institutional Change', *Studies in Public Policy*, no. 91, Glasgow, Centre for the Study of Public Policy, University of Strathclyde, 1981.

a Welsh translation of the Bible should be available in every Welsh chapel,[28] contributed to the continuing sense of Welsh identity. Over the course of the twentieth century, the use of the Welsh language was extended in public and official business through the Welsh Courts Act, 1942, Hughes-Parry Report 1965 and Welsh Language Act 1967.

The Conservatives were weak in Wales and the split in the Liberal Party over Irish Home Rule in the late nineteenth century had little impact in Wales. Only Wrexham in Wales was won by a Liberal Unionist at the 1886 general election, and that was only because the seat was uncontested, though nearly a quarter of Welsh Liberals opposed Gladstone's Home Rule bill. According to Kenneth Morgan, Liberal Unionism was 'always a lost cause in Wales'.[29] Welsh Liberalism's base in nonconformism might have been expected to make unionism attractive. As Morgan noted, 'In Wales truly the Orange card seemed the one to play.'[30] Whether it was Welsh loyalty to Gladstone or 'organizational deficiencies and image problems'[31] Liberal Unionism failed to take hold.

Tensions existed between 'particularism' and 'assimilationalism' though Wales, as elsewhere in the UK, experienced particularism within particularism. Efforts to create all-Wales institutions had to address diversity within Wales, not least between Welsh and non-Welsh speaking areas.[32] This was carried through into the twentieth century. The Labour Party's dominance of twentieth century Welsh politics brought evidence of continuing tensions between particularism and assimilationism represented, respectively, by two giants of post-1945 Welsh Labour, James Griffiths and Aneurin Bevan.[33] The Attlee Government rejected proposals for a Welsh Office. Labour Deputy Prime Minister Herbert Morrison had argued that Wales was an integrated part of the British economy and there was no tradition of a separate Welsh legal and administrative tradition as existed in Scotland.[34] In a Commons debate in 1946, Nye Bevan as Minister of Health articulated a theme that

---

[28] Williams, D., *Modern Wales* (London: John Murray, 1950), p. 76.
[29] Kenneth Morgan, 'The Liberal Unionists in Wales', *National Library of Wales Journal*, vo.15, 1969, p. 168.
[30] Ibid, p. 163.
[31] Naomi Lloyd-Jones, 'Liberal Unionism and Political Representation in Wales, c.1886–1893', *Historical Research*, vol.88, 2015, p. 468.
[32] Sir Percy Watkins, *A Welshman Remembers* (Cardiff: W. Lewis Ltd., 1944).
[33] Morgan, Kenneth (1989), *The Red Dragon and the Red Flag: The Cases of James Griffiths and Aneurin Bevan* (Aberystwyth, National Library of Wales, The Welsh Political Archive Lecture 1988).
[34] Kenneth Morgan, *Wales: Rebirth of a Nation, 1880–1980* (Oxford: Oxford University Press, 1982), p. 377.

would be echoed down the years in expressing opposition to the 'psychosis' that developed too far which, he maintained, would 'see in some of the English speaking parts of Wales a vast majority tyrannised over by a few Welsh speaking people'.[35] Bevan opposed the establishment of a Welsh Office whereas his colleague Jim Griffiths, who also served in Attlee's Government, was a leading advocate of a Welsh Office modelled on the office of Scottish Secretary, and became the first holder of the office when established by Labour in 1964. As Labour's British Deputy leader, Griffiths had drawn up a Welsh Labour manifesto for the 1959 election that had included a commitment to establish a Welsh Office.[36] These competing visions of socialism would play out both within the Labour Party in Wales and Scotland.

Scotland

Colin Kidd has argued that unionism was the dominant political ideology in Scotland for 500 years.[37] Much of unionism's constitutional content was obscured by the fact that it became so banal that it was largely unquestioned. The two most significant 'unionist' moments in Scotland were the 1603 Union of Crowns and the 1707 Treaty of Union. Both occasioned vigorous debate about the purpose and nature of Union and about the forms union might take.[38] Both unions continue to provoke debate on the causes and nature of union. These different interpretations have reflected contemporary concerns and viewpoints of the authors.[39] Unionists in the sixteenth and seventeenth centuries debated various forms of union and looked at other European examples, including Denmark and Lithuania.[40] A Scottish

---

[35] Aneurin Bevan, Hansard, Commons, 28 Oct. 1946, vol.428, col.401.
[36] Labour Party, *Britain Belongs to You* (London: Labour Party, 1959).
[37] Colin Kidd, *Union and Unionisms: Political Thought in Scotland, 1500–2000* (Cambridge: Cambridge University Press, 2008). Colin Kidd and others have contributed to a 'Unionist turn in Scottish history', offering refreshing and challenging interpretations of Scotland's past. See Alasdair Raffe, '1707, 2007, and the Unionist Turn in Scottish History', *The Historical Journal*, 53, 2010, pp. 1071–1083. Works identified by Raffe include Kidd, *Unions and Unionism*; Whatley, *The Scots and the Union*.
[38] There is a considerable literature on the reasons and nature of the unions of 1603 and 1707 with different explanations and emphases. Much of this is polemical and partisan. The tercentenary saw a number of new interpretations of the 1707 union. The two most significant academic works were Allan MacInnes, *Union and Empire* (Cambridge: Cambridge University Press, 2007); and Christopher Whatley, *The Scots and the Union* (Edinburgh: Edinburgh University Press, 2006).
[39] MacInnes, *Union and Empire*, p. 12.
[40] Colin Kidd, *Union and Unionisms: Political Thought in Scotland, 1500–2000* (Cambridge: Cambridge University Press, 2008), p. 72.

Parliament might continue to exist and protect Scottish distinctiveness within the union or a more incorporating and assimilationist union might exist. Federal ideas were rejected but Scottish institutions, including the Church of Scotland, were protected.

Scotland and England each had Protestant reformations though different established churches. Given the role played by the church this was significant in ensuring continuity of Scottish distinctiveness. In Bulpitt's terms, having achieved the goal of assimilation in matters of high politics (defence, foreign policy, trade, the Empire), 'low politics' of everyday justice, local government and education could be left to bodies in Scotland.[41] The Scottish economy was weaker and some elites stood to gain through its integration into a larger economy and access to new trading routes. Post-Revolutionary France increased security concerns. There was, however, a view that the Union of the Crowns had disadvantaged Scotland and largely served English needs.[42]

In the late nineteenth and early twentieth century, the idea of unionism was understood as supporting the Union with Ireland. The split in the Liberal Party had a much greater impact in Scotland than it had in Wales. Scottish Liberal Unionists created a distinct organisation after 1886 and worked closely with local Conservatives. Urwin noted that 'Conservative' was a term of abuse in nineteenth century Scotland. Liberalism's 'greatest driving force' had been Presbyterianism.[43] This would prove fertile ground for the development of support for Irish unionism and a realignment of Scottish politics. In 1912, the Scottish Liberal Unionists and Scottish Conservatives formally amalgamated to form the Scottish Unionist Association. The new party was organised into Eastern and Western Divisions with remarkable levels of autonomy, each raising its own income and organisation. It had close ties to the Orange Order in Scotland which had seats on the party's Western Division. The Scottish Unionist Party was replaced in 1965 when it was reorganised and renamed Scottish Conservative and Unionist Party but remained distinct from its sister party in England.[44]

Over the course of the twentieth century, in response to challenges posed by Scottish nationalism, Conservative unionism in Scotland emphasised defence of the 1707 union with England, without discarding sympathy for

---

[41] Jim Bulpitt, Territory and Power. [42] Jackson, 'The Two Unions', p. 46.
[43] Derek Urwin, 'The Development of the Conservative Party Organisation in Scotland until 1912', *Scottish Historical Review*, vol.44, 1965, p. 91.
[44] D. W. Urwin, 'Scottish Conservatism: A Party Organization in Transition', *Political Studies*, vol.14, 1966, pp. 145–162.

Irish unionism. Conservative unionists played their part in establishing and developing the Scottish Office.[45] Edward Heath, as British party leader, proposed to establish a Scottish Assembly in 1968 in reaction to the rise of the Scottish National Party (SNP).

But Conservative Unionism took a new turn when Margaret Thatcher became leader and especially Prime Minister in 1979. Mrs Thatcher's view of the union differed markedly from that of her Conservative predecessors. In her memoirs she conceded that there had been 'no Tartan Thatcherite revolution' and that the 'old Glaswegian Orange foundations of Unionist support which had in earlier times been so important had irreparably crumbled'.[46] She saw the Scottish Office as an impediment to her reforms.[47] Hers was a more assimilationist unionism as it related to Scotland though her unionism evolved differently as it related to Northern Ireland. This ideology would haunt the Conservatives in Scotland though the party accepted the establishment of a Scottish Parliament after opposing it to the last moment. The model of socialism pursued by the Attlee Government gave the centre a dominant role. Nationalisation involved centralisation. The term 'nationalisation' was itself significant and used in preference to the 'socialisation' of industry and referred not to the component nations but the state. Herbert Morrison, Labour's key thinker on nationalisation, was a staunch supporter of Parliamentary sovereignty and not keen on administrative devolution. Conservatives were quick to argue that nationalisation 'de-nationalised' much Scottish industry by removing control of private industry from locally based businesses in Scotland. Separate Scottish boards for the nationalised industries were only conceded after pressure.[48] The concession was justified from a Labour unionist perspective by Herbert Morrison, 'We have retained essential economic and managerial control, while giving Scotland all the concessions we can without endangering the undertaking.'[49]

Labour remained theoretically committed to Home Rule under Attlee but it was a low priority alongside nationalisation and developing the welfare

---

[45] See for example the pamphlet written by Ian Lang and Barry Henderson, *The Scottish Conservatives: A Past and a Future* (Edinburgh, Scottish Conservative and Unionist Association, 1975). Lang and Henderson were then aspiring Scottish Conservative MPs, elected in 1970. Lang became Secretary of State for Scotland, 1990–95.
[46] Margaret Thatcher, *The Downing Street Years* (London: HarperCollins, 1993), pp. 619–619.
[47] Ibid, p.619.
[48] Sir Norman Chester, *The Nationalisation of British Industry, 1945–51* (London: HMS, 1976), p. 432.
[49] Herbert Morrison, Hansard, Commons 6 May 1946 vol.422, col.613.

state, each viewed as requiring centralisation and a fair degree of uniformity across the state. During the 1950s, most socialists abandoned Scottish Home Rule following the experience of being in government, perceptions that socialism and equality required central demand management and central imposition of standards and policies. In 1957, Labour's Scottish executive came out against a Scottish Parliament on 'compelling economic grounds'.[50] Socialism and social democracy, for many, were deemed to be incompatible with Scottish nationalism or devolution though support for Home Rule existed on Labour's fringe.

This was the backdrop against which the Wilson Government confronted the rise of the Scottish National Party and Plaid Cymru and agitation for Home Rule in the 1960s and 1970s. Labour's conversion was a response to the electoral threat of the Scottish National Party (SNP). Labour's need for a response to the SNP explains Labour's return to the 1970s support for Home Rule. Opposition to the perceived imposition of Conservative policies on Scotland deepened that commitment in the 1980s. In the 1997 devolution referendum, Labour, Liberal Democrats and SNP campaigned for a devolved Scottish Parliament (but with different endpoints in mind) allowing unionists, federalists and nationalists to combine forces. But this coalition collapsed once the Parliament was established. By the time of the 2014 Scottish independence referendum, unionists in Scotland fought together against independence. They may have agreed on little else but the integrity of the state, unionism's core belief, was under threat.

Unionism in Scotland has not been a static ideology but evolved, taking account of wider changes in state and society. In the nineteenth century a combination of the Irish Question and a Parliament at Westminster perceived to be congested with a burgeoning range of issues contributed to a sense of grievance that Scotland was neglected. This early form of Scottish nationalism, as some historians referred to it,[51] can also be seen as unionist in so far as these grievances made no demands for a separate state. The concession of a Scottish Secretary, eventually with a seat in the cabinet, was supported by Conservative and Liberal parties. Where there were differences, these focused on the competences of the office. Conservatives, as staunch Unionists, would play a singular part in the growing competences of the Scottish Office over the course of the following century right through

---

[50] *Glasgow Herald* 28 January 1957.
[51] Sir Reginald Coupland, Welsh and Scottish nationalism: a study, London, Collins, 1954; H. J. Hanham, *Scottish Nationalism* (London: Faber, 1969).

to the establishment of the Scottish Parliament.[52] But unionism could accommodate support for an elected Scottish Parliament within the UK highlighting ideological flexibility.

Ireland

Linda Colley's *Britons: Forging the Nation, 1707–1837* argued that British nationalism was 'forged above all by war' with the Protestant religion playing an important part.[53] The 'invention of Britishness' had been so bound up with Protestantism, war with France and the acquisition of an Empire that Ireland was 'never able to play a satisfactory part in it'.[54] The 1800 Acts of Union passed by Parliaments in Ireland and Britain asserted that the 'said kingdoms of Great Britain and Ireland' shall 'for ever, be united into one kingdom, by the name of "the united kingdom of Great Britain and Ireland"'.[55] But the union was never consummated and would be contested from the outset. In 1881, Dicey argued that the union with Scotland was a work of great statesmanship but 'English policy has never so nearly failed of attaining any part of its objects than in the union with Ireland'.[56] This has become a standard trope in comparisons.

Irish unionism mirrored Irish nationalism in the form and force it took. It could be conciliatory and constitutional or militant and extra-constitutional. When threatened, unionism in Ireland (and its support in Britain) would become as belligerent as the threat was assumed to require. Unionist militancy was supported by and at other times aimed at Conservatives in Britain. Conservatives tended to be allies of Unionists in the nineteenth and early twentieth centuries but became less trusted over the course of the twentieth century. This relationship has been a key dynamic in understanding (Northern) Irish unionism.

While Irish Unionism can be dated from the union with Britain, it became a 'popular war cry' when unionism came under threat. Unionism linked an amalgam of interests and ideas.

---

[52] James Mitchell, *Conservatives and the Union* (Edinburgh: Edinburgh University Press, 1990), pp. 17–37.
[53] Linda Colley, *Britons: Forging the Nation, 1707–1837* (London: Yale University Press, 1992), p. 5.
[54] Ibid, p.8.   [55] Act of Union (Ireland) 1800, Article 1.
[56] A. V. Dicey, 'Two Acts of Union: A Contrast', *Fortnightly Review*, 1881, vol.36, pp. 168–178.

Unionism linked Protestant landlords across the island, Protestant professionals and business elite of Belfast and its neighbourhood, the Orange working class in the Lagan valley, and Protestant farmers and labourers demographically concentrated or dispersed depending in accordance with the strength of colonial settlements of previous centuries. Its core organizational strength lay in Irish Toryism, the Church of Ireland, and the Orange Order, but was joined by Presbyterian Liberalism after disestablishment, and by organised working class sectarianism, reinvigorated during disestablishment.[57]

Unionist leaders such as Edward Saunderson challenged the Tory leadership in London.[58] Saunderson's anti-Catholicism contributed to the 'evolution of an exclusivist Protestant political alliance'[59] that would be carried over into the Northern Ireland polity. The Irish Unionist Party, founded in 1891 and led by Saunderson, was an all-Ireland body with headquarters in Dublin but also had an Ulster Unionist Council from 1905.

The *Irish Times*, founded in 1859, modelled itself on the London *Times* and pursued a unionist editorial line. After independence, it 'helped to supply an essential narrative of continuity, easing the unionists into a tolerance – often begrudgingly – of the new Ireland'.[60] Within a decade, Southern Protestants and unionists would no longer feel the need to be politically organised. Southern unionists might have been electorally weak, representing about a quarter of the Irish population (though only 10 per cent under Dublin rule, but had strength in key institutions. Bryan Cooper, who briefly served as a Southern Unionist MP between the two Commons elections in 1910 and was returned to represent the same area in the Dáil in 1923, had sought assurances including to prevent the 'Hibernianization or Tammanization' of the civil service.[61]

Militant unionism asserted itself even before Sinn Fein's brand of militant republicanism had pushed constitutional nationalism aside. King George V corresponded with Irish Unionists when its leaders were proposing armed insurrection which, as Iain McLean noted, was 'an odd reason for His Majesty to accord them special attention'. In 1913, the King's advisers were 'instinctive Unionists', offering advice that was hostile to that being given by

---

[57] O'Leary, *Northern Ireland: A Treatise vol.1. Colonialism* (Oxford: Oxford University Press, 2019), p.293–294.
[58] Ibid, p.244.   [59] Ibid, p.247.
[60] Ian d'Alton, 'A Protestant Paper for a Protestant People: The *Irish Times* and the Southern Irish Minority', *Irish Communications Review*, 12, 2010, p. 65.
[61] R. B. McDowell, *Crisis and Decline: The Fate of the Southern Unionists* (Dublin: The Lilliput Press, 1998), kindle edition loc.1057.

the Liberal Government advising on Home Rule.[62] In opposition, Conservatives at Westminster condoned this extra-constitutional strand of unionism. The 'Ulster Solemn League and Covenant' combined with separate declaration for women, was signed by around half a million people in 1912 pledging opposition to Irish Home Rule and rejecting the authority of any Home Rule parliament. War interceded and transformed Carson from being a 'patron of illegality in Ulster to a law officer [Attorney General] at Westminster'.[63] Such could be the ambiguous nature of unionism.

The relationship between Irish unionists and the main parties in Britain would be important in the development of unionist thinking. Gladstone's conversion to Home Rule and the split in the Liberal Party created an opportunity for the Conservatives to emphasise their unionism and draw support from the Liberals. But the Conservatives would prove unreliable allies. The Conservative Government between 1895 and 1905 tried to 'kill Home Rule with kindness', pursuing policies that sought to address economic grievances. It was thought that grievances fuelled demands for Home Rule and by offering loans to allow tenants to purchase land would undermine Home Rule demands. In addition, the Conservatives thought that embarking on a programme of infrastructure investment, including building roads, railways and harbours would suffice. But legislation proved complex and few farmers took advantage of any opportunity. It failed to take account of the importance of what James Kellas referred to as 'psychic income', that is what satisfies the 'mental and spiritual needs of human beings' that are as important as 'material income' which are 'readily quantifiable in cash terms, such as incomes and jobs'.[64]

Ulster Unionism was initially a tactic to undermine Irish Home Rule. It was assumed that if some part of Ireland was excluded then Home Rule would become untenable. At various stages before the creation of Northern Ireland, 'Ulster' was conceived by unionists as consisting of between four and nine counties. Ulster in this sense, as Oliver MacDonagh wrote, was 'more than a province, less than a state; it constituted a people'.[65] In 1911, as Home Rule was once more under consideration at the centre, Edward Carson,

---

[62] Iain McLean, *What's Wrong with the British Constitution?* (Oxford: Oxford University Press, 2010), p. 262; David Cannadine, *George V: The Unexpected King* (London, Penguin) p. 105.
[63] Alvin Jackson, *Ireland 1798–1998* (Oxford: Blackwell Publishers, 1999), p. 196.
[64] J. G. Kellas, *The Politics of Nationalism and Ethnicity* (Houndmills: Macmillan, 1991), pp. 66–67.
[65] Oliver MacDonagh, *Ireland, the Union and Its Aftermath* (London: Allen and Unwin, 1977), p. 16.

leading Irish Unionist, believed that Home Rule would be 'impossible for Ireland without Belfast and the surrounding parts' and later declared that Unionists should assume responsibility for governing the 'Protestant province of Ulster'.[66]

The transformation of tactical Ulster unionism into a practical constitutional option was a measure of unionist desperation. This 'Ulsterisation' of unionism gained ground in tandem with militancy when Asquith's Liberal Government, dependent on Irish nationalist support, prepared for Irish Home Rule. The Government of Ireland Act, 1920 made provision for two Parliaments in Ireland: one in Dublin and the other in Belfast. After the establishment of the Free State and Irish Republic, Southern unionists were left to go 'into internal exile, while many contrived to play an active part in the economic and social life of the country'.[67] Many felt that a commitment to the United Kingdom and strong local affections could co-exist. 'Ireland was a country not a nation' to them.[68] The sense of abandonment would be a recurrent theme in (Northern) Irish unionism.

On resigning from the Ulster Unionist Council in 1921 before the first elections to the Northern Ireland Parliament the following year, Edward Carson warned, 'From the outset let us see that the Catholic minority have nothing to fear from the Protestant majority. Let us take care to win all that is best among those who have been opposed to us all in the past. While maintaining intact our own religion let us give the same rights to the religion of our neighbours.'[69] The success or failure of devolution would depend in part on whether Unionists heeded this advice. The Belfast Parliament was set up under the terms of the 1920 Government of Ireland Act and the Irish Free State was established under the terms of the Anglo-Irish Treaty of December 1921. Born out of opposition to Home Rule, it would become the only part of the UK with Home Rule for half a century presided over by a succession of Unionist Prime Ministers with inbuilt and apparently impregnable majorities. The motivations behind its establishment were varied: it affirmed Northern Ireland as a separate entity and as part of the British Empire and it sustained the distinct ethos and ideology of the majority Protestant community which included landowners and shipyard workers. The unionist-nationalist/ republican divide undermined the development of class politics and alienated the minority community.

---

[66] Quoted in O'Leary 2019, vol.1, p. 300.
[67] McDowell, *Crisis and Decline* kindle edition loc.33.   [68] Ibid. loc.334.
[69] A. T. Q. Stewart, *Edward Carson* (Belfast: Blackstaff, 1981), p. 120.

The response of James Craig, Northern Ireland's first Prime Minister, in 1934 to an Irish nationalist would become intimately associated with unionism,

> The hon. Member must remember that in the South they boasted of a Catholic State. They still boast of Southern Ireland being a Catholic State. All I boast of is that we are a Protestant Parliament and a Protestant State. It would be rather interesting for historians of the future to compare a Catholic State launched in the South with a Protestant State launched in the North and to see which gets on the better and prospers the more. It is most interesting for me at the moment to watch how they are progressing. I am doing my best always to top the bill and to be ahead of the South.[70]

Having failed to get the reassurances on 'Ulster's independent rights' from Irish President de Valera, Craig concentrated on institution-building,[71] an unusual case in UK constitutional development of state building *following* the existence of a 'nation'.

Like other nationalisms, unionism defined itself as much by what it was not or what it opposed as by what it stood for. Opposition to Dublin rule was core. This opposition had three major considerations, 'an independent Ireland meant Rome rule because of its Catholic majority; the Republic was monocultural, and therefore unattractive, at least compared to the multinational UK; and the Republic was poorer than Northern Ireland and Great Britain, partly because it pursued (or used to pursue) an isolationist and irrational economic policy' but, as O'Leary has argued, none of these arguments 'passes muster today'.[72] The Ulster Unionist Party (UUP) emphasised this core belief, allowing it to appeal across classes dispensing patronage and favouring its own community. But direct rule 'reduced overnight the Unionist Party from a party of government with patronage at its disposal, to a body of incoherent and effectual protest.'[73]

Unionisms, as practiced by successive UK (Conservative and Labour) Governments, had turned a blind eye to Stormont policies and practices until civil unrest and violence forced intervention. A few backbench Labour MPs raised awkward questions but for the most part, unionism at the centre took a self-denying ordinance. Northern Ireland was a place apart. The Heath Government created a major rupture in Conservative-Unionist relations

---

[70] Sir James Craig, Northern Ireland House of Commons Official Report, vol.34, 24 Apr. 1934, col.1095.
[71] Alvin Jackson, *Ireland, 1789–1998* (Oxford: Blackwell, 1999), p. 340.
[72] O'Leary, *Northern Ireland: A Treatise. vol.3: Consociation and Confederation*, p. 352.
[73] Graham Walker, *A History of the Ulster Unionist Party: Protest, Pragmatism and Pessimism* (Manchester: Manchester University Press, 2004), p. 212.

when Stormont was prorogued. Ulster Unionist Party (UUP) MPs had taken the Tory whip at Westminster until then and remained affiliated to the National Union of Conservative and Unionist Associations until the Anglo-Irish Agreement in 1985 which marked a further rupture in relations.

Northern Ireland's Unionist administrations were led by a landed gentry and aristocrats from 1922 until 1971. Business and professional classes were dominant amongst UUP representatives at Stormont before direct rule.[74] This would change after direct rule as its leadership became more representative of the party's base.[75] The mix of social backgrounds of UUP elites, alignment with the Conservatives and the culturally conservative milieu of Northern Ireland inclined the UUP to the right. A study of UUP members published in 2019 found that members themselves placed the party firmly on the right[76] but that did not preclude the possibility of being a unionist on the left.

Attlee's Government election in 1945 had 'caused consternation among those Unionists for whom the spectre of nationalisation was anathema'. The Northern Ireland Prime Minister warned his colleagues that 'more socialistic measures' would have to be copied.[77] This led to some discussion of seeking Dominion status for Northern Ireland, a further loosening of the union. Decades later, David Trimble advocated Dominion status in a pamphlet published by the Ulster Clubs, a network of Unionists associated with what has been called 'Ulster nationalism'.[78] Trimble considered the range of options from complete integration (advocated by Enoch Powell who moved from senior positions in the Conservative Party in England to become an Ulster Unionist MP in 1974) to independence, and concluded in favour of Dominion status within the Commonwealth.[79] Trimble argued that the 1985 Anglo-Irish Agreement involved Britain withdrawing the 'birth-rights' of Ulster British and that this required greater independence. That supporters of Dominion status or independence could be referred to as Unionists tells us much about their core beliefs. Objection to the Irish Republic having any voice in Northern Ireland's affairs appeared more significant than union with the UK. Loyalty to the Crown was the overriding issue. Jennifer Todd

---

[74] J. F. Harbinson, *The Ulster Unionist Party, 1882–1973* (Belfast: Blackstaff Press, 1973), ch.10.
[75] David Hume, *The Ulster Unionist Party, 1972–1992* (Lurgan: Ulster Society, 1996), pp. 18–19.
[76] T. Hennessy, M. Braniff, J. McAuley, J. Tonge and S. Whiting, *The Ulster Unionist Party: Country before Party* (Oxford: Oxford University Press, 2019), p. 106.
[77] Walker, *A History of the Ulster Unionist* Party, p. 104.
[78] Peter Taylor, *Loyalists* (London: Bloomsbury, 2000), p. 180.
[79] Dean Godson, *David Trimble* (London: HarperCollins, 2004), p. 91.

distinguished between Ulster loyalist and Ulster British traditions.[80] Each had its own traditions, values and 'Other' against whom it defined itself.

Other Unionist parties and organisations exist and existed. The most notable was Ian Paisley's Democratic Unionist Party (DUP), founded in 1971. At its foundation, one of its leaders described it as being 'right wing in the sense of being strong on the constitution, but to the left on social policies'.[81] It was deeply illiberal. It launched a 'Save Ulster from Sodomy' campaign in 1982 against decriminalisation of homosexuality and has been a staunch opponent of abortion. Whether its policies were left wing, its electoral support tended to be younger and more working class[82] than the UUP's though it may be better understood as populist than left wing. Northern Ireland was, for Paisley, the 'last bastion of evangelical Protestantism in Western Europe'.[83] Paisley always maintained that he opposed political violence but his rhetoric was seen by critics as demagogic, contributing to the escalation of tensions. Though the Church he established is tiny (only 1 per cent of the Northern Ireland population are members), his political reach was considerable and fed off fears that the Unionist Party could not be trusted to protect Northern Ireland's besieged Protestants. Two significant constitutional shocks had affected the prospects and outlook of the UUP and DUP: direct rule and the Good Friday Agreement. The DUP became the largest party in Northern Ireland in the 2003 elections to the reconstituted Stormont Parliament and became the largest Northern Ireland party at Westminster the following year when a Unionist MP defected. The key event that allowed the DUP to replace the Unionists was the Good Friday Agreement. By 2014, almost a quarter of DUP members had been members of the UUP,[84] including Arlene Foster who would become DUP leader in 2015 and was a member of the Church of Ireland, broadening its religious and social bases.

One of the key tensions in Irish unionism was that between its pluralist and integrationist wings. Isaac Butt had been a staunch opponent of the repeal of the Act of Union but would become an equally staunch supporter of federalism. His support for what Colin Reid has called 'national

---

[80] Jennifer Todd, 'Two Traditions in Unionist Political Culture', *Irish Political Studies*, vol.2, pp. 1–26.
[81] Jackson, *Ireland, 1789–1999*, p. 409.
[82] James Tilly and Geoffrey Evans, 'Political generations in Northern Ireland', *European Journal of Political Research*, vol.50, 2011, pp. 583–608.
[83] J. Tonge, M. Braniff, T. Hennessy, J. McAuley and S. Whiting, *The Democratic Unionist Party: From Protest to Power* (Oxford: Oxford University Press, 2014), p. 11.
[84] Ibid, p.67.

unionism'[85] blurred the distinction between nationalism and unionism. This unionism has been evident in Scotland too and served to challenge 'basic categories of political analysis.'[86] The integrationist wing would have no truck with increasing distinctiveness, fearing that concessions would encourage opponents. Both the DUP and the UUP have had devolutionist and integrationist strands. Ian Paisley adopted an integrationist position for a period after direct rule. Enoch Powell gave ballast to the integrationist wing of the UUP.

While much attention is paid to popular unionism in Northern Ireland, it would be wrong to ignore more intellectual contributions. Arthur Aughey's *Under Siege: Ulster Unionism and the Anglo-Irish Agreement*[87] makes the case for viewing unionism as a constitutional rather than a cultural ideology and rejects the associations with identity and religion. He argued that all citizens of Northern Ireland should owe allegiance to the UK state. Membership of the state, he maintained, should not be connected with identity but unionism should offer 'equality of rights and citizenship within a just political order'.[88] He contrasted unionism with nationalism and rejects any notion that unionism is a form of nationalism (as argued here).

Conclusion

Three key features of unionism are discernible from an overview over the many decades and centuries: flexibility, ambiguity, and contingency. Unionism has reflected the challenges it has faced, often mimicking but sometimes offering a mirror reflection of nationalist and other challenges. Unionists have supported diverse means of maintaining the UK state of unions. They have campaigned vigorously against devolution, in favour of devolution and some have insisted that a fully federal constitution is the only way to keep the UK together.

Encapsulating unionism is at once easy and challenging. Unionism is a thin ideology with a core but little agreement amongst the myriad forms of unionisms beyond this core. Indeed, even the core is at times unclear.

---

[85] Colin Reid, '"An Experiment in Constructive Unionism": Isaac Butt, Home Rule and Federalist Thought during the 1870s', *The English Historical Review*, vol.129, 2014, p. 337.
[86] Colin Kidd, *Union and Unionism* (Cambridge: Cambridge University Press, 2008), p. 304.
[87] Arthur Aughey, *Under Siege: Ulster Unionism and the Anglo-Irish Agreement* (Basingstoke: Palgrave, 1989).
[88] Ibid. p. 203.

While that core appeared to be a support for different unions that contributed to the constitution of the United Kingdom, loyalty to the Crown has been an inner core for some. But it is possible to find unionists who are republicans and, indeed, many Scottish and Welsh nationalists have been supporters of the monarchy. Even more perplexing when considering unionism is the case of Northern Ireland where the core for some appears to be loyalty to Northern Ireland, whether this means to all the people or the majority, over union with Britain. But we should not expect to find that unionism has any clearer set of beliefs or values than any other nationalism or indeed many other ideologies and the translation of ideas into policies and practice takes adherents on a journey that can be unpredictable.

22

Nationalism

MICHAEL KEATING

State and Nation in the United Kingdom

The concept of nation in the United Kingdom is famously ambiguous. It has no juridical value but is a central element in constitutional debates. It can refer to either the whole state or to one of its component parts, England, Scotland, Wales and a part of Ireland. The name of the state, United Kingdom of Great Britain and Northern Ireland, lacks a corresponding adjective; as Richard Rose remarks, 'No one speaks of the "Ukes" as a nation'.[1] 'Nationality' is sometimes used as a synonym for citizenship but even this is quite recent. My first passport, issued in 1967, describes me as: British subject: Citizen of the United Kingdom and Colonies. Only in 1981 was a clearly defined British citizenship specified. This includes people from Northern Ireland which, strictly speaking, is not part of Great Britain, although the majority community there staunchly regard themselves as British. These legal categories cut across the nationality of the component parts. My mother and father, married in India in 1945, signed themselves in the church register respectively as Scottish and Irish; although carrying different passports, both were formally British subjects.[2]

The term 'national' is used freely and, to outsiders, confusingly across the public domain and civil society. Wales has a national library, university and museum, just to name three items. Scotland has national theatre, opera and library. England has a national opera and orchestra but the Royal National Theatre in London is known internationally as the National Theatre of Great Britain. England, Scotland, Wales and Northern Ireland have their own international teams in football and at the Commonwealth Games but not

---

[1] Richard Rose, *Understanding the United Kingdom. The Territorial Dimension in Government* (London: Longman, 1982), p.11.
[2] Following the Declaration of the Irish Republic and the British Nationality Act, my father later had to claim to remain a British subject.

at the Olympics. There is just one national rugby team covering both Northern Ireland and the Republic of Ireland. Foreigners have to be instructed in the concept of a 'home international'.

The recognition of nationality in the paraphernalia of the state is similarly confused. While the late monarch was almost invariably referred to abroad as Queen of England, at home great care was taken to represent her as presiding over a union of three kingdoms. This arises from the circumstance that Scotland and Ireland (since 1922 just Northern Ireland) were joined with England under union treaties, having been discrete kingdoms. Wales, on the other hand, was incorporated into England in the sixteenth century and features neither on the union flag nor in the royal coat of arms. Yet, few would deny Wales the status of a nation within the union.

Given this multiplicity of meanings and uses, it is hardly surprising that the nation has not featured as a working concept in constitutional law and practice, the way it has in other countries. Yet there has long been a 'national question', which periodically erupts in constitutional crises. The underlying issue is whether the UK is to be seen as a nation-state or a plurinational union and whether its constitution should be unitary or federal. In the twenty-first century, it has become so acute as to threaten to fracture the polity. Rival conceptions of the nation have come to structure politics in the peripheral parts of the UK, while departure from the European Union has removed a structure that helped to manage internal territorial tensions.

Nations, Nationality and Nationalism

Scholarship nowadays largely concurs with the proposition that nations are constructed politically in modernity, albeit often on the basis of ancient materials.[3] Nationality is not derived from any particular objective fact, as Renan[4] argued long ago. Nor, however, is it a purely objective notion, an idea in the heads of individuals, since for me to feel national it is necessary for others to feel the same way. It is, rather, an intersubjective sentiment, connecting people in multiple ways and providing a common set of references. Nationalism, in turn, is not simply the outgrowth of nationality; it can

---

[3] Umut Özkirimli, *Theories of Nationalism. A Critical Introduction*, 3rd ed. (Basingstoke: Palgrave, 2017).
[4] Ernest Renan, *Qu'est-ce qu'une nation?* (Conférence prononcée le 11 mars 1882 à la Sorbonne) www.iheal.univ-paris3.fr/sites/www.iheal.univ-paris3.fr/files/Renan_-_Qu_est-ce_qu_une_Nation.pdf.

also create the nations whose cause it pleads.[5] As these are often contested, nationalism must be seen as a claim. Specifically, it is a twofold claim. The first is an ontological claim, that the nation exists as a social reality. The second is a teleological and normative claim, that it is destined to be self-governing and has a right so to be. Neil Walker makes a similar distinction between reflexive nationalism, concerned with reproduction of the nation and teleological nationalism.[6] The ultimate expression of this would be an independent nation-state. The ideal-type of nation-state, in turn, aligns the nation with the sovereign state within clear territorial boundaries.

At one time, it was common to write of the United Kingdom as such a state. For sociologists and political scientists, this was the culmination of a once-dominant modernisation paradigm of territorial integration and functional differentiation.[7] For the Whig historians, it represented the triumph of liberalism and progress over the backward forces of the periphery. More commonly, and increasingly in recent years, the United Kingdom is seen as a plurinational polity in which competing conceptions of nation and state have played out historically. This is a common experience in composite states such as Canada, Spain or Belgium. What is different in the British experience is that those defending the integrity of the state have not generally contested the ontological claims of the Scottish, Irish, Welsh and (occasionally) English nationalists. By contrast, they do not accept the teleological claim that self-government is the logical consequence of nationality. The contrast with Spain is dramatic. There, governments and the Constitutional Court have steadfastly refused to concede the term 'nation' to Catalonia, the Basque Country and Galicia, precisely because they think that would entail a right of self-determination and, ultimately, secession. Instead, these are allowed to call themselves 'historic nationalities', a term whose meaning has been further diluted by allowing other regions to adopt it. Unionism in the United Kingdom, on the other hand, has been able to draw on local traditions of 'patriotism' embedded in the nations, to balance out assimilationist tendencies.

Nationalists in the peripheral nations of the United Kingdom have drawn teleological conclusions from the fact of nationality but these have not been

---

[5] Ernest Gellner, *Nations and Nationalism* (Oxford: Blackwell, 1983).
[6] Neil Walker, 'Teleological and Reflexive Nationalism in the New Europe', in Jacint Jordana, Michael Keating, Alex Marx and Jan Wouters (eds.), *Changing Borders in Europe. Exploring the Dynamics of Integration, Differentiation and Self-Determination in the European Union* (Abingdon: Routledge, 2019).
[7] Michael Keating, *State and Nation in the United Kingdom: The Fractured Union* (Oxford: Oxford University Press, 2021).

straightforward. In particular, they have only occasionally pointed to secession. There was always a separatist current in Irish nationalism but it did not become hegemonic until after the Easter Rising in 1916 and the subsequent violence. Secessionism in Scotland surfaced between the two world wars but only became a significant political movement in the 1970s. In the twenty-first century, independence has become the official policy of the Welsh nationalist party Plaid Cymru, but only as part of a transformed state system within an integrated Europe. Challenges to the union in the early years took the form of 'repeal', which would have undone the parliamentary union but left the monarchical one intact. Such was the policy of Scottish Jacobites in the eighteenth century and Daniel O'Connell in Ireland in the mid nineteenth century. This later gave way to the concept of Home Rule, an ambivalent concept which would have provided for parliaments in the constituent nations but subordinate, in various ways, to Westminster. There was ambivalence on two fronts. The first was whether Home Rule was a right inherent in nationhood or an act of decentralisation by a sovereign UK Parliament. The second was whether Home Rule was a route to the union or to secession. The Irish nationalist Charles Stewart Parnell is well-known for his aphorism that 'no man can set the bounds to the march of a nation' but he did accept the Home Rule Bill of William Ewart Gladstone as a final settlement.[8] In the late twentieth century, the term Home Rule was replaced by devolution, another ambivalent term but which has come to suggest more strongly that Westminster retains ultimate control.

The political opposite of nationalism has long been known as unionism but that is equally ambivalent.[9] There is an assimilationist unionism, which is itself a form of nationalism focused on the larger state. Yet other conceptions of unionism can embrace diversity and decentralisation, on condition that the principle of parliamentary sovereignty is not undermined. This means that, while nationalism and unionism have framed the debate about the territorial constitution of the United Kingdom for a century and a half as polar opposites, they have in practice overlapped in numerous ways.[10] If assimilationist and centralising unionism stands at one pole, Irish republicanism, insisting on the integrity of the Irish nation and absolute independence, stands at the other. In between, there has been a large area in which differing

---

[8] Charles Stewart Parnell 1886, Speech on Second Reading Government of Ireland Bill, *Hansard*, 07-06-1886.
[9] Keating, *State and Union*.
[10] Colin Kidd, *Union and Unionisms. Political Thought in Scotland, 1500–2000* (Cambridge: Cambridge University Press, 2008).

conceptions of the nation co-exist without having to deny the presence or validity of the other. Nationalism and unionism have been most at odds in Ireland but, even there, compromises have been tried in the late nineteenth century and from the late twentieth century. Tensions in Scotland and Wales have been recurrent but less acute. Why, in the twentieth century, they should have shaped Irish and Scottish politics into antagonistic camps is something to which we will return at the end. Before that we must consider the origins of nations and nationalism in the United Kingdom and the way the UK's particular model of state and nation-building has both fostered nationalisms and provided for their accommodation. Three elements were critical: the lack of unified state religion; Empire; and monarchy.

A Non-Westphalian State

International relations scholars often employ the term 'Westphalian state' to refer to the unified and sovereign European nation-state. Historically, this is misleading and the term itself was invented in the late nineteenth-century to legitimate the sovereignty claims of that era.[11] Westphalia[12] was of more importance in establishing the principle of religious uniformity within the domain of every ruler, that being a more important division than nationality. Religious homogeneity was, in turn, an element in nation-building in many states. Linda Colley in a much-cited thesis, has argued that the Protestant religion was a key factor in creating a British nation after the Anglo-Scottish union of 1707.[13] The argument is problematic in two respects. First, religion actually also prevented the formation of a nation corresponding to the United Kingdom, as Ireland remained defiantly Catholic and, even after the Union of Britain and Ireland in 1801, UK governments delayed the removal of Catholic civil disabilities. Second Protestantism was not uniform within Great Britain; the distinct religious settlement in Scotland sustained a strong national identity and union with England was agreed only on condition that there not be a single British church. Non-conformist religion later became a badge of an awakened Welsh national consciousness.

The concession of ecclesiastical self-government for Scotland in the settlement of 1689, guaranteed in the union of 1707, removed a potential

---

[11] Anders Osiander, 'Sovereignty, International Relations and the Westphalian Myth' *International Organization*, 55 (2001), 251–287.
[12] The treaties of Münster and Osnabrück, which ended the Thirty Years War in 1648.
[13] Linda Colley, *Britons. Forging the Nation 1707–1837* (London: Pimlico, 1st ed., 2nd ed. 1992, 2003).

national grievance while at the same time while the religious settlement was an important factor in maintaining a sense of national distinctiveness. Concessions to Ireland came too late. The Anglican Church of Ireland[14] was disestablished only in 1871 and the state missed the chance to make allies with the Catholic Church, which came to shape the Irish nationalist movement. Following lengthy campaigns, the Anglican Church in Wales was disestablished in 1920.

Empire to Commonwealth

The constitutional history of the United Kingdom is deeply marked by the circumstance that, as it became a state, it simultaneously became an empire.[15] In the 1970s, Michael Hechter used the then-fashionable concept of 'internal colonialism' to argue that the UK was created by conquest from England and the subordination of the periphery in an ethnic division of labour.[16] Scholars have generally dismissed this as misconceived as an analysis of Scotland,[17] but some Welsh nationalists have pursued the theme.[18] It is, however, at least a useful perspective on the experience of Ireland[19] even if a literal comparison with African and Asian colonies is not apt.[20] Ireland was governed by rulers sent over from England and its Parliament (before the Union of 1800) represented only the Protestant population, alienated from the mass by religion and allegiance. After Union, direct rule from London continued, in alliance with the old elites. Only from the late nineteenth century did British governments seek to coopt the nationally inclined middle class into the regime. Nationalists in the Irish diaspora in North America and Australia, tended to be republican and anti-imperialist.

---

[14] Which had amalgamated with the Church of England as part of the union of 1801.
[15] It is not unique in this respect. The same happened to Spain, where the end of Empire in the aftermath of the Napoleonic Wars and again in 1898, also had severe repercussions on the domestic territorial constitution.
[16] Michael Hechter, *Internal Colonialism. The Celtic Fringe in British National Development, 1536–1966* (London: Routledge and Kegan Paul, 1975).
[17] Hechter himself so modified his account of Scotland as to turn his original conclusions on their head. Michael Hechter, 'Internal Colonialism Revisited', in Edward Tiriakian and Ronald Rogowski (eds.), *New Nationalisms of the Developed West* (Boston: Allen and Unwin, 1985).
[18] Adam Price, *Wales: The First and Final Colony* (Talybont: Y Lolfa Cyr, 2019).
[19] Brendan O'Leary, *A Treatise on Northern Ireland, vol. I. Colonialism* (Oxford: Oxford University Press, 2019).
[20] Stephen Howe, *Ireland and Empire. Colonial Legacies in Irish History and Culture* (Oxford: Oxford University Press, 2000).

Scotland's experience was quite different. The union abolished the Scots Parliament but left intact the administrative infrastructure. Scotland was managed by local elites under the aegis of union and, while some of these were Anglicised in accents and habits, they were not alienated by religion or perceived nationality. Scots were disproportionately present in the Empire, in trade, finance, medicine, civil administration and the military.[21] They took their national ways with them so that, in Cairns Craig's formulation, what in other European countries was a defensive nationalism gave way to a 'projective nationalism', reproducing the nation but in a loyalty to the Empire.[22] Wales was also deeply involved in Empire, including trade, missions and colonisation.[23] There was some anti-imperialism in more radical circles in Scotland and Wales, and sympathy with the Boers as a small, European nation under attack.[24]

Monarchy

A similar story could be told about monarchy. The lack of a principle of popular sovereignty in the British constitutional tradition may have annoyed democrats and modernisers but it enabled the state to sidestep the question of who the demos (the people) were. Vesting sovereignty instead in the monarch-in-parliament did allow the constitution to embrace differing conceptions of nationality so long as all recognised what Rose identified as the mace.[25] Since it was the king of Scotland who united the crowns in 1603, there was little suggestion that the monarchy was a foreign imposition.[26] From the nineteenth century, the monarchy established a strong presence in Scotland and even took to worshipping in the Church of Scotland. In the early twentieth century, the ceremony of investing the monarch's eldest son as Prince of Wales was re-established. While the monarchy was not always resented in Ireland, it was never able to command instinctive loyalty, except among the Protestant minority.

The United Kingdom thus came into the age of nationalism as a complex, plurinational union embedded into a wider polity. Its peculiarity is that, unlike

---

[21] T. M. Devine, *Scotland's Empire* (Harmondsworth: Penguin, 2004). Michael Fry, *The Scottish Empire* (Edinburgh: Birlinn, 2002).
[22] Cairns Craig, *The Wealth of the Nation. Scotland, Culture and Independence* (Edinburgh: Edinburgh University Press, 2018).
[23] Martin Johnes, *Wales: England's Colony?* (Cardigan: Parthian, 2019).
[24] Rather than the native African people. [25] Rose, *Understanding the United Kingdom*.
[26] There were, of course, dynastic revolts seeking the restoration of the Stuart deposed in 1689 but these did not seek to divide the crowns again.

other European states, it retained many of these features into the modern age, so conditioning nationalism both at the state and the sub-state level. There was a strong sense of Britishness directed outside, in the name of Empire and country but less of an inward-looking project to create a homogeneous British nation. There was never, for example, a single UK-wide department for education or state-wide school curriculum. Instead, the constitution was founded on the principle of the sovereignty of the Monarch-in-Parliament.

The Age of Nationalism

While the view that nationalism is a modern phenomenon is widely shared, there is less agreement on exactly to when it should be dated. It is clear, however, that the last half of the nineteenth century was a critical period, witnessing the rise of the modern administrative state and the extension of its competences. It also saw European states penetrating and incorporating peripheral territories while establishing fixed external borders. National markets were created, turning places that were central in former maritime trading systems into peripheries, while former peripheries became centres.[27] Education, military service and other means of socialisation were used to forge nationally aware populations. Such nationalising projects often encountered opposition within territories that were culturally distinct or with competing economic interests. There was a similar nationalising impulse in the United Kingdom but with crucial differences from the continental experience.

One difference was that there was no project for the creation of a protected British national market but rather two choices.[28] On the one hand was a global free trade regime enforced by the United Kingdom as a hegemon or, if necessary, unilateral free trade. On the other hand was protectionism within the wider British Empire. A second difference was that the UK never established a single state-wide education system. Rather, separate systems emerged for England-and-Wales, Scotland and Ireland with a strong element of local control. A third difference was that British elites never sought to monopolise the concept of nation and were relaxed by the ontological nationalism of the periphery, as long as it did not disturb politics at the centre. The capital never became locus of plurinational constitutionalism but retained the prerogatives and ethos of the old English Parliament. In the dominant Whig history, British

---

[27] Michael Keating, *Rescaling the European State. The Making of Territory and the Rise of the Meso* (Oxford: Oxford University Press, 2013).
[28] David Edgerton, *The Rise and Fall of the British Nation* (Harmondsworth: Penguin, 2018).

constitutional evolution was presented as a continuous process centred on the monarch and Westminster, with the smaller nations getting walk-on parts after which the main narrative resumes. Scottish and Welsh intellectuals, indeed, often embraced the idea.[29] Anglocentrism, however, was mitigated by the wider frame of Empire, which was one of the few institutions that were always called British and not carelessly referred to as English.

It is in this context that the contemporaneous nationalisms of the periphery were born and shaped. Until the late twentieth century, they were always pioneered by Ireland, which had by far the largest nationalist movement and the only one with the capacity to pose a political threat to the regime. Irish nationalism was divided into two streams, although there was a lot of coming and going between them. One was radically separatist and republican and focused on the Irish Republican Brotherhood (the Fenians), which was committed to revolutionary means and sporadic violence. The other was constitutional nationalism organised around the Irish Parliamentary Party, whose ostensible aim was Home Rule within the union and Empire, to be achieved by parliamentary action in alliance with British parties. It is one of the great failures of British statesmanship that unionism was unwilling to accommodate this version of nationalism. While the Gladstonian Liberals had conceded Home Rule by 1886 and were to make two further attempts, their opponents in Parliament regularly frustrated them. The outcome was armed rebellion in 1916, a subsequent armed struggle and a new constitutional agreement in 1922.

Yet this was not the end of the matter. The British were prepared to go beyond Home Rule but not all the way to an Irish Republic. The answer was found, instead in the Empire and in monarchy. Ireland would have a Free State, with powers equivalent to the Dominion of Canada, and recognise the British monarch as head of state. This was before the Statute of Westminster (1931), which was to make the Dominions effectively independent, although it was not to become obvious for some years after that. The treaty provoked a civil war within the new state, won by the pro-Treaty side but the concept of the Republic survived in successive versions of the Irish Republican Army mostly (but not entirely) aimed at the province of Northern Ireland, which remained in the United Kingdom under unionist domination. In the event, the limitations on Irish sovereignty imposed by the treaty proved illusory, as the Free State was able to work around them in a new constitution in

---

[29] Colin Kidd, *Subverting Scotland's Past: Scottish Whig Historians and the Creation of an Anglo-British Identity, 1689–1830* (Cambridge: Cambridge University Press, 1993).

1937 and in 1948 renounced the monarchy, established a republic and left the Commonwealth (as the Empire had now become).

Scottish nationalism, apart from a radical fringe, was by contrast constitutional and monarchist. There was no distinct Scottish Party but Liberal and Labour MPs presented fifteen Scottish Home Rule bills between 1885 and 1924, with four of them gaining a second reading. All except one were supported by a majority of Scottish MPs.[30] There were numerous Home Rule motions and one Home Rule bill for Scotland and Wales.[31] These were all inspired by the Irish bills and were usually presented as a step in a wider process of federal reform or, as it was called, Home Rule All Round. In this way, it was argued, union could be cemented rather than sundered, and the Empire could be bolstered. Following the Irish settlement, the last two Scottish bills of this era provided for Dominion status but this, too, was seen as far from separatism. The failure of these bills and the loss of interest in Home Rule on the part of the Labour Party (once it had established a foothold in Westminster), provoked a split among supporters of self-government, some breaking away to form the Scottish National Party committed to Dominion status while others were assimilated into the practices of Westminster politics. Yet the boundary between supporters of Home Rule and independence remained a fluid one, as it still does.

A Welsh national movement also arose in the late nineteenth century.

Its initial concerns were with ontological nationalism, seeking recognition for Wales as a constituent nation of the union rather than an integral part of England, which was its legal status. This matured into a demand for Home Rule on similar lines to Scotland but there was lesser momentum in Wales. As in Scotland, the movement split after the First World War, with Plaid Cymru being formed in 1925, committed to full national status for Wales. Inspired by communitarian ideas, Plaid Cymru de-emphasised the idea of a separate state and for many years was ambivalent about the concept of independence.

The British Nation

While historians have traced the idea of Britain back to ancient times and the term was in use well before the unions[32] the British national project is also

---

[30] Nathan Kane, *A Study of the Debate on Scottish Home Rule, 1886–1914* (PhD thesis, University of Edinburgh, 2015).
[31] James Mitchell, *Strategies for Self-government. The Campaigns for a Scottish Parliament* (Edinburgh: Polygon,1996).
[32] Kidd, *Unions*.

the product of modernity, in this case linked to the end of Empire and the rise of the developmental welfare state. It was in the twentieth century that the working class were incorporated into the political nation (with universal suffrage arriving in 1928) and issues of national efficiency, welfare and trade were posed in a British framework. David Edgerton dates it as late as the post–Second World war period of state intervention and mobilisation.[33] Beginning in the 1930s but taking off in the 1960s, regional development policy sought to assure territorial cohesion by redistributing economic growth. It appears to have been in these period that politicians in Westminster started using the terms Britain and British instead of England and Empire. The term 'nationalisation' was used for the expansion of state-owned industry. The new social citizenship underpinning the welfare state[34] was certainly British. The National Health Service referred to the British nation. Momentum drained from the Home Rule movements as the Irish question was taken off the political agenda by the independence of the south of Ireland and a far-from-benign neglect of the condition of Northern Ireland under the devolved Stormont regime.

What was left could plausibly be presented as a unitary nation-state. Indeed, that is exactly how political scientists and legal scholars saw it.[35] Home Rule movements in Scotland and Wales survived only in the margins. Yet efforts to harness this British national sentiment to constitutional reform failed almost completely. Sovereignty remained vested in the monarch-in-parliament rather than the British people. Reform of the House of Lords curtailed its powers and reduced the hereditary element but in the twenty-first century it remains otherwise intact. The royal prerogative remains the basis for much of ministerial power. The electoral system channels electors into the main blocs and fails to reflect voters' preferences.

This modernising British national strategy began to falter from the 1970s. From 1979 there was a sharp change in direction. The welfare state remained a token of national identity but failed to expand as in other European countries. From the 1980s, the language of social citizenship was replaced by that of dependency and the revival of ideas of the deserving and undeserving poor. Social security gave way to 'welfare'. The developmental state ran out of steam at the same time, with a reversion to a strategy of insertion of

---

[33] David Edgerton, *The Rise and Fall of the British Nation* (Harmondsworth: Penguin, 2018).
[34] T. H. Marshall (ed. T. Bottomore), *Citizenship and Social Class* (London: Pluto, 1992).
[35] Jean Blondel, *Voters, Parties, and Leaders. The Social Fabric of British Politics*, rev. ed. (Harmondsworth: Penguin, 1974).

British business into international capitalism. Regional policy was wound down to the minimum required to draw down European moneys dedicated to territorial cohesion. What was left was a strident rhetorical nationalism but without a substantive national social and economic project to bear it.[36]

The greatest failure of the British national project was in forging a relationship with the new economic and political order emerging in Europe after the Second World War. Other countries re-founded their nationalities within the European frame. Germany regained its sovereignty by sharing it with other European nations. France embraced the *Europe des patries*. Italy, Greece and Spain used Europe to rebuild democracy. Central and Eastern European countries spoke of a 'return to Europe' as a metaphor for escaping the Soviet embrace. For the United Kingdom, however, Europe was always the 'other' against which the nation could be defined. The UK reluctance to join the project was attributable to a number of considerations, mostly linked to conceptions of the nation. On the right was a lingering imperial nostalgia and transatlanticism which was to re-emerge later in the shape of the Anglosphere. On the left a 'little England' conception envisaged national self-reliance, protectionism and social security. A right-wing version of little England drew on an imagined a nation of small businesses and sturdy citizens. While other European countries incorporated Europe into the very redefinition of their national projects, for the UK, Europe remained the foreigner, a threat to a certain idea of sovereignty. Eventually, both British parties agreed to join what became the European Union but continued to regard it as an intergovernmental order and refused to accept that national sovereignty had been transformed. Instead, the issue was side-stepped for decades.

Neo-nationalism

To the surprise of many observers, peripheral nationalisms revived from the 1960s in the United Kingdom and other European states. In some interpretations, this was a reversion to the past, a case of retarded modernisation or even a 'revolt against modernity'.[37] They should more properly be regarded as part of the latest phase of modernity, linked to the rescaling of political

---

[36] Perhaps best epitomised by the picture of Margaret Thatcher holding a handkerchief over the tailfin of a British Airways plane in protest against the removal of the union flag, although she herself had privatised the firm.
[37] Seymour Martin Lipset, 'The Revolt against Modernity', in *Consensus and Conflict. Essays in Political Sociology* (New Brunswick: Transaction, 1985).

authority and political mobilisation in the fact of transformations of the European state.[38] Like all nationalisms, they were steeped in references to history but their appeal lay in what they had to say about the present. Far from rejecting modern British norms, their claim was often to defend the social democratic, inclusive welfare state and model of managed capitalism which British governments appeared to be abandoning. The ontological claim was that the nation existed, not just in historic memory, culture or sport, but as a relevant unit for addressing economic and social questions. The teleological claim, to self-determination, remained but this was increasingly framed by new understandings of statehood and sovereignty in an interdependent world.

The classical nation-state formula relies on the coincidence of nation and state within a single bounded territory, underpinned by the principle of sovereignty. As scholars down the ages have complained, it is impossible to apply this universally, because claims to be a nation are too many and overlap. Recent conceptual developments can, if not resolve, then reframe these dilemmas. Traditional conceptions of territory are linked closely to boundaries, so that a fixed line encloses the relevant physical space. Modern understandings of territory see it not as a purely topological concept – about lines of maps – but also as a sociological one.[39] The alternative to the bounded conception of territory is the relational one, in which what matters is the temporal and spatial connection among social processes. Borders, in the old sense, give way to less well-defined boundaries, in which territories fade into each other. Sovereignty is understood now less as a fact than as a claim, less as an attribute of institutions than a relationship.[40] This opens the way for new and open understandings of how state, nation, territory and sovereignty can be negotiated in a changing world. The essence of the post-sovereignty thesis is that, while sovereignty remains an important principle of authority, it does not necessarily reside in one place. Rather, there may be multiple sources of legitimate authority, which combine in various ways. Sovereignty can, moreover, be divided and shared.[41] Such ideas have had great traction in places where the concept of sovereignty has always been

---

[38] Keating, *Rescaling*.   [39] Keating, *Rescaling*.
[40] Martin Loughlin, 'Ten Tenets of Sovereignty', in Neil Walker (ed.), *Sovereignty in Transition* (Oxford: Hart, 2003).
[41] Neil MacCormick, *Questioning Sovereignty. Law, State and Nation in the European Commonwealth* (Oxford: Oxford University Press, 1999). Michael Keating, *Plurinational Democracy. Stateless Nations in a Post-Sovereignty Era* (Oxford: Oxford University Press, 2001).

contested, such as the historic nationalities of Spain and the nations of the United Kingdom and Ireland. It represents a stark alternative to the Westminster view of the constitution, as articulated by A. V. Dicey,[42] according to which parliamentary sovereignty is the fount of all authority and cannot be limited.

The challenge in Northern Ireland arose initially from the failure of the British state to secure the civil rights that should have stemmed from shared citizenship and nationality. This rapidly transmuted into a revived nationalist movement with, as before two strands. A republican element insisted on the unity of the whole Irish people and its necessary realisation on the form of a republic. This was accompanied by a campaign of violence. A moderate element, grouped in the Social Democratic and Labour Party, favoured Irish unity only by consent, while being influenced by post-sovereigntist ideas for transforming the conflict.

Scottish nationalism also revived from the late 1960s in the form of the Scottish National Party (SNP). Unlike the old Home Rule movements, the SNP has always been committed to Scottish independence but this has taken different forms. Initially, the aim was Dominion status, then seen as less than independence. SNP figures like John MacCormick were prepared to join the cross-party Home Rule movement of the 1940s. From the 1960s, the party was divided into 'fundamentalists' and 'gradualists', with the latter accepting devolution as a first stage in the constitutional journey. Some, like the late Neil MacCormick[43] have embraced post-sovereignty fully. While its early appeal was to the small-town middle class, by the second decade of the twentieth century, the SNP had taken over from Labour as the defender of universal benefits and the post-war welfare settlement.

Welsh nationalism shares a similar centre-left perspective although Plaid Cymru has not had the electoral success of the SNP. Historically ambivalent about what form self-determination would take, it has come out for independence, but with a strong post-sovereigntist hue.

Devolution, finally conceded by the Labour Government at the end of the twentieth century, was intended to satisfy mainstream opinion in Scotland and Wales and isolate the pro-independence element in nationalism; Labour politician George Robertson was quoted as saying that it would kill

---

[42] A. V. Dicey, *Introduction to the Study of the Law of the Constitution* (Basingstoke: Macmillan, 1959).
[43] MacCormick, *Questioning Sovereignty*. Neil MacCormick was the son of John MacCormick, professor of constitutional law, and sometime Member of the European Parliament.

nationalism stone dead. Initially, devolution did seem to clarify matters and make a sharp distinction between nationalists and unionists. With devolution won, some in the SNP adopted the slogan 'we are all fundamentalists now', meaning that the party was united on the next stage of the journey. Plaid Cymru, similarly, adopted independence as the logical next goal. The Northern Ireland settlement eventually embraced nearly all of nationalism and unionism except for republican dissidents and a loyalist fringe. The term nationalist in Northern Ireland no longer has the same teleological implications as in the past but the division between nationalism and unionism was formally entrenched. Members of the Northern Ireland Assembly are invited to designate themselves with these labels and power is shared between them accordingly.

In practice, matters were not so simple. In Scotland, a middle ground, consisting of more devolution or 'devolution-max' emerged, alongside proposals for federalism and stronger guarantees for the devolved institutions, which were still officially creatures of Westminster. In 2011 the SNP won an absolute majority in the Scottish Parliament and Westminster conceded their demand for an independence referendum. While both sides agreed that the question should be clear, the meaning of independence was not. With many voters grouped in the middle-ground of more devolution, both sides sought to get themselves there. In the last stages of the campaign, the unionist parties pledged an extensive package of more powers in the event of a No vote. The SNP, for its part, offered what critics called 'independence-lite', promising to remain in five unions with England (monarchical, monetary, defence, European and social) while withdrawing only from the sixth. Following the loss of the referendum, the old division between fundamentalists and gradualists re-emerged. Plaid Cyrmu's independence prospectus continued to be informed by post-sovereigntist thinking. While the Northern Ireland settlement left open the teleological question of Irish unification or remaining within the UK, moderate nationalist opinion moved strongly in favour of a mixed solution of power-sharing within Northern Ireland combined with an all-Ireland dimension to politics and institutions. Sinn Féin, while committed to Irish unity, advanced politically by embracing the post-sovereignty ideas of its moderate rivals.

The post-devolution period saw some nationalist stirrings in England. As the majority, English nationalists hardly needed a separate vehicle for their aspirations and English people were historically unvexed about the confusion between England and the United Kingdom. They were also secure in the knowledge that the constitutional principles embedded at Westminster were derived from their own unitary parliamentary tradition. There is, according to surveys, little opposition in England to devolution for the periphery and nor is there significant support for an English Parliament. Movements in favour of English independence are almost non-existent. Yet there is a certain ontological nationalism, concerned for the first time with the status of England as a constituent nation within the union. Surveys asking people in England about their identity show an increase in those identifying as English after devolution but with the proportion stabilising after that. The new English nationalism is a contested project. There is a stereotypical depiction of it as the preserve of the populist right, anchored in left-behind post-industrial communities. Yet there is also a progressive strand, seeking to rescue Englishness from the right and drawing on traditions of community and solidarity.[44]

In the absence of a teleological nationalism, there is an inchoate sense of grievance about England's place in the union. It finds expression when people are reminded that Scottish, Welsh and Northern Irish MPs at Westminster can vote on purely English matters and are told about the financial settlement for the devolved territories. A short-lived provision was brought in for English Votes on English Laws (EVEL) in the House of Commons, allowing English MPs an effective veto on legislation applying only to England, but this could be of use only in the extremely rare times when UK governments do not have a majority of English MPs. This is more a matter of democracy and accountability than of English nationalism. One matter on which there is a distinct English constitutional sensibility, however, is Europe.

The European Question

European integration has sometimes been presented as the antidote to nationalism and at others as the saviour of the nation-state.[45] In practice, it has been both, as post-war European states used the European context to re-position their national ideologies and use the European institutions as an external support system for states whose viability was otherwise in doubt. The United Kingdom never managed this trick. Modernising sections of the

---

[44] Michael Kenny, *The Politics of English Nationhood* (Oxford: Oxford University Press, 2014).
[45] Alan S. Milward, *The European Rescue of the Nation-State*, 2nd ed. (London: Routledge, 2000).

British establishment saw Europe as spur to economic change and some were committed to a transnational future. For the most part, however Europe was either an economic project devoid of constitutional implications, or else a threat to the British national identity and self-government. The nationalisms of the periphery were equally ambivalent, but by the time of the 2016 referendum on membership of the European Union they were all on the pro-Remain side, seeing Europe as the frame for self-government, often with a post-sovereigntist flavour. Scottish nationalism always had a pro-European element but at the time of the 1975 referendum on the European Community, the SNP was opposed to membership. This position changed in the 1980s as Europe was seen as an external support system for an independent Scotland, replacing the Commonwealth. Like the Labour Party, the SNP was also influenced by the European social dimension, seen as a mechanism for protection against British neo-liberalism. Plaid Cymru travelled in the same direction, from strong opposition during the 1975 referendum to more reluctant support a few years later and then enthusiasm. Moderate nationalism in Northern Ireland was an early supporter of the European project, which it saw as a means of bringing the two parts of Ireland together and opening the border. Republicanism, in the form of Sinn Féin, was strongly opposed to European integration and opposed every referendum held in Ireland on the question. Only when the question of withdrawal was proposed in the 2016 referendum did it change its position, arguing that Brexit would 'repartition' Ireland and undercut the peace agreement.

The result of the 2016 referendum on EU membership gave some credence to this connection between peripheral nationalism and the European project. While England voted Leave by 55 per cent, Scotland and Northern Ireland voted Remain by 62 per cent and 56 per cent respectively. Wales voted much like England. Further examination reveals that the Northern Ireland vote was divided on national lines, with 85 per cent of nationalists voting Remain and a majority of unionists voting Leave, following the lead of the Democratic Unionist Party; Euroscepticism has always been stronger on the unionist than the nationalist side. In Scotland, on the other hand, there was no clear relationship between supporting Europe and supporting independence. This was to change in the following years, so that the issues of independence and Europe came into line. The option of independence outside the EU was supported only by a minority within the SNP while the Scottish Conservative Party doubled down on support for Brexit and a resolute opposition to another independence referendum.

If nationalism in the periphery has embraced Europe, the opposite is true of the emerging English nationalism. Surveys have repeatedly shown that feeling strongly English, as opposed to British, is associated with supporting the UK's departure from the EU. Moreover, the essence of the Brexit project, about restoring sovereignty, whether the Parliament or to the people, is consistent with an English or unitary vision of the constitution, as opposed to the vision of it as a plurinational union. Indeed, a majority of English pro-Leave voters would give up on the United Kingdom if that were the price of obtaining Brexit. English nationalism, it appeared, had found its cause.[46]

Neo-unionism

Nationalisms on the periphery have, thus, come back in new forms, as adaptations to modern transformations of the state and of sovereignty. Like their predecessors, they are often ambivalent about the teleology of independence and can now rationalise this in the language of post-sovereignty and of European integration. It is not nationalism but unionism that faced the greatest challenge after devolution at the end of the twentieth century. Having been largely defined for over a hundred years by opposition to devolved legislatures, it accepted what was in effect the old Home Rule project almost overnight, defining itself in opposition to separatism. This did not prove as easy as might have been thought. As we have seen, a middle ground soon opened around propositions for a looser union. More fundamentally, unionism, which had hitherto been largely taken for granted and 'banal'[47] felt the need to articulate itself as a coherent ideology. Previously, it had consisted of diverse strands including assimilationism, local patriotism, contractualism and conditional loyalty, coexisting under the umbrella of monarch in parliament. Unionists could always claim that that formula was unchanged, given that the devolution acts expressly stated that Westminster remained sovereign, but this was not enough. Faced with ontological and teleological nationalisms at the periphery, unionism had to become a nationalism itself, the mirror image of its rivals.

The first challenge is the ontological one, the idea of a unitary British people. Traditional unionism provided different routes to belonging, mostly direct in England but mediated by local patriotisms in the other parts of the

---

[46] Future of England Survey (2019), www.cardiff.ac.uk/__data/assets/pdf_file/0010/1708624/Copy-of-Wales-16-Oct-AH.pdf.
[47] Kidd, *Union*.

union. Neo-unionism tackles this problem by evoking a superordinate and singular British identity, below which are local and sectoral variations. This is a formula used to address both territorial nationalism and the challenges of multiculturalism arising out of recent migration. This differs from traditional unionism, which could accept that Britishness (not that the term was used then) is a polyvalent term and itself differs from one part of the union to another. Nor is Britishness the only space in which multiculturalism can thrive; the constituent nations are also sites of their own multicultural compromises. Britishness as a superordinate identity encounters particular difficulties in Northern Ireland, where the settlement explicitly allows people to identify with different national communities and provides for their institutional expression. The UK is pledged to support this, not to promote the British over the Irish identity.

Another move is to attribute higher ethical norms to the UK level in the form of 'British values'. The problem is not, as is sometimes argued, that these are invariably universal values such as liberty, democracy and tolerance – many nationalisms do that. The problem is that these are the very same values espoused by the peripheral nationalisms and so provide no basis for preferring one level over the other. It is significant that the only part of the UK where the teaching of British values is compulsory in schools is England.

These ethical arguments about the value of union have been accompanied by instrumental arguments focused on specific policy fields. One is the economy, with the argument that the UK offers large internal market'; but this argument is not available to the Conservative and Unionist Party, committed to leaving the European Single Market. Another persistent theme is of the UK as a 'sharing union' based on common social citizenship. It is true that the social welfare system is mostly financed at UK level and provides for citizens regardless of location. On the other hand, devolution was not accompanied by any system of fiscal equalisation and the financing of the devolved governments owes nothing to need but rather to the incremental effects of the Barnett Formula. Indeed, unionist appeals in Scotland are often based on the idea that Scotland gets more than its due share, an argument that by definition cannot be universalised across the union. Because of its strong support and emotive appeal, the National Health Service has been adopted as a symbol of union, but this is in fact completely devolved to the nations and organised in ways that differ significantly.

Finally, the most explicit assertion of British nationalism, leaving the European Union, has not been available to neo-unionists as many of them supported Remain. Prime Minister Theresa May's insistence that 'the British people' voted to leave the EU amounts to a claim that that particular political community or *demos* has more value that the individual nations, two of which voted the other way.

Nationalism against Nationalism

Nationalisms in the United Kingdom have taken multiple forms, both ontologically and teleologically. It is not merely that there are different nations and national projects within the same state as in multinational unions. The UK is rather an example of what I have called plurinationalism in which the meaning and implications of nationality differ from one part to another, and in which some people are content with one national identity while others can live with several overlapping ones. This ontological complexity means that the United Kingdom is not destined to fragment into its constituent nations since they themselves are not clearly bounded entities with shared identities. Nor, on the other hand, is a neo-unionist nationalising project, predicated on a single over-arching identity, likely to succeed. Our constitutional predicament is altogether more complicated than that. Within the European Union, these tensions could be managed. The entire European project is based upon post-sovereign premises about shared sovereignty, which provided a good fit with the plurinational understanding of the UK itself. It lowered the stakes in the Irish conflict and allowed for the Irish border to be taken largely out of contention. It permitted an independence referendum in Scotland in which both sides were committed to maintaining a common market in Europe and thus among the home nations. Brexit is predicated on a single British nation and a single locus of sovereignty; if such a nation ever existed it does not exist in the twenty-first century.

At one time it was widely believed that nations and nationalism would disappear with modernisation as differences in substantive values were transcended. The idea reappeared again at the end of the Cold War with volumes on the end of territory,[48] the end of history[49] and the end of nations and nationalism.[50] The United Kingdom is not the only place where that did not happen. On the contrary, politics in Northern Ireland, Scotland and, in a

---

[48] Bertrand Badie, *La fin des territoires. Essai sur le désordre international et sur l'utilité sociale du respect* (Paris: Fayard, 1995).
[49] Francis Fukuyama, *The End of History and the Last Man* (New York: Free Press, 1992).
[50] Eric Hobsbawm, *Nations and Nationalism since 1780. Programme, Myth, Reality* (Cambridge: Cambridge University Press, 1990).

different way Wales and England are increasingly, but not exclusively, organised on national lines. This is not because substantive values are diverging – they are not. The argument, rather is over the political and institutional framework in which these values are expressed. The very fact that both peripheral and British nationalisms are claiming the same normative space makes accommodation more difficult than would be the case where they looking for mutual tolerance of divergent cultures. This is what Stéphane Dion has called de Tocqueville's paradox, of political diversity and cultural convergence.[51] Nationalism and unionism in the United Kingdom are rival siblings, condemned to live together but ever seeking to emphasise their essential differences.

---

[51] Stéphane Dion, 'Le nationalisme dans la convergence culturelle. Le Québec contemporain et le paradoxe de Tocqueville', in R. Hudon and R. Pelletier (eds.), *L'engagement intellectuel. Mélanges en l'honneur de Léon Dion* (Sainte-Foy: Presses de l'Université de Laval, 1991).

Index

A. v Secretary of State for the Home Department (Belmarsh Prison) [2004], I. 84
Aberdeen Doctors, II. 245
absolute authority, I. 68, 262, 266, 343
absolute sovereignty, I. 261, 339
abuse of power, I. 25, 70, 469
Act in Restraint of Appeals of 1532, II. 142
Act of Parliament, I. 7, 47, 70, 154, 184, 215, 223, 320, 374, 423
Act of Renunciation, II. 307
Act of Restraint of Appeals of 1533, I. 125
Act of Security, II. 327–28
Act of Security of 1704, I. 294
Act of Settlement, I. 305, 342, 347
    1701, I. 18, 39, 137, 144, 294, 318, 376
Act of Settlement, II. 184, 253, 259–63, 266, 270–72, 274–76, 278–79, 284, 286
    1701, II. 184, 424
Act of Succession, I. 125
Act of Supremacy
    1534, II. 142
    1558, II. 470
Act of Supremacy of 1534, I. 25, 125, 127
Act of the Westminster Parliament, II. 326
Act of Uniformity, I. 139
    1549, I. 126
    1552, I. 126
    1662, I. 135
Act of Union, I. 330, 537
Act of Union, II. 175, 209, 218, 227–28, 386, 398
    1536, I. 310
    1536, II. 142
    1707, II. 430
    1800, I. 531
    1800, II. 329
    1801, I. 492
    1840, II. 508
    Ireland 1800, I. 149

Act Rescissory, II. 234
Acts and Monuments, II. 144
administration, I. 55, 58, 105, 335–36, 339, 349, 357–58, 506
    aspects of, I. 40
    central, I. 305, 339
    history of, I. 352
    local, I. 305
    local government., I. 345
    of justice, I. 38–39, 188, 304, 512
    poor law, I. 153
    property rights, I. 153
    royal finance, I. 361
    royal justice, I. 197, 302
    supervise, I. 302
administrative law, I. 48–49
Ælle of Sussex (king of the South Saxons), II. 5
Æthelbald (king of Mercia), II. 8, 10–11, 14, 17
Æthelbald (king of Wessex), II. 3, 10, 17
Æthelberht (king of Kent), II. 4–5, 17
Æthelflæd, Lady of the Mercians, II. 20, 23
Æthelred I (king of Wessex), II. 2, 17–18
Æthelred II (king of the English), II. 25, 27
Æthelstan (king of Anglo-Saxons), II. 20, 23–25
Æthelwulf (king of Wessex), II. 15–17
Afrikaners, II. 512
Agrarian Law, I. 66
Agreement of the People, II. 173, 175
Air Force Act of 1955, I. 389
Alcuin of York, II. 13, 20
Alexander III, Pope, I. 119
Alfred (king of Anglo-Saxons), II. 3, 16, 18–20, 22, 25, 28, 210–11
Alfred the Great. *see* Alfred (king of Anglo-Saxons)
Aliens Restriction (Amendment) Act of 1919, I. 22
amateur, I. 23, 25

INDEX

amateur, I. (cont.)
    electorate, I. 23
American revolution, II. 488
Amery, Leopold Charles Maurice Stennett, I. 28
An Historical Disquisition Concerning the Knowledge Which the Ancients Had of India, II. 500
anarchy, I. 63, 261, 266–67, 361
ancient constitution, II. 164, 175–80, 185, 198, 204, 206, 254, 256, 474, 482
    concept, II. 134
    defence, II. 182
    dialogue, II. 165
    failure, II. 161, 171
    inadequacy, II. 170, 173, 175
    notion, II. 236, 255–56, 473
    origins, II. 199
    primacy, II. 160
Angevin, I. 25, 369
    dynasty, II. 55
    kings, II. 63–64, 94
    procedures, II. 59
    succession, II. 64
Angles, II. 2–3, 22, 25
Anglican, II. 178, 181, 264, 280, 327
    church, I. 158
    church, II. 259, 281, 287, 330, 450
    clergy, I. 137
    communion, II. 279
    elites, I. 136–37, 141
    establishment, I. 142
    establishment, II. 183
    gay, I. 159
    monopoly, I. 140
    supremacy, I. 440, 450
Anglican Church in Wales, I. 525
Anglican Church of Ireland, I. 545
Anglican missionary, I. 147
Anglicans, I. 154, 158, 166, 490
Anglo-Irish Agreement of 1985, II. 466
Anglo-Irish Union, II. 312, 320, 338
Anglo-Saxon
    England, II. 1
    kingdom, II. 19–21, 23, 26
    legacy, II. 27
    period, II. 28
    predecessors, II. 63
    royal diploma, II. 7
Anglo-Saxon Chronicle, II. 1, 8, 21, 28, 36–37
Anglo-Scottish Union, II. 164, 285, 312, 320, 328–29

Anisminic Ltd v Foreign Compensation Commission, I. 358
Anne, Queen, I. 17, 140, 319, 377
Anne, Queen, II. 234–35, 253, 259–63, 266–69, 429
Anson, William Reynell, II. 446, 497
anti-Catholicism, I. 149, 491, 532
anti-slavery
    agitation, I. 157
    campaign, I. 150, 156
    campaigns, I. 19
    legal cases, I. 147
    movement, I. 147–48
anti-union campaign, I. 172
Appellants, II. 89, 94, 107
Appellate Jurisdiction Act of 1876, I. 317, 327
Aquinas, Thomas, I. 256, 464
Aquinas, Thomas, II. 87
aristocracy, I. 56, 62–63, 74–76, 78, 264, 408, 485
aristocracy, II. 30, 172, 313, 349, 407, 413, 470
Aristotle, I. 65, 116, 221
armed forces, I. xviii, 386–88, 442
    abroad, I. xviii, 392–96
Armed Forces Act
    2006, I. 389, 392
    2011, I. 389, 391
    2016, I. 389
Army Act of 1955, I. 389
Arnold, Thomas, I. 153
Arthur of Brittany, II. 65
Articles of Agreement, II. 461–62
Articles of the Barons, II. 57, 60
Ashby v White, I. 378
Ashby v White, II. 276
Asquith, Herbert Henry, I. 31, 227, 442, 449, 491, 534
Asser, John, II. 1, 17, 20–21, 28, 211
assize, II. 53–54, 68, 71, 93, 103, 128, 153, 401, 406
Assize of Clarendon, II. 54
Attlee government, I. 182, 503, 507–8, 511, 514, 526, 529, 536
Attlee, Clement Richard, I. 159, 231, 507, 513, 518, 529
Attlee, Clement Richard, II. 382, 499, 526
Aughey, Arthur, I. 538
Austin, John, I. 23, 280, 493–94
authoritarianism, II. 234, 247, 345
authority of parliament, I. 61

Bacon, Francis, I. 374
Bacon, Sir Francis, II. 131

Index

Bagehot, Walter, I. 14, 44, 77, 79–80, 97, 224, 279, 296, 436, 438, 489
Bagehot, Walter, II. 318, 372, 396, 446, 498
Baldwin, Stanley, I. 228, 435
Balfour of Denmilne, James, II. 244, 246
Balfour, Arthur James, II. 456–57, 518
Ballot Act of 1872, I. 325
Bancroft, Richard, I. 132
Baner Ac Amserau Cymru, II. 409
Bank of England, I. 92, 99
Bank of England Act
    1946, I. 92
    1998, I. 92
Bannockburn, II. 88, 101
barons, II. 43–46, 61, 73–74, 215, 224, *see also* Twenty-Five barons of the realm
    and freeholders, II. 255
    concessions, II. 66
    of England, II. 40, 80
barons and freeman, II. 201
Basset, Ralph, I. 361
bastard feudalism, II. 85, 104–5, 110
Battle Abbey Chronicle, II. 52
Battle of Hastings, II. 3, 31
Battle of Worcester, II. 426
Baxter, John, I. 19
Bayly, Christopher Alan, II. 514
Becket, Thomas, I. 119
Beckett, James Camlin, II. 307
Beckett, John Vincent, I. 425
Beckford, William, I. 146
Bedchamber Crisis, I. 296
Bede the Venerable, II. 1–2, 4–8, 10–11, 14, 18, 28
Belfast Agreement, II. 357, 359, 368, 370, 372–73, 379–80, 383–84, 394, 466
Benkharbouche v Secretary of State for Foreign Affairs, II. 393
Bentham, Jeremy, I. 75, 79, 276, 489
Beowulf, II. 207
Berlin, Isaiah, I. 6, 433
Bevan, Aneurin, II. 1612 416
bicameralism, I. 71
Bishopric of Manchester Act of 1847, I. 326
black chattel slavery, I. 146, 148, 380
Black Death, I. 370
Black Death, II. 84, 93, 97, 103–4, 106
Black Lives Matter, I. 399
Blackstone, Sir William, I. 13, 40–41, 204–5, 276, 324, 337, 343–49, 358, 379, 451
Blair
    era, II. 369
    government, II. 388, 395

Blair government, I. 7, 189, 250, 281, 384, 449
Blair, Anthony Charles Lynton, I. 82, 214, 243, 429, 449
Blair, Anthony Charles Lynton, II. 352, 362
blasphemy, I. 162, 164
Blasphemy Act, I. 142, 145, 150, 162
bloodless revolution, I. 10
Board of Trade, I. 108, 177–78
Bobbitt, Philip Chase, I. 431
Bodin, Jean, I. 261, 338–40, 343, 345–46, 357
Boer War, II. 327, 512
Boethius, Anicius Manlius Severinus, II. 21
Bogdanor, Vernon Bernard, I. 450–51
Boleyn, Anne, Queen, I. 125, 432
Boleyn, Anne, Queen, II. 138
Bolingbroke, Henry St John, I. 30, 273, 289, 433, 447, 462, 468, 473, 475
Boniface, Saint, II. 10
boroughs and counties, I. 418
Bourchier, Thomas, I. 123
Bracton, I. 254, 257, 260, 262, 365
Brexit, I. 108, 112, 243, 250, 431, 449, 497, 557, 559
Brexit, II. 375, 377, 380, 383, 394, 396–97
    aftermath of, I. 334
    agreement, II. 389
    campaign, II. 382
    deal, II. 390
    hard, I. 86
    opponents, I. 443–44
    party, I. 247, 444
    party, II. 390–91
    pre-, I. 101
    process, I. 321, 332–33, 374–75
    process, II. 377, 385, 440–41, 466
    prorogation affair, I. 296, 301
    referendum, I. 246
    referendum, II. 383
    schism, I. 429
    soft, I. 86
    support, I. 556
Briggs, Asa, I. 24
British constitution, II. 385, 395, 421, 448, 468–69, 494, 496–98, 506–7, 524, 527
    Brexit, II. 396
    defective, II. 498
    flexibility, II. 318
    India, II. 490
British identity, I. 22, 558
British Nationality Act of 1948, II. 504
British North America Act of 1867, II. 508

British-Irish Council, II. 373, 380
British-Irish Union, II. 328
Britishness, I. 22, 466, 531, 547, 558
Britons, II. 4, 484, 490, 510
Brown, James Gordon, I. 393
Bryce, James, I. 12, 248, 493
Buchanan, George, I. 30, 132
Buchanan, George, II. 237, 239, 249–50
Bulpitt, James Graham, I. 524, 528
Burials Act
  1880, II. 411
Burials Act of 1880,
  I. 162
Burke, Edmund, I. xix, 6, 8–9, 30, 295, 353, 427, 432, 464–67, 469, 483, 489, 522
Burke, Edmund, II. 161, 185, 315, 489
Burkean, I. 477
  ideal, I. 428
  member, I. 430
  scholar, I. 451
Burmah Oil v Lord Advocate, I. 393
Burnham, Andrew Murray, II. 382
Burns, Robert, I. 8
Butt, Isaac, II. 324, 413, 450, 453

Calamy, Edmund, I. 141, 146
Cameron, David William Donald, I. 228, 241, 243, 248, 439
Cameron, David William Donald, II. 370, 380, 389, 391, 435
Campaign for a Scottish Assembly (CSA), II. 418, 433
Campbell v Hall, II. 277, 488
Canning, George, I. 15, 150
canon law, I. 38, 115–16, 119, 125, 152, 255, 371
Carlyle, Thomas, II. 2
Caroline, Queen, I. 19
Carr, Edward Hallett, I. 11
Carson, Edward Henry, II. 446
Castile, II. 202
Catherine of Aragon, Queen, I. 124–26
Catherine of Aragon, Queen, II. 138
Catholic emancipation, I. 149–51, 160, 166
Catholic Emancipation, II. 449
Catholic Emancipation Act, II. 452
Catholic Relief Act
  1778, II. 307
  1782, II. 307
  1792, II. 314
  1793, II. 314
Catholic Relief Act of 1791, I. 149
Catholicism, I. 9, 138, 144, 164, 432
Ceawlin (king of Wessex), II. 5

centralisation, I. 354, 407, 411–12, 429–30, 529–30
  of economic management,
  I. 111
  of the rule of law, I. 26
centrality, I. 417, 422, 447, 492
Ceolwulf I (king of Mercia), II. 23
Ceolwulf II (king of Mercia), II. 18–19
Chamberlain, Austen, II. 518
Chamberlain, Joseph, II. 323, 326–27, 382, 455
Chamberlain, Joseph Austen, I. 8, 227, 229, 410, 430
Chancellor of the Exchequer, I. 184, 189
Chancellor of the Exchequer, II. 381
Charlemagne, II. 13, 20
Charles I, King, I. 62, 86, 132–35, 203, 270–71, 291, 303, 318, 374, 422, 432–33, 437
Charles I, King, II. 132, 166, 170, 172–73, 175, 181, 183, 233–34, 246, 251, 337
Charles II, King, I. 135–36, 292–93, 299, 318, 375, 433
Charles II, King, II. 177–80, 233, 246–48, 262, 291, 426, 476–77
Charles V, King, I. 124–26
Charles, Prince of Wales, I. 166, 523
Charter
  1215, I. 37
  1362, I. 37
  1838, I. 20
Charter I. 82, 214
Charter of Fundamental Rights, I. 194
Charter of Fundamental Rights, II. 392, 394
Charter of the Forest, II. 77, 124
Charter of the Fundamental Rights of Workers, I. 190
Chartism, I. 20, 157
Chartist
  attacks, I. 157
  demands, I. 21
  demonstration, I. 503
  leadership, I. 157
  Movement, I. 325
Chartist movement, II. 334, 450, 467
Chartists, I. 20, 157, 204, 278, 280, 488, 492, 503
Chaucer, I. 23
Chequers Estate Act 1917, I. 15
Christian, Edward, I. 3
Christianity, I. 114–15, 117, 142, 148, 162
Christianity and the Social Order, I. 159
Church of England, II. 142–44, 184, 262–63, 279, 329, 411, 443
Church of Ireland, II. 330, 443, 450

Index

Church of Scotland, II. 238, 321, 328–31, 431
Churchill, Sir Winston Leonard Spencer, I. 231, 505, 510, 517, 519
Churchill, Sir Winston Leonard Spencer, II. 324, 345, 362
Cities and Local Devolution Act 2016, II. 371
Cities and Local Government Devolution Act of 2016, I. 236
Civil Authorities (Special Powers) Act of 1922, II. 464
Civil Contingencies Act of 2004, I. 390
civil law, I. 47, 172, 265
civil service, I. 24, 224, 300, 339, 349, 353–55, 357, 504–5, 532
Civil War, II. 166, 170, 318, 407
  English, II. 474–76
Claim of Right, II. 251, 253, 379, 428
Claim of Right for Scotland, A, II. 433
Clarendon, Edward Hyde, II. 160
Clark, Jonathan Charles Douglas, I. 439
Clement VII (pope), II. 138
Clement VII, Pope, I. 25, 124
Cnut (king of England), II. 2, 25, 27, 31–32, 40–41
Cobden, Richard, II. 410, 511
codified constitution, II. 378, 386, 396–97
Coke, Daniel Parker, I. 425
Coke, Sir Edward, I. 28–29, 39, 42–43, 67, 199, 201, 263, 270, 368, 373–74, 450
Coke, Sir Edward, II. 28, 136, 154, 164, 168, 189, 200, 337, 472–73
Cold War, II. 346
Coleridge, Samuel Taylor, I. 15
collective agreements, I. 168, 180, 507
collective bargaining, I. 168, 180, 190–91
Colley, Linda Jane, I. 6, 8, 41–42, 51, 531, 544
Colonial Laws Validity Act of 1865, I. 329
Colonial Laws Validity Act of 1865, II. 503
colonialism, I. 316, 513, 545
Commentaries, I. 205, 223, 324, 343, 345
Commentaries of the Laws of England, I. 13, 73
Commentaries on the Laws of England, I. 204, 379
Common Bench, I. 362–64, 367–68, 382
Common Bench, II. 67, 73
common law, I. 26, 29, 269–70, 379
common law, II. 165, 197
  and the constitution, I. 30
  court, I. 38, 43, 199, 201, 219, 303–4, 366, 369, 371
  court, II. 128, 200, 266, 276
  judiciary, I. 359

jurisdiction, I. 364, 373
liability, I. 173, 186–88
offence, I. 162, 171
principles, II. 165
procedure, I. 37
restraint, I. 185
rights, I. 50–51, 217, 373
rules, II. 111–12
theories, I. 265, 269, 373
common law constitution, I. 55, 67, 83, 86, 269
Common Law Procedure Act of 1854, I. 382
common law system, I. 370
Common Pleas, II. 93, 276, 289
Commonwealth, I. 135, 216, 292, 329, 340, 433, 477, 500, 549
  countries, I. 82
  Games, I. 540
  immigration, I. 163
Commonwealth Franchise Act, II. 526
Commonwealth Immigrants Act, I. 163
Commonwealth of Oceana, The, I. 271
Competition Act of 1998, I. 109
Composition for Tithes (Ireland) Act of 1832, II. 450
Comprehension, I. 141
Comprehension Scheme, I. 140
Compromise of Avranches, I. 119
concepts of law and the constitution, I. 44
conservatism, I. 457–65, 467, 469, 475, 477
  British, I. 458–60, 464–65, 467, 473
  concepts of, I. 458
  moderate, I. 470, 474
  modern, I. 463, 468, 470
  role of, I. 473
conservative constitutionalism, I. 477–78
Conservative Party, I. 85, 244, 247, 281, 440–41, 473–74, 495, 525, 536
Conservative unionism, I. 528
Consolation of Philosophy, II. 21
Conspiracy and Protection of Property Act of 1875, I. 171
Constantine I (Roman emperor), I. 114, 116
Constitution Act
  1791, II. 489
  1852, II. 515
Constitution of 1782, I. 414
constitution of rights, I. 195
constitutional
  community, I. 408, 414, 416–17, 419, 430
  conservatism, I. 459, 461–62, 470–71, 478
  conventions, I. 45, 48, 393
  crisis, I. 42, 291, 448, 473, 479, 496

565

constitutional (cont.)
  hagiography, I. 8
  history, I. 3–5, 15–19, 21, 23–29, 32–34, 301, 330, 336, 451, 487
  monarchy, I. 70, 285, 461, 501
  norm, I. 31, 54, 88, 320, 322, 436, 439, 501, 506
  revolution, I. 25–26, 101, 493
  scrutiny, I. 101
  statutes, I. 51
constitutional convention, II. 351, 377, 383
constitutional crisis, II. 92, 106, 170, 319, 360, 444, 518
Constitutional History, I. 16
Constitutional History of England, I. 12, 76, 279
Constitutional History of England, II. 110
constitutional reform, II. 352, 357–58, 370–71, 395, 447, 456, 513
Constitutional Reform Act, II. 387
  2005, II. 352, 371, 386
Constitutional Reform Act of 2007, I. 307
constitutional union, II. xxv, 422–25, 441
constitutionalism, I. 463–64, 466–71
Contagious Diseases Act of 1864-66, I. 158
contestatory model
  of economic constitution, I. 91
Continental law, II. 192, 201
control of power, I. 58
Convention of Estates, II. 252
Convention Parliament, I. 293, 318, 376
Convention Parliament, II. 428
Convention rights, I. 50, 212, 215, 384
Conway v Wade, I. 186
Co-operative Party, I. 515–16
coronation
  oath, II. 88, 182, 241, 250–51, 263, 469
  proclamation, II. 45, 47–48, 52, 55
Coronation Charter, II. 42, 48, 51, 54, 57–58, 60
Coronation Oath Act, II. 263
Corporation Act, II. 278
  1661, II. 279–80
  1718, II. 279
Cortes of Castile, II. 203, 205
cosmic order, I. 114
Council in the Marches, II. 147, 404, 406
County and Borough Police Act of 1856, I. 424
County Police Act of 1839, I. 397
Court of Common Pleas, I. 38–39, 104
Court of Exchequer, I. 38, 93
Court of Exchequer Chamber, I. 368, 378, 383
Court of Great Sessions, II. 406

Court of High Commission, II. 170
Court of King's Bench, I. 38–40, 302, 364
Court of Star Chamber, I. 38, 40, 303
Courts of Great Session, II. 408
Covenant, II. 233, 245–46, 426
Covenant Chain, II. 478, 483, 485
Covenanter, II. 245, 247
  constitution, II. 247
  elite, II. 245
  leadership, II. 243, 246
  parliament, II. 247
  political theory, II. 256
  propaganda, II. 245, 250
  revolution, II. 244
  Scottish, II. 233
Covid-19, I. 202
Cragoe, Matthew, II. 331
Craig of Riccarton, Thomas, II. 250
Criminal Justice (Scotland) Act of 2016, I. 400
Criminal Law Amendment Act of 1871, I. 171
criminal liability, I. 171–72
Criminal Procedure (Scotland) Act of 1995, I. 400
Crofter case, I. 187
Cromer, Evelyn Baring, II. 511
Cromwell, Oliver, I. 10, 68, 135, 139, 222, 262, 271, 292, 324
Cromwell, Oliver, II. 177, 208, 233, 312, 475
Cromwell, Thomas, I. 125, 262, 438, 453
Crossman, Richard Howard Stafford, I. 14, 413
Crown Proceedings Act
  1946, I. 306
  1947, I. 513
Crown Prosecution Service, I. 398
Cumann na mBan, II. 459
Custance, George, I. 461
customary law, I. 43–44, 257, 269
customary law, II. 188, 192–96
Cymdeithas yr Iaith Cymraeg, II. 417
Cymru Fydd, II. 322, 413
Cymru, Plaid, II. 417–20

Dalrymple, James, II. 250
Danby, John, II. 115, 160
Darcy v. Allen, II. 157
David I, King, I. 115, 117
Davies, Andrew, II. 417
Davies, John, II. 406
Davies, Richard, II. 407
Davies, Robert Rees, II. 213, 398, 400
Davies, Ronald, II. 419–20
De Bracton, Henry, I. 29, 365

Index

De Jure Regni Apud Scotus, II. 249
De la Mare, Sir Peter, I. 313
De Laudibus Legum Angliae, II. 133
De Lolme, Jean-Louis, I. 28, 276
De Montfort, Simon, I. 310–11
De Natura Legis Naturae, II. 112
De Republica Anglorum, II. 133
De Smith, Stanley Alexander, II. 506
De Tocqueville, Alexis, I. 28, 463, 560
Deakin, Alfred, II. 508
Death of British Democracy, The, II. 346
decentralisation
    of British institutions, I. 28
    of EU competition law, I. 109
    of power, I. 521
Declaration for Liberty of Conscience, II. 180
Declaration of Rights, II. 181, 183
Declarations of Indulgence, I. 136
Declaratory Act, II. 299, 306, 309, 489
    1719, II. 286, 481
    1720, II. 300, 306
    1766, II. 304, 486
decolonisation, I. 21, 329, 495, 513
decolonisation, II. 348, 502, 507, 523, 527–28
democracy, I. 473–74
    direct, I. 72, 221, 238–40, 248
    representative, I. 72, 77, 85, 87, 221, 240
    social, I. 79, 169, 194, 530
Democracy in America, I. 235
democratic
    accountability, II. 420
    legitimacy, II. 458, 460
    mechanism, II. 357
    norms, II. 521
    perspective, II. 346
    principle, II. 339, 344, 350
    rights, II. 494
    status, II. 343
democratic political constitution, I. 86
democratic representation, I. 333
democratic scrutiny, I. 92
democratic system, II. 345
democratisation, I. 58, 219, 323, 418, 420, 473–74
democratisation, II. 231, 332, 337, 345, 520
    of the Commons, I. 329
    process of, I. 324
Denning, Alfred Thompson, I. 188, 305
Despensers, II. 88–89, 106
devolution, I. 7, 86–87, 100, 232, 333, 430, 488, 553–55
devolution, II. 326, 370, 372, 378–80, 385, 442
    boundaries of, I. 332

England, II. 380
    legislation, II. 366, 372, 375–76
    Northern Ireland, II. 317, 372, 439
    of power, I. 324, 422, 478, 495, 497
    referendum, I. 230, 235, 244, 246, 530
    Scottish, I. 331–32
    Scottish, II. 357, 422, 439
    settlement, I. 331–32
    settlement, II. 373–74, 376–77, 394
    structure, II. 466
    system, I. 233, 310
    to Scotland, I. 80, 82, 214
    Wales, II. 420
    Wales and Scotland, II. 356
devolved
    assemblies, I. 449
    governments, I. 64, 558
    institutions, I. 554
    legislatures, I. 310, 333–34, 557
    national assemblies, I. 498
    nations, I. 99, 215
    power, I. 332, 421
    Scottish Parliament, I. 530
    state, I. 520
    territories, I. 555
Dialogue on the Exchequer, II. 41
Dicey, Albert Venn, I. 27, 42, 44–49, 73–74, 103, 206–8, 219, 223, 229, 279, 322–23, 356–58, 452, 493, 498
Dicey, Albert Venn, II. 325, 354, 373, 378, 429, 439, 448, 457, 497–98, 506, 525
Diceyan
    analysis, I. 46
    approach to rights, I. 212
    constitutional actors, I. 100
    constitutional dualism, I. 102
    view, I. 212
dictatorial powers, I. 32
Dilke, Charles Wentworth, II. 510
direct taxation, I. 288
Disarming Act of 1746, II. 283
Disarming Act of 1747, I. 522
disestablishment, II. 329–31, 411–12
Disestablishment of the Church, II. 414, 452
Disraeli, Benjamin, I. 225–26, 436, 446, 469, 473, 475, 483, 491
Dissenters, I. 135–36, 140–44, 146, 148, 491
Dissenters Relief Act
    1779, II. 281
divine law, I. 200, 261–62
divine law, II. 87, 110, 250
Dogmas of the Constitution, I. 278
Domesday Book, II. 31, 33–36, 41, 43, 47, 50

Domesday Inquiry, II. 33, 38, 41–42, 46
Du Bois, William Edward Burghardt, II. 512
Dufferin, Frederick Temple Hamilton-Temple-Blackwood, II. 511
Dundas, Henry, II. 314–15
Dunsaetan agreement, II. 211–12
Duverger, Maurice, I. 175

East India Company v Skinner (1666), I. 293
Ecclesiastical History of the English People, II. 1, 6, 11, 28
Ecclesiastical Titles Act of 1851, II. 452
Ecgberht (king of Wessex), II. 14–15
ECHR, I. 50–51, 82, 84, 90, 211–13, 215–19, 392, 394–96, 404, 511, 517–18
ECHR, II. 364, 465–66
economic constitution, I. 88–92, 95, 99, 106, 110
  contestatory model of, I. 91
  substantive, I. 89
economic democracy, I. 169, 178, 180
economic liberalism, I. 103, 170, 186, 194, 478
economic management, I. 88, 90–92, 97, 102, 109–12, 182, 495
economic regulation, I. 88, 104, 109
ECtHR, I. 50, 82, 193, 212, 215, 217, 392, 394–96
Edgar II, King, II. 32, 40
Edict of Nantes, I. 137
Edmund, Burke, II. 490
Education Act
  1902, I. 228, 411, 491
Edward I, King, I. 7, 26, 93, 121, 125, 197, 204, 298, 311, 366
Edward I, King, II. 66, 73–75, 90, 99, 102–3, 105, 112, 213, 406
Edward II, King, I. 259, 287, 289, 311
Edward II, King, II. 85, 88–93, 95, 99, 102–3, 105, 217, 225
Edward III, King, I. 121, 288, 313, 341
Edward III, King, II. 86, 89–96, 98–100, 103–4, 106–7, 113
Edward IV, King, I. 323, 370
Edward IV, King, II. 111
Edward the Confessor (king of Anglo-Saxon), II. 15, 32–34, 39–40, 48, 52, 56–57
Edward the Elder (king of Anglo-Saxons), II. 20–23, 37
Edward the Exile, II. 27
Edward V, King, I. 289
Edward V, King, II. 108, 111
Edward VI, King, I. 126, 129–30, 290
Edward VI, King, II. 136, 138–39, 153

Edward VIII, King, I. 523
Edward VIII, King, II. 463
Edwardian
  administrative machinery, II. 401
  charters, II. 49
  Conquest, II. 210
  constitution, II. 106
  England, II. 34, 46
  period, II. 327
  reformation, II. 139
  settlement, II. 399, 401
  suffragette activity, II. 336
Edwards, John Goronwy, II. 223
Edwin (king of Northumbria), II. 5
Eleanor of Brittany, II. 65
election
  1802, I. 425
  1868, I. 226
  1880, I. 161
  1886, I. 526
  1906, I. 227
  1910, I. 78, 227, 229, 442, 532
  1918, I. 412
  1922, I. 228
  1945, I. 536
  1959, I. 163, 527
  1970, I. 233
  1979, I. 192
  1997, I. 449
  2001, I. 85
  2003, I. 537
  2005, I. 85
  2010, I. 99
  2015, I. 247
  2017, I. 443
  2019, I. 87, 242
Elections and Referendum Act of 2000, I. 244
Elections Ireland Act, II. 449
elective dictatorship, I. 79, 213
Elizabeth I, Queen, I. 93, 128, 133, 138, 146, 264, 290–91, 314, 372
Elizabeth I, Queen, II. 131, 137–38, 140–42, 144, 148, 155, 157, 161, 232, 470–71
Elizabeth II, Queen, I. 296, 306, 308, 523, 541
Elizabeth II, Queen, II. 377, 385, 387, 430
Elizabeth of York, Queen, II. 137, 404
Elizabethan
  common law judges, II. 150
  parish, I. 406
  period, II. 151, 406
  Reformation, I. 128
  statutes, II. 169

Index

Ellis, Thomas Edward, II. 412–13
Elton, Sir Geoffrey Rudolph, I. 312, 314, 316, 450
emancipation of organised labour, I. 169
Employment Act of 1988, I. 82
Empress Matilda, II. 48–50, 139
Encomium Emmae Reginae, II. 2
English common law, II. 69, 80, 113, 219, 224, 289, 401, 469, 482
English Constitution, II. 372, 498
English Constitution, The, I. 14, 76, 279, 489
English Mutiny Act, II. 292
English polity, I. 36, 433
English revolution, II. 170, 172–73, 177–78, 184
English Riot Act, II. 293
Enterprise and Regulatory Reform Act of 2013, I. 109
Entick v Carrington, I. 378
Entick v Carrington, II. 277
e-petition, I. xvi, 241, 243
equality
　of rights, I. 212
　principle of, I. 106
Equality Act of 2010, I. 165, 213
equality legislation, I. 216
Essay towards an History of the Laws of England, An, I. 30
ethos, I. 441, 515, 534, 547
　constitutional, I. 24
　rule-of-law, I. 365
EU. *see also* European Union
　law, I. 50, 84, 88, 109, 190, 194
　legislation, I. 216
　membership, I. 85, 189, 556
　referendum, I. 243, 443
　settlement, I. 449
European Communities Act, I. 49, 435
　1972, I. 51, 216, 281
　1972, II. 365
　1972, II. 368
European Convention of Human Rights, II. 371, 392
European Convention on Human Rights. *see* ECHR
European Convention on Human Rights (ECHR), II. 364, 465
European Court of Human Rights, II. 364, 466, *see* ECtHR
European Court of Justice, II. 392–93
European Union, I. 111, 551, 559, *see also* EU
　exit, I. 332, 541, 558
　membership, I. 235, 431, 439, 556
　referendum, I. 248

　withdrawal, I. 282
European Union (Notification of Withdrawal) Act of 2017, II. 440
European Union (Withdrawal) Act, II. 440 2018, II. 374–75, 440
Evolution of Parliament, The, I. 28
Exchequer, I. 341, 361, 364–65
Exchequer, II. 67, 73, 75, 90, 167, 268, 274, 276, 285
Exchequer and Audit Department, I. 98
Exchequer and Audit Departments Act of 1866, I. 97, 354
Exchequer Chamber, I. 368, 374
Exchequer of Pleas, I. 361–62
Exclusion Crisis, I. 140, 272, 432, 439
Exclusion Crisis (1679-81), II. 162, 178, 184
executive power, I. 8, 18, 40, 61, 206, 337, 343–45, 347–48, 353, 358
Expansion of England, II. 498

Fabian Society, I. 507
federalism, II. 323–26, 378
federative power, I. 69
female suffrage, I. 504
female suffrage, II. 337, 355
feudal system, I. 68, 256, 387
feudalism, I. 26, 408
First World War, I. 158, 161–63, 177, 181, 230, 391, 412, 434, 503, 506, 515, 549
Fisher, Herbert Albert Laurens, I. 11
FitzGeralds, II. 148
Fixed Term Parliaments Act, II. 389 2011, II. 389
Fixed-Term Parliaments Act of 2011, I. 296
Fleming, Sir Thomas, II. 166–67
Fletcher of Saltoun, Andrew, II. 240, 254–56
Forbes of Corse, John, II. 245
Fortescue, Sir John, I. 14, 260, 263
Fortescue, Sir John, II. 109–10, 113, 117, 119–21, 133, 470
Fox, Charles James, I. 15, 75, 440
Fox, Charles James, II. 269, 310–11
Foxe, John, II. 144
Francis I, King, I. 124
frankpledge, II. 45, 47, 54
Freedom of Information Act 2000, II. 366, 371
Freeman, Edward Augustus, I. 16, 357, 494, 496
Freeman, Edward Augustus, II. 320, 498
freemen, II. 47, 87, 104, 125, 151, 237, 298
French Revolution, I. 9, 43, 75, 250, 465, 467–69, 481, 485

569

fundamental constitution, II. 251–52
fundamental law, II. 134, 159, 164, 172, 181, 185, 240, 249–51, 397, 429, 431

Gascoigne, Sir William, II. 116, 127–28
Gauci, Perry, I. 425
Gee, Thomas, II. 409
gender equality, I. 19
General Council of Hauts de Seine, II. 382
George I, King, I. 18, 143, 315, 377
George I, King, II. 263–69, 283, 285
George II, King, II. 263–65, 267–69, 301
George III, King, I. 13, 145, 149, 295, 300, 434, 440
George III, King, II. 28, 263, 268–70, 302, 304, 311, 314, 449, 484
George IV, King, I. 19, 151, 295, 523
George V, King, I. 7, 227, 286, 532
George VI, King, I. 163
George, David Lloyd, II. 361
Geschichte des Römischen Rechts im Mittelalter, I. 12
Gilroy, Paul, I. 22
Gladstone, William Ewart, I. 21, 160–62, 429, 445–46, 481, 492–93, 526, 533, 543
Gladstone, William Ewart, II. 322–23, 325–26, 329–30, 333, 338, 358, 413, 455
Glanvill, II. 54, 56
Glorious Revolution, I. 39, 94, 138, 140, 196, 203, 304, 376, 388, 409, 433, 484, 486, 494
Glorious Revolution, II. 180, 183–84, 260–62, 287, 293, 407–8, 478, 481–82
Glyndwr, Owen, II. 404
revolt of, II. 402–3
Godden v. Hales, II. 180
Goldsworthy, Jeffrey Denys, I. 319, 330
Gooberman, Leon, II. 419
Good Friday Agreement, II. 357, 359, 368, 370, *see also* Belfast Agreement
Gordon, George William, II. 505
Governance of England, II. 110, 386
government administration, I. 49
Government of India Act
1858, II. 509
1935, II. 525
Government of Ireland Act, II. 458, 461
1920, II. 317, 464
Government of Ireland Act of 1920, I. 233, 534
governmental power, I. 54, 56, 58, 107, 200, 308, 335, 472
Grand Assize, II. 54
Great Charter, I. 156
great council, II. 78, 120, 136, 288

Great Famine, II. 452
Great Irish Famine, II. 338
Great Northern War, II. 265
Great Reform Act
1832, II. 408, 493
Great Reform Act of 1832, I. 21, 204, 324, 409, 415–16, 425, 483
Greater London Council, II. 382
Greater Rome and Greater Britain, II. 499
Gregory I, Pope, I. 115
Gregory the Great, Pope, II. 4, 10, 21
Gregory VII, Pope, I. 118
Grey, Jane, Queen, II. 139–40
Griffith, John Aneurin Grey, I. 52, 54, 80–82, 336
Griffiths, Ralph Alan, II. 400
Groundwork of British History, The, I. 17
Gruffudd ap Cynan, II. 214
Gruffudd ap Gwenwynwyn, II. 224
Gruffydd ap Llywelyn (king of Wales), II. 212
Guthfrithsson, Olaf, II. 25
Habeas Corpus, II. 151, 153, 293
Act, II. 302, 305, 307–8, 315, 445
bill, II. 294

Habeas Corpus Act, I. 207, 375
1679, I. 201, 375
Hadrian, II. 6
Hadrian I, Pope, II. 12
Hailsham of St Marylebone, Lord, I. 79–81, 83–84, 184, 213
Hailsham, Quintin McGarel Hogg, II. 351, 367, 395
Hale, Matthew, I. 30, 268–69, 272
Hale, Matthew, II. 199, 449
Hall, Catherine, II. 500
Hamilton, Alexander, I. 41
Hancock, William Keith, II. 507
Hanoverian
bishops, I. 166
Chancery, II. 264
Crown, I. 351
domain, I. 143
dynasty, I. 18
kings, II. 481
line, II. 429
monarchs, I. 295
period, I. 18, 299
royal influence, I. 297
settlement, I. 433, 477
succession, I. 407, 423
succession, II. 162, 184
territory, II. 265

Index

Hanoverians, I. 294, 342, 522
Harcourt, Sir William, I. 25
Harold II (king of Anglo-Saxons), II. 27, 31, 33
Harrington, James, I. 68, 72, 465
Harrington, James, II. 175
Harringtonian republic, I. 68
Harriss, Gerald Leslie, II. 86, 100
Hastings, Warren, II. 489–91, 500
Head of
    Government, I. 57
    Government (the Prime Minister), I. 308
    State, I. 57, 308, 329
    State (the monarch), I. 308, 548
    the Church, I. 25, 124, 261
Heads of the Proposals, II. 173, 175
Health Act of 2007, I. 236
Hearn, William Edward, I. 5
Heath government, I. 183, 233, 535
Heath, Edward Richard George, II. 389, 417
Heath, Sir Edward Richard George, I. 228, 443, 529
Hengham (de), Sir Ralph, I. 367
Hennessy, Peter John, I. 508
Henrician Reformation, I. 262–63, 496
Henry I, King, I. 118, 360–62
Henry I, King, II. 42, 44, 48, 50–51, 53, 57
Henry II, King, I. 26, 118–20, 129, 362
Henry II, King, II. 51–53, 57–58, 60, 64, 68, 70–71, 87, 112, 191, 222, 296
Henry III, King, I. 120, 197, 204, 311, 364
Henry III, King, II. 64–66, 68, 70, 72, 74, 76–77, 79–80, 89, 215, 220
Henry IV, King, I. 93, 122, 289
Henry IV, King, II. 110–17, 123–24, 128
Henry V, King, I. 123, 312
Henry V, King, II. 102, 105, 111, 116, 123, 128, 402–3
Henry VI, King, I. 123, 289
Henry VI, King, II. 109–11, 115–16, 119, 125, 128
Henry VII, King, I. 123, 289
Henry VII, King, II. 109, 111, 113–14, 117, 131, 137, 145, 147, 149, 161–62, 404, 470
Henry VIII, King, I. 25, 123–26, 129, 261, 264, 290, 312, 371–72, 432, 438
Henry VIII, King, II. 114, 130, 138–39, 142, 148, 156, 285, 405–7
Heptarchy, II. 4, 19
Her Majesty's Inspectorate of Constabulary, I. 402
hereditary monarch, I. 71, 224, 316, 322–23
hereditary monarchical succession, I. 10
Heuston, Robert Francis Vere, II. 457

Hewart, Lord Gordon, I. 30, 208, 357
High Court of Justice, II. 176
Hill v Chief Constable of West Yorkshire, I. 404
Himmelfarb, Gertrude, I. 465
historical constitution, I. 4, 15, 33
History of England, I. 13, 17, 432, 485
History of Scotland, I. 7
History of the Rebellion, II. 160
Hobbes, Thomas, I. 61, 204, 266, 464–65
Hobbes, Thomas, II. 134, 176, 476
Hobbesian, I. 464, 477
Hobson, John Atkinson, II. 344, 508
Hollis, Patricia, I. 420
Home Rule, I. 492–94, 529, 543, 548–50, 553, 557
Home Rule, II. 358–59, 454, 457–58, 492–94
    Irish, I. 496, 498, 526, 533
    Scottish, I. 530, 549
Home Rule Bill, II. 326, 454–57
Home Rule League, II. 413, 452
Hooker, Richard, I. 128–29, 138, 153, 263, 464–65, 475
Hooker, Richard, II. 143
House of Commons, I. 28, 98, 208, 225, 232, 234, 270, 277, 305, 323, 353
    democratisation, II. 316, 323, 326–27
House of Hanover, I. 294, 318, 440
House of Lords, I. 232, 306, 323, 325–28, 367, 384, 441, 474, 496, 500
House of Lords Act
    1999, II. 352, 371, 388
House of Lords Act of 1999, I. 326
Housing Act of 1919, I. 411
HRA, I. 84–85, 215–17, *see also* Human Rights Act
human law, II. 166, 250
human rights, I. 211, 405, 478, 497–98, 518
    breaches, I. 50
    commitments, I. 384
    compliance with, I. 404
    concept of, I. 210
    law, I. 471
    regime, I. 218
    violation of, I. 393
Human Rights Act, I. 404, 435, *see also* HRA
Human Rights Act, II. 386, 393–94
    1998, I. 50, 82, 194–96, 214, 395, 404
    1998, II. 364, 371, 466
Humble Petition and Advice, II. 177
Hume, David, I. 7, 62, 74, 275, 277, 432, 464, 467, 475, 477
Hume, David, II. 185, 242
Hundred Years War, II. 89, 100, 103

571

Hundred Years' War, I. 121
Hyam, Ronald, II. 505
Hywel ap Cadell. *see* Hywel Dda
Hywel Dda, II. 211–12, 229

immemoriality, II. 179, 196–99
Immigration Act of 1971, II. 504
impeachment, I. 313, 353, 469
    jurisdiction, I. 368
impeachment power, I. 347
imperial constitution, II. 146, 468, 485, 490–92, 494, 503
Improvement Act of 1844, I. 424
Income Tax Act (1842), I. 21
Indemnity Act, II. 279
independent representation, I. 414–15
Indian Councils' Act of 1861, II. 510
individual rights, I. 213–14, 278, 518
indivisible Crown, II. 462–63
Innocent III, Pope, I. 119, 197
institutional scrutiny, I. 98
institutional-functional balance, I. 56
Instrument of Government, The, II. 174
Interpretation Act of 1850, II. 336
Introduction to the Study of the Law of the Constitution, II. 378, 429, 458
Introduction to the Study of the Law of the Constitution (1885), I. 44, 279
Investiture Controversy, I. 118
Ireland, I. 531–32
Ireland Act
    1949, II. 463
Ireton, Henry, II. 174
Irish Act of Union, II. 316
Irish Church Act, II. 452
Irish Convention, II. 459–60
Irish Declaratory Act of 1720, 1433 304
Irish Free State Constitution Act of 1922, II. 462
Irish Home Rule, II. 319, 322–26, 355, 358, 384, 413, 451, 456
Irish land Act
    1881, II. 412
Irish Mutiny Act, II. 292, 306, 308
Irish War of Independence, II. 317, 461
Islamophobia, I. 165

Jackson case in 2006, I. 321
Jackson v Attorney-General [2005], I. 83
Jackson, Alvin, I. 450, 521
Jacobitism, I. 143–44, 166, 447, 522
James I, King, I. 29, 93, 102–3, 199, 291, 350, 373–74, *see also* James VI, King

James I, King, II. 131, 146, 149, 162, 169, 184, 240, 259–60, 425, 471, 473
James II, King, I. 9–11, 136–37, 140, 293, 299, 338, 375–76, 440, 482, 485, 487, *see also* James VII, King
James II, King, II. 162, 180–81, 183, 185, 234, 260, 294, 427, 429, 477–78
James III, King, I. 297
James III, King, II. 240
James V, King, I. 130
James VI, King, I. 30, 131, 144, 291, 304, 350
James VI, King, II. 131, 141, 146, 149, 162, 184, 232, 250–51, 423, 425, 471
James VII, King, I. 136, 140, 293, *see also* James II, King
James VII, King, II. 234, 426
James, Cyril Lionel Robert, II. 520
Jeffreys, George, I. 375
Jenkins, Roy Harris, I. 234, 427
Jennings, Sir William Ivor, I. 11, 22, 27, 198, 208, 224, 228, 310, 318, 432, 436, 451
Jewish
    community, II. 67
    subjects, II. 82
Jewish Relief Act, II. 452
John of Salisbury, I. 256–57
John, King, I. 195–97, 204, 214, 311, 335, 363–64, 438
John, King, II. 55–58, 64–68, 73, 77–78, 215, 222, 224, 470
Johnes, Martin, II. 419
Johnson government, I. 86
Johnson, Alexander Boris de Pfeffel, I. 56, 86, 242, 445
Johnson, Alexander Boris de Pfeffel, II. 381–82, 390
Joint Ministerial Committee EU, I. 64
Judicature Act of 1873, I. 329
judicial assertiveness, I. 56
judicial independence, II. 115, 153, 276, 387
judicial power, I. 70, 73, 269, 272, 301, 308, 359, 363
judicial scrutiny, I. 382
judicialisation
    of politics, I. 58
judiciaries, I. 359, 376
judiciary, I. 80, 305
Jurisdiction in Liberties Act, II. 149
Jus Regium, II. 249
Jutes, II. 2, 4

Index

Khan, Sadiq Aman, II. 381
King Æthelred the Unready. *see* Æthelred II (king of the English)
King Alfred the Great. *see* Alfred (king of Anglo-Saxons)
King in Parliament, I. 67, 86, 262–63, 270, 273, 319
King Philip's War, II. 477
King's Bench, I. 198–99, 305, 350, 364, 368, 370, 372–73
King's Bench, II. 68, 73, 93–94, 103, 116, 123, 127–28, 149–51, 276, 289
King-at-Arms, Lyon, II. 244
kingly succession, I. 289
Kingship Act of 1541, II. 290
Kinnock, Neil Gordon, II. 419
Knox, John, I. 130–31

Labour Party, I. 78, 174–77, 413, 506–7, 509, 515, 517, 527, 549
  election manifesto, I. 183
Labour Representation Committee, I. 174, 503, 509
labour rights, I. 193–94
Ladies Elect, I. 420
Lady Jane Grey. *see* Grey, Jane, Queen
Lambert, John, II. 174
Lancastrian
  constitutionalism, II. 110, 113
  experiment, II. 109
Lancastrians, II. 117
Land League, II. 412, 453
Land League courts, II. 453
Land War, II. 460
Latham, Richard T E, II. 504
Laudianism, I. 133, 135
law I. 35
  as artefact, I. 57
  as norm, I. 35, 57
  as norm and artefact, I. 36, 58
  rights and wrongs, I. 41
Law and Custom of the Constitution, II. 497
law and the constitution, I. 35
Law and the Constitution, The, I. 225
law of King Edward, II. 32, 34, 36–37, 40, 43–44, 57
Law of the Constitution, I. 97, 100, 208
Law, Andrew Bonar, I. 228, 442
Laws of Edward the Confessor, II. 198
Le May, Godfrey Hugh Lancelot, I. 31
Learned Commendation of the Politique Lawes of Englande, A, I. 14
Lectures on the Law of the Constitution, I. 73

Lee v. Ashers Bakery (2019), I. 165
legal aid, I. 511–12
Legal Aid and Advice Act of 1949, I. 511
legal constitution, I. 36, 45–46, 54–55, 57, 60–61, 69, 79, 82–84, 87
Leges Anglorum, II. 60
Leges Edwardi Confessoris, II. 39–42, 44, 49–50, 56, 60
Leges Henrici, II. 42, 44–45, 56, 60
legislative competence, II. 429, 437, 441, 445
legislative power, II. 270, 272, 329–33
  delegation of, I. 208
  dispersal of, I. 329
  distribution of, I. 40
  of Parliament, I. 249, 321, 453
legislative sovereignty, I. 309
legislative supremacy, II. 300, 304, 424–25, 430–31, 438, 442
legislatures, I. 40, 54–55, 69, 71–72, 153, 224, 272, 276, 309–19, 329–34, 402
  dissolve, I. 24
Leveller
  doctrine, I. 222
  proposals, I. 341
  tract, I. 222
Levellers, I. 149, 203, 222–23, 271, 323, 499–500, 503
Levellers, II. 174
Leviathan, II. 176
Liberal Party, I. 77–78, 157, 238, 446, 480–81, 496–98, 526, 528
liberalism, I. 446, 462, 467, 470, 480–82, 495, 498, 528, 542
  classical, I. 470
Liberation Society, II. 411
liberty
  absolute, I. 205
  natural, I. 205
  relative, I. 205
Licensing Act
  1961, I. 235
  1976, I. 235
Life of Alcuin, II. 20
Life of King Alfred, II. 1, 20–21, 28
Life of King Edward the Confessor, II. 2
Life Peerages Act
  1958, II. 350
Life Peerages Act of 1958, I. 326
Lilburne, John, I. 203, 222
Lindsay, David, II. 243
Livingstone, Kenneth Robert, II. 381–82
Llewelyn the Great, II. 404
Lloyd, John Edward, II. 208

Llywelyn ap Gruffudd, II. 213, 215, 224, 399
Llywelyn ap Iorwerth, II. 215, 222, 224, 227–28
local government, I. 224, 235–41, 406–9, 411–14, 416, 423, 426, 429, 525
local government, II. 257, 280, 390, 417, 456, 461
   administration, I. 416
   elections, I. 418
   evolution of, I. 421
   reform of finance, I. 506
Local Government (Ireland) Act of 1898, II. 456
Local Government Act
   1894, I. 239
   1929, I. 411
   1972, I. 237, 240, 398, 413, 416
   2003, I. 237
Local Government and Public Involvement in Health Act of 2007, I. 236, 240
Local Government and Rating Act of 1997, I. 240
Local Government Finance Act of 1992, I. 240–41
Localism Act of 2011, I. 237
locality, I. 350, 406–7, 417, 422, 427
   centrality of, I. 426
   constitutional, I. 416
   constitutional ideal of, I. 430
   constitutional role of, I. 407, 430
   constitutional status, I. 414
Locke, John, I. 10, 32, 40, 69–70, 142, 204, 266, 272–74, 324, 346, 465
London Collection, II. 56, 60
London County Council, II. 382
London Working Men's Association, I. 20
Long Parliament, I. 29, 68, 94, 133, 303, 375
lords spiritual, I. 288, 326, 349
lords temporal, I. 288, 326, 349
Louis XIV, King, I. 135
Louis XIV, King, II. 180, 183, 234, 258
Low, Donald Anthony, II. 505
Low, Sidney James Mark, I. 23, 33, 450
Low, Sidney James Mark, II. 386
Lowe, Rodney, I. 177, 419
Lowell, Abbott Lawrence, I. 9, 79
Lucas, Charles, II. 304, 499
Lugard, Frederick John Dealtry, II. 514
Lynch, Philip, II. 415

Macaulay, Catherine, I. 13
Macaulay, Thomas Babington, I. 16, 428, 485–88, 494

MacCormick v Lord Advocate, I. 331
MacCormick v Lord Advocate, II. 430
MacCormick, John MacDonald, II. 415
Mackenzie of Rosehaugh, George, II. 248, 250
Mackintosh, James, I. 428, 483–84
Macmillan government, II. 522
Macmillan, Maurice Harold, II. 363
Maddicott, John Robert Lewendon, I. 312
Madison, James, I. 63
Madog ap Llywelyn, II. 401
Magna Carta, I. 6, 36, 58, 119–20, 195–201, 203–5, 363–64, 438, 484
Magna Carta, II. 57, 66, 68, 70, 87, 124, 135, 200, 470, 526
Maine, Henry James Sumner, II. 318, 510
Maitland, Frederic William, I. 5, 11, 15, 93, 95, 111, 290, 346–47, 388, 450, 494
Maitland, John, II. 249
Maitland, Thomas, II. 514
Major, John, I. 228
Major, John, II. 382, 386
Manley, Norman, II. 516
manorial court, II. 96, 189–91
March of Wales, II. 213
Marsiglio, I. 256, 262–63
martial law, I. 201, 387, 389
Martin, Ged, II. 507
Mary I, Queen, I. 126–27, 130–31, 371
Mary I, Queen, II. 138–41, 143, 153, 157, 241, 291, 427
Mary II, Queen, I. 9, 10, 137–38, 203, 294, 318, 338, 376, 482
Mary II, Queen, II. 181–82, 234, 240, 251, 259, 262, 426, 428–29, 479
Mary of Guise (queen consort Scotland), I. 130
Mary of Modena (queen consort England), I. 137
Mason, Roger Alexander, II. 241
Matilda of Scotland, Queen, I. 361
May, Theresa, I. 84, 86, 444, 559
May, Theresa, II. 382, 389, 392
May, Thomas Erskine, I. 76, 452
McFarlane, Kenneth Bruce, II. 85–86, 107, 110, 127
McKechnie, William Sharp, II. 343–44
McLean, Iain, I. 452, 521, 532
Merriman, John Xavier, II. 508
Metcalf, Thomas R, II. 509
Methodism, I. 147, 149, 157
Metropolitan Police Act of 1829, I. 424

574

Index

Middleton v. Crofts, I. 144
military law, I. 387, 391–92
Military Service (No 2) Act of 1918, II. 460
Mill, John Stuart, I. 235, 489
Miller case, I. 333
Milton, John, I. 271
Milton, John, II. 176
Mining Act (1842), I. 21
ministerial responsibility, I. 91, 102, 105, 107, 109, 111, 347
mixed constitution, I. 65, 74–75, 77–78, 87, 275, 484–85
mixed government, I. 62–67, 71–73, 87, 262, 270
mixed monarchy, I. 14, 70, 269
Moir, William, II. 249
Molasses Act, II. 486
  1733, II. 482
Molyneux, William, II. 295–97, 304, 308
monarchical power, I. 67, 422
monarchy, I. 63, 198, 203, 264, 294, 298, 308, 318, 489, 546
  abolition, I. 500, 549
  absolute, I. 145
  constitutional history of, I. 286
  French, I. 121, 408
  future of, I. 308
  Ireland, I. 376
  Norman, I. 360
  personal, I. 290
  restoration of the, I. 135, 249, 271, 293, 318, 375
  supporters, I. 539
monopolies, I. 103, 113, 199
Monopolies and Restrictive Practices (Inquiry and Control) Act of 1948, I. 108
Monopolies and Restrictive Practices Commission, I. 108
Montagu, Edward, II. 153
Montagu, Edwin, II. 518
Montesquieu, I. 6, 13, 40, 42, 47, 53, 62, 70–73, 77, 215, 465
Morgan, Kenneth Owen, II. 414
Morley, Vincent, II. 305
Morrison, Herbert Stanley, II. 382, 502
Mortimer, Edmund, II. 111, 220
Mortimer, Roger, II. 102–3, 229, 399
Movement for Colonial Freedom, I. 513
municipal
  boroughs, I. 409
  corporations, I. 406, 410, 413–14, 416, 418, 420
  elections, I. 428

electors, I. 417
socialism, I. 410–11
Municipal Corporations Act of 1835, I. 397, 409
Municipal Corporations Act of 1835, II. 381
Municipal Franchise Act of 1869, I. 420
Munro, Colin R, II. 428
Muslim, I. 143, 163–65, 167
  population, I. 162
  presence, I. 164
Mutiny Act, I. 388
Mutiny Act, II. 305, 307

National Assembly of Wales (NAW), II. 376, 420
National Audit Office, I. 98, 101, 106–7, 402
National Council for Civil Liberties, II. 464
national health service, I. 511
National Health Service. *see* NHS
National Health Service model, I. 512
National Regulatory Authorities, I. 108
nationalism, I. 520, 535, 541–44, 547
nationality, I. 540–43
natural law, II. 87, 94, 110, 112, 117, 134, 242, 476
Naval Discipline Act of 1957, I. 389
Navigation Act
  1660, II. 477
  1696, II. 479
Nedham, Marchamont, I. 271
New and Impartial History of England, I. 19
New Democracy and the Constitution, The, II. 343
New Poor Law Amendment Act of 1834, I. 409
Newman, Sir Kenneth, I. 22, 475
NHS, I. 495, 510, 550, 558
Nine Years' War, II. 263, 471
Nippel, Wilfried, I. 64
Nonconformist movement, I. 525
Nonconformists, I. 142, 150, 154, 156–58, 162, 491
non-constitutional law, I. 46, 51
norm and artefact, I. 36, 54
Norman Conquest, I. xxi, 16, 29, 36, 40, 117, 224, 386, 408, 435
Norman Conquest, II. 1, 15, 25, 27–28, 64–65, 187, 198, 473
Norman kings, II. 47, 63, 94, 469
Norman kingship, II. 56
North Wales Liberal Federation, II. 414
Northcote-Trevelyan report, I. 24, 355, 504

Northern Ireland
  police service, I. 400, 402–3, 405
  polity, I. 532
  settlement, I. 554, 558
  terrorist, I. 82
  troubles, I. 165, 213, 435
Northern Ireland Act
  1998, II. 379
Northern Ireland Act of 1998, I. 246
Northern Ireland Constitution Act of 1973, I. 249
North-South Ministerial Council, II. 372–73
Northumbrian revolt, II. 40

O'Connell, Daniel, II. 447, 449–52
O'Sullivan, Noël, I. 468–70, 472
Oakeshott, Michael Joseph, I. 464, 469, 474–77
Oceana, II. 175
Octennial Act, II. 302
Of the Lawes of Ecclesiastical Politie, II. 143
Of the Laws of Ecclesiastical Polity, I. 263
Offa (king of Mercia), II. 3, 9, 11–15
Offences Against the Person Act of 1861, I. 159
oligarchy, I. 21, 28, 63, 65, 448
Operation Banner, I. 390
Ordinance of Labourers in 1349, II. 97
Osborne v Amalgamated Society of Railway Servants, I. 174
Osborne, George, II. 381
Osborough, William Nial, II. 446
O'Shea, Katharine, II. 454
Oswald (king of Northumbria), II. 5
Oswiu (king of Bernicia and Northumbria), II. 5–6
Othman (Abu Qatada) v. the United Kingdom [2012], I. 84
Owain Glyn Dŵr, II. 218–20, 225–27

Padfield v Minister of Agriculture and Food, I. 358
pagan
  convertion, I. 117
  practice, I. 116
  traditions, I. 117
Paine, Thomas, I. 19, 73, 75, 276, 324
Pannikkar, Kavalam Madhava, II. 514
papal
  aggression, I. 160
  authority, I. 261
  bull, I. 25, 125, 127
  courts, I. 122

  curia, I. 124
  dispensation, I. 124
  grant, I. 129
  interference, I. 122
  jurisdiction, I. 438
  legal jurisdiction, I. 25
  legate, I. 123
  simony and corruption, I. 121
  support, I. 123
  supremacy, I. 26, 256
Papists Act, II. 449
  1778, II. 281
Papists Act of 1778, I. 145
Paris, Matthew, II. 28, 214
parish, I. 115, 141, 151
  churches, I. 157
  clergy, I. 152
  council referendums, I. 236
  councils, I. 237, 239–40, 430
  meetings, I. 238–39
  register system, I. 153
  structure, I. 131
  system, I. 115
  vestry, I. 127, 238, 416, 420, 422
Parish Councils Act, I. 239
  1894, I. 417
Parliament Act, II. 353, 358
  1694, I. 294
  1695, I. 294
  1911, I. 328, 496
  1911, II. 347, 349–50, 354, 356–57, 363–64, 367
  1949, I. 328
  1949, II. 350
Parliament Recognition Act of 1689, II. 428
parliamentarian theories, I. 264–65, 268–69
parliamentary
  authority, I. 95, 100, 312, 367
  democratisation, I. 322–23
  legislation, I. 49–50, 209, 439
  petitions, I. 243
  privileges, I. 265, 270
  reform, I. 156–57, 491–92
  representation, I. 121, 169, 325
  scrutiny, I. 80, 88, 98, 313, 423
  supremacy, I. 47, 206, 209
parliamentary government, I. 62, 76, 87, 262, 315, 482–83, 490
  characteristics, I. 85
  decline, I. 79
parliamentary sovereignty, I. 73, 206, 317–22, 331, 461, 493, 498, 525, 529, 543, 553
  constraints, I. 84

Index

defence, I. 86
doctrine, I. 309
origins, I. 83
principle, I. 27, 47
Parliamentary Standards Act, I. 242
  2009, I. 242
Parliamentary Voting System and Constituencies Act of 2011, I. 246
Parnell, Charles Stewart, II. 451, 453–54, 456
participation, I. 178, 180, 191, 503
  by labour, I. 170
  in government, I. 178, 181, 189–90
  of clerics, I. 371
  of the monarch, I. 39, 304
  trade union, I. 169
  of women, I. 19
Party Systems and Voter Alignments, I. 231
Paschal II, Pope, I. 118
patriarchal
  authority, I. 266
  preserve, I. 23
  underpinnings, I. 19
Patten Commission, I. 405
Paul III, Pope, I. 126
Peasants' Revolt, I. 122, 499
Peck, Linda Levy, II. 247
Peel principles, I. 397–98
Peel, Sir Robert, I. 21, 77, 151, 397, 428, 437, 446, 469, 473, 481, 483
Peelite, I. 446, 481
Peerage Act
  1963, II. 351, 367
Penal Laws, II. 329, 449
people and the constitution, I. 221
People's Charter, I. 503
  1838, I. 214, 325
Pergau Dam case in 1995., I. 101
Perils of the Nation, II. 335
Peterloo massacre, I. 325, 503
Petition of Right, II. 168
Petition of the Barons, II. 79
petitions, II. 81–83
Philip II, King, I. 126
Philip II, King, II. 140, 205
Pickin v British Railways Board, I. 320
Pitt, William, I. 15, 149, 381, 431, 437, 440
Pitt, William, II. 269, 309–11, 313–16, 484–85
Pitt, William the Elder, II. 265
Pius IX, Pope, I. 160
Plantagenet, I. 121, 287, 298
Plummer, Charles, II. 110

plurinational
  constitutionalism, I. 547
  state, I. 64
  understanding, I. 559
  union, I. 541, 546, 557
plurinationalism, I. 559
Pocock, John Greville Agard, I. 10, 29, 460
Pocock, John Greville Agard, II. 200, 450
police, I. 396–400, 404–5
  accountability, I. 402–4
  Ombudsman, I. 403
  powers, I. 400–2
Police Act
  1964, I. 397
  1996, I. 398
Police and Criminal Evidence Act of 1984, I. 213, 398, 400
Police and Magistrates' Courts Act of 1994, I. 398
Police Reform Act 2002, I. 400
Policing and Crime Act of 2017, I. 400, 402
Policraticus, I. 257
political
  equality, I. 78, 83
  institutions, I. 60, 66
  jurisdiction, I. 363
  laws, I. 42, 47
  participation, I. 23, 381
political constitution, I. 52, 57, 59, 62, 66, 68, 78–79, 82–87, 309, 484
political constitutionalism, I. 59–60, 62, 69–70, 83, 86–87
political parties and the constitution, I. 434–35, 439
Political Parties, Elections and Referendums Act
  2000, II. 371
Polity, I. 42, 65–66, 210, 255, 377, 379, 472, 541
  British, I. 436
  constitution of a, I. 61
  elements of the, I. 444
  freedoms of the, I. 452
  plurinational, I. 542
  stability of the, I. 433
  three basic types of, I. 63
Pollard, Albert Frederick, I. 28, 316
Pollock, Frederick, I. 223
Polybian
  argument, I. 65
  cycle, I. 66
  version, I. 65
Pontiac's War, II. 485
poor law, I. 127, 156, 239, 411, 510

poor law, I. (cont.)
  abolition of, I. 417
  concepts, I. 156
  guardians, I. 406, 414, 420
  provision, I. 151, 411
  unions, I. 406
Poor Law Amendment Act, I. 105
Poor Law Commission, I. 105, 347, 355
Poplar Rates Rebellion, I. 413
populist
  democracy, I. 87
  governments, I. 472
  ideas, I. 203
  reaction, I. 145
populist constitutionalism, I. 87
positive law, II. 87, 134, 488
power
  checks and balances, I. 63–64, 73, 77
  dispersal of, I. 63, 309
powers
  separation of, I. xxv, 62–64, 68–70, 72–73, 77, 104, 271, 358, 465, 485
Poynings' Law, II. 285–86, 290–94, 299, 301–3, 306–9, 312–13, 316
Poynings, Sir Edward, II. 290
Prerogativa Regis, II. 155
prerogative
  authority, I. 378
  courts, I. 371, 375
  powers, I. 57, 86, 198, 214, 296, 305–6, 345, 368, 387, 390, 503
  taxation, I. 201
  tribunal, I. 371, 379
Presbyterian
  church, II. 246, 328, 429
  critics, II. 239
  patriots, II. 243
  theory, II. 238
Presbyterianism, II. 248, 330
Presbyterians, I. 140–41, 146, 148
Prince of Wales, I. 546
Principles of Church Reform, I. 153
private armies, II. 108–9, 126
privatisation
  of public enterprises, I. 106
  of public services, I. 106
Privy Council, II. 156, 162, 171, 266, 287, 506
  British, II. 301, 307
  Great Britain, II. 262
  Irish, II. 294, 298, 303
procedural law, I. 41
Proclamations Act of 1539, I. 290

proportional representation, I. 214, 421
Proportional Representation (PR), I. 497
Protestant Constitution, II. 183
Protestant Reformation, II. 288
Pryce, Huw, II. 208
psephological equality, I. 416
psephological map, I. 415
public administration, I. 106, 505
  function, I. 169
Public Health Act of 1848, I. 424
public participation, I. 241, 244

Quadripartitus, II. 40, 42, 44, 51, 56
Quakers, I. 114, 143, 494
Quebec Act of 1774, II. 487
Quinn v Leathem, I. 173
Quinton, Anthony, I. 474

R v Mawbey, I. 171
R v Vaughan, II. 487
R. v. Home Secretary, ex parte Simms [2000], I. 83
R. (Jackson) v Attorney General, I. 328
race discrimination, I. 384
Race Relations Act of 1965, I. 213
Rædwald (king of East Anglia), II. 5
Rainborough, Thomas, I. 499, 503
Ramsay, James, I. 147
ratepayer democracy, I. 406–7, 409–10
Recall of MPs Act, I. 242
Redcliffe-Maud Commission, I. 239
redistribution, I. 230, 415–16, 426
  of constituencies, I. 415
  of parliamentary constituencies, I. 409
Redistribution Act of 1885, I. 325
Redistribution of Seats Act of 1885, I. 415
referendum, I. 244–53
referendum, II. 323, 326, 365, 369–71
  1967, II. 526
  1973, II. 357, 359
  1974, II. 433
  1975, II. 357, 359
  1979, II. 418, 433
  1997, II. 415, 433–34
  1998, II. 373
  2011, II. 420
  2014, II. 379–80, 383, 423, 435, 437–38, 442
  2016, II. 357, 374, 380
  EU, II. 389, 391
Reflections on the Revolution in France, II. 490
Reform Act
  1832, II. 336

Index

Reform Act of
  1832, I. 156, 224, 278, 325, 346, 381, 434, 474, 481, 483, 487, 503
  1867, I. 280, 325, 474, 491, 503
  1884, I. 21, 325, 474, 503
  1918, I. 474
Regency Act of 1705, I. 315
Regulating Act
  1773, II. 486
regulation of frankpledge, II. 45
regulatory agencies, I. 107
regulatory boards, I. 105
regulatory institutions, I. 88, 102, 104, 106
religion, I. 126, 129, 141
  disputes, I. 265
  folk, I. 131
  Protestant, I. 137, 531, 544
  reference to, I. 161, 163
  and race, I. 380
  role, I. 116
  social recognition, I. 160
  state, I. 293
Remuneration, Charges and Grants Act of 1975, I. 183
Rendel, Stuart, II. 413
Renunciation Act, II. 309
Reorganisation of Offices (Scotland) Act, II. 415
representation, I. 62, 176–77, 208, 280, 309, 311, 314
  of the aristocracy, I. 311
  for the nobility, I. 71
  in government, I. 180, 189
  and property rights, I. 324
  social, I. 170
  as workers, I. 194
  of worker interests, I. 177
Representation of the People (Equal Franchise) Act of 1928, I. 323
Representation of the People (Equal Franchise) Act of 1928, II. 343
Representation of the People Act, I. 224, 242, 323
representation of trade union, I. 169
restoration
  of the monarchy, I. 135, 249, 271, 293, 318, 375
  of Stuart monarchy, I. 292, 433
Restoration, I. 43, 69, 146, 203, 222, 271, 275, 433, 477
Restrictive Practices Court, I. 108
Restrictive Trade Practices Act of 1956, I. 108

Revolution Settlement, I. 55, 204, 305
Revolutionary War, II. 488
Rex v Bear, II. 277
Rex v Dammaree, II. 277
Rex v Francklin, II. 277
Rex v Hardy, II. 278
Rhodes, Cecil John, II. 456
Rhys ap Gruffudd, II. 214
Richard I, King, I. 118, 120, 362
Richard I, King, II. 53
Richard II, King, I. 122, 289, 313–14, 369
Richard II, King, II. 88–90, 94–96, 98, 105–6, 111–15, 117
Richard III, King, I. 289
Richard III, King, II. 111, 113, 137
Richard, Henry, II. 410, 412
Ridge v Baldwin, I. 358
right
  to asylum, I. 210
  to education, I. 212
  of personal liberty, I. 205, 207
  of personal security, I. 205
  of private property, I. 205
  to vote, I. 212
  to work and equal pay, I. 210
Rights of Man, I. 73, 324
Riot Act, II. 454
  1714, II. 283
Roberts, Peter, II. 407
Robertson, John, II. 254
Robertson, William, I. 7
Robertson, William, II. 500
Robson, William Alexander, I. 412
Roman Catholic Relief Act, II. 449
  1791, II. 281
Roman law, II. 133, 192, 194–95, 206
Rose, Richard, I. 520, 540
royal assent, II. 169, 171, 245, 261, 308, 363
royal authority, I. 126, 138, 254, 260, 314, 347, 422
  decline, I. 26
  exaltation, I. 122
  strengthening, I. 312
royal control, I. 38, 55, 118–19, 131, 299, 308
  over the Church, I.233 123
royal diploma, II. 26
royal power, II. 9, 89, 94, 113, 118, 129–30, 195, 233–35, 244, 311
Royal Proclamation of 1763, II. 485, 488
royal succession, II. 109, 116–17, 183, 259–60, 262, 287
rule of law, I. 47–48, 58, 69–70, 206–7, 280–81, 356, 386, 472, 476, 498

579

Rushdie, Salman, I. 164
Russell, John, I. 17, 150, 160, 416, 428, 491
Russell, Lord John, II. 331, 448, 506
Russell, Michael William, II. 377
Rutherford, Samuel, I. 30
Rutherford, Samuel, II. 239, 251, 254

Salesbury, William, II. 407
Salisbury, Lord, II. 350–51, 386, 415, 454
Salisbury, Lord Robert Arthur Talbot Gascoyne-Cecil, 3rd Marquess, I. 21, 226–27, 327, 483
Same Sex (Couples) Act, I. 228
Sandys, Samuel, I. 15
Satanic Verses, The, I. 164
Saxons, II. 4, 22, 25
Schmitt, Carl, I. 438, 445
Schmittian state, I. 444
Scotland, I. 403, 422, 449, 523, 527–31
referendum, I. 246
Scotland Act, I. 246
Scotland Act, II. 376, 379
1998, II. 423, 431–32, 434, 436, 438–39, 441
2012, II. 434–35
2016, I. 333
2016, II. 374, 435, 438–39, 442
Scotland and Wales Acts of 1978, I. 246
Scotland's Claim, Scotland's Right, II. 434
Scott, Walter, I. 523
Scottish
devolution, I. 247
enlightenment, I. 146, 277
Scottish Act of 1868, II. 334
Scottish Act of Security of 1704, I. 144
Scottish Board of Health Act, II. 415
Scottish Constitutional Convention (SCC), II. 379, 418, 434
Scottish Home Rule, II. 321–23
Scottish Liberal Unionists, I. 528
Scottish nationalism, II. 422, 431, 441
Scottish Unionist Party, I. 528
Scottish Universities Act of 1852, I. 12
scrutiny of public expenditure, I. 88
scrutiny of public spending, I. 98
Second Boer War, I. 388
Second Reform Act of 1867, I. 21, 420
Second Treatise of Government, I. 249, 272
Second World War, I. 52, 58, 89, 181, 391, 550–51
Seddon, Richard John, II. 513
Seditious Meetings Act of 17950, II. 284
Sedley, Stephen John, I. 142, 305
See of Rome Act of 1536
Seeley, John Robert, I. 3, 451

Seeley, John Robert, II. 498
Select Charters, II. 207
self-regulation, I. 99, 102, 104, 110–11
Semayne case, I. 373
separation of powers, I. 449
Septennial Act, I. 448
Septennial Act, II. 302
1716, I. 294
Seven Years' War, II. 304, 480, 486
Sewel convention, II. 374, 376–77, 439–41
Sewel, Lord John Buttifant, II. 439
Sex Discrimination Act of 1975, I. 213
Sexual Offences Act of 1967, I. 213
Sharp, Granville, I. 147
Sheppard, Katherine Wilson, II. 514
Sherlock v Annesley, II. 285
Ship Money case II. 94
Shirley v Fagg (1675), I. 293
Simnel, Lambert, II. 137, 145, 290
Simpson, Alfred William Brian, II. 522
Skinner, Quentin Robert Duthie, I. 83
slavery, I. 56, 118, 146–47, 156
abolition of, I. 243
Slavery Abolition Act of 1833, II. 493
Smith, Adam, II. 503
Smith, Jenkyn Beverley, II. 229
Smith, Joshua Toulmin, II. 341
Smith, Llinos Beverley, II. 209
Smith, Robert Haldane, II. 435
social constitution, I. 169–70, 177, 184–85, 190, 192
social constitutionalism, I. 169–70, 177, 192–94
Social Contract, I. 170, 181, 183–85, 187, 189–92, 204
social contract theory, I. 266, 464–65, 471
social democratic constitution, I. 168
Social Dialogue, I. 170, 190–92
Social Dialogue agreements, I. 190–91
social order, I. 114, 137, 142, 151–52, 158, 166, 453, 468
social security, I. 159, 507, 509–10
socialism, I. 410, 499, 501–2, 507, 515, 517, 519, 527, 529–30
Society of Antiquaries, II. 28
socio-political-economic balance, I. 56
Somerset v Stewart, II. 278
Sophia, Princess of the Palatinate, II. 259–62, 266
South Africa, II. 326–27, 462–63, 512
South Wales Liberal Federation, II. 414
sovereignty, I. 67, 86, 319, 493, 552, 557
in the Crown, I. 62

Index

legal, I. 322, 333, 464
legislative, I. 271, 319, 322, 330
monarchical, I. 75
of Parliament, I. 28, 55, 61, 82, 97, 184, 246, 273, 279
of the Monarch-in-Parliament, I. 547
of the people, I. 42, 222, 230, 249–51, 281
political, I. 322, 464–65
popular, I. 471–72, 546
unitary, I. 493, 497
Sowerby, Scott, II. 183
spending review, I. 99, 101
Staatswissenschaft, I. 11
Stamp Act
  1765, II. 304, 486
Stanley, William Owen, II. 412
State Immunity Act
  1978, II. 393
Statute of Acton Burnell of 1283, II. 80
Statute of Additions of 1413, II. 97
Statute of Mortmain of 1279, II. 81
Statute of Purveyance of 1362, II. 102
Statute of Quia Emptores of 1290, II. 80
Statute of Treasons of 1352, II. 89
Statute of Wales, II. 63, 209, 217, 222, 225
Statute of Waste, II. 81
Statute of Westminster II of 1285, II. 81
Statute of Westminster of 1931, II. 326, 504, 519
Statute of Winchester, I. 387, 396
statutes
  constitutional, I. 13
  Tudor, I. 261
statutory norm, I. 44
Stephen, King, II. 47–53, 56, 58, 60, 112
Stephenson, David, II. 226
Stopes, Charlotte Carmichael, II. 335–36
Stormont administration, II. 465
Stuart
  Catholic monarchy, II. 281
  conceptions of kingship, I. 286
  constitution, II. 165, 170
  dynasty, II. 423
  England, I. 265
  kings, I. 304
  kings, II. 166–67, 237–38
  line, II. 162
  monarchy, I. 292
  multiple kingdoms, II. 170
  period, II. 160, 162, 337
  periods, I. 102
  realms, I. 138
  restoration, I. 144
Stuart Scottish plot, I. 13
Stuart, Charles Edward, II. 260

Stuart, Elizabeth, II. 259
Stuart, James Francis Edward, II. 260, 429
Stuarts, I. 166, 298, 375, 377, 440
Stuarts, II. 131, 234, 258, 407, 525
Stubbs, William, I. 12, 451, 486
Stubbs, William, II. 84, 106, 110, 113, 207, 318–19, 501
substantive
  constitutional norms, I. 89–90
  economic management, I. 90, 110
  economic policy, I. 90
  law, I. 37
  law of liability, I. 306
substantive law
  of public and private wrongs, I. 41
succession, I. 10, 126, 136–37, 261, 271, 289
succession, II. 178, 201, 234
  agreed rules, II. 427
  apostolic, I. 135
  Catholic, I. 139
  by charter, II. 113
  contested, II. 131
  dispute, II. 50
  hereditary, II. 161–62, 178, 249
  laws of, I. 289, 294
  lines of, II. 44, 232
  order of, II. 144
  powers, I. 372
  principle of, II. 110, 184–85
  property, II. 403
  Protestant, I. 376, 433
  Protestant, II. 293, 429
  royal, I. 267, 272–73
  rules, II. 65
  statute, II. 113, 139
Succession to the Crown Act, I. 294
Sugar Act
  1764, II. 486
Sunday Closing Act of 1881, II. 411
Sunday Licensing Act of 2003, I. 235
Sunningdale Agreement, II. 384
Supreme Court, II. 257, 376, 378, 387, 440, 516
synthetic Constitution, I. 43, 58
synthetic sense, I. 35
system of law, I. 26, 81, 360

Tacky's War, II. 483
Taff Vale Railway Company v Amalgamated Society of Railway Servants, I. 172
Tamworth Manifesto, I. 437, 473
Tanner, Duncan, II. 416–18
taxation, I. 78, 120–22, 133, 201, 203, 209, 311, 510
  Church, I. 256
  indirect, I. 93

taxation powers, I. 5, 331, 492
Taylor case (1676), I. 142
Tea Act of 1773, II. 487
Teleologia, II. 207, 210
Temperance (Scotland) Act of 1913, I. 235
Temple, William, I. 158
Ten Articles, II. 32, 37, 41, 56
Ten Hours Act (1847), I. 21
tenants-in-chief, II. 35, 55, 61, 66, 78, 82, 237
Tennyson, Alfred, I. 485–86
tenurial
  caste, II. 55
  dependency, II. 33–35
  disputes, II. 45–46, 54
  law, II. 37
  redistribution, II. 36
  relationship, II. 35
  rights, II. 34, 50
  security, II. 36
  system, II. 43, 61
  terms, II. 52–53
  turmoil, II. 52
territorial governance, II. 367
Test Act
  1672, II. 184
  1673, II. 178, 279–80
  1678, II. 279
Test and Corporation Act, I. 137, 144–45, 150, 491
TFEU, I. 190, 194
Thatcher
  administration, I. 82, 180
  era, I. 83, 85
  government, I. 106, 155, 193
  regime, I. 189
Thatcher, Margaret, I. 81, 155, 177, 435, 529
Thatcher, Margaret Hilda, II. 418
Thatcherism, I. 214
Thatcherism, II. 419
Theodore of Tarsus, Archbishop of Canterbury, II. 6–8
third Agreement of the People, I. 222
Third Marquess of Salisbury, Robert Arthur Talbot Gascoyne-Cecil. *see* Salisbury, Lord
Third Reform Act, I. 325
Thomas of Lancaster, II. 85, 107
Thompson, Edward Palmer, I. 19
Thoughts on the Cause of the Present Discontents, I. 483
Tithe Act, I. 162
Tithe Commissioners, I. 355
Tithe War, II. 450

Tocquveille, Alexis Charles Henri Clérel, comte de, II. 385
Toland, John, II. 160
Toleration Act, II. 239
  1689, II. 183, 281
Tolkien, John Ronald Reuel, II. 207
Tomkins, Adam, I. 83, 92
Tonna, Charlotte Elizabeth, II. 335
tort law, I. 39, 47
Trade Boards Act of 1918, I. 179
Trade Disputes Act of 1906, I. 173, 186
trade union, I. 78, 168–90, 193, 435, 516
  action, I. 173
  as legitimate actors, I. 181
  demands, I. 169
  freedom, I. 188
  industrial action, I. 173
  leaders, I. 181
  legislative role for, I. 190
  membership, I. 168, 175, 192
  movement, I. 177, 503, 513
  organisation, I. 184
  participation, I. 182
  political levies, I. 175
  political representation, I. 177
  power of, I. 180
  protection, I. 172
  regulation, I. 496
  representation, I. 169, 179
Trade Union Act
  1913, I. 175
  1974, I. 188
  1976, I. 188
  1984, I. 82
trade unionism, I. 168, 176
Trades Union Congress. *see* TUC
Transportation Act of 1717, II. 282
Treasonable and Seditious Practices Act of 1795, I. 324
Treasonable Practices Act of 1795, II. 284
Treaty of Limerick, II. 294–95
Treaty of Paris, II. 64, 485, 489
Treaty on the Functioning of the European Union, I. 100, *see* TFEU
Trevelyan, George Macaulay, I. 16, 26
Trevelyan, George Otto, II. 325, 338
Triennial Act, I. 94
Triennial Act, II. 171, 244
Trinitarian
  dissenters, I. 142
  doctrines, I. 142
  Protestants, I. 141
  stipulations, I. 150

Index

tripartite, I. 181
  body, I. 178
  division, I. 70
  economic management, I. 189
  form of governance, I. 105
  legislature, I. 311
  separation of powers, I. 276
  trade boards, I. 179
tripartite structure, I. 407
TUC, I. 177, 182–85, 192, 509
Tudor
  borderlands, II. 145–46
  constitutionalism, I. 298
  crown, II. 407
  domains, II. 158
  dynasty, I. 372
  dynasty, II. 161
  education, I. 339
  government, I. 312
  governments, I. 314
  law-state, II. 151, 154
  legislation, II. 285
  legislatures, I. 28
  monarch, II. 131, 232
  monarchs, I. 297, 302–3
  nation-building project, I. 129
  parliaments, I. 286
  periods, I. 102
  predecessors, I. 291
  realms, I. 129
  regime, II. 148
  reigns of, II. 288
  rule, II. 141
  systems, I. 381
Tudor period, I. 18, 29, 198, 303, 312, 314, 407–8
Tudor predecessors, I. 291
Tudor, Henry, II. 130, 225, 227, *see also* Henry VII, King
Tudors, I. 93, 166, 290, 298
Tudors, II. 131–32, 137, 139, 143, 149, 450
Tudur, Owain, II. 404
Twenty-Five barons of the realm, II. 57–60, 70, 470
Two Treatises of Government, I. 10
Tyndale, William, I. 124, 126
tyranny, I. 63, 65, 67, 261, 264, 267, 274–75, 336, 343, 346, 358, 511
tyranny, II. 87–88, 106, 135, 140, 176, 210, 318, 336, 487, 491, 494
  definition, II. 88
tyrant, II. 85, 479
  definition, II. 88

UDHR, I. 209–10, 212, 218–19
unconstitutional
  acts, I. 275, 377
  oppressions, I. 262
Undertakers, II. 298, 301, 303–4
unionism, I. 520–25, 528, 537–39, 543–44, 557
  Irish, I. 528, 531, 534, 537
  militant, I. 532
  Scotland, I. 527, 530
  Ulster, I. 533
Unionists, II. xx, 321, 326–27, 329, 356, 372, 384, 455, 457
Unitarianism, I. 142
United Irishmen uprising, II. 444
Universal Declaration of Human Rights. *see* UDHR
universal female suffrage, I. 281
universal male suffrage, I. 178, 276, 281, 324–25, 503
universal suffrage, I. 67, 95, 210, 214, 230, 381, 426, 550
Unknown Charter, II. 57, 60

vernacular, II. 12, 21, 50, 56
  Bible, II. 407
  literature, II. 205
  revolt, II. 426
Victoria, Queen, I. 31, 77, 225, 296, 300, 523
Victoria, Queen, II. 330, 496, 509
Victorian
  age, I. 103
  constitution, I. 485
  discourse, I. 159
  era, I. 85
  local government, I. 410
  period, I. 407, 482
  system, I. 411
Victorian Constitution, I. 31
Viking case, I. 194
Volunteer movement, II. 307
Volunteers, II. 305–6, 309–11, 459–60
Von Braunschweig-Lüneburg, Georg Ludwig. *see also* George I
Von Gneist, Heinrich Rudolf Hermann Friedrich, I. 28
Von Ranke, Leopold, I. 11
Von Savigny, Friedrich Carl, I. 12
voting age, I. 21

Wakefield, Edward Gibbon, I. 355
Wales, I. 64, 86, 129, 162, 235, 237, 331, 525–27, 540, 546, 549–50

Wales Act
  2017, II. 374
Wales Act of 2017, I. 333
Wales and Berwick Act of 1746, I. 525
Walpole, Sir Robert, I. 15, 18, 143, 315, 433,
  447–48, 453, 473, 482
War Cabinet, II. 361–62
War Damages Act 1965, I. 393
War of Madog, II. 401
War of the Bavarian Succession, II. 265
Warbeck, Perkin, II. 137, 290
Wars of the Roses, I. 131–32, 123, 260–61, 370
Webb, Martha Beatrice, I. 409
Webb, Sidney James, I. 175, 409–10, 510
Wedderburn, Kenneth William, I. 170, 377
Weinstein, Benjamin, I. 412, 420
Welsh
  administration, II. 408
  constitutional development, II. 398
  constitutional history, II. 210
  devolution legislation, II. 379
  disestablishment, II. 322
  independence, II. 220
Welsh Courts Act of 1942, I. 526
Welsh Language Act of 1967, I. 526
Welsh Liberal Party, II. 413
Welsh Liberalism, II. 413
Wesley, John, I. 147–48
Western Mail, II. 415
Westphalian state, I. 544
Whigs, I. 225, 272, 486–87, 491, 494
  Court, I. 273–74
  Foxite, I. 75, 492
  Protestant, I. 487
Whitaker, Frederick, II. 515
Whitehouse, Constance Mary, I. 162
Wight, Martin, II. 503
Wilkes, John, I. 13, 145, 203
William I, King, I. 360–61
William I, King, II. 27, 30, 37, 40–42, 48, 50,
  56, 9–11, 117
William II, King, I. 251, 140, *see also* William
  III, King
William III, King, I. 9–11, 137–38, 140, 203,
  294, 318, 338, 376, 440, 482, 485, 487
William III, King, II. 160, 234, 259–63, 267,
  272, 275, 292, 426, 428, 479
William IV, King, I. 31
William of Orange. *see* William III, King
William the Conqueror. *see* William I, King

William, Mari Elin, II. 418
Williams, Eric Eustace, II. 513
Williams, Glanmor, II. 403–4, 407
Williamson, Arthur H, II. 236
Wilson reform programme, II. 363
Wilson, James Harold, II. 362
Wollstonecraft, Mary, I. 9, 19
Wolsey, Thomas, I. 123–24
women, II. 110, 238, 342
  authority, I. 131
  constitutional rights, II. 336
  council, II. 459
  and decision-making, I. 221
  elite and aristocratic, II. 334
  middle-class, II. 335
  partially enfranchised, I. 21
  political subordination, II. 140
  position of, I. 19, 380
  right to vote, II. 343, 360, 513
  rights of, I. 490
  suffrage, I. 490–91, 493, 498
  suffrage, II. 336
  voting rights, I. 322, 325, 420, 503
  working-class, II. 334
Women's National Anti-Suffrage League, I.
  503
Women's Social and Political Union, I. 504
Wonderful Parliament of 1386, II. 106
Wood, Charles, II. 510
Wood, Edward, II. 513
Woolf, Leonard Sidney, II. 416
Woollen Act, II. 297
  1699, II. 300
World War I, II. 319, 341–42, 359–61, 414, 456,
  459–61
World War II, II. 321, 339, 342, 346, 360, 362,
  366, 368, 415, 463
Wormald, Charles Patrick, II. 37
written constitution, I. xv, 42, 44, 48, 206,
  213–14, 222, 307, 453
written constitution, II. 173–74, 354, 364,
  366–67, 511
wrongs
  private (non-criminal or 'civil'), I. 41
  public (criminal), I. 41
Wyclif, John, I. 122, 124

xenophobia, I. 23, 451

Zines, Leslie, II. 504

A cumulative index of both volumes is available for download on Cambridge Core and via www.cambridge.org/constitutionalhistoryindex